THE YALE LIBRARY OF MILITARY HISTORY

Donald Kagan and Dennis Showalter,
Series Editors

FRANK McLYNN

The Burma Campaign

Disaster into Triumph 1942–45

Yale

UNIVERSITY PRESS

NEW HAVEN & LONDON

First published in the United States in 2011
by Yale University Press.
First published in hardcover in Great Britain in 2010
by The Bodley Head. First published in paperback by
Vintage Books in 2011.

Yale University Press books may be purchased
in quantity for educational, business, or promotional
use. For information, please e-mail sales.press@yale.edu
(U.S. office) or sales@yaleup.co.uk (U.K. office).

Library of Congress Control Number: 2011930214
ISBN 978-0-300-17162-4 (hardcover: alk. paper)
Printed in the United States of America.

A catalogue record for this book is available
from the British Library.

This paper meets the requirements of ANSI/NISO
Z39.48-1992 (Permanence of Paper).

10 9 8 7 6 5 4 3 2 1

To Pauline

Contents

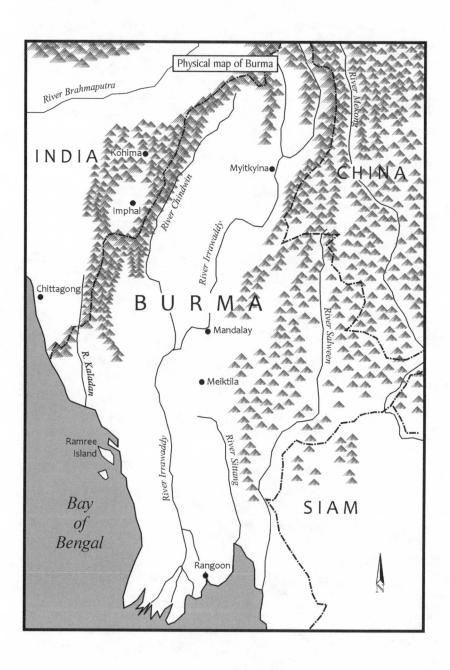

Physical map of Burma

Illustrations and maps

Illustrations

1. Burning camp © Keystone, Hulton Archive, Getty Images **2.** Archibald Wavell and Joseph W. Stilwell © William Vandivert, Time & Life Pictures, Getty Images **3.** W.J. Slim © Keystone, Time & Life Pictures, Getty Images **4.** Burma campaign © William Vandivert, Time & Life Pictures, Getty Images **5.** Strategy meeting on the Burmese border © William Vandivert, Time & Life Pictures, Getty Images **6.** Chindits in Burma © Hulton Archive, Getty Images **7.** Military briefing © Keystone, Hulton Archive, Getty Images **8.** Joseph W. Stilwell, Chiang Kai-shek and Madame Chiang © Fred L. Eldridge, Time & Life Pictures, Getty Images **9.** General Stilwell pictured with a group in the Burmese jungle © Haynes Archive, Popperfoto, Getty Images **10.** British forces behind Japanese lines © William Vandivert, Time & Life Pictures, Getty Images **11.** Cairo Conference © Keystone, Hulton Archive, Getty Images **12.** Louis Mountbatten © Central Press, Hulton Archive, Getty Images **13.** Wounded at casualty clearing station © William Vandivert, Time & Life Pictures, Getty Images **14.** Chinese infantry during Burma campaign © William Vandivert, Time & Life Pictures, Getty Images **15.** Dead Japanese soldiers lying next to road © William Vandivert, Time & Life Pictures, Getty Images **16.** General Slim in London © Keystone, Hulton Archive, Getty Images **17.** William Joseph Slim and Bernard Montgomery © Hulton Archive, Getty Images

Maps

1. Physical map of Burma; **2.** Political map of Burma; **3.** Japanese invasion of Burma 1942; **4.** Chindit operations 1943 & 1944; **5.** Battle of Kohima-Imphal 1944; **6.** 'Capital' & 'Extended Capital' 1944–1945

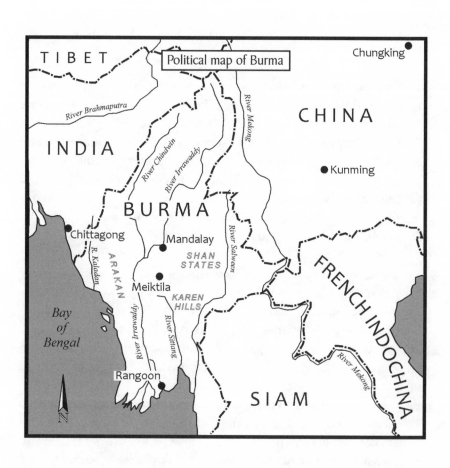

Political map of Burma

Preface

Go, tell the Spartans, stranger passing by
That here, obedient to their laws, we lie.

The famous words of the 300 Spartans at Thermopylae have been brilliantly used as the inspiration for the equally moving motto of the 14th Army in Burma in 1942–45:

When you go home, tell them of us and say
For your tomorrow we gave our today.

The story of the British and Indian soldiers who died in the Burma campaign has been told, partially at least, by many authors, but in my view it would take the combined talents of a Zola, a Dostoevsky and a Céline to do justice to the epic. It is certainly beyond my poor powers adequately to convey the pity and terror of this particular war. Nor is it my intention to provide a blow-by-blow, hour-by-hour slog through the warfare in jungles, mountains and rivers, a military history properly so called. My aim has been more modest: in an example of 'history from above' to tell the story of the campaign through the biography of four larger-than-life personalities: William Slim, Louis Mountbatten, Orde Wingate and Joseph Stilwell. In my more fanciful moments, remembering a childhood love of Alexandre Dumas, I think of them as Burma's 'Four Musketeers'. Mountbatten, the boastful royalist and self-publicist, is certainly the d'Artagnan of the piece; Slim, the soldier and man of integrity, is Athos; Wingate, with his Machiavellianism and vaulting ambition, is an Aramis *redivus*. Stilwell as Porthos, then?

Certainly the match does not work in physical terms, the one cadaverous, the other portly, but there is something about the dogged and ingenuous professional soldier that makes the pairing not entirely inappropriate. Readers may notice that my ultimate estimate of the four warriors in Burma accurately reflects what I imagine would be the consensus view on Dumas's quartet.

As always, I must thank my long-standing and dedicated collaborators, Will Sulkin, publisher at Bodley Head, Tony Whittome, editor at Random House, Paul Taylor, mapmaker, and my wife Pauline, the best critic and in-house editor an author could wish for.

Farnham, Surrey, 2010

In the terrible war in Burma in 1942–45, some 27,000 Anglo-Indian soldiers died out of a total British Commonwealth force of 606,000. Of these, 14,326 (fewer than 5,000 of whom were Britons) fell in battle and the rest succumbed to tropical disease. In all, the casualty roster amounted to 73,909. Japanese casualties (144,000 dead and at least another 56,000 wounded) were proportionately far, far greater, but perhaps the greatest toll of all was sustained by the Burmese civilian population, which may have lost one million dead to warfare, forced labour, Japanese war crimes and, above all, the famine and disease unleashed by the warfare.[1] One owes it to the fallen to try to understand how such a dreadful conflict took place, even within the greater horror of the Second World War. The older atlases, well known to schoolchildren in the 1940s and 1950s, used to divide countries into what they called 'political', with the emphasis on cities and national boundaries, and 'physical', with the emphasis on rivers, mountains, forests and plains. Any overall analysis of Burma is best conducted along such bifurcated lines. Why did the British and their Commonwealth allies – from all parts of India and Nepal, from West Africa and East Africa – plus their allies the Chinese and the Americans, fight the Japanese in Burma? What were the root causes of the conflict? What were the British doing there in the first place? Why did the Commonwealth provide over 600,000 troops to a total Allied force of 690,000 while the Americans contributed just 12,000 and the vastly more populous China only 72,000? What conditions did they fight in? This is an important issue, for many histories of the Burma campaign read almost as though the conflict was going on in Europe, with no appreciation or sensitivity to environment, habitat or milieu. Accordingly, in our 'physical' section some attempt will be made to point up the uniqueness or 'otherness' of Burma.

The war in Burma was part of a wider conflict waged in Asia and the Pacific by the empire of Japan against the Western democracies, principally Britain and the United States. Some historians go so far as to say that this was a geopolitical conflict inevitable once the great voyages of Cook, La Perouse, Vancouver and others opened up the Pacific in the eighteenth century, for such expansion was bound to bring Europe into collision with the mightiest powers in Asia. Others see the opening up of Japan in 1853–54 at gunpoint by the US Commodore Perry as the key event.[2] There had been commercial, political and even religious relations with the West for about one hundred years from the 1540s, but after 1637 Japan withdrew into isolation, with virtually no contact with the outside world for more than two centuries. Humiliated by the 'barbarians' in the 1850s, the Japanese quickly learned from them, overthrew the Shogunate, forged a modern state with modern armies and within 50 years of the end of its two centuries of isolationism had defeated both China and Russia in major wars; the latter victory in particular caused a world-wide sensation. For 20 years from 1902, Japan had a warm relationship with Great Britain and even fought on her side against the Germans in World War I.[3] All this came to an end with the Washington Naval Treaty of 1922, which attempted to rationalise the conflicting goals of US global hegemony with the powerful mood of isolationism following American rejection of the Treaty of Versailles and the League of Nations. The USA scored a great diplomatic triumph, but at a price. The treaty laid down that the ratio of capital warships possessed by the great navies of the world should be in the ratio of 5:5:3 – the United States, Britain and Japan respectively. Moreover, the British were bound by the terms of the treaty to abandon their existing alliance with Japan. The British agreed reluctantly to these steep terms, under the mistaken impression that as a quid pro quo Washington would cancel its war debts. This did not happen, and it occasioned such bitterness that by 1928 both nations were seriously considering the 'impossible' scenario of a war between the two English-speaking democracies. Resentment in Japan was even more grievous. Tokyo felt that it had been humiliated, not just by the infer-ior ratio of capital ships, but because the British had jettisoned its friendship in order to curry favour with their American cousin. Some historians see the 1922 Washington treaty as the decisive moment when Japan clearly began to perceive the United States as its mortal enemy.[4]

Japan was also increasingly outraged by what it considered the humbug of US foreign policy. As early as 1905, President Theodore Roosevelt thought that the way forward in the Far East might be for Japan to have its own Monroe doctrine. Just as the original Monroe doctrine laid down that the Americas were an exclusive sphere of influence for the United States, with the corollary that the USA would not interfere in other continents, so Roosevelt felt it would make sense if Asia was designated an exclusively Japanese sphere of influence.[5] Events in China destroyed this prospect. In 1911, following Japan out of the epoch of backwardness, China overthrew the Manchu dynasty and, under Sun Yat-sen and Yuan Shi-kai, aimed to become a modern state. Instead it became a bearpit of factionalism between warlords. Since 1898 and its intervention in the Philippines, the USA had abandoned the Monroe doctrine's corollary of non-intervention in other hemispheres while still keeping the Americas as its special preserve. The many American economic interests, not to mention their proliferating missionary societies, led Washington to become more and more involved in Chinese affairs. From this would develop the notorious US 'China complex', whereby, against all reason and empirical observation, a friendly China was perceived to be essential to the national security of the United States. The Japanese refused to accept that Washington could intervene massively in Asia, Nippon's own doorstep, while barring all other nations from the Americas. Still less could they accept the duality (which they read as hypocrisy) of economic protectionism, or the 'closed door', in US markets coupled with an insistence on 'open doors' everywhere else. Rocked by economic failure – there was a particularly bad bank collapse in 1926, followed by the nightmare of the Great Depression in 1929 – the Japanese considered their own form of customs union, with a tariff wall to match those introduced in the early 1930s by the USA (the Smoot-Hawley) and the British Empire (Imperial Preference). This was the genesis of the proposed economic autarky of the Greater East Asia Co-Prosperity Sphere. It was economic warfare, at root, that led to Pearl Harbor.[6]

As anger mounted against the perceived selfishness of the Western democracies, right-wing factions in business and the army came to the fore. While it would not be correct to characterise Japan in the 1930s as 'fascist', since the army itself contained a moderate faction and the navy was always dovish, it is undoubtedly true that after 1931 the militaristic hotheads made all the running. Most Western histories begin their account of the origins of the Pacific War with a sudden, unexplained act of aggression when Japan invaded Manchuria in 1931, as if the militarists in Japan had appeared out of nowhere and for no reason; the triggers and precipitants, sadly, were all too obvious, and not helped by an uncompromising and myopic Asian policy pursued by President Franklin Delano Roosevelt after 1933.[7] FDR decided at a very early stage that China was vital to the self-interest of the United States *and* that the emerging strongman in China, Chiang Kai-shek, represented the way of the future. By the 1930s, China was being torn apart by a three-way split: by the Kuomintang (KMT) party, founded by Chiang, allegedly representing liberalism and capitalism; by the plethora of old-style warlords with their private armies; and by the burgeoning Chinese Communist movement led by Mao Tse-tung. Roosevelt, partly out of sentimentality (his grandfather had made a fortune in China) and partly from faulty analysis, always backed Chiang uncritically.[8] In fact Chiang was very far from being the great hope of Western democracy. His true character may be gauged from his treatment of women. He abandoned his first wife, gave the second venereal disease on her wedding night and then discarded her in favour of a match with Soong Mei-ling, the youngest of the fabulously wealthy Soong sisters. Venal, corrupt, cruel and egomaniacal, he had far less control over the warlords than he always boasted of to his American contacts. The warlord Lung Yun of Yunnan, who had made a fortune from opium and ran his own mini-state, complete with a private army and a local currency, always insisted that Chiang's wife come to his headquarters as a hostage before he would consent to meet Chiang.[9]

With FDR so fanatically wedded to China, the Japanese move into Manchuria in 1931 was bound to mean eventual conflict with the USA. The sanest voices in Tokyo all counselled against an unwinnable war with the American colossus, with Admiral Yamamoto and the navy unceasingly vociferous in this regard. Even in the army, strategists divided into 'northerners' and 'southerners'. Northerners tended to be the fanatics of the 'Imperial Way' faction and advocated expanding into Manchuria and beyond, where they would inevitably come into

4

conflict with both the United States and the Soviet Union. The moderates in the 'Control' faction thought this policy was dangerous folly, and advised concentration on South-East Asia.[10] If Japan had been prepared to swallow its anger about US policy in China and simply let it go, it is unlikely that there would ever have been a Pearl Harbor or a need for one. The Greater East Asia Co-Prosperity Sphere, however, inevitably meant conflict with Britain. To achieve autarky and self-sufficiency, Japan needed not only a viable internal market, but also the oil of the Dutch East Indies (later Indonesia) and the rubber and tin of Malaya. That meant war with the British Empire and the powerful Royal Navy. With no other enemies, it would have been well within Tokyo's capability. The United States would never have intervened simply to help the British Empire; it did not do so even when Britain itself seemed likely to surrender to Hitler in 1940. Only when China was brought into the equation did war with the United States loom as a certainty.[11] Simply to safeguard their naval moves against Malaysia and the East Indies, the Japanese would be compelled to attack the USA in the Philippines, in order to pre-empt any US naval intervention. That in turn meant general war with the USA, and the only conceivable theoretical way that even a holding action could be waged was if the US Pacific fleet no longer existed; hence the eventual decision for the attack on Pearl Harbor. Yet instead of abandoning all ambitions in China and concentrating purely on South-East Asia, the 'northerners', in a classic exhibition of fanaticism, doubled their bets by expanding their military adventurism into China. A cause for war was trumped up, and Japanese armies rapidly overran eastern China, capturing Nanking and Shanghai and besmirching their reputation forever in a holocaust of slaughter, rape and genocide. Chiang simply withdrew his government to Chungking in western China, where he sustained himself with massive American aid. Between 1938 and 1941, the war in China quickly became bogged down in a stalemate.[12]

Such were the preconditions for the war that eventually broke out in December 1941, in circumstances too well known to require retelling. Not only was Burma not a primary target in the establishment of the Greater East Asia Co-Prosperity Sphere, it might have been left uninvaded but for the war in China. Closing the Burma Road, which ran from Rangoon to the Chinese border and was thus a primary artery for supplying Chiang in Chungking, soon became a strategic imperative. Thus the Japanese were inveigled into an unnecessary invasion of Burma simply because the hotheads in Tokyo could not leave China well alone. Japan's policy in China meant conflict not just with the Chinese but with the USA and the USSR as well; it was always a state version of hara-kiri. The 'southerners' were right: there should have been exclusive concentration on the Co-Prosperity Sphere in South-East Asia. By pursuing the northern and southern strategies simultaneously, Japan got itself into a situation for which 'overstretch' seems a euphemism. Not even Hitler ended up, as Japan did, fighting the United States, the British Empire, China and the Soviet Union simultaneously. But why were the British in Burma in the first place? As in India, they had acquired the country piecemeal, not quite in a fit of absence of mind, but by getting sucked into a succession of wars – the third and last was against King Thibaw in Upper Burma in 1885. Incorporated into the British Empire, Burma enjoyed a limited level of self-government from 1932 and was fully separated from the administration of India in 1937. After 1937 the country even had three 'prime ministers' (all strongly circumscribed in power by the British overlords), Ba Maw, U Pu and U Saw, all figures who wanted independence and were thus a running sore for the British government.[13] When Churchill as prime minister refused to promise dominion status for Burma in return for fighting the Japanese in the event of an invasion, U Saw made overtures to Tokyo and was promptly interned. The year 1940 indeed saw something of an epidemic of anti-British conspiracies, and the ultra-nationalists like Aung San got out of Burma and made their way to Tokyo, though Ba Maw told his Japanese contacts that the country was not ready for a general insurrection. It was simply the culmination of a decade of riots, civil disobedience and anti-British turmoil; there was even a serious strike by students at the University of Rangoon in 1936.[14] Europeans did not enjoy their postings to Burma. George Orwell, who served in the police there, confessed that his dearest wish was to stick a bayonet in the guts of some canting Buddhist monk.[15] Touring Burma in 1939, H.G. Wells met a party of Burmese nationalists and tried to interest them in his ideas for world government. He found them unpleasant, negative and peevish. When Wells suggested that Burma should help China against the Japanese invasion, he got a dusty answer from his interlocutor. Wells related:

'He cared no more for the freedom of the Chinese than he cared for the future of an ant-hill in Patagonia.'[16]

The British had only themselves to blame. In contrast to the excesses of US economic imperialism – all expatriated profits but no spending on government or administration – they built roads, hospitals and irrigation schemes while trying to educate the locals. Yet in the main they acted like naked exploiters. Their aim was to buy cheap in Asia and sell dear in Europe. They knew nothing of the language, culture or folklore and rarely met the 'natives'. In Burma purely for the money, they were guilty of racism, arrogance, aloofness and greed.[17] Burma was rich in rice, timber, oil and minerals, with particularly valuable oil wells at Yenangyaung and a wolfram mine at Mauchi in the Karen hills that produced one third of the world's wolfram. Yet few of the country's 17 million inhabitants saw any benefits from this. After 1914, foreign capitalists began to rationalise the Burmese economy on a superefficient basis. Between 1914 and 1942 British investment in the country tripled – in oil, timber, mining and rubber.[18] Tens of thousands of entrepreneurs turned rice-growing into an agribusiness in place of the old subsistence farming, but nearly all the landowners were incomers from India. Meanwhile some 300,000 Chinese immigrants cornered most of the middleman and middle-class occupations, especially in medicine and dentistry. The result was that traditional society began to disintegrate, social mobility for the locals was entirely downwards and the crime rate augmented.[19] Increasingly the hated Indians became the targets for violent race riots, especially in Lower Burma, where there was a particularly serious outbreak in 1930–31.[20] The British played their old game of divide and rule. Out of the country's 17 million population, only 10 million were ethnic Burmans. There were also four million Karens, two million Shans and hill tribesmen like the Kachins, Nagas, Mons and Chins; between these and the Burmans the state of relations rarely advanced beyond animosity. There was particularly bad blood between the Burmans and the Karens, dating from the last Burma war. When King Thibaw's defeated troops turned to dacoitry (banditry) after the war, it took 30,000 troops five years to suppress them, and instrumental in bringing the defiant ones under the British yoke were the Karens.[21] In 1939, the armed forces in Burma contained only 472 Burmans as against 3,197 Karens, Chins and Kachins. The reason was clear: the British did not trust the Burmans and considered that in a war with the Japanese, the old Shan states and the hill peoples would be loyal to the Raj while central Burma was likely to be treacherous.[22] The Burmans meanwhile were alienated on at least four different grounds. They could not share the dominant values and ethos of their political masters because of their Buddhism; they loathed the Chinese and the pro-British minorities; they entertained murderous feelings for the Indians; and they had an unquenchable desire for independence. The Japanese, it seemed, might be pushing at an open door.

Naturally, in the real world phenomena interpenetrate so that there can be no hard and fast distinction between the 'political' and the 'physical'. Military operations were profoundly affected by the monsoon, which falls from mid-March to mid-October and generates 200 inches of rainfall annually in the Arakan. The meld between the political and the physical can also be appreciated immediately when one correlates geography with ethnicity. Burma is striated by four great rivers, which all run roughly north–south: the Chindwin, marking the border with India; the Sittang, running along the frontier with Siam (Thailand); the Salween, which rises in China and is effectively the border with that country; and the great Irrawaddy, 1,300 miles long, which links northern Burma with the sea and is navigable as far as Bhamo, 800 miles of its length. Riverine Burma provides one geographical dimension, but another is altitude, linked to climatic zones. A country sharply differentiated into jungle, plains and hills, Burma has many upland regions at 3,000 feet, while the peaks ascend to 8,000 feet in the Chin hills and 12,000 in the so-called Naga hills (really mountains) on the Indian border. Apart from the Karens, whose heartland is the Irrawaddy delta, the highlands boasted all the pro-British minorities so loathed by the majority Burmans. The Kachins, in the most north-easterly corner of the country, have always fascinated anthropologists, while the Shan were of historical importance, as they provided most of the military manpower for the pre-colonial Burmese armies.[23] The differing altitudes in Burma are part of what makes it a paradise for rhododendrons, for different varieties grow in the tropical regions (up to 5,000 feet), the subtropical (5,000–9,000), the temperate (9,000–10,500) and the alpine (above 10,500); above 9,000 feet, apart from scrub, bamboo and rhododendron largely have the field to themselves.[24] Burma, with 7,000 species of flora, including

8

1,200 tree species, has always been a Shangri-La for botanists. Teak, acacia, bamboo, ironwood, mangrove, betel palm, *Michelia champaca* and coconut – with oak and pine in the north – are the most commonly encountered varieties, but one botanist found *all* the following in a single forest: oak, chestnut, maple, rhododendron, birch, cherry, laurel and magnolia, plus genera known only to botanists or enthusiasts such as *Sorbus, Rhodoleia, Illicium, Eriobotrya, Daphniphyllum, Schima, Zanthoxylum, Helicia, Bucklandia,* [*Eriobotrya*] *Acacia julibrissin* (a rare genus containg just one species), *Millingtonia hortensis* and *Manglietia caveania.*[25]

Soldiers serving in Burma in 1942–45 tended to be more interested in the 300 mammal species. Apart from elephants, tigers and leopards, found in all regions, there were the fauna encountered almost exclusively in Upper Burma – rhinoceroses, wild buffalo, wild boar, deer, antelope, tapirs, monkeys, gibbons and flying foxes. It was only those among the officer classes who had the leisure and financial surplus for ornithology who took an interest in the 1,000 species of birds.[26] Even so, it is remarkable that the fauna of Burma plays such a small part in the memoirs, reminiscences, anecdotes and autobiographies of those who fought here. As the first biographer of General Orde Wingate (of whom we shall hear much more) commented: 'In reading of 77 Brigade, or of events in Burma in 1944, one may be surprised at how little mention there is of perils from jungle animals in this country containing elephants, rhinoceros, tigers, panthers, leopards and snakes in abundance.'[27] Even the mentions there are tend to subsist at the level of imagination rather than reality, as witness this statement from a secret agent undergoing jungle training in Ceylon: 'Every tree, every creeper, every leaf had its message. We could interpret jungle sounds; we could identify jungle smells. We developed the quivering awareness of the beasts and the reptiles of the jungle, for were we not sharing this tangled luxuriance with wild elephants, rhinoceroses, man-eating tigers, buffaloes, deer, monkeys, cobras, chameleons and hamadryads twelve to fifteen feet long?'[28] The relative absence of wild-animal stories in the autobiographical literature can be explained in various ways. There was in some officers' messes the feeling that to mention the jungle and its inhabitants was somehow infra dig, not quite the thing for a gentleman.[29] Then there is the obvious consideration that many animals dangerous to man tend to give him a wide berth even in peacetime conditions; with the blast of war, the stutter of machine guns and the din of exploding bombs and napalm around the advancing armies, it can well be imagined that an even greater distance was kept. Visitors to Burma frequently comment (complain) that although the numbers of tigers are large, they are rarely seen.[30] J.H. ('Elephant Bill') Williams, who knew Burmese wildlife better than most, thought that in the 1920s and 1930s there were 'too many' tigers and leopards in the jungle.[31] Studies done during the Vietnam War of 1965–75 tend to indicate that in conditions of jungle war, tiger populations tend to become even larger, as there are so many dead bodies to feed on. Yet sightings in the war zone remained rare. One of Wingate's men did have an unexpected encounter while relieving himself in the jungles of Saugur while the Chindits were training there. He bolted at high speed and told his boss about the experience. Wingate rounded on him: 'Why did you run away? Don't you know that when you find yourself face to face with a tiger, all you have to do is to stare him out.'[32] It was fortunate indeed that the man did not put Wingate's daft theory to the test.

The animal the troops saw most of in their campaigning was the elephant, invaluable for carrying heavy loads, rolling logs and other onerous duties. At the start of the Burma war it was estimated that there were about 20,000 domestic elephants and 6,000 wild ones, though the wartime mortality of the domestic ones was terrific, and by the end of hostilities only 2,500 were left alive.[33] J.H. Williams listed many of the attributes that made this behemoth so useful. Apart from snakebite, it had nothing to fear from other creatures, for not even a crocodile or a tiger could make any impression on an adult tusker. Even though the occasional elephant did succumb to the venom of a snake, they were unfazed by the reptiles and seemed unconcerned if they appeared.[34] The one animal the elephants disliked intensely was the dog, but the canine irritant in turn was reduced by the huge dog mortality, as they fell victim to tigers, bears, snakes and, especially, leopards, whose favourite food they were. Also disliked by elephants were ponies and mules. Mules were indispensable, but ponies were rapidly phased out, not just because of the elephant hostility but also because they became the prey of preference for tigers.[35] The other wild creature the troops saw most of was the Burmese rock python, a huge constrictor, usually in the 17–23 foot range (though even larger ones have been recorded). Python became one of the favourite dishes of Wingate's Chindits when they were living off the land in the jungle. The snakes seemed ubiquitous, and on one occasion Wingate was addressing his officers in the mess hall when one slithered in at the back; inevitably, the Bible-punching Wingate immediately used the incident as an excuse to digress on to the story of Adam and Eve and the serpent.[36] Large groups of soldiers treated pythons with justifiable disdain, although a one-on-one encounter would not have been so pleasant. 'Elephant Bill' Williams told a story about an acquaintance who tried to adopt a 17-foot Burmese rock python as a pet but then got a nasty shock when the pet tried to constrict the owner.[37] This is in line with other lore about these serpents. The psychologist C.G. Jung claimed that zoology had taught him one thing: rapport with all animals is possible except with reptiles. He cited the case of a man who reared a python and used to feed it by hand until one day, without warning, the constrictor wrapped itself round him and nearly killed him; it loosened its coils only when hacked to death by the man's friend.[38]

When it came to poisonous snakes, no one could afford to be so insouciant as men habitually were around pythons. Although fewer than 200 of the roughly 2,500 kinds of snakes in the world are dangerous to man, unfortunately many of them are found in Burma, which, for a country its size, has probably the largest concentration of venomous serpents in the world, except perhaps for Tanzania.[39] An estimated 10,000 people a year still die of snakebite in the modern Myanmar. An early survey by a colonial civil servant contains some particularly interesting statistics. In 1902 in Burma official records showed just 73 people killed by dangerous mammals, but 1,123 by snakes. A census of cattle revealed that 4,194 had been killed by tigers, 1,386 by leopards, 28 by wolves and six by bears but 4,986 by serpents – which meant that more cattle had succumbed to snakes in Burma than in all the rest of India (Burma was then administered as part of India).[40] The most spectacular of the elapid snakes was the hamadryad or king cobra, the largest venomous snake in the world, which can attain a length of 18 feet. Usually the king cobra avoids contact with humans but sometimes it is drawn into villages in pursuit of its favourite prey, the rat snake. Elephant Bill Williams told a story of a colleague who was chased by a hamadryad and confessed he was sceptical about the story until two years later he himself was chased in the very same place; he concluded it must have been a breeding location for king cobras. Magwe was another place reported by British troops as one of their haunts.[41] The only thing to be said in favour of the king cobra was that its diet was almost exclusively other snakes, including the ordinary cobra, so that its net effect was probably as a human ally. Far more dangerous than the fabled hamadryad were the 'normal' snakes, especially the monocled cobra and the Russell's viper. John 'Scarsdale Jack' Newkirk, a flyer with the American Volunteer Group, found and killed a seven-foot cobra in his barracks one day. Even more feared was the Russell's viper. This serpent had the peculiarity that the venom of the Burmese variety differed from that of the Thailand species, which in turn was different from the Indian and the Ceylonese variants. This made the preparation of an effective antitoxin and the provision of effective treatment fiendishly difficult.[42] Yet even the dreaded Russell's viper paled into a relative danger alongside the krait. No more than a foot long, the krait in all its species is supremely deadly; the banded variant is known as the 'two step' because that is as far as a man will walk after being bitten.[43] The peculiar horror of the krait was that it could hide in the dust, in a man's shoe or indeed in any unexpected nook anywhere; a red, yellow and black krait was found inside the radio set of a member of the 4th Royal West Kent Regiment.[44] General William Slim, the military genius of the Burma campaign, had his own close encounter with this tiny nightmare in January 1945: 'The Japanese had left behind a number of booby traps which were disconcerting, but my chief fright came from the snakes which abounded in the piles of rubble. They seemed specially partial to the vicinity of my war room which lacked a roof but had a good concrete floor. It was my practice to visit the War Room every night before going to bed, to see the latest situation map. I had once when doing so nearly trodden on a krait, the most deadly of all small snakes.'[45] The American general Joseph Stilwell was also troubled and wrote to his wife in July 1944: 'The damn snakes are starting to appear. One got into the office and one tried to get into my tent. Now I look around before I put my bare feet on the floor and shake my shoes before I put them on.'[46]

The danger from snakes was real enough, but this does not seem to have been enough to satisfy some lurid imaginations. During the final stages of the campaign to take the Ramree islands, in February 1945, the British trapped about a thousand Japanese, cutting off their escape routes to the east. In a typical samurai decision, the commander decided not to surrender but to take his troops out by an unblocked route across ten miles of mangrove swamps. It was a nightmarish scenario because these swamps were essentially acres of thick and impenetrable forest, dark even in the daytime, just miles of deep black mud, infested with snakes, mosquitoes, scorpions and other malign insects. Nine hundred men went into the mangrove swamp, but many were already dying or wounded and most were suffering from malaria, dysentery or dehydration. Only about 500 emerged at the other side; the losses were about what one might have expected in such a situation. That was not good enough for the sensationalists and mythmakers, who concocted a wild and improbable story that except for 20 men taken prisoner by the British, all the others were killed by crocodiles.[47] It is well known that the best way of telling a lie is to tell the truth, and the story has a certain specious plausibility, for the estuarine or saltwater crocodile, which can attain a length of 20 feet, is both a known man-eater and an opportunistic killer.[48] Many who saw these great saurians basking on the banks of the Irrawaddy shuddered with horror, and the thought of death by crocodile is one of mankind's abiding nightmares. The following purports to be an account of what happened on the night of 18 February 1945, as the Japanese troops hacked their way through the mangrove swamp: 'That night was the most horrible that any member of the ML [motor launch] crews ever experienced. The scattered rifle shots in the pitch black swamp punctured by the screams of wounded men crushed in the jaws of huge reptiles, and the blurred worrying sound of spinning crocodiles made a cacophony of hell that has rarely been duplicated on earth. At dawn the vultures arrived to clean up what the crocodiles had left . . . Of about 1,000 Japanese soldiers that entered the swamps of Ramree, only about twenty were left alive.'[49]

This story, which was solemnly entered as fact in the *Guinness Book of Records* as the greatest ever human loss to dangerous animals, offends every single canon of historical verifiability. We are told that the observer sitting parked at the edge of the swamp in a motor launch was one Bruce Wright, a naturalist, but diligent research has turned up no trace of him nor of the book or journals in which this account was written. As in all urban myths, close investigation involves one in a vicious circle, where one comes back to the same, single, unsubstantiated, anonymous and unverifiable source. So much for provenance. What about internal coherence? Are we seriously to believe that Japanese firepower, which tore such holes in British tanks and armour, was helpless against crocodiles? That none of the Japanese who failed to emerge from the swamp was hit by British strafing fire or bitten by snakes, or succumbed to dehydration and disease? Most of all, there is a simple zoological problem. If 'thousands of crocodiles' were involved in the massacre, as in the urban (jungle) myth, how had these ravening monsters survived before and how were they to survive later? The ecosystem of a mangrove swamp, with its exiguous mammal life, simply would not have permitted the existence of so many saurians before the coming of the Japanese (animals are not exempt from the laws of overpopulation and starvation).[50] Finally there is the issue of external evidence. The official British military records for the occupation of Ramree contain no corroboration or even mention of the story, Japanese survivors of Ramree knew nothing of it, and there is no record in the oral tradition of the Ramree islanders themselves.[51] The indefatigable professional researcher W.O.G. Potts and other interested parties conducted minute investigations into the story, interviewing elderly Ramree islanders, Japanese survivors of Ramree and members of the Anglo-Indian armed services. All of them denied that any such incident took place.[52] We are left, then, with two possibilities. Either nothing remotely like the horror described by 'Bruce Wright' ever took place. Or, more plausibly, a few of the Japanese wounded may have fallen prey to some saltwater crocodiles (certainly not 'thousands'). What we confront here is not an authentic wartime memory but a version of the Bermuda Triangle syndrome or a variant of the Angel of Mons legend transmogrified in diabolic fashion.[53]

Stories like the Ramree crocodile 'massacre' or an overemphasis on the menace from poisonous snakes carry the danger that the real experiences of the fighting men in Burma may be distorted. Overwhelmingly, the memoir and anecdotal evidence suggests that what the troops feared most were leeches and mosquitoes and insects of all kinds. When the British irregulars the Chindits were marching north from Mogaung on 9–10 June 1944 through marshes and mud, what oppressed them was not snakes or crocodiles but large vicious striped mosquitoes, biting flies and leeches.[54] Yet even with all these natural hazards and afflictions, not all the British who served in Burma perceived it as a green hell. The hill stations were especially prized as oases, and before the great battle there in 1944, Imphal was viewed as something of a paradise, with its cornucopia of plant and bird life. Peach trees, oaks, teak, wild banana and bamboo mingled with irises, jasmines, marigolds, lilacs, primulas and asters. Wagtails, pigeons, orioles, parrots, peafowl, pheasants, crows, herons and paddy birds competed for space on the lake and its islets with snipe, ducks and geese.[55] In January 1945, the Gurkhas' own newspaper tried to put the beauty and terror of Burma into proper balance:

> Much has been written on the horrors of Burma warfare, of rains and leeches and snakes, of unseen enemies and deadly ambushes. This time we experienced none of these things. The Burma hills in January are cool and fresh, and when in the sunset the hillsides turn to all the greens and browns of an English woodland in autumn, their beauty is unsurpassed ... Who can convey on paper the charm of the little pagodas, standing in clusters large and small, guarded on their hill tops by the chinthes, and with their tinkling, silver-voiced wind bells that never stay silent? How clean the villages are, so unlike those of India, where the sanitary arrangements are nil and a circus of hawks wheel above. The livestock seemed in first-class condition, small sleek cattle and poultry that would rival the pride of English farmyards. It was indeed delightful to trek through in those January days.[56]

Given the perennial motif in Japanese poetry of the juxtaposition of beauty and death, it could be argued that warfare in Burma had a certain organic functionality to the homeland culture. Their successes in the early months of the war certainly seemed to support that view.

The man who would later be hailed in some quarters as the greatest general of the twentieth century had obscure and unpromising beginnings. This, coupled with his unpretentious and self-deprecating manner, often made people think he had risen from the ranks. The truth is a little more complex. Born in 1891, the son of a struggling Birmingham ironmonger, William Slim won a scholarship to a grammar school and showed academic promise, but the family's financial plight forced him to leave school early. He began as a trainee schoolteacher in a primary school in the Birmingham slums. Undoubtedly his later famous rapport with the ordinary soldier and his instinctive understanding of his abilities and limits derived from that experience, which gave him insights into the life and mentality of the working class most conventionally educated officers could not dream of. Faced with boys who were routinely thrashed and brutalised by their fathers, and for whom violence was almost a way of life, Slim tried kindness and affection, which he found worked wonders. But he always had to temper this with firm discipline; he was shrewd enough to realise that the slum kids would eat a 'do-gooder' alive and were likely to interpret too much compassion as weakness. Exhausted by the emotional toll of such a tightrope act, he became a clerk in an engineering works.[1] At 23 he was in a dead end, with no apparent way out. War was his saviour, then as always. In 1914 he applied to enrol in the Birmingham University Officers' Training Corps, despite not being a student at the university. The urgent demands of wartime meant that the usual rules were waived, and in August 1914 he was commissioned as a temporary second lieutenant in the Royal Warwickshire Regiment. The following year he was badly wounded at Gallipoli, but fought his way back to fitness through sheer willpower. He was then granted a regular commission as second lieutenant in the West India Regiment, reputedly the only one in the British army where an officer could live on his pay. In October 1916 he joined another battalion of the Royal Warwickshires in Mesopotamia, where General F.S. Maude was trying to rebuild British strength after the shattering defeat by the Turks at Kut the year before. Promoted full lieutenant in March 1917 and wounded a second time, he was awarded the Military Cross in February 1918 and given the temporary rank of captain.[2]

Ever since Gallipoli, Slim had nursed an ambition to join the Gurkhas, and after the war he got his wish. In November 1918 he was given the temporary rank of major in the 6th Gurkha Rifles, formally promoted captain and transferred to the British Indian Army. Even for the chosen ones of Sandhurst, military promotion was painfully slow in the interwar period, and most of Slim's next 20 years were spent in routine administration or education. In 1926 (the year he married his wife Aileen), he was sent to the Indian staff college at Quetta. It took him until 1933 to reach the formal rank of major, though he had been breveted with this rank before. His performance at the staff college led to appointments first to army headquarters in Delhi, then to staff college at Camberley back in England, where he taught from 1934 to 1937. In 1938, at the age of 47, he was promoted lieutenant colonel and given command of the 2nd Battalion, 7th Gurkha Rifles. So far he had enjoyed a steady though far from spectacular career. Money worries were never absent, to the point where he moonlighted as a fiction writer under the pseudonym of Anthony Mills, churning out adventure stories obviously influenced by his early reading of tales of Victorian military glory, but also evincing a shrewd notion of human nature and many shafts of dry wit.[3] In June 1939, he was promoted colonel with the temporary rank of brigadier and appointed head of the Senior Officers' School at Belgaum, India. On the outbreak of the war he was given command of the Indian 10th Brigade of the 5th Infantry Division (India) and sent to the Sudan, where he took part in the campaign to liberate Abyssinia (Ethiopia) from the Italians. He was wounded for a third time in the fighting in Eritrea during an air attack; the surgeon removed not just a large bullet but chunks of Turkish ammunition he had carried with him since Gallipoli. For this and other exploits he came to the notice of General Archibald Wavell, then commanding in the Middle East. Wavell gave him the acting rank of major general, and in this capacity he commanded forces in the Anglo-Iraq war of 1941 (the insurgency of Rashid Ali), the Syria-Lebanon campaign and the invasion of Persia (Iran). Because the commander of the 10th Indian Division fell sick, it was a stroke of luck for Slim to lead it against the Vichy French in Syria, and he acquitted himself well and was mentioned twice in dispatches in 1941. When Wavell, since transferred to Burma, was looking for a corps commander with fighting spirit, he remembered Slim and sent for him.[4]

To make sense of this development, we have to rewind the historical reel and glance for a moment at Slim's boss, Archibald Wavell. His career had been very different from Slim's, starting with his privileged educational background at Winchester and Sandhurst. Commissioned into the Black Watch in 1901, he fought in the Boer war and then saw service in India until 1908. Seconded to staff college in 1909, he made an unusual career move in 1911 when he was appointed military observer to the Russian army for a year and took the time to learn Russian. After being staff officer at the War Office and promoted captain, he became brigade major of the 9th Infantry Brigade and in 1915 was wounded at the second battle of Ypres, losing his left eye.[5] Having won the Military Cross, he was made acting lieutenant colonel and once again sent as liaison officer to the Russian army, this time in the Caucasus (1916–17). In 1917 he was liaison officer with the Egyptian Expeditionary Force. After a short spell at the Supreme War Council at Versailles (between January and March 1918), he was appointed temporary brigadier general and sent out to Palestine, where he came heavily under the influence of General Edmund Allenby. Wavell and Allenby were both intellectual officers, lovers of poetry and literature, and Wavell admired his boss to the point where he would later write his biography.[6] Promoted full colonel in 1922, Wavell held a number of general staff appointments and by 1933 had been promoted major general. Having previously been identified as a Russian specialist, he was now regarded as an expert in the Middle East and was sent out to Palestine in 1937 as General Officer Commanding British Forces in Palestine and Transjordan. Promoted lieutenant general in 1938, after a short spell as General Officer Commanding the United Kingdom Southern Command, in 1939 he was promoted to full general and given command in the Middle East.

He made his name in the wider world by defeating the Italians in East Africa in 1940–41, though heavily outnumbered, but fell foul of Churchill when he showed himself reluctant to intervene immediately in the Rashid Ali rebellion in Iraq.[7] Churchill at once replaced him as commander in the Middle East with Claude Auchinleck and gave him the consolation prize of commander-in-chief in India (July 1941).

Burma in 1941 was a neglected area even within a neglected wider military sector. Although India was responsible for Burma's defence administration, operationally it came under the control of the British Commander-in-Chief Far East, Sir Robert Brooke-Popham, who had been appointed three months before Wavell became the military supremo in India. Wavell's position in Burma was ticklish, since he was in a particularly impossible situation within a generally impossible one. Brooke-Popham immediately saw the lamentable state of defence in both Singapore and Malaya and asked for reinforcements, but Churchill, preoccupied with the war in North Africa, made it clear that none would be forthcoming.[8] In early 1941, Churchill was adamant that a Japanese attack on Singapore was chimerical, but the truth was that Britain could not afford war with Japan and hoped that the totemic power of the British Empire and the Royal Navy would scare the yellow race away. Meanwhile the Foreign Office backed US policy on China, and in particular the idea of supplying China via the Burma Road, as a *pis aller* for a realistic policy. The Americans paid back this timid approach by isolationism, dislike of the British Empire and suspicion of being gulled by the 'Limeys'.[9] Faced by official myopia, chronic shortages in every area and a confused chain of command, Wavell returned to London in September 1941 and requested that Burma be placed under his operational command. The then Chief of the Imperial Staff Sir John Dill, who was later to prove the linchpin of the Anglo-American alliance in Washington, told him bluntly that British support for the American line in China and the consequent need to assuage the susceptibilities of Generalissimo Chiang Kai-shek, meant that Burma would have to remain under operational control of Singapore.[10] This was part of the deep subtext that would always bedevil Anglo-American cooperation in Burma. For the USA, China was always the priority; for the British, it was India, and both sides regarded Burma as a kind of subculture to their own predilections and aspirations.

It must be emphasised that Wavell largely shared the complacent view of likely Japanese intentions in the British-held parts of South-East Asia. The General Officer Commanding Burma, Major General D.K. McLeod, discounted a possible threat from Siam (Thailand), while the Governor-General of Burma, Sir Reginald Dorman-Smith, believed that if the Japanese invaded his territory, the Burmese would rise up against them as one man.[11] After a visit to Rangoon in October 1941, Wavell convinced himself that these were correct judgements: indeed his optimism went further and he stated that not only would the Japanese not invade Malaya, but that if they did, they would 'get it in the neck'.[12] His concern was chiefly administrative. He signalled Dill that since the defence of Burma was not vital to that of Malaya but was vital to the defence of India, it made no sense for Burma to continue to be under the operational command of Brooke-Popham; this arrangement was 'the cardinal mistake'. Perceptions changed rapidly after Pearl Harbor. On 10 December, Prime Minister Winston Churchill sent Wavell a signal, finally putting Burma under his command and advising him: 'You must now look East', meaning that Malaya was in danger. On 15 December, Churchill further signalled Wavell to expect a Japanese invasion of Burma.[13] He was appalled and alarmed by the sensational gains made by the Japanese in just over a week since the 'day of infamy' in Hawaii. US airpower in the Philippines had been destroyed by the raid on Clark airbase; the pride of the Royal Navy, the *Repulse* and the *Prince of Wales*, had been sunk off Singapore; Hong Kong's fall was imminent; and the Japanese were already making major inroads in Malaya, where Penang fell to them on 16 December. The sole consolation for Wavell was that the lacklustre Brooke-Popham was replaced by the more energetic General Henry Pownall as Commander-in-Chief, Far East. Yet there was not much Wavell could do apart from general exhortation. He flew to Calcutta to meet Pownall on 18 December, then, not having any reinforcements to offer Rangoon, he flew down and tried to impress the senior personnel there with his force of personality, as 'compensation' for lack of any clearer ideas.[14]

From Rangoon Wavell flew to Chungking for what would be a disastrous meeting with Chiang Kai-shek. Wavell was scarcely charmed: Chiang, he wrote, 'was not a particularly impressive figure at first sight: he speaks no English but makes clucking noises like a friendly hen when greeting one. Madame [his wife] of course speaks perfect English. We had long discussions until midnight.'[15] Chiang offered two Chinese 'armies' (roughly equivalent to a weak British division) to help Burma, but Wavell turned down the offer. Quite apart from scepticism (warranted) as to whether Chiang would make good on his offer, Wavell did not want the Chinese in Burma for a number of reasons. Their presence might possibly encourage the nationalists in India; they might revive their ancient claims to parts of Burma, and anyway, how could he be sure of getting rid of them; there was certainly not enough food and transport in the country to accommodate foreign troops; the Chinese were deeply unpopular in Burma where they were viewed both as the exploitative 'Jews of the East' and, by their investment in banking and shipping, as supporters of British imperialism. Most of all, though, Wavell was still convinced that the Japanese would never invade Burma, since they were already overstretched in Malaya and the Philippines.[16] Wavell's demurral caused grave offence. Chiang construed the refusal as loss of 'face' for him and raged in private. He was anyway always deeply anti-Britain both as the major power in South-East Asia and as the nation that had historically humbled China in the Opium Wars. He suspected that Pearl Harbor would be used by the British as an excuse to pre-empt the US Lend-Lease materiel being routed through Burma.[17] His anger was compounded when Wavell told him that the British would indeed need all the Lend-Lease supplies reaching Burma and he would therefore not be sending any on to Chungking. Wavell reckoned that Chiang would be grateful if the British kept the Japanese out of Burma for him, but failed to realise that part of the point of Lend-Lease for Chiang was personal enrichment. It was a notable non-meeting of minds. The Americans in China meanwhile were gravely disappointed and feared that Wavell's action would encourage Chiang to make a separate peace with the Japanese and thus release the 15–20 Japanese divisions bogged down in China for action elsewhere.[18] It was somehow symbolic of the way things were going in general that Wavell flew back to Rangoon and landed there on Christmas Day in the middle of a raging air battle.

When news of the Chiang–Wavell contretemps reached Washington, there was predictable consternation. President Franklin Roosevelt had a genuine 'complex' about China: he regarded it both as part of the

US sphere of influence and as an indispensable means of promoting American hegemony in the Far East, despite a wealth of evidence that Chiang was both unable and unwilling to deliver these particular goods. In vain did General George Brett, the US commander in Chungking, who shared Wavell's low opinion of Chinese capability, point out that Wavell had in the end accepted the offer of one Chinese division, provided that all supply and commisariat were done from China. In vain did the British argue that Chiang's Chinese were mere dogs-in-the-manger: they had an inexhaustible hunger for Lend-Lease materiel but never used it effectively. Meanwhile in Burma, matters were becoming explosive. Chinese supply officers there refused to hand over the Lend-Lease supplies to the British and were threatened with confiscation in return. A furious Chiang, in what he thought was a studied insult but which probably passed Wavell by, offered the British 20 machine guns from his store in Rangoon. In Chungking he refused to see the British ambassador and threatened total non-cooperation with the British Empire. At a deeper level, Chiang was alarmed at the rapid reverses suffered by the Anglo-Saxons in the first month of war with Japan, and even more so by Roosevelt's adoption of a 'Europe First' grand strategy, which appeared to sideline Asia.[19] Roosevelt's military chief of staff, General George C. Marshall, became seriously concerned. He shared the President's view that Chiang might pull out of the war, and that if China collapsed all Asia would defect to the Japanese. Roosevelt considered that humouring Chiang was the number one priority in the Pacific war, for a Chinese defeat might well lead to the Japanese conquest of India, and then would follow the nightmare scenario of a German–Japanese link-up somewhere in the Middle East, cutting off the Soviet Union completely.[20] Quite unfairly, both Marshall and Roosevelt saw Wavell as a blinkered blimp and determined to bring him to heel by studied Machiavellianism. The first step was to lean on Churchill to get him to agree to force Wavell into a kind of fusion with Chiang. To the considerable anger of the new Chief of the Imperial General Staff, Alan Brooke (later Viscount Alanbrooke), Churchill agreed to the establishment of a new command, to be known as ABDACOM (American, British, Dutch, Australian and Chinese Command).[21] At first it was proposed to 'sweeten' Chiang by offering him command of the entire body, but Roosevelt soon had second thoughts. Knowing Chiang's relish for grandiose titles, he appointed him Supreme Allied Commander of the Chinese Theatre (which he effectively was anyway) and made Wavell Supreme Commander of ABDACOM.

There was little Wavell could do once Churchill had agreed to the American proposal, but he must have seen that he was being offered a genuine mission impossible. After all, Japanese triumph in this precise area was all but complete. Burma was included in the new command, which stretched 5,000 miles in a crescent to New Guinea – a line three times as long as the Russian front. ABDACOM was divided into three sectors: Burma and Malaya; the archipelago of the Dutch East Indies (modern Indonesia); and the south-eastern islands extending down to Australasia. Only in Burma was there a realistic chance of defence even on paper. ABDACOM was formally set up on 15 January 1942 and from its inception suffered from predictable problems: the Dutch were peeved about not having been consulted; the Australians, becoming increasingly anti-British, were worried about the possible invasion of their homeland and having their forces deployed so far from home; while the US naval commander in South-East Asia, Admiral Thomas Hart, resented having to take orders from a 'Limey'.[22] Yet Wavell did all that could reasonably be expected of him. He replaced the overcomplacent commander in Burma, General Donald Kenneth McLeod, with General Thomas Hutton, but this was a poor appointment, as Hutton was no fighting general. Much of January was taken up with a futile attempt to shore up the fighting spirits of senior personnel in Singapore. None of the troika there was impressive. The commanding officer, General Arthur Percival, was out of his depth (he was said to be so 'wet' you could shoot snipe off him), as were the governor, Sir Shenton Thomas, and the colonial secretary, Stanley Jones.[23] Wavell should have had the determination to sack all three and impose martial law, but he let matters drift. As is well known, the British defence of Singapore was conducted on the assumption that any attack must come from the sea, for the landward route through jungle was 'impenetrable'. Wavell was too busy in January 1942 to challenge this absurd assumption, for he spent much of the time in a plane, flying between Java, Malaya, Singapore and Calcutta, almost as if mere energy might make up for military planning.[24]

The British defeat in Singapore on 15 February 1942 and the loss of this jewel of the British Empire in the East, together with the surrender of 100,000 able-bodied British troops, does not form any part of our story, but it clearly demonstrated that supreme command of ABDACOM was a poisoned chalice. Wavell duly informed the American Pacific commander General MacArthur that it would fall to him henceforth to keep open the supply link to Australia while he concentrated on Burma. After handing over Java to the Dutch on 25 February, Wavell returned to India. ABDACOM was wound up, military responsibility for Burma reverted to India and Wavell took the blame for failure in South-East Asia even though halting the Japanese there, with exiguous airpower, was beyond Allied capability.[25] In any case Wavell had his hands full elsewhere, for despite the sanguine forecasts he and others had made, the Japanese launched their attack on Burma in mid-January, far earlier than anyone expected. The rotten apple in this barrel was Siam (Thailand). After initial resistance when a Japanese invasion force landed, the Thais signed a treaty with Japan, agreeing to become her ally.[26] This allowed Japanese forces to mass on the Siam/Burma border. General Shojiro Iida had clear-cut aims: first seize Rangoon and Mandalay, then the oilfields at Yenangyaung. Wavell was wrong-footed by the speed of the Japanese advance and in any case had guessed wrongly at their strategy. He had expected that any Japanese thrust into Burma would come in the centre of the country via the Shan states and had put his main line of defence there. He ordered General Hutton to place his fighting formations well forward so that all possible approaches could be pre-empted.[27] But when the attack came in the south, Wavell was seriously alarmed. He flew to Rangoon, recalled the 7th Armoured Brigade from Singapore and advised the commander of the Rangoon garrison, Major General Sir John Smyth, who commanded 7,000 men of 17th Division. Unfortunately these were raw and unreliable troops, with one half of the division having been trained for desert warfare and the other half not trained or equipped at all. Facing them now were 18,000 crack Japanese troops.[28]

The Japanese began their campaign against Rangoon with a series of 'softening-up' air raids on the Burmese capital. The first one, on 23 December 1941, killed 1,250 souls (and a further 600 subsequently died of their wounds), largely because there was no civil defence or air-raid precautions. By the time of the third raid, the casualties were down to 60 killed and 40 wounded, mainly because large numbers of the population had already fled.[29] When the invasion proper began in mid-January, the first Japanese target was Moulmein, a town with a population of 50,000 on the western bank of the Salween river. Wavell was reasonably confident of halting the enemy on the approaches to Rangoon, since the way was barred by three rivers, the Salween, the Bilin and the Sittang. Smyth and his troops were well dug in and there was much wild talk about making Moulmein a second Tobruk, although the civilian population deserted in droves, not willing to await the outcome.[30] But the omens were scarcely propitious: the British wildly understimated their foe; Hutton and Smyth did not get on; and Wavell was rarely available to advise and conciliate his warring commanders, since at this stage he was still shuttling around South-East Asia as commander of the ill-fated ABDACOM. The Japanese began by outwitting their opponents, infiltrating the jungle with small parties. Displaying astonishing mobility, they used bicycles or animals for transport, going lightly equipped with small arms, dressed in trainers (sneakers), shirts and gym shorts and carrying iron rations (four days' supply in a single pack). The British by contrast moved around in trucks, with full equipment and large weapons, and were kitted out with helmets, gas masks, heavy boots, tinned food, etc, etc. Some observers later remarked that they made the very same mistakes the redcoats had made against the American colonists in the war of 1775–83.

The fighting around Moulmein was bitter but one-sided.[31] To Wavell's disgust, the Japanese rolled up their opponents with surprising ease, and by 30 January the defenders had been driven out in humiliating circumstances. Wavell stormed down to the front and raged at the commanders of the luckless 2nd Burma Brigade who had just lost Moulmein. 'Take back all you have lost,' he thundered.[32] Hutton promised him he would hold Martaban to the west of the Salween. On 10–11 February the Japanese, reinforced by two new divisions of 18,000 men, crossed the Salween in force and quickly outflanked Martaban. In danger of being encircled, Smyth asked Hutton for permisson to retreat again, which was reluctantly granted. In London, Alanbrooke fulminated at the endless stories of British defeat. Such a lack of fighting spirit was, he declared, incomprehensible, but if it continued, the British would deserve to lose their empire.[33] The second river, the Bilin, proved no obstacle at all, since it was at low water and easily fordable. Smyth retreated all the way to the Sittang and pleaded with Hutton for reinforcements. Hutton, though, at this juncture came close to mental collapse. In desperation he signalled that his position was impossible, that he was overstretched and that he desperately needed two things: a corps commander to conduct operations and a liaison team to deal with the intractable Chinese. Incredibly, he received no answer to the signal, for its recipient, Wavell, had just sustained one of those bizarre accidents in which the careers of Allied commanders in Burma abounded. On 11 February, he got out of his car on the wrong side and toppled over a barbed-wire sea wall, sustaining serious injuries. He was in hospital for four days in Java, incommunicado.[34]

By the time he was on his feet again, more terrible news had come in. Smyth had suffered a devastating defeat on the banks of the Sittang, in a bloody battle that seemed to confirm the military superiority of the Japanese at all levels. In despair, Wavell signalled Churchill: 'We have got to fight REPEAT fight these Japs sometime somewhere. Burma is not ideal geographically but represents almost our last chance to show the Japs and the world that we do mean to fight.'[35] The disaster at Sittang made Rangoon's evacuation inevitable, and the British carried it out in stages. By 24 February the capital was a ghost town, as the Burmese vanished en masse and the Indian police abandoned their posts. Everywhere there were scenes of chaos as law and order broke down. Criminals and lunatics, released from their cells, roamed the streets, looting and raping.[36] Wavell, returning from convalescence, took a swift revenge on Hutton and Smyth, both of whom he held responsible for the recent disasters. Smyth was replaced by Major General David Cowan on 1 March, while Hutton suffered an even greater humiliation. It was announced that he was to be replaced but that until further notice he would be the new man's chief of staff. Churchill had never had full confidence in Wavell ever since the Iraq affair in 1941, and now he suspected him of not being on top of the situation in Burma. He announced that the new corps commander in charge of operations, under Wavell, would be his favourite general Harold Alexander. Maybe in response to the implied rebuke, Wavell's normal urbanity deserted him and he lost his temper in public at a reception, accusing all and sundry of incompetence.[37]

'Alex', as he was generally known, arrived in Burma on 4 March.

A child of privilege, educated at Harrow and Sandhurst, he was commissioned in the Irish Guards and wounded four times during the 1914–18 war on the Western Front. A great favourite with the men, he held a trench against sustained machine-gun fire and was awarded the Military Cross and the DSO. In 1919–20 he commanded Latvians successfully against a threatened Bolshevik takeover and then served in Turkey and Gibraltar before being appointed to the staff college at Camberley in 1926. Gaining rapid promotion, he attended the Imperial War College in 1930–31 and saw action on the North-West Frontier in 1934–36, as a result of which he was made a Companion of the Order of the Star of India and mentioned in dispatches. In October 1937, after a brief spell as ADC to King George VI, he was posted back to India and became the youngest general in the British army. In 1940 he took part in the retreat to Dunkirk and was again mentioned in dispatches. After a tour as Officer Commanding in Chief, responsible for the defence of south-west England, he was picked by Churchill as the ideal person to pull imperial chestnuts out of the fire in Burma.[38]

Whether 'Alex' was the right man for the job must be debatable. Although incontestably brave and a keen sportsman, he was not, in majority opinion, very bright.[39] He had certain attributes, however, that endeared him to most observers. Even more than Wavell, he was imperturbable and unflappable, the quintessence of that 'cool' so admired in officers of the Second World War. As soon as he arrived he cancelled Hutton's orders for a withdrawal and ordered an advance on Rangoon with all the heavy armour he could muster. The luckless Hutton lingered on until April, when at his own request he was transferred to India. He was not given another command. Wavell meanwhile advised Alexander that he must fight hard for Rangoon but not sacrifice his men needlessly; if, after they had given all they could give, Alex still thought the situation was impossible, he should pull back. Alexander accordingly ordered the advance. As his troops approached Rangoon there was an eerie silence, with vultures wheeling in the sky overhead.[40] His men entered the city and began destroying anything that could be of conceivable use or value to the enemy. On 7 March the sky was lit up as £11 million worth of installations belonging to the Burmah Oil Company was blown up – an action that would lead to 20 years of high court litigation after the war.[41] The fall of Rangoon was also a disaster for Lend-Lease stores, with

972 unassembled trucks and 5,000 tyres being put to the torch. The squabble between Chiang and the British about the destination of 900 trucks and jeeps and 1,000 machine guns was thus rendered academic. Next day Alexander came under Japanese counterattack and was close to being surrounded and his entire command wiped out; escaping just in time, he then found that the enemy had cut off the route north to Prome with a roadblock. A massive tailback of marching columns and vehicles built up and catastrophe seemed imminent when the Japanese suddenly took the cork out of the bottle and opened the road north.[42] Why they removed their roadblock is still disputed. Some say they did not realise the extent of the victory they could have won simply by standing pat; in a word, their intelligence was faulty. Others say that General Sakurai Shozo, the Japanese field commander, was determined above all to take Rangoon and did not want to be sidetracked; bitter resistance was expected from the encircled British army and he preferred to consolidate his gains rather than be sucked into a slugging match that was irrelevant to the capture of Rangoon. Whichever interpretation is correct, 'Alex' had had a lucky escape. By rights he should either have been taken prisoner or killed in the fighting. The Japanese meanwhile entered Rangoon on 9 March to find it completely deserted.[43]

Such was the lamentable state of affairs when Slim arrived on 19 March to take up his corps command.

He made an impression immediately. He was one of those people so quietly confident of his own abilities that he saw no need to make a splash or throw his weight around. Unlike so many other generals, he did not bring with him to the new appointment an entire cadre of favourite staff officers. 'I don't travel with a circus,' he said – a palpable hint at the prima donna antics of 'Monty' (Field Marshal Bernard Montgomery was famous for the gallery touch).[44] Slim had a look of bulldog tenacity and was squarely built, with a heavy, slightly undershot jaw and short greying hair.[45] With his famed lucidity – doubtless honed in his secondary occupation of writing adventure stories – he made a brilliant multicausal analysis of why British forces had performed so disastrously hitherto. Undoubtedly the root cause was that British commanders in South-East Asia had had no real guidance from London. The complacent assumption had been that Singapore was impregnable and therefore the scenario of a Japanese invasion of

Burma was chimerical and need not be addressed. It followed from this that all the second-order 'on the ground' factors militated against British success in the event of an actual invasion. British intelligence was extremely bad, particularly about the situation in Siam and its possible knock-on effects; British troops were ill-trained and ill-equipped for jungle warfare; the combat units were below strength in men and materiel and had been deployed ineptly; morale was low.[46] The British administration of Burma was atrocious at every level. Burma had been neglected and shunted from one governing body to another – to India until 1937, to the British chiefs of staff from 1937 to 1940, to Far Eastern Command in 1940, and finally to Wavell's ill-starred ABDACOM in 1941–42; in 16 months there were five separate headquarters responsible for the country's defence. As for civilian administration, what could be of poorer quality than the Burmese civil service? As soon as the Japanese invaded, there was mass desertion of personnel in the police, local government and utility companies. The so-called administrative class of civil servants was no better. Later in the 1942 campaign a delegation of top Burmese bureaucrats approached Slim and asked him not to fight in the exclusive residential district of the Sagaing Hills (in the bend of the Irrawaddy opposite Mandalay). Slim replied crisply that he would oblige provided the Japanese did likewise. Privately he shook his head in stupefaction, wondering what planet these Burmese mandarins were on.[47]

At a deeper level Slim pondered how the British could make progress in a country where the population was either profoundly apathetic or overtly hostile. Perhaps only 5–10 per cent of Burmese were anti-British in the strong sense of being pro-Japanese, and the hill tribes such as the Karens had a long tradition of supporting the British, often to the fury of the mainstream Burmans, but the peoples of the plains and valleys were notably neutral and insouciant about the outcome of the war. Yet Slim felt that all these adverse structural factors could in the end be overcome if only Britain and her allies could attain superiority in airpower. In 1940 the chiefs of staff in London had calculated that Far East Command needed at least 14 squadrons or a minimum of 336 planes to be fully secure in the area, but no action was taken. It was the same story when Wavell reported in December 1941 that the entire area from Hong Kong to the Indian border was covered by just 200 aircraft, none of them long-range fighters, and pleaded for more as a matter of urgency.[48] Once again nothing significant was done. The dribble of reinforcements consisted mainly of obsolete planes, of more danger to their pilots than to the Japanese. Although the Japanese Zero fighter was, plane for plane, inferior to both the RAF Hurricane and the P-40 Tomahawk fighter of the American Volunteer Group based in Rangoon, the Japanese knew they would win in a war of attrition, and began the way they meant to go on by destroying a number of Blenheims on the first day of the invasion. Thereafter they systematically demolished all cities and major towns by pattern bombing. From 23 to 26 January the skies over Rangoon were thick with dogfighting aircraft. The Japanese lost this first full battle in the air (Slim, with some hyperbole, claimed they lost 200 planes), but even the more sober estimate of 17 Japanese aircraft downed as against 12 Allied was ominous, since the Japanese could increase their numbers and the Allies could not.[49] Quite what the disparity in planes was has always been disputed. Slim reckoned that on 31 January 1942 there were just 35 Allied aircraft against 150 Japanese, but that the gap had widened to 45 and 400 respectively by the time he arrived in Burma. Others say the true figures for February were 140 as against 900 Japanese.[50] It is quite clear that the ratio was heavily in Japan's favour and that the gap was becoming a crevasse. Slim took heart from a successful RAF bombing raid on 21 March when Hurricanes shot down 27 Japanese planes, but his solace was short-lived, since the enemy hit back by bombing Magwe non-stop (there were six raids in 24 hours with 250 planes) and extending their raids to the Akyab peninsula in the far west of Burma. Battered into submission and with most of their planes caught on the ground and destroyed, the RAF finally quit Burma at the end of March, with 3,000 airmen withdrawn to India. So low was air morale that the RAF did not even bother to notify Alexander of their withdrawal. This meant that Slim's corps, already in retreat, was totally without air support.[51]

The loss of Rangoon and the surrender of Java on 8 March gave the Japanese a great naval opportunity on which they failed to capitalise. Off Sumatra on 2 April, Vice Admiral Nagumo Chuichi proceeded to Ceylon with five of the six carriers he had commanded on the Pearl Harbor operation and shelled Colombo. With army cooperation he could easily have captured both Ceylon and Mauritius, giving Japan mastery not just of the Bay of Bengal but the entire Indian Ocean;

certainly Allied sea contact with India would have been severed. Yet the army, displaying the stolidity and lack of imagination it so often evinced in the 1941–45 war, muffed this glittering opportunity.[52] Meanwhile on land in Burma the disaster that was to disfigure the land in 1942 saw its opening chapters, as the first of the country's million Indians, despairing of their future under a Japanese occupation, began the trek north. Hated by the ethnic Burmans for their wealth and privilege, many of these Indians fell victim to dacoits and even casual violence from the envious, resentful and racially prejudiced Burmese; the sickening litany of rape, murder, robbery, looting and violence was now heard on all sides.[53] Slim had no time to listen to such tales, for his mind was concentrated entirely on saving his soldiers from destruction. After his initial consultation with Alexander at Prome, he was now based at Maymyo, the summer capital of Burma, pleasantly cool at an altitude of 3,500 feet, a kind of Simla transplanted and described by one observer as looking like a village in Kent or Connecticut.[54] Here he set up the headquarters of the Burma army. Unlike Hutton, who had never got on with his second in command Smyth, Slim was singularly fortunate in that his closest collaborators were Major General J. Bruce Scott, commanding 1st Burma Division, and Smyth's replacement Major General David Cowan, nicknamed 'Punch' because he resembled the choleric figure on the cover of *Punch* magazine.[55] Not only were Slim, Cowan and Scott all Gurkha officers who thought alike, but they had been friends for 20 years and more. Slim told his officers that the newly constituted BURCORPS would be an amalgam of 1st Burma Division, 17th Indian Division and 7th Armoured Brigade. He explained the difficulties involved in fighting alongside the two Chinese divisions, which by this time Wavell had reluctantly accepted into Burma as allies. He warned them that heavy, severe and taxing fighting lay ahead, for it was clear that Japanese strategy would be to try to push the Chinese 5th Army back to Mandalay, capture the oilfields of Yenangyaung and then cut off the British and Chinese retreat west of Mandalay.

Slim's first task was to relieve the Chinese army at Toungoo; Wavell had made this a priority. From 24 to 28 March the Chinese there fought grimly and gave a good account of themselves, but the Japanese gradually flushed them out, and in the confusion of the retreat the Chinese neglected to blow the bridge over the Sittang river. Meanwhile Cowan, commanding the would-be relieving force, took heavy casualties at Schwedaung, losing 10 tanks and 350 dead and wounded. The mission was pointless on two counts, both because the two Allied armies had to retreat and because resources were diverted from the more important objective of defending Prome.[56] The Wavell–Alexander notion of defending both the Sittang and the Irrawaddy valleys simultaneously was clearly doomed. Alexander compounded the error by insisting that Slim hold *both* banks of the Irrawaddy, not only at Allanmyo but also at Taungdwingyi, 50 miles to the north-east. Disregarding this, Slim pulled back from Allanmyo and concentrated at Taungdwingyi, where he would have the Chinese under General Tu Lu-ming to support him. Marching south to meet him, the Chinese laid waste the town of Meiktila, looting, destroying and stealing, even from their allies.[57] The Burmese campaign seemed to be rapidly deteriorating into a war of 'all against all'. The Japanese shocked their opponents, who expected warfare to be waged in accordance with the Geneva Convention and were stupefied to learn that they were hanging prisoners upside down and using them for bayonet practice; they also strafed columns of refugees as target shooting. The Burmese, sensing that the Japanese were winning, began acting treacherously towards the retreating British, murdering foraging parties and stragglers. In response, attitudes hardened on the British side. There was a reluctance to take Japanese prisoners, and in revenge for the treachery of the ethnic Burmans, British troops took to burning settlements and, in at least one case, massacring an entire village.[58] With even tame Burmese preying on Indian refugees, the cycle of atrocities escalating in the formal war, and organised dacoits taking their chances against all and sundry, it hardly needed the Chinese to add another wheel to this wagon of war crimes. However, they contributed a refinement of their own by shooting Buddhist monks in the belief that they must be spies since they were 'in disguise'.[59]

Slim's first contacts with the Chinese led him to have the same exasperated feelings towards them that the US general Stilwell always had. He had arranged to rendezvous with them at Taungdwingyi but they failed to arrive on time, the first of many such contretemps that led Slim to remark exasperatedly: 'It was rather like enticing a shy sparrow to perch on your windowsill.' He gave an order to a Chinese colonel who said he could do nothing without the express orders of General

Sun Li-jen. Slim explained that since he was General Sun's superior, an order from him was ipso facto an order from General Sun. He repeated the command. 'But I cannot move until I get the orders of General Sun,' the man protested doggedly.[60] Alexander had a similar experience. He saw a battery of Chinese field guns one day, well dug in and expertly camouflaged. Next day they were all gone. When he asked General Tu Li-ming what had happened to them, Tu said they had been 'withdrawn'. In which case, said Alexander, what is the point of having them? Tu explained that the Chinese 5th Army was Chiang's best division only because of those field guns. It followed that he could not afford to lose them in battle, because if he did, the 5th Army would no longer be the best division.[61] Slim claimed that he soon learned two vital lessons about the Chinese: timekeeping and punc-tuality meant nothing to them; and they would steal anything that came within range – stores, rations, lorries, trains, even noticeboards. On one occasion they tried to steal a British train to steam north in, and Slim faced the ticklish problem that he might have to open fire on an ally to stop them. He solved the problem by having the engines uncoupled and taken 10 miles up the line. When the Chinese poured aboard the train, they found there were no engines to pull it.[62] But when the Chinese did finally get into action, Slim was impressed by their fighting qualities and even more by the talents of General Sun. 'I had expected the Chinese soldier to be tough and brave,' he wrote, 'but I was, I confess, surprised at how he responded to the stimulus of proper tank and artillery support, and the aggressive spirit he had shown. I had never expected, either, to get a Chinese general of the calibre of Sun.'[63]

Yet with Toungoo lost, there was little point in trying to defend Prome. At a tripartite conference at Allanmyo, Wavell, Alexander and Slim all agreed that they had to abandon it. It was at this meeting that Alexander made the bizarre suggestion that 7th Armoured Brigade should retire to China. He said nothing about how the tanks were to be supplied with petrol in that case, but logistics was never Alex's strong point.[64] Slim resisted this suggestion and clearly was not over-impressed by his chief at any level. He found his legendary 'cool' embarrassing and inappropriate, as when he was machine-gunned from the air but refused to dive for a trench, instead taking shelter under a tree. Instead of admiring his sangfroid, Slim was annoyed with him for setting a bad example. As Japanese pressure mounted, Slim moved his headquarters back to Magwe. It was now April, which was the cruellest, and certainly the hottest, month in Burma, and at this very moment Slim's troops were entering the most arid regions in the central plains. They were mired in heat and dust and permanently short of water – a nightmare for the physically fit but certain death for the wounded and pack animals.[65] Two days before the move to Magwe, Japanese bombers blitzed Mandalay, reducing it to a smoking crater (6 April). It was said that a city that had taken a thousand years to build was destroyed in an hour. Masses of bloated dead bodies lay crawling with flies, picked over by crows, kites and hawks.[66] As Japanese airpower progressively devastated all the urban centres, cholera and smallpox spread quickly. Assailed by heat, thirst and disease, beset by an enemy that seemed unbeatable, the British troops became despondent and morale plummeted to rock bottom. One unit suffered 59 suicides and desertions in four hours, reducing its strength from 220 to 161, after being ordered forward once more.[67] And in an awful symbiosis with the retreating army there came a wretched line of refugees, suffering even worse travails than the troops. The progress of the army was reported as follows: 'Men, mules and horses were strung out across the dusty hills under a white blazing sun. They were collapsing dog-tired in the sand for a brief rest, then heaving themselves to their feet again and marching forward. Bearded, dust-caked men, with the sweat salt dried white across their shirts, their waterbottles clacking dry against their hips.'[68]

For four days from 10 April, BURCORPS's 48th Brigade was engaged in desperate fighting as the Japanese in a lightning move got between them and the British 13th Brigade on the road between Magwe and Taungdwingyi. Slim wanted to unite all sections of his army as soon as possible, but Alexander reasoned that to pull his troops out of the nodal point at Taungdwingyi would demoralise the Chinese and might make them start retreating pell-mell for the Chinese border. For this reason the decision was taken to stand and fight the enemy outside Yenangyaung. What followed was the most brutal battle of 1942 in Burma. First Slim ordered the vital oil wells destroyed so that they could never fall into the hands of the Japanese. In a rerun of the Rangoon explosion (and with similar post-war legal consequences), a million gallons of crude oil soared skywards in flames reaching 500 feet high; the black cloud of smoke blotted out the sun. That was on 15 April.[69] Next day, 1st Burma Division went into action against the enemy but were decisively routed. On 17 April, Slim tried to relieve the pressure on the badly mauled 1st Burma Division by launching a counterattack by 17th Indian Division, but this too was swatted aside. A further counterattack by the Chinese failed when, supposed to be catching the Japanese in a pincer movement, they simply failed to arrive at the rendezvous at the required time. At this point British morale cracked, and the men broke ranks in disarray, interested only in slaking their thirst. All in all, the four-day battle of Yenangyaung on 15–18 April was one of the blackest periods in the history of British arms to that date.[70] Far too late the Chinese got into the battle, and although they acquitted themselves well, they were swimming against an unstoppable tide. Faced with the prospect of bloody hand-to-hand fighting in the smoking ruins, Slim ordered the Chinese out of the firing line. He conveyed the atmosphere well: 'The temperature that day was 114; the battlefield was the arid, hideous, blackened shade of the oilfield, littered with wrecked derricks, flames roaring from the tanks, and shattered machinery and burning buildings everywhere. Over it all hung that huge pall of smoke. And there was no water.'[71] But Slim did, in a sense, have the last word. When the victorious Japanese entered Yenangyaung, his sappers bade a defiant farewell by dynamiting the power station.[72]

While they drew the knot tighter and tighter over the British windpipe in the west, the Japanese suddenly played their trump card by appearing in force in the east, moving with amazing speed through the Shan states and brushing aside all opposition. They reached Mauchi, with its valuable wolfram mines, on 13 April. They next attacked the Chinese 6th Army in the hills between the Mandalay–Rangoon railway and the Sittang river. After another easy victory, they seized Taunggyi, capital of the southern Shan states, on 20 April. This city had huge petrol stocks, and its seizure was timely, as the Japanese were running out of gasoline.[73] With the British in full retreat and vast numbers of civilians in danger of not being evacuated fast enough, Slim addressed his officers and tried to find the proverbial silver lining. 'Well, gentlemen, it might be worse,' he began. A sepulchral voice said: 'How?' Slim takes up the story: 'I could have murdered him but instead

I had to keep my temper. "Oh," I said, grinning. "It might be raining." Two hours later it was – hard.'[74]

Soon it was time for more serious conferences. On 19 April, Slim met Wavell and Alexander to lay contingency plans for a retreat into India and China should the situation in Burma become untenable, as it showed every sign of doing. Slim still hoped that the Chinese 6th Army could hang on grimly but began to change his mind when it was put to him that in that case, the British would have to stay on too, and the end of the road might be that they would have no option but to retreat with the Chinese into China. Slim was alarmed. 'Personally, I did not like this plan at all. Above all, I disliked sending a British formation into China. Their administration in a famine-stricken area would be practically impossible, they would arrive in a shocking state and be no advertisement for us, while the men, both British and Indian, would be horribly depressed at the prospect.'[75] It was therefore with some relief that he heard, at his next conference with Alexander six days later at Kyaukse, that Burma would definitely be abandoned but that no British troops would withdraw into China. The troops would leave for India in two general directions, via Imphal to Assam and to India through the Hukawng valley. Slim agreed with Alexander that if BURCORPS got out fast, General Iida would be denied the decisive battle he sought around Mandalay.[76]

Morale in the army improved miraculously once it was known that there was a general retreat to India. Perhaps this factor accounts for the splendid actions fought by British units in the closing weeks of the campaign. While a holding action was fought in the eastern sector around Meiktila (and later at Wundwin when Cowan retired there) to stem the Japanese advance as the main Chinese forces retreated, BURCORPS regiments reached the west bank of the Irrawaddy on 30 April and blew up the great Ava bridge once their Chinese allies were safely across. They were able to get to the bridge before the enemy because of a valiant Rorke's Drift-style stand by 48th Indian Brigade at Kyaukse on 28–29 April. Meanwhile other units ceded the crucial area around Monywa inch by inch, buying more valuable time.[77] However, what Alexander had hoped would be the *pièce de résistance* failed to come off. He sent Major Mike Calvert with guer-rillas of the so-called Bush Warfare School to 'hold' the 825-foot-high Gokteik viaduct, 30 miles east of Maymyo between Mandalay and

Lashio, making it clear with many a wink and nod that he would like it destroyed, while formally ordering Calvert (for what he mysteriously refers to as 'political reasons') not to blow it. He hoped Calvert would read between the lines and disobey his orders, especially as the major had a reputation for being insubordinate, but the literal-minded Calvert abided by the letter of his instructions.[78] The Japanese therefore secured the Gokteik gorge intact. The martial glories of the last days of April were somewhat dimmed by anxieties about river transport for the retreating divisions. The ferries for crossing the mighty Irrawaddy were found to be woefully inadequate. Slim rationalised his disappointment with an 'old soldier' anecdote, referring to the 'blanket' system of army administration: 'And we says to 'im, "Jump and we'll hold the blanket." And he jumped and there weren't no blanket!' It was in this context that the crossing of the Ava bridge across the Irrawaddy must be accounted crucial. Moreover, the corps of Royal Engineers performed brilliantly, utilising bridge-building skills that enabled the river crossing even of 13-ton tanks.[79]

The next stage of the campaign turned into a race for Monywa, a vital town as it dominated the Chindwin and had a railway north to Yeu. If the Japanese managed to get there first, they would cut the retreating British off from India. It was touch and go, but Slim's men just pipped the enemy to it.[80] General Scott then dug in at Yeu for another rearguard action to hold up the pursuing Japanese. Slim had his last ever meeting with Alexander there on 1 May, where they discussed the unexpectedly determined efforts of the enemy to intercept them. There were three major anxieties for the military leaders: that the Japanese would cut them off; that food supplies would give out before India was reached; and that the monsoon would break while they were still struggling over the mountains in the border country.[81] By the first week of May, most of the British troops had already reached Kalewa, but on 10 May there was bitter fighting between the pursuers and the Gurkhas in the rearguard at Shegwyin. That night the Gurkhas broke off and made a swift march along a track to Kaing, opposite Kalewa, then joined the mass exodus north from Kalewa to Tamu, a 90-mile trek through the Kabaw valley. With their inimitable gallows humour, the troops soon nicknamed this 'Death Valley' because of the high mortality from malaria. The Japanese broke off the pursuit after Kalewa, realising that they could not overhaul their prey. But 2 Burma Brigade, taking a different route up the west bank of the Irrawaddy and then north-west to follow the Myittha valley, ended up fighting not the Japanese but large forces of Burmese dacoits.[82] By 9 May, however, most of BURCORPS was west of the Chindwin. Now began the slog to the Indian border. A popular story had the soldiers querying how they were supposed to get back to India, eliciting the grim reply: 'You walk, mate. You walk or you die.'[83] Entire histories have been devoted to this, the longest retreat in British military history, but the horrors of the trail never diminish in rereading. All who were there agreed that the trek through the jungle and across razor-backed mountains seemed unending. Food drops from planes operating out of India and Assam eased the worst pangs of starvation, but there was a permanent shortage of water, and disease – malaria, typhus, blackwater fever and cholera – was rampant. One of the worst problems was vitamin C deficiency, which engendered jungle sores that reddened, suppurated and would not heal.[84] The entire tatterdemalion army looked like a bunch of ragged scarecrows. Beards were ubiquitous; even Slim tried to grow one, but gave up when a glance in the mirror convinced him that the corps commander looked like Santa Claus; he resumed shaving with the rusty relic of a blade.[85]

On 12 May the monsoon burst on the column of retreating soldiers and the clouds of refugees who clung close to them for imagined safety. Those who dropped dead were simply washed away and those who remained were made even more vulnerable to disease. The one consolation was that the monsoon halted both the Japanese pursuit and the constant air attacks. There were no proper roads, only jungle tracks, and many cursed the name of the Assam–Bengal railway and the tea companies who had deliberately impeded the building of proper infrastructure so that they could enjoy a transport monopoly. But the army never degenerated into an indisciplined rabble, owing largely to the example set by Slim from the top. After describing the misery his men endured, he then spoke with pride of their *esprit de corps*.

> Ploughing their way up over slopes, over a track inches deep in slippery mud, soaked to the skin, rotten with fever, ill-fed and shivering . . . their only rest at night was to lie on sodden ground under the dripping trees, without even a blanket to cover them . . . All of them, British,

Indian and Gurkha, were gaunt and ragged as scarecrows. Yet as they trudged behind their officers in groups, pitifully small, they still carried their arms and kept their ranks, they were still recognizable as fighting units. They might look like scarecrows but they looked like soldiers too.[86]

At last, on 15 May, the vanguard began entering Assam, and by the 28th nearly all the troops of BURCORPS had crossed into India, having accomplished a 900-mile retreat. Parties of refugees continued to dribble in until October. No reliable estimate has ever been attempted of fatalities on this grim march. Altogether over a million fled from Burma, and at least 100,000 Indians (some say 200,000) died on the trek north.[87] Slim estimated that he sustained casualties of 13,000 dead and wounded in BURCORPS, that he took only 38 out of 150 big guns from Burma into India, and that he was left with just 50 lorries and 30 jeeps.[88] Some humanitarian attempts were made to feed the starving columns of refugees, but most of these foundered on the irreducible rock of human nature. The RAF dropped supplies, but these were largely looted by gangs of armed Punjabis and Sikhs.[89]

Everything Slim saw on the retreat convinced him that his initial diagnosis of the ills of Burma had been correct. Even if only 5 per cent of Burmese could be counted actively hostile to the British, there were just too many self-seeking groups, too many bandits and dacoits, and too few Burmese fighting men who had been trained to be of the right calibre. The lack of preparation on the British side – since no one had expected an invasion of Burma – was woeful, compounded by poor and overlapping civil administration. There was an overall lack of clarity over British aims, with neither Slim nor Alexander being given lucid guidelines: they were told neither to conduct a fighting retreat nor to slug it out to the bitter end. Inadequate airpower virtu-ally told its own story, as did the poor and inadequate British intelligence about Burma. Worst of all, the British had been consis-tently outpointed and outgeneralled by the enemy. Although it was a myth that the Japanese were 'naturals' at jungle warfare, they had trained their troops thoroughly in this aspect of fighting and the British had not; all foreign-theatre training had concentrated on the very different conditions of campaigning in the desert. Moreover, the Japanese tactics of using roadblocks had demoralised the British, giving their foes a clear psychological advantage. Most impressive of all was the Japanese use of the 'hook', whereby they would use river transport to appear suddenly in BURCORPS's rear.[90] Worst of all aspects of the terrible defeat in Burma was the blow to Britain's imperial prestige. After the sinking of two of its capital ships, the fall of Hong Kong and the ignominious surrender of Singapore, the rout in Burma was the very last thing the reputation of the empire in Asia needed.[91] Beaten in preparation, execution, strategy and tactics, Slim was quite prepared to put himself down as well: 'For myself I had little to be proud of; I could not rate my generalship high.'[92] Here he protested too much, for the situation he faced in Burma in March–May 1942 was beyond the reach of even the most consummate military genius. In the face of stresses and strains that nearly derailed even the 'laid-back' Alexander, Slim had remained unflappable and imperturbable, never lurching into panic, even at the most perilous moments, like the encounter at Shegwyin or the race for Monywa. And it was his grip on the disciplined retreat that enabled the cream of his fighting troops to retain their morale and hope for a return match with the enemy. The success of the withdrawal from Burma was Slim's work and Slim's alone.[93]

Neither Alexander nor Wavell, his immediate superiors, gained much kudos from the Burma campaign in early 1942. Alexander was always overrated as a commander and did so well in the Second World War largely because he was one of Churchill's pets. It is highly significant that he devotes just three pages in his memoirs to his unhappy five months in Burma (he was transferred to the Middle East in July); in his heart he knew that that episode in his career did not redound to his credit.[94] Slim skirts carefully around the question of Alexander's performance, but it is clear from the subtext that he was not impressed.[95] In some ways Wavell appears in an even poorer light, initially complacent and overconfident, then consistently jumping the wrong way, as when he proposed that the British army retreat into China.[96] When Churchill blamed him for the fall of Rangoon, Wavell tried to shift the blame on to Alexander, insinuating that he should have fought on and not destroyed the oil installations in the city. Alexander very properly retorted by pointing to Wavell's own order that he should pull back if he feared the imminent destruction of the whole army.[97] Wavell always had a very high opinion of his own abilities, but the suspicion arises that he was far too much *au-dessus de la mêlée* to be a really effective commander-in-chief. His severest critics accuse him of trying to be a Marcus Aurelius, maintaining a posture of Olympic detachment while the heavens fell around his ears. There is a suspicion of unjustifiable levity in the poem he wrote at the very moment the British army was plodding along the via dolorosa to Assam. It is a pastiche based on Kipling's famous poem about Mandalay.

> By the old Moulmein Pagoda, at the corner of my map
> There's no Burma girl awaiting, but a nasty little Jap.
> Yet the cipher wires are humming, and the chiefs of staff they say
> Get you back, you British soldier; get you back to Mandalay.
> Get you back to Mandalay
> Where mosquitoes fall in May:
> And the Jap comes up through jungle like a tiger after prey.
>
> The anopheles is buzzing, and his bite is swift and keen,
> The rain falls down in torrents, and the jungle's thick and green;
> And the way back into Burma is a long and weary way
> And there ain't no buses running from Assam to Mandalay.
> On the road to Mandalay
> Where the flying Zeros play
> And the Jap comes up through jungle like a tiger after prey.[98]

No one could ever accuse Slim of not having a sense of humour, but unlike Wavell, he was more sensitive to the right time and place for levity.

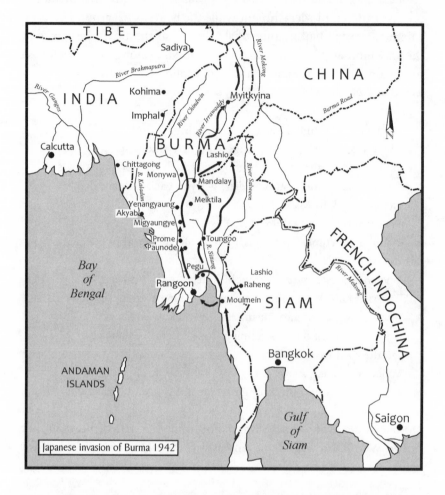

Japanese invasion of Burma 1942

To put the disaster of early 1942 in Burma into wider perspective, we have to flash back to General Joseph Stilwell's arrival in the country, just a few days before Slim. Born in 1883, Stilwell was a West Point graduate with a talent for languages, a hard-working professional soldier but also a genuine eccentric with a pronounced contempt for all formality, including army uniforms, a sincere commitment to the interests of the enlisted man and a caustic tongue. It is alleged that he was for a long time held at the rank of brigadier general because of his habitually insulting attitude to military superiors, but he had many powerful backers in the corridors of power in Washington, most notably General George Marshall, who rated him very highly and considered him the best corps commander in the whole US Army.[1] The two men had served briefly together in China and were family friends. Marshall had a notoriously short fuse, and Stilwell has been described as 'one of the few officers willing to test Marshall's sense of humour . . . the only theater commander who dared rib him occasionally'.[2] Highly intelligent and well read, Stilwell was also an outstanding linguist, who had been top of the class in French at West Point and later taught both Spanish and French there. Even more impressively, he had set himself to master Chinese over the years and was universally regarded as the army's senior Chinese expert. He had other peculiarities, among them an avidity for movies that would later make him more than a match for the cinephile Louis Mountbatten. In December 1941 he went to see Walt Disney's *Dumbo*, and enjoyed it so much that he sat through it twice.[3]

Physically Stilwell was unprepossessing. He looked prematurely old, with grizzled grey hair that made him seem an uncanny ringer for the playwright Samuel Beckett. Part of the problem was that he was half blind, having sustained serious injuries in World War I when an ammunition dump exploded. His left eye was so badly impaired that he could not count the fingers of a hand at a distance of three feet, while his right eye needed constant correction. With a squint, a strong nose and a scrawny neck, he looked like a wise old turtle, but constantly strove to surmount and minimise his physical frailties: at one time he was army handball champion in the Orient.[4] While commanding at the staff college in Fort Benning, Georgia, Stilwell acquired the nickname 'Vinegar Joe'. One of his students drew a caricature of the waspish commander rising out of a vinegar bottle. So far from feeling insulted, Stilwell was delighted and had multiple copies of the cartoon made.[5] Stilwell had observed at first hand, often at great personal risk, every phase of the Chinese revolution since 1911, when the Manchu dynasty was thrown out by Sun Yat-sen. Fluent in Chinese, he was a veteran of three long military tours in China, most recently as military attaché at the US Legation in Peking (1935–40). During 1940–41 he commanded the 7th Infantry Division at Fort Ord, California, and was in charge during the notorious post-Pearl Harbor panic in Los Angeles in December 1941, when the Japanese were falsely reported to have landed on America's West Coast. Commanding the whole of the Californian coastline as far as the Mexican border, Stilwell famously telephoned the War Department in Washington to say that he was desperately short of ammunition with which to repel the invaders. The officer at the end of the line promised to do the best he could. 'The best you can?' Stilwell roared. 'Good God, what the hell am I supposed to do? Fight 'em off with oranges?'[6] He was initially selected to command the Allied forces in North Africa in what later became Operation TORCH, but the pressure of events brought him back to China.

It was a perennial worry of President Roosevelt that his 'Europe First' policy would disenchant Chiang Kai-shek to the point where he would sign a separate peace with Japan. This was the genesis of FDR's cable to Chiang on 31 December 1941 to tell him that Britain, Australia, New Zealand and the Netherlands had 'agreed' to the formation of a China Theatre of War, including parts of Siam and Indo-China, with Chiang as supreme commander. The reality of course was that this arrangement, like the associated ABDACOM, was simply a fait accompli Roosevelt had imposed on unwilling allies. But Chiang, duly flattered, went for the bait. On 2 January he cabled Washington to ask for a suitable US general as his chief of staff. It was considered that Brigadier General John Magruder of the American Military Mission to China was not senior enough, and anyway he was already disenchanted with the Chinese. Lieutenant General Hugh A. Drum was offered the post but turned it down as not prestigious enough.[7] As the hunt for a suitable candidate went on, Stilwell's name came up. The Army Chief of Staff, General George C. Marshall, FDR's strong right arm in the prosecution of the war of 1941–45, was always a fervent admirer of Stilwell, and viewed him as 'immensely capable and remarkably resourceful'.[8] Perhaps to sweeten the pill, Marshall decided that the new post would combine the functions of Chief of Staff, China Theatre, with those of US Commander, China-Burma-India Theatre, and also supervisor of Lend-Lease materiel in South-East Asia and the Far East. This multiple role was to be the source of much confusion, bitterness and misunderstanding during the next three years. It was a bad mistake both in terms of lack of clarity of the overall chain of command and because Chiang himself never really understood it. Initially suspicious, he asked his brother-in-law T.V.

Soong (Soong Tze-vun) to investigate the implications of the tripartite role, but Soong, an inveterate intriguer who always had his own agenda and who may even have aspired to replace Chiang as leader of the Kuomintang, reassured the generalissimo that the other two roles the new man would fill were entirely subsidiary to that of Chiang's chief of staff. In other words, Chiang, worried that the British would pre-empt 'his' Lend-Lease materiel, would always get his way.[9]

Meanwhile Marshall pressed hard for the appointment of his protégé. He summoned Stilwell to Washington and told him flatly: 'Joe, you have got twenty-four hours to think up a better candidate, otherwise it's you.'[10] Mischievously Stilwell suggested that General Drum, as the army's senior-ranking officer, should be approached again. It is an interesting pointer to the warmth between Marshall and Stilwell that Marshall was prepared to listen to his friend's slanderous diatribe about Drum, whom he despised as pompous, self-important and an overpromoted nonentity. Since Chiang was the original stuffed shirt, Stilwell argued, the best bet would be for the USA in turn to send out its own biggest stuffed shirt, i.e. Drum. At another meeting three weeks later, the army chief said: 'It's hard as hell to find anybody in our high command who's worth a damn. There are plenty of good young ones, but you have to reach too far down.'[11] Another Stilwell admirer was the Secretary for War, Henry L. Stimson, who had a number of meetings with him in January. Stimson impressed on Stilwell that there were two immediate priorities for the new chief of staff. One was ensuring that Chiang was really prepared to let an American take operational charge of his armies; without this the mission would be a flop. The other was to patch up the appalling collapse in relations between the Chinese and the British, the result of Wavell's refusal of Chiang's help at the Lashio conference in December, which had caused the generalissimo to lose face.[12] Under American pressure the British relented and invited Chiang to take up the defence of the Shan states on Burma's eastern border, thus freeing up 1st Burma Division for the defence of Rangoon. Churchill was the next leader to have to save face: he told FDR that of course Burma was more important strategically than Singapore but that he had to concentrate on Singapore to keep the Australians happy. On 19 January 1942, Stimson formally asked Chiang to approve a US commander for Chinese troops in Burma. Chiang appeared to agree but, as ever, hedged his bets with a form of wording that was deliberately ambiguous. However, it satisfied Washington. On 23 January Marshall told Stilwell that he was definitely going to China. The dour 'Vinegar Joe' used the same words to him he had previously used to Stimson: 'I'll go where I'm sent.'[13]

There followed an interview with Roosevelt, who tried out on Stilwell the usual brand of easy charm he used for all comers. Vinegar Joe refused to buy the bill of goods; the truth was that he disliked and despised the President. He found FDR 'very pleasant but very unimpressive'. Roosevelt was one of those people who was arrogant, overconfident and, in his own mind, all knowing, but also shrewd enough to realise that such attributes would make him unpopular. As a good politician therefore he masked his character under a carapace of frivolity and banter. He had other weaknesses, such as a tendency to make policy on the wing. When Stilwell asked the President if he had a personal message for Chiang, FDR at first stalled and then came up with what he thought was a clever bromide: 'Tell him we are in this thing for keeps and we intend to keep at it until China gets back all her territory.'[14] This was an unwise commitment, comparable to J.F. Kennedy's 'pay any price' promise in his inaugural address, or FDR's own 'unconditional surrender' announcement at the Casablanca conference in 1943. Stilwell would have been still more astonished to learn the President's attitude to Burma. He confided to Churchill in April 1942 as follows: 'I have never liked Burma or the Burmese, and you people must have had a terrible time with them for the past fifty years. Thank the Lord you have He-Saw, We-Saw, You-Saw under lock and key. I wish you could put the whole bunch of them into a frying pan and let them stew in their own juice.'[15] He was even less impressed by Roosevelt's *éminence grise*, the ubiquitous (in White House terms) Harry Hopkins – 'a strange gnomelike creature (stomach ulcers) . . . He had on an old red sweater and crossroads shoes and no garters, and his hair hadn't been cut for eight weeks' according to Stilwell.[16] This from a man who was notoriously careless of his own appearance. Hopkins promised he would commandeer the *Normandie* for use as a troop transport in South-East Asia. Next morning Stilwell heard that the *Normandie* had been gutted in New York Harbour. 'Is that Fate?' he confided to his diary.[17]

In retrospect the appointment of Stilwell created the classic situation of an accident waiting to happen. The person sent out should have been someone with deep sympathies for both Chiang and the British, someone prepared to use the dual sympathy to build bridges between these uncertain allies. But Stilwell detested both the people he was supposed to work with. A convinced 'Pacific-firster' who saw the war with Japan as a conflict representing the USA's true interests, as opposed to the war in Europe, which was primarily of concern to the British, in the privacy of his journal Stilwell poured out all his bile against the hated 'Limeys'. He despised Roosevelt for being (allegedly) Churchill's dupe, and wrote witheringly about the President: 'The Limeys have his ear, while we have his hind tit . . . the Limeys want us in with both feet . . . The Limeys want us in, committed. They don't care what becomes of us afterwards because they will have shifted the load from their shoulders to ours . . . And by God the Limeys now say it is impossible for Great Britain to produce even the munitions she needs for herself, and we must keep up our offerings or else. I don't know what 'or else' means, but I would like to ask them. And tell them what they can do.[18] No one has ever satisfactorily explained why Stilwell was such an Anglophobe. Partly it was an idiom of the time, a relic of the very strong undercurrent of isolationism in the USA, and the conviction that Europe liked to use the Americans as a 'cash cow'. Partly it was the widely held belief that 'Europe first' was a big mistake; this was the stance taken by another notable military Anglophobe, Admiral Ernest King.[19] It has been suggested that in Stilwell's case it may have had something to do with his deep resentment of his parents' love of pomp, ritual and strict hierarchy, which he always associated with the 'Limeys.'[20] With Vinegar Joe, visceral distaste of a 'fee-fi-fo-fum' kind was linked with contempt for Britain's military policies, and in his journal he liked to inveigh at some favourite targets. He claimed that a unified Allied command in the Far East was impossible because the Brits could not even agree among themselves, with high levels of inter-service rivalry and factionalism. 'The "Senior Service" sits disdainfully aloof. No one can command them – it is not done. The arrogant RAF will have none of it'.[21] Moreover, Wavell's snubbing of Chiang and his subsequent forced recantation showed the calibre of Britain's top brass. According to Stilwell, Wavell simply 'didn't want the dirty Chinese in Burma'.[22]

But if he detested the British, Stilwell was no more enamoured of the Chinese. He spoke of their leaders as 'oily politicians . . . treacherous quitters, selfish, conscienceless, unprincipled crooks'. Their generals had an 'inherent distaste for offensive combat' because of their tradition of winning campaigns by outlasting the enemy.[23] Chiang Kai-shek was the past master of the doctrine of outlasting. Cynical about Chinese casualties, on the grounds that with her vast population China could always absorb them, Chiang had the fixed purpose of inveigling the West into his conflict with Japan so that they would do his fighting for him. He saw the Western powers as actuated by mirror-image motives. The Anglo-Saxons, in his view, wanted to deflect the full might of Japan against *him*, so that they would not have to fight to defend Singapore, Hong Kong and the rest of the British Empire in Asia. He noted that in the past, Britain and the United States had warned Japan off from Indochina, Siam, the Dutch East Indies and even Siberia, but never from China. To Chiang, 'Europe first' was simply a slogan masking the West's desire that China should do all the fighting in the Far East. The Chiang military doctrine, then, if we can call it that, came down to three main propositions. One, attrition: China had the manpower to outlast Japan. Two, the long game: in the end, he and the Kuomintang would be bailed out by the West when it was forced into all-out war with Japan. Three, and this went to the heart of Chiang's world view: his real enemy was the Chinese Communists, not Japan; it followed that he must soft-pedal in the fight against the Empire of the Rising Sun and conserve all his resources for the eventual reckoning with the Communists.[24] That was why in January 1941, to Roosevelt's consternation, he had attacked Mao Tse-tung's New 4th Army instead of fighting the Japanese.[25] Whether at this stage Stilwell was aware of Chiang's complete grand strategy is doubtful, but he had already met the man, taken his measure and formed a strong dislike for 'the Peanut', as he would ever afterwards refer to him. The first meeting between the two was in Chungking in December 1938. After a superficially cordial encounter, Stilwell wrote afterwards: 'Chiang Kai-shek is directly responsible for much of the confusion that normally exists in his command . . . his first consideration is to maintain his control over the best troops and material so that his position cannot be threatened.'[26] Chiang's aim was to keep all his subordinates in the dark: if they know nothing, then by definition they cannot plot against him. For instance, he never gave top-class artillery to his divisions, so that its generals would not have the power to oppose him. Stilwell's 'take' on Chiang was unerringly accurate, and he was to prove a true prophet. Chiang's defenders then and since like to say that Stilwell 'lacked real knowledge of Chinese culture, politics, the aspirations of the Chinese and the ability to evaluate them'.[27] It seems more likely that what engendered his many critics was simply that he saw the reality of China under Chiang only too clearly.[28]

Stilwell's mood in the weeks before his departure was singular, and inappropriate for the role he had been assigned. He read everything he could lay his hands on, including confidential material Marshall made available to him, but it merely depressed him further. It now transpired that one of the reasons Wavell turned down Chiang's offer of two Chinese divisions at Lashio was fear of upsetting the ethnic Burmans, who loathed the Chinese, if anything, even more than they hated the Indians. So, mused Stilwell, what confronts me is a hostile native population who detest both the British and the Chinese, the people who are supposed to win a war in Burma. 'Archie [Wavell] now claims he never refused help. Said he'll take two [Chinese divisions] and for the time being leave the other division where it was. Somebody is a liar. Archie misled Peanut at Lashio and now they are both sore, each thinking the other ducked out on him.'[29] On 28 January he noted despondently: 'The very uncertain nature of the job, the unknown conditions and situation, all go to make it a heavy mental load. Will the Chinese play ball? Or will they sit back and let us do it? Will the Limeys cooperate? Will we arrive to find Rangoon gone?'[30] Sensing his mood, pessimistic about British ability to hold the line in Burma and privately agreeing with Stilwell that Rangoon would probably have fallen by the time he arrived, Marshall made a number of important concessions to his friend. First he extended his remit by making it a quadripartite affair: Stilwell was to be the commander-in-chief of US forces in the CBI (China/Burma/India) area; chief of staff to Chiang; supervisor of all Lend-Lease materiel and US representative on any Allied war council. Marshall seemed unconcerned that this would produce the anomaly that Stilwell could end up with inferior ranking to a British general while wearing one of his hats and superior to the very same person while wearing one of the others. In addition, although Marshall had previously promised Chiang that his personal favourite Claire Chennault would be ranking air commander in China, to please Stilwell he announced that the Americans would have their own independent air commander, Colonel Clayton L. Bissell, with whom Chennault was known to have an ancient feud. Finally, Marshall promised Stilwell that if Rangoon had fallen by the time he arrived in Burma, he would have the option of transferring to Australia.[31]

Stilwell and his Washington-recruited staff flew to Miami on 11 February and left the USA three days later, at first on a Pan American seaplane. With a stopover in the Caribbean, he headed first to South America, then across the Atlantic to West Africa, thence to Cairo, Palestine, Iraq, Iran and Delhi, the later stages flying in Douglas DC-3s. The first lap of the journey was enlivened by a friendship he struck up with the wealthy and powerful newspaper proprietor Clare Boothe Luce, who became an immediate fan.[32] While he was in the air, Singapore fell and 80,000 British troops were taken prisoner. On landing in India, Stilwell attended his first conference with his British allies, where he was appalled by their ignorance about Burmese geography and politics. Predictably he found General Alan Hartley, commander-in-chief of the Indian army, a figure of fun, and mocked his 'far-back' accent: 'Miracles do happen in wah, don't they. One does enjoy a cawktail, doesn't one. It's so seldom one gets the chawnce. In my own case, I hardly have time for a glass of bee-ah.'[33] It has to be said that if Stilwell was an a priori Anglophobe, the British officer class certainly provided him with plenty of circumstantial ammunition. He then flew down to Calcutta to meet Wavell, who had just arrived from Java, and found him 'a tired, depressed man, pretty well beaten down'.[34] On the day of their meeting, Rangoon was being evacuated, but Stilwell did not take up Marshall's contingent offer of a move to Australia. Then it was on to Lashio for a conference with Chiang (3 March). This involved a four-and-a-half-hour flight over the Brahmaputra delta and into Burma. The generalissimo did not reveal his true colours at first and was in relaxed mood after what he considered a triumphant visit to India the month before. As Stilwell noted: 'The Limeys thought they were impressing their guests but the Chinese were laughing most of the time. Actually Chiang Kai-shek was much more impressed with Gandhi and Nehru than with the whole damn British Raj.'[35] Stilwell was right about that, for Chiang's visit, however much it pleased him personally, had turned into a public relations disaster. Officially encouraged by FDR to visit India and talk recalcitrant Congress leaders round to the Allied cause, Chiang had done no such thing but instead delighted in Gandhi's anti-Western jibes. Gandhi pointed out that the fact that the Allies deliberately excluded Chiang from summit conferences hardly made a compelling case for India to back the West. Charmed by Gandhi, Chiang then went public with a plea for Churchill to make concessions to the Indian nationalists. Churchill, who had famously declared that he had not become prime minister to preside over the liquidation of the British Empire, predictably saw red.[36] But Stilwell's worst fears about Chiang were confirmed when he asked what the generalissimo's plans for operations in Burma were; Chiang replied stony-faced that there were none. On 9 March Stilwell went for dinner with the Chiangs and was asked to stay behind afterwards for a private session that lasted two hours. Chiang reiterated his favourite line about the long view and defence in depth, making it clear he had no intention of sacrificing Chinese divisions for the defence of Mandalay.[37]

Like all Western visitors, Stilwell was charmed and intrigued by Chiang's beautiful wife, Soong Mei-ling, still something of a beauty though already in her forties. Brought up in comfort by a wealthy family and US-educated, she spoke perfect English with a Georgia accent, which helped her popularity with Americans. Married to Chiang since 1927, she was the original trophy wife, Chiang's fourth. Rather than outright polygamy, Chiang favoured serial monogamy with a bevy of mistresses on the side, but he relied heavily on his wife's ability to read American culture and attitudes. Her union with Chiang was not so much a marriage of convenience as a demonstration of the aphrodisiac of power. To amend a phrase about another famous couple, he gave her power and she gave him sex appeal. Destined to live to the age of 105, Soong Mei-ling was in her younger years a perfect example of what the psychologist C.G. Jung called a 'power devil'.[38] At her meetings with Stilwell, Madame Chiang liked to make caustic remarks about the British, which he relished. Less to his taste was her penchant and favouritism for Colonel Claire Lee Chennault, an adventurer overdrawn on his military bank account, so to speak. In 1937 Chennault, an amateur aviator, was living in pauperised retirement in Louisiana, having been invalided out of the

US Army Air Corps for partial deafness. For a while he kept the wolf from the door and even gained a measure of short-term fame by running a flying circus known as 'Three Men on a Flying Trapeze'.[39] When Japan invaded China in 1937, Chennault had the ingenious idea of forming a band of aerial mercenaries that would fight for Chiang. Using undercover slush funds made available by the US government in its clandestine bid to halt Japanese ambitions, Chennault was able to offer his volunteer pilots between $600 and $750 a month plus a bonus of $500 for every Japanese plane shot down.[40] The so-called 1st American Volunteer Group (AVG) was formed and began taking on Japanese fighters in dogfights long before Pearl Harbor. The AVG were popularly known as the 'Flying Tigers', from a Chinese proverb – 'Like tigers with wings, their strength is irresistible.' Flying fighter planes painted over to resemble the toothed maw of a shark, dressed in leather jackets and Hawaiian shirts, they acted like playboys and buccaneers, but Madame Chiang adored them: 'They were my angels,' she said, 'with or without wings.'[41] As a high-placed member of the Kuomintang, she naturally had a very complaisant attitude to corruption, and the US aid given to the Tigers led to a plethora of scams and rackets, ranging from payroll padding to gasoline hoarding. Fortunes were made, by both US and Chinese 'entrepreneurs' on 'enterprises' that had very little to do with any conceivable war effort.[42] Presiding over this cornucopia of corruption was Claire Lee Chennault. Although many of the individual fliers were brave and dedicated men, everything to do with Chennault was essentially false. His own claim to be a fighter ace was apocryphal; many of his recruited pilots lied about their previous experience in fighters; the 'dive and zoom' tactics he favoured were not his own original invention but filched from the Russians; and the tally he claimed of 297 Japanese planes downed by the AVG before July 1942 was bogus: the true figure was 115.[43] Nevertheless, for the Chiangs Chennault could do no wrong, and he was held to have strategic insights far superior to those of General Stilwell.[43]

It has been suggested that Stilwell and Chennault were destined not to get on, being the proverbial chalk and cheese. Stilwell was a Yankee and Chennault a southerner. Stilwell was an introvert and a West Pointer where Chennault was an extrovert and a military iconoclast. Most of all, Stilwell had a deep feeling for the ordinary Chinese people while

Chennault loved his niche among the Chinese elite and joined in their corruption and peculation with avidity.[44] One of Stilwell's first tasks, then, was to put Chennault in his place and re-emphasise that he was subordinate to Bissell. A two-hour flight took him over the route of the Burma road to Kunming, where he had a long talk with Chennault, who at this stage appeared friendly and cooperative.[45] Then he flew back to Chungking, this time in the kind of heavy turbulence that all travellers over the Hump so feared, and tried to settle in at the house once occupied by the well-known leftist Sinologist Owen Lattimore. Chungking, battered by years of Japanese bombing, overpopulated, crowded with refugees, insanitary and ill-provisioned, was certainly no Shangri-La, with humid heat in summer and rain and mud the rest of the year. Every night an army of rats appeared, and everywhere was filthy, feculent, noisome and stinking; it was said there were enough bad smells in the city to last anyone a lifetime.[46] Hyperinflation, the black market and every form of corruption was rampant; at the apex of the triangle of graft, peculation and defalcation stood Chiang's dreaded secret police force and its sinister chief, Tai-li.[47] Stilwell's intention was to put distance between himself and all the unsavoury manifestations of the Kuomintang by building his own enclave of staff and headquarters. Some say that he was more a Montgomery than a Slim by having a massive staff, but the difference was that in China he could not select cadres from officers in situ, as there were none. This is the explanation for the 400 technicians who gradually arrived in Chungking after passage from the USA by sea. Stilwell had brought with him by air a core staff of 35 officers and five enlisted men – the officers partly old China hands and partly hand-picked aides from 3rd Corps at Fort Ord.[48] One of his instructions – which was why he needed the technicians to train the Chinese – had been imposed on him while he was flying to Asia after one of FDR's hurriedly convened cabinet meetings. This was to build a 'back country' route between India and China. Fearing the loss of Burma, Chiang wanted a road from Ledo to Assam that would cut through the mountains, forests and rivers of northern Burma to link with the Burma road at Lungling on the Chinese side.[49] One of the problems was that Chiang, so often ensconced in his own dream world, thought this could be built in five months. Stilwell's own experts reckoned the road would take two and a half years to build; hence the need for so many technicians.

Stilwell began his mission with an enthusiasm that was soon damp-ened. He had bright ideas for an ambitious campaign to retake Rangoon, together with a 'failsafe' fallback plan for a retreat to high ground east of Mandalay where he could threaten the flank of any Japanese army and thus prevent a breakthrough into northern Burma. He believed he had sold the idea to Chiang by coupling it with a follow-up plan for an offensive in China once he had thrown the enemy out of Burma. But Chiang was cautious and said he wanted to know whether the Japanese were increasing their forces before he ordered an all-out offensive; in any event, he added, the best divisions in 5th and 6th Army would not be ordered south 'in case the British ran away'. Refusal to commit his best troops or to allow any concentra-tion in depth effectively stifled Stilwell's more ambitious plans at birth. Stilwell wrote mournfully in his diary: 'What a directive! What a mess! How they hate the Limeys! What a sucker I am . . . Maybe the Japs will go at us and solve it for us.'[50] He was not exaggerating the Anglophobia, for Chiang actually cabled FDR to request that Stilwell be made supreme commander of all Allied forces in Burma. Sensing his chief of staff's deep disappointment about the veto on his plan to retake Mandalay, the generalissimo sugared the pill on 11 March by telling him he could take three armies south: the 5th, 6th and 66th.[51] Stilwell, however, remained sceptical that his orders would be obeyed, for he had heard of Chiang's devious methods. Each divisional general was always informed that whatever orders he received from a super-ior, he was always to seek confirmation from the generalissimo himself, for Chiang thought this the best way to make ineffective any plotting by ambitious generals.[52] Such was the genesis of the move south by the Chinese 5th Army to Toungoo on the Sittang, on the same latitude as the 17th Indian Division at Prome. On paper, the Allied strategy of holding the Prome–Sittang line 150 miles north of Rangoon made sense, but it ignored geography. It required opera-tions to be conducted on a horizontal grid, but all communications in Burma were longitudinal, depending on the great rivers that ran north–south.

Stilwell set up his Burma headquarters at Maymyo, 'the Burmese Simla', where the British were already ensconced. He suffered initially from a severe shortage of staff officers, and contrasted his own 'can-do' attitude with the (alleged) laziness of the British, who had 70,000 men on their ration list but only 12,000 at the front.[53] Stilwell's always rampant Anglophobia was kindled anew when he contemplated the 'all chiefs and no Indians' hierarchy of the British army, for so he construed it when he calculated that there was one full general, one lieutenant general, five major generals, 18 brigadiers and 250 staff officers for 15,000 men. The fact that many of the senior officers conformed to the blimpish stereotype Stilwell so detested did not help matters. He evinced particular animus towards the civilian governor Sir Reginald Dorman-Smith, whom he predictably referred to in his journal as 'Doormat Smith'. He tried to rile the governor by stating uncompromisingly that he would open fire on any Burmese who gave him trouble, but Dorman-Smith spoiled his fun by agreeing without demur.[54] Stilwell found the British full of contempt for the Chinese, both as soldiers and because of their race. The 'Limeys' were also highly amused when both Stilwell and General Tu Li-ming presented credentials as commander of the Chinese armies. Dorman-Smith got revenge of a kind when Tu told him in confidence that Chiang had given Stilwell a mere paper command, but the real power was his. It would not be the last time that Stilwell would be bedevilled by such blatant duplicity. As has been well said: 'the problem [of who was in charge] caused his command in Burma to take on the complexities of a Pirandello play'.[55] According to the traditions of the Chinese army, a supreme commander had to possess a certificate signed by the head of state (in this case Chiang), complete with a six-inch-square seal with archaic Chinese characters and stamped in vermilion ink. The only man in Burma who had such a document was a general named Lo Chin-ying, whose speciality was stealing trains from the British.[56]

On 13 March General Alexander arrived, and his meeting with Stilwell was, predictably, a non-meeting of minds. The American's diary entry says it all: 'Very cautious. Long sharp nose. Brusque and standoffish. Amazed to find an American commanding Chinese. "Extwawdinery!" Looked me over as if I had just crawled out from under a rock.' Distinctly unimpressed, Stilwell was positively infuriated when he was woken at midnight that same day with a message that Alexander and his no. 2, General Edwin Morris, wanted to see him at ten o'clock sharp next morning. 'Can you beat it? I wonder what those babies would have said if I had sent Dorn on a similar errand to them? It's just a superior race complex, for which they will pay dearly.'[57] Stilwell's bark was always worse than his bite, so the conference next morning passed without acrimony. By the 15th, Alexander was becoming cordial, and confided to Stilwell that he had only 4,000 really good fighting men. He massaged his bubbling paranoia effectively. 'Alex says he now perfectly understands and we will cooperate with each other.'[58] The Alexander–Stilwell entente was further cemented when the American made it clear he would put Anglo-American objectives ahead of any loyalty to Chiang. Further shuttle diplomacy, including a two-day conference with the generalissimo, a meeting with Chennault at Kunming and a terrifying flight over the Hump in a snowstorm to Lashio, found Stilwell more disillusioned than ever. Chiang insisted that his 5th and 6th Armies could not be allowed to be defeated (Stilwell wondered how he was supposed to guarantee that) and that they should concentrate on the defence of Mandalay (which, however, he thought was a walled city) instead of 130 miles south at Pyinmana, as Stilwell wanted. Stilwell reflected that Chiang was a 'stubborn bugger', but the more he saw of Chinese ways, the more he found it a source of wonderment that his own status was accepted, since it was the first time since General 'Chinese' Gordon in the 1860s that a foreigner had commanded regular troops in China.[59] Since duplicity was a way of life, Stilwell found nothing untoward about disregarding Chiang's wishes and detaching the 22nd and 96th Divisions for an attack at Pyinmana. This gesture delighted Alexander, who was favourably impressed: he became 'a new man, all smiles and jokes about how I'd gotten his Chinese troops away from him'.[60]

Tired of Chiang's stalling and procrastination, Stilwell virtually stole away from Chungking and based himself at Toungoo, where he hoped to make a stand. In the week of 24–31 March he made a desperate attempt to reinforce his troops, both to prevent a threatened encirclement and to hold the flank of the British at Prome. But the situation at Toungoo was perilous, for he had few radios, other communications were poor and his medical facilities were non-existent at the very time that malaria and blackwater fever were rampaging through his army. A particular headache was Japanese airpower, as the enemy was virtually unchallenged in the skies since the RAF withdrew to India. If he could mobilise his few American pilots to fly night and day, Stilwell could perhaps put 45 planes in the air, but the Japanese could send 260 planes against them without difficulty.[61] Worst of all was the lack of cooperation from Chiang. Rail delays – deliberately engineered by the generalissimo, Stilwell thought – made it impossible for reinforcements to arrive at the front. When Stilwell asked Chungking for trucks, he was sent 50 out of 700 available, since the rest were being used to move materiel to private stashes deep inside China, ready for the future war with the Communists. Chiang, tired of face-to-face confrontations with his turbulent chief of staff, devised ever more Byzantine ways of holding him at arm's length. He forced Stilwell to communicate with him indirectly through two liaison officers who were primed to be obstructive. Meanwhile Madame Chiang bombarded Stilwell with air mail, sometimes three letters a day, possibly as a deliberate campaign of obfuscation, for the missives contained self-contradictory messages and sometimes countermanded orders Stilwell had already given. Stilwell was so appalled by all this that he signalled Stimson in Washington that Chiang's delaying tactics had destroyed any chance the Allies had in Burma.[62] The last straw was when he learned on 27 March that the British intended to withdraw from Prome, exposing his own flank.[63] Almost the only consolation he had in those dark days at Toungoo was the companionship of Frank Merrill, a soulmate both as a linguist and as a fighting officer. Tall, heavyset, short-sighted, 'with glasses perched on a sunburned peeling nose', 41-year-old Merrill was shrewd, genial and, above all, courageous. Enlisting in the army at eighteen, he took the West Point exams six times before the academy agreed to overlook his astigmatism and admit him. A Japanese-language specialist who was acting as liaison with the British, Merrill was the exact opposite of an armchair officer. When the Japanese strafed Maymyo, he jumped into a trench and opened fire on the Zeroes with a Bren gun.[64]

It was through Merrill that Stilwell first made contact with Slim – a contact that would produce a notable entente. When Slim arrived at Prome to command 1st Burma Corps, Merrill went to see him. Slim asked what Stilwell's objective was, to which Merrill replied: 'Rangoon.' 'Tell Stilwell he can count me in,' said Slim.[65] This promising beginning was followed by a meeting between the two commanders that was highly successful. Slim was certainly not the stereotypical British officer, and Stilwell appreciated his qualities, not least the fact that he had come up the hard way if not quite the whole way. Slim recorded his impressions of Stilwell at length:

> These were my first contacts with Stilwell, who had arrived in Burma a few days before me. He already had something of a reputation for shortness of temper and for distrust of most of the world. I must admit he surprised me a little when, at our first meeting, he said, 'Well, general, I must tell you that my motto in all things is *buyer beware*,' but he never, as far as I was concerned, lived up to that old horse-trader's motto. He was over sixty [not quite] but he was tough, mentally and physically; he could be as obstinate as a whole team of mules; he could be, and frequently was, downright rude to people whom, often for no good reason, he did not like. But when he said he would do a thing, he did it. True, you had to get him to say that he would – quite clearly and definitely – and that was not always easy – but once he had, you knew he would keep his word. He had a habit, which I found very disarming, of arguing most tenaciously against some proposal and then suddenly looking at you over the top of his glasses with the shadow of a grin, and saying, 'Now tell me what you want me to do and I'll do it.' He was two people, one when he had an audience, and a quite different person, when talking to you alone. I think it amused him to keep up in public the 'Vinegar Joe, Tough Guy' attitude, especially in front of his staff. Americans, whether they liked him or not – and he had more enemies among Americans than among British – were all scared of him. He had courage to an extent few people have, and determination, which, as he usually concentrated it along narrow lines, had a dynamic force. He was not a great soldier in the highest sense, but he was a real leader in the field; no one else I know could have made his Chinese do what they did. He was, undoubtedly, the most colourful character in South East Asia – and I liked him.[66]

The understanding between Slim and Stilwell led to what, it was hoped, would be the first outstanding feat of Anglo-Chinese collaboration. Slim agreed to stand and fight at Taungdwingyi if the Chinese under General Tu would back him up. Stilwell was delighted: 'Limeys will attack in force with all tanks. Good old Slim. Maybe he's all right after all.'[67] But the plan misfired badly. The Chinese failed to arrive – reliable reports said they had simply run away – and Slim's armoured brigade had to pull back quickly to avoid being encircled. Trying to make some sense of his embarrassment, Stilwell learned that the root of the problem was that Chiang had issued secret orders forbidding Tu to advance with the British. Stilwell was therefore in the impossible position of a commander whose troops refuse to obey him, and meanwhile he could neither shoot them, replace them nor even talk to them, as that was a waste of breath.[68] It was quite clear that every time he tried to take offensive action and Chiang agreed, the generalissimo would simply go behind Stilwell's back and sabotage everything. Chiang's defenders make three points, none of them very cogent. One is that in Chinese culture confrontation is to be avoided, so that if pushed into a corner a leader will agree to anything to save 'face' and then undo the agreement clandestinely. A second is that Chinese martial culture believes that war is a game of chess where you try to avoid decisive encounters. A third is that a leader does not have sufficient respect for his generals and military advisers because, unlike the scholar, bureaucrat or mandarin, the warrior has no secure place in Chinese culture.[69] The refutation of all these points, whatever their internal validity, is that unless he was terminally stupid, Chiang could not have imagined that he could carry these tenets into international relations and dealings with the West. To stand firm on such a set of credos could be justified in a leader who sought nothing at all from the West, but Chiang's greed for American money and materiel knew no bounds. Stilwell, therefore, was perfectly justified in his rage against the generalissimo. He considered three options: doing nothing, resigning, or once again confronting Chiang. It was obvious that for a person of Stilwell's temperament, only the third option was really viable. He stormed up to Chungking for a showdown.

Arriving on 1 April without notice, he ranted to Chiang about the insubordination of Chinese commanders, especially the general in charge of 22nd Division, and announced that he intended to resign forthwith as chief of staff in order to concentrate on a special training programme for 30 divisions in India. To use Stilwell's own words: 'At 12 o'clock went down and threw raw meat on the floor . . . I have to tell Chiang Kai-shek with a straight face that his subordinates are not carrying out his orders, when in all probability they are doing just what he tells them.' But he acknowledged that Madame Chiang was helpful and noted that she usually influenced her husband along the right lines. She was 'a clever, brainy woman. Sees the Western view-point . . . Direct, forceful, energetic, loves power, eats up publicity and flattery, pretty weak on her history.'[70] Since Chiang was about to fly to Maymyo to meet Alexander and Slim, the last thing he wanted was a sensational development with Stilwell. Madame suggested that Chiang go to Lashio to make it clear to the Chinese generals that Stilwell really was in charge. Once again Stilwell allowed hope to triumph over experience.[71] In the event it was he himself who flew to Lashio while Chiang went directly to Maymyo for his conference with Alexander. The generalissimo assured his allies that Stilwell had his full confidence and was vested with plenipotentiary powers. To 'prove' this he offered to send Stilwell the famous seal that had such talis-manic effect with Chinese commanders, stating that his chief of staff was Commander-in-Chief of the Chinese Expeditionary Force in Burma. Needless to say, when the seal arrived, it said nothing about plenipotentiary prerogatives but referred to Stilwell simply as chief of staff. Moreover, contrary to the agreement with Alexander at Maymyo, he did not send Stilwell a letter of authority, allowing him to punish recalcitrant Chinese generals. Madame meanwhile sent Stilwell the usual deluge of letters, trying to flatter and cajole him into accepting the unsatisfactory state of affairs; Stilwell concluded that she evidently thought all Westerners idiots.[72]

The Japanese were now preparing for the next phase of the campaign: the capture of Mandalay. To achieve this, they brought in two new divisions and two rank regiments and planned a three-column drive up the river valleys to smash the Allies between Lashio and the Chindwin before the monsoon came. First they softened up Mandalay in the devastating air raids that reduced the city to a charnel house (see p. 34). Even the cynical Chiang, visiting Mandalay after his confer-ence with Alexander, was shaken by what he saw and wrote to Churchill: 'I have seen nothing to compare with the deplorable unpre-pared state, confusion and degradation of the war area in Burma.'[73] To try to hold on to Mandalay, the generalissimo sent the 38th Division under General Sun Li-jen, generally considered the best of the Chinese generals. With the Japanese beginning to break through on the Mandalay front, another top-level military conference was held at Maymyo on 15 April, with Alexander, Slim and Stilwell all present. Whatever Alex's original feelings about Stilwell, he was by now fully convinced of his value as a fighting general, and there was no more sardonic talk in the officers' mess about 'Stilwell's great Chinese offensive'. 'He calls me "Joe" now,' Stilwell reported contentedly. When Alexander admitted that his troops seemed mesmerised by the enemy and genuinely afraid of the Japanese, Stilwell noted: 'Did Aleck [sic] have the wind up! Disaster and gloom. No fight left in the British. Afraid of the Japs who dress as natives and live openly in the villages.'[74] During the next few days Stilwell saw a good deal of Alexander, and his comments grew more and more patronising: 'Alexander impressed me as sucking a lot of moral support about of [sic] being around us' (17 April); 'Alexander will do anything I tell him to. Had him radio Wavell for two reconnaissance planes' (22 April).[75] Such astringent remarks probably reflected a growing feeling among the American military that Alexander was under secret orders from Churchill to cut and run, giving up the fight for Burma. Ironically, Mrs Luce Booth, energetically promoting the legend of 'Vinegar Joe' and even interviewing Chiang to that end, reported that Alexander had said to her: 'I do hope Joe doesn't go. I would find it very difficult to command the Chinese without him.'[76] Yet the military situation went from bad to worse. In mid-April the Japanese seized key points on the route to Lashio, cutting the Burma road and the escape route by which Stilwell planned to withdraw to China. To Stilwell's consternation, Slim informed him that he had issued contingency orders for the destruction of the oilfields at Yenangyaung. 'Good God, what are we fighting for?' was Stilwell's appalled response.[77]

The brutal battle for Yenangyaung on 17–20 April saw Stilwell and the Chinese at their best. The 38th Division under General Sun Li-jen took Twingon on 19 April after a hard slugging match, penetrated Yenangyaung on the 20th and fought off a vicious Japanese counter-attack in which heavy losses were taken by both sides. Slim eventually took the decision to pull the Chinese out to avoid the likely blood-bath in house-to-house fighting among the smoking ruins. Stilwell remained keen for yet another counterattack on Yenangyaung, as Slim recorded: 'I found him, as he always was, ready to support an offensive move and prepared to go a long way to help me.'[78] Yet Stilwell's capacity for offensive operations was limited by the need to keep substantial forces in the north to protect the Chinese 5th Army against flank attacks from Japanese forces on the Irrawaddy. Moreover,

Alexander was not keen on a counteroffensive, further increasing Stilwell's contempt for his 'defeatism'. 'Are the British going to run out on us? Yes' was a diary entry for 20 April.[79] In any case, all such ruminations appeared academic when the terrible news came in that the Japanese had severely routed the Chinese 6th Army in the hills behind the Mandalay–Rangoon railway and the Sittang. This was the defeat that enabled the Japanese to gain control of one of the world's most valuable wolfram mines (see p. 35). Having cowed the 6th Army, the Japanese began hooking around them to the north, taking Hopong and Loilem in a rapid move. Any chance of reinforcing Slim and his own 5th Army was gone, and Stilwell had to concentrate on the developing crisis in the north. Using 200th Division from the 5th Army, he headed for Taunggyi, hoping to retake it, but the Chinese at first refused to obey his orders. He then secured their cooperation by outright bribery, offering not only a bonus for every man who fought but a collective reward of 50,000 rupees if the town could be taken by 5 p.m. that day. They achieved that goal and then, flushed with victory, drove the Japanese out of Loilem and Hopong as well. As Slim recalled: 'It was a magnificent achievement, and only made possible by Stilwell's personal leadership.'[80] But it was too little, too late. It was the last hurrah of the Chinese, and both the 5th and 6th Army were exhausted and at the end of their resources.

The great Japanese eastern push through the Shan states was a total triumph. The Chinese withdrew to Lashio, but the Japanese advanced and took it on 29 April; they then pressed on to further triumphs in the north, capturing Bhamo on 4 May and Myitkyina on 8 May. By the time of the next Slim–Stilwell–Alexander conference, at Kyaukse, 25 miles south of Mandalay, on 25 April, all were agreed that the only recourse was to get out of Burma with as many divisions intact as they could manage. The conference was reported by one onlooker as follows: 'Slim dominated the scene, and made certain once and for all that no British or Indian troops would withdraw into China. Alexander gave me, at any rate, the impression of being rattled. I think he needed Slim to help him compete with Stilwell.'[81] The last week of April was the grimmest possible time, with bitter fighting around Meiktila and General Cowan falling back with great speed to Wundwin and beyond. By now all was chaos and confusion. In their retreat the Chinese behaved very badly – 'their necessities knew no law and little mercy', in Slim's graphic words, but as the scale of the Allied defeat became clear, war crimes and atrocities increased exponentially on all sides. British soldiers who drove jeeps with open tops were sometimes found decapitated by wires stretched across roads at neck height.[82] In the panic and rumour of war, it came to Stilwell's ears that the British, instead of covering the Chinese retreat north of Wundwin, were trying to get ahead of them in a Gadarene rush to safety. This was all the Limey-hating Stilwell needed. Without pausing to verify the report, he sent Slim a blistering message, accusing him in highly emotional terms of having failed to carry out his duty as the rearguard. Slim takes up the story:

> I dare say my nerves were nearly as stretched as his – we were neither of us having a very good time – and I was furious at this injustice to my troops who were at that moment fighting briskly far to the south of his Chinese. I replied with a very stringent refutation of the charge. This was the only time Stilwell and I fell out, but a few days later he sent me a message withdrawing the accusation and coming as near to an apology as I should think he ever got.[83]

Here it is appropriate to remark that Stilwell had a near obsession about the alleged cowardice of his allies and a conviction that practically everyone in both the British and the American armies was 'yellow'.[84] Stilwell's convictions about Chiang's duplicity and perfidy were quite correct, but it may be that he transferred these feelings, appropriate in that quarter, into areas where they had no validity at all. This is another way of saying that Stilwell, despite his great talents and impressive insights, was also a flawed individual.[85]

Meanwhile Stilwell's relations with the generalissimo, never great, reached rock bottom. The trigger seems to have been a fatuous decree by Chiang that water melons should be distributed to his troops, one for every four men.[86] Railing at this idiocy, Stilwell incautiously used his secret code word for Chiang – 'the Peanut' – in a public context and the contemptuous nickname was passed on to the generalissimo, who would certainly have assassinated any of his own generals for so impugning his honour. From that day on in Chiang's eyes Stilwell was a marked man, and he would intrigue against him tirelessly for the next two years. The first fruit of this new antipathy was Chiang's refusal to discipline his generals for gross insubordination, cowardice and dereliction of duty. Stilwell had wanted action taken against both Ch'en of the 55th Division, who deserted during the battle for Taunggyi, and Tu, whom he fingered as an egregious scrimshanker.[87] But Chiang pointedly ignored these requests. Chiang's anti-Western animus was increasing all the time, fuelled partly by Stilwell and partly by FDR's 'Europe first' policy. Particular offence was caused to Chiang, and for once Stilwell agreed with him, when Wavell suddenly ordered a bombing raid on Rangoon by US bombers, ostensibly to take the pressure off India. Having been told repeatedly that there were no fresh Allied resources to spare in Burma, Chiang now received the most blatant proof that Britain, not China, would always be the number one priority with Washington. In vain did the US ambassador in Chungking explain that General Marshall had had to assign US planes to help the British in South-East Asia as a quid pro quo for getting Churchill's agreement to a cross-Channel invasion in 1943 (which never happened), since the British wanted to postpone direct strikes at the heart of Europe, thinking them premature.[88] To Chiang all this had as much relevance as if it were happening on Mars. His enemy was the Japanese and his only concern was the Japanese (or so he said; actually his only real concern was the Chinese Communists).

To Stilwell it seemed that Chiang was becoming more imbecilic and more impossible by the moment, especially when he sent a message saying that Mandalay must be defended at all costs and then immediately another one countermanding the first order. Stilwell replied with a radio signal to say that he also wanted General Lu of the 28th Division court-martialled; again this request was ignored.[89] Despairing of his so-called boss, Stilwell was no happier with the British, whom he repeatedly accused in his diary of running from a fight. 'Alex has 36,000 men to take out [of Burma]!' he thundered. 'Where the hell have they all been?' In Stilwell's view, laziness and incompetence in the British upper class extended even to an insouciance about their own nationals. He went to confer with British headquarters about the British families still in his war zone. 'Dumb Limeys sitting around. Got a captain finally. Not interested, don't you know. "Our people are all out, I believe."'[90] At the beginning of May his anger became near apoplectic when he listened to a BBC broadcast that tried to put a positive 'spin' on the shambles of the long

64

retreat into India: 'General Alexander, a bold and resourceful commander, has fought one of the great defensive battles of the war. And a lot of crap about what the Limeys have been doing.'[91] In despair at both Chiang and Alexander, Stilwell decided that the only credible future lay in getting to India with six Chinese divisions, so that he could train them like Western soldiers, and they could eventually return to Burma and defeat the Japanese. 'God, if we can only get those 100,000 Chinese to India, we'll have something.'[92] Amazingly, given his hatred of Stilwell, Chiang gave approval in principle to the plan to train six of his divisions in India, subject to the sole proviso that the troops should not be used to put down risings by Indian nationalists. It may be that Chiang's thoughts were elsewhere. Late in April, FDR had joined Stilwell and the British on his hate list as a result of the Doolittle raids. On 18 April, USAAF commander James H. Doolittle led a daring raid on Tokyo by B-25 bombers – a brilliant propaganda coup to show that Japan was vulnerable to air attack.[93] Although the aircraft took off from the carrier *Hornet* some 700 miles off the Japanese coast, the plan was that they would then fly on to land at Chinese airfields. In the long term Japan responded by trying to take out all US aircraft carriers, and their disastrous defeat at Midway in June was the result. In the short term they vented their ire against China and its airfields. They launched ferocious attacks on the coastal areas of China where the Doolittle fliers had crash-landed and committed many atrocities and massacres of entire villages with women and children. Since Chiang had not even been informed about the raid until it was too late to cancel it, he felt both slighted and angry that, as he saw it, the Chinese people were having to pay the price for a futile American propaganda gesture.[94]

But now it was time for Stilwell to get out of Burma. On 1 May he had radioed for a plane to take him to India when he learned that Chiang's favourite general Lo Chin-ying had vanished or deserted; it later transpired that he had stolen a train at gunpoint with the intention of escaping north to Myitkyina but had crashed it 25 miles up the line. It suddenly seemed to Stilwell that if he departed by air, the Chinese soldiers would think that he too had decamped in panic and would never trust him again. He therefore took the decision, worthy of the samurai warriors of his Japanese opponents, that he would trek out overland. Decanting most of his headquarters staff on to the waiting C-47 transport plane, he announced that he intended to march out with the rest. He assembled a party of 140 people who seemed to represent all parties on the Allied side: there were 26 Americans, 13 Britons, 16 Chinese, some Burmese nurses and civilians, plus Indian cooks and mechanics. As his right-hand man on this perilous expedition he had the trusty Frank Merrill. 'By the time we get out of here, many of you will hate my guts, but I'll tell you one thing: you'll all get out.'[95] There was a choice of routes: either to India or north to Yunnan via Myitkina, but Stilwell initially kept his options open. From Kathaw the party set out for Indaw on 4 May, following a northern tributary of the Chindwin. They managed 14 miles a day in dreadful conditions in the hottest month of the year, just before the monsoon, prey above all to malaria and dysentery. They were beset by soldier ants, thorn bushes, sores, blisters and sundry infections; at one point they encountered a rogue elephant.[96] At one stage Frank Merrill, who never enjoyed robust health and had a weak heart, fainted of sunstroke in the middle of a river and had to be pulled over on an air mattress and afterwards carried by bearers; he was unconscious for two hours.[97] Stilwell's journal conveys the flavour of the terrible journey: 'May 8. Start ordered for 5.00. Off at 5.45. Delay in kitchen. Made Dorn mess officer. No guard on food. No check. Did four marches to Saingkyu. Arrived 10.15. Limeys' feet all shot. Our people tired. Damn poor show of physique. Chattering monkeys in the jungle. Bombers over, reminder that we are not yet out.'[98]

They crossed the Chindwin on rafts on 13 May. At Indaw Stilwell decided to turn west for India, taking a little-known route to avoid the mass exodus of Chinese and refugees. At this point the monsoon burst on them with full fury, but at least that alleviated all thoughts of Japanese pursuit. At Kawlum, reached on 14 May, there was good news: 'Heavy rain caught us just as we arrived. Soaked. Well, we were met at Kawlum by the British from Imphal. Food, doctor, ponies and everything. Quite a relief. Had chow with the British. Canned sausage, while our people had pig. Jones, Sibert and I struggled up the mountain and back to be polite. Rained like hell.'[99] The convoy was now relatively safe, but there was a further week of strenuous hiking over the Manipur hills in the monsoon before journey's end. The daily mileage improved: on 19 May the party covered 21 miles, but nothing could ever quite dampen Stilwell's epistolary Anglophobia: 'Two thirds of Limeys on ponies. None of our people.'[100] The Limey-bashing got worse when they reached Imphal the next day, with Stilwell in his diary initially praising his allies and thus setting them up for the 'sucker punch': 'Cordial reception by the Limeys. The provincial administrator failed to send our messages. The colossal jackass. "Oh, were they to be forwarded," he says. The colossal jackass.'[101] From Imphal the party was taken by lorry and train to Tinsukia, where there was a meeting with Wavell and Alexander, and then flown to Delhi. Stilwell was jubilant about his exploit and told his wife it had given him a new lease of energy with which to confront 'the Peanut'. One of his aides commented admiringly: 'Hell, that was a picnic excursion for him. He's just made of steel wire, rubber and concrete for guts.'[102] The general was certainly in gung-ho mood at his press conference in Delhi, where he made a famous announcement: 'I claim we got a hell of a beating. We got run out of Burma and it is as humiliating as hell. I think we ought to find out what caused it, go back and retake it.'[103]

Stilwell received the plaudits of President Roosevelt, a personal commendation from Stimson, a cordial message from General Marshall and even a eulogy from Madame Chiang. But her husband did not join in the chorus of praise. Apart from the pre-existing reasons for enmity and hatred towards Stilwell, Chiang fumed that his Chief of staff had not sent him a single message in May, in which time he had managed to transmit at least half a dozen to Washington. He was also angry about the losses to his beloved legions, for not only had thousands been killed in bitter fighting with the Japanese, but tens of thousands more had perished or gone missing on the retreat north. The first the generalissimo learned of Stilwell's arrival in India was when Brigadier General John Magruder of the American Military Mission in Chungking casually mentioned it to him. Chiang was furious and made clear to all within listening range that he had no confidence in his chief of staff. 'Stilwell deserted our troops and left for India without my permission,' he thundered, once again ignoring the fact that Stilwell's role as his aide was only one of four positions he filled.[104] Nevertheless Chiang at once mobilised his friends, allies and stooges to make a maximum propaganda onslaught on his favourite hate figure. Prominent in the lists was Chennault, who finally threw off the mask of affability and used Stilwell's jungle trek as 'proof' that his superior officer did not understand airpower. 'If

Stilwell had been a company, battalion or regimental commander whose primary responsibility was for the troops in his immediate command, his walkout would certainly have been commendable. But of a man with the tremendous burden of ranking American officer in Asia and Chief of Staff of the Chinese Republic, it was a startling exhibition of his ignorance or disregard for these larger responsibilities.'[105] The considerable anti-Stilwell faction in the USA also tried to make political capital out of Stilwell's 'eccentric' and 'inappropriate' decision to trek out of Burma instead of flying out. One of FDR's key assistants, Thomas Corcoran, minuted that Stilwell's decision was wrong on at least three counts: he was disobeying Chiang; his trek might have failed and he might have become the prisoner of the Japanese; and what he did was inconsistent with the dignity of a commander-in-chief.[106] These were the opening shots of a brutal anti-Stilwell propaganda campaign, waged either by the generalissimo's conscious minions or by Roosevelt's more Right-thinking or unthinking acolytes. The Chiang–Stilwell quarrel, which was to poison and bedevil Allied efforts in Burma, was destined to run and run.

To understand the actions of Slim and Stilwell in Burma it is enough to concentrate on their distinguished military careers before the coming of World War II. This is not the case with Orde Wingate, the third of the four larger-than-life personalities in the Burma war. With him the roots of his controversial personality and behaviour must be sought in early childhood. Wingate was born into a military family in February 1903. His father was a religious fundamentalist who had become a member of the Plymouth Brethren and then, aged 46, married the eldest daughter of another family in the Brethren. When the young Orde was two, his father reached retirement age and returned to England from India with his family. Wingate and his six siblings experienced the most austere and repressed childhood. They were kept away from other children for fear of spiritual 'contamination' and instead endured a regime of religious mania, spending whole days reading and memorising the Old Testament. Robert Louis Stevenson had a childhood suffused with gloomy thoughts of hell-fire and damnation, but was otherwise a pampered and much-loved child. In Wingate's case, added to the religious indoctrination was a spirit-shrinking spartan regime, a kind of secular boot-camp.[1] When the family moved to Godalming, Surrey, in 1916, Orde was finally sent as a day boy to Charterhouse school, but he was always an outsider who did not mix and played no sports. In 1921 he was accepted into the Royal Military Academy, Woolwich, training as an officer in the Royal Artillery. It was here, according to his recollections, that he endured a salient trauma. Freshmen who broke the rules or the code – and Wingate habitually broke all rules, whether social or hierarchical – had to undergo a ritual known as 'running'. First a howling mob of military students summoned the culprit from his room; then he was stripped naked; then he had to run between lines of senior students who whacked him with knotted towels; finally the victim was thrown into a tank of icy water.[2] By force of personality, Wingate fixed his eyes on his tormentors and defied them to do their worst. Taken aback by the 'unhinged' response to their ceremony, the students declined to chastise him. He then showed his contempt for the proceedings by plunging into the water tank himself. He had thus shown himself to be 'one to note' at an early age, for other trainee officers at Woolwich described this particular form of fazing as singularly terrifying.[3]

In 1923 Wingate received his commission as a gunnery officer. Posted to Salisbury Plain, he soon established a reputation as a skilled horseman, particularly keen on fox-hunting and point-to-point. But already observers noted a dark side: the contempt for rules and conventions extended to a Skimpole-like insouciance about paying his mess bills. The personality flaws became more overt: when posted to the Military School of Equitation in 1926, he alienated his peers and superiors by a brash and arrogant insubordination. But Wingate always enjoyed powerful patronage, and at this juncture he was rescued from a career cul-de-sac by his father's first cousin Sir Reginald Wingate, former Governor-General of the Sudan and High Commissioner in Egypt. 'Cousin Rex', as he was known, nudged Wingate into a future as an Orientalist. Obtaining leave, Orde studied Arabic at the London School of Oriental and African Studies and then served in Sudan and Ethiopia.[4] During leave periods in Britain, he carried on a five-year affair with a young woman named Enid 'Peggy' Jelley, to whom he was secretly engaged. Wingate seems to have been ambivalent about Peggy, valuing her for 'maternal' qualities but fobbing off her desire for marriage with vague mumblings about the hardship of garrison life. However, as the sixth year of the affair approached, he evidently felt he could stall no longer, and a public notice of the engagement appeared in the London press. Then fate lent a hand. Shortly after boarding the P & O liner *Cathay* at Port Said, returning to England for his marriage, Wingate met and fell heavily in love with a 16-year-old named Lorna Paterson, who was travelling home from Australia with her mother. This time it was not a case of a mother substitute but a genuine *coup de foudre*. As soon as he got to London,

Wingate told Peggy he was in love with another. His official biographer claimed that the jilted Peggy took the news in her stride and bore up stoically. But later research has revealed that she was devastated, to the point where she never married.[5] To her family's disgust, she remained loyal to Wingate. He repaid her self-denying fortitude by rationalisation, in effect blaming her for his early traumas by a weird psychological process of transference whereby she was conflated with his mother and thus accused of unacceptable weakness and inadequacy. It was arranged that Wingate would marry Lorna when she was 18. Instead of thanking the stars for this happy outcome to a knotty emotional crisis, Wingate rounded on his future mother-in-law, writing her a quite outrageously rude, hectoring and domineering nine-page letter, staggering for the vehemence of its language and its breathtaking, insulting contempt.[6]

Still, Wingate got his way, as he usually did, and, whatever his in-laws' opinion, he married Lorna in 1935. It is a curious example of a kind of family repetition compulsion that he married a woman 13 years younger than himself while his father had been 14 years older than his mother. Next year he became an intelligence officer with the British Mandate in Palestine and very soon became an ardent Zionist, in many ways *plus royaliste que le roi* since he was not himself Jewish. Palestine was at this point seething with unrest. There had been only 55,000 Jews in Palestine at the end of the First World War, but following the famous Balfour Declaration and, particularly, the Nazi persecution of Jews in Germany, a further 135,000 had arrived, and were perceived (rightly) by the indigenous Arabs as a threat to their future. In 1936 the Arabs declared a general strike, holy war was proclaimed by Haj Amin, the Grand Mufti, and there were attacks on Jewish settlements.[7] Arab guerrilla groups were ubiquitous. Supported by Wavell, the newly arrived commander-in-chief in Palestine, Wingate formed the so-called Special Night Squads (SNS) to combat Arab terrorism. Wingate was an early exponent of 'shock and awe', believing that paramilitary activity at night induced a unique and singular terror in an enemy. He spiced the SNS up with the use of slavering dogs, a calculated piece of cruelty since the animal was regarded as unclean by Muslims. This was another controversial episode in his career. The Special Night Squads were simply a legitimation of Zionist counter-terrorism, with Jewish thugs striking back at Arab ones. Mainly formed of Haganah members led by British officers, the squads appealed mightily to Wingate's Old Testament belief in the efficacy of 'smiting'. He was essentially retreading the tactics of the infamous 'Black and Tans' in Ireland in 1919–20, unleashing a private army to mete out random killings, beatings and other atrocities. Many of the unsavoury methods later adopted by the state of Israel were pioneered by Wingate, including the apparatus of collective punishment.[8] He set up phoney 'courts' and 'trials' followed by executions; he liked to raid villages, line up the inhabitants and order every tenth man executed.[9] Sometimes he would punish Arabs by smearing mud in their faces, and sometimes he would shoot them out of hand. On one occasion he exhorted his Jewish soldiers to dress up as Arabs, enter the Arab market at Haifa and begin shooting.[10] On another, after killing four Arabs in a raid on a suspect village, Wingate took five prisoners and grilled them about an alleged arms cache in the village. When the men pleaded ignorance, he took some sand and pushed it down the throat of one of the men until he choked and puked. When he still protested ignorance, Wingate ordered him shot and ordered a Jewish squad member to carry out the execution.[11]

It is beyond any doubt that Wingate was guilty of war crimes, and his actions were particularly outrageous given that Britain was in Palestine simply as a trustee for the indigenous people according to a League of Nations mandate. There could be no question here of compelling necessity or the defence of vital national interests. It is yet another strike against the record of Archibald Wavell that he should have allowed Wingate such a free hand.[12] Moreover, war crimes apart, Wingate allowed his Zionism to override his loyalty to his own country and his oath as an officer. He leaked confidential information from British army files to his Jewish friends, and in any conflict between the interests of the British Empire and those of Zion, he always opted for the latter.[13] Although the accusation that he later advised Haganah leaders to take up arms against the British and blow up the Haifa oil refinery have never been proved in a sense that would satisfy the legal definition of proof, it would be entirely in character for him to have done so, and many good witnesses allege that he did just that.[14] Chaim Weizmann, the leader of the Zionist movement, adopted him as a 'son' ; his own two natural sons had renounced the faith.[15] Wingate's head of intelligence in Palestine, Wing Commander A.P. Ritchie, said that his attachment to the Zionists made him worse than useless to the intelligence service.[16] It is amazing that he was not court-martialled for some of his activities, but he always had powerful protectors at court and in this instance he had the purblind Wavell as his patron. Nonetheless, by 1938 his almost blatant attachment even to the anti-British wing of the Zionist movement was becoming an open scandal and led to his recall. The obvious question arises: what animated his Zionist fanaticism? The usual answer is that his dark and gloomy background among the Plymouth Brethren is to blame, allied with his fervent belief in certain eschatological doctrines: in short, he believed he was doing God's work.[17] Others say that he became a Zionist because he identified the Jews with himself, as joint victims of bullying. Still others assert that Wingate was a contrarian, that because his brother officers were pro-Arab, he automatically had to be pro-Jew.[18]

Wingate was recalled because of his overidentification with one side in a conflict where he was supposed to be ringmaster. For many men it might have meant the end of an army career, and it is true that for two years Wingate was in the doldrums. In this interim period both Wavell and a new champion, Sir Edmund Ironside, kept his name before the high command and made interminable excuses for him, even when he recklessly criticised superior officers and deliberately went outside the chain of command. Ironside, who became Chief of the Imperial Staff, was initially attracted to him because he seemed to be a genuine version of the T.E. Lawrence legend; Ironside detested Lawrence, thought him a charlatan and wanted to raise up a true example of the guerrilla leader as a counterpoise.[19] Wavell, too, was irresistibly drawn to the Lawrence comparison. He pointed out that both Wingate and Lawrence had intellectual interests, were widely read and had retentive memories. In military terms, as regards supply, logistics, etc., Wingate the professional soldier had the edge over Lawrence the amateur, but Lawrence had the advantage of being both restful and humorous, whereas Wingate had no real sense of humour at all.[20]

It was the support of Wavell and Ironside that saw Wingate back in the martial saddle in early 1941. Wavell was waging his very successful campaign against the Italians in Ethiopia, and Wingate, once again with his commander's backing, attempted a rerun of the Special Night Squads. This time his band of irregulars was to be called Gideon Force and was a motley assemblage of British, Sudanese and Ethiopians and even some ex-Haganah men. Gideon was the Old Testament patriarch (featuring in the book of Judges) who led 300 men against superior numbers and defeated the enemy by discomfiting them with trumpets. Wingate's methods proved spectacularly successful, and this time there was no controversy, because he was fighting an accredited foe in wartime.[21] Yet by his tactlessness and insubordination, he engineered a situation where the high command whisked him out of Ethiopia at the end of hostilities with what even his critics thought was unseemly haste. Even without his alienation of his colleagues, Wingate had managed to be controversial. The psychologist C.G. Jung remarks that a fanatic, deprived of his initial outlet, will soon find another, even a glaringly contradictory one. Removed from the ambit of Zionism, Wingate conceived an equally irrational obsession with the Ethiopian emperor Haile Selassie and became, in effect, a kind of Rastafarian. For him the unkindest aspect of his sudden expulsion from the country was that he could not say goodbye to his adored and revered potentate.[22]

In Cairo, Wingate composed an angry 9,000-word report on the campaign in Ethiopia, criticising almost every aspect of it: the calibre of British army officers, the NCOs, signals officers and technicians, the equipment and rations, the weapons and armaments, the disdain shown for the native Abyssinians and, most bruisingly, the attitude of the general staff. Alarmed by the state of mind evinced by the report, Wavell went to the trouble of interviewing his turbulent junior. Initially sympathetic, he was gradually repelled by Wingate's almost pathological egotism. Both men went away angry. Shortly afterwards Wingate was informed that his report was impertinent in tone and unwarranted in its charges. Not only was it rejected, it was actually burned.[23] All that early summer Wingate had been sinking deeper and deeper into depression, possibly aggravated by malaria and the drug (atrabine) he took to combat it. The rejection of the report seems to have been the last straw, convincing Wingate that he was in a battle against Satan and that the Evil One had prevailed. Early in July 1941, he checked into the Continental Hotel in Cairo and attempted suicide. Lacking his Biretta revolver, which had been left behind in Addis Ababa when he was bundled out of Ethiopia, he had as his sole instrument of self-slaughter a rusty Ethiopian knife (a kind of variant on the bowie), with which he tried to cut his throat. He botched the job of severing the carotid artery, and the man in the adjoining room heard the sound of a body slumping heavily to the floor. Left alone, Wingate would have died within the hour, but he was rushed to hospital and operated on. For 24 hours he hovered between life and death but finally recovered.[24] Wingate was always subject to bipolar disorder or cyclothymia – there had been another acute episode in the Sudan – and it seems that it was a severe downswing in the manic-depressive cycle that led him to try to take his life. Both the syndrome and its particular manifestation in Wingate's case can be convincingly traced to the obsession with hell inculcated in his childhood.[25] His many enemies delighted in his supposed downfall, thinking he would either be court-martialled or sent to a lunatic asylum. But the army had enough problems without a cause célèbre of this kind, and anyway Wingate had many powerful backers. Either through ignorance or because he was leaned on, the army psychiatrist attributed the suicide attempt almost entirely to malaria and the unsupervised use of atrabine. The most bizarre aspect of the incident was that Wingate's wife and his friends tried to explain it away as 'justifiable self-homicide', the action of a man spurned by envious and inferior spirits. Wingate was often compared to Clive of India, and Lorna reminded him that Clive attempted suicide three times and finally succeeded.[26]

A general assessment of Wingate's character and attributes is essential if his career in Burma is to make any sense. Unfortunately, his biography is peculiarly problematical since he has become the object of a cult, a hero who, in the eyes of his admirers, did no wrong. As with many other cults of personality, where the subject is in effect deified, true believers will not tolerate *any* criticism of their totem; the case of C.G. Jung comes to mind. The historian, though, has to deal with incontestable facts, however unpalatable, and Wingate's career is full of pointers to a very dark personality indeed. He was rude, pushy, opinionated, bad-tempered, egotistical and self-promoting, an 'all or nothing' personality whose motto was 'Either you are for me or against me.'[27] His admirers have also compared him to Stonewall Jackson, Lawrence of Arabia and Gordon of Khartoum, though the only Gordon comparison that really works is that with Stilwell, for both were Westerners who commanded Chinese armies. Even more hyperbolically, the comparison has sometimes been extended to Cromwell and Napoleon.[28] Most emphatically not a team player – a serious drawback in a professional army officer – Wingate had a contempt for rank and authority, or at least for those superior to him in the hierarchy. When it came to those lower in the pecking order, he was a ferocious martinet who would brook no questioning of his orders and insisted they be carried out to the letter. But there was usually some 'compelling reason' why he could not be so meticulous about orders issued to him from above. To make matters worse, he frequently cheated by going outside the chain of command and appealing to powerful protectors several rungs above his 'line manager' in the hierarchy. Inevitably, words like 'humbug' and 'hypocrite' were frequently used about Wingate. There can be few more unsavoury spectacles than the habitual insubordinate who is also a ferocious disciplinarian.[29] Not surprisingly, most of his colleagues tended to lose their temper with him, which Wingate then used as self-validating proof that he was an object of envy for his superior talents. Even Wilfred Thesiger, himself a pitiless egotist, dedicated to violence and primitivism, fell foul of Wingate in Ethiopia and referred to him as 'ruthless and uncompromising, an Old Testament figure, brutal, arrogant and assertive.[30] The only colleague who seemed capable of handling him was Captain Douglas Dodds-Parker, his assistant in Ethiopia, later an SOE executive and a distinguished post-war Tory politician. Two of Dodds-Parker's bons mots are worth citing. Once, when Wingate had been delivering one of his interminable jeremiads about Haile Selassie as David with the Italians in Ethiopia as Goliath, Dodds-Parker interjected: 'I can't help thinking, Orde, that you are making a sob-story out of necessity. I am all for human courage and David versus Goliath, but I wish we could get just enough elastic to provide David with a sling.' Dodds-Parker also remarked that he had lived too close to Wingate to take him entirely seriously, and on another occasion brought him down to earth as follows: 'Come on, Orde, you are not Napoleon yet, nor even T.E. Lawrence.[31]

Few public figures have ever been more overtly and blatantly arrogant than Wingate. He assigned himself the status of 'great soldier' on the basis of his work in Ethiopia; he habitually used the word 'shall' in his orders, implying that the command came from a godlike figure; when he could not get from the Indian army 100 per cent of what he had demanded, he wrote back: 'Inability is a sign of incapability.'[32] Part of this stemmed from a genuine belief that he was doing God's work and engaged in a daily battle against Satan. Wingate exhibited most of the classic signs of paranoia, from delusions of grandeur to a feeling that there was a general conspiracy to do him down and minimise his talents. If he did not get the promotion he sought and thought he deserved, he never reflected that this might be because of some personal shortcoming or because he was not yet ready for higher office or rank; it was always because he was being victimised by envious nonentities of superior rank. If he was officially reprimanded or otherwise visited with official disapproval, the paranoia would reach storm force.[33] Another classic sign of religious mania, apart from paranoia, is a relish for violence, in line with the activities of the 'smiting' Yahweh of the Old Testament. Here as in other other areas Wingate aligned more properly with the explorer H.M. Stanley than with Gordon or Lawrence. Like his colleague in Ethiopia Wilfred Thesiger, Wingate thought human life had no intrinsic value, and would have guffawed at those who spoke of it as 'sacred'. Not content with reducing officers who disagreed with him to the ranks, he would sometimes physically assault them. In this regard he made no distinction between officers and enlisted men, lashing out at all who annoyed him. The most notorious assault on a brother officer was that on Captain Brian Franks, of a cavalry regiment, who happened to make a derogatory, though entirely justifiable, remark about Zionists.[34] The religious mania, paranoia, propensity to violence and underlying cyclothymia unquestionably made Wingate a suitable case for treatment. As Churchill's personal physician Lord Moran wrote in his diary: 'Wingate seemed to be hardly sane . . . in medical jargon a borderline case.'[35]

As if all this was not enough, Wingate was both an exhibitionist and a sartorial eccentric. Careless of dress, unkempt, slatternly and slovenly, he evinced disrespect for military convention and hierarchy while expecting his superiors to satisfy his every whim. During his period of deep gloom just before the suicide attempt in Cairo in July 1941, he asked for an interview with General Auchinleck, who had just succeeded Wavell as commander-in-chief in the Middle East. Auchinleck was appalled to find a slovenly figure in his office, looking both swarthy and sallow, with wrinkled thighs visible below his shorts, wearing a dirty solar topi and a greasy bush jacket. Auchinleck, a stickler for proper dress, roared at him to get out and return only when he was properly dressed.[36] Curiously for one who set so much store by physical prowess, Wingate was a weedy physical specimen and not very practical; by common consent he was a hopeless driver.[37] He seems to have 'compensated' for this with deliberate exhibitionism, often going around camp naked, or appearing out of a shower, nude, to bark an order at his men, still wearing a shower cap and scrubbing himself with a shower brush as he spoke. He liked to wear an alarm clock around his wrist that would go off on odd occasions for no particular reason that any onlooker could discern. He was rarely seen without his trademark Wolseley helmet and fly whisk, and carried on a string around his neck a raw onion on which he would occasionally munch as a snack.[38] He would dictate letters while parading around naked, and even experimented with the method later made famous by Lyndon Baines Johnson, carrying on conversations while sitting on the lavatory. Notoriously absent-minded about practical matters, he often went on trips without basic necessities like soap or shaving kit, rarely cleaned his teeth and was careless about hygiene, for example using a bidet as a urinal. There were frequent food fads too, which he imposed on his men and his staff: he tinkered with vegetarianism and, like many men of a monomaniacal bent, believed in the virtues of copious mugs of hot tea. He also saw no point in unnecessary laundry and rarely changed his clothes.[39] Eccentricity is a mild word to use.

The limbo period Wingate spent in London, in semi-despair, in the autumn and winter of 1941 is a crucial part of his biography but not really relevant to his time in Burma. The salient fact was that at the beginning of 1942, his champion Wavell remembered him from Ethiopia and asked for his services in South-East Asia. Wingate was originally told he would be training Chiang's Chinese in guerrilla warfare, and he was unenthusiastic on two grounds. First, such an endeavour would be like teaching one's grandmother to suck eggs. Second, what was the point of sending a Middle East expert to the China-Burma-India theatre?[40] But on 27 February he found himself on a Liberator bound for Delhi, still with the rank of major. A lengthy stopover at Cairo meant that his journey took three weeks, and it was 19 March before he met Wavell for a briefing. By this time Rangoon had fallen. Wavell told him that his remit had changed, that he would now be in charge of all guerrilla operations against the Japanese in

Burma. What this meant was not immediately clear, for at least four bodies of irregulars were already operating in and around Burma. There was the Special Operations Executive (SOE), with whom Wingate had declined to serve in London in his limbo period.[41] There was the American forerunner of the CIA, the Office of Strategic Services (OSS), operating in Assam and north Burma and vainly trying to persuade Stilwell of the efficacy of irregular operations.[42] There was V-force, supposedly specialising in liaison with the Kachin and Naga hill tribes and with the Muslim traders of the Arakan peninsula and mainly recruited from Anglo-Burmans and Anglo-Indians.[43] Finally there was the British-run Bush Warfare School, designed to train Chinese guerrillas for sabotage operations inside Burma. At the head of the Bush Warfare School was a colourful roistering character named Michael ('Mad Mike') Calvert.[44] Wavell suggested that Wingate should begin by assuming command of the Bush outfit, and accordingly he flew down to Maymyo, east of Mandalay. On paper this should have been a disastrous move, for the fire-eating Calvert was just then returning from an embarrassing fiasco that nearly precipitated 'friendly fire'. Determined to drown his sorrows once back at Maymyo, he was astounded to see a stranger sitting at his desk. Calvert takes up the story: 'I glared at him and said, "Who are you?" He was quite calm and composed. "Wingate," he replied. In spite of my unpleasant mood I was impressed. He showed no resentment at this somewhat disrespectful treatment by a major. He began talking quietly, asking questions about the showboat raid. And to my surprise they were the right sort of questions. Tired as I was I soon realised this was a man I could work for and follow.'[45]

Soon Wingate and Calvert were close friends. They decided their first task should be to go down to see Slim at Prome, 250 miles away. Calvert openly deferred to his new friend by suggesting that, with his mandate from Wavell, he should be the one to be closeted with Slim. This was April 1942, just before the retreat from Burma, at the point where Slim was trying to see whether anything could be salvaged at the eleventh hour. Slim had already met Wingate once, in East Africa in 1940, when both were serving under Wavell and fighting the Italians. The talks went well, with 'several lively discussions on the organisation and practice of guerrilla warfare'. While agreeing with some of Wingate's theories, Slim doubted if his Ethiopian experience was strictly relevant, since there the indigenous population had been actively hostile to the enemy, unlike the situation in Burma, and jungle warfare was a much tougher proposition than campaigning in mountains or deserts. Nevertheless he paid the newcomer a handsome compliment: 'Wingate was a strange, excitable, moody creature but he had fire in him. He could ignite other men. When he so fiercely advocated some project of his own, you might catch his enthusiasm or you might see palpable flaws in his arguments; you might be angry at his arrogance or outraged at so obvious a belief in the end, his end, justifying any means; but you could not be indifferent. You could not fail to be stimulated either to thought, protest or action by his sombre vehemence and his unrelenting persistence.'[46] Wingate too was impressed and told Calvert that Slim was the best man, bar Wavell, east of Suez. Later he amplified: 'There is only one soldier worthy of the name East of Suez. He is a bad-tempered little terrier by the name of Slim.'[47] What particularly impressed him was Slim's coolness and aplomb, his failure to react with irritation or indeed any strong emotion to Wingate's outlandishness. Slim was concerned solely with how effective an officer would be in Burma; he was uninterested in Wingate's colourful past or his suicide bid. He was capable of differentiating between a man's character and his military talent, and was prepared to give Wingate the chance to see what he could do. This was, however, the high-water mark of the Wingate–Slim accord; each was gradually to become disenchanted with the other.

When Alexander replaced Hutton at the end of March, Chiang flew down from Chungking to meet him (see p. 60). When they returned to China, Wingate wangled a seat on the plane alongside the generalissimo, hoping to learn about warfare in Burma from the horse's mouth. But the flight turned into a nightmare: first the aircraft was chased by Japanese fighters and had to take evasive action, and then it ran into severe turbulence, which ended with Madame Chiang throwing up violently.[48] With consummate naivety, Wingate had imagined Chiang as a second Hailie Selassie, and was presumably quickly disillusioned. He was certainly taken with the feminine charms of Madame Chiang, but failed to make much headway with her husband. Stilwell scathingly remarked (for Chiang had at one time converted to Methodism and studied the Good Book) that the meeting between Wingate and the generalissimo was 'the clash of two Bible thumpers'.[49]

In any case, when he reached Chungking, General J.G. Bruce, head of the British military mission there, told him that for a twofold political reason it would not be possible to transfer the Chinese Bush Warfare troops to his command: Burma was on the point of being lost, and the Chinese irregulars had already been assigned to Stilwell and the American allies.[50] Frustrated, Wingate returned to Maymyo on 15 April to find the chaos principle reigning supreme. Calvert told him that over 100 of his Bush Warfare people had just been ambushed on the Irrawaddy and only 11 had survived. Perhaps even more seriously, it was clear that Wingate's advent was bitterly resented not just by senior officers in the Indian army but by the irregulars of the Bush school themselves, who understandably regarded him as an unproved Johnny-come-lately. Wingate decided to take Calvert with him on a week-long car tour of the Burmese frontier. Calvert claimed that his new friend enabled him to see Burma with fresh eyes and to point out details that had previously escaped him. In his obsessive, quasi-scholarly way, Wingate made a careful note of animals, insects and reptiles and even details like the sogginess of the ground and the space between the trees.[51]

In Delhi from 24 April, Wingate announced that he had clarified his ideas to the point that he now made a clear distinction between guerrilla warfare, which was a reactive matter, and the more proactive notion of long-range penetration (LRP); he no longer had any interest in the former but only in the latter. He had not yet developed the extreme or radical theory of LRP he was later to propound, but at conferences in May–June 1942 he hammered away at three main motifs: that Japanese troops behind the lines must perforce be inferior to those at the front; that a British force should get behind them, communicate with base by radio and be supplied from the air; and that cutting supply lines and destroying arms dumps would tie up a disproportionate number of enemy troops.[52] He spent eight weeks in a long battle of attrition with army authorities, particularly the Director of Staff Studies, who allotted troops to various theatres. Against Wingate's urgent pleas, the army hierarchy made many telling points: it was foolish to think that men could be trained for jungle warfare in just eight weeks, as Wingate seemed to think; the Ethiopian analogy, which he was fond of pushing, was misleading as the Burmese population was very far from being uniformly pro-British; LRP groups should be formed solely from volunteers, not secondments from regular regiments as Wingate was suggesting; and the numbers Wingate was proposing were unrealistic given general shortages – he wanted a minimum of 3,000 men but the army would be stretched to provide a maximum of 1,300. These were powerful arguments, especially that relating to manpower shortage, but Wingate tried to counter them by talking up the role of the hill tribes and talking optimistically about recruiting Pathans to his standard. He tried to obfuscate by introducing a somewhat otiose distinction between tactical and strategic penetration,[53] but what it came down to was that his special units would have to be supplied by airdrops. The idea of supplying irregulars from the air was not a new one, although Wingate's more gung-ho supporters later claimed that no one had thought of it before.[54]

Wingate endured a tense few months. As time went on, he began once more to slip into depression. The long game was not really his style and patience was not one of his virtues. Only the influence of Wavell stood between him and the outright rejection of his ideas. However, his spirits were boosted by the support he received from a cadre of like-minded officers, initially just Calvert but soon to include men like Bernard Fergusson, on the Joint Planning Staff at GHQ. Fergusson was just the sort of British officer Stilwell detested, a monocled Old Etonian with a patrician drawl who had served in the Black Watch, but he was a genuine man of action who welcomed the excuse to escape the secretariat for battleground bravado. He describes the impact of the 'broad-shouldered, uncouth simian officer', who 'used to drift gloomily into the office for two or three days at a time, audibly dream dreams, and drift out again . . . As we became aware that he took no notice of us . . . but that without our patronage he had the ear of the highest, we paid more attention to his themes. Soon we had fallen under the spell of his almost hypnotic talk; and by and by we – some of us – had lost the power of distinguishing between the feasible and the fantastic.'[55] With Calvert, Fergusson and Captain George Dunlop, another veteran of the recent retreat from Burma, on his side, Wingate had the credibility to press his commander-in-chief harder. Wavell responded by agreeing to the numbers requested and redesignating the various LRP groups as the 77th Indian Brigade.

The new brigade was a motley collection. The elite troops were the volunteers from the infantry regiments and the Royal Engineers who had been in the original Bush Warfare School. The other main British component was the 13th Battalion of the King's Liverpool Regiment, raised in Glasgow, Manchester and Liverpool in 1941. These were mainly older, married men with no dreams of martial glory, previously employed in the coastal defence of Britain and suddenly shipped to India after Pearl Harbor in December 1941. Assigned to Wingate in June, they not surprisingly displayed a marked lack of enthusiasm for his schemes, and in any case most of them were too old and too unfit for jungle warfare.[56] Wingate rejected 250 of them at first sight, including the colonel, and got Wavell's permission to fill the gaps by ad hoc drafts from other units. The rest of the new LRP force was made up from two Oriental units. With the first of these, the 2nd Battalion, Burma Rifles, Wingate always enjoyed good relations. They were mainly warriors from the anti-Japanese hill tribes – the Karens, Kachins and Chins – who seem to have been affected by the Wingate magnetism. They imbibed his ideas eagerly and he learned much from them about jungle warfare.[57]

Yet with the other Asian component of 77th Indian Brigade, 2nd and 3rd Battalion, Burma Rifles, Wingate always had the most antagonistic and unsatisfactory relationship. Although the Gurkhas were universally held in high regard, Wingate thought they were arrogant, ill-disciplined and overrated. Quite why he thought that is a mystery, but it may be that at root he shared Noel Irwin's pride in the British army in India and a corresponding disdain for the Indian army, which he once described as 'the largest unemployed relief organisation in the world'. Certainly he was 'pathologically opposed' to the close and almost mystical family relationship that existed between officers and men in most Indian regiments, and above all in the Gurkha Rifle regiments.[58] The Gurkhas in turn found Wingate arrogant and domineering, a know-all who would not listen to men who had actually fought in Burma. Reasonably enough, they thought they knew far more about jungle warfare than a man whose previous experience had been entirely in deserts and mountains. They had their own traditions and tactics and viewed Wingate as an amateur who had nothing to teach them. Moreover, they disliked him personally, for his rude and autocratic treatment of their officers led to loss of 'face' for the entire regiment.[59] He was also too impatient to recruit liaison officers with a proper mastery of the Gurkhali tongue. Needless to say, Wingate and his close associates like Calvert believed as an article of faith that any resistance or opposition to a Wingate ukase was fomented or engineered among the Gurkhas by senior officers in the Delhi hierarchy. But the Gurkhas needed no goading from the Indian army to loathe Wingate cordially. As one Indian army general who had been a Gurkha officer put it: 'He brought off what must be an all-time record in rotting out a Gurkha battalion, a young one withal.'[60] Or, as the historian of the Gurkhas has expressed it: 'Wingate was the only officer in 130 years of service ever to criticise the performance of Gurkha soldiers, characterising them as mentally unsuited for their role as Chindits. Of course the same might be said of Wingate.'[61]

Welding such heterogeneous elements into a cohesive fighting force was a Herculean task, but the energetic Wingate began his tough training programme in July 1942. He divided his force into eight columns, each commanded by a major and each with 15 horses and 100 mules. Since the columns would be sustained by airdrops, there was also an RAF signalling section attached to each unit. The columns trained in the Central Provinces of India, in the Saugur jungle south of Gwalior, where Major General Wilcox of Central India Command was, fortunately, a Wingate supporter and gave him every assistance. The idea was to simulate every contingency the columns might encounter, short of contact with the enemy himself. Wingate believed that human beings underrated the horrors and trials they could endure, and his spartan training programme was accordingly designed to push his men to the limit and beyond. As Calvert put it: 'Most Europeans do not know what their bodies can stand; it is the mind and willpower which so often give way first. Most soldiers never realised that they could do the things they did, and hardly believe it now. One advantage of exceptionally hard training is that it proves to a man what he can do and suffer. If you have marched thirty miles in a day, you can take twenty-five miles in your stride.'[62] Every conceivable privation was visited on the men of the LRP. They endured encounters with snakes, mosquitoes and leeches, learned to deal with exhaustion as a daily fact of life and were deliberately kept on half-rations in preparation for the ordeals to come. If men collapsed under the heat of long marches with full pack, they were simply put under the shade of trees and received no further comforts. When the monsoon broke they slogged through mud, rivers and teeming rain. The training day began at 6 a.m. with half an hour's bayonet drill, and then unarmed combat. Breakfast was followed by woodcraft lectures and exercises, map-reading, use of the compass, instruction in distinguishing useful plants from poisonous ones. The daily exercises would include route marches, blowing bridges, laying ambushes or simulating attacks on airfields. After a rest during the noonday heat there would be fatigues, such as digging latrines, mule-tending and jungle-clearing, from 3 to 5 p.m. Then there would be further strenuous tasks until dusk.[63]

It seems quite clear from contemporary accounts that at Gwalior Wingate was widely disliked by his men and popular only with an inner circle, especially Calvert, Fergusson and Dunlop. It must be said that the mental processes of this trio were uncannily like Wingate's own. Calvert was a ferocious disciplinarian, though he could maintain order by personal magnetism and authority, whereas Wingate usually needed to mete out punishments. Fergusson was obsessed with the view that in the Middle East he and Wingate had been living in a golden age among elite personnel and that now they had somehow been relegated to a second XI.[64] Some said that 'Mad Mike' was as crazy as his boss, and the idea gained ground when he and Wingate ordained that everything was to be done at the double, with even his officers having to run everywhere to keep up with him, expected to hear every word he said as he jogged furiously.[65] Fergusson had been repeatedly warned by his colleagues at GHQ Joint Planning to have nothing to do with Wingate, including this gem from a departing major at Saugur: 'My advice to you is to turn round and go straight back to Delhi. Wingate's crackers and I'm off.'[66] The issue of reporting sick became especially contentious. At the beginning of the training programme there were sickness levels as high as 70 per cent. Wingate dealt with this in typically ruthless fashion, decreeing that attending sick parade without very good reason was a punishable offence. In the case of those claiming to be suffering from dysentery, he ordered his officers into the latrines to inspect the men's stools to see if they were lying.[67] Like H.M. Stanley, whom he resembled in so many ways, Wingate accepted that he could be genuinely sick himself but did not really believe in anyone else's illnesses, which he regarded as hypochondria or malingering. Among the multitude of enemies he made by his attitudes was the Medical Corps, who largely regarded him as a barbarian. He also had a positive mania about the so-called Tactical Exercises Without Troops. A massive sandpit, some 40 yards square, was used to simulate the relief conditions in a stretch of territory, complete with rivers, hills, gun emplacements etc., done on a scale of 100 yards to a foot. Wingate then had his officers lie prone in the sandpit to visualise the terrain – literally the lie of the land. Because the men were tired from their normal duties, they did not always build the model with the precision their martinet commander required, but he brooked no excuses.[68] And he came close to public explosion when he held the first full-scale manoeuvre at the end of September, witnessed by Wavell and other top brass, and it fell far short of his expectations; there were particular problems about handling the mules. Nevertheless, Wavell's continuing favour meant that Wingate was promoted to the rank of brigadier during the training of the LRP groups.

Throughout this period Wingate evinced singular insensitivity about public relations and self-image and, by his arrogance, alienated further swathes of people in the Indian army. When one senior officer came to a meeting and said that because of other commitments he could stay no longer than an hour, Wingate swept up his papers, stormed from the room and said he would return when the officer had sufficient time to take his duties seriously.[69] At another conference he demanded to know why certain equipment had not been supplied and was then interrupted by a protest from another senior officer that this was the first he had heard of the request. 'I have been told nothing about this whatsoever,' said the officer. 'Why should you have been?' Wingate answered scornfully. 'I'm telling you now.'[70] He particularly antagonised Major General S. Woodburn Kirby, Wavell's Director of Staff Studies. When Wingate was incensed that there had been a delay in sending him smoke grenades, he signalled to GHQ that 'those responsible should be sacked for iniquitous and unpatriotic conduct'. His rudeness to Kirby was egregious and he treated him (again, his superior) 'as if he were the inefficient manager of a rather unsatisfactory multiple store'.[71] But the high point of his arrogance came in a self-assessment in 1942 where the real man is finally on full view, in a way that even his defenders cannot mitigate or attenuate. Self-pity, delusions of grandeur and paranoia manifest themselves in a singular fashion.

I must be exceptional, even today, when an officer who has defeated and destroyed nearly 40,000 enemy troops, strongly supported by aircraft and artillery, with 2,000 troops, without either aircraft or artillery, and in complete isolation from any other operations, who, as scarcely ever happens in war, has not only been in sole command of the forces engaged, but has also planned the whole campaign, organised, trained and equipped the troops, and brought the whole to a satisfactory conclusion, that such an officer on his arrival home should not even be asked to see the men who are responsible for the army's hitherto not highly successful campaign; that as soon as they hear he is not fit to fight the only response should be an order to join the regimental depot at Woolwich with the rank of major. Even if it were only for a day, it would be a waste of a day.'[72]

Notable also in this screed are the outright lies and the failure to tell the whole truth. His description of the Ethiopian campaign is a self-regarding travesty; he was granted interviews with generals like Wavell and Ironside far beyond what his rank and achievements warranted; and so far from being consigned to obscurity, he was transferred to Burma through a notable act of favouritism. Truly in Wingate's world no good deed went unpunished.

Wingate's paranoia is underlined by his curious decision to have Calvert spend much of his time not at the training camp but in Delhi as 'brigade liaison', or in other words, as Wingate's spy in the corridors of power. One wonders why, instead of expending so much energy on finding out what his critics were saying about him, he did not make some attempt to humour them, conciliate them or meet them halfway. At any rate Calvert heard enough to become alarmed, and wrote to Wingate on 6 August that he was generally considered 'not fit to command'.[73] Wingate's reply, containing not an atom of reflection or self-criticism, was entirely predictable: 'Before I took command in Ethiopia people were saying exactly the same things they are reported as saying now. If there is any difference, I am a good deal more moderate now than I was then, having learned some valuable lessons in the interim. The personal attacks cannot be answered by argument but they can be, and are, answered by the facts. It is because I am what I am, objectionable though that appears to my critics, that I win battles.'[74] That reply implied that Wingate had learned some humility, but there was little evidence of this. He misinterpreted the Burmese word for lion – *chinthe* – as *chindit* and declared that from now on the lions of the LRP would be called Chindits. His Burmese aide Sao Man Hpa told him that the word made no sense in Burmese, but Wingate replied that *chinthe* made no sense in English (but Chindit did?) and he would therefore continue to call his men Chindits. Wingate always had a cavalier way with local cultures, customs and languages, as his treatment of the Gurkhas reveals. He appointed two Burmans – Sao Man Hpa and Aung Thin – to be his experts on Burma even though they protested that as Western-educated oligarchs they knew little about the country and were barely literate in the language.[75] Wingate overrode their objections as he always overrode inconvenient truths. Yet on certain men he made a profound impression, and indeed it would be impossible to explain his posthumous fame otherwise. His clear, carrying voice obviously helped, as did the piercing, unblinking stare usually associated with fanatics, faced with which most sensible men simply backed down. By all accounts he had the rare gift of being able to remind his men of death and the unlikelihood of their returning from missions without demoralising them. This is a faculty usually associated with men with an innate gift for leadership like Ernest Shackleton, who could make his men believe he was their brother or father, as appropriate. There was no 'band of brothers' quasi-kinship motif in Wingate's brand of leadership. What seems to have riveted those he appealed to was his very quality as an Old Testament prophet, the sense that he was not quite of this planet or this dimension.[76]

After the unsatisfactory first manoeuvre, Wingate ran his men through a fresh series of hoops. This time there were night marches as well. Gradually his ruthlessness forged a corps with self-belief and a sense of self-reliance.[77] But there were significant costs. He reduced the sickness level to 3 per cent (from 70 per cent at the beginning of the training), but only by brutal methods whereby even the genuinely ill were too afraid or browbeaten to go on sick parade and behaved like the inhabitants of Samuel Butler's *Erewhon*, in denial even about the most palpable maladies. Such behaviour, complete with periodic tirades about the Western world's effete reliance on physicians and doctors, further alienated the medical profession, who universally 'thought Wingate was mentally unstable. We couldn't write it down of course, but we all agreed amongst ourselves. We couldn't understand why he was kept on.'[78] Even sympathetic observers agreed that Wingate acted barbarously. John Masters, who later commanded a Chindit brigade and went on to become a best-selling novelist, wrote: 'I believe Wingate lacked humanity. He thought in great terms, and worked for great ends, among great men. For that huge majority which is less than great he had little sympathy.'[79]

Beneath the surface, however, even the Ahab-like Wingate had doubts. Was it not true, as everyone kept insisting, that so far he had beaten only weak and mediocre enemies (the Italians would be no one's first choice as a warrior race) but that he was about to come up against a truly martial people, man for man easily the superior of Westerners? It is probable that this underlying tension accounted for the increasingly eccentric behaviour in the autumn of 1942. He obsessed about the necessity of wearing shorts in the rain and the branding of numbers on the mules, about the efficacy of raw onions, for whose qualities he was now proselytising througout the brigade, and about the salubrious qualities of buffalo milk; he kept four of the beasts tethered for personal milking.[80] But he lacked concern for the truly relevant details: he ordered that all non-swimmers should be taught to swim, but then failed to follow this up and enforce the ruling.[81] The obsessive, finical concern with unimportant details seems to have been transferred also to Fergusson, for he began complaining that his men could never keep quiet and that they were irremediable litter louts.[82] This jittery period finally came to an end in November. The training ended with two full-scale exercises: the first, lasting five days, around Saugur, to sharpen up on signalling, was widely considered a success; but the second, involving streamlined handling of the mules, was less so, and the incompetent management of the animals at one point bade fair to diversify into general indiscipline and defeatism.[83] Wingate's military machine was by no means perfect, but his credibility meant that he could not turn back now, whatever his doubts. Wavell told him that he should expect to be in action by January 1943. Wingate's personal Rubicon had already been crossed.

When Slim arrived in India ahead of his troops, he was appalled by the attitudes he encountered among his so-called colleagues. The defeated soldiers were treated not as heroes but as men who had shirked their duty, and this from officers who had been enjoying comfortable billets while the men of BURCORPS suffered and died. He himself almost immediately fell foul of Lieutenant General Noel Irwin, who commanded 4 Corps, responsible for the defence of north-east India, and was one of the most trenchant critics of the fiasco in Burma.[1] Irwin was one of those overpromoted nonentities who compensate by dictatorial egocentricity. When he spoke to Slim harshly and with barbed criticism about the retreat from Burma, Slim quite rightly replied: 'I never thought an officer whose command I was about to join could be so rude to me.' The incomparable Irwin riposted: 'I can't be rude. I'm senior.'[2] It seems that he was paying off an old score. Irwin had been commissioned into the Essex Regiment. During the Sudan campaign of 1940, 1st Essex Regiment broke and fled at Gallabat, and Slim subsequently sacked the commanding officer, an old friend of Irwin's. Burma was thus payback time.[3] With no under-standing of what the troops had suffered on the retreat, blimpish officers complained vociferously about the lack of discipline and break-down in morale among the new arrivals. The immaculately turned-out administrative staff at army headquarters in Delhi became known to the exhausted survivors as the 'gabardine swine', and the same general perception held good wherever the returnees were dispersed, whether at Imphal, Ranchi or elsewhere.[4] The most intelligent observers concluded that the failure in communication between those who had seen active service at the front and those who had not was at root Alexander's fault, and his lack of proper leadership was especially reprehensible. His sudden decision to cut and run, it was said, engendered a devil-take-the-hindmost, *sauve qui peut* mentality among those fleeing Burma. Wavell, too, and the viceroy must take some share of the blame, for there seemed to be no overall mind directing affairs from the top, with so many welfare efforts being carried out ad hoc or privately. The Indian Tea Association, for example, ran trucks with relief supplies as far as Imphal but not beyond, and soon ceased doing even that after complaints from Indian civil servants and journalists that the rescue efforts were racist, with Europeans and Anglo-Indians being favoured.[5]

Slim, always cautious about pointing the finger at figures superior in the hierarchy, later remarked blandly and without naming names that no preparations had been made to welcome the Burma veterans back into India, as no foresight had been applied at any level. It did not help that India itself was in crisis in 1942, and that Japanese bombing raids reached as far as Imphal, with heavy aerial attacks there on 10 and 16 May. The best-case scenario was that everyone returning from Burma should either have gone on immediate leave or been taken to hospital at speed, but the woefully inadequate transport facilities in India did not permit this. Yet there was worse to come, for, as Slim said: 'If our welcome into India was not what we expected, the comfort provided was even less.'[6] Basically, there was no housing available for the wretched and tempest-tossed of Burma, and the troops were simply told to bivouac in the open. The 'luckier' ones were herded into makeshift camps originally designed to take one tenth of the numbers that were eventually shoehorned into them. As an eye-witness reported of one of these 'health resorts' north of Imphal: '[it was] uncomfortable, not only because it was raining hard ... but because we had no shelter or unsoiled ground on which to lie, thousands of people having previously occupied it, with surprisingly primitive ideas for soldiers, on the most elementary rules of sanitation'.[7] Even when trains did become available for onward transport, the suffering soldiers soon realised they had merely swapped one version of hell for another. The three-day rail journey from Dimapur to Ranchi, where there were proper camps, took three days, a wearisome ordeal by train, as the rolling stock chugged slowly across Assam and Bengal into Bihar. There were no carriages, only steel cattle trucks with no bedding; with no medical help or drugs, those already suffering from cholera, dysentery or malaria often succumbed en route, infecting others and raising the death toll exponentially. The roistering guerrilla leader Colonel Michael Calvert rememered that 'There were no blankets and no food. We had cholera, dysentery and malaria cases on the train but there were no medical or even toilet facilities. The lavatory accommodation consisted of ropes to which the user clung while hanging over the side of his truck . . . We would have suffered more had it not been for the planters and their wives . . . As we slowed or stopped at stations they threw us food and other supplies.'[8]

All the surviving troop accounts tell the same story: campsites where the rain teemed down, there were no tents, and men bivouacked in the mud. There were rarely groundsheets or blankets to be had, though sometimes mosquito nets were available. In some units ingenious engineers were able to construct rude shelters out of brushwood and tarpaulins, yet even if they avoided the pitiless pelting of the monsoon, they could never get their clothes dry. It has been estimated that 90 per cent of those who trekked out of Burma suffered from malaria and 20 per cent were eventually hospitalised with serious maladies.[9] It was routine to hear of men who had lost up to a third of their body weight after just a month of marching and 'recuperating' in India.[10] Yet, incredible as it may sound, the British soldiers did better than the Indian refugees or their counterparts in the Chinese army. The British response to the Chinese troops who got through to India was especially crass and boneheaded. The 38th Division, which had fought so valiantly at Yenangyaung and won the plaudits of Slim, was treated as a pack of banditti when it began to arrive in India between 25 and 30 May. General Sun Li-jen was that rare animal, a superb Chinese general, a graduate of the Virginia Military Academy, an excellent English-speaker, a humane and sensitive man with something of Stilwell's concern for the enlisted man, and a handsome and charismatic individual withal.[11] Arriving on a more southerly itinerary than that taken by Stilwell, Sun was alarmed to find himself under suspicion and in danger of internment. The egregious General Irwin, who added racism to his other less attractive attributes, regarded Sun with contempt, and he had the backing of Alexander, who had complained publicly that the Chinese were a pack of parasites, 'pusillanimous bastards')[12] wanting to be fed and pampered at British expense. Fortunately, for once, Wavell exerted himself and overruled

Irwin, thus avoiding a public-relations catastrophe, especially given Chiang's pre-existing Anglophobia.[13] In Sun's case this would have undone all Slim's good work. Stilwell had warned Sun that the 'Limeys' would try to manipulate him and make him over, but Slim had won his trust. It was the peculiar evil genius of Irwin to be forever ignoring his good advice.

On 20 May Slim handed over all his troops to 4 Corps and the old Burma Corps ceased to exist. He said goodbye to his close friends Scott and Cowan and then took an emotional farewell of his troops, receiving an accolade that would have heartened a Marlborough or a Wellington and induced in him the irrational feeling that he was deserting them. As he said: 'To be cheered by troops whom you have led to victory is grand and exhilarating. To be cheered by the gaunt remnants of those whom you have led only in defeat, withdrawal, and disaster, is infinitely moving – and humbling.'[14] Already Slim had won hearts and minds by his common touch, his utter simplicity and his complete lack of pretension and humbug. With a deep under-standing of human nature, he possessed in abundance common sense, the soldier's bluff humour and a down-to-earth wisdom. In many ways he was the very finest kind of Englishman, tough, blunt, unflappable, but sensitive and insightful too.[15] The affection in which he was held by his troops was remarkable and bears further examination. Patrick Davis, a Gurkha officer, had this to say: 'We trusted him not to embroil us in a major botchery. We accepted the possibility of death, and the certainty of danger, discomfort, fatigue and hunger, provided that our fighting was constructive and with a reasonable chance of success. Moreover, Slim had been weaned with the 6th Gurkhas, so we had an extra reason for liking him.'[16] Slim's salty humour was another reason for his popularity. Later, when the British in Burma became known as the 'Forgotten Army', he caused riotous laughter in the ranks when he poked fun at the sobriquet: 'Forgotten Army. They've never even heard of us!' A similar sensibility is evidenced by an anecdote from the dark days after the retreat, when Slim and Stilwell shared a joke while sitting dejectedly on a wall. Stilwell said: 'Well, at least you and I have an ancestor in common.' 'Who?' said Slim. 'Ethelred the Unready,' replied Stilwell.[17] Slim's laughter reinforced Stilwell's convic-tion that he was the only 'good Limey'. Given his almost monomaniacal regard for fighting generals, it is no mystery why he should have so prized Slim. This explains the rare homage Stilwell paid his British counterpart when he presented Slim with an American M11 carbine – which Slim ever afterwards carried as his personal weapon.

From Imphal, Slim was transferred to Calcutta, in command of the newly formed 15 Indian Corps, where his immediate concern was to take precautions against a possible seaborne invasion across the Bay of Bengal and in particular to guard against amphibious operations by the Japanese in the Sunderbans, that complex delta of waterways through which the combined Ganges and Brahmaputra rivers pour into the sea across a 200-mile front. To this effect he held man-oeuvres in July with the RAF and Royal Navy. In fact the threat of Japanese invasion was non-existent, for their carrier force had been destroyed in the great American victory at Midway on 4–6 June, though of course this was not known at the time.[18] Although at one level the pressure on Slim was eased when Noel Irwin was replaced by Geoffrey Scoones as commander of 4 Corps (Irwin was transferred to the newly formed Eastern Command), this serendipity was more than upset by six weeks of serious rioting throughout India. The British government had effectively promised India independence in the 1935 India Act, but Indian nationalists, represented in the powerful Congress party, remained suspicious and resentful.[19] After Pearl Harbor it was thought particularly important to enlist Congress in the Allied cause, and Sir Stafford Cripps, Lord Privy Seal in the Churchill government, went out to India in March 1942 on a mission to gain the support of Gandhi, Nehru and other leading lights among the Indian nationalists. As an austere left-winger, Cripps was looked on favourably by Congress, but when he offered what was tantamount to virtually immediate self-government, he was effectively disowned by Churchill and the viceroy Lord Lithlingow. Cripps was caught in the crossfire and blamed by Nehru and his other friends in Congress, who thought this yet another example of 'perfidious Albion' at work. Gandhi made a point of dismissing the gelded Cripps proposals as 'a postdated cheque on a bank that is obviously failing.'[20] He was not confident that the British Empire would win the struggle with Japan, so what, he reasoned, was the point of signing up to an agreement the other side might not be able to deliver? The machinations underlying the Cripps mission are still controversial, with Lithlingow and Wavell, as commander-in-chief, fundamentally opposed to any real change in wartime, while American diplomats, at FDR's urging, exerted pressure behind the scenes to get virtual Indian independence. Yet another problem was that the British proposed to give individual provinces an 'opt-out' right from the new nation, which raised the fear of 'Balkanisation' and separatist and racial enclaves.[21]

Cripps returned to London with his mission a failure. The suspicion arises that many parties to a would-be agreement, especially Churchill, were secretly pleased at this outcome. But Gandhi reacted with indignation to what he now saw as an elaborate charade. Unmoved by the reservations of some in Congress, who thought that his actions might be construed as giving comfort to Japan, and heedless of the global military implications, he launched a 'Quit India Now' movement and announced that there would be a new wave of satyagraha, or non-violent civil disobedience – the tactic he had used so effectively since 1930. Gandhi and the entire Congress executive committee were arrested in Bombay in August 1942 and imprisoned; Gandhi stayed in jail for two years.[22] The predictable response to this on the streets was anger, followed by violence. Strikes, demonstrations and mass absenteeism quickly escalated to military mutiny, bomb outrages and the burning alive of policemen. The authorities cracked down hard in response: hundreds of thousands were arrested, including 30,000 Congress activists, and thousands of demonstrators were killed or injured by police gunfire. So far British military personnel had not been targeted, and warnings were always given in advance about railway sabotage. But as the indigenous death toll mounted, the popular mood turned ugly and troop trains were attacked, especially in the bandit country of central Bihar on the line to Assam and the Burmese border.[23] There were also serious disturbances in the coal- and iron-producing areas of the north-east. There was immense disruption to transport and industry, to the production of munitions and to the building of airfields. From Calcutta Slim reported that the riots there were not serious, but it was a different story in the countryside, and the destruction of the railways was particularly serious. There could be no thought of offensive action in Burma with such a grave situation in the home base. Wavell was forced to deploy no fewer than 57 infantry battalions in the worst hotspots, and it is estimated that the entire war against Japan in South-East Asia was put back a good two months by the troubles.[24] Incredibly, having shown himself as much out of his depth in India as in Burma, Wavell had the gall to petition Churchill at this very juncture for promotion to field marshal. Over the very reasonable protests of the Secretary of State for War, P.J. Grigg, Churchill, abetted by Alanbrooke, approved the promotion. In October Wavell received his baton. Perhaps in recognition that he was the real worker in the India-Burma theatre, Slim was given the consolation prize of a CBE.[25]

Slim's nemesis Irwin got in touch with him in July to say that since he proposed to take direct control of a forthcoming offensive in the Arakan peninsula, he and Slim would be swapping headquarters at the end of August. Slim was delighted to switch from Calcutta to Ranchi, for as he said: 'Its climate was vastly preferable to the steaming heat of Bengal, malaria was much less, and the tawdry distractions of Calcutta were absent.'[26] But he found that the insurgency in India had seriously affected morale and *esprit de corps*, with a particular unwillingness on the soldiers' part to go on parade; even his own Gurkha orderly proved recalcitrant. The new 15 Corps comprised the 70th British Division, 50 Armoured Brigade and some assorted corps units, and some of the battalions were work-shy to the point where they would have fulfilled all Stilwell's anti-Indian-army strictures. Slim had to spend a good deal of time whipping his army into shape, insisting on regular parades and physical fitness. Having surmounted the first hurdle, he instituted his own training programme, based on his grim experiences earlier in the year. His eightfold credo was eventually turned into a pamphlet summarising his findings; Slim claimed he never deviated from them and that adhering to them would eventually win the war. The principles were as follows: soldiers must learn that the jungle is not hostile but merely neutral; patrolling is the key to jungle fighting; when you find Japanese units in your rear, do not panic but reason that it is the enemy who is 'surrounded'; don't hold long continuous lines in defence; there should never be frontal attacks but always responses to hooks or assaults on the flank and rear; tanks are useful but always in a pack and always in a cloud of infantry; there are no non-combatants in jungle warfare; never allow the Japanese to hold the initiative.[27] All these tenets were conveyed to the recipients with dry humour. Slim discovered that his men were unnerved by the screams and ululations produced by the Japanese in night attacks, demoralising inexperienced troops and leading them to blast away into the darkness in terror, thus giving away their positions. He had a simple solution: 'The answer to noise is silence.'[28] He liked to sit down beside young, greenhorn officers with a mug of tea and an avuncular manner and 'shoot the breeze'. Colonel James Lunt remembers such a 'fireside chat': 'You know, Jimmy, we haven't got a snowball's hope in hell of beating those buggers – but the point we must make to everyone is that we mustn't give up. Because once we give up, they will just corral us like cattle. We've got to fight . . . and maybe, who knows, we may suddenly find their weak spot or something of that nature, that will give us the opportunity, because we've still got a lot of fight left in us.'[29]

In the long run the Japanese in Burma did much of the Allies' work of reconquest for them by a brutal, blinkered and exploitative occupation that gave the lie to the much-trumpeted Greater East Asia Co-Prosperity Sphere – the Japanese project for a common market. Although they were supposed to have liberated Burma from British oppression, the Japanese imposed a tyranny that made Western colonialism seem small beer. Almost all the country was under direct military rule, and Hideki Tojo in Tokyo proclaimed that because of its proximity to India, the 'economic independence' promised to Burma would have to be deferred until the end of the war. The anti-British Burma Independence Army, which had aided the Japanese invaders, was considered insufficiently loyal to the new masters; its ranks were winnowed, and the slimmed-down version became the vehemently pro-Japanese Burma Defence Army, led by Aung San, just 4,000 strong, so incapable of emerging as a third force.[30] A joint policy of political indoctrination and re-education on one hand with terror on the other saw the rise of a Gestapo-like force, the Kempeitai, universally feared. Evincing contempt for Burmese culture and religion, Japanese commanders routinely desecrated Buddhist temples and insulted village elders. Inflation and other forms of financial distortion warped the agricultural economy, disgorging a flood of unemployed labourers and peasants. These were used by the Japanese as a gigantic corvée, and to this forced labour were added the unfortunate British prisoners, pressed into labour gangs and virtually starved to death.[31] The prisoners of war were the focus of an especial rage in Burma, beyond the normal contempt expressed by the bushido code for men who had allowed themselves to be taken alive. This was because the retreating British had been so successful in destroying the infrastructure, tearing up rail track as they went, and in particular blowing up the Ava bridge, whose repair was considered unfeasible in wartime. All in all, the years 1942–45 were grim ones for Burma, but Japanese myopia meant there would be no regrets from the Burmese when the tide eventually turned in favour of the Allies. Almost the only group to be temporarily swayed from their normal pro-British stance was the Karens, whom the Japanese treated with extreme favour, thus increasing the hatred for them among ethnic Burmans. It is sometimes said that the Japanese achieved a masterpiece of social control in Burma by using just 300 civil servants from Tokyo and 540 Kempeitai, thus rivalling the British feat in the Indian Raj, but this is to discount the coercive effect of an army of occupation.[32]

If the Japanese position in Burma was essentially brittle and unstable, there was, however, little the British and Americans could do in 1942 to take advantage of this. Amazingly, Wavell, who always underestimated the Japanese military capability, was making plans for the reoccupation of Burma even as his troops retreated in disarray in May. This was the genesis of his notion of abolishing the peacetime commands of the Indian army, organised along administrative lines, and 'transforming' them into operational centres; Irwin's appointment as head of the Eastern Army was the first fruit of this new bearing.[33] But it was not possible to effect change by waving a magic wand or simply reshufflling the existing deck of cards, and additionally, Eastern Army had the serious internal security situation in Bengal, Bihar, Orissa and Assam to deal with. Training and recruitment for supposed new units was painfully slow, and only Slim had a real grip on what confronting the Japanese would really mean. Yet both public opinion in Britain and, more seriously, in America, demanded that something be done immediately. A campaign was needed both to raise morale in India and to show the world that Britain was not beaten.[34] This was the context in which Wavell on 17 September 1942 ordered Irwin to begin operations in the Arakan pensinsula of Burma. The ultimate aim was to seize Akyab island, from which bombing raids could be launched at Japanese-held Rangoon. But a campaign in the Arakan meant challenging nature at its most difficult, even before the Japanese were encountered.[35] From the Indian frontier to a point just short of Akyab island ran the Mayu hills, 90 miles long and 20 miles wide.

Down the centre ran a ridge of razor-sharp scarps some 2,000 feet high, jungle-clad and precipitous. The narrow strips of land on either side of the hills were striated by numerous streams or *chaungs*, which on the western side were tidal, with treacherous mudbanks at low tide. This coastline was beautiful when observed by the traveller or tourist[36] but pretty poison in wartime. From October to May, with chill evenings, campaigning was feasible, but with the monsoon season in May came 200 inches of rain. The menace of leeches, mosquitoes and malaria knew no seasons and in some ways posed more of a problem than the Japanese defenders.

Irwin's animus towards Slim was such that, as far as possible, he tried to marginalise him during the Akyab campaign. The original conception of the campaign, under Wavell's direction, called for a threefold approach: direct infantry attacks in the Mayu hills; guerrilla activities that in some ways anticipated the later long-range penetration strategy; and amphibious landings at Akyab island to coincide with this. Slim, who was not asked for his opinion, thought it a bad mistake to try to combine all three approaches, and favoured going for the penetration option.[37] Wavell was at first inclined to put most weight on the amphibious approach, but soon discovered that he was woefully short of landing craft, simply because there was such heavy demand for them in other theatres, especially for the US Marines' island-hopping campaigns in the Pacific, and Operation TORCH, the Allied landings in North Africa scheduled for November 1942. On 17 November he therefore abandoned his more grandiose scheme and ordered Irwin to blast a passage to Akyab island overland, through the Mayu hills.[38] The next unexpected obstacle was heavy, unseasonal rains, which further delayed operations. Finally, in December, the advance got under way, led by Major General W.L. Lloyd. Since Slim was a corps commander, this was the point where he should have been brought into the picture. Lloyd had nine brigades under his control, a force three times the size of a normal division, and in all usual circumstances this would have entailed corps control, especially with Irwin overseeing everything from Calcutta to Fort Hertz in northern Burma and trying to control a domestic insurgency at the same time.[39] Yet Irwin's dislike of Slim overcame reason and expediency. Even worse, Irwin was a compulsive micromanager, who should never have become bogged down in the tactical minutiae of Lloyd's battalions. Yet this is precisely what happened. It was a classic case of the wrong man in the wrong job. As one modern critic has pointed out, Irwin was a man of 'dictatorial and egocentric temperament' who treated subordinates 'like indentured coolies deserving neither trust nor consideration'.[40] Another student of Arakan has put it even more strongly: 'Irwin was also, by nature, a meddler. He trusted no one but himself, and involved himself constantly in detail which should have been of no concern of an Army Commander. He gave little or no latitude to his subordinates to use their own initiative and ensured that in every point of detail his orders were carried out without discussion or deviation. This made him dangerously inflexible, finding it difficult to change his mind and approach when the situation demanded it.'[41]

Nevertheless, at first the Arakan offensive seemed to go well. Despite appalling transport difficulties – 'like fighting a modern war along stone-age tracks'[42] – Lloyd enjoyed the advantage of both air mastery and considerable numerical superiority. The brilliant Japanese defence took all this into consideration. They made no attempt to hold the line between Maungdaw and Buthidaung, or to resist when outlying parties of British troops were flung out as far east as Kyauktaw. There was even more optimism at Lloyd's HQ when his men reported, as a Christmas Day present, that the enemy had pulled out of Rathedaung on the eastern bank of the Mayu river. As this river enters the Bay of Bengal, it forms a long 'sea loch' between which and the Indian Ocean is a narrow peninsula in the form of an inverted triangle, with the apex at Foul Point, temptingly only five or six miles away from Akyab island across the Mayu delta. A few miles north of the point, at Donbaik on the coast of the Bay of Bengal, the talented Japanese general Koga dug in and waited. Having excelled in jungle warfare in gym kit, the roadblock and the amphibious 'hook', the enemy was about to reveal yet another unsuspected weapon: the bunker. Slim describes it thus: 'For the first time we had come up against the Japanese "bunkers" – from now on to be so familiar to us. This was a small strong-point made usually of heavy logs with four to five feet of earth, and so camouflaged in the jungle that it could not be picked out at even fifty yards without prolonged searching. These bunkers held garrisons varying from five to twenty men, plentifully supplied with medium and light machine guns.'[43] The bunkers were formidable defensive positions, impervious to field guns or medium bombs and sited so that any attacking force came under fire from at least two other bunkers. The redoubt at Donbaik was situated alongside a *chaung*, in itself a natural anti-tank position, with steep sides up to nine feet high up to the bunker. On 7 January 1943, the attacking forces had their first taste of trying to assault these positions. They were thrown back with heavy losses, and the same pattern continued for four successive days. Wavell and Irwin, both in high alarm, visited Lloyd on the 10th and told him that he must at all costs take Donbaik.[44] He asked for tanks, and was granted them. But to Slim's stupefaction, he was asked to supply just one troop from 50 Tank Brigade, part of his 15 Corps. He objected strenuously, pointing out, in accordance with his central tenets, that tanks should always be used en masse, that 'the more you use, the fewer you lose'. His objections were overruled, and the decision was taken to deploy half a squadron of tanks on a narrow front. As Slim had predicted, eight tanks made no impression at all; at least a regiment of the armoured monsters should have been used.[45]

Massive British attacks were beaten off, with heavy casualties, in February and again in March. Koga knew that the reinforcements he wanted would not be fighting fit until the end of March and was determined to hold on until he could counterattack. Irwin meanwhile believed in overwhelming infantry power on narrow fronts – 'an idea rich in casualties', as one analyst has commented sardonically.[46] Early in March, sensing that defeat was staring him in the face, he tried to coopt the detested Slim to share some of the blame,[47] sending him to Maungdaw to see Lloyd and report on the situation there. When Slim queried whether that meant he was now in operational control, Irwin said no: he just wanted Slim's assessment of the situation. He might be in operational control in the future, he added, but only when he, Irwin, said so, and even in that case Irwin would retain administrative control. This was dog-in-the-manger with a vengeance. As one historian has remarked: 'Alice came across nothing more extraordinary in Wonderland; it was a Mad Hatter's contrivance.'[48] Slim found morale at an all-time low. He advised Lloyd to abandon the pointless frontal assaults and make a flank attack through the jungle. Lloyd replied that this was unfeasible and of course, because of Irwin's absurd orders, Slim had no power to overrule him. He returned to Irwin and wrote a pointless report.[49] For a while Wavell, completely out of touch with reality, urged just one more effort. Under pressure to make another attack, Irwin so ordered Lloyd, and the result was another disaster. By 20 March Wavell, Irwin and Lloyd were at one in accepting that they would have to withdraw to the Maungdaw–Buthidaung line.[50] But Wavell secretly fumed and decided to make Lloyd the scapegoat. Lloyd was dismissed and replaced by Major General C.E.N. Lomax, who simply tried more of the same. But by this time Koga was ready to launch his counteroffensive. His troops quickly rolled up the British and annihilated 47th Brigade.[51] Irwin, in a frenzy of blame-shifting, said that the brigade, not his own tactical ideas, was alone to blame and once more tried to inveigle Slim. This time he told him to hold himself in readiness to take over operational control and move his corps head-quarters to Chittagong. Even so, he was to have neither administrative control of operations, nor even operational direction, until such time as Irwin gave him the nod. Irwin's hatred of a superior talent meant he would rather burden one of his forward divisions with adminis-tration than give Slim a free hand. Slim saw Irwin in Calcutta on 5 April, having been (typically) recalled from leave in the small hours by his superior. In the evening he dined with Lloyd at the Bengal Club and heard his side of the story; remarkably, he found, without any bitterness at his shabby treatment.[52]

There followed a meeting at Chittagong with the surprisingly phleg-matic Lomax. With Koga sweeping all before him, they agreed that the Japanese general's next logical step must be an assault on the Maungdaw–Buthidaung line. As expected, this came on 20 April. Slim and Lomax devised a stratagem for catching Koga in a 'box' on the Mayu peninsula. The box would involve six battalions, two on the ridges of the Mayu hills, two along the Mayu river and two in hills just south of the Maungdaw–Buthidaung road, which would form the bottom of the box. The idea was that the Japanese would be bound to utilise the tunnels on a disused railway track, dismantled many years before because a shipping company disliked the competition (in Burma always the same monopolistic story). They would be allowed to enter the box on their way to the tunnels and the lid would be provided by a force of brigade strength.[53] Ever since Hannibal's victory over the Romans at Cannae, generals have sought to compass the perfect encirclement, but it always eludes them. So it was here. Slim and Lomax were using tired and demoralised men to carry out a scheme of geometrical perfection, when their only chance would have been with fresh, well-motivated ones. The Japanese walked into the trap, Lomax gave the order, but the bottom fell out of the box when the two battalions in the south failed to hold. By 8 May the triumphant Japanese had taken both Maungdaw and Buthidaung. Slim was bitter: 'It was too much like 1942 over again, with the added bitterness that this time we had been defeated by forces smaller than our own.'[54] It was only Slim's incessant pressure that led to the order being given for Lomax to abandon Maungdaw; Irwin's first instincts were to throw away further men in a pointless siege. In London Churchill noted: 'This campaign goes from bad to worse, and we are being completely outfought and outmanoeuvred by the Japanese. Luckily the small scale of the operations and the attraction of other events has prevented public opinion being directed upon this lamentable scene.'[55] He wrote at a time, after the Anglo-American victory in North Africa and the crushing defeat of the German army at Stalingrad, when it was becoming obvious to all but the purblind that the Allies would win the war in Europe. But he was furious with Wavell, whom he had always disparaged, and the feeling of distaste was shared by the Americans. Irwin refused to accept a scintilla of the blame, and, in lengthy correspondence with Wavell, blamed everyone but himself, and especially the cowardly behaviour of his troops.[56] His final absurdity was a signal recommending that Slim be removed from command of 15 Corps. But Wavell, under severe criticism himself, was determined that Irwin would carry the can. Slim was informed that he should report to Irwin's headquarters, and with stoical resignation told his staff that this had to mean he was about to be dismissed. But the very same day Irwin sent another signal: 'You're not sacked. I am.'[57] When he heard this, Slim remarked: 'I think this calls for the opening of a bottle of port or something if we have one.'[58]

Everyone remarked on Slim's mental toughness and his extraordinary ability to resist stress. The frustrations of defeat were not the only strains he had to bear, as he was constantly shuttling between his headquarters and the front. On one occasion his pilot landed on an airstrip that the British had already abandoned but which the Japanese, fortunately, had not yet taken over. To make matters worse, the pilot switched off the engine before realising his error and then could not start it again for a very long time, while Slim reconciled himself to spending the rest of the war in captivity.[59] Always an optimist, he even found things that were encouraging about the disastrous Arakan campaign. British battle casualties amounted to 2,500 but could easily have been far higher, given the nature of the warfare and the frontal attacks. On the other hand, the British had learned about Japanese methods and the precise areas in which British military training and tactics were deficient.[60] There had been 7,500 cases of malaria, but much had been learned about the disease. Troops were now routinely issued with mosquito nets and repellents, and by the autumn of 1943 a 'wonder drug', mepacrine, was developed, which made malaria less of a menace. By 1944 the pesticide DDT and the febrifuge sulphaguinidine had been added to the arsenal of weapons deployed against the anopheles mosquito.[61] Yet the most important long-term development in 1942–43 was the gradual reassertion of Allied air superiority. By the end of 1942, 150 new airfields had been built, RAF pilots and aircraft began to arrive in large numbers, and the United States had sent 10,000 air force personnel to serve in the China-Burma-India (CBI) theatre. Heavy bombers – B-24 Liberators – appeared at the battlefront for the first time, and in November 1942 staged a spectacular 2,760-mile return trip to bomb Bangkok.[62] The Japanese soon realised that all of their proposed Burma–Siam railway was vulnerable. When the war in the Middle East was finally wrapped up early in 1943, the USAAF transferred many of their heavy bombers to the Far East; there were substantial bombing raids on Bangkok, Rangoon and Mandalay over the Christmas period 1942–43. Gradually the Japanese were forced to cede air superiority, and this worried them. During the Arakan campaign a Japanese colonel issued the following telltale order: 'There must be no fear of aircraft. As long as you are not discovered you must seek to remain so. If once our position is revealed, the enemy planes must be shot down. It is not permissible to suppose that our soldiers are no match for aircraft.'[63] Even more significantly, the Japanese were forced to yield the skies above Arakan to the Allies even though they had been victorious on the ground. The RAF conducted search-and-destroy missions over Sinho, Thaitkido, Buthidaung and Akyab island, and in June, six Hurricanes of 17 Squadron escorted Blenheim bombers on a long-range raid on Ramree island. Allied air superiority would eventually become almost *the* crucial factor in the struggle for Burma.[64]

For Slim's biographer perhaps the most significant thing about 1942–43 is what it reveals about the general's deep character and that of his bitter enemy General Irwin. It seems that Irwin was hostile to Slim on three separate grounds. The most obvious was that Slim had sacked his old friend Lieutenant Colonel G.A.M. Paxton because of his discreditable performance at Gallabat in 1940.[65] But Irwin genuinely thought that Slim was partly responsible for the defeat in Burma in early 1942. Moreover, he entertained a snobbish attitude towards a man who was a product of the Indian army, a mere 'sepoy general'. He, by contrast, belonged to the allegedly infinitely superior British army in India.[66] People had been known to come to blows because membership of the latter body was confused with that of the former. Yet beyond this there was the visceral antipathy felt by the inadequate human being for the superior one. Irwin has been described as lacking in moral courage, of an aggressive temperament, outspoken, egocentric, dictatorial, inflexible, unimaginative, conservative and reactionary. With a penchant for acerbity, he inspired neither loyalty nor affection. A sycophant to those above him and a bully to those below, he had a deep-seated reverence for rank, hierarchy and authority. He would accept no questioning by subordinates but would not himself query the orders of his superiors.[67] He was, in short, exactly the blimpish officer so loathed by Stilwell and often thought to be a mere caricature. That he should have been chosen for high command in Burma is yet another nail in the coffin of Wavell's reputation, for it was Wavell who insisted on having him. To add to all his other faults, Irwin was a micromanaging control freak. Irwin was also, by nature, a meddler, as has already been pointed out.

Slim, by contrast, was both brilliant as a military strategist and a deeply impressive human being. No one reading his memoir *Unofficial History* could doubt his wisdom or his ability to read human nature. He also had a great sense of humour and a very good ear for dialogue. He knew how the official military mind worked and he also knew how the army was perceived by the enlisted man. As has been well said, he had the head of a general with the heart of a private soldier.[69] He had seen plenty of Irwins in his early life, as is apparent from some of the reminiscences he provided to the journalist Frank Owen. He spoke of seeing in his early years in Birmingham 'Men who were fathers of families cringing before a deputy-assistant-under-manager who had the power to throw them out of their jobs without any other reason than their own ill-temper or personal dislike'[70] and claimed that one reason he liked the army was that there were fewer cringers and fewer martinets than in civilian life. But they certainly existed. In August 1914, he was a lance corporal on a three-week training course in Yorkshire. Slim takes up the story:

> It was a sweltering, dusty day and the regiment plodded down an endless Yorkshire lane. At that time British troops still marched in fours, so that Lance Corporal Slim, as he swung along by the side of his men, made the fifth in the file, which brought him very close to the road-side. There were cottages there and an old lady stood at the garden gate. I can see her yet, she was a beautiful old lady with her hair neatly parted in the middle and wearing a black print dress. In her hand she held a beautiful jug and on the top of that jug was a beautiful foam, indicating that it contained beer. She was offering it to the soldier boys.

Slim took one pace to the side, grasped the jug and took a swig. There came a bellow from the front of the column, and the colonel rode back on his horse to 'bust' Slim to private on the spot. By mere chance he had looked back just as Slim put the jug to his lips. The colonel bellowed at him: 'Had we been in France you would have been shot.' Slim commented: 'I thought he was a damned old fool – and he was. I lost my stripe, but he lost his army.'[71] It is hard not to imagine that in Burma Irwin became for Slim a transmogrified version of that blink-ered colonel. Yet when Slim was given command of the newly constituted 14th Army in May 1943, it turned out that Wavell, whether he knew it or not, had appointed a commander with unique and excep-tional qualities.

Slim is still probably underrated today simply because, as a modest meritocrat, he believed that talent would speak for itself and be recog-nised as such. He despised the gallery-touch antics and histrionics of the Montgomerys, Pattons and MacArthurs. Sadly, such is human nature, the meretricious and the self-advertising will always score over the merely talented. That is just one reason why men like Slim are scarce, but it is not the only one. It is rare to find a keen intellect coexisting with down-to-earth affability and humour, and rarer still to find such intellectual powers in harness with absolute personal integrity and uprightness of character.[72] Yet human excellence was far from exhausting Slim's exceptional traits. It has been pointed out that as a master of warfare he provided a 'practical bridge' from the theory of 'indirect approach' expounded by J.F.C. Fuller, Sir Basil Liddell Hart and others of the 'English school' of military strategy between the wars. Indirect or 'manoeuvre' warfare was dedicated to the proposition that strategy meant undermining an enemy's strength and skill to win via a concentration of forces based on surprise, psychological shock, moral dominance and physical momentum. It is opposed to the idea of meeting strength with strength and force with force, as in the discredited approach of men like Field Marshal Douglas Haig; there would be no Sommes or Passchendaeles in Slim's curriculum vitae. Instead of slogging and attrition, a 'manoeuvrist' commander relies on cunning, guile, tricks and deceit, working always on the enemy's weaknesses. Because Slim did this on a battlefield and not in a book of theory, and left no treatise on general principles, his originality has been lost sight of.[73]

Events began to move significantly in Slim's favour in May 1943, not just with the sacking of Irwin following the Arakan fiasco but as a result of decisions taken at the Washington TRIDENT conference that month. In the first place, the man who replaced Irwin was especially welcome. Although General George Giffard would later have many vociferous critics, and even Slim eventually backtracked on his initially favourable estimate, at first he seemed like a breath of fresh air after Irwin.

The new Army Commander had a great effect on me. A tall, good-looking man in the late fifties, who had obviously kept himself physically and mentally in first-class condition, there was nothing dramatic about him in either appearance or speech. He abhorred the theatrical, and was one of the very few generals, indeed men in any position, I have known who *really* disliked publicity ... But there was much more to General Giffard than good taste, good manners and unselfishness. He understood the fundamentals of war – that soldiers must be trained before they can fight, fed before they can march, and relieved before they are worn out. He understood that front-line commanders should be spared responsibilities in the rear, and that soundness of organisation and administration is worth more than specious short-cuts to victory.[74]

Even more welcome was the replacement of Wavell as Commander-in-Chief, India, by Sir Claude Auchinleck. 'The Auk' had always been a Slim supporter and recommended him to Wavell for advancement when Wavell was Commander-in-Chief, Middle East, in 1941. Indeed 'the Auk' had wanted to retain Slim in the Middle East and had fought hard to try to dissuade Wavell from taking him to Burma.[75] Auchinleck was appointed basically because Churchill, who never held Wavell in high regard, was tired of his quasi-academic effusions and wanted a 'fighting general' in command in Burma. Moreover, a unique conjuncture allowed Churchill to get rid of Wavell without humiliatiing him. The Prime Minister had had great difficulty finding a new viceroy of India after Lord Linlithgow's retirement. Wavell's 'promotion' to viceroy and his replacement by 'the Auk' semed a perfect solution. Now the commander in India was a man respected by both Slim and, more surprisingly, Stilwell.[76]

Implicit in Slim's enthusiasm for Giffard and Auchinleck was an implied criticism of the old guard of Alexander and Wavell. While Slim liked Alexander personally and found him charming, he had no great opinion of his abilities. The subtext is there in his own account of the 1942 campaign, when he complains that no real counter-offensive against the Japanese was attempted. Typically, Slim turns this into self-reproach: 'Thus I might have risked disaster, but I was more likely to have achieved success. When in doubt as to two courses of action, a general should choose the bolder. I reproached myself that I had not.'[77] But any perceptive reader would realise at once that Slim lacked the power and authority to be bolder, that he was compelled to follow orders. Alexander's time at the helm in Burma (February–July 1942) was characterised by mindless optimism and an unwillingness to face reality. His refusal to take risks grated on Slim, who always thought that the Japanese would never be disturbed by conventional responses but could be thrown off balance by the unexpected. Even Alexander's biographers and champions concede that his brief, unhappy stay in Burma was not his finest hour.[78] Later in life Slim allowed his true opinion of Alexander to emerge: 'I don't believe he had the faintest clue what was going on.'[79] His opinion of Wavell was not much higher. Wavell had consistently underrated the Japanese at every level, even before Pearl Harbor, and in Burma had evinced a blinkered, unimaginative stolidity. This enabled the Japanese to take risks and use new methods against which the outdated tactics employed by Wavell were powerless. Chief among these were the roadblock and 'hook' methods, not really formidable in themselves if countered by a talented general. But in the ethos presided over by Wavell, they easily could, and did, lead to panic, confusion and chaos and to a defeatist mindset according to which the Japanese were invulnerable military supermen.[80] The Japanese scored heavily in 1942 by engendering in the British army a sense of psychological dislocation and a devastating sensation of being trapped in a nightmare. The switch from facile optimism to equally fatuous pessimism was part of a culture that Slim implictly laid at Wavell's door. Now with Auchinleck and Pownall at the helm, there was every chance that the British could finally turn the corner.

The tireless Stilwell barely broke stride after his gruelling trek through the jungle. He departed from Delhi for Chungking at the end of May 1942 but arrived only on 3 June, after an enforced five-day stopover at Kunming because of bad weather. In the next seven months he would make the 2,200-mile journey between Chungking and Delhi no fewer than seven times. First there was a 450-mile flight from Chungking to Kunming; then 650 miles over the Hump to Sadiya in Assam; finally another 1,100 miles from Assam to Delhi. It must be emphasised that he had to fly over the Hump section of the Himalayas at 17,000–20,000 feet to get clear of the 15,000-foot peaks, through turbulence so bad it could tear a plane apart. The old, slow transport planes he flew on were not designed for such conditions, which meant that passengers had to carry their own oxygen, and there were no navigational aids or any defence against prowling Japanese fighters. If he was very lucky, Stilwell could get a ride in a B-25 bomber, which cruised at 250 m.p.h. – much faster than the transports.[1] He went to see Chiang while depressed and ill, suffering from jaundice, and underweight after the ordeal in the jungle. He told his wife he was 'like the guy in the medical book with his skin off, showing the next layer of what have you'. But the old martial spirit was never quenched. In the same letter written to his wife from Delhi, he expressed his bitterness about the Japanese: 'I have hopes that some day we can step on these bastards and end the war, and if I am lucky enough I can go back and have a few days at a place called Carmel, where there are a few people I know who will welcome a vulgar old man, even though he has proved a flop and has been kicked around by the Japs.' But his more immediate target was the generalissimo: 'Tomorrow or next day I'll be going back to report to G-mo and I sure have an earful for him. He's going to hear stuff he never heard before and it's going to be interesting to see how he takes it.'[2]

The mood in Chungking was sombre and barely polite. Chiang blamed the British for the debacle in Burma but could not break with them openly for fear of alienating the USA and thus losing the crucial Lend-Lease materiel. He lobbied behind the scenes to get the Americans to recall Stilwell but as yet by means of winks and nods.[3] To Chiang, the defeat of his armies had proved the truth of his credo that one should never attack; in the words of the old Chinese proverb: 'One hundred victories in a hundred battles is not the best of the best; the best of the best is to subdue the enemy without fighting.' Chiang's mood was one of sullen non-cooperation. As he saw it, with the loss of the Burma road and with the Doolittle raids having precipitated a renewed offensive by the Japanese in China, his country was effectively blockaded. Meanwhile China was not treated as an equal by the Anglo-Saxon nations, who were obsessed with their 'Europe first' policy, and China had to endure routine humiliations like being refused membership of the US Munitions Control Board. Chiang's basic attitude therefore was that the Western powers should now do the rest of the fighting in South-East Asia; after all, ancient wisdom dictated that the great leader should encourage one set of 'foreign devils' to fight another.[4] At their conference with Stilwell on 3 June, Chiang and his wife tried to lay on the machiavellianism with a trowel, claiming that China was on the brink of collapse and thus hoping to suck even more aid and Lend-Lease out of the United States. Such was the barefacedness of the Chiangs that they even invented a 'peace party' within the Kuomintang, which aimed to sign a separate peace with Tokyo and by whom Chiang claimed to be threatened. For Chiang, Stilwell had a simple role: he was his chief of staff and should therefore get from the United States whatever Chiang wanted. Naturally, Stilwell did not see it at all that way: Lend-Lease was a quid pro quo for hard fighting, not a personal perquisite of the generalissimo. The conference was therefore the predictable dialogue of the deaf. Stilwell made good on his promise to tell his boss the truth, the whole truth and nothing but the truth and revealed some of the more singular scandals in the brief campaign in Burma. He actually recommended to Chiang that some of his generals be shot, the officer corps purged and the army streamlined to 60 really effective and well-trained divisions.

The Chiangs feigned astonishment at these revelations. Historians are divided on whether this was simple two-faced deceit or whether Chiang genuinely was ignorant of the worst excesses of his generals because his 'face' had to be saved.[5]

It became obvious that Chiang intended to do nothing about his rebellious or recalcitrant officers, and Stilwell's frustration became evident. After the main meeting, Madame Chiang took Stilwell aside and tried to brief him on what she called the nuances of Chinese culture but which Stilwell regarded as a string of fatuous and disingenuous excuses. The generalissimo, she said, was ignorant of the true state of affairs in the army because Chinese 'good news' culture overwhelmingly accentuated the positive. To keep up the pretence that no one in China was ever discontented, and also to save the leader's face, the truth was kept from him; Stilwell's words had therefore come like a douche of cold water. This was doubtless the source of Stilwell's self-congratulatory gloss on the meeting as confided to his diary: 'I told him the whole truth, and it was like kicking an old lady in the stomach. However, as far as I can find out, no one else dares to tell him the truth, so it's up to me all the more.'[6] When Stilwell pressed the point about army reform, Madame replied inconsequentially: 'Why, that's what his German advisers told him.'[7] She added mysteriously that Chiang was under pressure from 'certain influences' (this was doubtless a riff on the fictional 'peace party'), that he was not the free agent he appeared to be and not even master in his own house. There was a scintilla of truth in this. Many of Chiang's generals were de facto provincial governors. Chiang had in effect 'solved' the endemic Chinese problem of warlordism by transmogrifying his own generals into warlords, and they would rebel if pushed too hard. But Madame insinuated that the problems between Stilwell and her husband were not insoluble. Chiang was reluctant to use his army against the Japanese, but might change his mind if the trickle of Lend-Lease materiel became a flood. Here Madame was being both clever and obtuse. She was clever in that she emphasised her husband's pragmatism. As has been well said: 'Chiang's resistance to Stilwell's proposals was never fixed or solid but changeable and vacillating in proportion to what he thought Stilwell could obtain for him from America.'[8] But she was obtuse in that she failed to realise that even if Stilwell was prepared to indulge Chiang at all points (he was not), as the more pliable Chennault was, he was not a free agent himself. The needs of the Russian front and the contingency planning for a cross-Channel invasion, to say nothing of the war in the Pacific, meant that Chiang's war theatre had a very low priority. Nonetheless, Stilwell always incurred blame and vituperation from the Chinese when a cornucopia of material did not flood their way.

By this stage of his mission Stilwell was already frustrated, deeply angry and profoundly contemptuous of 'the Peanut' and his corrupt clique in Chungking. As he clearly saw, the Kuomintang's grip on power was shaky, with hyperinflation, sky-high rents and taxes plus incipient famine compounding the malaise of a string of military defeats. Worst of all was the all-pervasive corruption, the graft, profiteering, landlordism, peculation and defalcation, with a pro-Western business elite practically flaunting their extravagant wealth and conspicuous consumption in the faces of starving peasants. As Stilwell saw it, the KMT leaders dealt with all this by burying their heads in the sand. He commented on Chiang that he was 'the most astute politician of the twentieth century . . . he must be or he wouldn't be alive'.[9] The only people Stilwell really got on well with in Chungking were those who shared his own low opinion of Chiang, men like General Shang-chen, in charge of military liaison with China's allies and one of the few fluent English speakers in the higher echelons. On the other hand, he detested the head of Chiang's press and public relations, Hollington Tong, 'oily and false, mouthing delight at my arrival'. The chief of police, Tai-li, was another of Stilwell's pet hates. Then there was Chiang's Chinese chief of staff General Ho Ying-chin, conversations with whom were described as 'double talk and tea'.[10] The other Americans in Chungking largely shared Stilwell's distaste for Chiang, with attitudes ranging from cynical indifference to positive loathing, but the US ambassador Clarence Gauss was a major ally. Gauss considered that China was a very minor asset to the USA but a major liability, and in his reports was implictly critical of FDR's obsession with the country. In private he and Stilwell expressed their opinions more forcefully. They could not understand the mental block, a mixture of a priori fixed ideas and psychological denial of reality, whereby Roosevelt construed Chiang's corrupt regime as vital to the Allied war effort.[11]

What disgusted them most was Chiang's lust for money and the Kuomintang lies that were accepted uncritically. One of Chiang's most notorious 'big lies' was his claim to have attacked the Japanese army besieging Hong Kong in December 1941 and killed 15,000 of them. Needless to say, no such engagement ever took place, but such was Washington's 'will to believe' that no one questioned Chiang's Walter Mitty propensities, and the propaganda about Chinese 'victories' was accepted as fact. FDR's cant about 'democracy' was particularly repulsive when applied to a fascist dictatorship like the Kuomintang. He was able to get away with it because foreign journalists self-censored and concealed the truth about Chiang's China so as not to give comfort to the Japanese. And so in the press Chiang was always presented as an heroic paladin, his wife as a peerless beauty and the Chinese as noble and courageous.[12] In such a context it was not difficult for Chiang to pull off his most breathtaking and outrageous coup. In January 1942 he managed the blatant extortion of $500 million from the US government, claiming it was necessary for China's survival. Although many in Washington warned that this 'aid', if granted, would simply disappear into the bank accounts of Chiang and his cronies, Roosevelt felt that Chiang could not be refused. Treasury Secretary Morgenthau and others tried to attach conditions to the 'loan', but Chiang adamantly refused to accept them.[13] With the abiding fear in Roosevelt's circles that Chiang would throw in his lot with the Japanese, forming a bamboo curtain of yellow races against the whites, the President granted Chiang all he asked for. Morgenthau admitted to a Senate committee that the money was an explicit bid by the USA to outbid Tokyo for Chiang's services. When Secretary of War Stimson testified before the House Foreign Relations Committee on 3 February 1942, the House voted unanimously for the 'loan'; Stimson then repeated the trick with the Senate Foreign Relations Committee. The outcome was that a huge loan had been made without security, control, conditions or any means whatever of getting the money back.[14] What infuriated Stilwell was that 'the Peanut' had blackmailed his (Stilwell's) own country. Even though by now he knew that Chiang would never launch a major offensive against Burma, he had to look on while FDR bought into a pack of lies, all based on the dubious premise that Chiang would withdraw from the war. Not while there was Lend-Lease materiel to acquire, Stilwell reflected bitterly.

Further contacts in the month of June left Stilwell convinced that Chiang wanted him merely as a pro-Chinese stooge, someone useful for blocking and sidestepping the hated British and as a conduit to Lend-Lease. He brooded that Chiang had double-crossed him in China, had never officially endorsed him as commander-in-chief of the Chinese army, consistently went behind his back or even, so far as he could, over his head in Washington, never answered his memos and refused to clean up the rampant corruption in the army. It was quite clear that he had confirmed Stilwell's command of the 5th Army units who had been evacuated to India simply so that he would not have to meet Wavell or any other Britons. But he refused to budge on the issue of the generals Stilwell wanted court-martialled or executed: 'Tu to remain,' Stilwell wrote bitterly. 'His face is to be saved, the hell with mine.'[15] At a conference on 24 June, with Madame's support, Stilwell got Chiang to agree to having significant units of the Chinese army trained in India. However, Chiang insisted as a quid pro quo that Stilwell procure an airlift of 5,000 tons of supplies a month over the Hump and 500 combat planes. This was a very steep request because, with bad weather and a shortage of planes, only 100 tons a month was currently being delivered.[16] Chiang of course had no idea and no interest in how the materiel reached him, and seemed to have thought it could be conjured up by a magic wand. In fact the transport of the Lend-Lease materiel meant a journey of 12,000 miles by sea from the USA to the west-coast ports of India, then 1,500 miles by railway to Calcutta, and thence by the narrow-gauge Assam–Bengal track to the airfields of Assam for the flight across the Hump. Even when the supplies had reached Kunming, they still had to be taken several hundreds of miles further to the military bases. It was estimated that the USAAF burned a gallon of fuel for every gallon it delivered to China and had to deliver 18 tons of supplies to enable Chennault's Flying Tigers to drop one ton of bombs on the enemy.[17] Heedless of all this, Chiang was so pleased with the hard bargain he had driven with Stilwell that he went over the top, tweaking his requests a further notch by expanding them into his famous 'Three Demands': this time it was not just 5,000 tons of materiel and 5,00 combat planes but three US infantry divisions as well. This was pure pie in the sky.[18]

As if all this pressure was not enough, Stilwell also had to deal with the gadfly antics of Chennault. In July 1942 the renamed Flying Tigers became the China Air Task Force. Chennault was promoted to brigadier general but was then placed under the command of General

Clayton Bissell, who now commanded all US planes in the CBI sector. Since Bissell was Chennault's bête noire and since Chennault had impressed the Chiangs by his absurd but reiterated argument that he could win the war with airpower alone, this new appointment infuriated Chiang, who started to intrigue to have Bissell removed. But Chiang was as impotent in the case of Bissell as with Stilwell, for just as Stilwell was General Marshall's favourite, so was Bissell the hand-picked appointee of the father of the American air force, the hugely influential General Henry 'Hap' Arnold, the only man ever to be a five-star general in both the US army and (after 1945) the newly formed US air force.[19] Arnold cordially detested Chennault as a show-off and a charlatan. Chiang fumed about this fresh humiliation, for he had wanted Chennault as the air supremo, believing in the far-fetched theory that with 500 planes he could win the war. This total fantasy suited Chiang, for it meant he would not have to send his army into battle, reform his officer corps or upset his warlords/generals in any way. Meanwhile Chennault continued to drip poison into the ear of Madame, whose special favourite he was. On one occasion she wrote to him: 'If we destroy fifteen Nippon planes every day, soon there will be no more left.'[20] Meanwhile the USA, having to subvent China over such a long supply chain, often cut what it could offer Stilwell and Chiang, as new global emergencies arose. The particular crisis triggered by the fall of Tobruk to Rommel in June 1942 meant that US air resources were overwhelmingly switched to the Middle East. This evoked in Chiang a twofold reaction. On the one hand it increased his Anglophobia. He complained that the British were always the Americans' senior partner, that every time they faced a crisis, China had to carry the can.[21] He was also deeply resentful that he could not control the allotment of Lend-Lease within China as the British did within Britain. The reason was obvious. Washington knew that what it supplied to Britain would be used in the global struggle against fascism but that what was sent to Chiang would not. Chiang, presiding over a snakepit of corruption in Chungking, wanted equal treatment with an advanced Western democracy governed by the rule of law. But he was interested neither in the special relationship nor in political theory or logistics. For him the failure of his demanded monthly quota to arrive meant either that Stilwell was lazy and not exerting his influence or that he was deliberately sabotaging China. Chiang always operated in a cloud cuckoo land where Stilwell simply had to ask for something to be given it at once. While under pressure from such absurd demands, Stilwell was being harangued by the War Department for not being conciliatory enough. Reasonably, he concluded that he was being made a whipping boy: 'In a jam blame it on Stilwell.'[22]

On 1 July, Stilwell attended yet another conference with the Chiangs; present also were the two top generals in the Chinese air force. Chiang now formally tabled his infamous 'Three Demands', this time with timetables attached. The three US divisions were supposed to arrive by September to open the Burma road, while the 500 planes and the 5,000 tons of supplies over the Hump were to start at the beginning of August. Stilwell found the demands outrageous but agreed to forward them to Washington. Writing bitterly in his diary that night about the sheer ingratitude of Chiang, he noted: 'utterly impossible, but they're so dumb, they think we'll promise it'.[23] He did, however, baulk at Madame's further requirement, that he endorse the Three Demands. Patiently he explained that he could not support an ultimatum to his own government. Madame allowed him to leave and then phoned him in a furious rage. 'She got hot on the phone and started to bawl me out, so I said I should like to see her . . . Obviously mad as hell. She had snapped the whip and the stooge had not come across.'[24] Once again Stilwell controlled himself and explained patiently that he wore four hats, and three of them entailed absolute loyalty to Washington; being the generalissimo's chief of staff was just one in his portfolio of activities. 'If she doesn't get the point,' he wrote, 'she's dumber than I think she is.'[25] Although both Stilwell and ambassador Gauss advised FDR that Chiang was bluffing when he spoke of 'making other arrangements' (i.e. peace with Japan) if the Three Demands were not met, Roosevelt once again proved surprisingly weak and flaky on this issue. He knew perfectly well he could not give Chiang what he wanted, but indulged his usual instincts as a politician by stalling. He sent a soothing letter to the generalissimo to say that things would be better in the future and promised to send out his personal representative to sort out 'misunderstandings'. This was to have been his *éminence grise* Harry Hopkins, but in the end he dispatched Lauchlin Currie to China. As Stilwell sardonically commented: 'Apparently now that stooge [Hopkins] won't come across, Soong [Chiang's ambassador in Washington] is sending someone that will.'[26]

Stilwell kept pressing to get Chiang to commit to a campaign to reconquer Burma. This became his abiding ambition in Chungking. On 19 July he submitted a three-point plan, which envisaged a land offensive by 20–30 Chinese divisions and the opening of Rangoon to shipping, by which means the generalissimo could receive an extra 30,000 tons of supplies. Stilwell called this the X-Y plan, for he had in mind a two-pronged invasion, with X-force invading from India and Y-force operating from Kunming in Yunnan.[27] The third element was a British landing at Rangoon in concert with the Chinese, once they had reasserted naval control in the Bay of Bengal and retaken the Andaman islands. Curiously, and quite independently of Stilwell, the British chiefs of staff were at that very moment considering the recapture of Rangoon in an operation to be codenamed ANAKIM. But this project was largely chimerical, for it was scheduled for November, whereas Wavell had warned the War Cabinet that he would not have built up the necessary forces, and especially airpower, by that time. Besides, the chiefs of staff made ANAKIM contingent on developments in other theatres, especially the Middle East, gave it a very low priority and then added the near-impossible proviso that all depended on Japan's being drawn into a war with the Soviet Union.[28] Chiang's immediate response was to stall; he hoped that the Lauchlin Currie mission might lead to Stilwell's recall. He refused to reply to Stilwell's memos or requests for interview. In his diary Stilwell fumed at the stupidity of an uneducated and friendless man and said that Madame would make a more effective leader if she was generalissimo. He concluded: 'This is the most dreary type of maneuvring I've ever done, trying to guide and influence a stubborn, ignorant, prejudiced, conceited despot who never hears the truth except from me and finds it hard to believe.'[29] Lauchlin Currie duly arrived, his talks with Chiang went well, and the generalissimo was thereby encouraged to another piece of machiavellianism. On 1 August Chiang finally replied to Stilwell and accepted his ideas for an offensive, subject to two conditions. One was full and effective British cooperation, and the other was the support of a proper air force. What Currie had revealed to him had made it clear that the British would not be attempting to retake Burma in the near future and Stilwell's ideas did not have top priority in Washington.

This meant Chiang could accept the idea of an offensive, knowing it would never come to pass.[30]

Chiang was initially buoyed by the visit of Lauchlin Currie, a Canadian-born economist who had risen fast during the New Deal to become one of FDR's 'Young Turks'. He would later become semi-famous through being suspected of being a Soviet spy, and had to spend the last 40 years of his life in exile in Colombia. He had been to China the year before on a dual mission, trying to expedite the Flying Tigers and attempting (futilely) to reconcile Chiang and the Communist leader Mao Tse-tung.[31] An arrogant 'know-all' on China, Currie was easily duped by Chiang, who pressed either for Stilwell's recall or the separation of Lend-Lease adminstration from his powers. Chiang was very pleased with the way he had gulled Currie, but when the envoy returned to Washington, the generalissimo's hopes and plans unravelled. Influenced by Currie's report, which ascribed most of the problems in Sino-American relations to the personality clash between Chiang and Stilwell, FDR toyed with the idea of replacing Stilwell immediately. But Marshall and Stimson would have none of it and told the President forthrightly that Stilwell was unquestionably the right man for the job. Marshall, who knew the true picture from his signals to Stilwell, summoned Chiang's ambassador and told him brusquely that all his master's machinations were in vain, for even if Stilwell himself was replaced, US policy on Lend-Lease would remain the same. He followed up with a memorandum to this effect.[32] The slippery T.V. Soong doctored this, expurgating everything negative, and sent it on to Chungking. It took another two years for FDR to realise that Soong applied this treatment to all his correspondence with Chiang. Yet Marshall suspected the ambassador was not to be trusted and sent on the original to Gauss in Chungking for transmission to the generalissimo. When Chiang saw Marshall's original, he was outraged and insulted, having suffered the most massive loss of face. Stilwell recorded on 1 August: 'Snafu with Peanut. He's having a hell of a time with his face.'[33] The trio of Marshall, Stilwell and Gauss never had any illusions about the Kuomintang and its illustrious leader, which was why in later years they became marked men in the eyes of the McCarthyite 'China lobby'.[34]

By this time Stilwell's thinking on China had advanced well beyond his visceral dislike of Chiang, who now seemed like a particularly sickly icing on top of a rotten cake. He raged that Washington seemed to condone the most barefaced corruption and profiteering. A particular Kuomintang scam was the so-called 'pegged rate'. When the United States imported from China it had to pay in Chinese currency, which was pegged at a ludicrously high artificial rate against the dollar. This allowed Chinese profiteers to pocket the difference between the pegged rate and the true market rate; there were times when the pegged rate was 20 times the value of the market rate.[35] The entire rotten edifice of the KMT meant that Chiang would never countenance a disciplined army, as this might come under a new commander and challenge his rule, and sacking incompetent commanders meant removing most of those who owed him favours or were beholden to him. Above all else, Chiang was always more concerned about Mao and the Communists than about the Japanese. As Stilwell noted: 'Chiang would prefer to see Germany win than to end up with a powerful Russia at his door, backing up the 18th Army Group [the Chinese Communists].'[36] As for the Communists, Stilwell sometimes expressed the wish that he could have them at his side as combatants, for at least they were genuinely committed to fighting and killing the Japanese. In his clear-headed analysis of Nationalist China, Stilwell was at one with Clarence Gauss, who in his own quiet way hammered away in his diplomatic dispatches at the terminal sickness of the KMT and the inadequacy of Chiang. Neither man could ever understand how, in a war supposedly waged to rid the world of fascism, the United States could not just aid and abet an openly fascistic regime but almost treat it as most favoured nation.[37] Stilwell deplored the stupid US propaganda about a 'gallant ally' when the alleged gallant ally was simply taking his country to the cleaners. He was disgusted with the way Americans had been 'forced into a partnership with a gang of fascists under a one-party government similar in many respects to our German enemy . . . there is sympathy here for the Nazis. Same type of government, same outlook, same gangsterism (except that the Kuomintang is incompetent) . . . Chiang is not taking a single step forward or doing anything to improve the position of China.'[38]

Disillusioned as he was, Stilwell was also in poor health, with bad eyesight (he was blind in one eye), jaundice and worms to contend with. There were continual Japanese air raids over Chungking. Additionally, he had just received news of his mother's death in the

USA. Finally there came a ray of light. It seemed that Wavell had been strong-armed into approving Stilwell's training camp for Chinese troops in India. With Chiang having already given his approval (albeit for machiavellian motives), the way was now clear for Stilwell to return to India and escape the miasma of Chungking. Marshall told him that the British did not want to use the Chinese in the reconquest of China, fearing the possible effect on Indian and other Asian nationals, but that pressure from Washington had finally done the trick.[39] Stilwell accordingly prepared to fly to India for a month. The Chiangs gave him a farewell dinner, at which the generalissimo was bland and affable. Having concluded that confrontation with Stilwell was pointless, he contented himself with vapid remarks about how Chinese psychology was different from that of the West and could never be understood by Westerners. Stilwell found greater consolation from the company of Madame and her two sisters, Madame Kung and Madame Sun Yat-sen. Always ambivalent about Madame – Stilwell considered she was a 'power-devil' who wished she was a man – by now he had no great opinion of her intelligence, despite his earlier praise, and noted particularly how she accepted any old rumour as fact, without testing or verifying anything. Allied to this was a tendency to shoot from the hip: to take decisions first and consider the reasons for them later. He liked her sisters better. 'Madame Sun is the most *simpatica* of the three women, and probably the deepest. She is most responsive and likeable, quiet and poised, but misses nothing, would wear well.'[40] Stilwell was a shrewd judge. Soong Ching-ling (Madame Sun Yat-sen) had always been sympathetic to the Communists and lived in Moscow in the 1930s. After a temporary reconciliation with Chiang and the KMT during the war with Japan (1937–45), she threw in her lot with Mao and became (after 1949) *the* great female figure of the Chinese people's republic.[41]

Next it was on to Stilwell's battered DC-3, with his regular pilot Captain Emmet Theissen, for another 2,200-mile journey to Delhi via the Hump and Assam. As more and more American fliers had to make the perilous run over the Himalayas, the Hump came to be known as 'the Skyway to Hell' and flying it as 'Operation Vomit' or 'the Aluminium Trail', from the number of crashed planes. The worst peril in the Hump was the banks of cumulonimbus clouds, which could reach a height of 25,000 feet. Mired in these, pilots spoke of being tossed about like an egg in a tin. It was difficult and often impossible to control the plane in these circumstances, so crashes into the mountainside were frequent.[42] Even when Stilwell got safely through this and proceeded to Assam from Kunming, he still had to reckon on the fact that ditching meant almost certain death. There were no emergency airstrips, only paddy fields and jungle into which a stricken plane would disappear without trace. Stilwell and Theissen simply hoped for the best, flying in all weathers, fair and foul, without radio aids or military security. The travails of this particular trip were even greater, for even when he had completed the 2,000-plus miles to Delhi, Stilwell had to fly another 500 miles from Delhi to the training ground at Ramgarh in Bihar province or another 700 if he wished to visit the chief Lend-Lease supply port at Karachi. It was yet another ordeal that would have taxed a man half his age. Leaving on 7 August, he flew to Delhi, then on to Karachi on the 12th, back to Delhi and then on to Ramgarh on 16 August. India was then at the height of the 'Quit India' insurgency, but on top of this there was severe flooding in the whole of the north. Ramgarh itself was no picnic: Stilwell reported to his wife that tigers prowled the artillery range at night.[43]

Stilwell had always felt that, man for man, the Chinese soldier was a superb fighting instrument. It was the useless officers, lack of morale, indiscipline and corruption that were the problem. In China, under Chiang's watchful eye, there was nothing he could do about any of that, except to intrigue and give discreet backing to the more enlightened clique of officers, which included his protégé General Ch'en Ch'eng. Here in Ramgarh he was a free agent and he could introduce genuine and radical reforms. The first thing was to reform the organisation of the Chinese army, which was responsible for much of the blinkered mindset among its generals. Among Chiang's many eccentricities was a quasi-Confucian obsession with triads. So, he had three million men organised into 300 divisions; each division had three regiments; there were three divisions to an army and three armies to a group army.[44] When the Chinese had entered Burma, Chiang had ordered it divided into 12 distinct war zones, each with a virtually independent command, so that the Japanese could never eliminate more than a small part of his army. Three group armies were then assigned to each of the war zones. There was no uniformity of arms and materiel in the armies, as Chiang had 'pets' among his divisions, which he favoured hugely with special issues of food, arms and ammunition. Of the 300 divisions, 40 per cent were under strength, but since army pay was disbursed en bloc to the officers commanding the divisions, who naturally enough pocketed most of the payroll for themselves, the commanding officers continued to draw pay for the full strength – payroll padding with a vengeance. The upshot of this corrupt system was that officers got rich – some of them even sold their arms on the open market and traded overtly with the Japanese for their own enrichment – while their men died of malaria, dysentery and cholera. One general (Lan Yang) decreed that all two-wheeled carts must be equipped with rubber tyres, then sold off the 'inadequate' tyres he had previously confiscated; he then capped the exploit by taxing all carts with rubber tyres.[45] The block payment system actually made it a matter of self-interest for generals to keep their divisions under strength, for otherwise their 'profit margins' would be cut. As for those who were recruited, these men were secured mainly by press gang, with those who could afford it buying their way out of the draft. Not surprisingly, the desertion rates were astronomical – some 44 per cent in 1943, or 750,000 out of 1,670,000 recruited. In the 8th Division of the 8th Army (thought to be one of the better units), 6,000 men out of 11,000 disappeared, either through death or desertion, in 1942.[46]

Stilwell wanted to train an entirely new army, where all this misery and corruption would be a thing of the past. He began with the problem of sickness. Since losses through disease and malnutrition ran at about 40 per cent annually in Chiang's army, this meant a 7,000-strong division would need 3,000 new recruits to maintain its strength. He did not find them. Out of eight million troops recruited in the war years, one in every two could not be accounted for, having either deserted or died from non-battle reasons; an incredible 500,000 actually deserted to the Japanese.[47] Epidemics of dysentery, smallpox, typhus and relapsing fever swept through the ranks, all exacerbated by virtually non-existent medical care, hygiene and sanitation. 'The reason for digging latrines was not understood; fuel for boiling water was just another expense.'[48] Such military hospitals as existed were understaffed and ill-equipped. Everyone seemed to think that since China had limitless manpower, a high wastage level could be tolerated, but the reality was that if Chiang kept his huge army and at the same time fed his people adequately, the manpower base was not large enough for both. Stilwell began tackling the problem of disease and desertion by a tripartite approach of drugs, good diet and regular pay. All the Chinese at Ramgarh were vaccinated against cholera, typhoid and smallpox and fed three good meals a day – which produced an average weight gain of 21 pounds in three months. They were also properly equipped and outfitted, so that the previously starving and ragged soldiers were transformed. Stilwell's reforms produced their own black comedy moments, as when Chiang's generals began sending men to be trained at Ramgarh stark naked or clad only in shorts (many died of cold in the planes en route). Chiang and his cynical henchmen reckoned that it was stupid to clothe soldiers if the USA was going to provide them with a new uniform anyway.[49] Yet it would be wrong to insinuate the idea that Ramgarh was some kind of Shangri-La. Stilwell's reforms engendered new and acute cross-cultural problems. All training was done by American officers and instructors, but they could not lord it over their trainees as over home-grown GIs, and many were resentful. The Chinese officer class was outraged by the financial reform, whereby each man was paid on the parade ground after stepping forward and being identified, as in the American army. This cut out all the officers' chances for graft and corruption. On the other hand, Stilwell alienated many of his own officers by his order that Americans were not to lay hands on the Chinese, no matter how insubordinate, nor (contradictorily) to intervene if Chinese officers ordered draconian punishment for their own men. The worst clashes and tensions between Chinese and Americans came about because Stilwell was determined to avoid the British Empire pattern of white officers and native troops. This handed the initiative to the Chinese officers, who were in competition and often conflict with Stilwell's US liaison officers (the equivalent of political commissars).[50]

Some of the problems Stilwell encountered at Ramgarh were an inevitable consequence of the way the Kuomintang army was run. The 11 armies he hoped to mould into 30 crack divisions turned out to be short of 185,000 men (because of both desertion and payroll padding). They had only 50 per cent of the arms they were supposed to have, and half of those weapons were useless for lack of parts.[51] Nevertheless, Stilwell worked tirelessly to ensure that he would have real, creditable divisions to his name by 1943. Slim, based at Ranchi, just 40 miles away, often had occasion to observe the training of Stilwell's New Model Army and commented as follows:

> Stilwell, indomitable as ever, planned to raise on this nucleus a strong, well-equipped Chinese force of several divisions that would re-enter Northern Burma and open a road to China. Only Stilwell believed that was both possible and worth the resources it would demand. The Chinese themselves were by no means enthusiastically cooperative; the Indian government, not without justification, felt considerable apprehension at the prospect of thousands of Chinese about the countryside . . . Stilwell was magnificent. He forced Chiang Kai-shek to provide the men; he persuaded India to accept a large Chinese force and the British to pay for it, accommodate, feed, and clothe it. . . . The two Chinese divisions were reconstituted. Good food, medical care, and regular pay achieved wonders. I have never seen men recover condition as quickly as those Chinese soldiers . . . I was very impressed by the rapid progress of the infantry who were converted to artillery, and who in an astonishingly short time were turned into serviceable pack batteries. No doubt they were apt pupils, but the major credit went to their teachers, under Colonel Sliney, one of the best artillery instructors any army has produced. Everywhere was Stilwell, urging, leading, driving.[52]

Slim omitted to mention the very considerable tensions between some Americans, who regarded the Chinese as craven 'slopeys', and the Chinese, who saw the Westerners as arrogant barbarians. Imbued with the culture of defence and non-engagement, the Chinese regarded as realism what the Americans saw as cowardice. The lack of adequate Chinese-speakers was another problem at Ramgarh. American instructors liked to teach in a populist way, using movies and Disney cartoons, but now had to find other methods. The man so highly praised by Slim, Colonel G.W. Sliney, summed it up thus: 'Thank God we don't speak Chinese and we don't have interpreters. We demonstrate and they copy. They are the greatest mimics in the world and are learning very fast.'[53]

After two weeks' hectic work on the new Chinese army, Stilwell suffered something like culture shock when he returned to Delhi to see the opulence at the headquarters of both the British and American military. The cynics said there were so many brass hats in Delhi that a plane could land there in the fog. The 'too many chiefs, not enough Indians' motif was a constant one in Stilwell's letters home to his wife, as in this one: 'The Limey layout is simply stupendous, you trip over lieutenant-generals on every floor. Most of them doing captain's work, or none at all.'[54] He found time for a quick meeting with Wavell and dinner with the viceroy Lord Linlithgow on 30 August before flying back to Chungking on 9 September. Next day there was a conference with Madame and then an unwontedly quiet period until 21 September, when there was a formal dinner with the Chiangs, where the generalissimo seemed delighted with the photographic evidence of his new divisions at Ramgarh. 'Why shouldn't he be, the little jackass,' Stilwell confided to his diary. He consoled himself with a minor triumph: 'For the first time I carried on a conversation with the G-Mo without any help.'[55] For the next few days Stilwell contented himself with mutterings in his journal about KMT graft and corruption, but then on 27 September came really serious news from Washington. The Allies had agreed to a limited war in northern Burma, to open a new road from Ledo in Assam that would connect with the Burma road and force it open; Stilwell's project for a full campaign, objective Rangoon, was set aside. Yet even the limited campaign represented victory of sorts, for the British were not keen on an offensive in northern Burma. They had no interest in China and considered Chiang a military dead weight. Besides, in addition to the critical state of affairs on the Russian front and the plans for a cross-Channel invasion, Operation TORCH, the Allied landings in North Africa, was looming as a priority. FDR now gave a definitive answer to Chiang's Three Demands, telling him that while there could be no question of any American divisions in Burma, beginning in 1943 100 transport planes would bring 5,000 tons of supplies over the Hump, and 265 combat planes would be delivered; to Chiang's delight, no quid pro quo was mentioned.[56]

Roosevelt's highly conciliatory attitude to Chiang explains his next move. Baulked by Stimson and Marshall when he tried to remove Stilwell after the Lauchlin Currie report, FDR next sent out a bigger gun, Wendell Wilkie, the man he had beaten by a landslide in the electoral college in the 1940 presidential election. Wilkie was something of a curiosity. Elected as the Republican candidate that year as a complete dark horse with no significant political experience (he was a corporate lawyer), he initially campaigned on an isolationist platform.

The 1940 election campaign was considered the dirtiest ever to date, with FDR's vice-presidential nominee Henry Wallace accusing Wilkie of being 'the Nazis' candidate'.[57] Wilkie performed creditably in terms of the popular election, winning 22 million votes to Roosevelt's 26 million, but after his defeat he performed a complete volte-face and became an ardent supporter of his erstwhile opponent. In this capacity he had already been sent as the President's personal representative to Britain and the Middle East in 1941. Some thought there was machiavellian method in the timing of the visit, and that FDR wanted Wilkie out of the country during the run-up to the mid-term Congressional elections; apparently he suspected that Wilkie might be preparing to 're-rat' and run against him again in the 1944 presidential elections. But Chiang saw a unique opportunity to get rid of Stilwell and replace him with the biddable Chennault. Accordingly he arranged Wilkie's visit with full pageantry, laying out the red carpet as if he were royalty or one of those 'friends of the Soviet Union' Stalin used to entertain so lavishly. Wilkie took the bait and swallowed Chiang's propaganda whole. His six-day visit was something of a tour de force of gullibility, which predictably excited Stilwell's scorn.[58] He noticed that Wilkie seemed particularly influenced by Madame, and if the Des Moines newspaper publisher Gardner Cowles can be believed, there was more to it than mere charm and flattery. According to Cowles, who had been special adviser to Wilkie in the 1950 election and knew him intimately, Wilkie and Madame had an affair, first consummated in China during this visit and later continued in the USA, during which the 'power devil' Madame conceived the notion of divorcing Chiang and marrying Wilkie. The idea was that she would use China's wealth to get Wilkie elected in 1944 and then, as husband and wife, they would rule the world as a more successful Antony and Cleopatra, with Wilkie assigned the West as his sphere of influence and Madame the East.[59]

All one can say is that in the madhouse atmosphere of Chungking in October 1942, anything seemed possible. The egregious Chennault, at Madame's bidding, buttonholed Wilkie and completely sold him on the idea of winning the war by airpower alone. Chennault portrayed Stilwell as a stick-in-the-mud diehard general, still fighting the battles of the American Civil War with infantry alone, and ignoring the dimension of airpower. He complained to Wilkie that Stilwell used all the Lend-Lease materiel on expensive infantry projects, and claimed that if he, Chennault, was given just 105 fighters and 42 bombers, he could promise victory over Japan in a mere six months. The absurdity of Chennault's ideas will be apparent when it is realised that in 1945 the USA was deploying no fewer than 14,847 combat aircraft against Japan and scarcely putting a dent in the defensive capacity of the Japanese homeland; only the use of the atom bomb finally compelled the enemy's surrender. As Stilwell often pointed out, an attempt to win the war by airpower alone would simply lead the Japanese to overrun all those airfields within striking range of their armies – airfields that in turn could be defended only by the despised infantry. The document Wilkie came away with, virtually dictated by Chennault after being closeted with the envoy for two hours, has rightly been called 'one of the extraordinary documents of the war'.[60] Chiang played his part, promising Wilkie that if Chennault was made commander-in-chief in China, he would wield real power, thus virtually conceding that he had been sabotaging Stilwell. What he promised was true as far as it went, for nothing would have given Chiang greater pleasure than an American chief of staff who made no demands on his precious armies while bringing in masses of Lend-Lease materiel. Small wonder that Stilwell referred to the generalissimo as 'the little dummy' and remarked 'thank God' when he heard that Wilkie was leaving.[61] But he was unaware that he was harbouring another serpent in Chungking in the form of the US naval attaché James McHugh, who was in on the plot to oust him. McHugh wrote to Navy Secretary Frank Knox to say that Stilwell's plans for the recapture of Burma were simply a piece of quixotry by a glory-hunter and were an obstacle to Chennault's 'brilliant' ideas. Knox showed McHugh's communiqué to Stimson, who in turn showed it to the Chief of the Army. Marshall was predictably enraged and suggested that McHugh be disciplined, describing Chennault's ideas as 'just nonsense; not bad strategy, just nonsense'.[62] The problem was that FDR continued to have a sneaking regard for Chennault, whom he considered a man with a 'can do' attitude. But he could do nothing against the combined opposition of Marshall and Stimson. Meanwhile Marshall put Stilwell fully in the picture about all the plots and machinations against him.

Confident that his enemies would not prevail, Stilwell vented his anger on the generalissimo and cited a recent incident to show how woefully incompetent Chiang was as a general. 'Peanut "directed operations" from Chungking, with the usual brilliant result. The whole thing was a mess. Peanut ordered two armies to hide in the mountains and attack on the flank when the Japs paused. The Japs simply blocked the exit roads and went on.' But Chiang was in good spirits, thinking that Stilwell's days were now numbered. Stilwell's diary entry for 11 October captures the mood: 'Date with Peanut at noon . . . He was quite blithe and cheerful.'[63] Three days later, Chiang committed to a campaign in Burma provided the British also committed fully and that the Allies had air and naval superiority in the Bay of Bengal. It was time for Stilwell to make another of his long flights to Delhi. His visit had a dual purpose. On the one hand he had to get formal British agreement to the Chiang proposals to prevent him using their non-compliance as an excuse to welch on the commitment. On the other, he was concerned about negative reports reaching him about the Raj's attitude to the training of the Chinese at Ramgarh. One report was that Wavell had approved his recent request to increase the numbers of Chinese at Ramgarh, not wishing to oppose Stilwell openly, but had then got the viceroy Lord Linlithgow to write to Churchill to complain of the dangers of having so many Chinese in India.[64] It was quite clear that Wavell did not really like the Ramgarh training project and kept finding various reasons why it should be wound up. One was that Chinese–Indian cooperation would be an entering wedge for nationalism, further weakening the hold of the Raj on India. Another was that the Chinese had still not formally waived their traditional claim to northern Burma. Yet another was that the presence of the Chinese caused railway congestion, shortage of trucks and transport for animals; the Ramgarh project, in short, stymied all other operations. Stilwell thought this attitude smacked of humbug: 'Well, to hell with the old fool . . . They don't want Chinese troops participating in the retaking of Burma. That's all (it's OK for US troops to be in England, though).'[65] He took the precaution of signalling Marshall in Washington to alert him to Wavell's attitude and suggest bringing pressure to bear on London.

The flight over the Hump on 15 October was noticeable for severe turbulence, and Stilwell's pilot climbed to 20,000 feet to try to avoid it. Stilwell arrived in Delhi on the 17th and at once plunged into conferences, encountering all the above objections. Suddenly on the 19th the atmosphere changed, and Stilwell guessed that Marshall's pressure had borne fruit in London. His guess was correct. Around this time Wavell wrote to the chiefs of staff: 'We must accept with good grace and willingness this American-Chinese cooperation in recapture of Burma . . . Stilwell is pretty close and does not give away much, but I like him and think him cooperative and genuine.'[66] Wavell and Stilwell agreed that the campaign would start in February 1943, though the 52 air squadrons originally envisaged would not be ready until two months later. Stilwell told Wavell that his Chinese armies would be aiming primarily at the Hukawng valley of northern Burma and in particular Myitkyina. A joint planning staff was set up, with the faithful Merrill as Stilwell's representative.[67] On 26 October Stilwell declared that he intended to operate from a base at Ledo, from which he planned to build a road along the Hukawng valley to link with the old Burma road near Bhamo. This would have a twofold purpose: to support his campaign in northern Burma and to supply China over an old caravan route.[68] The British were always uneasy about the Ledo road, on the grounds that it destroyed the private shipping monopoly and allowed the Chinese road access to India. Though forced by Washington to accept it, they secretly obstructed it and even agreed to attempt the recapture of Rangoon by amphibious assault in hopes of diverting resources from the road; they were not really that interested in Rangoon, for Singapore was always their prime objective. Wavell and his men argued that even if such a road were built, it would absorb most of its capacity in simple maintenance.[69] This was meant to be an ace card, but the Americans promptly trumped the ace by accepting full responsibility for the Ledo road and all its costs. This was an amazing move on Stilwell's part, for it is normally thought to be an axiom of military campaigns that planning precedes logistics and logistics precede fighting; here the planning, the fighting and the logistical preparations were all going on simultaneously.[70]

Stilwell was never at his best in planning conferences, and by 21 October he was bored and irritable after four days' non-stop negotiations. He recorded his reactions: 'In general we're getting along – our Limey friends are sometimes a bit difficult, but there are some good eggs among them . . . the British don't know how to take me – I catch them looking me over occasionally with a speculative glint in their eyes . . . Some of them that I had thought most hidebound and icy prove to have a good deal of my point of view and take delight in watching me stick the Prod into the Most High.'[71] Here Stilwell made a rare admission that his judgement of men was not always peerless or perfect. But soon he was reverting to a more familiar cynicism: 'Hell, I'm nothing but an errand boy. I run up to Chungking and jerk the Gimo's sleeve. I tell him to better be ready to move into Burma from the south . . . The Chinese are going to lose a lot of face if the British do it alone. Then I fly down to India and jerk Archie's sleeve [and tell him] the Gimo is going to move down the Salween and you better get going too. You Limeys are going to have a hell of a time with the white man's burden if the Chinese have nerve enough to fight and you haven't.'[72] By the end of the month it was time to report to Chiang. After another bumpy passage over the Hump (this time at 17,000 feet – 'cold as hell', Stilwell reported), the two men conferred on 3 November. Stilwell was frank about the difficulties he had encountered with the British and the problems over a united command. 'I said if Slim could command the Limeys it would work fine.'[73] At this conference Chiang was unusually affable and claimed he would have 15 divisions ready by 15 February. After buoying Stilwell's spirits immeasurably by saying that the American could pick the divisions for the campaign, name the commanders and have the power to sack them at any time, he brought him down to earth with the ominous proviso that all was contingent on the Allies having *total* sea and air superiority, by which Chiang seemed to mean a guarantee that his troops would never once be attacked from the air. It seems that his new benevolent attitude was the result of talks he had held with T.V. Soong, who had returned from Washington to brief him. Soong told Chiang that the best chance of getting increased Lend-Lease might be to cooperate with Stilwell, since the Marshall–Stimson axis in Washington meant that he was in effect irreplaceable. Yet even so there were limits to what Chiang would do. For a moment Stilwell hoped he could get rid of General Tu, the lacklustre commander of the 5th Army and his bête noire. His biographer explains why this would never be: 'In the case of Tu Li-Ming, the inner obligations of Chinese relationships were stronger than promises, and each time Stilwell thought he was rid of him, he reappeared in another capacity.'[74]

Yet in another sense Chiang had shot himself in the foot. In his eagerness to get hold of 4,300 tons of supplies by 15 February 1943 (with no guarantee, of course, that he could use them properly), he forgot that this would mean a cut in fuel for his ally Chennault, who protested vociferously. Stilwell, who had bent over backwards to conciliate Chennault, encouraging him and even ordering him to speak his mind to Wilkie, however crazed Stilwell thought his ideas, had now had enough. He noted: 'Chennault with his squawk. He's a pain in the neck. Still sore at Bissell. Told him to shut up and take orders.'[75] Yet for most of November Stilwell was in unusually good spirits, commenting on the departure of Madame Chiang (whom he now took to nicknaming 'Snow White') to the USA, but without talking about the reasons.[76] Some said she had had a blazing row with Chiang about his mistresses and was leaving for a cooling-off period; others that she was following her new lover Wendell Wilkie to the Land of the Free; still others that she was going on a goodwill mission to bolster the Kuomintang's flagging image in the USA.[77] But on 21 November Stilwell was back down to earth with a bump. At the Anglo-American planning conference in Delhi on the 19th, Wavell had announced both that the larger three-pronged plan for the capture of the Akyab peninsula had been scaled back *and* that operations in northern Burma must be postponed in favour of the purely overland offensive towards Akyab island.[78] Predictably, Stilwell returned to Limey-bashing. This time the focus of his rage was a speech by Churchill, which the BBC claimed had 'encouraged' his American allies. Stilwell raged that the BBC always used the formula 'British planes' when the RAF was in action but 'Allied planes' when the USAAF took to the skies.[79] But this time the British were as irritated with Stilwell as he was by them. Wavell complained that he was effectively communicating with Stilwell via Washington, and that Chiang's chief of staff continued to plan operations independently when there was now supposed to be a joint Allied command. Stilwell, he went on, even kept his own men in the dark and made decisions 'without much reference to his staff here [Delhi] who seem to know little . . . His senior staff here give me the impression of being overawed by Stilwell and afraid of representing the true administrative picture.'[80]

Stilwell raged impotently at the new situation: 'Ominous stuff from India. Limeys thinking on limited lines. Their objective is a joke – Arakan Hills, Chin Hills, Kalewa . . . on the whole they want to dig in in north Burma and wait till next fall before going after it seriously . . .

Peanut and I are on a raft, with one sandwich between us, and the rescue ship is heading away from the scene.'[81] The British hesitancy was more than understandable, with the TORCH landings in North Africa, the battle for Guadalcanal and the struggle to supply Russia on the seaborne Murmansk run straining the resources of even the mighty United States. But Stilwell would have none of it and thought all such talk defeatism. In December he made a brave, but unsuccessful, attempt to persuade Wavell to undertake an offensive in northern Burma. At a conference with Wavell on 17 December in Delhi, he insisted that an attack on Myitkyina was essential, since the economic situation in China meant that the Ledo road had to be opened with all speed. This time Wavell was well briefed and made some telling points in rebuttal. He pointed out that there was currently no hope of Royal Navy action in the Bay of Bengal – which Chiang had stipulated as a prerequisite for his cooperation – that it was impossible to fight in the monsoon season, and that the Japanese had the advantage of interior lines.[82] He also had some arguments that Stilwell found impossible to deal with, precisely because he found administration and logistics so boring. Since the railway ended at Dimapur and thereafter everything had to go to the front by road, Wavell demonstrated that to move the Chinese divisions from Ramgarh to Ledo to start the offensive would require 800 lorries and 200 tons of supplies a day over a 350-mile line of communication; but the lorries were unavailable and the infrastructure impossible, since to support Chinese operations a road would have to be built in the monsoon season.[83] When Stilwell returned to Chungking to report to Chiang, the generalissimo launched a screaming tirade about perfidious Albion; whether real or simulated does not appear from the evidence. Chiang then cabled FDR on 28 December to urge the British to do more, and Roosevelt replied that he would raise the matter with Churchill at the forthcoming Casablanca conference. When he did so, Churchill brushed aside the accusation of bad faith, saying that all military promises must almost by definition be contingent on developing events.[84]

Yet Churchill probably was acting in bad faith, for slightly different reasons. With his obsession with India, he was determined to prevent Chinese forces operating on the subcontinent, and this time he was prepared to ride out the storm of American pressure. By saying he could not guarantee Royal Navy supremacy in the Bay of Bengal in the near future, knowing that this was one of Chiang's preconditions, he hoped to trigger a Kuomintang walkout.[85] This is exactly what happened. When FDR could not get Churchill to change his mind at the famous conference at Casablanca on 14–23 January, Chiang said that in future he would take no account of Western promises but simply assume that campaigns in northern Burma were impracticable. In vain did Stilwell try to persuade T.V. Soong that if Chiang did not cooperate, Lend-Lease might be cut. Soong had seen enough of FDR to know about his 'China complex'. It followed that all threats of ending Lend-Lease were the most obvious bluff. Stilwell was left in a military cul-de-sac, hating Chiang but hating the British even more. With Chiang reverting to the default position of Chennault and his doctrine of unaided superiority, Stilwell dubbed the first Friday after New Year's Day 'black Friday'. His frustration is obvious from his diary: 'Peanut screams that the British Navy hasn't appeared and the Limeys will use only three divisions instead of seven. The Limeys squawk that "it can't be done" and look on me as a crazy man, as well as a goddam meddler stirring up trouble. If anything goes wrong, I am sure to be the goat. Both Chinese and Limeys want to sit tight and let the Americans clean up the Japs.' As for Chennault and his idle boasts: 'What a break for the Limeys! Just what they wanted. Now they will quit and the Chinese will quit, and the goddam Americans can go ahead and fight.'[86] At Casablanca FDR was proclaiming his controversial doctrine of 'unconditional surrender', now confident, after the success of TORCH and the victories at Alamein and Stalingrad, that the Germans were on the run. But in South-East Asia, with the Arakan campaign about to run into the sand, the Allies in disarray and the Japanese seemingly impregnable, the outlook was grim. Whatever 1943 had in store for Stilwell, it surely had to be better than the dark days of 1942.

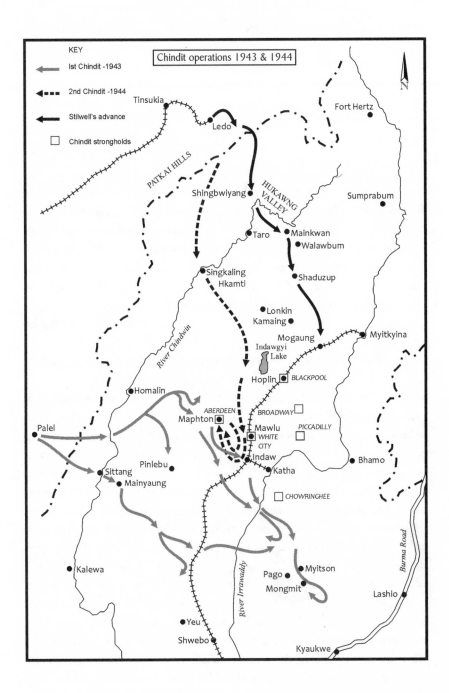

KEY

← 1st Chindit -1943

◀▪▪▪ 2nd Chindit -1944

← Stilwell's advance

☐ Chindit strongholds

Chindit operations 1943 & 1944

N

Tinsukia

Fort Hertz

Ledo

PATKAI HILLS

Shingbwiyang

HUKAWNG VALLEY

Sumprabum

Taro

Mainkwan

Walawbum

Singkaling Hkamti

Shaduzup

Lonkin

Kamaing

River Chindwin

Mogaung

Indawgyi Lake

Myitkyina

Homalin

Hoplin ☐ BLACKPOOL

Palel

ABERDEEN

Maphton ☐

BROADWAY ☐

Mawlu

WHITE CITY

PICCADILLY ☐

Pinlebu

Indaw

Bhamo

Sittang

Katha

Mainyaung

☐ CHOWRINGHEE

Kalewa

River Irrawaddy

Myitson

Pago

Mongmit

Burma Road

Lashio

Yeu

Shwebo

Kyaukwe

135

It was now December 1942 and Wingate and the Chindits were ready for action. Wingate had held a kind of aqueous 'passing-out parade' by swimming past treetops in 30-foot-high flood water as a fillip to his troops. His prejudice against the Gurkhas continued as they proved hopeless at watermanship, whereas the Burma Rifles excelled at everything and could live off the country, even knowing which frogs and pythons were good to eat. The Chindits had been trained to carry 70-pound loads on the march – tropical uniform, army boots, mosquito net, mess tins, sterilising kit, rifle or Bren gun plus 50 rounds of .303 ammunition and six days' iron rations (12 wholemeal biscuits, two ounces of nuts and raisins, two ounces of cheese, four ounces of dates, two ounces of chocolate, 20 cigarettes, tea, sugar, powdered milk, salt and vitamin C tablets). The mules carried the three-inch mortar, extra ammunition, wireless sets and battery chargers.[1] Wingate divided his 3,000 men into eight columns of about 400 men, each of which comprised three rifle platoons and a support platoon with two three-inch mortars and two Vickers medium machine guns, with a mule transport platoon and an RAF air liaison detachment. Only seven columns actually operated, since the original No. 6 Column was broken up to replace casualties sustained in training. In addition, as the 'eyes and ears' of the columns, Wingate had 10 platoons for reconnaissance, scouting and sabotage; he was convinced that he did not need proper commandos, that his men could do the job just as well.[2] Wingate's idea was that to maximise confusion each column would march independently, carrying a week's rations, to be resupplied by airdrop. The Chindits accepted that their leader was a courageous and resourceful man and kept their wider reservations to themselves. What they thought of the constant bible-thumping can only be surmised. Wingate was particularly fond of quoting Ecclesiastes 9:10 in his speeches: 'Whatever thy hand findeth to do, do it with thy might.' The men whispered to each other about 'Tarzan' (their name for Wingate) or, when he played the angry prophet with his baleful, thundering looks, 'Brigadier Bela Lugosi'.[3]

At the end of 1942, the Chindits went by road and rail to Dimapur, then marched up the Manipur road by night (by day it was used by motorised convoys) through pelting rain, taking nine days to cover the 120 miles to Imphal, where they rested for 12 days, told to await further orders. Advance Headquarters of 77th Brigade at Imphal was a 25-foot-square operations room papered with maps and photos, with a one-inch-to-the-mile map on the floor. Here for 12 hours a day and five days non-stop they pored over the details of Burma's geography. Wavell came to see them and spent an unusually bibulous and talkative evening with Wingate and Calvert, apparently enjoying the 'return-to-nature' feel about their primitive accommodation, and generally in good spirits now that Churchill had made him a field marshal.[4] But there was little relaxation for the Chindits. Wingate had deliberately bivouacked seven miles to the north of Imphal, and the men were allowed into the town strictly and solely to attend briefings in the operations room. The puritanical Wingate had decided there would be no last-minute visits to brothels, and even considered that going to the cinema had a 'softening' effect. Instead of last-minute pleasures, those who were about to go into combat had to spend time on final training and exercises, including a supply-drop manoeuvre with the RAF.[5] Suddenly, however, all Wingate's dreams and ambitions were threatened. It will be remembered that the LRP operation was originally designed as part of a three-pronged offensive, with conventional British forces attacking Akyab and the Arakan, while the Ledo and Yunnan forces under Stilwell swept down from the north and north-east to secure northern Burma and reopen the land route to China. A series of mishaps now occurred. It was originally planned that 4 Corps would assault Sittang and Kalewa while 15 Corps tackled Akyab and Arakan, but shortages of labour, transport and even the wherewithal to build new roads led to the cancellation of the project. Even worse, Chiang Kai-shek, angry about the decisions taken at the Casablanca conference, refused to sanction a Chinese advance from the north. With all hopes for a 1943 campaign of reconquest gone,

Wavell had to consider whether the LRP project was any longer relevant. The case for abandoning it was strong, but Wavell, always partial to Wingate, told him that it was being postponed.[6]

On 7 February, a crucial date in Wingate's biography, Wavell arrived at Chindit headquarters with his mind, on balance, inclined towards cancellation. In a two-hour interview Wingate fought his corner tigerishly. Having heard Wavell state that he could not be a party to the pointless waste of lives, Wingate hit back with six main arguments. First, cancellation would boost the defeatist blimps in the Indian army who had always opposed Wingate and LRP. Second, it was essential for the British to overcome their current ignorance of Japanese methods of fighting in the jungle. Third, Fort Hertz – the one remaining British outpost in Burma, 60 miles south of the Chinese border, manned by Karen levies – was in desperate need of relief. Fourth, without a Chindit crossing, the Japanese would dominate the jungle on either side of the Chindwin river. Fifth, 77 Brigade was now pitch perfect and any delay or cancellation would have a catastrophic impact on morale. Sixth, an attack by 77 Brigade would impair and set back Japanese preparations for an offensive.[7] Actually, these arguments were not that powerful except for the point about Fort Hertz. But psychologically Wavell was looking for ways and means to be persuaded so that he could 'sell' the operation, and Wingate pressed all the right buttons. It was a classic case of giving bad reasons for what was believed on instinct. Impressed by Wingate's enthusiasm and his absolute conviction that the venture was worthwhile, Wavell made a Pilate-like gesture by referring the final decision to the man who had accompanied him to the conference, Lieutenant General Brehon Somervell of the US army. Somervell said: 'Well, I guess I'd let them roll.'[8] Wavell then mounted the reviewing stand, saluted the Chindits as they marched past and made a short speech: 'This is a great adventure. It is not going to be an easy one. I wish you all the best of luck.' Such brevity, reminiscent of Lincoln at Gettysburg, was not Wingate's style. His highly rhetorical order of the day issued to his men reads like a speech from Caesar or Thucydides.[9]

By sheer determination and perseverance, Wingate now had what he wanted. Since the previous year he had held the rank of brigadier, and both Calvert and Fergusson had been promoted to lieutenant colonel. Wavell had laid down few provisos or qualifications. It has never been satisfactorily explained why, particularly in the light of the collapse of the Chinese offensive, Wingate's columns were not directed south-east to help the Arakan operation, where such an intervention might just have tipped the balance. The Chindits' main assignments were to cut two railways, that between Myitkyina and Mandalay in northern Burma and also the Mandalay–Lashio line. The only thing that annoyed Wingate was the code name given to his first Chindit expedition: Operation LONGCLOTH, which did not have the grandiloquence he sought.[10] In the week after 6 February, the seven columns marched south-east from Imphal to Moreh on the Assam/Burma border. Once across the border the brigade was to split into two groups. The first or Southern Group, comprising Columns 1 and 2 (1,000 men and 250 mules) was to feint and sow disinformation so as to throw the Japanese off the scent. Northern Group (Columns 3, 4, 5, 7 and 8), comprising 2,000 men and 850 mules, was to carry out the railway demolitions. Small patrols of 77 Brigade had already crossed the Chindwin and travelled some 30 miles into enemy territory, returning without mishap, but a crossing by 3,000 men and more than a thousand animals would be an entirely different matter. This was why the disinformation strategy employed was of almost labyrinthine complexity. On 13 February, an advance party of the Northern Group crossed at Tonhe, 50 miles to the north. This was an elaborate double bluff. The Japanese were meant to conclude, when the Southern Group crossed farther south, that this advance party was a feint to divert attention from the traverse of the Southern Group, whereas in fact Southern Group was itself the feint to mask the crossing of the bulk of Northern Group. As a further refinement of deception, a disinformation party split off from the Southern Group, marched south and ordered a huge quantity of supplies from a village known to be pro-Japanese, mentioning various places on a supposed southern itinerary. The ruse was a great success. The second wave, 2,000 men of Northern Group, crossed the Chindwin unopposed on 14 February.[11]

Yet Wingate was far from satisfied. There were several unforeseen problems. He had poured scorn on the Gurkhas for being such inept muleteers, but in the field, facing the great rivers of Burma in conditions unlike those they had trained in at Saugur (where there were no wide rivers), not even the so-called expert mule-drivers proved capable of handling the animals efficiently. While elephants and bullocks swam the Chindwin with ease, the mules proved skittish, recalcitrant and even hysterical, perhaps fearing crocodiles. Getting them to the far bank was a nightmare of braying, bucking and stampeding animals.[12] Mules also played a part in the mixed fortunes of the Southern Group. Supposed to be two days ahead of the Northern Group, they soon fell behind schedule. Their first task was to ambush a 250-strong Japanese garrison at Maingnyaung on 18 February, but there was a skirmish between the three Gurkha platoons and a Japanese patrol before the objective was reached, which left six Japanese dead. Alerted, the enemy opened up with mortars. This spooked the mules, and the panic-stricken muleteers added to the stampede. The mules were missing for several days and some of them never returned. More importantly, the element of surprise was lost, and the fiasco cost the Southern Group a delay of three days.[13] The group then made painfully slow progress from Maingnyaung out of the hill country east of the Chindwin but the remaining mules, existing on bamboo leaves, became increasingly emaciated and the men found that the loss of the grain in the fracas on the 18th cut down on their rations. Wingate continued to fulminate about the excessive noise the mules were making and ordered that if they whinnied they were to be given a sharp poke on the nose. This disconcerted the British drovers, who had formed a sentimental attachment to their charges. Soon the well-disciplined Chindits were beginning to turn into something of a rabble, discharging their kit and anything that could be construed as surplus baggage.[14]

The Southern Group then slowly pulled away from the hill country east of the Chindwin, making for the Mandalay–Myitkyina railway. On the night of 3–4 March, they were ambushed in the Mu valley in the dark. The result was disaster. Radios, ciphers and most equipment was lost, and No. 2 Column came close to being annihilated. The battered remnants of No. 1 Column limped on to the banks of the Irrawaddy, awaiting final orders from Wingate, who naturally blamed the commander, Major Burnett. 'The disaster to No. 2 Column,' he wrote later, 'was easily avoidable [he did not say how] and would never have taken place had the commander concerned understood the doctrines of penetration.'[15] Meanwhile Wingate and the Northern Group rendezvoused five miles inland from the Chindwin in pelting rain, having successfuly received their parachute drops. Wingate then dithered about his choice of options: to make for Tonmakeng, where intelligence reported no enemy presence, and wait for the next supply drop; to attack the 200-strong Japanese garrison at Sinlamaung; or to bypass it and head into the Mu valley.[16] Keeping his options open for the moment, Wingate made for a very pleasant teak forest, with the leaves still on the trees providing a canopy from the sun and an umbrella from the rain. But in this idyllic setting the men grew over-confident and forgot that they were in enemy country; Wingate was angry to see discipline lapse, to see his Chindits dawdling and neglecting elementary precautions and even leaving a trail for the enemy to find by dropping litter.[17] After giving the officers a tongue-lashing, he decided that what would restore *esprit de corps* was a real firefight. His scouts reported that there was a Japanese garrison in a gold-mining village called Metkalet between Myene (15 miles east of the Chindwin) and Tonmakeng. He accordingly ordered No. 3 and No. 5 Columns, under Calvert and Fergusson respectively, to attack at once. Another fiasco soon developed. Fergusson found his column floundering in a swamp, still far from his objective, when a courier arrived to tell him that he was on a fool's errand anyway, as there was no Japanese garrison in Metkalet after all.[18] He and Calvert took their columns back on to the main Tonmakeng track, where they found Wingate again uncertain and dithering, not knowing whether to call in another supply drop near Tonmakeng or divert into the Mu valley and get one there. Eventually he opted for the Tonmakeng option, on the basis that no one knew Japanese strength in the Mu valley. He was taking a risk on two grounds. They were making slow progress, only 10 miles a day instead of the scheduled 15, which meant that enemy pursuers might even then be gaining on them. Worse still, if there was a strong Japanese garrison at Tonmakeng, Northern Force's adventure would perforce come to an abrupt end.[19]

All this time the Chindits were trekking through the most difficult country, alternating stiff uphill climbs with precipitous descents, crossing the Zibyu range, down into a wide valley, then up again across the Mangin range at 4,000 feet and down once more into the valley of the Meza, a tributary of the Irrawaddy. They reached Tonmakeng without further incident on 22 February. Learning that there was a Japanese garrison at Sinlamaung, 10 miles away, Wingate decided that three of the columns would attack there while the rest waited for a massive supply drop, expected to take three days. His idea was that if the attack on Sinlamaung ran into trouble, it could be reinforced from Tonmakeng. There ensued a further comedy of errors. The attackers could not even find Sinlamaung for three days, and when they finally located it on 25 February, having marched round in circles, they discovered that there had been a garrison there but it had just pulled out. Heartened by the success of the three-day supply drop, Wingate called a conference of senior officers, at which it was decided to march on to Zibyutaungdan, with No. 3 Column under Calvert operating independently. On 26 February, Wingate delivered a pointless harangue to his officers about the British cult of gallant losers – how it was a sign of corruption and degeneracy that the British celebrated a terrible defeat like that at Dunkirk in 1940 as if it were a glorious victory.[20] Doubtless everyone was glad to get under way next day, but the initial relief at not being on the receiving end of a lecture turned to gloom as the men found themselves marching single file along a narrow jungle track; once again the muleteers performed wonders in extremely difficult going. Wingate did not enhance his reputation among the marchers by issuing a deeply unpopular prohibition on brewing up morning tea at first light.[21] On 1 March the trekkers came to the Zibyutaungdan escarpment and began the descent into the Mu valley. Wingate now decreed that the Northern Group would disperse into its individual columns and rendezvous later at the Irrawaddy or beyond. He sent an advance party across the Irrawaddy to the Kachin highlands north-east of Mandalay to raise a guerrilla force among the notably pro-British people. On 2 March he marched his men 20 miles down a motor road in broad daylight and in teeming rain to a bivouac area in the forest about 10 miles north-east of Pinlebu. Since this was against all his carefully inculcated principles, eyebrows were raised, but Wingate explained that he had decided on the easy progress on the metalled road as there would be no vehicles on it in the torrential rains; also, he added, a good commander always knew when to break his own rules.[22]

The dispersal of the Northern Group into individual columns was always a risk, but Wingate could hardly have expected disaster as complete as that on the night of 3–4 March. At the very same time as Southern Group was being ambushed and No. 2 Column wiped out, No. 4 Column also walked into an ambush, two miles west of

Pinbon. Major R.B. Bromhead, a descendant of the Bromhead famous for the defence against the Zulus at Rorke's Drift in 1879, did his best but was stymied when panicking Gurkhas stampeded the mules. He gave the order to disperse and regroup at a rendezvous point where they could get help from No. 7 and No. 8 Columns, but while trying to reach the rendezvous, the men were attacked again, and by the time they arrived at the rallying point, 7 and 8 had moved on. With no food or radio, low on ammunition and with just a handful of animals left, Bromhead had no choice but to order a retreat to India.[23] And so in just 24 hours, both No. 2 and No. 4 columns were out of the picture and on their way back to Assam. Needless to say, Wingate did not accept this setback as part of the fortunes of war. Since his own credibility and that of LRP in general was at stake, responsibility had to be fastened on the luckless Bromhead. Fortunately the Japanese believed that in wiping out No. 2 Column they had destroyed the entire invasion. Meanwhile Wingate began to have secret doubts about the whole operation. He had seen himself as a knight-errant, delivering Burma from tyranny, but there were two main problems. One was that the Burmese population was apathetic, had no interest in the war and just wanted to be left alone. The pro-British tribes of the north and east were not national but separatist movements; the only national movement was headed by the morally and politically ambivalent Aung San, a man distinguished only by 'great cleverness and Hitlerite fixity of purpose'.[24] In Burma there was no equivalent of Haganah or Haile Selassie's liberation movement, but only Aung San's pro-Japanese Burmese Independence Army. Lacking an ideological or emotional focus for his military ambitions, Wingate often seemed detached or half-hearted about the struggle he was engaged in. As has been well said, 'nothing that he wrote on Burman affairs is comparable with his impassioned and assertive pleadings on behalf of Ethiopia and Israel'.[25]

However, the Chindits were about to score a great success, under the aegis of Calvert and Fergusson. By 6 March both their columns were within striking distance of the Wuntho–Indaw railway. Calvert was in his element, sowing disinformation wherever he went, euphoric, manic, fond of lethal practical jokes, with a macabre sense of humour and a hatred of all Japanese.[26] He and Fergusson hatched a daring and ingenious plan for an assault on the 800-strong garrison at Pinlebu.

Making contact with Major Walter Scott, who was leading No. 8 Column, they agreed that Scott would attack Pinlebu while they supervised a massive supply drop north-east of the town. The idea was that the attackers and the supply collectors could support each other. To this end they set up roadblocks to the north and east of Pinlebu to guard the approaches to the supply drop, while calling in the RAF to bombard the town, making the Japanese think they were facing a huge force. The attack on Pinlebu turned out to be a notable success, which at once confused the Japanese about exactly what was going on and masked a supply drop. The battle itself turned into a grim and bloody affair. On the afternoon of 6 March, Calvert and Fergusson ordered the demolition of the railway line. Calvert's men reached the tracks after heavy fighting and set the charges. The line was blown up in several places as a fitting birthday present for Calvert, who was 30 that day.[27] The Japanese then counterattacked in force to try to stop the demolition. The main battle raged around the outlying village of Nankan. While this was going on, Calvert's men also mined two railway bridges, one of them a three-span 120-foot monster. No. 3 Column saw the bulk of the fighting. In a bloody night's work, Calvert and Fergusson's men killed about one third of the Pinlebu defenders, aided by a lucky mortar shot, and cut the railway line in several places (some say in more than 70 separate locations) without taking significant losses themselves. In the evening, Fergusson's No. 5 Column blew the 40-foot rail bridge at Bongyaung gorge and also exploded the gorge's overhanging rock walls, dropping hundreds of tons of rubble on to the railway track. The explosions at Bongyaung railway station lit up the night sky and announced to all of Northern Group that the main LRP mission had been accomplished.[28]

Ten miles north of Wuntho, Wingate had established his headquarters in the Bambwe Taung hills. Now he had to make one of the salient decisions of his life: should he retire to India or press on and cross the Irrawaddy? He was faced with the dilemma that so often afflicts commanders, revolutionaries and even thinkers. What happens when the theoretical framework surrounding events collapses and the individual is left without pointers, guidance or rudders? The theory of LRP posited that once the severing of the railway had occurred, the main force of the regular army would invade, but it was obvious this would not happen. Wingate therefore had to invent a refinement or secondary development of his theory. Without being too fanciful, one might compare it with Lenin's adaptation of classical Marxism to form Marxist-Leninism. In other words, it was time for the theory of LRP Mark Two. But what form should this take? Wingate toyed with the idea of turning his headquarters at Bambwe Taung into a second Fort Hertz; this would allow him to be supplied by air and to sortie at will, forcing the Japanese to give up the Indaw and Irrawaddy towns immediately to the north and south of his operating ambit. There was even the hope that eventually all of northern Burma could be reclaimed.[29] But this assumed that everything would continue on an 'as is' basis. The Japanese, however, were determined to cut out this cancer in their midst. It may seem extraordinary, especially after the ostentatious early antics of Southern Group, that the Japanese were at first unaware that the Chindits were being systematically resupplied by air, but such appears to be the case. Once they realised they were not dealing with small raiding parties but with something more serious, they strengthened their land forces and commenced a search-and-destroy operation.[30] The success of the railway demolition had created its own perils. The Japanese were now present in numbers in the rear of the Chindits, while their strength in the country across the Irrawaddy was unknown. It was conceivable that if Wingate crossed the Irrawaddy, he would deliver the entire brigade to destruction. On the other hand, the same fate might await them if they tried to retreat. Wingate has been much criticised for the decision to press on, but in fairness it must be stressed that there were no easy options. This explains his indecisiveness. After another attack of the dithers, he effectively left the decision to Calvert and Fergusson. They both said they wanted to cross the Irrawaddy and Wingate finally gave them the nod, rationalising his decision on the grounds that the terrain on the other side of the river was better suited to jungle warfare. His decision to go on 'was the most difficult, the most dangerous, and the most expensive in men of any which he took at any time'.[31]

Perhaps his decision was influenced in part by the news that No. 1 Column, the surviving rump of Southern Force, had also blown up a railway bridge, at Kyaikthin, and then crossed the Irrawaddy at Taguang on its own initiative (but with the sanction of the original general order) on 10 March. But with the Japanese on their trail, there was no time to lose. The people of Tigyaing welcomed the British and made boats available for the crossing. Fergusson and No. 5 Column got across by nightfall just before a Japanese column arrived on the west bank to intercept them.[32] Learning that the enemy had occupied Tigyaing, Calvert and No. 3 Column crossed five miles downriver, where the western shore is divided into islands stiff with elephant grass. The column was able to approach the river under cover of this tall and thick grass, using an elephant and mahout as guide. But on the shoreline on the morning of 13 March they ran into a serious ambush. Calvert tried to hold the attackers off with the rearguard while the main body crossed to an island in midstream. If the Japanese had pressed their attack, they would have destroyed the whole of No. 3 Column. But, uncertain of British numbers, they probed hesitantly. Sensing how the Japanese commander's mind was working, Calvert bluffed heavily by launching a temporary counterattack with the rear-guard, simulating a large force. The Japanese drew off to reconsider, allowing Calvert to get his force across by midnight. To have crossed the mile-wide Irrawaddy while under attack was a major military achievement. The cost was seven men killed and six wounded, who were left on the island with a note from Calvert asking the Japanese commander to treat them according to the code of bushido.[33] Wingate and the main body of Northern Force (1,200 men) left Bambwe Taung and came to the confluence of the Irrawaddy and its principal northern tributary, the Shweli, on 17 March. Here the river was so wide that their ropes and dinghies were useless, and the crossing had to be made in boats. The danger was that the approach to the stream was over open paddy fields, where they could easily be spotted. A further problem was that intelligence revealed the far shore was held by units of the Burmese Liberation Army. But when Wingate sent across an envoy to treat with them, the fearless warriors of the BLA promptly decamped. The crossing commenced but once again the mules proved difficult. Forty were left behind, and those that crossed were tethered to boats that were paddled while the animals swam. The crossing began at nightfall on 17 March and was complete by sunset on the 18th.[34]

With Calvert and Fergusson well ahead of him, Wingate signalled them to make for the Gokteik viaduct and destroy it, thus severing the Mandalay–Lashio road. This was the structure Alexander had hoped Calvert would destroy in 1942, and now, it seemed, he had another chance.[35] Calvert and Fergusson turned south towards Mytison, but shortly afterwards Fergusson was ordered by Wingate to abandon his back-up for Calvert and instead rejoin the rest of the brigade. Calvert, unaware of this order, approached Mytison, concluded it was too strong to take and switched tactics to an ambush. While the RAF pounded the town, Calvert laid a trap along the Nam Mit river. A Japanese patrol walked right into the ambuscade and lost 100 men killed. Calvert reported: 'We let fly with everything we had and a lot of Japs could never have known what hit them. It was one of the most one-sided actions I have ever fought in.'[36] Calvert's boast that he had not lost a man was, however, sheer vainglory. Perhaps half a dozen Gurkhas died in this action.[37] Although his men were now very tired, Calvert was buoyed by the success of an airdrop on 19 March – a 10-ton aerial dump of supplies that was the biggest drop in the entire expedition. Up in the hills he made final preparations for the assault on Gokteik, the glittering prize that had eluded him in 1942 and which he still yearned for. But he was to be disappointed yet again. Suddenly he received an order to return to India; as he was then far to the south of the main body, he would have to achieve this on his own initiative. Bitterly disappointed, he showed his contempt for the orders by carrying out further railway demolition on the retreat. Reading his chief acolyte's mind, Wingate sent him a further signal to say that he should get out as fast as he could and not attempt any more derring-do. It was now crucial to bring out as many survivors as possible, for 'we can get new equipment and wireless sets. But it will take twenty-five years to get another man. These men have done their job, their experience is at a premium.'[38] No. 3 Column reached the Chindwin on 14 April, crossed it without opposition and were the first out of Burma. This column and Calvert himself were the real success stories of Operation LONGCLOTH. The combination of proper training and Calvert's natural talent as a leader of irregulars had created a formidable unit.[39]

Meanwhile Wingate seems to have entered another 'down' period in the bipolar cycle, for many accounts refer to him at this juncture as a *luth suspendu* – highly strung, irritable, irrational. During the crossing of the Irrawaddy, an officer had reported a snag, and Wingate threw himself on the ground with a cry of exasperated despair. With what his biographer calls 'one among a hundred evidences of his impersonality at continual variance with his egotism' he left no record of exactly where he crossed the Irrawaddy. He seems to have concentrated on the negative and discounted the amazing run of luck the Chindits had enjoyed so far – crossing the Chindwin, cutting the railway in 70 different places, crossing the Irrawaddy, all without significant losses – suspecting that, in the words of one of his sergeants, 'there must be a catch somewhere'.[40] Maybe Wingate was actually more perceptive than his many crazed utterances would suggest, for at a deeper level he might have been aware how many bad mistakes he had already made and was continuing to make. At war with the deep, irritable pessimism was a countervailing facile optimism. He was complacent about being able to link up with friendly tribes in the Kachin hills, unaware that between him and them lay a hot, dry belt of waterless forest, criss-crossed by crude motor roads heavily patrolled by the Japanese. He seemed not to realise that after all their exertions, his men were at the limit of their endurance. And he had made the cardinal mistake of in effect funnelling his columns together in a possible death trap. Instead of spreading them over a wide area, he had compressed them within 15 miles of each other in a kind of peninsula surrounded by the Shweli and Irrawaddy rivers, making it easier for the Japanese to find them. The Chindits were now concentrated on the base of this triangle, and as the terrain was mainly paddy fields rather than jungle, they were peculiarly liable to discovery by the enemy.[41] A spotter plane did in fact detect No. 5 Column at one stage, and all the Japanese needed to do was man the roads from Mytison to Male and they would have the whole 77 Brigade in a trap. Suddenly aware of his predicament, Wingate ordered his men to break out of the 'Shweli loop'. It was easier said than done. The men marched slowly because of hunger, thirst and disintegrating boots, and they had to wait for supply drops, which were intermittent and inadequate – to the point where No. 5 Column went 48 hours without food. It became apparent that Wingate's force was really too large to be supplied by air. The logic of that was that by taking 77 Brigade east of the Irrawaddy, Wingate had made a serious mistake.[42]

Back in Imphal, 4 Corps, providing the logistical back-up for the Chindits, were puzzled by Wingate's plans once he had crossed the Irrawaddy. They signalled to know what his intentions were, and he replied that his destination was the Kachin hills, from where he would strike at the Lashio–Bhamo road. Gently 4 Corps reminded the visionary commander that at such a distance they would be unable to supply him by air. It was suggested that he try instead for an attack on Shwebo, west of the Irrawaddy; the clear implication was that that was where they wanted him. Obstinately Wingate responded that he could not get back across the Irrawaddy as the Japanese had commandeered every boat and barred all access routes. At this, the commander of 4 Corps ordered him to end his operations and withdraw to India.[43] This was the trigger for Wingate's message to Calvert. At the same time he ordered Fergusson to rendezvous with him at Baw, where all columns save Calvert's would assemble to receive the supply drop that would enable them to attempt the return journey. Fergusson's column was by now suffering badly. With little water, they sucked the fluid from whatever green bamboo stems they could find. They butchered the mules for meat and then made stews of monkeys, rats, locusts and cockroaches. They were crawling with lice and leeches. Leeches were a particular problem, for when they were pulled off, the leech's head tended to stay embedded in the skin, creating open, infected, oozing sores. Gazing at his cadaverous men, Fergusson felt impelled to radio Wingate with a bitter Bible verse: 'I can count all my bones: they stare and gloat over me. (Psalms 22:17).' It was a mistake to trade quotations with a bible-thumper like Wingate. He flashed back a bowdlerised quote from St John's Gospel: 'Consider that it is expedient one man should die for the greater good of all people.'[44] But Wingate's original signal to Fergusson engendered a twofold error. Not only did it draw the columns back into the Shweli loop, but it also indicated overconfidence about the airdrops. The ploy of attacking garrisons with one part of the force while overseeing the aerial drops with the other (allowing mutual support between the sections) had hitherto worked so well that the Chindits had begun to take its efficacy for granted. But at Baw the inevitable happened and things went wrong. Wingate launched his ground attack but the RAF pilots, seeing a confused battle going on in the jungle beneath them, flew off after dropping only one third of the needed supplies. Wingate's reaction to this was to scapegoat a junior officer and reduce him to the ranks.[45]

Fergusson finally rendezvoused with Wingate at the Shaukpin Chaung river bed on 25 March and found his leader despondent, arguing that the Japanese commander must now do his utmost to annihilate them in order to save face. Fergusson later nostalgically recalled the final conference of Wingate and his officers as 'the last reunion of a very happy band of brothers before setting out on the perilous homeward journey, which many of them did not survive'.[46] Knowing that the Japanese would contest the passage of the Irrawaddy, Wingate decided to try bluff: he would march back to Inywa and cross at the identical point of the eastward crossing. It would be necessary to kill all remaining animals and make the traverse lightly armed; once across, they should disperse into small groups and try to sabotage more railway installations on their way back to Assam. Fergusson suggested that they would do better to stick together. That way they could keep their beasts and weapons and would be more likely to prevail if they encountered the Japanese, who would be unlikely to be in one place in similar strength. The itinerary would be a round-about one: crossing the Shweli, then striking north to re-enter India in a huge loop via Bhamo and the Hukawng valley. Wingate vetoed the idea on the grounds that supply drops would be too difficult, particularly after the monsoon. Many officers were secretly stupefied that he had ordered all his units back into the Shweli loop for the rendezvous. Should he not have arranged airdrops south of the loop for No. 3 and No. 5 Columns and ordered them to make their own way back thence to India? Wingate's supporters said that this option was ruled out when he decided to use the RAF for a classic piece of deception. He arranged for drops to be made south of the loop in hopes of persuading the Japanese that that was where the brigade was, thus buying time. As a further and controversial piece of disin-formation, he sent No 1. Column on eastwards to the Kachin hills; he was sending them to their doom to save the rest of the brigade.[47]

All columns endured a dreadful march back to Inywa. The mules were slaughtered as they went, which caused great grief to the mule-teers. It soon became clear that the Japanese were following them, and all the indications were that this was part of a master plan for interception. Colonel Tomotoki Koba had set up three defensive lines between the Chindits and the Indian border, the first at the Irrawaddy, the second along the Mu valley and the third following the line of the Chindwin. Meanwhile the pursuers who dogged the Chindits were supposed to drive them into the trap as if this were a wild beast hunt.[48] Wingate tried to throw the enemy off the scent by feints and decoys, including an attack by Fergusson's No. 5 Column on the village of Hintha, halfway between Baw and Inywa.[49] The feints seem to have worked, for the bamboozled Japanese never caught up; they thus missed their best chance by not trapping the Chindits in the Shweli loop. The main body of the raiders reached Inywa at 4 p.m. on 28 March, and once again their luck was in. Although the Japanese had commandeered all boats on the Irrawaddy, they had neglected to do the same on the Shweli. After collecting a number of country boats, the Chindits began to cross the river. No. 7 Column went first, followed by No. 2 and No. 8, but No. 8 was fired on by the enemy when halfway across. By the time No. 7 embarked, they were having to repel the Japanese from the landing area. It was fortunate for the Chindits that the Japanese had only a small force and lacked heavy machine guns. Even so, they did so much damage with mortars, rifles and light auto-matics that Wingate called off the embarkation and left No. 7 to its own salvation while he and the others melted away into the forest.[50] He moved to a 'secure bivouac' 10 miles east-south-east of Inywa and 10 miles south of the Shweli, right at the top of the 'loop'. Here he divided his columns into five 'dispersal groups' and arranged for supply drops. From now on it was *sauve qui peut*. Wingate's own group was 43 strong and the rest of the groups had similar numbers. With the remnants of the Southern Group on its mission impossible in the Karin hills, Northern Group also seemed in imminent danger of destruction.[51]

The first to suffer from the disintegration was Fergusson's No. 5 Column. After the fight at Hintha, Fergusson sent his second in command to Wingate, who advised him about the rendezvous and airdrop. But by the time Fergusson got there, the rest of the brigade had gone and he had missed both drop and supplies. Since his radio had been destroyed during the fast and furious encounter at Hintha, he was on his own in every sense. He decided to make for the Kachin hills and likely sanctuary. But the crossing of the raging Shweli turned out to be a nightmare. Some of his men were swept away by the flood, as were some of the animals. Another 46 men were abandoned on a sandbank in the middle of the river, since the Japanese were arriving on the far bank and Fergusson had no time to rescue them: 'the decision which fell on me there was as cruel as any which could fall on the shoulders of a junior commander'.[52] Fergusson's group staggered on, half crazed with hunger and thirst, all the men obsessed with thoughts of food and particularly the sugary kind. Fifteen days after crossing the Shweli, they reached the Chindwin on 24 April and limped in to Imphal two days later. No. 5 Column suffered grievously, with only 95 survivors out of an original complement of 318; the toll would have been higher had some fortunate individuals not made their way to China or Fort Hertz.[53] Major Ken Gilkes and No. 7 Column managed to get to China with 150 survivors and then flew back to India. All the dispersed groups had terrible tales to tell about Japanese atrocities, the treachery of Burman villages, the constant battle to stay awake, the snatched shards of sleep in trees or caves while the enemy hunted for them, and the agony of hunger and thirst. Rice and buffalo meat were rare luxuries for the refugees; more often the menu would be python and nettles.[54]

Later some bitterness was evinced among Chindit veterans that Wingate and his group had taken the easy way out, holed up in a secure billet while the rest of the dispersed columns were used as decoys. Certainly Wingate's party found themselves a secure eyrie in the neighbourhood of the supply drop (which made it all the more ironic that Fergusson had not found them). Here they stayed put for a week, sleeping, resting and eating (which meant the silent slaughter of horses and mules so as not to alert the enemy by gunshots), gathering strength for the long march back to the Chindwin. Wingate was never a taciturn man, but during this week he became positively loquacious and expansive, talking about a wide range of subjects: Plato's *Republic*, H.G. Wells, Shaw, world government, the League of Nations, eighteenth-century painting, Leonardo da Vinci, the symphony versus the concerto, detective fiction, contemporary cinema and especially the psychology of strip cartoons, with special reference to Popeye and Jane.[55] On one occasion the hidden Chindits had to take a big risk by starting a fire to scare away wild elephants. But the real hazard of this week's stopover was the incessant plague of mosquitoes. At last, on 7 April, Wingate and his group started for the Irrawaddy, by now with no mules and no radio. Wingate thought the trek to India would take two weeks, but it took 22 days. For two days the party tried to find a way across the Irrawaddy but were always frustated by enemy patrols. Finally on 13 April, with the help of friendly locals who provided them with rowers, they built bamboo rafts and began floating across. They intended to cross in relays of three parties, but before the third could embark, the Japanese arrived; the luckless rearguard was left to its fate. Marching north-west, the survivors reached the Meza and again found friendly locals who got them across. By dusk on 11 April they had marched 70 miles on just eight hours' sleep and had put two river crossings behind them. Always heading north-west or west-north-west, they reached rocky country, at its driest in this period just before the monsoon. They were dispirited, hungry, thirsty, and plagued with mosquitoes now that they had lost both veils and ointment, but Wingate tried to keep their spirits up with mini-lectures on Beethoven and the Italian Renaissance during rest periods.[56]

They began to approach the Wuntho–Indaw railway and were once again in a teak forest, though a far cry from the pleasant sylvan surroundings of two months earlier. Now that the great leaves had fallen in the dry season, the men found the experience like walking through crockery, and Wingate fumed at the din, audible 300 yards away. Still, there was nothing to do but trust to luck, and it held. They emerged from the teak forests on descending foothills and debouched on to the plain, where they hit the railway line. It was fortunate both that they arrived at midnight and that the teak petered out a long way before the railway so that their approach was not heard by the Japanese patrols. Once they managed to slip across to the teak forests on the other side, Wingate was heard to express contempt for the low stan-dard of Japanese patrolling.[57] Then it was uphill again as between the railway and the Mu valley they crossed the Mangin range, sometimes having to make mountaineers' ropes out of their rifle slings. By now they had run out of all food, even biscuits and dates. It did not seem possible, but the men looked forward each night to python stew, which became the staple. Conscious that the Japanese might be dogging them, they never rested more than three or four hours at any time. At one village they bought rice, but at once the pro-Japanese villagers rang great gongs to summon the Japanese. At another village they fared better with apathetic neutrals and were able to buy a quantity of buffalo meat. On one occasion Wingate broke his own golden rule about sickness and stopped for 48 hours to tend a Lieutenant Spurlock, who was suffering from dysentery. His unwontedly humane gesture paid no dividends, however, as Spurlock was still too ill to go on and had to be abandoned. As they marched on through the dry uplands of the Mangin range, Wingate controversially prevented his men from collecting ripe limes on the grounds that the Japanese were close behind them.[58]

Near the end of their strength, the Chindits had a stroke of luck when their Burmese interpreter contacted a monastery and bought a veritable cornucopia of victuals: chickens, tomatoes, rice, bananas and five sucking pigs.[59] Refreshed, the party crossed a river in the Mu valley and climbed up the Zibyutaungdan escarpment – a rock wall 1,500 feet high. By now convinced they would be overhauled or intercepted, they took a chance and accepted an offer from a hermit to lead them over the scarp by backtracks unknown to the Japanese. Despite Wingate's natural suspicions, the guide proved as good as his word. But stragglers were dropping behind all the time. A lance corporal who could not keep up walked off into the wilderness, Captain Oates style, so as not to slow his comrades up. On 23 April the marchers reached a high point from which they could see the Chindwin below. Wingate uttered one of his quasi-Biblical effusions: 'Behold the Chindwin. It is a poor heart that never rejoices.'[60] But Odysseus had long ago learned that the hardest part of any voyage is when journey's end is sighted. The 30 miles to the Chindwin was the most gruelling experience yet, with Japanese patrols seemingly ubiquitous, in reality keyed to a high pitch of alertness by the recent passage of No. 3 Column. On 27 April Wingate and his men finally got to the river, about 20 miles south of where they had crossed 10 weeks before. With Japanese troops thick, fast and assiduous and all boats along the Chindwin commandeered, the travellers once more seemed to have reached impasse. But the resourceful hermit was not yet done. He located a friend who was able to provide exact details of the patrols' timetable. Now it was a question of finding boats.[61]

First Wingate divided his men into those he deemed strong enough to swim across the river and those who needed a boat. Then he set them to cut down 12-foot-high stalks of elephant grass in a massive copse by the riverside. By this time they were heedless about the noise they made. It took five men seven hours to hack a 700-yard path through these reeds. Once again their luck was in. It turned out there was no wide beach between river and copse; the Chindwin began virtually where the reeds ended. It was 3 p.m. Wingate decided to take to the water instantly. The swimmers took off their boots and cut off their trousers to form shorts. The Chindwin was 500 yards wide at this point, with a vicious current running, and even strong swimmers were in danger of drowning, only avoiding this fate by taking turns at floating on their backs. Wingate himself was one of those who came close to being swept away, and stayed afloat only because of the bamboo sticks that had been thrust into his pack for buoyancy.[62] All who reached the far side of the river lay on the bank utterly exhausted, too tired to run for cover. To their great relief they learned from the locals that there were no Japanese on this side of the river. They devoured a meal in the first village and were then guided to a post manned by a company of Gurkha Rifles. It was then a question of finding boats to paddle back across the Chindwin to rescue the non-swimmers. By this time these men had had to move to a fresh location to avoid Japanese patrols and there was no way to contact Wingate. It was a do-or-die situation. Two unsung heroes who supposedly lacked the skills to breast the raging Chindwin somehow got across and alerted their comrades about the new location. Wingate sent his rescue party with a strong protecting contingent of the Gurkha Rifles. The Japanese spotted the flotilla of boats and opened up with mortars, but the Gurkhas gave as good as they got. Soon the survivors were safely on the far side of the Chindwin.[63] Wingate's dispersal group was the fourth to reach Assam; of the 43 who started the journey, 34 survived.

So ended Operation LONGCLOTH, or Chindit One, as it came to be called. Two issues immediately present themselves: Wingate's character and behaviour on the expedition; and the quite separate issue of the military value of the LRP probe. On the first point, it is not surprising that extreme stress often showed up the brittle personality that had already manifested itself in 'black dog' episodes and a suicide attempt. Since in his own mind Wingate could never be at fault, and his mindset did not really admit mere contingency, it followed that after untoward episodes, mishaps or setbacks there had to be a search for a culprit. At the river crossing at Inywa he complained that his men were floundering about. But as General Julian Thompson has pointed out, it will not do to blame soldiers for incompetence if after six months' training they do not meet one's required standards. The correct deduction is that there is something wrong with the training or the leadership. In this case Wingate had simply failed to factor in the importance of river crossings – unpardonable, given Burma's riverine systems. If Gwalior did not provide the geographical where-withal for such training, he should have taken his recruits somewhere else, at least for that part of the Chindit course.[64] The crossing of the Irrawaddy has also been taken as an example of Wingate's glory-hunting, an exploit that served no purpose and was meaningless. Wingate justified it by saying that he had the enemy between him and the Chindwin, but this was always going to be the case. Not only would the Japanese still be between him and the Chindwin when he returned from across the Irrawaddy, but on any conceivable war-gaming of the campaign this was always going to happen anyway, whatever Wingate did or wherever he went. Another controversial incident is the 'busting' of the officer after the unsuccessful airdrop at Baw (see p. 149), which seems like simple scapegoating, though Wingate's supporters pedantically insist that the punishment was for failing to reach an assigned position in time.[65] But Wingate's punish-ments were always draconian. He thought nothing of striking enlisted men and even officers in one of his rages, confident that King's Regulations could not be applied in the jungle. He told his men that he would shoot anyone who pilfered from comrades, raided villages or even grumbled and that he would expel anyone who lost his rifle or equipment.[66] It must be emphasised that this went beyond the normal army code, that Wingate had never been given such authority and that he was taking it on himself to assume such powers. Of course, when sentries fell asleep, as happened, something drastic had to be done or the security of the entire column was at risk. On one occa-sion a sleeping sentry was given three choices: he could be shot, sent into the wilderness alone to make his own way back to the Chindwin, or be flogged. Not surprisingly the man opted to be flogged. There was at least one other flogging for a similar offence. Needless to say, Wingate's supporters attenuate these punishments by claiming that the beating was not so much an eighteenth-century cat-o'-nine-tails ordeal but more like a regular caning at an English public school.[67]

Wingate had virtually made a career out of thumbing his nose at regulations and doing things that, with a less fortunate individual, would certainly have led to a court-martial or dismissal from the service. A more salient issue is whether Operation LONGCLOTH achieved anything of significance. The casualty figures were appalling.

Of the 3,000 men of 77th Brigade Wingate took into Burma, only 2,182 returned to India. About 450 had been killed in action and the rest 'went missing' or died in captivity. Only 260 men of the 1,000-strong Southern Group survived. The 13th King's lost over a third of their 721 men. Even worse, of those who came back, only 600 were fit for active soldiering thereafter. The others, sick and broken, had fought their last campaign and were invalided out.[68] What had been achieved to justify such losses? Most judgements have been harshly negative. According to the official Indian history of the Burma campaign, 'the strategic value of the operation was nil'. The Gurkha official history endorses this: 'Never have so many marched so far for so little.'[69] Slim saw the whole venture as simply a modern version of the old-style cavalry raid, and summed up the operation as follows:

> They had blown up bridges and cuttings on the Mandalay–Myitkyina railways that supplied the Japanese northern front, and attempted to reach across the Irrawaddy to cut the Mandalay–Lashio line. Exhaustion, difficulties of air supply, and the reaction of the Japanese, prevented this, and the columns breaking up into small parties made for the shelter of 4 Corps. About a thousand men, a third of the total force, failed to return. As a military operation the raid had been an expensive failure. It gave little tangible return for the losses it had suffered and the resources it had absorbed. The damage it did to Japanese communications was repaired in a few days, the casualties it inflicted were negligible, and it had no immediate effect on Japanese dispositions or plans.'[70]

Even Wingate's own supporters admitted that the operation was a failure. 'An engine without a train' is how one of them described it.[71] Perhaps even more damning is this assessment from Fergusson: 'What did we accomplish? Not much that was tangible. What there was became distorted in the glare of publicity soon after our return. We blew up bits of railway, which did not take long to repair; we gathered some useful intelligence; we distracted the Japanese from some minor operations, and possibly from some bigger ones; we killed a few hundreds of an enemy which numbers eighty millions; we proved that it was feasible to maintain a force by supply dropping alone.'[72]

Wingate's admirers claim that this is 'battle accountancy of the wrong kind',[73] that because Wingate's exploits were talked up for propaganda purposes and because they lifted morale and raised the British public from a general atmosphere of gloom, LONGCLOTH was justified and can be judged a success. One can only reply that this is moral accountancy of the wrong sort. The sacrifice of 800 men on a pointless operation that was later used to promote a lie is a dubious proposition. The problem about lying propaganda is that it is ultimately self-defeating. Once the exaggerations and hyperbole are detected, and later events make them sure to be detectable, the cumulative effect on public morale is even worse, for people realise they have been lied to and will not trust government assurances again. And it is even difficult to see why the British government felt in such desperate need of favourable publicity. A year before the case might have seemed compelling, but this was 1943, when it was already obvious to any thinking person that the Allies were bound to win in the long run. Had not President Roosevelt already called for unconditional surrender in absolute confidence of victory? The answer seems to be that Wingate became the beneficiary of a 'perfect storm' of propaganda, with Churchill demanding quick and dramatic results on one hand, and the press eager for good, morale-boosting copy on the other. Churchill's gloss on LONGCLOTH is famous. On 24 July 1943 he announced: 'There is no doubt that in the welter of inefficiency and lassitude which has characterised our own operations on the Indian front, this man, his force and his achievements stand out; and no question of seniority must obstruct the advance of real personalities in their proper station in war.'[74] Wingate's press conference on 20 May was 'spun' by Allied propaganda into a glittering triumph. Reuters referred to 'The British Ghost Army'; the *Daily Mail* hailed Wingate as 'Clive of Burma'; and a glowing encomium by the then well-known columnist Alaric Jacob appeared in the *Daily Express*.[75] Wingate in Burma had fulminated at the British habit of turning obvious defeats into glorious victories, instancing Dunkirk. But he had no objection when his own failures were transmogrified by propaganda. The global legend of Wingate, superhero, was already in the making.

The dawning of 1943 saw Stilwell in the doldrums. Very bitter about Roosevelt's doctrinaire support for Chiang and the KMT, no matter how much damning evidence was produced, he said that even Russia under Stalin compared favourably with the nationalist regime in China, which he characterised as 'A gang of thugs with the one idea of perpetuating themselves and their machine. Money, influence and position the only considerations of the leaders. Intrigue, double-crossing, lying reports.'[1] Even the consolation prize of the Distinguished Service Cross, which Marshall had engineered for him, and which was celebrated by the generalissimo with a congratulatory dinner on 26 January, did nothing to dispel the gloom. 'The whole thing is bunk,' he wrote to his wife, 'pumped up out of a very minor incident and entirely undeserved. It is embarrassing but luckily time moves on, such things are forgotten.'[2] To console himself, he clung to the idea that Madame Chiang's mission in the USA had been a flop – a mistaken idea that he seems to have extrapolated from some negative personal remarks by Marshall. Sadly for him, the reality was that Madame's American trip, which would go on until May, was a great triumph. By clever public relations and spin, abetted by FDR, she managed to create the greatest sensation of any conquering celebrity since Lindbergh in 1927. She cleverly projected a smiling, bubbly public persona quite at odds with her irascible, arrogant, prima-donna-ish behaviour in private, which eventually alienated even Roosevelt.[3] FDR too was in public a very different creature from the irritated and exasperated private figure. Even though Chiang had just run up the white flag in Burma, the US president continued to churn out cant and humbug about the glorious and risky defiance of the generalissimo. He remained inflexible on the four cardinal points of his China programme: that US policy in the

Far East had to hinge on a close China–USA rapport; that the Kuomintang alone could unify China; that China must retrieve all the territory lost to Japan; and that the Soviet Union should play no part in the destinies of post-war China. No one in the State Department thought the KMT a viable option for the future, but nothing could shake Roosevelt's *idée fixe*.[4] The journalist Theodore White's famous description of the terrible famine in Honan in 1942–43 was censored by the authorities in Washington to make sure neither Chiang nor the Kuomintang were held to blame. Historians have always considered US blindness over nationalist China well-nigh incredible – the triumph of received opinion and the a priori over truth and reason. US press censorship on this issue was as complete as anything in the Axis countries. 'Probably never before had the people of one country viewed the government of another under misapprehension so complete.'[5]

The year would be one of conferences – summits in which both Stilwell and Wingate would play a significant part. British reluctance to fight a war in Burma, especially with Chinese help, was highlighted at the Casablanca conference when both General Marshall and the head of the US navy, Admiral Ernest King, announced that ANAKIM, laid aside by Wavell, was a vital part of the grand strategy in the war against Japan. Marshall indulged in some crude but very effective arm-twisting by telling his British counterparts bluntly that unless they signed up to ANAKIM, the Americans might pull out of planning for the invasion of Europe. The British tried to counter that providing the numbers of boats required for the amphibious side of ANAKIM would cut down on what was available for a cross-Channel invasion of Europe, but King checkmated the objection by offering to provide all the necessary landing craft from the US Pacific fleet. ANAKIM was then scheduled for 15 November 1943, with a final decision to be taken no later than 15 July.[6] Because Chiang was sulking about not being invited to Casablanca, it was decided to send a top-level delegation to Chungking, headed by General 'Hap' Arnold. FDR was secretly beginning to agree with Churchill that the reconquest of Burma was like 'munching a porcupine quill by quill'[7] and increasingly felt it should be abandoned in favour of the cross-Channel invasion of Europe, thus bringing the inter-Allied arguments full circle. FDR's secret, machiavellian motive in sending General Arnold to China was in hopes that Arnold would approve the Chennault airpower strategy and so appease the disaffected Chiang. But if he hoped the Arnold mission would follow the pattern of the Currie and Wilkie visits, he was soon severely disappointed. Arnold found both Chiang and Chennault every bit as quixotic and chimerical as Stilwell did, and was particularly disgusted with Chiang's oily slipperiness.[8] Chiang asked him for an independent command for Chennault, 500 combat planes by November and a pledge to fly 10,000 tons a month over the Hump. Stilwell, who attended the talks with Arnold, tried to pin Chiang down to support of ANAKIM, at which point the generalissimo, losing face in the presence of Arnold, lost his temper. When Stilwell asked if Chiang would still take part in the reconquest of Burma even if Allied naval support was limited, Chiang snapped: 'Didn't I say I would?' Later he complained that Stilwell had embarrassed him publicly. Stilwell noted in his diary: 'He can go to hell. I have him on that point.'[9]

Stilwell judged it was time for a cooling-off period and on 1 February departed for India. While he was en route, Chiang wrote to FDR (7 February) agreeing to ANAKIM but adding riders that would easily enable him to back out later. A full-scale planning meeting convened in Delhi on 9 February – a kind of tripartite conference, with T.V. Soong and Ho Ying-chin representing China, Wavell and Field Marshal John Dill representing Britain, and Arnold, Stilwell, Bissell and Somervell defending the American corner. Stilwell enjoyed particular rapport with Arnold and Dill, who had a positive genius for getting on with Americans. Both told him that negotiations with the Chinese had given them some idea of what Stilwell was up against in Chungking. Arnold told him: 'You ought to get a laurel wreath ... You have one son of a bitch of a job ... If at any time you think I can help, just yell.'[10] Stilwell would need all the help he could get, for FDR, irritated that Arnold had not reported as he wanted, dispatched yet another fact-finding mission to Chungking, this time sending the journalist Joe Alsop, who was close to Harry Hopkins. Needless to say, the 'facts' Alsop brought back were merely a specious confirmation of FDR's a priori belief in the Chennault doctrine of airpower and yet another recommendation that Stilwell be removed. But the Chennault doctrine gave Roosevelt the fig-leaf justification he needed to abandon ANAKIM (an even more problematical enterprise after the British defeat in the Arakan). He could now switch resources to

Europe while pretending to be doing something for Chiang. Accordingly, on 8 March he signed an order for an independent air force under Chennault's command and no longer subject to Bissell's orders; the snag for Chennault was that he would still have to obey Stilwell. FDR also told Chiang he would have his 500 combat planes and 10,000 tons of supplies a month, once again without any quid pro quo.[11] In a masterpiece of ignorant nonsense, Roosevelt told Marshall that Chiang was entitled to more respect, since he had come up the hard way. The most fatuous of his fantasies about China and the Kuomintang was his assertion that Chiang had created in a very short time what it had taken the USA two centuries to achieve.[12] Either FDR was conceding what anti-American critics habitually say – that the USA was a snakepit of corruption comparable to an Oriental despotism – and this is an impossible reading of his remark –; or he was evincing the most grotesque and lamentable ignorance of a truly fascistic society.

Stilwell continued in near-despair over his President's myopia. He pointed out that although Chiang had the 'negative' power to countermand positive orders to the army by his chief of staff, elsewhere he was a paper tiger, unable to control the endemic corruption of the KMT, knowing that any order he issued to control graft and racketeering would be ignored. Stilwell himself could make no headway as FDR readily imbibed the most barefaced lies from the Kuomintang propaganda machine about 'victories'; to feed his wrath, Stilwell made a list both of the phoney military 'successes' claimed by Chiang and of his broken promises. As he wrote to Marshall: 'If the Chinese army is so full of fight and so well led, what am I here for?'[13] Marshall and his colleagues in the War Department were furiously angry about FDR's continued attempts to sideline Stilwell and the absurd promotion of Chennault to major general. In pointed memos to the President, Marshall underlined the fatuity of Chennault's ideas. If US airpower really did make a significant impact on the Japanese, they would retaliate by overrunning the Chinese airfields, and since Chiang was habitually and pathologically unwilling to release his divisions to fight, who would stop them?[14] Stilwell evinced his contempt for Chungking and all its works by staying in India during February–March, overseeing the training sessions at Ramgarh and the agonisingly slow building of the Ledo road, and conferring with his British counterparts in Delhi. This left the field clear for Chiang and Chennault to intrigue for Chennault to be called back to Washington by FDR, hoping that he could then cut Stilwell out of the loop and be assigned responsibility for Lend-Lease. When Roosevelt seemed happy to accommodate the request, Marshall once more intervened. He insisted that if Chennault was to be recalled for talks, then Stilwell must be also.[15] The two men left China on 21 April and were in Washington on the 29th. Stilwell planned to counterattack at his meeting with the President, not just repeating Marshall's arguments about the limitations of airpower but extending the discussion to a general strategic overview of the entire South-East Asia and South-West Pacific area; he also hoped to persuade FDR to use American troops in Burma.

Unfortunately, when Stilwell was invited to speak at a meeting at the White House on 20 April, he turned in a mumbling, lacklustre, low-key performance. In an aside to Marshall, Roosevelt commented that Stilwell was obviously ill and should be replaced. Marshall knew his man better. Unlike the MacArthurs, Pattons, Chennaults and others – the type with whom FDR mainly dealt – Stilwell was temperamentally incapable of boasting and bragging. He made the mistake so many talented but modest men make, of thinking that merit will speak for itself without the megaphone of self-publicity. Alas, it almost never does. Unable to be vainglorious, openly ambitious or in any way to talk himself up – significantly his *Who's Who* entry was a mere six lines as against 15 for Eisenhower, 33 for Patton and 55 for MacArthur – Stilwell managed to come across as a journeyman mediocrity.[16] Additionally, he and FDR never got on well at that mysterious visceral level that determines the chemistry between individuals, and Stilwell found it hard to conceal his contempt for the President's backing of Chiang and Chennault. On 2 May, FDR told Marshall that he was going to overrule the objections of the War Department and give Chiang what he wanted without any caveats or preconditions. He completely accepted Chennault's boast that with 500 planes and 10,000 tons of Lend-Lease materiel a month he could sink one million tons of Japanese shipping by the year's end. So bowled over was Roosevelt by this that he told Chennault he could correspond with him directly, without going through Stilwell, Marshall and the usual channels. Stilwell saw in his own discomfiture the malign hand of Madame Chiang, who, he said, had 'put it over FDR like a tent . . . [Chiang was] a one man joke. The KMT is his tool. Madame is his front. The silly US propaganda is his lever. We are his suckers.'[17]

Stilwell was invited to stay on for the forthcoming TRIDENT conference, which would be an Anglo-American overview of the entire global conflict, with special reference to strategy in the Mediterranean and the much-touted cross-Channel invasion. From the Burmese viewpoint the prime problem would be that Churchill's only real interest in the East was Singapore, regaining which he viewed as vital for the prestige of the British Empire. He was broadly in favour of bypassing Burma, which he saw as being of advantage only to China, and on that subject none of the British could ever understand FDR's obsession with China nor what was the point of replacing Japan with China as the dominant power in the Far East. Once again FDR's view of the hemisphere can be seen as fatuous, since he regarded China only as a Pacific power, ignoring or unaware of her claim to Tibet, Mongolia and northern Burma, to say nothing of Hong Kong. Even if FDR's tunnel vision of a 'Pacific' China were accepted, why would anyone like the idea of the country as the area's hegemon or, as the British Foreign Secretary Anthony Eden put it, of China running up and down the Pacific?[18] Faced with FDR's pro-Chiang mania, the British adopted the machiavellian stance of supporting the Chiang/Chennault airpower idea, knowing it would fail anyway. Unaware of all these cross-currents, the honest Stilwell prepared his own memorandum for the conference. He felt he needed to get across that the President completely underrated the cunning and evil personality of the generalissimo. He wanted to stress the danger of the USA becoming a solitary Atlas bearing the burden of the world because the British were too clever for FDR. A forthright attack on the Chennault air strategy and its likely consequences would need to be reiterated. Most of all, he had to underline Chiang's ambitions to get rid of his present chief of staff, replace him with a 'yes man' and acquire the Lend-Lease materiel for his own ends without let or hindrance. Specific recommendations included an end to the ludicrous exchange-rate scandal, the sending of US troops to the CBI theatre, and the need to nail down Chiang to specific commitments, with dates and figures and no supplementary clauses enabling him to wriggle out of his promises; most of all, back-door, stab-in-the-back secret diplomacy

164

had to stop, and the endless stream of Curries, Wilkies, etc. extinguished.[19]

Clear in his own mind about his objectives, Stilwell spent a pleasant five-day break in his native Carmel before returning to Washington for TRIDENT on 14 May. Again he found the British negative and unimpressive, but this time he identified his mirror image in the Americanophobe Field Marshal Alanbrooke, Chief of the Imperial Staff. Stilwell regarded it almost as a point of honour to lock horns with him, but by all accounts came off second best. Even Marshall was disappointed and told Stimson that 'Stilwell shut up like a clam and made an unfavourable impression.'[20] Sometime in the course of TRIDENT, Roosevelt asked Stilwell what he thought of Chiang, and Stilwell replied: 'He's a vacillating, tricky, undependable old scoundrel who never keeps his word.' By contrast Chennault, when asked a similar question, replied: 'Sir, I think the generalissimo is one of the two or three greatest military and political leaders in the world today. He has never broken a commitment or promise made to me.'[21] With Chiang's representatives (including his wife) still crying wolf – threatening that he would pull out of Burma and make a separate peace with the Japanese unless the British moved against Rangoon – it was decided to increase supplies flown over the Hump and shelve ANAKIM. Against this Stilwell argued the contrary case: that if the Allies waited another year before launching a land-based campaign, nationalist China really would collapse. It seemed, though, as if the Chennault 'airpower alone' thesis, absurd as it was, had won the day. But Marshall found a way to save the northern Burma campaign by telling FDR that the Hump route could not increase its deliveries unless Myitkyina and its air base was taken. When Roosevelt pledged to deliver 7,000 tons of goods a month over the Hump, with the first 5,000 earmarked for Chennault, a lesser man than Stilwell might have given up and handed in his resignation. Not only was he in an impossible situation with both FDR and Chiang against him, but the cuts in his materiel were more savage than those experienced by any other major US commander.[22]

The atmosphere at the TRIDENT conference was certainly chaotic. Admiral King pounded the table violently in support of Marshall and Stilwell, disconcerting FDR. Marshall was icy towards the President and refused even to speak to Harry Hopkins because of his 'treachery' over Chennault. King and Marshall wanted the land route to China open but the British opted for the Hump. Alanbrooke's patrician disdain was palpable, but then this was a man who claimed that human beings were a pretty bad lot and that only birds merited admiration. 'Wavell was called upon followed by Somervell who contradicted him! Then Stilwell who disagreed with both and with himself as far as I could see! He is a small man with no conception of strategy. The whole problem seemed to hinge on the necessity of keeping Chiang Kai-shek in the war. Chennault was then called upon followed by more Stilwell and more confusion.'[23] The one bright spot in Washington was that Stilwell conferred privately with Churchill and got on well with him. Churchill agreed with the American's blunt criticism that the high command in India was listless, and it may even be that this was the final trigger for his decision to replace Wavell, with whom he had been unhappy for some time. Churchill spoke of the 'great respect and liking he had for General Stilwell'.[24] After this meeting Stilwell penned his own reflections:

> With Wavell in command, failure was inevitable; he had nothing to offer at any meeting except protestations that the thing was impossible, hopeless, impractical. Churchill even spoke of it as silly. The Limeys all wanted to wait another year. After the Akyab fiasco, the four Japanese divisions in Burma have been scared to death. The inevitable conclusion was that Churchill has Roosevelt in his pocket. That they are looking for an easy way, a short cut for England, and that no attention must be diverted from the Continent at any cost. The Limeys are not interested in the war in the Pacific, and with the President hypnotised they are sitting pretty. Roosevelt wouldn't let me speak my piece. I interrupted twice but Churchill kept pulling away from the subject and it was impossible.'[25]

Yet Stilwell gained a minor victory. Churchill had been looking for a new viceroy and finally decided that the ideal solution was to kick Wavell upstairs by promoting him to viceroy and replace him as commander in India with Sir Claude Auchinleck. Stilwell was pleased: 'If they give the Auk a free hand and real authority, things will look up.'[26]

Stilwell returned to China via London, North Africa and Cairo. In London he went on a celebrity tour arranged by Marshall to heighten his profile, including a state luncheon where he was honoured by a toast from the Deputy Prime Minister Clement Attlee. But once back in China he was profoundly depressed. 'Better an hour in Carmel than a cycle of Cathay,' he wrote. 'Back to find Chiang same as ever – a grasping, bigoted, ungrateful little rattlesnake.'[27] His diary entries for late June are a long, agonised shriek of splenetic abuse:

Any Jap threat will put the Peanut in an uproar, and if they are wise they will repeat their attempt, for this if for no other reason. And if they seriously want to gain the game, they can attack Kunming or Chungking, or both, with five divisions on either line and finish the matter. If we sting them badly enough in the air, they are almost sure to try it . . . The Peanut's promise of picked men for India is so much wind; last year 68% of the men sent were rejected for trachoma or skin disease . . . This is going beyond all bounds. This insect, this stink in the nostrils, superciliously inquires what we will do, who are breaking our backs to help him, supplying everything – troops, equipment, planes, medical, signal, motor services, setting up his goddam SOS, training his lousy troops, backing his dastardly chief of staff, and general staff, and he the Jovian dictator, who starves his troops and is the world's worst ignoramus, picks flaws in our preparations and hems and haws about the Navy, God save us.'[28]

Stilwell's frustration was understandable. By early July Chiang had still made no reply to FDR about any of the currently pressing issues: Operation SAUCY; the date for the beginning of the Burma campaign; whether he consented to General George Stratemeyer as air commander of all CBI units. The generalissimo replied to all exhortations about collaboration with the Chinese Communists by saying that they must first give cast-iron guarantees that they would obey him at all times. Stilwell continued to be baffled about why the USA was supporting a fascist regime in China while fighting another one in Europe. 'To reform such a system, it must be torn to pieces,' he remarked. He wanted FDR to make him field commander in China, with the proviso that if his orders were not carried out, Lend-Lease would stop immediately. Obviously this was what Roosevelt should have done but equally obviously, given his myopia over China, this was the one thing he would never do.[29]

As an inducement to Chiang to declare his hand, FDR decided to award him the Legion of Merit, as well as gongs for his right-hand men such as Stilwell's bête noire Ho Ying-chin, the man most responsible for the corruption and disarray in the Chinese army. Stilwell was supposed to pin the medals on both men – a prospect that was distasteful to both sides: 'It will make me want to throw up,' Stilwell admitted. For his part Chiang, alerted by his spies that such an award from the US President was in the offing, manoeuvred so that he did not have to accept it from Stilwell and suggested informally that it be sent to him by messenger – a proposal Stilwell regarded as a mortal insult to himself and the American people. Both sides had to endure the unendurable. At a ceremony on 7 July, the two men went through the charade with gritted teeth. Stilwell recorded: 'Peanut was half an hour late . . . Everyone anywhere near him turned to stone . . . When I grabbed his coat and pinned it on him, he jumped as if he was afraid I was going to stab him.'[30] Even more distasteful was the award to Ho Ying-chin. And at first Roosevelt's gesture seemed to have been in vain. Stilwell had another pointless conference with Ho, which he thought marked a new low, especially when he learned Ho had been trying to subvert the Ramgarh innovations as they showed up his own incompetence and venality. Word had got back to troops in China that their colleagues in India were actually being paid individually at a public roll call to avoid the 'lump sum' scam, and the men were beginning to query why the system could not be applied back home. While it was the money aspect that most concerned Ho, it was becoming clear that Chiang disliked the Ramgarh experiment as the end of the road might be elite troops under a rival commander.

On 12 July the clouds lifted momentarily and FDR's manipulation appeared to have borne fruit when Chiang committed himself in writing to go along with the strategy of the combined chiefs. Stilwell wrote triumphantly: 'After a year of constant struggle we have finally nailed him down. He is committed in writing to the attack on Burma. What corruption, intrigue, obstruction, delay, double-crossing, hate, jealousy and skulduggery we have had to wade through. What a cesspool . . . What bigotry and ignorance and black ingratitude. Holy Christ, I was just about at the end of my rope.'[31] He then sat down to write a memorandum predicting that the Kuomintang would not be able to stay in power once the war ended. The essential problem was Chiang himself, an uneducated villain living in a dream world, a man to whom the truth was alien and if anyone told it to him he would fly into a rage. 'He is afraid of the crowd and what people will say, so he tries to stop them talking. This is very foolish. It is like trying to stop the sound of a rattlesnake's rattle while leaving the poison in his fangs . . . The Peanut, fifty years ago, would have been an acceptable leader, but his lack of education handicaps him under modern conditions . . . Obstinate, pigheaded, ignorant, intolerant, arbitrary, unreasonable, illogical, ungrateful, grasping.'[32]

Yet even as the pressure about Chiang eased once he signed up to the Allies' strategy, Stilwell found other irritating problems annoying him. There were three main ones. In the first place, his own countrymen seemed to be 'going native' and becoming sucked into the vortex of corruption and inhumanity in the CBI theatre. Stilwell raged in private: 'Officers pimping. Hauling whores in our planes. Sent for Chennault. He *knew* . . . more dope on the gas-stealing ring.'[33] Apart from the fiddles and scams practised by his own officers, he found their attitude to Indians disconcerting. Initially sympathetic to the subcontinent's people as 'victims' of British imperialism, the Americans soon came to agree with their British cousins that the Indians were 'wogs' and even more despicable than the Chinese. With such attitudes, how could the USA take the moral high ground about colonialism? Second, morale among pilots flying the Hump seemed to be plummeting. One obvious factor was the danger. Nearly 400 US crewmen went down over the Hump in 1943, of whom only 125 were rescued. Another was that the 'flyboys' were cynical about the whole operation. Why, they asked, should they risk life and limb so that shady KMT entrepreneurs could sell supplies on the black market? The official line that they were flying vital materiel to China was believed by almost nobody.[34] Stilwell looked into this, and found that the fliers' complaints were warranted. Relations between American servicemen and the Chinese they dealt with on the ground were at rock bottom. Even worse, the 'skinny' that the Hump operation was all a giant scam led to increasing corruption and a thriving black market among the Americans themselves. One plane, which in fact had flown just four hours, was logged as having been refuelled eight times for a total of 700 gallons of gasoline.[35]

If that kind of corruption was unacceptable, it was more difficult to brush aside the core complaint that the chore of flying the Hump was simply too exhausting. Hundreds of planes made a 600-mile crossing of the Himalayas daily, and sometimes pilots clocked up three times that mileage. Mainly the aircraft were C-46 and C-47 cargo planes, but with an increasing presence of converted B-24 Liberator bombers. Takeoff was often in heavy weather with no radar, no air traffic control and inadequate radios. After fighting through zero visibility, the pilots would often get above the cloud canopy into clear air and find another plane flying straight at them; mid-air collisions were frequent.[36] Faced with such conditions, US pilots became more hardline, refusing to fly if there was a cloud in the sky and baling out immediately an engine missed once. Stilwell had to steer a difficult course between insisting on proper discipline and accepting that the pilots had legitimate griev-ances. Part of their grumbling concerned objective reality, for there was nothing anyone could do about the fog, ice, storms and severe turbulence over the Himalayas. But much of the grousing was well warranted. It was clear that the fliers were overworked, and Stilwell tried to compensate for this by high salaries and lavish allowances.[37] He was furious when he discovered that Chiang's regime, lacking the paper to print their own currency, were having it printed in other countries and then flown in via the Hump. He decided to allay the pilots' anger by scapegoating his own side, since there was nothing he could do about Chiang and the KMT. At Chabua he staged a piece of rabble-rousing theatre. After joining the mess line with his GIs and finding the food inedible, he incited a riot in the mess hall, then summoned the commander to see the resulting destruction. 'There's your mess,' he told him.[38]

The third problem was the agonising slowness of the Ledo road construction. It took all of 1943 for the road to be cut from Ledo in Assam to Shingbwiyang in Burma – just 103 miles in all. This was hardly surprising, since 100,000 cubic feet of earth had to be removed along a track that ran as high as 4,500 feet over the Patka range through thick forests, up steep gradients and around hairpin bends; from the air the road looked like a gigantic snake. Moreover, the engineers had to work 'by guess and by God' when it came to soil analysis, river barriers and general topography; there could obviously be no prior studies in enemy-held territory. Even a workforce of 15,000 US troops (60 per cent of them black African-Americans) and 35,000 locals could make little progress against such obstacles. Churchill famously described the Ledo road as one that would be open only when there was no longer any need for it, and most observers shared his scepticism.[39] Chennault, eager to make propaganda for airpower at every opportunity, argued that the road used up precious resources and would never provide the 65,000 tons of supplies over the Hump that his pilots could deliver. In fact, he was very far from fulfilling his boast, for tonnage over the Hump was only 3,000 in May, 5,500 in July, 8,000 in September and 13,000 in November (when the monsoon ended).[40] And he neglected to mention that conveying such tonnage by air cut down on the resources available for the Ledo road. Nevertheless, most Allied analysts agreed with Chennault, and even Slim, always Stilwell's doughtiest defender on the British side, argued that the reconquest of Burma by conventional military means would mean that China could be supplied far more liberally even than by a completed Ledo road. But he understood that pressing on with the road was one of the few means Stilwell had to force the recalcitrant Chiang to play a more active part in the war. His analysis of the Ledo road showed Slim at his most fair-minded and judicious:

> I agreed with Stilwell that the road could be built. I believed that, properly equipped and efficiently led, Chinese troops could defeat Japanese if, as should be the case with his Ledo force, they had a considerable numerical superiority. On the engineering side I had no doubts. We had built roads over country as difficult, and with much less technical equipment than the Americans would have . . . Thus far Stilwell and I were in complete agreement, but I did not hold two articles of his faith. I doubted the overwhelming war-winning value of this road, and, in any case, I believed it was starting from the wrong place. The American amphibious strategy in the Pacific, of hopping from island to island would, I was sure, bring much quicker results than an overland advance across Asia with a Chinese army yet to be formed. In any case, if the road was to be really effective, its feeder railway should start from Rangoon, not Calcutta.[41]

It is a fair inference that Stilwell was glad to shake off the dust of China. He left for India on 14 July and remained there until September, even taking a holiday in Kashmir. While his fortunes dipped,

Wingate's soared astronomically. After reaching Imphal on 3 May, he went through an initially fallow period, annoyed that Fergusson had pre-empted him by writing a report on LONGCLOTH, and finding affairs in limbo, with Wavell still nominally commander-in-chief but actually phasing out pending his replacement by Auchinleck. Before he went, Wavell left behind a shirt of Nessus by setting up a second Long Range Penetration Group (111 Brigade) under the command of Brigadier William Lentaigne and composed mainly of Gurkhas. Wingate liked neither this rival in principle nor Lentaigne in person (Lentaigne vehemently detested Wingate), nor the idea of the despised Gurkhas looming so large in LRP.[42] Yet there was worse to come. Auchinleck, the incoming commander-in-chief, did not believe that LRP groups were much more than glorified patrols – an attitude that put him on a collision course with Wingate. Staying at Maiden's Hotel in Delhi for a fortnight, Wingate ran into a blizzard of criticism for the conduct of LONGCLOTH and in particular the level of casualties. The widespread perception that he was an irresponsible maniac was reinforced. Then came the famous press conference in the third week of May and the press furore about 'Clive of Burma'. Even though Wingate's prickly personality should not have made him a favourite with reporters, the media's appetite for heroes and sensational copy overrode this. By the time he left for Calcutta at the end of the month, after three weeks in Delhi, he was a household name. But he was exhausted and went back to Imphal, where he checked into the military hospital under the care of the formidable matron Agnes MacGeary, who was a favourite of his and always treated him as 'teacher's pet'.[43] While he rested and recovered under her regime, he wrote his own report on LONG-CLOTH. This was indiscreet and highly critical of the military hierarchy. Irwin, also on his way out, was predictably furious and summoned Wingate to Delhi for a dressing-down. On 21 June Wingate flew in to the Indian capital and began by meeting Lentaigne. The two men were superficially cordial but too unlike in personality and temperament for real rapport. Then it was on to the meeting with Irwin, who told him that the entire 4 Corps regarded his report as a disgraceful act of disloyalty and that it would be suppressed. Irwin's real problem was that by this time Wingate was a national hero. In any case Wingate had already outwitted him, getting a friend in high circles to smuggle out a copy, which was sent to Churchill and read enthusiastically.[44]

Wingate withdrew in a sulk to the balmy breezes of Simla, while in Delhi the controversy continued to rage. The opposition to and dislike of Wingate seemed to grow exponentially, with the officers of 13th King's particularly bitter about the casualties their regiment had sustained. But in London Churchill and his close aide Leo Amery came to see Wingate as the last great hope of the British Empire. Always fighting his one-man campaign against the 'defeatist' military, and with Alanbrooke counselling a postponement of all major operations in Burma until the winter of 1944–45, Churchill viewed Wingate as the man of the hour, a hero whose 'can do' attitude would overhwelm the caution of his generals. Making policy on the wing as so often, he suddenly announced that he wanted Wingate to return to London for consultations, and on 25 July an official order of recall was issued.[45] Wingate left Delhi on 30 July and flew to London in hops via Karachi, Basra, Kallia (on the Dead Sea) and Cairo, arriving in England on 4 August. There was a brief meeting with Alanbrooke, then on the evening of 4 August Churchill invited Wingate to dinner and decided on the spur of the moment to take him with him to the Quadrant Conference at Quebec. Improvising hurriedly, Wingate swept up his wife Lorna, took the train to Glasgow and sailed from Clydeside on the *Queen Mary* on 5 August.[46] Alanbrooke was appalled at this further example of Churchill's eccentricity: 'To my astonishment I was informed that Winston was taking Wingate and his wife with him to Canada. It could only be as a museum piece to impress the Americans! There was no other reason to justify this move. It was sheer loss of time for Wingate and the work he had to do in England.'[47] The passage was a reasonably calm and uneventful one, and Wingate was frequently summoned to attend the Prime Minister in his stateroom. After reading Wingate's report, Churchill criticised his prose but said he liked the content. Wingate asked for six LRP brigades, arguing that the Japanese were very slow at counteroffensives, and Churchill, in one of his periods of euphoria, made favourable noises. In vain did Alanbrooke point out that accepting Wingate's ideas meant that Britain would have to put all its Far Eastern eggs into the Burma basket. Some of Churchill's entourage were more critical of Wingate's social gaucherie, his inability to mix freely, engage in small talk or even dress properly. Wingate held himself aloof from social life on the liner and was judged stand-offish and incapable of real friendship.[48]

On 9 August the *Queen Mary* reached Halifax and the Prime Minister's party proceeded by train on the evening of the 10th to Quebec, where they were housed at the Chateau Frontenac Hotel. While Churchill left for Hyde Park to spend a few days with Roosevelt, Alanbrooke introduced Wingate to the Canadian chiefs of staff and told him that he would be expected to address the combined chiefs of staff when the Americans arrived in a few days.[49] Wingate got down to work and produced one of his better memos, shorn of the usual Biblical quotations. He proposed an invasion of Burma with three LRP groups, each of eight columns – some 26,500 men in all – as a pre-emptive strike against a predicted Japanese offensive against the Arakan in 1944. The memo was dispatched immediately to Auchinleck in India. When the American service chiefs arrived on the 13th, they were enthusiastic about Wingate's ideas, as they wanted swift action from the British in Burma and this new man (to them) looked likely to provide it. A cable from Auchinleck on the 14th put the first dent in the plan, since he reported disastrous floods in Bengal that seemed likely to delay any operations involving the Indian army. A further problem was that Churchill, always a devotee of the indirect and peripheral approach, had conceived a positive obsession about a campaign in northern Sumatra that Allenby suggested recalled his similar mania about Trondheim in 1940.[50] For three days (14–17 August), Wingate was sidetracked into helping Dickie Mountbatten (another of Churchill's personal favourites) plan Operation CULVERIN, the seizure of the Andaman islands, part of the Sumatra strategy. When he was not working, he again spent no time socialising but closeted himself in the Frontenac hotel with Lorna. Finally, on 17 August, he got his chance to pitch his ideas directly to the Americans. After a closed session with only chiefs of staff attending, Alanbrooke then opened up the meeting and introduced Wingate. Estimates of his performance that afternoon differ. Some say he addressed his super-iors as if they were his column commanders, showing no sensitivity to rank or status. But Alanbrooke was pleased and described Wingate's performance as 'first class'. Finally, on 18 August, Churchill introduced Wingate to FDR and asked him to give a presentation of his ideas to the President. Again he seems to have performed well. Afterwards

Churchill thanked him for his lucidity, to which Wingate replied, 'Such is always my practice, sir.'[51]

But on 19 August a cable came in from India, expressing dismay that the chiefs of staff were backing Wingate. In a private communication 'the Auk' told Alanbrooke that there was a danger that Wingate was becoming absurdly overrated; he was fine as a battlefront inspirer but would be a disaster in any senior position, such as corps commander. Then, in a formal memo for transmission to Churchill, he outlined in detail his objections to Wingate's new LRP proposals. Wingate's plans, he pointed out, took no account of transport requirements, called for vast numbers of aircraft that would be far better used in conventional warfare, allowed no time for proper training and made it impossible to carry out the traditional LRP tasks such as destroying oilfields and arms dumps. Moreover, Wingate's ideas took for granted Chinese participation, when this was very doubtful, as Chiang would not make a move until he saw a *general* British offensive in Burma with conventional forces, which could not take place before March 1944 at the earliest. But the biggest problem would be manpower. Wingate's requirement of 26,500 men could be provided only if all other operations were disrupted; divisions would have to be broken up, and even then only 60 per cent of those earmarked would survive the training. Moreover, Wingate's plans would also impair Stilwell's advance from Ledo and use up the reserves of animals and motor transport currently earmarked for the attack on the Ramree islands.[52] Auchinleck's riposte to Wingate was devastating and, on paper and other things being equal, should have killed his ideas stone dead. The problem was that Churchill had already given too many hostages to fortune. He could not now withdraw support from the Wingate proposals without provoking a backlash from the Americans.[53] Typically, the Prime Minister dealt with inconvenient facts with an emotional outburst and was indiscreet and even disloyal to Auchinleck in his private assurances to Wingate. 'The Auk', a model of compromise, suggested just three LRP brigades in his cable of 19 August, as against Wingate's eight; he did not mention that his own staff in India wanted none at all. Faced with Churchill's intransigence, he signalled again on 21 August, proposing five brigades. But Wingate, typically 'all or nothing', rejected even this statesmanlike compromise and composed a 3,000-word memo in effect accusing Auchinleck and the top brass in Delhi of having supplied him with second-rate troops for LONGCLOTH, which now enabled them to claim that the Chindits were evaders, not true fighters. Wingate pretended that he in turn was being reasonable by suggesting the West African Division as one of the extra brigades. The upshot was that he got most of what he wanted. On 23 August the Joint Planning Staff gave approval to the new, improved LRP group with six brigades, to be formed by breaking up 70 Division and reorganising 81 African Division.[54]

When the Quebec conference finished on 24 August, it was obvious that Wingate had scored a great personal triumph, thanks to the resolute backing of Churchill and the Americans. The only cloud in an otherwise blue sky was that he had not impressed FDR, who took against him personally and much preferred Wing Commander Guy Gibson, the leader of the famous 1943 Dambuster Raids – another of the war-hero celebrities Churchill had taken across the Atlantic to impress the President. In high spirits nonetheless, Wingate accompanied Mountbatten to Washington, where they met General 'Hap' Arnold, commander of the USAAF, who was a Wingate enthusiast and promised full backing to the Chindits. Arnold really took to Wingate at an individual level, in contrast to FDR, showing once again that the mystery of personal chemistry and interaction can never be pinned down. Arnold's testimony was eloquent: 'You took one look at that face, like the face of a pale Indian chieftain, topping the uniform still smelling of jungle and sweat and war, and you thought: "Hell, this man is serious." When he began to talk, you found out just how serious.'[55] After Washington, Wingate flew back to England while Lorna sailed back on the *Queen Mary*. The parting of the couple, who had been inseparable throughout most of August, was caused by the sudden death in England of his mother, a genuine religious maniac who believed that prayer could move not just mountains but everything else in life too. Influenced by her, Wingate's time in London was marked by a return to the devotional ethos he had laid aside in the secular atmosphere of Quebec. He told his sister that even great actions without faith were no good. 'One must have faith and by that I mean faith in God.'[56] In London too he had to make good the boasts with which he had spellbound his audiences in Quebec. He set about recruiting more officers for his columns and at first enjoyed limited success; the word was that Wingate alienated many by his Jamesian inability to give a simple answer to a simple question. Among the staff officers he did recruit were Philip Cochran and Derek Tulloch. He batted aside an offer of help by SOE, fearful that he would lose his independence, but he hardly needed them as, aided by Churchill, Alanbrooke and continuing glowing press publicity, he enjoyed a halcyon period in London. Finally, after visiting Chaim Weizmann in the Dorchester, he prepared to return to India.

On 11 September, together with Tulloch and four other newly recruited staff officers, he flew to Lisbon. The party was there a day and a night and then proceeded to Cairo, where there was a 24-hour stopover before an onward flight to Karachi, two nights in Agra, and finally journey's end in Delhi on the 19th. Wingate has been accused of shiftiness in thus delaying his return to Delhi to meet Auchinleck, but the atmosphere in the Indian capital was poisonously hostile. Wingate was considered to have double-crossed his colleagues in India by his grandstanding in Canada, and there was deep resentment that a man who had come out 18 months earlier as a major was now hobnobbing as a strategical adviser with the world's leading statesmen. It was quite clear that Wingate was going to receive minimal co-operation in India. No accommodation, office, private aircraft, car or even stenographer had been provided for him. At a meeting with the deputy chief of staff on 20 September, the atmosphere was icy and the attitude of the hierarchy was clearly that Wingate 'was regarded as a vulgar go-getter who had gone behind the backs of his superiors in India to indulge in audacious intrigues with politicians, on the strength of a very questionable achievement'.[57] Everyone who spoke mentioned the near-insuperable difficulties of the operations Wingate proposed. He responded with fury, threatening to report them to Churchill for obstructionism. He was the proverbial bull in a china shop if anyone tried the 'good administrator' tactic of trying to cut through or shorten meetings. Acting even more the prima donna after his triumph in Quebec, he alienated many who might have been inclined to support him. One senior officer took Tulloch aside and told him that his career was at an end if he continued to associate with Wingate. Naturally Wingate's supporters insist that if he had been conciliatory, the army bureaucracy would have buried the Chindits under a mountain of paper and a Fabian campaign of stalling, procrastination and tergiversation.[58]

Gradually Wingate wore down the opposition. In Delhi he was given the office, car and stenographer he had been promised at Quebec, but only on loan, and his staff were forced to work in the corridor. He countered by demanding the hotel in Gwalior as his headquarters and moving 70th Division to Bangalore. The divisional commander, Major General george Symes, agreed to serve under him as deputy, even though he was angry that the Quebec decision meant the break-up of the division. Meanwhile his enemies scored a minor victory by refusing to allow the Chindits to be called 'Gideon Force'. At this juncture Wingate's habitual rudeness was observed to reach new heights. When Fergusson came to Delhi to meet him, Wingate noticed that he was wearing the Palestine medal. 'A badge of disgrace,' he growled, reverting to his Zionist persona; pointedly he did not congratulate Fergusson on his recently awarded DSO.[59] The beginning of October found him both restless and ill. The restlessness found expression in a meeting in Assam with General Geoffrey Scoones and General G.E. Stratemeyer, US Chief of Eastern Air Command.[60] The illness was incipient typhoid, which he had contracted by drinking water from a flower vase in Cairo. The incident was classic Wingate. Impatient when drinks were not delivered fast enough at an Egyptian airfield, he quenched his thirst by draining the vase. Although he was daily becoming sicker, he forced himself to form part of the reception committee when Louis Mountbatten arrived as Supreme Commander South-East Asia on 7 October (see p. 195) His enemies took advantage of his failing health to deny him the Gwalior hotel as his headquarters on the grounds that it was needed to accommodate BOAC passengers. At first refusing to admit he was ill, Wingate was finally rushed to hospital, where, luckily for him, an expert diagnosis of his illness was made. He came very close to death and was in hospital for a month. Once again the invaluable Matron MacGeary took personal charge of his nursing.[61]

While Stilwell and Wingate enjoyed such mixed fortunes in the summer and autumn of 1943, Slim's activities were far less flamboyant and pyrotechnical but ultimately more significant. In early June he returned to Ranchi from the Arakan front and resumed command of 15 Corps with responsibility for East Bengal. He was in good spirits, relieved that Irwin and Wavell were on their way out and that Giffard and Auchinleck had taken their place. Giffard ordered him to prepare for operations in the Arakan at the end of the monsoon and gave him three months to prepare a suitable army while the monsoon raged. The planned offensive was to be with three divisions and its objective was the capture of the Maungdaw–Buthidaung road by January 1944.[62] Slim was promised two brigades of 81 West African Division when it arrived in India in August, with the further promise that they would be supplied entirely by air. Here was the first clear evidence that military affairs in the India–Burma theatre were no longer plagued by factionalism and petty jealousy. Slim worked in a smooth, streamlined way with Giffard and he in turn got all the necessary approvals from Auchinleck by August. Slim's notion of a campaign was based on a fourfold premise: it should be simple in conception; offensive in intention; it had to be given absolute and undeviating priority over all other operations; and it should always contain the element of surprise. His first problem was morale: had not the disgusted Irwin declared that the fighting spirit of his men was so poor that the Japanese could simply hike their way to Delhi?[63] Slim knew all about the mistakes of 1942–43 but considered them contingent mistakes, based on the inadequacies of Irwin, Alexander, Wavell and their underlings. There was no intrinsic reason why the British, Indian or Nepalese fighting men should consider themselves inferior to the Japanese, and indeed the recent defeat of the Japanese by the Australians in New Guinea proved this beyond dispute. Slim hammered away at this theme in his many speeches to his men, the content of his addresses always emphasising the spiritual, intellectual and material foundations of military morale.'[64] The main practical way he went about overthrowing the myth of Japanese military supermen was by sending out elite groups on special patrols into the Arakan into the monsoon, then carefully escalating operations to aim at Japanese outposts north of the Maungdaw–Buthidaung road. The successful patrols would return to hearten the rest of the men with tales of how they had trounced the enemy in the jungle. Naturally Slim omitted to mention that he had sent out only the crème de la crème.[65]

It was part of Slim's military credo that morale, motivation and training were mutually reinforcing, so he sought practical ways to combat the tactics the enemy had used so successfully in 1942–43. Offensively the Japanese relied on envelopment and infiltration. Slim thought these could be stymied by the formation of a 'box' – a development of the infantry squares of old. When threatened by envelopment and infiltration, the British and Indian units should go into a defensive posture but ready to strike back, imitating the action of a snake when cornered. All troops should form themselves into 'boxes' or self-contained strongholds, to be supplied by air, ready to counterattack and sever the enemy's supply lines. Strongholds would in effect be the anvil against which the hammer of the reserves would strike. Slim thought the 'box' idea was peculiarly likely to work, since he observed that the Japanese had the fatal flaw of being too pigheaded to realise when they had failed and of throwing good resources after bad.[66] The codes of bushido, 'face', obedience to hierarchy and even kinship made them inclined to flog a dead horse. The Japanese, with their banzai charges, had a fanatical will to win, but this could be blunted and destroyed by really good troops. The key idea was to get them to exhaust themselves by battering away at the anvil until the hammer was ready to descend on them. Defensively, the Japanese bunkers posed a more ticklish problem, but they were static and were therefore vulnerable to envelopment and the cutting of communications. It must be emphasised that all this was relatively unconventional thinking at the time. But Slim's ideas called for top-class troops and commanders who could hold their nerve. He aimed to turn all his men into tough professionals by training during the monsoon and putting them through rigorous manoeuvres, covering every conceivable contingency in every conceivable terrain.[67] Slim's talent can be seen especially in the way he transformed 5 Indian Division, which returned from Iraq in June 1943. Using his methods he very soon turned a force expert in desert warfare into a unit specialising in the jungle variety. He taught them to regard the jungle as more than a neutral, a potential friend even. He inculcated woodcraft and calmness under pressure; there should never be any panicky shooting in the direction of unidentified noises, for example.[68]

For his battlefield commanders Slim would rely on Harold Briggs and Frank Messervy. Commanding a division each, these two generals had the great advantage of being popular with the men. Briggs was perhaps unimaginative but was reliable, phlegmatic and unflappable; Slim could provide the military brainpower.[69] Briggs soon acquired a Stilwell-like reputation for being a fire-eater, and had five commandments that every member of his division had to learn: kill every Jap you meet; don't let him trick you with ruses or ambushes, but read his mind and turn the tables on him; always hold fast until ordered otherwise, whatever happens; carry out to the letter and in detail every task assigned to you, with no half-measures; be determined and even fanatical.[70] Messervy by contrast was a dynamo of energy, with something of the quality of the Confederate cavalry commanders in the American Civil War, full of ideas and imagination.[71] With the right men trained in the right way and led by the right commanders, Slim then needed to ensure that transport and supply was first class. Realising that all modern warfare must be a combination of airpower and infantry fighting, he dinned airmindedness into his men. All thoughts of inter-service rivalry were banished as he built up a mutually respectful relationship with the RAF. Additionally, he turned himself into an expert on railways. The route from Calcutta to the front at Assam ran first on a broad-gauge track for 235 miles, then on a metre-gauge train from the Brahmaputra valley to Pandu, 450 miles from Calcutta. All goods wagons were then unloaded on to barges for a slow river crossing, reloaded and taken to Dimapur from the central front, now 600 miles from Calcutta; if bound for the northern front, there were another 200 miles to reach Ledo. The railway system had low capacity, as it was originally built to service the Assam tea gardens, but the peacetime daily capacity of 600 tons had already been increased to 2,900 tons by 1943. Eventually the Americans put in 4,700 trained railwaymen so that by October 1944 capacity had been raised to 4,400 tons and by January 1945 to 7,300 tons. The railway was vulnerable to bombing, floods, landslides, train wrecks and earthquakes that buckled the line, but against this could be set the vast US input; not just the manpower and the more powerful locomotives but the sheer 'can do' elan.[72] It will be appreciated that Slim was not just concentrating narrowly on the Arakan campaign but was already thinking ahead to an invasion of Burma via Assam.

Not content with all this, he worked hard to solve the problems of food supplies and disease. The armies at the Burma front consumed 500,000 rations daily, even though most of the personnel were non-combatants. Feeding such a host would have been difficult in any circumstances, but in 1943 India was stricken by a famine in which more than a million died. It was fortunate indeed that Auchinleck proved to be such a good administrator and that he was so responsive to

Slim's concern about food supplies, even to the point of holding a kind of summit conference on the issue in Delhi in November.[73] As Slim would so often point out in his bluff way, without meat a soldier could not fight, and without fresh fruit and vegetables at the front, a host of diseases, from scurvy to scrub fever, would break out.[74] In some ways an even more serious problem was that of malaria, which had an incidence rate of 84 per cent in the Indian army in 1943, though it was far from the only scourge, with typhoid, cholera, dysentery, skin diseases and a special kind of jungle typhus caused by mites also rampant. In his darker moments Slim sometimes thought that his army would simply melt away, without any help from the Japanese.[75] Chronically short of everything, guns, ammunition, food, Slim experienced particular scarcity with medical staff, doctors, paramedics, nurses and the most basic medical equipment. He took a fourfold approach to disease and illness. While not having Wingate's obsession that all illness was hypochondria or malingering, he was not unaware of the psychosomatic origin of some maladies, and thought that the enhancement of morale would in itself cut down the sickness rate. In the case of the many genuinely ill soldiers, he advocated treating them as far as possible at the front instead of evacuating them instantly to India, which he thought a somewhat knee-jerk response. But he accepted that some serious cases would have to be evacuated. He was also very keen on following all the latest medical research and introducing any alleged wonder drugs as soon as possible. The most-used drug of the Burma war was mepacrine, which regimental officers had to ensure their men took daily.[76] At first the men were cavalier and resisted taking their medicine. The barrack-room lore was that the drug was simply another bromide and was designed to make randy soldiers impotent. The officers initially tended to be sympathetic to the men and complaisant or lackadaisical about the orders concerning mepacrine. A few dramatic sackings and demotions changed attitudes. By 1945 the daily sickness rate was down to one in 1,000.[77] By the time Mountbatten arrived as supreme commander in October 1943, Stilwell was in limbo and Wingate near death. It was Slim, the least flamboyant of the three, who was on an upward curve.

Although he acknowledged him as a great war leader, Alanbrooke was frequently exasperated by Churchill's impetuous, irrational and unthinking irruption into military affairs of which he knew little or nothing. One of the best examples of this was the Prime Minister's decision to appoint a 43-year-old career naval officer as supreme commander in South-East Asia. Yet this was no ordinary naval officer. The future Lord Louis Mountbatten had been born as His Serene Highness Prince Louis of Battenberg, a great-grandson of Queen Victoria and uncle of the present Duke of Edinburgh, and became Mountbatten when the royal family, of which he was a scion, dropped all German styles and titles in 1917 and became the House of Windsor. Although it may not necessarily be saying very much, Mountbatten was the most talented member of this house, and was always chillingly ambitious. He was almost impossibly charming, ferociously energetic, a power-seeker with a talent for intrigue, and he was intelligent – though not nearly as intelligent as he imagined himself to be. Against this he was egocentric, vain, reckless, eccentric and unreliable, with a marked talent for blame-shifting. In love with the sea and matters naval, from an early age he aspired to become First Sea Lord – an ambition he would eventually fulfil. He contracted a glittering marriage in 1922 to Edwina Ashley, heiress to the huge Cassel fortune, and moved in all the highest circles, one moment in Buckingham Palace, the next in Hollywood with Charlie Chaplin and Mary Astor. Edwina was a promiscuous woman who flitted from one affair to another; her husband followed suit, though less enthusiastically, for there is compelling evidence that he was bisexual; in certain circles he was known as 'Mountbottom'.[1] The marriage was consequently an unhappy one, and Mountbatten was thus the odd man out among Burma's 'Four Musketeers'. Wingate, Slim and Stilwell, though very different personalities, were all deeply uxorious.

Although his official biographers and hagiographers strenuously deny it, there is no question but that Mountbatten owed his meteoric rise in the Royal Navy to his royal connections. He worked hard at becoming a naval signals expert but even harder at being a playboy and socialite. At the outbreak of war he became commander of the 5th Destroyer Flotilla, with his flagship HMS *Kelly*, and almost immediately displayed his flaky side. On the way home through the North Sea after an operation on the Norwegian coast, the *Kelly* was struck by a giant wave, which caused the ship to heel over 50 degrees to starboard. The Norwegian coast is one of the most dangerous locations in the world for the dreaded 100-foot wave, and Mountbatten can be considered unlucky to have encountered one of these monsters. But his captaincy was just plain incompetent, since he was pushing a destroyer through high seas at a rate of 28 knots when a speed of at most half that would have been appropriate for the conditions. By a miracle the ship survived that terrifying roll and did not capsize. Even his official biographer, always sympathetic to his foibles, remarks: 'If Mountbatten had a purpose in pushing on at such a reckless speed, it is not apparent. It seems more likely that, as was his wont, he was ordering full steam ahead out of sheer impatience to reach wherever he was heading to start on something else.'[2] Seemingly having learned nothing about the risks of being a bull at a gate, in the next 18 months he collided with another destroyer, was mined once and torpedoed twice. His cavalier way with the physical universe also contributed to the loss of the *Kelly* in May 1941 during the Battle of Crete, when German bombers sent it to the bottom within minutes. The Royal Navy commander-in-chief Andrew Cunningham blamed Mountbatten for the loss, and posterity has largely concurred. His biographer remarks: 'Mountbatten was not a good flotilla leader, or wartime commander of destroyers. It is perhaps not too fanciful to equate his performance on the bridge with his prowess behind the wheel of a car. He was a fast and dangerous driver. His maxim was that, if you were shaping up to pass and saw another car approaching, it was always better to accelerate and press on.'[3]

Any other man would probably have seen his career effectively finished after his incumbency on the *Kelly*, but Mountbatten was the kind of person who always bounced back. The loss of his ship was transmogrified by his friend Noel Coward into an epic of inspirational courage in the film *In Which We Serve*, in which Coward played a barely disguised Mountbatten and even used verbatim some of his pep talks to the crew. Mountbatten's vanity may perhaps be most easily conveyed by the simple statistic that he watched the movie at least a dozen times.[4] Moreover, he always had the powerful support of Churchill and other figures in the Establishment, even if his brother officers and superiors in the navy resented him for his wealth, his glamorous connections, his queue-jumping career advancement, his instant access to the highest elite circles and the quite manifest fact that he was over-promoted because of his royal connections. A sober estimate of his naval abilities concludes thus:

> If a destroyer could leave skid-marks, *Kelly* would have disfigured the sea in which she sailed. Mountbatten was impetuous. He pushed the ship fast for little reason except his love of speed and imposed unnecessary strain on his own officers and the other ships in the flotilla. He allowed himself to be distracted from his main purpose by the lure of attractive adventures. Above all he lacked that mysterious quality of 'sea sense', the ability to ensure that one's ship is in the right place at the right time. Mountbatten was as good a captain as most and better than many of his contemporaries but among all his peers who have expressed an opinion the unanimous feeling is that, by the highest standards, he was no better than second-rate.[5]

An even more serious stain on Mountbatten's reputation came when he was promoted to the role of Chief of Combined Operations in 1942 and personally pushed through and oversaw the disastrous Dieppe raid on 19 August that year, in which 4,000 Allied casualties (mainly Canadians) were sustained in a single day. His reputation in Canada never recovered from this fiasco,[6] and even his admirers find it hard to argue round the palpable truth that his direction was deficient at a number of levels simultaneously: the substitution of commandos for paratroops; the cancellation of a preliminary air bombardment; his faulty intelligence, especially about the scale of German fortifications; and his promise of naval support artillery that never came. Inevitably, his defenders claim that lessons were learned at Dieppe that proved invaluable two years later at the D-Day landings, but it would be amazing if a raid on such a scale did not reveal something. The key issue is whether vital lessons about cross-Channel operations could be learned only with such a colossal loss of life. The overwhelming consensus is that such an end did not justify such bloody means.[7] Against such vague bromides used as a 'defence' of Mountbatten, his harshest critics add two more barbed criticisms. One is that he exceeded his authority in conducting the entire raid, but this is palliated by the consideration that his superiors knew all about his plans but did nothing to stop them.[8] The other is that he deliberately gave the operation the nod when he already knew that the vital prerequisite – amphibious artillery support from destroyers – would not be forthcoming. The presence of the Luftwaffe in the skies above Dieppe, the insufficient broadside of British naval guns and the strength of the German coastal batteries together presented an almost unanswerable case for calling off the operation, yet Mountbatten went ahead. It is this that has led some critics to say that the Canadians were sacrificed to his megalomania. Nigel Hamilton, the biographer of Field Marshal Montgomery, has this to say: 'a master of intrigue, jealousy and ineptitude, like a spoilt child he toyed with men's lives with an indifference to casualties that can only be explained by his insatiable, even psychopathic ambition'.[9]

By all normal rules the tragedy of Dieppe should have finished off Mountbatten for good, yet because of Churchill's support he was irrepressible and was soon once again in conclave in the highest military circles. 'The difficulties in which he found himself were caused by his own errors and impetuosity' is a recent, very charitable assessment.[10] Even the professional soldiers who liked him personally found him a trial as a planner and thinker. Alanbrooke, who was fond of him, frequently expressed exasperation in his diary. 'Dickie's visits were always dangerous moments and there was no knowing what discussions he might be led into and what he might let us in for!' (28 March 1942). 'One of those awful COS meetings where Mountbatten and Dudley Pound drive me completely to desperation. The former is quite irresponsible, suffers from the most desperate illogical brain, always producing red herrings' (8 January 1943). 'Very heated argument at COS with Mountbatten who was again putting up wild proposals disconnected with his direct duties. He will insist on doing work of Force Commanders and does it infernally badly! Both Portal and I were driven to distraction by him' (10 March 1943).[11] Mountbatten was one of the party Churchill took with him to the Quebec conference on the *Queen Mary*, and on this occasion his eccentricity was to the forefront. Alanbrooke related a bizarre incident when Mountbatten was trying to persuade the Anglo-American combined chiefs of staff that aircraft carriers could be built of ice.[12]

Dickie now having been let loose gave a signal, whereupon a string of attendants brought in large cubes of ice which were established at the end of the room. Dickie then proceeded to explain that the cube on the left was ordinary pure ice, whereas that on the right contained many ingredients which made it far more resilient, less liable to splinter, and consequently a far more suitable material for the construction of aircraft carriers. He then informed us that in order to prove his statements he had brought a revolver with him and intended to fire shots at the cubes to prove their properties! As he now pulled a revolver out of his pocket we all rose and discreetly followed behind him. He then warned us that he would fire at the ordinary block of ice to show how it splintered and warned us to watch the splinters. He proceeded to fire and we were subjected to a hail of ice splinters! 'There,' said Dickie, 'that is just what I told you; now I shall fire at the block on the right to show you the difference.' He fired, and there certainly was a difference; the bullet rebounded out of the block and buzzed round our legs like an angry bee![13]

By May 1943 Churchill was angry and disillusioned about the course of the war at the CBI front. His tactless, booming open criticism nearly led a thin-skinned Wavell to resign and thus miss the chance of being kicked upstairs to the viceroyalty. Alanbrooke got Wavell to withdraw his letter of resignation by pointing out that if he took offence at Winston's charmlessness he would be resigning on a daily basis.[14] Yet Churchill somehow got it into his head that the key to success in Burma would be a revival of the old ABDACOM idea, in which Wavell had so signally failed. Churchill secretly agreed with the Americans that as a quid pro quo, the command of OVERLORD, the cross-Channel invasion, would go to an American and that a new supreme command in South-East Asia would go to a Briton. Next he had to find an appropriate person to fill the spot. There was no shortage of candidates with strong claims, but all were eventually discarded because of either opposition from Washington or a veto from General 'Pug' Ismay, Churchill's chief of staff. Leo Amery, the Secretary of State for India, was an ardent champion of the South-East Asia command idea, possibly to get Churchill off his back. Although he admired the Prime Minister and thought him a great man, Amery had no illusions about Churchill, especially when it came to India. His judgement was as follows: 'Churchill knew as much of the Indian problem as George III did of the American colonies.'[15] While Churchill and Amery waited for the formal approval of the chiefs of staff, not given until June, they made a long list and then a short list. On paper, Wavell had claims to be considered, especially as he had virtually occupied the post once before, but both Churchill and Amery concurred in finding him inert, lacklustre and defeatist; additionally he quite manifestly did not get on with Stilwell.[16] An even wilder idea was that the hero of the hour, Wingate, should be given the appointment. Churchill, a mindlessly gung-ho Wingate enthusiast, was initially keen on the idea until it was pointed out that it would cause consternation and possibly mass resignations in the army. According to Oliver Harvey, Anthony Eden's secretary, Wingate was at one time a serious candidate, but Amery and Pug Ismay persuaded Churchill that Wingate was needed as a fighter at the front. This was when the idea of a Mountbatten–Wingate 'dream ticket' first took root.[17]

Churchill was not at first particularly keen on the idea of Mountbatten as Supreme Commander in South-East Asia. He considered him not 'big' enough as a military or political figure and was concerned about his poor health. For a while the front-runner was Air Chief Marshal Sholto Douglas, Commander-in-Chief, RAF, Middle East (having been Commander-in-Chief of Fighter Command, 1940–42), but he was detested by the Americans and personally vetoed by FDR. Another distinguished airman at one time in the running was Marshal of the RAF Arthur Tedder, Sholto Douglas's predecessor as commander of the RAF in the Middle East, but the Americans considered him irreplaceable as a Middle East expert. Then the idea gained ground that the post was not appropriate for an airman.[18] Accordingly, naval candidates were sought, of whom by far the strongest was Admiral Andrew Cunningham, aka 'ABC', the hero of the naval battles of Taranto in 1940 and Cape Matapan in 1941 and unquestionably the most talented admiral in the Royal Navy. Cunningham, who had many American admirers, including the rising star General Dwight D. Eisenhower, declined the offer of the job as he had his sights set on becoming First Sea Lord – a position he attained later in the year.[19] When Alanbrooke persisted in pressing the claims of ABC, Churchill cut through the argument by declaring that the post was not suitable for a sailor. For this reason, and because of opposition from Washington, Admiral Sir James Somerville was also rejected. There were many more names submitted to the chiefs of staff: General Henry 'Jumbo' Wilson, Commander-in-Chief, Middle East, 1943–44;[20] Marshal of the RAF John Slessor (Commander-in-Chief, RAF, Middle East, 1943–44); and three men who had already or soon would swim into Slim's ken in Burma: Generals Oliver Leese, George Giffard and Henry Pownall, of whom Pownall was tainted in Churchill's eyes for having been chief of staff to Wavell until the fall of Singapore. The last five candidates were all rejected because 'Pug' Ismay regarded them as mediocrities. Churchill seldom went against Ismay's advice, for it was on him, even more than on Alanbrooke and Eden, that the Prime Minister truly relied.[21]

It was on the way across the Atlantic to the Quebec conference that Churchill finally decided he was going to appoint Mountbatten as Supreme Commander in South-East Asia, doubtless forgetting his earlier stricture that the post was not suitable for a sailor. Second thoughts had supervened, and he now concluded that all Mountbatten's supposed disadvantages (his poor health, playboy image, youth, lack of gravitas) were not after all major problems. He summoned General Ian Jacob, Ismay's deputy, and General Leslie Hollis and asked them who they thought should be the new supreme commander. When Jacob mentioned Giffard, Churchill grimaced, then, 'with a face like a naughty schoolboy', produced Mountbatten's name.[22] All the chiefs of staff were unenthusiastic but acquiesced reluctantly. Alanbrooke remarked tartly that he would need a very efficient chief of staff to pull him through but did not oppose him strongly, allowing himself to be argued round to the proposition that Mountbatten might make up for what he lacked in experience by sheer energy, drive and arrogant self-confidence.[23] Admiral of the Fleet Dudley Pound was much more vociferously opposed to the appointment, arguing that it was just another example of Churchill's making a mockery of the traditions of the Royal Navy. Pound had always beeen concerned about the blatant favouritism accorded to Mountbatten in his accelerated rise through the navy. When Churchill made him Chief of Combined Operations in 1942 against the unanimous advice of the Admiralty, Pound complained bitterly that he had been put in a false position: on the one hand it was thought that *he* had approved the leapfrog promotion, and he had to support it publicly; whereas the truth was that no one but a royal would have been promoted three grades at the premier's whim. Pound made his negative feelings plain with a *de haut en bas* comment that doubtless Mountbatten was 'as likely to make a success of the job as any other junior officer'.[24] If the reaction in military circles was lukewarm to put it mildly, that in the political arena was closer to stupefaction. In London Eden and Attlee, thoroughly alarmed, put in an eleventh-hour bid for Cunningham once more. P.J. Grigg, the Secretary of State for War, denounced to all comers the 'ludicrous' promotion of a mere aristocratic playboy. But once Churchill had one of his 'bright ideas' there was no stopping him. Few arguments though could be weaker than Churchill's fatuous 'apologia' that Mountbatten's youthfulness would make the appointment go down well with public opinion. Churchill, a movie-lover, was confusing fact with fiction, illusion with reality.

It is an astounding fact that no serious or reputable person could be found to approve the appointment. Cunningham denounced it but consoled himself with the thought that it must surely be the end of the upstart Mountbatten's naval career. Universal criticism within the Royal Navy had a threefold basis: senior officers were naturally jealous of an overpromoted junior; there was resentment that royal influence had been allowed to override the interests and traditions of a professional service; and there were genuine doubts about Mountbatten's abilities. In the army there was also understandable resentment. Auchinleck was very displeased with the appointment, though publicly he sent Mountbatten a generous letter of congratulation.[25] Most bitterly disappointed was Alanbrooke, who had reluctantly supported Mountbatten for the job on the understanding that his loyalty would secure him the post of Supreme Commander of OVERLORD. Suddenly, and in a cavalier aside, Churchill told him that that job was going to an American, even though he had explicitly promised it to

Alanbrooke on no fewer than three occasions. Alanbrooke was eloquent in his disappointment: 'It was a crashing blow to hear from him that he was now handing over this appointment to the Americans, and had in exchange received the agreement of the president to Mountbatten's appointment as Supreme Commander for South-East Asia! Not for one moment did he realise what this meant to me. He offered no sympathy, no regrets at having had to change his mind, and dealt with the matter as if it were of minor importance! . . . [The alleged necessity] did not soften the blow, which took me several months to recover from.'[26] Meanwhile Churchill cabled the news of Mountbatten's new job to the premiers of Australia, New Zealand and South Africa, disingenuously (and with typically Churchillian hyperbole) claiming that everyone was delighted with the appointment. Oliver Harvey, Eden's secretary, said that all people of any substance and importance were opposed to Mountbatten except Churchill and the Americans. A Wingate admirer himself, Harvey consoled himself with the much-touted idea that the Mountbatten–Wingate 'dream ticket' would be a huge improvement on the Wavell–Auchinleck axis.[27]

One of Churchill's unique selling points for Mountbatten was that he was the one British officer who could get on easily with Americans, charm them and talk to them in their own idiom, a kind of military version of David Niven, as it were. Like all Churchill's hyperbole, this claim was overdone. Actually, even Harvey was, albeit unknowingly, exaggerating. The Americans were very far from pleased with Mountbatten as an Asian panjandrum. Although Marshall had given his approval as part of the inevitable give-and-take imbricated in Allied discussions, he was privately displeased and said that the Mountbatten appointment was part of a plot by the British to divert landing-craft to South-East Asia to regain their colonies.[28] The American press was never keen on the idea of a Brit as Supreme Commander in South-East Asia, and queried the wisdom and propriety of having an effete princeling giving orders to American GIs. Some saw the move as a slap in the face to General MacArthur and a conspiracy to keep him out of the highest roles in Allied decision-making.[29] A few observers connected this with Eisenhower's known partiality for Mountbatten and his corresponding detestation of MacArthur. When asked if he knew MacArthur, Eisenhower famously replied that he not only knew him but had studied dramatics under him for many years in the Philippines. Privately, his animadversions were even more ferocious: 'I just can't understand how such a damn fool can have gotten to be a general,' he said. 'MacArthur could never see another sun or even a moon for that matter in the heavens as long as *he* was the sun.'[30] In this context it is interesting that Ike constantly 'talked up' Mountbatten and said that he was much more able than his detractors claimed. And it is true that, initially at least, Americans responded well to Mountbatten's brio and charisma, even though they tended to see through him after a while. His American deputy chief of staff at South-East Asia Command (SEAC), Major General Albert Wedemeyer, is a good barometer of this transatlantic ambivalence. Wedemeyer, who began by agreeing with Eisenhower, to the point where he thought Mountbatten capable of gulling the impressionable FDR, soon cooled in enthusiasm once he worked with the boy wonder, and remarked cynically that he was unreliable 'away from salt air'.[31]

Perhaps the most surprising American ally of Mountbatten was the US Navy Chief Admiral Ernest King. Another complex character, King aimed to be the complete mariner, a kind of Renaissance man of the oceans. Having served on destroyers and battleships in World War I, he set out to master all aspects of naval warfare, and was in turn a submariner and a naval aviator. He commanded the US Atlantic fleet in 1940–41, when the USA was still neutral in the war, but was of the aggressive tendency who wanted to take the war to German U-boats even before Pearl Harbor. After war with Japan was declared, he devoted all his energies to the Pacific theatre and was a vehement opponent of Roosevelt and Marshall's 'Europe first' strategy. In addition to all this, he was a dedicated Anglophobe, who matched Stilwell in his contempt for the 'Limeys'. He disliked everything about Britain, especially the Royal Navy, but was equally intolerant and suspicious of the US army.[32] He was especially dismissive of civilians, who, he said, should be told nothing about a war while it was being waged and afterwards only who had won. Two other aspects of King are worthy of note. He was notoriously irascible and described himself as a 'sonofabitch'. He claimed that charm was a virtue that should be reserved strictly and only for wives of US naval officers. FDR described him as 'a man who shaves with a blowtorch'. His own daughter said of him: 'He is the most even-tempered man in the Navy. He is always in a rage.'[33] He was also a deep-dyed alcoholic. The famous incident at the Casablanca conference when he allegedly tried to climb across the table to hit Alanbrooke was in fact a drunken outburst.[34] Such a man would have seemed an unlikely ally for Mountbatten, particularly in the perfervid atmosphere of the Quebec conference. If we posit that the conference was trying to square a circle, or rather a triangle, one can see how unlikely the Mountbatten–King entente was. The main allies had contrary interests, with the British obsessed with India and trying to regain their lost empire in South-East Asia, the Americans similarly preoccupied with China, and Chiang pursuing his own agenda, which had very little to do with the war aims of the English-speaking nations. Yet King correctly intuited that Mountbatten was Churchill's 'teacher's pet' with a vengeance, and may have seen an unexpected opportunity to advance his 'Pacific first' designs. Certainly there is not much extant evidence to warrant King's assertion that Mountbatten was the most impressive officer at the Quebec conference.[35] This was not an attitude shared by Americans without an axe to grind. When 'Hap' Arnold was told of Mountbatten's ice-and-sawdust composite for the creation of iceberg aircraft carriers (HABBAKUK), he showed his contempt by attacking the exhibit with an axe.

All in all, it could not be said that the appointment of Mountbatten was one of Churchill's wiser decisions. Perhaps this accounts for the slightly *opéra bouffe* quality of the many anecdotes about Mountbatten both on the trip across the Atlantic and in Quebec. On 15 August 1943, Churchill, having decided to appoint Mountbatten, had a private talk with him to sound him out about his ambitions. When the Prime Minister mentioned South-East Asia, Mountbatten at first thought he was referring to a tour of inspection. He replied that he would of course go where he was sent, but what he really wanted was to go to sea. 'Go to sea?' bellowed Churchill. 'Don't you understand I am proposing you should go out as Supreme Commander?'[36] With no sense of irony, in his letters to his family Mountbatten compared himself to Eisenhower and MacArthur, the only other supreme commanders. He wrote a gushing and sycophantic letter of thanks to Churchill, calling him 'the greatest master of strategy and war this century has produced'.[37] To the fury, bitterness and consternation of his colleagues in the Royal Navy, he was promoted to acting admiral, though even Churchill drew the line when his protégé proposed that he be given an equivalent rank in the two other services. But the vain and self-loving Mountbatten found a partial way around this proscription, as Alanbrooke relates:

> Just after he had been informed of his selection as Supreme Commander for South-East Asia Command, Dickie had come up to me and asked if I could give him one of my tunic buttons! He said that he intended to put a similar request to Portal [Head of the RAF, Marshal Charles Portal] and that the reason was that he wanted to have them sewn on his tunic. He would then have on him buttons of the three services on his jacket and felt that such an arrangement was a suitable one for a Supreme Commander. I only quote the story as an example of the trivial matters of outer importance that were apt to occupy Dickie's thoughts at times when the heart of the problem facing him should have absorbed him entirely.'[38]

Although the choice of supreme commander was an unwise one, there are grounds for saying that the very creation of the post was even more ill-advised. Stilwell accurately described it as 'a Chinese puzzle, with Wavell, Auk, Mountbatten, Peanut, Alexander [the ATC commander] all interwoven and mixed beyond recognition'.[39] Stilwell was to add the role of deputy supreme commander to his three existing roles (head of US forces in China, Chiang's chief of staff, and director of Lend-Lease in the CBI theatre), so that he now fulfilled a fourfold function and had to satisfy three different chiefs: Marshall, Chiang and Mountbatten. It is not surprising that even the participants in the Chinese puzzle were confused and uncertain about the demarcation between the overlapping responsibilities. The most ticklish problems concerned Mountbatten's relations with the British service chiefs in the CBI theatre. The chiefs of staff in London fudged the issue of whether he was to be a mere coordinator or whether he could overrule his commanders-in-chief.[40] This in turn was a consequence of the failure to define 'supreme commander' adequately. There were two existing models, divergent and almost diametrically opposed. The Eisenhower model stressed conciliation and teamwork, while MacArthur functioned more like an Asian generalissimo or a Roman proconsul, reluctantly acknowledging the distant authority of

Washington. Since MacArthur answered only to Marshall but Ike to both Marshall and Alanbrooke, Mountbatten drew the convenient inference that he should be like MacArthur and answer only to Alanbrooke, cutting Washington out of the loop just as MacArthur and King had cut the British out of the Pacific. The British commanders-in-chief naturally thought that the Eisenhower model was the only sensible and realistic one. In Mountbatten's desire to be another Chiang or MacArthur lay the waters of a sea of further troubles. Even Churchill eventually tired of Mountbatten's imperial pretensions. When he began to complain vociferously about the 'recalcitrant' commanders-in-chief, he was told tersely that Churchill had more important things on his mind. Moreover, it was intimated, if he could not run things without antagonising Royal Navy high-ups, he would have no chance of ever becoming First Sea Lord. Churchill had in the end to dispatch a special envoy to India to persuade Mountbatten to toe the line and accept the Eisenhower model of supreme commander.[41]

If all these problems may be said to have been intrinsic to the very notion of a supreme commander, Mountbatten compounded the difficulties by his attitudes, managing within a short time to alienate all his important collaborators except Wavell. Dismayed that the wayward Edwina did not deign to join him on his tour of duty, he left Northolt airport on 2 October, made a stopover in Baghdad and arrived in Delhi on 6 October. The scope of his command (much of it *in partibus infidelium*, since it was Japanese-occupied territory) comprised Burma, Ceylon, Siam, Sumatra and Malaysia. Mountbatten's vanity is fully in evidence in this diary entry for 6 October: 'I could not help getting a certain thrill at the moment when we crossed the coast of India, to feel that it had fallen to me to be the outward and visible symbol of the British Empire's intention to return to the attack in Asia and regain our lost empire.'[42] But his first days in India were scarcely propitious. Auchinleck received him icily and made it clear he wanted absolutely no interference in his domain as Commander-in-Chief, India.[43] By this time 'the Auk' had heard Wingate's disparaging comments about the Indian army as an immense system of outdoor relief and was incandescent about the Zionist upstart he regarded as a 'churlish bully'. And now here was Mountbatten, whom Churchill had sent out expressly to be Wingate's 'minder'. One raging prima donna in his bailiwick was intolerable for Auchinleck, but now here was a second.[44] Wavell was always much more sympathetic to Mountbatten and welcomed him cordially, but his powers as viceroy were not really designed to assist the younger man in his new role.[45]

Matters deteriorated when Mountbatten made the disastrous and insensitive decision to evict General Giffard and Admiral Somerville, the army and navy commanders-in-chief, from their offices in Faridkot House, a maharajah's palace in Delhi, to make way for his own staff. Though exasperated by such impudence from a man many years his junior (Giffard 58, Mountbatten 43), Giffard did not at first make his displeasure felt and tried his best to accommodate himself to the new situation, though the personality clash was evident to outsiders. It was hardly surprising that the publicity-hating Giffard would not hit it off with publicity-hungry Mountbatten.[46] The secret enmity of Giffard was to some extent compensated for by the surprising commitment shown to the new supreme commander by General Henry Pownall, who had once been in the running for the job himself. Alanbrooke thought he was being very subtle in appointing Pownall as Mountbatten's chief of staff, hoping that he would be both Dutch uncle and mentor to his younger superior *and* combat the scheming of the Admiralty, elated that they had 'their' man as supremo, even if ABC Cunningham detested him. Unfortunately Pownall very quickly 'went native' and became a staunch Mountbatten ally. Some have speculated that because he loathed Churchill, Pownall deliberately tried to put a spoke in the wheel of his key aide, Alanbrooke. When the issue of the Eisenhower versus MacArthur model for leadership came up, Pownall weighed in on his chief's side with a decisive statement: '"Supreme Commander" means just that – he's not just the chairman of a committee.'[47] Pressure from London soon made Mountbatten climb down, and he announced that he was amalgamating his own war staff with the planning staffs of the commanders-in-chief. This 'statesmanship' (actually action taken under duress) persuaded Giffard and Auchinleck that Mountbatten should be given a second chance, so that a 'honeymoon' period ensued.[48] But Mountbatten, secretly piqued by the directive from London, took his revenge by breaking his pledge to Alanbrooke. He had promised that he would govern in a down-to-earth manner, with a small staff and without any trappings of proconsular grandeur. Soon, to the consternation of Alanbrooke,

Auchinleck, Giffard and all interested parties, the Supreme Commander's staff had expanded to mammoth proportions.[49] Moreover, Mountbatten was guilty of blatant cronyism and appointed all his old friends from Combined Operations to senior positions. ABC Cunningham raised the issue of the 'gravy train of the Mountbatten appreciation society'. Once again Mountbatten was reprimanded, but nothing serious was done. When Alanbrooke mentioned the question of the bloated staff at the Supreme Commander's HQ, Mountbatten simply asserted that his staff was small (a howling lie) and Alanbrooke expressed his delight, saying that this was the sort of sacrifice all commanders had to make at the present juncture.[50]

If Mountbatten had temporarily managed to find a modus vivendi with Giffard, the problems with the other two commanders were more intractable. Air Chief Marshal Richard Peirse was temperamentally unsuited to working with a risk-taker like Mountbatten, since 'safety first' was his motto and he always liked to plan every military operation with huge margins of safety.[51] Even worse, Peirse was carrying on an indiscreet affair with Auchinleck's wife, which the gossip-mongers of Delhi claimed as the Eastern version of the notorious affair between Harold Macmillan's wife and Robert Boothby. By the end of 1943, Peirse's affair was virtually public knowledge. Mountbatten, no stranger to affairs himself, had always considered that sex had the potential to ruin a career, and now he proved it by cabling London and asking the head of the RAF, Marshal Portal, to recall Peirse once his tour ended in early 1944. The luckless Peirse, unaware that his fate was being decided, asked for a six-month extension of his tour (to prolong his amour), but Portal coldly rebuffed him. Peirse's career ended in disgrace virtually overnight. A much tougher proposition in every way was Admiral James Somerville, the naval commander-in-chief, a combative character who despised Mountbatten and had the secret (and sometimes not so secret) support of ABC Cunningham.[52] There was open warfare between the staffs of Somerville and Mountbatten, and Somerville spent much of his time minuting complaints to Cunningham that Mountbatten was trying to set himself up as a second MacArthur. When Mountbatten tried to make an official complaint about Somerville, Alanbrooke in effect told him to shut up and get on with the job. This was the occasion when even Pownall lost patience with his boss, whom he described as 'highly strung, inconsequential and temperamental, his tongue runs away with him'.[53] The vendetta with Somerville irked everyone on both sides. Somerville's secretary Alan Laybourne wrote that both men behaved like schoolboys at times, and many other observers commented that they acted pettily, childishly and like prima donnas.[54]

Mountbatten had a variety of tasks to perform as supremo. One was to protect and cherish Churchill's great favourite Wingate, so one of his first stops was the hospital where the Chindit leader lay ill; accompanying him on this visit were Giffard and Wedemeyer. Mountbatten was puzzled by Wingate's behaviour: 'he refused to report sick in his mad desire to see me personally on my arrival, as he wished to get certain things cleared up. Now he is out of action for some weeks at a most unfortunate moment.'[55] Churchill had high hopes of the Mountbatten–Wingate ticket as both men were his hand-picked protégés, both in their early forties, both impatient, reckless dynamos of energy who tended to act first and think later. In reality the two were totally different types. Nothing more clearly illustrates the gulf between them than their attitudes to illness. Wingate took a Shavian approach to doctors and was reluctant to admit that anyone could ever really be ill; he was prepared to make an exception in his own case, but maladies in others were always construed as instances of malingering or hypochondria. With Mountbatten the case was the exact opposite. He really was a hypochondriac, or as his biographer puts it, 'he treated his health with the utmost seriousness and summoned a doctor for causes that to others sometimes seemed trivial'.[56] Yet in the first two weeks of October Wingate was not his prime source of worry; Stilwell was. Although Stilwell had flown down to Delhi for Mountbatten's arrival on 7 October and stayed for a week, the contacts between the two men had been superficial, and he was not au fait with the latest developments there. So, the day after the hospital visit, Mountbatten travelled down to Assam and then took a plane for Chungking, crossing the Hump at night to avoid the intense Japanese fighter sweep. It is somehow typical of his tactlessness that the first person he went to visit on his arrival in Chungking was Chennault, Stilwell's bete noire.[57] Perhaps he was seeking clues to the psychology of monomania, for Chennault was in many ways the American equivalent of Wingate. Where Wingate had a tunnel vision whereby LRP operations alone could win the war, Chennault had a similar obsession about unaided airpower. Some observers have remarked that the true soul partner for Wingate would have been the founder of the Flying Tigers.

Mountbatten cannot have relished the impending meeting with Stilwell, for the American general was in a particularly sour mood now that Marshall had communicated to him all the decisions and implications of the Quebec conference. Marshall related that he had had to fight hard to keep the Ledo road project going, and did so mainly by pointing out that it took a ton of petrol to deliver a ton of cargo to China over the Hump. When someone suggested an oil pipeline, Marshall deftly used this as a point in favour of the road, pointing out that the Japanese were not at present concerned about the Ledo highway but certainly would be if an attempt was made, however impracticable, to run an oil pipeline along it.[58] Further bad news was that Roosevelt remained blind to the faults of Chiang. Despite all contrary evidence, he was certain that Chiang would maintain his position after the war, and was committed to China as the fourth of the Big Four post-war powers. In the short run China still loomed large militarily, as it was the only place from which the USAAF could bomb Japan – for the advance to the Gilbert and Marshall islands and the use of B-29s with a 1,500-mile range was still some way in the future. Ominously, FDR continued to discount the obvious evidence that the Kuomintang was a fascist regime and to insist that the only real problem in China was the personality clash between Stilwell and the generalissimo. But worst of all the news Marshall had to impart was that the 3,000 US troops finally earmarked for service in the CBI theatre under the codename GALAHAD would be under Wingate's command. This information produced a state of near-apoplexy in Stilwell, who had fought so hard and so long to get American ground troops into Burma. 'After a long struggle we get a handful of US troops and by God they tell us that they are going to operate under WINGATE! We don't know how to handle them but that exhibitionist does! He has done nothing but make an abortive jaunt to Katha, cutting some railroad that our people had already cut, get caught east of the Irrawaddy and come out with a loss of 40%. Now he's an expert. That is enough to discourage Christ.' Marshall mournfully replied to Stilwell's strictures: 'We must all eat some crow if we are to fight the war together.'[59]

Stilwell too saw Wingate as another Chennault, forever diverting resources from important objectives to pursue his own private fantasies. But whereas Wingate was still riding high, Stilwell had hopes that the Chennault bubble was about to burst, for the lavish promises the hyperbolic airman had made to FDR had come to nothing. 'He has been screaming for help,' Stilwell wrote triumphantly. 'The Japs are going to run us out of China! It is to laugh [sic]. Six months ago he was going to run them out.'[60] He therefore was less than pleased at Marshall's suggestion that the deficiencies of both Chennault's and Wingate's thinking could be remedied if the two mavericks cooperated. Marshall's concern was not Wingate's reputation but anxiety about casualties. Washington would scarcely tolerate GALAHAD losses at the level Wingate had sustained on Operation LONG-CLOTH, and the way to avoid this, he thought, was to use Chennault's fliers as a shield. But all Chennault's hyperbolic requests for hundreds of aircraft had to go through Stilwell, who either spiked them or truncated and doctored them before sending them on to Marshall.[61] Sooner or later, though, Chennault was bound to prevail, simply because of FDR's purblind and complaisant attitude to anything that concerned China and the generalissimo. Stilwell's slender hope, encouraged by Marshall, was that eventually the weight of expert military and public opinion would force Roosevelt to change tack. At the military level Marshall confided the absurdity to Stilwell that although the USA had broken the Japanese codes and knew from this that the Japanese in turn had broken the Chinese codes, none of this could be passed on to the sieve-like Kuomintang for fear of compromising Allied sources. Meanwhile, bit by bit and agonisingly slowly, the American public were finding out the truth about FDR's absurd propaganda on Chiang's China. By late 1943 it was public knowledge that simply keeping China nominally in the war on a supine basis was using up 95,000 US servicemen. Indeed, some sections of informed American opinion were ahead even of Stilwell. The view was becoming more pronounced in some circles that China was a busted flush and that Japan could be beaten only in the Pacific, or on land by the Russians.[62] Such views tended to leave Stilwell trailing, for he still believed in China and still envisaged an eventual pincer strategy in collaboration with MacArthur. But it was difficult for him to make common cause with FDR's critics, for incredibly, he believed in notions like truth and merit. He could have lobbied his friend Marshall much more assiduously to promote his own views, as MacArthur and Chennault did on a virtually daily basis, but he refrained on the grounds that 'he's running a war all over the world'.[63]

Such was Stilwell's state of mind when, as newly appointed Deputy Supreme Commander, South-East Asia, he met his boss in Chungking. As for Mountbatten, it would be surprising if he did not go into the meeting with some preconceptions, for with the exception of Auchinleck, all the people he had spoken to so far had characterised Stilwell as a fire-eating, Limey-hating wild man. Pownall described him as 'offensive, ignorant and obstinate'.[64] When Alanbrooke met him in Washington in May 1943 he described him thus:

> Stilwell was a strange character known as Vinegar Joe, a name that suited him admirably. One of Marshall's selections, and he had a high opinion of him. Except for the fact that he was a stouthearted fighter, suitable to lead a brigade of Chinese scallywags, I could see no qualities in him. He was a Chinese linguist, but had little military knowledge and no strategic ability of any kind. His worst failing, however, was his deep rooted hatred of anybody or anything British! It was practically impossible to establish friendly relationships with either him or the troops under his command. He did a vast amount of harm by vitiating the relations between American and British both in India and Burma.[65]

As it happened, the basic disharmony between Stilwell and Mountbatten was masked by yet another crisis in Chungking, when Chiang again tried to oust his turbulent chief of staff. Stilwell returned from his long leave in India to find himself in the middle of a firestorm that he could not have anticipated, since the causes were external and essentially nothing to do with him. In short, Chiang was in a state of fury because of loss of face at the hands of the Americans and a power struggle within the KMT. Washington had long been pressing hard for some kind of truce or treaty between Chiang and the Chinese Communists so that the full military resources of China could be directed against the Japanese. Chiang had always refused such a popular front unless Mao and the Communists explicitly submitted to his authority – an impossible demand, as he must have known. In

September FDR finally put the generalissimo on the spot, stating that without the desired united front between KMT and Communists, he would have to insist that Chiang renounce the use of force against the Reds. Fuming, but facing the loss of Lend-Lease if he did not come to heel, Chiang agreed (13 September). But from that moment he was looking around for a scapegoat for his fury, and Stilwell was the obvious candidate.[66]

In addition to his loss of face with the Americans, Chiang became embroiled in a power struggle with the Soong family. T.V. Soong, ambassador to the USA, had accomplished what he considered a miracle by energising his close contacts with Harry Hopkins and getting FDR, in principle, to recall Stilwell. Under direct orders from the President, Marshall actually prepared a cable dismissing his old friend. He told Stilwell that the poor relations with Chiang gave him no choice and he had wanted to recall him two months earlier but Admiral King had objected strongly. He said he was particularly sorry to be ending his mission now, since everybody would think Mountbatten was behind it; he even asked Stilwell's advice on his successor.[67] Marshall tried to smooth over the awkward transition by suggesting that Stilwell was tired and needed to go on extended leave; he even fixed him up with a luxury two-week holiday at the palace of an Indian maharajah. Stilwell defeated that ploy by saying that he had just taken two weeks' leave and in any case needed to 'sit on the eggs for a while longer'.[68] Meanwhile Soong noticed that he had been cut out of the loop in Washington, but misread the reasons; actually it was because the Americans did not want the enemy to know that they had broken their codes and were on to them. Soong was loose-mouthed, as were some members of the State Department, and if he remained in the inner circles, it was possible that a bibulous bureaucrat at some reception might blurt out the truth. Construing his ostracism as machiavellianism emanating from the generalissimo, Soong mobilised his powerful extended family in an attempted coup in Chungking. When Chiang decided not to press for Stilwell's withdrawal, Soong in a rage declared that the generalissimo was a capricious despot who had changed his mind 'like the chief of an African tribe'. [69] Primed by Soong, Madame Chiang and her sisters, supporting their brother, thought that Stilwell would make a reliable ally and accordingly made honeyed overtures to him.[70] Stilwell, unaware of the deeper currents, thought this was a disguised olive branch from the generalissimo. Soong wanted to replace Chiang as head of the Kuomintang and saw himself as a kind of Meiji emperor, whereas Chiang always struck a more reactionary pose, taking his inspiration from Confucius and the Boxers. There followed a month of bitter infighting, with Stilwell baffled as former enemies (like Soong) appeared as friends and vice versa. When Chiang finally decided to ask for Stilwell's recall, the Soong sisters moved by reflex action to his defence. Madame had many secret meetings with Stilwell, which he reported as follows: 'May let out that she has a hell of a life with the Peanut . . . no one else will tell him the truth so she is constantly at him with the disagreeable news.'[71] The details of the Soong plot are still far from clear, and it is particularly uncertain whether they coordinated their efforts with an army revolt. The sinister Tai Li uncovered a plot by a cabal of young generals to seize the generalissimo when he arrived at Chungking airport; the generals were all executed. A more serious show of defiance, about which Chiang could do little, came from a junta of southern generals led by the Cantonese Li Qi-shen; these officers made a kind of unilateral declaration of independence and set themselves up as virtually autonomous warlords.[72] A further complication was that the Kuomintang veteran He Ying-quin allied himself with the Soong sisters in autumn 1943, trying to weaken the generalissimo and himself aiming for supreme power.[73] All the plots came to nothing and Soong, lucky not to be liquidated, was placed under house arrest. Stilwell was unaware of all these deeper currents and never trusted Soong or Madame, suspecting that their amity might simply be a devious ploy. His interpretation was that Soong was encouraging the generalissimo to get rid of him (Stilwell) so that he would fall foul of Washington and further weaken his position, but that Madame was secretly loyal to her husband rather than her brother and was playing her own machiavellian game. Meanwhile pro-Chiang aides were briefing Stilwell that he was alienating 'the Chinese people' (!) by his friendship with the Soongs. Actually the falling out between Chiang and the Soongs may have saved Stilwell from dismissal, for the generalissimo had graver matters on his mind than a recalcitrant chief of staff. The attempt by the Soongs to use Stilwell as a patsy seemed anyway doomed when he, in typically mulish fashion, declared that he had no intention of staying where he was not wanted.[74]

This was the maelstrom Mountbatten now entered. His first call was on Soong, who told him that Chiang was absolutely determined on Stilwell's ousting, that Stilwell no longer had his confidence nor that of any other Chinese and that he was in effect *persona non grata*.[75] Mountbatten then proceeded to talk to Stilwell and found him in cynical and jaundiced mood. Whereas at the first meeting in Delhi on 7 October Mountbatten had been at his most charming, prompting the curmudgeonly Stilwell to record: 'Louis is a good egg . . . full of enthusiasm and also of disgust with the inertia and conservatism . . . energetic and willing to do anything to make it go . . . a nice informal guy . . . He and the Auk are not hitting it off any too well'[76], now he was suspicious and guarded, thinking the British too were working for his dismissal: 'Mountbatten called me and we had a long talk. He is burned up. Feels the doublecross himself, because he'll have to work with a brand-new man. Wants me to stay over and break him in.'[77] Despite the suspicions, the British were very keen to have Stilwell stay on. Mountbatten had been accused of trying to steal MacArthur's thunder and, if he now got rid of Stilwell, it would seem that his critics were right: Mountbatten was trying to do down all the top American generals. He was therefore keen to have Stilwell stay on and showed talent and skill in talking Chiang round. 'If you want your job back, I'll get it for you,' he told Stilwell, who was sceptical and said there was nothing anyone could do: 'You should not be shaking hands with me; it will be bad for you.'[78] Next Mountbatten bearded Chiang in his lair, sending General Brehon Somervell as his emissary, and stressed the absolute necessity for Stilwell to continue. He could not use any units of the Chinese army without Stilwell, he averred, knowing that this would be a terrible loss of face for the generalissimo.[79] Not only were the entire Anglo-American plans for future campaigns in the CBI theatre predicated on Stilwell's presence but, he confided, as to a close friend, FDR could not continue to function without General Marshall at his side, and Marshall had explictly stated that if Stilwell was removed from China, he himself would resign. The issue of a possible suspension of Lend-Lease to China was left hanging in the air. Finally it was the generalissimo who ate crow. He sent for Stilwell and said that he was concerned that the American did not fully understand the duties of a chief of staff but that if he desisted from his 'superiority complex' they could continue to work well together. Primed by the Soong sisters, Stilwell made the necessary token gestures.[80] How much influence Mountbatten's intervention had, or whether Chiang had had second thoughts when he realised the extent of the Soongs' manoeuvrings, is uncertain. But Mountbatten was happy to take the credit. As he wrote to Churchill: 'I am glad that he is not being sacked immediately on my arrival, as I am quite certain that the American forces out here would have felt that I had been the cause.'[81] In his own diary he had an amusing anecdote about the case, involving General Brehon Somervell. 'About midnight he [Somervell] came into my room and said: "This is the gosh-darndest country I have ever had any dealings with. Would you believe it? After the generalissimo had told me categorically that Stilwell was out, he sent for Stilwell this evening, kissed him on both cheeks and said he loved him more than ever and said he was right in again."'[82]

Stilwell was temporarily jubilant and said that Chiang's climbdown was 'a terrific loss of face for the Peanut'. Probably most of all Stilwell had been lucky: deeply embroiled in the power struggle with the Soongs, Chiang could not at the same time get bogged down in a potentially disastrous showdown with the Americans. The real loser was T.V. Soong, who, failing to topple Chiang, was in disgrace for a year.[83] Meanwhile, glad that he had cut the Gordian knot on the Stilwell affair, Mountbatten tried to impose himself on the Chinese sector of the war with some manipulative conferences with Chiang. From the first moment of his arrival in Chungking, Mountbatten had been engaged in a subtle game of 'face' or oneupmanship with the generalissimo. His plane had arrived five hours late and he was full of apologies at having kept the reception committee of Chinese generals waiting. But his Chinese expert, Lieutenant Colonel Dobson, told him this was excellent, as he had 'outfaced' the generals.[84] Dobson was less pleased when the Supremo, evincing Western courtesy, allowed himself to be ushered in to dinner ahead of another general, and cautioned his boss to take a tougher, ruder, more Chinese line. But there were swings and roundabouts in this game of face, as Mountbatten soon discovered. Finding the reading light in his bedroom inadequate because his hosts had enclosed it with a porcelain bowl, he asked to have the bowl removed, but Dobson pointed out that this would be construed as a grave criticism of the Chinese for not having provided an efficient light and they would accordingly lose face.[85] The training in the subtle nuances of Mandarin society paid off when Mountbatten had his first face-to-face interview with Chiang on 18 October. Chiang kept him waiting for 15 minutes, so in retaliation Mountbatten spent an unconscionable time rifling through his attaché case, 'trying to find' the credential prepared by George VI. Very impressed by Madame, as Westerners tended to be ('she has a beautiful figure and the most lovely legs and feet imaginable'), he found that flattery got him everywhere in China. Keeping a straight face, he told Chiang that he was hoping to learn from his wisdom and experience. 'I made a few more complimentary remarks of this type which, had they been made to me, would have made me squirm, but they went down like a dish of hot green tea with the generalissimo.'[86]

Genuinely flabbergasted at the sycophancy and servile deference exhibited at the court of this secular Chinese emperor ('I have never come across such awesome reverence as they showed towards the generalissimo. I very much doubt whether devout Christians could show any more reverence for Our Lord if He were to appear on earth again'), Mountbatten decided to get Madame to coach him in some more fine points of etiquette. She pulled the time-honoured but still effective Chinese trick of telling him that he was the only 'foreign devil' who really understood China, that he was different from other foreigners, etc. He responded by presenting her with a Cartier vanity case set. At his second meeting, on 19 October, Mountbatten scored a notable diplomatic triumph. He promised Chiang 10,000 tons a month over the Hump and in return Chiang agreed that Mountbatten could send guerrillas into Indochina, in an arrogant assumption that that area was within the Chinese sphere of influence.[87] That night, on the eve of Mountbatten's departure, the generalissimo paid him the unprecedented compliment of coming to his quarters to tell him that he had formed the highest possible opinion of his new friend. When the supremo left next day, a delighted Chiang wrote to George VI to shower compliments on his kinsman and ambassador. Mountbatten noted in his diary: 'I must say I left the Chiang Kai-sheks with a real feeling of affection and regard, and I am sure that this is reciprocated since I was told on my return that he had been ringing up constantly to make certain that I had arrived back safely.'[88] Pownall expressed scepticism about how much

Mountbatten had really achieved, though he conceded that he had probably done much better than Wavell on his disastrous visit to Chungking in December 1941.[89] But the gung-ho Mountbatten was full of his 'triumph' and wrote enthusiastically to FDR about his visit. The President replied that he was 'really thrilled over the fact that for the first time in two years I have confidence in the personality problems in the China and Burma fields – and you personally are largely responsible for this'.[90]

The coded reference to Stilwell was significant, for Mountbatten also thought he had made a great hit with the American. Highly vulnerable to flattery, Mountbatten thought it a singular compliment when Stilwell told him he admired him uniquely as a fighter, unaware that he had already said the same thing to Slim and would say it again to the future Field Marshal Sir Francis Fasting. Writing to Field Marshal Dill in Washington about Stilwell, Mountbatten opined: 'I feel you should know that all the British I have met have the lowest possible opinion of his intellect and cooperativeness, and I am told that 90% of the Americans hate his guts. Nevertheless he and I are getting along surprisingly well and so far I have no complaints about his relationships with me, and I have every intention of trying to make a success of them.'[91] He was being naive about both Chiang and Stilwell. Always polite and rarely saying no to anyone's face, Chiang was a master at telling people what they wanted to hear, though he lived in an eternal present in which words were not supposed to have any future consequences. Stilwell had seen it all before and laughed at Mountbatten's naivety. 'He thinks they will do everything . . . The Chinese politeness has fooled Dicky [sic].'[92] And, despite his initial good impressions, Stilwell was already disillusioned with his new boss, though taking a leaf out of the Chinese book, he was always scrupulously polite in public, never giving a hint that he increasingly detested Mountbatten. So convinced was the Supremo that he had tamed Vinegar Joe where so many stuffed-shirt Brits had failed that he invited him back with him to Huang Shan, where Mountbatten announced his intention of setting up an Allied high command in which British, Americans and Chinese would function as one staff, in the manner of Eisenhower's HQ in the Mediterranean. Later, in Delhi, the two men discovered they had a common interest in the movies, and Mountbatten recorded the unique experience of 'going to the pictures' with Vinegar Joe.[93] Stilwell, however, had cause to be grateful to Mountbatten. He was still in his job in Chunking, with both Chiang and the Soong sisters geniality itself. 'The Peanut is now affable again ... May calls me Uncle Joe now.'[94] But the honeymoon was not destined to last long. Already the looming spectre of another Allied conference was casting its shadow.

Having at least temporarily settled relations with Stilwell and patched up the Chinese end of his operation, Mountbatten turned his attention to Slim and Wingate. On 16 October he designated Slim commander of the new 14th Army – the new version of the old BURCORPS. On 22 October he met Slim for the first time, at Barrackpore. In the absurd confusion of ranks that characterises the British army – and many other armies as well – Slim's official rank was still colonel, though he had the wartime rank of major general and the temporary rank of lieutenant general by virtue of his command of the new reorganisation of his units into the 14th Army – the official nomenclature under which the 'Forgotten Army' would win fame. Slim, never a complainer, nevertheless thought he had been given the toughest of hands to play, for the new 14th Army was deployed along a 700-mile front from the Chinese border to the Bay of Bengal. The new commander described the terrain:

> Along the Indo-Burmese border, in a shallow curve, sweeps the wide belt of jungle-clad, precipitous hills, railless, roadless and, for six months of the year, during the monsoon rains, almost trackless. Sparsely populated by wild tribes, disease-infested and even unmapped in places, much of this area has been penetrated only by occasional Europeans and then only in the dry season. It could fairly be described as some of the world's worst country, breeding the world's worst diseases.[1]

Slim asked Mountbatten to address his troops, knowing of his reputation as a morale-booster and possibly also hoping to size up the new commander. It was one of Mountbatten's least attractive qualities that he was a magpie, appropriating other men's bright ideas and presenting them as if they were his own original thoughts. On this occasion he managed to filch two of Slim's best thoughts. One was a variation on the 'Forgotten Army' as a misnomer, for no one in England had ever heard of them (see p. 93). The other was Slim's original contribution to Burma warfare, the suggestion that the British army could fight on during the monsoon.[2] Slim seems to have taken the 'plagiarism' in his stride. He realised that Mountbatten was above all a histrionic and a showman. Indeed the Supremo was known to prize Frederick the Great's advice that to make a hit with their troops commanders should behave like actors on the stage.[3]

In his books and speeches Slim never had anything but praise for Mountbatten.

> Youthful, buoyant, picturesque, with a reputation for gallantry known everywhere, he talked to the British soldier with irresistible frankness and charm. To the Indian he appealed equally. The morale of the army was already on the upgrade; he was the final tonic . . . His comparative youth . . . was something of a stimulant to most of us, and certainly to our troops . . . From the very start, no one could fail to like the Supreme Commander – even Stilwell, in a picturesque phrase once admitted that to me – and his quick brain, backed by a remarkable memory and tireless vitality, enabled him to grasp the intricacies of the whole vast organisation of which he was the head.[4]

Later, as his knowledge of Mountbatten deepened, he began to see his flaws and described him to confidants as a playboy who liked to be liked, tried to please everybody and therefore agreed with the last person he spoke to: 'the only way to get anything done is to ensure that you see him last'.[5] Nevertheless he always worked well with Mountbatten and kept out of the rancorous disputes between the staffs of the Supreme Commander and those of the commanders-in-chief. Slim could see no personal reason for envy and dislike of the new Supremo, while fully understanding why senior navy personnel resented him. Privately, though, there is good reason to believe that he sympathised more with the 'Auk' and the old India hands than with the brash and bumptious Combined Ops staff Mountbatten had brought to India with him. It tended to be a golden rule that those who operated at arm's length from Mountbatten disliked him while those who worked closely with him admired and idolised him. On the other hand, Slim's own plans were in jeopardy from the tension between the commanders-in-chief's planners and the Supremo's: 'It was rather like a game of tennis,' he remarked ruefully.[6] By the end of 1943 the Mountbatten–Slim entente was firmly established and was clearly the key aspect of the new command dynamic, confounding those who had thought that Mountbatten–Wingate would be the significant axis. Slim, in a word, was lucky with his boss, for he would not have fared so well under any of the other men who had originally been suggested for this command – Sholto Douglas, Tedder and Cunningham being obvious cases in point.[7]

The talks at Barrackpore were full and frank, though on Mountbatten's side unacceptably vainglorious. Slim told the Supremo that he disliked Barrackpore as it was too close to Calcutta yet 550 miles from the front and 400 miles even to Imphal, with the Chinese front still farther away: 'It was as if I was controlling from London a 700-mile battle front in the Italian Alps.' Mountbatten took the point and authorised a move to Comilla, 200 miles east of Calcutta, which would make it easier to visit his forward units in Assam. He warned, however, that Slim would be required at frequent SEAC conferences in Delhi, which would mean extra travelling.[8] When Mountbatten produced documents to confirm Slim as the new commander of the 14th Army, Slim queried whether he should not have asked Giffard first. Mountbatten's response was typical: 'No, I am the Supreme Commander and Giffard is my subordinate.' Mountbatten assured Slim that there would be no trouble with Giffard, but Slim knew his man better than the Supremo did. When Mountbatten informed Giffard, he was angry and resentful about the Supremo's 'interventionism' and said grudgingly that he would have to think about it. Mountbatten at once cabled Alanbrooke to ask if Giffard had to obey his direct order if given one. Alanbrooke replied in the affirmative, further deepening the rift between supreme commander and commander-in-chief.[9] Yet if he backed Slim to the hilt at a personal level, Mountbatten's strategic views (really those of Churchill, which he was parroting faithfully) bade fair to make Slim's position otiose, for he told him that he was in favour of any offensive in Burma taking place in the south rather than the north. Churchill's continuing obsession with peripheral campaigns, preferably amphibious ones, put him on a collision course with his American allies and had been one of the reasons for his appointment of Mountbatten, whom he described as 'young, enthusiastic and triphibious [*sic*].'[10] Mountbatten painted an altogether fantastic picture of the coming combined operations in the south, claiming that SEAC would soon have so many ships that the harbours of India and Ceylon would not be big enough to contain them.[11] This was of course an idle Churchillian boast, for by January 1944 the D-Day operation and that in southern France would take all the landing-craft. Churchill, Alanbrooke and Mountbatten were forever hankering after Rangoon, the Andaman islands, Sumatra or Singapore, but the much-vaunted amphibious operations against these targets never happened because the European and Pacific wars consumed all available resources. Slim's eventual success in northern Burma happened, ironically, solely because FDR was determined to bolster China.

Mountbatten went away from his talks with Slim elated and recorded his favourable opinion of the new commander of the 14th Army: 'I thought him absolutely splendid in every way and never changed my point of view from beginning to end. I have reason to believe he liked me too from the beginning. Nothing could ever come between us. I saw Bill Slim whenever I could and never missed a chance of seeing him on any visit to the front. We talked over everything with the utmost candour and he and I saw eye to eye all the way through.'[12] Now it was time to turn his attention to Wingate, meant to be his strong right arm but still lying seriously ill in hospital. On 1 November Mountbatten reported his progress:

> He has been terribly ill with typhoid and is still very weak, but he is now well on the road to recovery. This he owes to the fortunate fact that his wife, hearing he was ill, informed someone at COHQ that the only person who could manage him was Sister MacGeary, the matron of the Imphal hospital, who had looked after him the last time he came out of Burma. This they telegraphed to me in Chungking and I arranged to have her flown down. From the time she arrived, Wingate took a turn for the better and this week has been able to sit up in bed and take an interest in his important work.[13]

Wingate proved his boast that he had a special hotline to Churchill when the Prime Minister sent him a personal 'get well' cable, to the consternation of his enemies. He was finally released from hospital into the Supremo's personal care in the second week of November, though the doctors warned he would not be fully fit until the New Year. Determined to prove them wrong, Wingate enjoyed a threefold convalescence. First he stayed with Mountbatten at Faridkot House, ate ravenously and began to put on weight at the rate of two pounds a day. Then he transferred to the viceregal lodge as Wavell's guest, over the protests of Lady Wavell, who did not like him. As a compromise she agreed to take him if MacGeary came too, and she exercised such an iron control over her patient that Lady Wavell was won over. On 17 November he moved from the viceroyalty for the third part of his convalescence, with the family of Sir Humphrey Trevelyan, who noted, as the Wavells had, that Wingate had 'an anxiety not to disobey Matron MacGeary that seemed part affectionate and part fearful'.[14]

Mountbatten just had time to reply to a letter from Edwina, who warned him against Madame Chiang (simple jealousy or dog-in-the-mangerism?) before flying out for the Cairo conference, which Stilwell was also to attend. Despite his secret and never healed antipathy to Stilwell, Chiang, primed by the Soong sisters, was convinced he needed him to speak on his behalf at the coming conclave of top Anglo-American generals so as to increase his share of Lend-Lease and to present a coherent strategic and logistical plan of future Chinese army operations – something his own generals were not competent to do. After a very cordial meeting with the generalissimo on 6 November, Stilwell commented sourly: 'the rattlesnake was affable as hell'. Chiang told his sister-in-law that his talk with Stilwell was the most satisfactory he had ever had.[15] Yet once again Stilwell's position was complicated and to an extent undermined when FDR sent out yet another of his personal representatives to Chungking. Roosevelt was still working on his idea that the post-war Big Four would be the USA, Soviet Union, Britain and China, and against very strong Soviet opposition had managed to get China included in a four-power declaration on the shape of the post-war world. At the same time he was trying to get the USSR to enter the war with Japan. Stalin, willing to aid FDR over Japan but not over China, was lukewarm at the prospect of meeting Chiang, but the generalissimo solved his problem for him by telling Roosevelt he would attend a four-power meeting only if the President met him first. Stalin was unwilling to agree to these terms, so FDR's four-power meeting was off. The only way he could salvage something of his vision was to have *two* conferences, the first with Chiang and the British, the second with Stalin and the British. It was agreed that the first meeting would be in Cairo and the second in Tehran.[16] To finalise the details of the Cairo conference and to smooth out any diplomatic wrinkles in advance, FDR sent to Chungking his faithful aide Brigadier General Patrick Hurley.

It remains a mystery why Roosevelt should have entrusted so many delicate missions to Hurley, who was both an extreme right-winger and generally regarded as a bit of a joke. He had been Secretary of War in Herbert Hoover's 1928–32 administration and had been employed by General Marshall in early 1942 to investigate the feasibility of evacuating American troops trapped by the Japanese on the Bataan peninsula in the Philippines. Thereafter he had acted as FDR's roving ambassador, in New Zealand, the Soviet Union and the Middle East. No more disastrous choice as a China envoy could be imagined, for Hurley was rabidly anti-Communist in a mindlessly ideological way and thus a priori committed to Chiang and the Kuomintang, whatever corruption he uncovered.[17] Stilwell knew him and despised him, and assigned his star military attaché and expert linguist, Colonel Barrett, to put him in his place. When the absurd Hurley arrived at Chungking airport as the classic beribboned buffoon, Barrett remarked scathingly: 'General, I see you have every campaign ribbon but Shay's rebellion.'[18] Apart from his other deficiencies, Hurley was a 'stirrer' and quickly put it about that Stilwell had lost Mountbatten's confidence. Stilwell took the bait and was soon writing furiously in his diary:

> Hurley talked with Louis [Mountbatten] who is after my scalp. I stand between him and dominance in China and he wants to get rid of me. Hurley warned him about my status in the United States and told him that he could expect plenty of trouble, and that if he got me, I would go after him. Said that I had kept China in the war at a very critical period and was considered in the US as the 'saviour of China' ... The old doublecross is going strong. Louis is playing the 'Empah' game and won't take chances. All he wants is something that can be labelled a victory, and if the Chinese can be left to take it on the nose, so much the worse for them – and me. Louis is

working up the 'controversy' between me and Chennault and spoke of it to Hurley.'[19]

This was all a fabrication, as was Hurley's solemn assurance that he had warned Mountbatten against playing 'divide and rule'. The only one playing games at this juncture was the machiavellian Hurley, and in this he was aided by the shadowy Wedemeyer, who was, however, less circumspect in covering his tracks as a 'stirrer'. Although Stilwell bought Hurley's mendacious bill of goods about Mountbatten, he saw through Wedemeyer and commented: 'The young man sure does appreciate himself. Gave him my idea of the tactical plan and now he's giving it back to me as his.'[20] Thus did Wedemeyer play with Stilwell the role Mountbatten had already played with Slim.

With the Soong sisters on the sidelines still stressing the importance of Stilwell at Cairo, Hurley met Chiang on 12 November and summarised Roosevelt's vision. He wanted to maintain Britain as a first-class power while dismantling her imperialism and clearing her out of Asia; he believed in a strong China as a dominant force in Asia; he intended to defeat Japan in the Pacific and the Japanese homeland, not Singapore, as the British would like; and he was committed to the triumph of democracy worldwide.[21] Stilwell had no quarrel with any of that, but he objected vehemently to the idea that B-29s should be based in China without demanding any quid pro quo from Chiang, not even a ritual and meaningless obeisance to the principle of democracy. His old hatred of FDR was rekindled and he took to referring to him in his diary as 'Rubberlegs' – a reference to the President's incapacitation by polio. In his own mind, Stilwell now thought that the only way to break the everlasting circle of Chiang's stalling and tergiversation was to imitate the Bolsheviks in 1917 or Bonnie Prince Charlie in 1745 – that is, to go it alone. If he got control of the Ledo force and invaded Burma with it, the generalissimo would be checkmated. This became Stilwell's primary aim at Cairo.[22] Almost as if reading his mind, Chiang started cutting down on the fresh troops he was prepared to assign to the Ledo force: first it was 50,000, then 25,000, then 20,000, finally only 14,000. There were times when Stilwell became so desperate that he contemplated intriguing with sympathetic Chinese generals to stage a kind of internal coup that would maintain the generalissimo as a figurehead while he and they could have a free hand in waging war. He and his friends all agreed that Chiang would not survive six months in peacetime, but how could he be unseated in wartime if FDR and his acolytes continued to give him such massive, blinkered support? There is historical irony here. Stilwell was plotting to cut Chiang out of the loop at the very moment that Roosevelt was in effect boosting the generalissimo, since for the first time he would meet the Allied leaders as an equal.[23] Moreover, both men approached the coming conference from diametrically opposite perspectives. For Chiang this was the climax of his career, the moment when he was finally taken seriously as an international statesman.[24] For Stilwell, the conference (and its sequel in Tehran) was the apogee of cant and humbug, the *reductio ad absurdum* of the Alice-Through-the-Looking-Glass world in which he had lived for the past two years. As he noted sourly: 'What a gag the Big Four will put on: Stalin the Communist, really approaching the democrat, with capitalist tinges. Roosevelt the Democrat backing Imperialist Britain. Churchill the Imperialist, giving lip-service to the Atlantic Charter. Chiang Kai-shek the Fascist, posing as a democrat.'[25]

On 15 November Stilwell left Chungking and made a five-day journey to Cairo, with stopovers at Delhi, Karachi, Abadan, Basra and Jerusalem. On 20 November he checked into the Mena House hotel near the Pyramids, where a huge contingent of Allied generals was staying, engendering what Harold Macmillan called 'a scramble for bathrooms'.[26] Chiang and Madame had already arrived, and Stilwell scrupulously checked that the generalissimo's position was still as they had discussed at Chungking, even though he thought it pure cloud cuckoo land. Chiang was proposing to offer FDR 90 divisions, of which the first 30 would be ready by January 1944, the second 30 by August 1944 and the final 30 by January 1945. In return for this, and full Chinese cooperation in the invasion of Burma, Chiang wanted not just 10,000 tons a month over the Hump and B-29s based in China (which was feasible), but 13 US divisions with which to launch an offensive against the Japanese in central and northern China (which was not).[27] Chiang's lack of realism was the principal factor that would turn the Cairo conference into fiasco and make it the least successful of all the wartime summits, but Alanbrooke thought a serious mistake had been made in allowing the generalissimo to arrive early, dominate the agenda and distort the meeting's general purpose, which was supposed to be discussion of the war in Europe. As Alanbrooke correctly stated, the order of business should have been Europe, discussions with Stalin on points of difference, and a general communiqué on the Second Front; only then, as a coda, should Chinese affairs have been discussed. 'The whole conference had been thrown out of gear by Chiang Kai-shek arriving here too soon. We should *never* have started our conference with Chiang; by doing so we were putting the cart before the horse. He had nothing to contribute towards the defeat of the Germans, and for the matter of that uncommonly little towards the defeat of the Japanese. Why the Americans attached such importance to Chiang I have never discovered. All he did was to lead them down a garden path to a communist China!'[28]

With all participants in Cairo by 21 November (Chiang and Mountbatten had come from Delhi by a more direct route), an attempt at serious work began. But the element of farce that was never far away from the proceedings was immediately apparent when Churchill decided to pay a courtesy call on Chiang, whom he had never met (FDR had never met an upper-class Oriental of any kind) before a cursory encounter in the hotel lobby. Speaking through an interpreter, Churchill told the generalissimo he would call on him next day at noon. The 'interpreter' replied: 'The generalissimo is delighted and says when will you call?' A puzzled Churchill tried again with different words: 'Tell his Excellency that when the sun is at its zenith I will come.' Chiang then replied that he would expect the premier at ten the next morning. 'Impossible. I never get up as early as that,' replied Churchill, before proceeding to give the interpreter an angry tongue-lashing.[29] On the 21st, the British and Americans kept themselves apart, with Churchill holding court at dinner with Alanbrooke, Portal, Dill, Jumbo Wilson, Sholto Douglas and Mountbatten. On the 22nd, there was a combined meeting of the American and British staffs to discuss their approach to Chiang. Dinner saw Churchill and FDR in conclave with the Allied chiefs of staff, Harry Hopkins, Mountbatten, Stilwell (whom Alanbrooke persisted in regarding as a crank) and Chennault. There was disagreement both between the British and Americans and within both parties. The British chiefs of staff felt the priority must be Europe; Alanbrooke said that he was not about to strip the Mediterranean of shipping just to equip Mountbatten for ventures in Sumatra.[30] This predictably annoyed Churchill, who had laid elaborate plans for Operation CULVERIN, the assault on North Sumatra, or the TORCH of the Indian Ocean as he absurdly called it.[31] Alanbrooke tried to be diplomatic with Churchill (secretly he was exasperated) and mentioned Brian Horrocks as a possible task force commander for CULVERIN but gradually made it clear that the plan was anyway quixotic as no resources had been allocated to what was agreed to be a difficult undertaking. Mountbatten proposed as a compromise another operation, codenamed BUCCANEER, involving an advance along the Arakan coast to Akyab and an amphibious attack on the Andaman islands. Churchill, in a sulk that CULVERIN had been rejected, then switched his attention entirely, to Rhodes and the Dodecanese, and Mountbatten to his consternation even saw some of his beloved landing-craft diverted to this theatre.[32]

When the Americans joined the discussion, further complications arose. As far as Burma was concerned, it was basically the same old tug-of-war, with the British taking an imperial perspective and wanting to aim for Singapore while FDR and his acolytes were obsessed with China. The cross-cutting complexities can be appreciated when it is realised that the Americans backed Mountbatten on BUCCANEER as a prelude to an assault on Rangoon, while the British military planners thought that retaking the Burmese capital made little sense strategically and that the objective should be Singapore, as its recapture would 'electrify the eastern world'.[33] Roosevelt, initially cool on BUCCANEER, came round to it strongly, perhaps especially when he sensed the vehemence of Churchill's opposition to it. Mountbatten looked for, and to some extent got, the support of the US admirals for amphibious operations, though this was limited to 'in principle' approval without any offer of resources. But the Americans concurred in feeling that Mountbatten had performed well and his champion at Quebec, Admiral King, was again impressed.[34] Alanbrooke's impatience with Mountbatten and BUCCANEER again led to some spirited and even acrimonious verbal spats between him and King. As usual Stilwell reported the encounter in melodramatic terms: 'Brooke got nasty and King got good and sore. King almost climbed over the table at Brooke. God, he was mad at Brooke. I wish he had socked him.'[35] Field Marshal Dill, whose heroic work in Washington was the most valuable link in the entire Anglo-American alliance, tried to be statesmanlike and praised the Mountbatten–Stilwell combination as the 'dream ticket'. This was passing interesting, as Mountbatten–Wingate had originally been talked up in these terms, Mountbatten–Slim was actually as close as anything ever came to such an actuality, and now here was Dill proposing yet a third permutation, conveniently over-looking the fact that Mountbatten was entirely British Empire-centred and Stilwell an unregenerate Sinophile.[36] All in all, it is not surprising that the Anglo-Americans were ill-prepared for the Kuomintang tsunami that hit them next day, given how divided they were them-selves.

At 11 a.m. on 23 November, a distinguished cast assembled at the President's villa for the meeting with Chiang. Apart from FDR and Churchill, all the chiefs of staff plus Harry Hopkins, Mountbatten, Stilwell, Chennault and 'a full house of Chinese generals' were present. Alanbrooke was bemused by the presence of Madame Chiang, who had not been invited but simply gatecrashed on the reasonable assump-tion that no one would dare to turn away the generalissimo's wife. He described the scene:

> She was the only woman amongst a very large gathering of men, and was determined to bring into action all the charms nature had blessed her with. Although not good looking she certainly had a good figure which she knew how to display at its best. Also gifted with great charm and gracefulness, every small movement of hers arrested and pleased the eye. For instance at one critical moment her closely clinging black dress of black satin with yellow chrysanthemums displayed a slit which extended to her hip bone and exposed one of the most shapely of legs. This caused a rustle amongst those attending the conference and I even thought I heard a suppressed neigh come from a group of some of the younger members!'[37]

The real problem was that no one quite knew whether they were dealing with Madame or her husband. Whenever the official inter-preter translated Chiang's words, Madame would intervene to say that he had not quite conveyed the nuance of what the generalissimo had said. Alanbrooke commented that it left one wondering who was running the show, and that although Madame appeared to be the leading spirit, she was not to be trusted. She was, he thought, 'a queer character in which sex and politics seemed to predominate, both being used indiscriminately individually or unitedly to achieve her ends'. As for Chiang himself, he 'reminded me more of a cross between a pine marten and a ferret than anything else. A shrewd foxy sort of face. Evidently with no grasp of war in its larger aspects but determined to get the best of the bargains.'[38] Chiang's only contribution was to reiterate that the Chinese contribution to the Burmese war depended entirely on naval operations in the Bay of Bengal. Since everything he said had to be translated twice, once by his interpreter and then by Madame, the meeting turned into a painfully slow performance.

The afternoon was even worse. Alanbrooke and King soured the atmosphere still further with a slanging match about the Andaman islands while the British and Americans waited for the Chinese delegation to arrive. Earlier Stilwell had arisen to make a presentation on Chiang's behalf, only to receive a message that the generalissimo was going to come to the afternoon session and speak in person. He then changed his mind and cancelled that decision, then cancelled his recantation too, restating his intention to come in person before finally recancelling.[39] At 3.30 p.m. three Chinese generals came in sheepishly with their staff and took their places. Alanbrooke asked them to speak but they declined, saying they merely wished to listen. It was obvious that since Chiang had finally decided it was beneath his dignity to attend, he had sent his aides along to save 'face'. But since he had not briefed them or authorised them to negotiate about anything, their presence was totally pointless. An embarrassing silence followed. Alanbrooke, in the chair, in vain coaxed and even goaded them to say something. Some 60 to 70 British and American officers looked on in stupefaction as the dozen or so Chinese sat whispering together. They then repeated that they simply wished to listen.[40] Patiently Alanbrooke said that the Allied opinion was well known and position papers had been circulated; the point of the meeting was to have a discussion. This simply provoked a fresh round of whisperings and long silences, at the end of which the Chinese spokesman repeated the same weary mantra he had used all afternoon: 'We wish to listen to your deliberations.' Meanwhile the suppressed sound of amusement on the Anglo-American side threatened to become outright laughter at the gruesome farce. Fearing a diplomatic incident if the embarrassing comedy was allowed to continue, Alanbrooke quickly adjourned the meeting on the pretext that the Chinese had 'doubtless' not had enough time to study the Allies' proposals. They were glad to be able to slip out of the door. Alanbrooke blamed the Americans for the fiasco. 'Mopping my brow I turned to Marshall and said, "That was a ghastly waste of time!" To which he replied, "You're telling me!" Considering that it was thanks to him and the American outlook that we had had to suffer this distressing interlude I felt that he might have expressed his regret otherwise. These two episodes on one day went a long way to convince me that there was little to be hoped for from Chiang's China.'[41] The Chinese had been infuriating and exasperating, but even Stilwell thought that Alanbrooke had chaired the meeting in too Mandarin a matter. 'Terrible performance. They couldn't ask a question. Brooke was insulting. I helped them out.' In fact he had had to save Chinese face by answering questions Chiang's generals dared not. Stilwell's biographer, curiously, thinks Alanbrooke was more to blame than the dumb Chinese. 'Brooke, the type of Englishman who considered a foreigner something to be snubbed and, if non-white, to be stepped on, pressed the embarrassed Chinese further.'[42]

On the morning of the 24th, the chiefs of staff went to the President's villa for a session with him and Churchill. FDR made it plain that he wanted to press on with BUCCANEER to appease Chiang, who, however, was already beginning to try FDR's patience by insisting on his 10,000 tons a month over the Hump while reserving his position on Burma. Churchill made it equally clear that he did not want BUCCANEER because he wanted landing-craft for an invasion of Rhodes – in pursuit of his current will o' the wisp, an obsession with prising Turkey out of its neutrality.[43] Marshall expressed his dislike for the Rhodes operation on the grounds that it would detract not just from BUCCANEER but, much more seriously, from OVER-LORD. Marshall departed for lunch with Chiang while FDR discussed Chinese affairs informally with Madame. She told him that Chiang was adamant that as part of the post-war settlement China should be given the Bonin islands east of Japan and regain Manchuria and Formosa (Taiwan); most of all, though, he needed to see Allied amphibious operations in the Indian Ocean so that he did not have to take the full weight of a Japanese onslaught. She brushed aside Roosevelt's queries about the likelihood of civil war between the Kuomintang and the Communists.

That afternoon the chiefs of staff held another pointless meeting with the Chinese generals. Since Chiang had been briefed that their inability or unwillingness to answer questions the day before had made them a laughing stock, he had issued new orders. In effect they were told to filibuster. When Alanbrooke asked for their comments and queries they responded by raising the most pointless and absurd nit-picking details, asking for the proportion of Indian troops as against British in the forthcoming campaigns. In the end an exasperated Alanbrooke gave up.[44] He, Stilwell and Mountbatten were all in the deepest gloom. But suddenly there came news that heartened them tremendously. Chiang had got away with so much in the past because of FDR's supine attitude that he thought he could order up American materiel at will. He had reckoned without the fiery Marshall, never a man to cross, who had no illusions about Chiang, the KMT or China. When Chiang laid out all his demands without offering anything in return, Marshall lost his temper and told him some long-overdue home truths. The generalissimo, he said, seemed to be in a world of his own and overlooked the fact that there was a war going on in Europe. If he was really committed to the Allied cause, there should be no more shilly-shallying and he should exert all his efforts to reopen the Burma road. Finally, and with brutal bluntness, he told the generalis-simo that he did not care for his attitude. He was making demands for supplies as if they were his by right. He seemed to forget that these were *American* goods, *American* planes, *American* troops and he had no automatic right to them. 'There must be no misunderstanding about this,' was his parting shot.[45] Stilwell was especially delighted that Marshall, of all people, had finally had a taste of the real Chiang, not the 'great leader' of Roosevelt's imagination. 'A grand speech for the G-Mo to hear,' he wrote, 'and incidentally for the Limeys. Louis [Mountbatten] told to go fix it up with the G-Mo. Welcome change from telling me to fix it up.'[46]

As soon as Roosevelt heard of Marshall's explosion, he reverted to his old, irrational anxiety about keeping China in the war and turned to Mountbatten for help. For the next two days the Supremo spent most of his time closeted with the recalcitrant generalissimo, using Madame as his interpreter. Trying a mixture of charm and sweet reason, Mountbatten impressed on Chiang that he could not have the 535 transport planes he was insisting on, and that the Allies could not supply China over the Hump at the level Chiang demanded *and* attack

Mandalay before the monsoon. At this point, whether deliberately putting on a 'dumb show' or simply woefully ignorant, Chiang claimed not to know what the monsoon was. When Mountbatten looked over to Madame, genuinely puzzled, she said: 'Believe it or not, he does not know about the monsoon.'[47] When Chiang repeated his usual mantra about the necessity for an amphibious operation in the Indian Ocean before he could commit his forces, Mountbatten patiently explained that this operation was not favoured by the Allied chiefs of staff. He then produced a highly detailed map and began to explain the problems. At this point Chiang's eyes glistened and he put his finger on the map. 'I like this plan, we will carry it out,' he said.[48] Patiently Mountbatten explained that the idea had been rejected by the Allied chiefs and repeated the reasons why, principally the lack of landing-craft. 'Never mind,' said Chiang, who had not a single boat in his army, 'we will carry it out all the same.' Not surprisingly, Mountbatten concluded that he was talking to a madman. 'I may say that he made several more illogical suggestions and I cannot help wondering how much he knows about soldiering.'[49] Nevertheless, as supreme commander he could not simply storm out and had to try to fulfil Roosevelt's wishes. Next day there was another meeting. 'I found the Generalissimo very difficult, although he kept on assuring me of his personal regard and told me he was protecting my interests as much as his own.' When they parted, Chiang promised to think over all that had been said to him. Mountbatten went off to an enjoyable lunch with Churchill, Pug Ismay, Jumbo Wilson and Churchill's daughter Sarah, who had caused something of a sensation by marrying the bandleader Vic Oliver. That afternoon, at 4. 15, Chiang and Madame gave a tea party. Alanbrooke decided he now disliked Madame more the more he saw of her. But when FDR and Churchill arrived, a triumphant Chiang announced that after talking to Mountbatten he agreed to all the points he had rejected the day before.[50]

Stilwell meanwhile had spent the day talking to FDR about the necessity for a proper US command structure for the American and Chinese armies, such that Chiang could not negate or subvert it. Most important of all was for the USA to take over the first 30 Chinese divisions entirely. Roosevelt responded by putting on one of his 'dumb shows', feigning ignorance and stupidity. Stilwell reported that he acted as if gaga, asking irrelevant questions such as 'Where are the Andaman islands?' then breaking in on Stilwell's explanations to say that it would be better if the US Marines rather than the US army were sent to Chungking, since the Marines were famous all over Asia. The only concrete thing Stilwell extracted was a presidential promise to equip all 90 divisions properly, though he knew in his heart Chiang would not allow them to be raised.[51] Roosevelt was displaying an almost fanatical refusal to alter course on China even though Chiang had over three days provided the most palpable and blatant evidence of his unreliability, and had confirmed in detail all the critical things Stilwell had ever said about him. It must be emphasised that over the five days of the Cairo conference Chiang on three occasions consented to support an Allied advance into central Burma and then on three other occasions recanted and withdrew his consent. On 25 November, after FDR had been given the generalissimo's agreement to operations, Chiang changed his mind. At 9 p.m. Stilwell was summoned to the presidential residence and given the bad news by Harry Hopkins. 'My God, he's off again,' Stilwell noted. On the 26th, Mountbatten reported his failure to shift him. 'Louis in at eleven to spill the dope. He's fed up on Peanut. As who is not?'[52] Then came Chiang's further change of mind at the tea party. On the 27th, Churchill, Roosevelt and all the senior commanders departed for the Tehran conference with Stalin. Now that he did not have to face the Allied leaders again and was himself on the point of leaving for China, the generalissimo finally revealed his hand definitively. He instructed Stilwell to hold out for 10,000 tons of supplies over the Hump and an Anglo-American airborne assault on Mandalay but in return refused to make any commitment whatsoever.

Mountbatten was meanwhile holding a conference of senior SEAC officers and described the upshot.

Joe Stilwell absolutely staggered me by coming in and saying that the G-Mo had that morning rejected all the points which he had agreed to at the last plenary meeting, and had instructed Stilwell to try to obtain a complete reversal of every point. I told Joe, 'I am rather hard of hearing. I am afraid I was unable to catch what you said. Please be good enough to send me a telegram at Delhi and also one to the Chiefs of Staff.' I really could not face staying another week and in any case my best hope will be in getting the G-Mo to myself as he passes through

India. I am delighted that the Prime Minister and President and the Combined Chiefs of Staff are at last being given first hand experience of how impossible the Chinese are to deal with. They have been driven absolutely mad and I shall certainly get more sympathy from the former in the future.[53]

The crafty Chiang thought he had outwitted the Westerners, but he reckoned without the energy and determination of Mountbatten. Taking the first plane out, he tracked the generalissimo down at Ramgarh, where he was inspecting his New Model Army. Predictably Chiang then did another volte-face (purely to get rid of his pursuer) and again conceded everything he had refused to Stilwell, assuring Mountbatten that he was his greatest friend and that this time he had been given a sacred pledge. Madame weighed in with the old dodge to the effect that the Supreme Commander was 'special' and unlike other Westerners. Mountbatten had been bitten once too often to take this entirely seriously, but there was nothing more he could do.[54] He gave himself a week's relaxation in Delhi but there was bad news at every level. His American director of public relations told him that SEAC was deeply unpopular with most Americans, who felt the British should be taking orders from a US supremo, not the other way around. Even his reliable ally Wavell disappointed him. Mountbatten the movie-lover could always be buoyed up by a good film, but when the two of them went to see *Casablanca*, which he adored, Wavell was dismissive and censorious.[55] His more acceptable partner at the pictures, Stilwell, was meanwhile sightseeing in Jerusalem and Luxor.[56]

The focus of international diplomacy had now shifted to Tehran. Although Churchill and Roosevelt have often been portrayed as close comrades in the defeat of the Axis powers, the truth is that they did not really see eye to eye either as private individuals or on grand strategy. Bruised by his experience at Cairo, where he felt FDR had neglected him and taken him for granted while he courted the pointless Chiang, Churchill was further enraged by Roosevelt's espousal of BUCCANEER over his strenuous objections. He made a note that he therefore did not consider himself bound by this decision.[57] At Tehran Churchill used Stalin's pledge to enter the war against Japan as soon as Germany was defeated as an excuse to pull out of BUCCA-NEER, which he said was therefore not needed. He favoured his own operation in Rhodes and the Dodecanese, but Stalin was adamant that nothing at all must detract from the earliest possible opening of the Second Front. Meanwhile the US Joint Chiefs denied that BUCCA-NEER would in any way impair or detract from the OVERLORD operation and insisted it must go on; if it was cancelled, Chiang would have just the excuse he wanted to do nothing. Both Marshall and King argued vociferously that cancellation of BUCCANEER would strengthen the Japanese hand in the Pacific, but the combination of Churchill and Stalin, both opposing the operation for their own different reasons, was hard to beat. FDR tried to make a decisive intervention by pointing out that BUCCANEER must go ahead, or else it would provide Chiang with spurious reasons to pull out also from the main assault on Burma planned for 1945 and at present codenamed TARZAN. Alanbrooke replied scathingly that whatever the generalissimo pulled out from was immaterial, as he was, in the idiom of the day, 'a dead loss'.[58] Mountbatten meanwhile unwittingly got across Roosevelt by using this precise moment to raise his own troop requirements to 50,000. Ismay told him that 18,000 was the maximum he would get, which was anyway a numerical ratio of three and a half to one over the inferior Japanese armies. Churchill grumbled that a request for 50,000 was an insult to the British army and minuted against Mountbatten's request: 'Noted. There is no doubt that a steam hammer will crack a nut.'[59] For all kinds of reasons FDR's hopes for BUCCANEER looked increasingly forlorn. Faced with Churchill's intransigence, he blinked first. On 5 December he sent the Prime Minister a laconic three-word message: 'BUCCANEER is off.' Wavell noted in his diary that he had never seen Mountbatten so depressed as on receipt of this intelligence.[60]

The Cairo conference marked something of a watershed in the purely military relations between Chiang's KMT and the United States. Although Roosevelt never abandoned his dream of China as one of the post-war Big Four and thought it important to keep Chiang in the war simply to tie up Japanese divisions on the Asian mainland, he increasingly discounted the generalissimo in his war planning, concentrating instead on the island-hopping strategy in the Pacific and on getting the Soviet Union into the war. He was far less starry-eyed personally about Chiang after the meetings and his disastrous performance at Cairo, viewing him as 'highly temperamental'. He was also prepared to pay more attention to the sophisticated reports of the State Department, which portrayed the Kuomintang as a regime riven with corruption. FDR's fading interest in Chiang was highlighted by his increasing concentration on the relationship with Stalin and is perhaps symbolised by his failure to meet the generalissimo at Cairo airport, with the loss of face for the Chinese that entailed.[61] Cairo had been a full-blown fiasco as a summit, the smiling faces at the photo opportunities notwithstanding. The mutual contact between East and West had simply resulted in China's augmented mistrust of the West and plummeting Western confidence in Chiang in grand strategy and geopolitical terms. The key event in the last week of November 1943 was not the opening of the Cairo conference but the successful landing of the US Marines on the Gilbert islands, confirming the success of the island-hopping strategy and hastening the day when Japan would come within range of the deadly B-29s.[62] But Chiang was not prepared to take his eclipse lying down. Humiliated by the cancellation of the very operation that was supposed to underline his importance, he responded by making extortionate demands. The request for 20,000 tons a month over the Hump and double the aircraft assigned to the CBI front could conceivably be regarded as bargaining positions, but his concomitant requirement of a $1 billion 'loan' as 'compensation' was merely ludicrous. Both Stilwell and Ambassador Gauss opposed this vehemently.[63] They had powerful allies in Washington. Secretary Morgenthau was determined Chiang would not get another cent after the fiasco of the 1942 'loan'. The KMT still had $460 million of unpledged funds in the USA, and everyone knew blatant cases of corruption; for example, Madame's nephew Kung had been given $867,000 for his personal use. FDR sent Morgenthau's exasperated comments on to the generalissimo. He responded by asking that the USA pay at an artificial rate of exchange (20 times the market rate) for the construction of the B-29 airfields in China. For Morgenthau this was the last straw. 'They're just a bunch of damn crooks,' he wrote.[64]

The reputation in Washington of Chiang and the Kuomintang had never been lower. Influential voices were heard demanding that Lend-Lease to China be cancelled, that Washington withdraw all its missions from Chungking and sever all contacts with Chiang, or at the very least that the US government find a new leader to replace the generalissimo.

It was pointed out that instead of the $1 billion Chiang was seeking, it would be far cheaper to spend a tenth of that sum in organising a coup that would overthrow him.[65] In this perfervid atmosphere Stilwell thought it worth sounding out FDR on his intentions. Did the cancellation of BUCCANEER signal a total change of policy towards China? Alas for Stilwell's hopes, the interview with Roosevelt on 6 December followed the same pattern as previous encounters. The President drawled on garrulously without coming to any point, and Stilwell went away disgusted and despising his commander-in-chief even more: 'the man is a flighty fool . . . hopeless outlook'. He did point out to FDR that it was now his unsavoury duty to follow Chiang back to Chungking and tell him that the Allies had reneged on their promise, which would of course then let him off the hook. All FDR could suggest was sweetening the pill by promising to fly more materiel in over the Hump, now that BUCCANEER was not competing for resources. A disillusioned Stilwell confided to his diary that after what he had seen of diplomacy close up, he would rather drive a garbage truck.[66] The plain fact was that after all that had happened – enough to discredit any other leader a dozen times over – Roosevelt was *still* not prepared to abandon his impossible dreams for China. But if Stilwell could not find a way of budging the intransigent Chiang and the President would not help him, his close contacts with Marshall at Cairo had won him some significant victories. The GALAHAD force, originally assigned to Wingate, had now been returned to him, and he still retained direction of the USAAF units in the CBI theatre, despite Mountbatten's insistence that they should be under his direct command.[67] He flew back to Chungking via Basra, Karachi, Delhi and Chabua, starting the journey on 8 December and arriving on the 12th.

It was now Stilwell's intention to take his army into action and spend as much time as possible at the front, away from the putrid atmosphere of Chungking. His first interview with Chiang was predictably sterile. The generalissimo refused to allow Yoke force [Y-force] to fight in Burma as long as the Allies would not make a landing in the south of the country. All the indications were that the Chinese Communists under Mao were gaining in strength and no longer feared Chiang's military capability. The Soong sisters confided to Stilwell that Chiang was becoming increasingly unpredictable and difficult to deal with, but neither they nor anyone else could put a dent in his obduracy.[68] On 16 December Stilwell saw for himself how bad things were. In a second, and longer, interview Chiang reiterated all his tired old tenets. He intended to stand on the defensive and let the Japanese attack him. His ideal scenario would be for the British to invade Burma, become bogged down and then for large-scale US forces to intervene to help their ally out; meanwhile Chiang would conserve Yoke force intact. When Stilwell pressed him on why he would never take the offensive, he said that he required a three-to-one manpower advantage over the Japanese to be sure of beating them. Stilwell pointed out that he already had that, as there were only five enemy divisions in Burma. No, eight, Chiang corrected him. Stilwell showed him chapter and verse from his intelligence reports, indicating no more than five Japanese divisions, but Chiang was adamant that there were eight, and would not be gainsaid on the point.[69] Seeing his chief of staff's dejection, Chiang for the first time proposed that Stilwell be given full powers to use the troops trained at Ramgarh and actually put this in writing. This meant Stilwell had total command of the two Chinese divisions trained at Ramgarh (X- or Ledo force). His plan was to cross the Salween and engage the enemy in eastern Burma. He prepared to leave for the jungle and wrote jubilantly to his wife: 'Put down December 18, 1943 as the day when for the first time in history a foreigner was given command of Chinese troops with full control over all officers and no strings attached.' On 20 December he left for the front. 'Off for Burma again. Under better auspices than last time. Can we put it over?'[70]

Despite Stilwell's sanguine attitude, a judicious conclusion on the events of autumn 1943 and the 'conference season' would be that he was only just holding his own against his many enemies, and that only the unwavering support of Marshall really sustained him. On the plus side, Roosevelt was definitely becoming disillusioned with Chiang; to an extent the debacle of the Cairo conference had opened his eyes. The generalissimo further blotted his copybook at the end of 1943 by truly asinine replies to FDR's post-Cairo memos.[71] There were distinct signs by New Year 1944 that the President was getting tough with the Kuomintang. He turned down contemptuously the generalissimo's request for a new loan, though as a face-saver he allowed him to send a delegate to Washington to discuss exchange rates and the artificial pegging of the Chinese currency against the dollar. More immediately

– and more worryingly for Chiang – he announced that US Army expenditure in China would henceforth be limited to $25 million a month.[72] Thus far events seemed to be swinging in Stilwell's favour. On the other hand, Vinegar Joe had narrowly escaped recall to Washington by the fortuitous coincidence of the Soong and Chinese army conspiracies. Stilwell's great qualities aside, he had no skill as a politician. Machiavellianism was not in his make-up, and he compounded his problems with Chiang by, so to speak, fighting on a second front against his British allies. The Limey-bashing continued apace, fuelled by a viscereral distaste for British colonialism. Stilwell confided to his associate Frank Dorn that the riot of starving refugees he had seen at Indaw in 1942 had permanently disgusted him and convinced him that he was witnessing the last days of the British Empire.[73] Yet a more circumspect, less call-a-spade-a-spade man might have decided that he could not realistically wrangle with the British and the generalissimo simultaneously. Marshall warned him at Cairo that calling Chiang 'the Peanut' might relieve his feelings but did little to advance his status with the generalissimo. When Stilwell protested that he never called Chiang 'the Peanut' openly, Marshall lost patience with his friend: 'My God! You have never lied. Don't start now . . . Stop talking to your staff about these things.'[74]

Moreover, Stilwell, a classic love-him-or-hate-him personality, seemed to make new enemies every day. The antipathy of Hopkins, Soong and Joseph Alsop might seem small beer alongside the support of Marshall, Stimson and Theodore White (an infinitely more talented journalist than Alsop), but this trio nonetheless constituted a deadly menace who directed a steady stream of misinformation and special pleading on China and Stilwell to the Oval Office.[75] Marshall did his best to offset Alsop's influence in the USA. When Roosevelt wanted to give Alsop a commission in the US Army, Marshall launched a blistering attack on him for arrogance and stupidity, vehemently opposing the presidential move. He may have thought that Roosevelt would not snub him by using his prerogative as commander-in-chief and appointing Alsop anyway, but that is precisely what FDR did.[76] Apart from this trio, Chennault was a daily gadfly but he was gaining adherents among US diplomatic personnel. Colonel James McHugh, US naval attaché in Chungking, was another enemy, who as far back as October 1942 had written to his superiors in Washington to press for

Stilwell's dismissal and his replacement as Commander-in-Chief, China, by Chennault.[77] And with Mountbatten's arrival had come another jealous rival in the shape of Al Wedemeyer. Initially reluctant to serve under Mountbatten as his US liaison officer, Wedemeyer was persuaded to accept the 'poisoned chalice' by promotion to major general.[78] Stilwell, to his own cost, always underestimated the wildly ambitious Wedemeyer and failed to spot the scope of his enmity. He minuted that Wedemeyer's skills were limited to staff work and he was useless as a putative field commander, but in fact Wedemeyer had achieved some success in combat operations in Sicily and had been singled out for praise by no less a figure than General Patton.[79] The most accurate criticism of Stilwell is that he was a polarising figure, who never truckled and therefore never went in for the grubby compromises that are the stock-in-trade of politics. If he really wanted to bring Chiang to heel, he had to make sure that all US political and military personnel presented a united front alongside him. Sadly, he never even attempted such a 'coalition of the willing'.

Before the Cairo conference the Allies had had ambitious plans for Burma and had envisaged an attack in seven places. The British and Indian forces would occupy the Maryu peninsula in Arakan, seize the Andaman islands, make airborne drops with India-based parachute regiments, promote large-scale LRP activity by Wingate and make a diversion across the Chindwin to distract Japanese attention from Stilwell's activities in the north. The Chinese meanwhile would advance from Ledo (with Myitkyina as the ultimate objective) while the army at Yunnan would penetrate into the Lashio-Bhamo area. Such an offensive would be bound to paralyse the four Japanese divisions in Burma. As a result of the decisions taken at Cairo and Chiang's peevish reactions, this super-ambitious strategy was whittled down to two immediate and two longer-term aims. The immediate objectives would be the attack on the Arakan and Stilwell's advance from Ledo, with the LRP and Chindwin operations scheduled for a little later.[1] Stilwell was accordingly the first into the fray. Buoyed by his position as absolute commander of the Ledo force, he was also delighted by the progress of the Ledo road. A new director of the project had been appointed in October 1943, a man after Stilwell's heart named Colonel Lewis A. Pick, known to his troops as 'Old Mud and Guts'; the road itself became known as 'Pick's Pike'. Establishing round-the-clock shifts and insisting that all personnel, whatever their expertise, do stints with pick and shovel, the aptly named Pick drove the project forward with ferocious energy.[2] The first US combat units also arrived, including a crack anti-aircraft battalion to provide the road-builders with protection from Japanese air attack. When Pick promised to complete a military highway to Shingbwiyang by 1 January, even Stilwell was sceptical, but Pick proved as good as his word. By fiendish willpower he had enthused the workforce and conquered mountain passes and gradients thought insurmountable. Pick was yet another unknown and unsung hero of the Burma campaign. It was his energy that ensured that by 27 December 1943 the road stretched 103 miles from Ledo and that the most difficult stretch of all, over the Patka mountains, had been conquered. The one snag with the Ledo road was that the longer it became, the more troops had to be detached to guard and maintain it, lessening the numbers of combatants at the front.[3]

In October 1943 the Chinese 38th and 22nd Divisions, under generals Sun and Liao, were transferred from Ramgarh to Ledo. Stilwell's strategy was to seize the airstrip at Myitkyina, the key to airpower in northern Burma, and to advance on 'Mitch', as the Americans called it, through the Hukawng and Mogaung valleys, to be coordinated with a British advance from Imphal to Indaw across the Chindwin. Stilwell was preoccupied with the negotiations that would culminate in the Cairo conference, so left the command of the armies to General H.L. Boatner, who unfortunately at once fell foul of Sun. The two men argued about the real strength of the Japanese in the Hukawng valley. Sun claimed that the Japanese forces there were formidable, but Boatner waved away his objections by airily remarking: 'My dear fellow, you don't have to fight; just march in!'[4] It turned out that Sun was right. Part of the problem was that, with the notable exception of Mountbatten, whose training had made him peculiarly sensitive to signals, the approach of the Allied generals to intelligence was amateurish. Stilwell relied almost entirely on OSS agents working with the Kachins, while Giffard despised information obtained by cracking codes, either because he did not believe in its efficacy or because, as someone else notably remarked, 'gentlemen do not read each other's mail'. Mountbatten received a constant stream of MAGIC (diplomatic) and ULTRA (naval and military) intercepts, but some authorities claim that decipherment played less of a role in the struggle with the Japanese than in the war in the West. On the one hand, the Japanese did not use enciphered messages nearly as much as the Germans, and on the other intercepted naval traffic, a vital tool in the US victories at Midway, Leyte Gulf and elsewhere, was of little importance in the CBI theatre.[5] This failure was serious in the case of the Hukawng valley, for in fact some of the Japanese crack regiments, veterans of the Singapore campaign, were there, preparing a bridgehead across the

Turung river, ready for a projected invasion of India. Whatever the exact reasons for the failure of intelligence, when Boatner's estimates of enemy strength proved false, Sun lost confidence in him and asked Stilwell to remove him. Stilwell at first thought Sun was playing games to mask a secret order from the generalissimo to go slow. But when he arrived at the front on 21 December, he found the advance already a month behind schedule and the Japanese at Yubang Ga, where the Ledo road would cross the Turung. The Chinese 112th Regiment (from 38th Division) had got itself into a trap, and Boatner and Sun had been unable to relieve it.[6]

The arrival of Stilwell transformed matters overnight. For the next seven months, apart from frequently intrusive SEAC meetings, he spent his time with his troops in the jungle. For this he was much criticised, just as he had been when he elected to trek out of Burma in May 1942. There were gibes about 'the best three-star company commander in the US Army' and the 'platoon war in Burma', but Stilwell was convinced that only his personal leadership would do the trick in this instance. All the best authorities agree that he was right. Slim noted that Stilwell's decision was controversial but was the right one, since the Chinese would fight hard under him but not other-wise.[7] Stilwell dismissed his lacklustre commanders, reprimanded Sun for putting personal animosity above the common struggle, exhorted his troops in a way only a Chinese-speaker could, and coordinated the hitherto ramshackle advance. The army surgeon Gordon Seagrave testified that wherever Stilwell went, something happened, or as Slim put it: 'The Chinese really began to get their tails up. For the first time they were attacking and defeating a modern army – something that had never before happened in the history of China.'[8] Slim was refer-ring to the dramatic events of the last week of December, when fierce fighting drove the Japanese out of Yubang Ga. The 38th Division lost 315 killed and 429 wounded, but their costly victory was their first in Burma.[9] And it was not gained against second-raters, since the crack Japanese 18th Division was commanded by one of its ace generals, Shinichi Tanaka. Stilwell, aping Richard the Lionheart as he so often did, was in the thick of the action and censured for it; he could have been hit by sniper fire. To the horror of the US advisers, the Chinese celebrated their victory with a parade of Japanese heads stuck on bamboo poles.[10]

Stilwell's tactics were to press the enemy frontally while the real attack came through the jungle from the flank, with a roadblock well behind. He liked to use a series of short hooks, arguing that the 'hook' was more efficacious than long-range penetration. His tactics were in a sense the mirror image of those used by the Japanese themselves in 1942, but then, as Slim pointed out, Stilwell 'was one of the Allied commanders who had learnt in the hard school of the 1942 retreat'.[11] He aimed to envelop the foe in packets and annihilate them, at this stage in proceedings using a sledgehammer to crack a nut (always sending an entire Chinese regiment against a single Japanese company) and ensuring that if a Japanese company was to be liquidated, one of the rawer Chinese regiments should be sent in to finish the job. But here he was up against the ingrained culture of the Chinese army, for military lore enjoined that one should respect Sun Tzu's dictum and leave a surrounded enemy an escape route.[12] For this reason the Chinese proved markedly reluctant to surround the enemy and fight a fierce battle to the death, preferring instead to form U-shaped ambushes with a way of escape. To encourage them to adopt his new methods, Stilwell attached US advisers or 'commissars' to each regiment; they had no powers of military veto but could influence what happened through the power to veto or delay supplies. Equipped with radio sets, the commissars kept Stilwell informed of what was really happening so that he could checkmate the lies of indolent Chinese commanders. Stilwell had hoped that the Chinese trained at Ramgarh would form a 'New Model Army', and to an extent his optimism paid off. But the improvements in Chinese morale were incremental and gradual. All the training and equipment in the world did not enable them to shake off a fundamental conviction that, man for man, the Japanese were markedly superior. And it was difficult in a short time to transform the attitudes and calibre of corrupt and scrimshanking officers. Moreover, at a deep psychological level, the Chinese would always opt for Sun Tzu over Stilwell, which was why, again and again, Stilwell's carefully baited traps were sprung by his own troops.[13]

The greatest boon Stilwell conferred on his own men was his personal presence. Never was leading by example so well illustrated. He had his combat headquarters in the woods in a bamboo hut or tent, where he slept on a hammock, and lined up for 'chow' like the rest of the men. Hearing of his presence at the front, the Japanese put a price on his head if taken alive. He won the Chinese over by his solicitous regard for the wounded, so unlike the practice of their own commanders; his medical officers reduced the death rate from wounds to 3.5 per cent. He seemed to be everywhere, bullying, flattering, cajoling, shaming, bribing, goading. He issued unit citations and decorations and encouraged his men to be prodigal with ammunition, telling them that airdrops would bring further supplies over and over again.[14] He involved his fliers intimately in the work of the army they were supplying by insisting that all pilots had to spend time on the ground at the front to learn how bad conditions really were. After a few days on a diet of Spam and water, the 'fly boys' took great risks to supply the men on the ground; they flew every day, in all kinds of weather, even when there were clouds on the treetops.[15] The previous friction between Stilwell and General Sun was soon forgotten, as Sun jubilantly recorded that 'the Chinese soldier has a tried and true record, now that he has been given a chance to prove what he can do when placed shoulder to shoulder with his ally and on equal terms with the enemy'. Neither Stilwell nor his commissars saw any reason to disagree.[16] By February 1944 the Chinese had cleared the Japanese out of the Taro valley on the east bank of the Chindwin and removed a potential threat to the Ledo road in the Hukawng valley, since the two valleys were separated only by a range of jungle-clad hills. They now pressed on to the head of the Mogaung valley. The objective was the main enemy base at Mainkwan in the Hukawng valley. Progress was slower than Stilwell would have liked. 'God give us a few dry days and we can go,' he wrote on 1 February. But the elements were against him. In this, the supposedly dry season, Burma experienced freak rainfall. There were 12 rainy days in January, 18 in February, and 10 each in March and April, providing a total of 175 inches in four months, and all this before the monsoon season proper opened.[17]

It was particularly frustrating for Stilwell, who was in his element with jungle warfare, to have to shuttle to and fro with Delhi on SEAC business. It was even more irritating that, having freed himself from Chiang and the spider's web of intrigue and inertia in Chungking, he should have been pitched into a series of conflicts with Mountbatten. The Supreme Commander's ambitions to be a second MacArthur and to have a streamlined Anglo-American organisation under him were largely to blame for engendering a series of clashes with his deputy. The largely unseen evil genius responsible for ratcheting up the tensions was Mountbatten's American deputy chief of staff Albert Wedemeyer, a frighteningly ambitious general in his forties. Secretly a dyed-in-the-wool Chiang supporter and after the war a prominent member of the China lobby, Wedemeyer was shifty, calculating and devious.[18] Initially reluctant to serve under Mountbatten, he was talked into it when he realised the post could be a springboard for his vaulting ambitions. Fundamentally anti-British, Wedemeyer had made his contempt for the 'Limeys' clear when General Carton de Wiart corrected his American pronunciation of 'schedule' ('sked-ule') and asked him where he had learned to talk in such a way. 'I must have learned it at shool,' Wedemeyer shot back.[19] But he was shrewd enough to see that there was purchase to be made from the deep underlying friction between Mountbatten and Stilwell. An ally of Chennault and secretly loathing Stilwell for his attitude to Chiang, Wedemeyer realised that Stilwell had a host of enemies (FDR, Chiang, Mountbatten, Giffard, etc., etc.) and that only General Marshall stood between him and disaster. With Pownall no great fan of Stilwell either, there was no one on Mountbatten's staff to argue the case for Vinegar Joe's considerable merits. The fact that Brigadier General Benjamin Ferris, chief of staff of Stilwell's rear echelon in Delhi, was also violently anti-British and disloyal to Mountbatten scarcely helped matters.[20] Wedemeyer therefore swallowed his anti-British feelings and impressed Mountbatten as a doughty ally: 'He is 100% loyal and straightforward,' the Supreme Commander wrote. Another to receive praise was the American general Raymond Wheeler, 'one of the nicest men I have ever met' according to Mountbatten.[21]

Mountbatten made many enemies by the way he tried ruthlessly to drive through his notion of an Anglo-American command where he would be a real supreme commander or generalissimo, and it is true that he sometimes behaved as if the CBI theatre was his own private war. But, with all his faults, he was never a negligible figure and proved it by his high talent for public relations. His contacts with Lord Beaverbrook enabled him to place favourable stories about SEAC in the British press. He tried to use his friendship with Eden to have a special Cabinet position created with responsibility for the war in Asia. This idea foundered on the rock of Churchill himself. The Prime

Minister was adamant that he wanted no publicity about SEAC until he was in a position to feed the public daily stories about glorious victories. Mountbatten even tried to bring pressure to bear on Auchinleck to visit the Burma front, but Auchinleck, unwilling to be a pawn in Mountbatten's publicity game, responded gnomically that the distance from Delhi to Assam was as far as from London to Leningrad.[22] But Mountbatten did score two signal successes. He took on Frank Owen, the brilliant young editor of the London *Evening Standard*, as the Delhi-based editor of a new newspaper for his entire command, named *SEAC*. A beguiling mixture of gossip from home and other-ranks chit-chat, *SEAC* became hugely popular and Owen himself a key player in the Mountbatten enterprise. The appointment of Owen even survived a spirited attempt by the Minister of War, P.J. Grigg – an old enemy of Mountbatten – to blacken the editor in Churchill's eyes by pointing to his known left-wing and anti-Conservative politics. On this occasion Churchill allowed expediency to overrule ideology, and Owen was confirmed.[23] The other area of public relations where Mountbatten evinced outstanding flair was in morale-boosting, or, as his enemies said, self-promotion. Taking a leaf from Monty's book, Mountbatten took to addressing the rankers from a soapbox, trying to take them into his confidence, cracking jokes and assuring them that their progress was being watched with loving interest by Churchill and the royal family; the Indian troops were particularly impressed by his royal blood and connections.[24] He turned the idea of the 'Forgotten Army' to advantage by telling the troops that the important thing in any race was to finish fast; they might be forgotten now, but by the end of the war their fame would eclipse that of the Desert Rats and the Eighth Army. He was convinced that their 'Forgotten Army' status was an important psychological reason for their conviction that the Japanese were invincible.[25] With his officers he tried the age-old Napoleonic stunt of having a file on every senior officer and memorising all their personal details before meetings, making each of them think he had a unique relationship with the Supreme Commander.

But alongside these talents Mountbatten had faults that perhaps outweighed them. The most fundamental was that he was restless and impatient – disastrous qualities in a commander whose role called for superlative diplomatic skills. The constant desire to press on and cut corners manifested itself in other aspects of his life. To his reputation as an appalling driver he now added that of an incompetent pilot. Thinking that there was nothing to flying and that aeronauts tried to cover their vocation in mystique, he foolishly tried to take over the controls of a USAAF plane in mid-flight and nearly crashed it. But it could not be denied that Mountbatten had style. He made good his pathetic performance in the air by sending a charming and perfectly judged letter to his American colleagues afterwards.[26] Another thing that incensed his co-workers was his hypocrisy. Flamboyant himself, he hated showmanship or larger-than-life qualities in others; one of the things he disliked about Admiral Somerville was that the man had a rapier-like wit. But he could charm people and make them think that his purposes were theirs. He took on Air Chief Marshal Philip Joubert de la Ferte as his chief of public relations and psychological warfare. Joubert was a stiff-backed RAF officer who had commanded the 'Cinderella' of the RAF, Coastal Command, in the first part of the war, and initial overtures to him were unpromising, with Joubert regarding Mountbatten as a jumped-up whippersnapper. But Mountbatten persevered, deeply impressed by the skill with which Joubert had had Coastal Command immortalised in wartime documentaries, with music by Vaughan Williams. Joubert finally agreed to take the job with the Supreme Commander, worked well with him and was accounted a great success.[27] Mountbatten's showmanship was also linked in some quarters with a somewhat sneering and depreciative stance on his movie-loving side. It is true that his diaries reveal a star-struck aspect that some might consider inappropriate. For instance, on 10 January 1944 he noted that one of his American pilots was Jackie Coogan, who starred as the child in Chaplin's film *The Kid* and with whom he and Edwina had made a home movie in Hollywood when Coogan was five. And on 25 February he positively salivated when recording the lunch he had just had with the beautiful Paulette Goddard on her way to entertain US troops in China.[28] But a lot of the criticism of him on these lines was plain snobbery, in an era when educated people did not yet appreciate the power or significance of the 'Seventh Art'. ABC Cunningham, for instance, always a man for a quip and who had remarked that the new admiral (Mountbatten) at the Cairo conference was certainly at sea, viewed the Supreme Commander's enthusiasm for the silver screen as simply a transmogrified version of his egomania. Cunningham went to see the propaganda film *Burma Victory* and reported: 'The Supreme Commander and his staff, and Slim and his staff, doing film-star work made me physically sick.'[29]

Mountbatten's aspirations to turn the job of supreme commander into something like a Roman proconsul brought him into almost daily conflict with his commanders-in-chief Peirse, Giffard and, especially, Somerville. But in such cases he could always appeal directly to Alanbrooke and beat down their opposition. With Stilwell it was different. Although he was in theory Mountbatten's deputy, it was an open secret that the real decision-maker in all things concerning Stilwell was Marshall, and Mountbatten had originally campaigned for Marshall to have no say in SEAC, just as Churchill had no say in the activities of MacArthur in the Pacific. The end of 1943 and the begining of 1944 saw Stilwell and Mountbatten locking horns over three issues, with Mountbatten emerging the victor by 2–1. For the first few months of Mountbatten's incumbency, the USAAF 10th Force under General George Stratemeyer was outside the SEAC system and reported not to Peirse but to Stilwell. On one occasion Mountbatten gave Stratemeyer an order, which Stilwell immediatedly countermanded, neglecting to inform the Supreme Commander of this for 24 hours.[30] Finding this intolerable, Mountbatten wrote to Field Marshal Dill in Washington to get Stratemeyer's independence annulled. This was formally agreed at the Cairo conference by Marshall and General 'Hap' Arnold, C-in-C USAAF, and in return Mountbatten agreed to switch control of GALAHAD force from Wingate to Stilwell. On his return from Cairo, Mountbatten insisted on immediate integration of the US air force, but both Stilwell and Stratemeyer claimed a right of appeal to Washington. Mountbatten refused to allow them to appeal over his head and insisted they cable him with their objections, which he would send on to Washington with rebuttals. 'It is time we had a showdown,' he wrote in his diary. 'I do not believe the US Chiefs of Staff will reverse my decision. I know it is really essential for the future conduct of the war.'[31] He sent on the correspondence to the American Joint Chiefs, together with supporting letters from Wedemeyer and Wheeler, so that Stilwell and Stratemeyer could not turn the issue into a Limey-bashing one; he also included his own proposal to appoint Stratemeyer as Peirse's second in command. This, together with the US chiefs' reluctance to reverse an explicit undertaking they had given at Cairo, did the trick. Stratemeyer, having proved his loyalty to Vinegar Joe, accepted the ruling happily and thereafter worked efficiently with Peirse. But he took a mild revenge of a kind by displaying in his office a cartoon showing himself at his desk surrounded by the pictures of seven men, all of whom could give him orders in one capacity or another: FDR, Marshall, Hap Arnold, Chiang, Mountbatten, Stilwell and Peirse.[32]

Stilwell was angry about the Stratemeyer decision, which he saw as one of Mountbatten's 'sly tricks'.[33] There was a confrontation waiting to happen and it came at a SEAC meeting where the partisans of the two men were fairly evenly split: Ferris and Merrill in Stilwell's corner and the three American 'apostates', Daniel Sultan, Wheeler and Wedemeyer in Mountbatten's. When Mountbatten suggested moving certain American units into the Hukawng valley to help the offensive there, Stilwell cut in brusquely: 'I should like it placed on record that I am responsible for the training of all American forces in this theatre and I am the person to decide when they are adequately trained and can move forward.' Mountbatten replied: 'I accept that in principle, but would remind you that these troops are being trained under British officers. I am responsible for operations and will decide when units move into the fighting lines. In other words, general, I should like to place on record that I am Supreme Commander out here and what I say goes.' This was fighting talk, but Stilwell took it good-humouredly and laughed. 'We none of us dispute that,' he said emolliently.[34] But in a letter to his wife, he revealed his real attitude. Referring scathingly to Mountbatten as 'the glamour boy', he went on: 'He doesn't wear well and I begin to wonder if he knows his stuff. Enormous staff, endless walla-walla but damn little fighting . . . And of course the Peanut is unchanged. The jungle is a refuge from them both.'[35] One of the problems was that whatever initial entente there was had gone. Stilwell was irritated by Mountbatten's compulsion to disagree with or qualify everything he said, and Mountbatten in turn was irritated by the reports of outrageous anti-Limey remarks and Stilwell's tendency to disparage absent British commanders. Stilwell had something of an obsession about generals who would not stand and fight, usually branding them as cowards, and on one occasion placed Alexander in this category. Mountbatten responded that all Alexander had done was retreat the length of Burma, which was precisely what he, Vinegar Joe, had done, yet nobody called him a coward.[36]

Irked by the Supreme Commander's attitude, Stilwell next produced a masterpiece of counteroffensive. In terms of Chiang's troops, Stilwell was a temporary corps commander of the newly formed Northern Combat Area Command (NCAC), while under the SEAC structure he was deputy supreme Allied commander. His biographer comments: 'The situation was like that of the Lord Chancellor in *Iolanthe* who tangled with himself as suitor to his own ward and wondered whether he could give consent to his own marriage, or marry without his own consent, and in that case could he cite himself for contempt of his own court?'[37] The situation was about to get even more tangled. When at the next January meeting Mountbatten announced that Slim would command in the Arakan and oversee the LRP operations while Stilwell continued his campaign in the north, with the proviso that both came under the operational control of General Giffard, Stilwell protested and dug his heels in. It was an open secret that he despised Giffard as exactly the kind of craven general he had so often denounced. Slim, who was at the meeting, described Stilwell's bitter resistance. 'When that old man resisted anything it was a dour business. Dour, yet not without its humorous side. To watch Stilwell, when hard pressed, shift his opposition from one of several strong-points he held by virtue of his numerous Allied, American and Chinese offices, to another, was a lesson in mobile offensive-defensive.'[38] Mountbatten scarcely knew what to do. He pointed out that if his own position meant anything, then logically Stilwell should come under Giffard. Stilwell riposted that as commander-in-chief of Chinese forces, he must be answerable only to the generalissimo. Moreover, he lacked President Roosevelt's consent to put himself under a British commander. While Mountbatten was digesting this, Stilwell produced his third argument, a trump card whose logic even Mountbatten could scarcely gainsay. This was that as deputy supreme commander of SEAC he was senior to anyone but Mountbatten and therefore could not possibly come under Giffard. 'The more Mountbatten, showing infinite patience, reasoned with him, the more obstinate and petulant the old man became,' Slim noted.[39] The real problem was that while Slim admired both Stilwell and Giffard, neither one could stand the other (and to add to the complications, Mountbatten cared for neither of them). Giffard, who was at the meeting and witnessed Stilwell's point-blank refusal to serve under him, behaved with dignity under provocation, and Slim kept out of the fight, which was not his, while disapproving of Stilwell's surly obstinacy.

The temperature in the room rose. The other American officers present were in a peculiarly uncomfortable position, for although officially on Mountbatten's staff, they believed in both patriotism and seniority. No American would want publicly to side with the British against his own countryman, and the American military were known to have a respect for rank and seniority rivalled only by the Royal Navy. Gradually Mountbatten became exasperated and red in the face; Slim thought he was on the brink of sacking Stilwell. 'Suddenly, with one of those unexpected gestures that I had seen him make more than once,' Slim wrote, 'Stilwell astonished everyone by saying, "I am prepared to come under General Slim's operational control until I get to Kamaing."'[40] Mountbatten, flabbergasted, queried how such an arrangement would work, while both Slim and Stilwell asked to be allowed to discuss it together in private. The two men agreed on tactical essentials: to get more Chinese divisions for the Ledo force and to use the Chindits to assist the push towards Myitkyina. Slim assured him that under the new direction Stilwell would have an entirely free hand. They shook on the deal. As Stilwell put it: 'I would fight under a corporal as long as he would let me fight.'[41] Slim later reflected: 'In practice this illogical command set-up worked surprisingly well. My method with Stilwell was based on what I had learnt of him in the Retreat – to send him the minimum of written instructions, but, whenever I wanted anything, to fly over and discuss it with him, alone. Stilwell, talking things over quietly with no one else present, was a much easier and more likeable person than Vinegar Joe with an audience. Alone, I never found him unreasonable or obstructive. I think I told him to do something he did not approve of on only two or three occasions, and on each he conformed, I will not say willingly, but with good grace.'[42] After the war, Slim added the following: 'I ought to add that Slim acted under my operational control from the end of November 1943 to the latter part of June 1944, i.e. throughout the most important part of his operations, and I never found him anything but an exemplary subordinate. I won't guarantee, however, that he didn't sometimes say hard things about me to his staff!'[43] Both men had a keen sense of humour and, on returning to the plenary session with Mountbatten, in effect turned the proceedings into comic opera or farce, doubtless reflecting their true opinion of Mountbatten's insistence on regular SEAC summits. At the end of the meeting Stilwell saluted Slim and said: 'Sir, as 14th Army commander, do you have any orders for me?' 'No, sir,' replied Slim. 'And, as deputy commander, do you have any orders for me?' 'Not on your life,' said Stilwell with a broad grin.[44]

There matters should have rested, but Mountbatten's ambitious restlessness brought on yet another crisis with Stilwell. Impatiently wargaming, he came up with another sideshow plan, dubbed PIGSTICK, which was to be a landing on the southern Mayu peninsula with the intention of cutting enemy communications with Akyab. He began assigning landing craft for an amphibious operation, but was immediately slapped down by Alanbrooke and told to return three fast tank-landing craft immediately for use in imminent Allied landings in Italy. There were two other, slower, tank-landing craft that Mountbatten hoped to retain, but his old enemy Cunningham spotted that these were still in the Supremo's possession; he requested their return and the Allied chiefs gave orders to Mountbatten accordingly.[45] Nothing daunted, the Supreme Commander simply fined down a few details of the original CULVERIN and rebranded it as an entirely new operation, to be named AXIOM. His now devoted and loyal ally Wedemeyer was sent on a mission to Washington to press the case, accompanied by another friendly US general (McLeod). The omens were scarcely propitious. On his way through London, Wedemeyer discussed AXIOM with Alanbrooke and found him less than keen. Alanbrooke employed a simple rule of thumb – will AXIOM shorten the war with Japan? – and concluded rapidly that it would not.[46] Meanwhile in Delhi Stilwell had got wind of Mountbatten's latest initiative – which he construed, not unnaturally, as an enterprise contradictory and inimical to his own offensive in China. There was another bad-tempered conference of the SEAC high command on 31 January, just before Wedemeyer left on his mission, where Somerville again annoyed Mountbatten by giving him lukewarm support and Wedemeyer exasperated Stilwell by backing Mountbatten against him. On general strategy Stilwell was infuriated to learn that AXIOM would not begin until the winter of 1944–45, when landing-craft could be

1. The British had already been fighting the Germans for more than two years when the USA entered the Second World War – the Chinese had been combating the Japanese for over four years by the time of Pearl Harbor. Japanese troops are pictured here in 1939 rushing in to attack the camp of Chinese soldiers at Vhangsha – one of Generalissimo Chiang Kai-shek's most important positions.

2. General Joseph Stilwell had as low an opinion of Field Marshal 'Archie' Wavell as of most other 'Limeys'. Their encounter in 1942 was scarcely a meeting of minds.

3. Not just the greatest British general of the Second World War but the finest commander-writer since Ulysses S. Grant. Field Marshal William Joseph Slim, 'Uncle Bill' to his troops, in typical bulldog mode.

4. Neither the British victory at Kohima-Imphal nor Major General Orde Charles Wingate's controversial 'Operation Thursday' would have been possible without massive Allied air supremacy.

5. The eccentric Wingate was probably the last leader of behind-the-lines forces who thought it necessary to dress for the part, rather like an old-style Hollywood director.

6. The jungle was supposed to be neutral but the hard-pressed Chindits rarely found it so.

7. Wingate with Colonel Philip Cochran. One of the more successful Anglo-American partnerships in Burma, the two men were nick-named 'the Wing and the Beard'.

8. 'Vinegar Joe' Stilwell grits his teeth and forces out a smile in a posed photograph with the detested 'Peanut', Chiang Kai-shek. The other rictus grin comes from Madame Chiang.

9. Stilwell was always a 'hands on' general who believed in leading his men at the front and fighting in the jungle rather than lolling at HQ.

10. 'There are no atheists in foxholes' – maybe especially in Burma where 'digging in' might mean excavating some of Burma's one hundred species of poisonous snake.

11. Made it. 'Top of the world.' Chiang Kai-shek basks in the (momentary) glory of having reached the top table. Pictured with Roosevelt and Churchill at the Cairo Conference, November 1943.

12. Admiral Louis 'Dickie' Mountbatten, here in full naval garb, was a controversial appointment as Supreme Commander, South-East Asia.

13. Treatment of the wounded in the jungle was perfunctory. Here one of the luckier victims takes a drink while he waits to be flown out to base hospital.

14. After years of being held back by the Generalissimo, Chinese forces finally crossed the Salween in May 1944.

15. The final stages of the Burma Campaign were the bloodiest, with the Japanese sustaining terrible casualties.

16. Slim at his moment of triumph. After his brilliant encirclement of the Japanese at the Irrawaddy, he returns to London to receive the nation's plaudits.

17. Another 'gritted teeth' moment. Field Marshal Bernard Montgomery wanted to be known as *the* British general of the Second World War, but in his heart 'Monty' knew Slim was the better man.

released from the European theatre. Moreover, Mountbatten urged him to abandon his ambitions to take Myitkyina before the monsoon and content himself with reaching the Mogaung valley.[47] It was all Stilwell could do to restrain himself and not explode with fury at decisions that seemed designed to avoid fighting – 'fancy charts, false figures and dirty intentions' was how he characterised the conference. Chiang had argued that he could not commit Y-force because the Allies had welched at the Cairo conference, but Mountbatten now argued that it was Chiang who was the betrayer and that it was his intransigence that precluded a credible campaign in north Burma. 'Louis wishes to welsh on an entire program' was Stilwell's gloss.[48]

Mountbatten remarked airily that if the Allied high command turned down AXIOM, he would resign and return to sea. Stilwell thought that all the talk about sea strategy via Malaya and Sumatra was simply an excuse to avoid hard fighting. He hit back by claiming that genuine cooperation between SEAC and Chiang (which emphatically meant no AXIOM) would see the generalissimo release Y-force, and that a real commitment of all Sino-British resources would mean that they could take the offensive in China in six months; it had to be realised, moreover, against AXIOM, that the European war might not in fact be over by the winter of 1944–45. At this point Wedemeyer intervened against his compatriot to say that Stilwell's projections were chimerical, that it would take at least two years to blast a passage to China.[49] There followed a series of ferocious clashes between Stilwell and Wedemeyer, whom he finally identified as a snake in the grass and a determined enemy. The Mountbatten–Wedemeyer claque greeted all Stilwell's proposals with cries of 'Impossible!' Goaded almost beyond endurance, Stilwell remarked scathingly that Clive had conquered India with just 123 men, which momentarily hushed the audience. 'Since the SEAC staff alone numbered ten times as many, this shaft was received, not surprisingly, in dead silence.'[50] Once again, the personality clashes reflected differential Anglo-American global perceptions. Almost all British politicians and generals by now regarded Burma as an expensive waste of time and Chiang as a waste of space. Churchill himself intensely disliked the idea of a campaign in north Burma, which he described as 'going into the water after the shark' or 'stripping a porcupine quill by quill'.[51] Meanwhile FDR remained adamant in his support for Chiang and had no interest in diversions to Singapore and Hong Kong, which he saw merely as Churchill's attempts to regain the British Empire. Stilwell tended to see the whole thing as simply the old Alexander–Wavell reluctance to fight: 'The Limeys take me more seriously now. But they won't fight if they can help it.'[52]

Learning of Mountbatten's plan to send Wedemeyer to Washington, Stilwell sent a rival mission of his own on ahead (five days in advance of Wedemeyer) 'to checkmate the Limeys', telling Mountbatten nothing of it and justifying it as action taken in his role as Chiang's chief of staff. He need not have bothered, for the Joint Chiefs opposed AXIOM as a colonialist venture and FDR vetoed it. As Alanbrooke had repeatedly pointed out to Mountbatten, scarcity of resources always meant that a US veto was final. Yet perhaps Stilwell's mission did achieve something, for his envoy Haydon Boatner had a private interview with Roosevelt and persuaded him to back Stilwell and the north Burma campaign to the hilt.[53] The realities of the war in the Far East dictated this. Since US strategy hinged on capturing the Luzon-Formosa-Canton triangle, and for this long-range bombers were needed, the capture of the airstrip at Myitkyina now seemed an essential goal. FDR sent a cable to Churchill to inform him that AXIOM and all its variants had been rejected. A sullen Churchill refused to accept this, and impasse loomed. The logjam was broken only with the Japanese attack on Imphal in March, which made all discussion academic: the British were forced to fight in Burma. It was to be a final irony that Mountbatten would end the war as Earl Mountbatten of Burma when he had never wanted to fight there in the first place. His immediate reaction to the Stilwell–Boatner mission was fury at what he considered treachery and disloyalty. He cabled Marshall to ask for Stilwell's dismissal. Marshall immediately contacted Stilwell and advised him to 'eat crow'.[54] To Mountbatten Marshall replied that he was prepared to go along with his request if that was what he really wanted, but he considered it ill-advised and counselled caution. Speaking of his protégé, Marshall made a determined attempt to pour oil on troubled waters: 'You will find, if you get below the surface, that he wants merely to get things done without delays . . . He will provide tremendous energy, courage and unlimited imagination to any aggressive proposals and operations. His mind is far more alert than almost any of our generals and his training and understanding are on an unusually high level. Impatience with conservatism and slow motion is his weakness – but a damned good one in this emergency.'[55]

A chastened Stilwell duly appeared in Delhi with a cable from Marshall stating that whether or not he kept his job was a decision for the Supreme Commander. Sheepishly he showed the cable to Mountbatten and one of his old cronies, General Wildman-Lushington, his chief of staff during the Dieppe debacle.[56] Mountbatten takes up the story:

> On this I came forward in as friendly a fashion as I could and fully accepted his apology and said that my chief regret at the various actions he had recently been taking behind my back was that they made the outside world think that we did not trust each other or work in close harmony. He was kind enough to say, 'I must have been mad not to take you into my confidence in the same way as you have always done to me, and I want you to know that I have always trusted you completely and I shall continue to trust you in the future.' After that we metaphorically kissed each other and went ahead and ironed out all the difficulties which had been cropping up since his departure.[57]

Soon Stilwell was free to return to his real love: jungle fighting. But the successes of January had meant heavy casualties and a drop in morale. A series of incidents convinced him that his commanders must still be receiving secret orders from Chiang to pull their punches. The most serious of these involved the 66th Regiment, which inexplicably 'went missing' for a few days and, when found, failed to execute the next orders Stilwell gave them, to block the Japanese retreat. Stilwell responded by sacking the regiment's commander.[58] Yet in general he revelled in the hardships of life at the front, as a letter to his wife makes clear: 'We eat straight rations or Chinese chow and we live where we have to and the trails are tough, but we sleep soundly and the food tastes good because we are hungry ... the jungle is everywhere and very nearly impenetrable. Yesterday on a cut trail I took three and a half hours to do three miles, tripping and cursing at every step.'[59]

Mountbatten, meanwhile, initially elated by having put Stilwell in his place, soon experienced a boomerang effect that made him realise how heavily he depended on the Americans to make his Supreme

Command meaningful. Mountbatten had made the fundamental error of supposing that US policy in the China-Burma-India theatre was simply rubber-stamping Stilwell's ideas, not appreciating that all Roosevelt's policies preceded Stilwell's appointment to China.[60] Although for the sake of amity and the alliance Marshall had ordered Stilwell to 'eat crow', he was greatly disillusioned with both Churchill and Mountbatten. To Mountbatten he sent an apparently friendly cable, which showered Stilwell with praise. He had diluted his order to Stilwell to come to heel with a terse minute to Dill, pointing out both that Stilwell had enormous merits as a fighting general and that Mountbatten had been unacceptably stirring things with Churchill out of his own megalomania. To distract attention from the British neglect of northern Burma in favour of the Prime Minister's quixotic Operation CULVERIN, Mountbatten had evidently decided to pick on Vinegar Joe. Dill passed these comments on to Churchill, who replied blithely that northern Burma would not miss out one iota because of CULVERIN.[61] This was true enough: Churchill was not doing anything for the northern Burma campaign anyway. Despite the apparent entente secured by Stilwell's eating crow on 6 March, Mountbatten brooded on the 'insult' both implicit and explicit in Vinegar Joe's independent ways and thereafter intrigued for his replacement. Stilwell now had two powerful enemies trying to oust him, Chiang in the north and 'Dicky' in the south. Much of Marshall's correspondence with the CBI theatre concerned diplomatic and subtle ways to detach Stilwell from SEAC and Mountbatten's orbit, possibly by making him commander-in-chief in China (if Chiang would allow that), with General Wheeler replacing him as Mountbatten's deputy and General Sultan as ground commander of US forces in Burma, so that 'Dicky' and Vinegar Joe would never have to come in contact. Marshall began by suggesting that Stilwell appoint Sultan to deal with Mountbatten on a day-to-day basis, and Stilwell, keen to be with his troops in the jungle, readily agreed.[62] Yet if Mountbatten thought he could intrigue to remove an American hero without the secret getting out, he was badly mistaken. Two articles in *Time* magazine in March 1944 revealed the scope of the Supreme Commander's machiavellianism and referred glowingly to Vinegar Joe, 'who probably knows China better than any brass hat in New Delhi'.[63] Within a matter of weeks Mountbatten, who prided himself on his rapport with the American cousins, became the most hated man in America. The situation became so embarrassing that Marshall had to write to 'Dicky' at the end of March 1944 like a Dutch uncle, gently suggesting that he be more diplomatic.[64]

While Mountbatten and Stilwell clashed and reclashed, Slim continued the patient process of building up the morale of the new 14th Army. As a man of some literary background he had an approach to morale very different from Mountbatten's. Where the Supreme Commander employed swagger, showmanship, dynamism and energy, Slim believed in spreading the gospel by word of mouth, patiently explaining his intentions to every unit in the army, platoon by platoon, almost man by man, adopting an approach that was both cell-like and holistic, in effect making every officer and NCO a public relations consultant.[65] Where Mountbatten was able to convey the feeling that the British Establishment and the royal family had Burma in their sights as *the* priority – necessarily an elitist approach – Slim aimed at a 'just folks' persona, stressing the simplicity, humour and credibility that would eventually make him 'Uncle Bill' in the eyes of his troops. He had a quasi-Biblical gift of evoking the faith that moves mountains, and often preached a kind of sermon based on the text 'From mud through blood to the green fields beyond' – the motto of the Royal Tank Regiment.[66] This worked well with the British-born troops, with whom he could communicate through shared language, culture, humour and general attitudes. The problem with 14th Army was that it was only one third British, with two thirds of the regiments consisting of Indians and Gurkhas in racially unmixed units, with their own NCOs but officered by Britons. To get through to the non-English-speaking troops, Slim took the trouble to learn a smattering of Urdu, Pushtu, Hindi and Nepali. He had the common touch: 'when speaking in English, Gurkhali, Urdu or Pushtu it was always as one man to another – never the great commander to his troops.'[67] The Mountbatten–Slim twin-track approach worked peculiarly well, for the caste-bound Indian troops were proud to be serving under a scion of the royal family as well as appreciative of Slim's humanity. Between them the two men raised the profile, prestige and reputation of the Indian army. There had always been a peculiar snobbery, and worse, evinced towards this body in Establishment circles. Churchill particularly disliked Indian troops, viewing them as intrinsically treacherous and disloyal. He hated to hear good things said about them, as he suspected they were merely awaiting a chance to rerun the events of the 1857 mutiny; for this reason he considered the Indian army in possession of modern weapons to be a kind of Frankenstein's monster.[68] The Indians decisively proved him wrong in Burma. Of the 27 Victoria Crosses awarded there, the Indian army won 20. Since they were intensely loyal to their officers, who in turn were imbued with Slim's 'can do' attitude, an ethos of success pervaded the entire 14th Army.

The one remaining psychological hurdle was the myth of Japanese invincibility in the jungle. To lay this to rest, Slim planned a campaign where he would enjoy such numerical superiority that he was bound to win; a single victory of this sort would prick the 'Japanese complex'. This was why he returned to the scenes of British humiliation in early 1943 and ordered another offensive in the Arakan. Stilwell and other American commentators thought this pointless, at least if there was no simultaneous amphibious operation farther south, but they missed the point, which was that Slim was seeking out an easy victory. The one obvious card the Allies had in Burma was numerical superiority. In 1943 the Japanese had five divisions there, which would increase to seven in early 1944 and later to eight, plus four divisions of their Thai allies. Thus far Slim was amply fulfilling one aim of Allied policy, which was to draw enemy manpower away from the Pacific theatre. Against this, even leaving Chiang's immobile Y-force out of the picture, the Allies could pit the three Chinese divisions Stilwell had trained at Ramgarh – 35,000 men in all – plus six British divisions and auxiliaries, not counting the Chindits and their auxiliaries. In the Arakan Slim was aiming at a two-to-one local superiority, which he hoped would be buttressed by a similar discrepancy in heavy armour and airpower.[69] His 15 Corps would attack the so-called 'Golden Fortress' across the Mayu range – a system of defences consisting of interlocking bunkers and built around three distinct bastions: a western approach at Razabil, an eastern approach at Letwedet, and the strongest position of all, the centre, based on the labyrinth of tunnels the British had encountered the year before and which had hitherto been considered impregnable.[70] Slim's plan was that 15 Corps would advance to the Maungdaw–Buthidaung road and would then bifurcate, with 5 Indian Division attacking Razabil while 7 Indian Division took Buthidaung and assailed the Letwedet bastion from the rear; both divisions would then unite for the attack on the tunnels in the centre. Careful preparations were laid. A road was built over the Ngakyedauk pass in the Mayu range, and where the pass entered the valley at Sinzweya, in a flat area of dried-up paddy fields some 1,200 yards square, corps headquarters was set up – a farrago of buildings, arsenals, petrol dumps, a mule station, an officers' shop, even a military hospital and soon dubbed the 'Admin Box'.[71]

Slim had gathered around him a cadre of trusted officers who knew his methods and had listened carefully to his lessons about concentration of force so as to have overwhelming local superiority, the crucial role of tanks, the importance of never attacking on a narrow front and the need constantly to be on the lookout for Japanese outflanking movements. A key part of his doctrine was the 'hammer and anvil'. Adopting the basic idea of the bunker, he aimed to construct defensive positions in places the enemy had to attack to keep their lines of communication open. Heavily defended, such positions would form the anvil against which the enemy would waste their forces in vain, until the time came for Slim to send in the reserves as the hammer that would deliver the *coup de grâce*.[72] Three additional factors made Slim confident of success: the Japanese habit of committing all their troops and not retaining a reserve; their reluctance to admit a mistake and cut their losses; and their appallingly idiotic habit of carrying their battle plans and marked maps into combat, so that when the British captured these documents they knew enemy intentions in detail. All these ideas Slim had often communicated to his inner circle, essentially 'Punch' Cowan, Philip Christison, Geoffrey Scoones, Frank Messervy, H.R. Briggs, C.E.N. Lomax, Douglas Gracey, Ouvry Roberts, Steve Irwin and Alfred Snelling, his supply and commissariat officer.[73] It was all the more amazing, then, that when the campaign opened in January 1944, Christison, commanding 5 Indian Division, launched exactly the kind of frontal assault on Razabil that had proved so disastrous the year before. Perhaps overconfident after a massive USAAF air assault and a huge tank and artillery barrage, he sent in the infantry, who made no progress against the bunkers. Barbed wire, bamboo stakes and withering fire from pillboxes halted the tanks and heavy artillery in their tracks. From their nests, Japanese machine-gunners doled out fearful damage.[74] Inwardly cursing Christison, Slim was in a difficult position, for if he intervened he would come across as a micromanager in the mould of Noel Irwin; he would be doing to Christison what Irwin had done to him in 1943. It was, he concluded, Christison's battle, and he just hoped and prayed he would see sense. Fortunately Christison and Briggs recovered from their mistake and on the second assault moved to the Slim orthodoxy of guile, hooks and encirclement, forcing the Japanese to counterattack. But after five days (26–31 January), the Japanese bunkers still stood firm.[75] At the end of January Christison switched his attentions from Razabil to Buthidaung and Letwedet.

Slim, who used to post photographs above his desk of the Japanese commanders he faced so that he might gain insight into their psychology by studying their faces, had always expected a counter-attack against 15 Corps. Indeed, he had worked out that the blow was almost certain to fall on the flank of 7 Indian Division on the left. But when the Japanese did launch their counterattack, he was taken aback by its size and the sheer speed of the enemy.[76] Where Slim had been tempting his foe to battle for his own short-term purposes, the Japanese counterpunch was part of a long-term, almost geopolitical objective. As some of Wingate's critics had feared, the main consequence of Operation LONGCLOTH was that it gave the Japanese ideas of their own and specifically raised the idea of an attack on India. Lieutenant General Mutaguchi Renya, victor of the Singapore campaign in 1942 and now commander in Burma, wargamed the possibility of an attack on India and won the support of his superiors in Tokyo. His thinking was that if he could brush past the British in Assam and thus reach the gateway into the subcontinent, all India would rise up to greet their deliverers, led by the pro-Japanese Subhas Chandra Bose and his so-called Indian National Army. The fall of India would mean the definitive end of the British Empire in Asia and would even allow the Japanese to link up with the Russians in Persia.[77] It must be said in passing that the Japanese geopolitical perspective was chimerical, for what was feasible in 1942 was, by 1944, after Stalingrad and Kursk, no longer so; by now the Germans were fighting for survival. Nonetheless, at the very moment Churchill was assuring Wavell that the Japanese would never invade India, Mutaguchi intended to achieve exactly that. Lieutenant General Hanaya Tadashi, commanding in the Arakan, was the stereotypical brutal Japanese officer of legend. His task was to make the British think that the counterattack in the Arakan was the appearance of the main army earmarked for the conquest of India, thus leading Slim to send up his reserves from Imphal. The operation in the Arakan was codenamed HA-GO and was intended as a feint to mask the real attack on Imphal, designated Operation U-GO. To mask U-GO convincingly, the assault in the Arakan had to be massive, and it was this that initially wrongfooted Slim.[78]

Faced with such huge and unexpected numbers, Messervy, commanding the British rear, withdrew into the Admin Box and 7 Indian Division dug itself in for what everyone knew would be a brutal, slugging encounter. Slim had no choice but to commit his reserves at Imphal to Arakan, but still hoped he could use them as the hammer if the Admin Box could hold out and provide the anvil. For 18 days battle ebbed and flowed around the Admin Box but the Japanese could make little impression, despite ferocious hand-to-hand fighting. They had expected that once the British saw their communications severed by the outflanking movement on their left, they would panic and flee, allowing the Japanese to pick off individual regiments at will and thus destroy the whole of 15 Corps. Instead, morale held and the British dug in and waited for a relieving force.[79] And now the scale of Japanese underestimation of the enemy became clear. Their arrogance and overconfidence was truly astonishing; it was almost as though they found it inconceivable that the British army could ever change its methods or tactics or that they might be facing an entirely different kind of opponent this time. Expecting to wind up the Arakan campaign in a mere 10 days, instead for 18 days they beat like oceanic waves against a towering cliff. Attacked by infantry and from the air, the garrison in the Admin Box never wavered, although casualties were terrific; the Box was so crammed with men and materiel that it was almost impossible for attackers not to find a target.[80] The Japanese came closest to success right at the beginning of the siege, when they broke into the hospital compound and shot or bayoneted many of the sick; when they were finally cleared out on 9 February, the bodies of 31 patients and four doctors were found.[81] The ferocity of the Japanese is explicable, though not pardonable, by their awareness of fighting the calendar as well as the British. Too late they realised the appalling risks they had been running with their chimerical 10-day timetable. Everything had been predicated on travelling light and seizing what they needed, but when the British did not roll over as expected, starvation loomed for the poorly supplied attackers.[82] Moreover, casualties began to mount exponentially. Yet as Slim had predicted, the Japanese refused to admit defeat and instead redoubled their effort. By 13 February Slim was confident of victory and soon 26 Indian Division began to arrive to deliver the blow from the hammer. The Japanese fought desperately during the final battles for the Box on 17–24 February, but when they withdrew they left behind them 5,000 dead.[83]

With the Japanese decisively defeated, Slim could proceed to his original objectives in the Arakan, to seize the Maungdaw–Buthidaung road and destroy the Golden Fortress. Serendipity played a hand, since the cancellation of all amphibious operations released 36 British Division for the final threefold assault. By 13 February Slim had definite intelligence from captured Japanese documents that HA-GO was a feint to draw resources from Imphal, so once Razabil and Letwedet were taken, he intended to withdraw 5 and 26 Indian Divisions to Imphal, leaving 25 and 26 Divisions to attempt the assault on the tunnels. Buthidaung fell to the British on 11 March, and soon they had severed the Japanese communications at the rear of Razabil by night infiltration by 161 Brigade. Now it was time to take the long-defiant Razabil.[84] By this time Slim had worked out how to deal with the heavily entrenched bunkers, and his system became part of 14th Army's normal practice. The problem essentially was that of trench warfare: how to achieve continuous fire, forcing the enemy to keep his head down, while your infantry gets within range. Slim's solution was to have his tanks fire surface-burst high explosives to clear the jungle around the bunkers, then delayed-action high explosives to break up the façades of the bunkers thus exposed; finally, as the infantry closed in, solid armour-piercing shot was used. As a further refinement low-flying aircraft covered the advancing foot-soldiers and tanks were used as snipers against the bunkers from the rear.[85] Even so, fanatical Japanese resistance had to be overcome before Razabil fell on 12 March after three days of inch-by-inch combat. The tunnels proved an even tougher nut to crack: the western one was taken by 36 British Division on 27 March and the eastern tunnel only after fierce fighting on 6 April. There remained one final Japanese stronghold, the so-called Point 551 – an 800-yard-long precipitous T-shaped ridge dominating the Maungdaw-Buthidaung road – which resisted three major assaults and was taken only on the fourth attempt on 4 May.[86] All Japanese opposition on the Akyab peninsula effectively came to an end. Because of the great battle of Kohima-Imphal which was still raging, it was decided to pull back from Buthidaung and concentrate around Taung Bazaar, Maungdaw and the mouth of the Naf river, where air supply would not be needed.

Slim had secured a signal victory. The battle of the Admin Box in particular was a great triumph, since the Anglo-Indian forces had for the first time decisively worsted the allegedly invincible enemy and had proved that there was an answer to Japanese infiltration and encircle-ment. The ensuing battles, moreover, had proved that the bunkers were not impregnable. All the aces the Japanese had hitherto held now looked like jokers. In their own way, as Mountbatten said, the battles in Arakan were as important as Alamein.[87] Slim was entirely justified in writing: 'It was a victory, a victory about which there could be no argument and its effect, not only on the troops engaged but on the whole Fourteenth Army, was immense. . . . The Arakan battle, judged by the size of the forces engaged, was not of great magnitude but it was, nevertheless, one of the historic successes of British arms.'[88] A British force had defeated the Japanese and followed up with a successful counterattack; the British and Indians had proved them-selves, man for man, the equal of the Japanese infantry; and most of all the myth of Japanese invincibility was shattered, leading to sky-high morale in the 14th Army. But, as always, Slim had his critics, who said that a minor victory had been talked up into a second Waterloo, that he had three-to-one numerical superiority over the enemy and therefore could scarcely have lost, and that the real winners of the campaign were the RAF and the USAAF.[89] The point about numbers can hardly be contested in aggregate, though it should be remem-bered that the 14th Army held its own even in local brushes where they did not have numerical superiority. The criticisms make no dent whatever in Slim's reputation when it comes to basic principles. The campaign vindicated his credo at every point, whether relating to a war of movement, the principle of hammer and anvil or the method for dealing with bunkers. He knew that the Japanese war of move-ment meant they had to travel lightly armed and lightly provisioned, and he calculated correctly that in a stand-off battle like that of the

Admin Box infantry and light artillery would make no impression against tanks and heavy armament. Most of all, it demonstrated that Slim's ability to take a calculated gamble was singularly well-judged. He was criticised for rushing his reserves from Imphal to Arakan just when Mutaguchi was about to strike in Assam, but he knew exactly what he was doing and had contingency plans to effect their return in time for the defence. He was a master of timing, and though committing six of the 12 SEAC divisions to the Arakan to deal with a feint, leaving only three at Imphal, looks like folly, the point is that Slim knew from his intelligence roughly when the blow on the Assam plain would fall. He calculated correctly that he could achieve the massive defeat of the enemy he needed in Arakan and still get his divisions back to Imphal in time to sustain the fresh onslaught. His management of risk was likewise outstanding, since he had acquitted himself with distinction while fighting a considerable battle in conditions of crisis management.[90]

The issue of airpower is complex and far-ranging. Slim's critics try to belittle his achievement at the Admin Box by saying that it could not have been achieved without massive Allied air support. Clearly the airlift of supplies to the Box was crucial, but airpower really came into the picture *after* the defeat of the Japanese at Sinzweya (the Box) and during the campaign to take the Golden Fortress. In the early stages of the Arakan campaign the Allies did not have that massive air superiority they were later to enjoy, and the Japanese made a spirited attempt to gain control of the air by putting up entire 100-strong fighter groups.[91] In the winter of 1943–44 the Japanese air force experienced something of a general revival, for the 7th Air Brigade and the Imperial Japanese Navy collaborated in a successful air raid on Calcutta, hitting the dockyards and destroying 10 British fighters. Buoyed by this, the Japanese put up large fighter sweeps along the entire Arakan front.[92] The RAF tended to be complacent about its superiority to Japanese fliers, and it was thought that little would disturb the even tenor of Allied airpower, with a troika in effective action: transport planes making airdrops to the armies, bombers providing support for ground operations, and Spitfires intercepting any enemy attempt to interdict either of the first two. But on 8 February a surprise Japanese attack on the planes supplying 15 Corps, which took out two of them, forced a rethink.[93] More and more Spitfires were assigned to deal with the enemy, and two days later the RAF defiantly made 60 airdrops to 15 Corps while RAF Wellingtons and USAAF Liberators raided Rangoon. By the middle of the month Japanese air units were forced to withdraw from the skies over Arakan. Three main factors contributed to Allied air superiority. One was numerical: in the Burma-India theatre the Japanese had 370 aircraft but the Allies could call on 719. A second was the calibre of Allied planes. The Japanese Zeros and Tojos were no match for the later models of Spitfire (the V and the VIII) and lost heavily in dogfights. In the first 13 days of the battle for Arakan, Spitfires accounted for 65 enemy planes for the loss of 13 of their own.[94] A third, and not unimportant factor was cultural. The bushido honour code meant that Japanese pilots tended to see themselves as samurai of the air rather than professional masters of a new way of fighting. Honour codes meant the pilots were unable to fit armour, take advantage of cloud cover or even adopt a professional attitude to take-offs, landings and air–ground communications. The World War I mentality that only gentlemen and aristocrats should fly planes led to a shortage of pilots and even of skilled mechanics.[95] Once the amateurs in their Zeros and Tojos were swept out of the skies, Slim could resupply his armies at will, while the Japanese continued to suffer from shortages of supplies. Mountbatten showed his continuing support of Slim by diverting 25 Commando aircraft from the Hump for three weeks.[96] Without doubt airpower was crucial to Anglo-American successes in Burma, and this would be proved in dramatic fashion when Wingate at last made a return to the fray.

It was December 1943 before the stricken Wingate was fully able to return to his usual regime of harrying, exhortation and bullying. A kind of early watershed was 17 November, the date he left the Wavells at the vigeregal lodge and moved on to convalesce with Sir Humphrey Trevelyan's family. To mark his semi-return to active duty, Mountbatten invited him to lunch that day to meet Stilwell, where the trio discussed aerial back-up for the Chindits. Stilwell made it plain he did not want this to involve any diversion of planes from the Hump. Wingate promised to integrate this caveat into his overall plans for LRP.[1] It was something of an irony that for the first time Stilwell could talk to a British officer who agreed with him that too many people in the British army were lazy and defeatist. To Mountbatten and others Wingate still seemed far from well, and there were suspicions that something more than just tropical diseases was involved. One suggestion is that he suffered from *arcus senilis* – a white ring at the outer edge of the cornea that indicates degenerative processes associated with premature ageing.[2] But there was little general sympathy for him in Delhi. He had succeeded in alienating almost everyone in the regular army command; as Major General George Symes said: 'He was an egomaniac and he revelled in offending others and creating difficulties for the sheer joy of overcoming them.'[3] Apart from his habitual rudeness, two things particularly incensed the authorities in Delhi. One was his notorious description of the Indian army as 'a system of outdoor relief', which by now was common knowledge.[4] Another was his perverse talent for feeding Churchill's crazed prejudices about the Indian army and particularly his insinuation that it was a million-strong force full of idlers. Auchinleck actually went to the trouble of refuting this by a detailed breakdown of numbers, which showed conclusively that there were only 413,000 men available to fight in India. Yet facts and figures made little impression on Wingate. When he returned from his triumph at the Quebec conference, Auchinleck and his officers were forced to live 'in the rancorous atmosphere of criticism when Wingate was in the full tide of his power'.[5] The long illness removed him from the scene, but on his return he was soon back to his old habits. He always refused to engage in point-by-point debate with Auchinleck's officers, but when confronted by irrefutable logic that rebutted his theories, he simply lost his temper and said he would appeal to Churchill.[6]

While Wingate was ill, most of the planning for the next stage of LRP and the Chindits was done by his faithful lieutenant Derek Tulloch. After four months, by early December, the organisational shape of Chindits Mark Two was complete. There were to be six brigades – originally seven, but the seventh, the US 5307th Provisional Unit, under Brigadier General Joseph H. Cranston, was transferred to Stilwell by Mountbatten after the American's vociferous complaints. It was remarked by many that Stilwell showed no gratitude to Mountbatten, but simply acted as if normality had been restored.[7] The elite corps was the original 77 Brigade under Calvert, drawn from battalions of the King's Regiment, the Lancashire Fusiliers, the South Staffs, the Burma Rifles and the Gurkha Rifles. The III Brigade, under W.D.A. Lentaigne, consisted mainly of Gurkhas, with a battalion each of the King's Own Royal Regiment and the Cameronians. Then there was 70 Division, which Churchill had ordered Auchinleck to break up and distribute according to Wingate's wishes. Major General George Symes, commander of 70 Division, had agreed to stay on as Wingate's deputy, even though he outranked him, in the clear expectation that he would take over command of the Chindits if anything happened to Wingate. This was not so much self-sacrifice on Symes's part as a desire by Auchinleck that he should have his own man inside the Chindits, to limit the damage he expected.[8] Symes's division was originally part of Slim's 15 Corps at Ranchi, but when Slim was appointed commander of the 14th Army, detached from Auchinleck's bailiwick, it was retained by Auchinleck and thus no longer under Slim's command. Slim felt bitter both that he had not been consulted about this and that Wingate was being allowed to eviscerate it, for 70 Division was the showpiece of 15 Corps. It was the only British formation trained in jungle warfare and was more effective than Wingate's 1943 Chindits, which were twice its size.[9] All this was to be sacrificed for a whim of Wingate's backed by a whim of Churchill's. The division was now to be carved up, mixed with other units and divided into three brigades: 16th Indian Infantry Brigade, led by Bernard Fergusson, would comprise the 1st Battalion Queen's Royal Regiment, 2nd Battalion Leicester Regiment and detachments from the Royal Artillery and Royal Armoured Corps; 14th Brigade, under Brigadier Thomas Brodie, would be made up of battalions of the Leicestershire Regiment, Bedfordshire and Hertfordshire Regiment, York and Lancaster Regiment and the Black Watch; 23rd Brigade, commanded by Brigadier Lawrence Perowne, would take in the Border Regiment, the Essex Regiment and battalions of the Duke of Wellington's Regiment. A sixth brigade was formed from the newly arrived West African Infantry.[10]

All in all Wingate had the equivalent of two divisions at his disposal. While he languished in hospital and convalescence, Tulloch and his other henchmen put the six brigades through the usual training: forced marches, mule-handling, 'watermanship', digging, column-marching, column bivouac, patrolling, Royal Engineers signalling exercises, medical and veterinary tests, weapons training. Most noteworthy was the emphasis given to training in air supply, air support, airfield construction and glider training, for the cynics and wiseacres said that Wingate had not just been given a private army but a private air force as well. This was an exaggeration. The RAF was firmly opposed to seconding trained personnel to the Chindits and resisted all pressure, Churchill or no Churchill. The airpower Wingate relied on was almost entirely that of the USAAF, the fruit of the conversion to his theories by General 'Hap' Arnold.[11] These American 'air commandos' were under the joint command of colonels Philip Cochran and John Alison, and it was their promise of gliders that enabled Wingate to write blithely to Stilwell shortly after the 17 November lunch meeting to say that the Chindits would not need to divert any planes from the Hump. Cochran was a genuine war hero and flying ace who had uncritically imbibed the Wingate doctrine during a meeting with him in London.[12] No. 1 Air Commando Group, as the wing came to be known, was a 500-strong outfit of supply planes, troop carriers, bombers and fighters. Altogether there were 100 light aircraft, 30 P-51 Mustang fighters,

20 Mitchell bombers, 20 C-47 Dakotas, 12 larger transport aircraft, six Sikorski helicopters and 150 gliders with the promise of another 50 to come.[13] The one snag was that the air commandos were mandated for just 90 days, and no one was sure what would happen after that. 'Hap' Arnold was a sincere Wingate admirer, but he was playing political games of his own, hoping for an expansion of the power of the USAAF without going through official channels in the Pentagon. Nevertheless, his role in Chindit 2 was crucial, and in this respect it is worth noting that Wingate had a peculiar appeal for Americans, even the curmudgeonly Stilwell, on the grounds that he was the one and only 'can do' Brit.[14] This was one of the few points of agreement between Churchill and his American cousins. As his faithful Pug Ismay said: 'The waffling which has gone on over our Far East strategy will be one of the black spots in the British higher direction of the war.'[15]

Things were working out well for Wingate, but he was irrationally annoyed that he had been out of action for so long and had been in semi-helpless convalescence while great decisions were being taken at the Cairo conference. His habitual rudeness and bad temper reached new heights in December 1943, and even loyal supporters like Tulloch found him almost unbearable.[16] The many tantrums Wingate threw at this time gave new meaning to the term prima donna. His erstwhile supporter General Wilcox, who had given him invaluable help when Wingate was under Central India command and thus under Wilcox, was one of the first to feel the verbal lash. Assuming that Wingate would not be fit to resume duties until January 1944, Wilcox had helpfully (as he thought) put into effect a contingency exercise code-named WASP. When Wingate came roaring back into action, he ordered the original Operation THURSDAY, code for Chindit 2, to be implemented, only to find that the army had done a lot of work on WASP and did not want all their efforts wasted. With supreme ingratitude both for this well-meaning effort and his previous generosity, Wingate denounced Wilcox to Giffard as an incompetent. Essentially a weak man, Giffard lacked the stomach for a fight with Wingate and let him have his way.[17] There were many other angry scenes and confrontations as 'all or nothing' Wingate gathered his strength. There was always bad blood between him and Lentaigne, and Wingate went out of his way to humiliate his brigade commander. After one exercise Wingate called his officers together in a cinema in

Gwalior to discuss what they had learned. He asked Lentaigne to take the meeting and Lentaigne presided diplomatically. Suddenly an exasperated Wingate decided that Lentaigne was not being 'tough' enough and impatiently announced he would chair the meeting himself. On another occasion, after flying back from Ledo to Comilla, he was enraged to find that his onward transport was not waiting for him. As the Dakota taxied forward to the dispersal pen, he suddenly assaulted his head of Operations, Lieutenant Colonel. J.F.C. Piggott and kicked him out of the open door of the moving aircraft. Even the lethargic Pownall had to do something this time, and Wingate was forced to apologise. He did so, but in a classic of the 'non-apology apology' made the following statement: 'I always used to kick my younger brother off moving buses and quite suddenly the old impulse came over me.'[18] Wingate had always thought of violence as the first, not last, resort in any situation, and the pro-Wingate clique in the Chindits had similar views. The cross-grained and intemperate 'Mad Mike' Calvert assaulted a senior officer (a lieutenant general) who had criticised the Chindits during drinks at the Delhi Officers Club. Waiting until he was leaving, Calvert charged the man and hurled him into a fountain, taking care that in the darkness he could not be properly identified.[19]

Pownall, who loathed Wingate, and Mountbatten, who at this stage thought he liked him, tried to find an outlet for Wingate's manic energies. On 17 December Mountbatten had him to stay with him and suggested a visit to Chungking to try to get Chiang to rethink his refusal to commit Y-force. On 29 December Wingate accordingly flew to China and had two meetings with the generalissimo, but was no more successful with him than any other Westerner had been; Chiang made it quite clear that there would be no Chinese advance in north Burma before November 1944, at the earliest.[20] Enraged by this, Wingate proceeded to what looked on paper as though it would be a furious encounter with Stilwell. Here after all were two men who were both notoriously abrasive – even one might say with atrocious manners – who were not prepared to be thwarted by anybody. When Wingate was told that the newly arriving American troops that had originally been assigned to him had been reassigned to Stilwell, he was incandescent. 'You can tell General Stilwell he can take his Americans and stick 'em,' had been his initial response.[21] Surprisingly, there were no fireworks at the meeting at Shingbwiyang on 3 January. It was a curiosity of Stilwell that although he habitually claimed to loathe 'Limeys' – as one commentator has put it, 'he entertained for the British people the kind of feelings a pious Nazi developed for the Jews: a spiritual disapproval informed by acute physical repulsion'[22] – and thought them systematically deceitful, effeminate but highly dangerous, with the exception of Alexander and a few others, he always found a reason to make an exception for the Brits he actually encountered, as though his repugnance was for a kind of Platonic Limey rather than the flesh-and-blood variety. On this occasion he took a shine to Fergusson, whom Wingate had brought along as an observer, and said of him drily: 'He looks like a dude but I think he is a soldier.'[23] It is thanks to Fergusson that we have a memoir of the Wingate–Stilwell meeting, highlighting the contrast between the bearded, strong-bodied, beetling-browed Wingate, who with his piercing blue eyes appeared every inch the prophet, and the wiry, gaunt Stilwell, looking quizzically from behind his steel-rimmed spectacles. Fergusson, who sat with them while the military future was discussed, thought that Stilwell too looked like a prophet and that the encounter was a kind of Biblical clash of thaumaturges, with the two men having many points in common: vision, intolerance, energy, ruthlessness, courage.[24] It worked in Wingate's favour that he was *persona non grata* with the British military establishment in India, and Stilwell knew this. So the meeting passed amicably, with Wingate promising to create a diversion soon with his LRP groups and almost hinting to Stilwell that he placed more credence in his operations than Slim's.[25]

It was Slim and Mountbatten rather than Stilwell that Wingate had in his sights during January–February 1944. The essential problem was that the Cairo conference had undone many of the decisions taken at Quebec, Wingate's high point of triumph. The encouragement and special powers Wingate had been granted then were contingent on an expected course of events, which did not materialise, but Wingate, absurdly, thought he had been given the green light for Chindit 2, unconditionally, whatever happened thereafter. It followed that any opposition or demurral to his plans had to be because of malice, envy, spite, incompetence, sabotage or Indian army *amour-propre*, not because Giffard, Slim or Auchinleck genuinely thought that LRP was an irrelevance in the changed circumstances. Many in the Indian army honestly thought that Operation THURSDAY was a chimera and would be suicidal.[26] Moreover, even some of those who suported Wingate had doubts about his leadership qualities. Major General Symes wrote in his diary: 'Wingate, although possessing boundless self-confidence, is lacking in administrative and organisation knowledge, and knowing it, has an inferiority complex on the matter.'[27] With Chiang refusing to move Y-force southwards because BUCCANEER had been cancelled, Wingate's LRP operations were now pointless. It was this that led Fergusson finally to snap and tender his resignation. He told Wingate that without the Yunnan offensive from Chiang, the second Chindit expedition would simply be a disastrous replay of the first. A shaken and angry Wingate remonstrated with him vociferously and finally prevailed on Fergusson to withdraw his resignation. Wingate saw clearly enough that if one of his own devoted lieutenants publicly expressed doubts about THURSDAY, its credibility would be irretrievably destroyed.[28]

Yet because the orders given him at Quebec had not been formally cancelled (doubtless through an administrative oversight), the self-centred Wingate, in defiance of all logic, continued to persist with them. At the same time, sensing the changed circumstances, the army and RAF bureaucracy, which had always loathed Wingate, revived its previous obstructiveness – hardly surprisingly since Wingate had virtually declared open war on them.[29] Suddenly Wingate found that the proposed Operation THURSDAY lacked most of the essentials for credible implementation: mules, supply-dropping aircraft, paratroops, transports and much else. His one chance was that Mountbatten, whatever his private feelings, was still on his side, as indeed he was obliged to be, since both were overpromoted Churchillian protégés and to an extent would sink or swim together. This did not stop Mountbatten complaining about Wingate and saying that he was the last thing he needed with all the other problems he had on his plate.[30] Moreover, Wingate as a 'can do' fighting general was the one clear point of agreement between Mountbatten and the Americans and a putative 'ace in the hole' in Allied attempts to get Chiang to resurrect Yoke force, whereas to disband the Chindits would appear to endorse the generalissimo's defeatism. In his attempts to patch up a peace between Wingate and the powerful bureaucratic forces opposing him, Mountbatten was helped by a foolish attempt by the RAF at overt obstructionism. At one conference RAF representatives opposed THURSDAY on the grounds that there were no radio sets in India capable of exchanging Very High Frequency messages with their planes. Tulloch broke in passionately to say that this was nonsense and that such sets did exist. At this the normally unflappable Mountbatten lost his temper and banged on the table: 'Someone here is talking nonsense.' He called in his signals officer, who confirmed Tulloch's version of the state of affairs. Angrily Mountbatten then faced down the RAF contingent: 'General Wingate has been promised certain things and while I am here I will see that he gets them. I want no more argument on the subject.'[31]

The three months December 1943–February 1944 saw Wingate locked in almost continual conflict with both Slim and Mountbatten. Slim met Wingate privately on eight separate occasions to discuss strategy, first at Delhi and later at Comilla and other locations. Wingate obviously chafed under the inconvenient circumstance that Slim was his immediate superior but acted with all the old arrogance, contumacity and contempt for hierarchy. Faced with myriad problems on all sides, Slim also had to contend with the most troublesome subordinate of his entire career.[32] The pattern was clear at a meeting at Comilla on 3 December, when Wingate demanded the use of Lomax's 26th Indian Division for his coming operations. When Slim flatly refused, Wingate replied that that could not be the end of the matter, since he owed loyalty to a higher commander. Slim queried who that might be. 'The Prime Minister of England and the President of the United States,' Wingate shot back. He told Slim that Churchill had given him secret instructions, if ever he was thwarted in his plans by a military superior, to go over their head and appeal straight to him; accordingly, he very much regretted that he must now report Slim's lack of cooperation to the Prime Minister. Slim then pushed a signal pad across the desk and said: 'Go ahead.' Wingate got up and took the pad with him, leaving Slim uncertain of his intentions.[33] It appears that Wingate decided not to contact Churchill on this occasion but stored up the refusal as ammunition for a future showdown in which he intended to involve the Prime Minister. For the rest of December Wingate was involved in work for Mountbatten, including the visit to Chiang in Chungking and, later, the conference with Stilwell. The next real contact with Slim came at an army commanders' conference on

4 January, when Chindit 2 was officially shelved as a result of the changed circumstances after the Cairo conference. Enraged, next day Wingate sent out two blistering memos, one addressed to Mountbatten, the other to 11 Army Group. The memo to 11 Army Group was a masterpiece of machiavellianism. It began by appearing to accept that the orders he had been given at Quebec could no longer be carried out, then changed tack and accused 11 Army Group of bad faith, obstructionism and withholding supplies. In both this and the intemperate memo to Mountbatten he threatened resignation if his force was disbanded.[34]

Slim's next encounter with Wingate was at Ranchi on 14 January. Again there was disagreement. Slim thought that Wingate's aerial needs should be supplied by the Americans and the planes detached from the Hump, but Wingate wanted them delivered by the Indian Parachute Regiment. Trying to lighten the tone, Slim explained that 4 Corps used a 'floater model' system by which every garrisoned base was served by a satellite mobile column trained to operate against the enemy's rear when he attacked.[35] Wingate accepted the idea with alacrity and soon passed it off as an original contribution of his own. In the course of the talks Slim was alarmed to find that Wingate's conception of LRP activities had undergone a massive change. Instead of envisaging the Chindits as a mobile super-guerrilla force, he was now arguing for seizing and defending enclaves or strongholds. His thesis was that if an offensive could not be launched across a broad front – and Slim explained why he did not have the resources for a trans-Chindwin thrust into Burma – the British could nonetheless create a series of battle-fields deep within enemy territory by establishing impregnable strongholds, backed by airpower and 'floater columns'.[36] He summed up his credo as follows: 'If we look upon the stronghold perimeter as the kid tied up to attract the enemy tiger, then we find the ambus-caded hunter in the shape of the floater columns on the grand scale and the floater companies on the minor scale. The floater columns are a strategical, the floater companies a tactical, ambuscade.'[37] In Wingate's mind the idea of strongholds came to have an almost mystical signif-icance, and the messianic fervour he once expended on Zionism was now transferred to the holy grail of enclaves. Not without many mental reservations, Slim agreed that on second thoughts he might be able to squeeze four battalions from 26 Division to garrison these strongholds, but all this would have to be on a contingency basis, with Slim reserving the right to dispose of the garrison battalions and Slim deciding when they were to be flown in – or even if they were to be flown in at all. Wingate, as usual, heard only what he wanted to hear and did not take note of these provisos and caveats. Sensing the mood of compromise in Slim, he tried to press his advantage by insisting that the four battalions train with him at Chittagong. At this Slim put his foot down and said they would stay where they were.[38]

Throughout January Wingate refined his ideas. His initial plan was for a three-brigade advance from the Central Provinces as the first wave of his assault. Calvert's 77 Brigade would proceed to the Kaukwe valley, where it would set up a stronghold blocking the Indaw–Myitkyina railway and the Bhamo–Lashio road. Lentaigne's 111 Brigade would strike out from Imphal to the country south of Pinlebu to set up a fortress that would dominate the valleys of the Wuntho and Mu. Fergusson's 16 Brigade would march from Ledo, establish a stronghold north of Indaw, from where they would attack the Bongyaung gorge and Meza bridge and seize the airfield at Indaw.[39] The idea was to establish three mutually assisting fastnesses right in the middle of enemy territory that would take the Japanese forces massive efforts to overcome. Wingate's ideas on strongholds became ever more fanatical, and he even managed to combine the language of the Old Testament with modern military phraseology. In his training notes he prefaced a mantra about the quasi-Platonic notion of enclaves with a quote from Zachariah 9:12: 'Turn you to the stronghold, ye prisoners of hope.' There followed a chant-like inventory:

> The Stronghold is a machan overlooking a kid tied up to entice the Japanese tiger. The Stronghold is an asylum for Long Range Penetration Group wounded. The Stronghold is a magazine of stores. The Stronghold is a defended air-strip. The Stronghold is an administration centre for loyal inhabitants. The Stronghold is an orbit round which columns of the Brigade circulate. It is suitably placed with reference to the main objective of the Brigade. The Stronghold is a base for light planes operating with columns on the main objective.[40]

Gradually Wingate's ideas became more and more ambitious, quixotic and chimerical. He saw no reason why eventually he should not have

100,000 men under his command. Having worn down the Japanese, who would have made repeated but futile assaults on the impregnable strongholds, his huge army would then march across Burma, into Indochina and reach the sea at Hanoi, whence it would turn north to pursue the enemy into China, possibly combining with Stilwell in a pincer movement to eliminate all Japanese forces on the Chinese mainland.[41]

It can be readily appreciated why both Slim and Mountbatten became alarmed by Wingate's progressive retreat into cloud cuckoo land. Slim's attitude to Wingate is difficult to pin down, but it is a theme that is worth pursuing, if only because too many historians have taken at face value his bland *nil de mortuis nisi bunkum* assessment in his autobiography:

> On the whole Wingate and I agreed better than most people expected, perhaps because we had known each other before, or perhaps we had each in our own way arrived at the same conclusions on certain major issues, the potentialities of air supply, the possibility of taking Burma from the north, and in our estimates of the strength and weakness of the Japanese. Of course we differed on many things. It was impossible not to differ from a man who so fanatically pursued his own purposes without regard to any other consideration or person.[42]

The true situation was rather more complex. The first thing to note is that Slim was not the normal hidebound British officer in 'Inja' who would have been troubled by eccentricity or unconventionality. Nor would he have been thrown off balance by Wingate's rudeness, for anyone who had endured Noel Irwin was well inured to that trait. Nor again did he have any objection per se to Long Range Penetration, provided it made sense in a given strategic context; Slim was, one might say, a 'horses for courses' man. And he did have a genuine appreciation of Wingate's talents, especially his ability to meld other people's ideas with his own so as to come up with a new 'emergent' synthesis (as in the synoptic vision of airpower and LRP). Part of it was that Wingate was that rare bird – a man both of thought and of action. Where Slim's theoretical mentor Liddell Hart was a pure theorist, while Mike Calvert was an unthinking man of action, Wingate was both.[43] Nonetheless, there were aspects of Wingate's thought that seriously perturbed Slim. He was bitter that Churchill had accorded the younger man such blatant favouritism, thus allowing Wingate to go outside the chain of command and appeal over the heads of his military superiors. He resented the break-up of the elite 70th Division at Wingate's whim. And he was stupefied that Wingate had been given two divisions to play with, to say nothing of the most massive air support in the form of fighters, bombers, transports, gliders and spotter planes; in other words, most of the Allied air strength in the Burma-India theatre had been allocated to him.[44] At root Slim disliked all that Wingate stood for, for he always despised the entire gallimaufry of private armies and maverick forces outside the normal military structure. As he said: 'We are always inclined in the British Army to devise private armies and scratch forces for jobs which our ordinary formations with proper training could do and do better.'[45]

Although Slim's attitude was full of nuance, fundamentally he was contemptuous of Wingate's abilities as theoretician, fighter, tactician and strategist. As he put it: 'I found Wingate stimulating when he talked strategy or grand tactics, but strangely naive when it came to the business of actually fighting the Japanese. He had never experienced a real fight against them, still less a battle.'[46] As General Symes pointed out, Wingate also lacked administrative experience or skill in logistical planning. Consequently he had not properly thought through the scale of provisions the strongholds would need to obtain by airdrop nor the heavy armament they would have to take in if they were to fight conventional battles. Slim thought that if Wingate's larger conceptions were given the nod and his brigades allowed to fight pitched battles, his Chindits would soon grow exhausted. By breaking up divisions and regiments for his own ends, he showed a lamentable lack of knowledge of human nature and the soldier's mentality, for everyone knew that regimental loyalty was primary. Slim also thought that Wingate did not learn from experience and was instead a devotee of the a priori or the *idée fixe*: 'In spite of his outstanding gifts of imagination, invention, exposition and leadership, Wingate, who had no staff training, was unsure in his control of forces in the field and too liable, having made his own picture, to read a tactical or strategical situation in its light.'[47] Worst of all, though, was the overall strategic thinking. Slim thought that the original LRP quasi-guerrilla notion of 1943 had had a certain validity in a context of low morale and Allied inactivity. But events had moved on since then, and the British army in India in early 1944 was quite unlike that of a year earlier. Auchinleck, Mountbatten and Slim himself had all contributed to the immense increase in morale and resources. Where the ideas of Chindit 1 would have been dubious in the changed situation, those of Chindit 2 were utterly fantastic.[48] Wingate justified his conceptions by claiming boastfully that he was the only Allied commander who could carry the fight to the Japanese, since Stilwell was stymied by Chiang and Slim lacked the resouces to get the 14th Army across the Chindwin. He overlooked a number of things. Slim's idea was to entice the enemy to come to him so that he could fight them on the Imphal plain, where he had the clear advantage. Instead of exploiting enemy weakness, Wingate proposed to attack the Japanese at their strongest, where communications, supply and reinforcements all favoured them rather than the Chindits. His new idea, that his Special Force should be primary and 14th Army secondary, was literally preposterous. As for the larger ambitions about extending the war to Indochina and China, Slim thought them almost self-evidently nonsensical.[49]

Beyond all this, Slim had severe reservations about Wingate as a decent moral human being. One can sense ambivalence, at least, in the following observation: 'To see Wingate in action on some hesitant commander was to realise how a medieval baron felt when Peter the Hermit got after him to go crusading.'[50] For Slim, Wingate was a bully, and he hated bullies, prima donnas, exhibitionists and those who deliberately went out of their way to give offence. That Wingate was such a man was admitted even by his friends and admirers: 'He seemed almost to rejoice in making enemies,' is how Bernard Fergusson remembered him.[51] Slim may not have gone all the way with those of his brother officers who considered Wingate an unspeakable specimen of humanity or thought him barely sane,[52] but he intensely disliked his love of confrontation, his arrogance and his assumption that only Special Force mattered, that LRP should be primary in strategy and that everything else should be subsidiary. He also considered him shifty, two-faced and unreliable, so pathologically secretive that he never confided his intentions or ambitions to anyone, including his commanders and chiefs of staff.[53] The two-facedness manifested itself in his compulsion to go behind Slim's back to Mountbatten and to go above both of them to Churchill, often taking their name in vain as he did so and claiming that they endorsed something when they plainly did not. Most of all, Slim loathed Wingate's almost reflex mendacity, which was noticed by others, including Wingate supporters. Fergusson said that often with Wingate the truth was whatever he wanted it to be at a given moment. Like Marcus Aurelius, Slim himself had a rare commitment to truth-telling, and his biographer has remarked: 'Slim was incapable of telling a lie, whether in his own defence or to harm another.'[54] As a corollary, Slim felt that all the valued items in his own moral code – trust, integrity and loyalty – were set at naught by Wingate, and after the war he said: 'In my opinion Wingate was deliberately untruthful in some of his statements, and most disloyal in the method he frequently pursued of passing such statements behind the backs of some commanders to others.'[55] Faced with this devastating appraisal, Wingate's many supporters have tried several tacks: Slim too went behind Wingate's back (Tulloch claimed he was approached in this way); Slim was devious and often illustrated the adage that the best way to tell a lie is to tell the truth (but not the whole truth); and the image of Slim the simple, ingenuous, straightbacked soldier without an ounce of guile is an obvious fraud.[56]

Whatever emphasis we finally put on the deep and even unconscious dynamic between Slim and Wingate, there is no doubt that background, context, policies and personalities all made for the most difficult of working relationships. There was another meeting at Ranchi on 19 January but it seems to have been another dialogue of the deaf, with Slim reiterating that he had the final say and the power of veto and Wingate somehow imagining that he had been given carte blanche over the four battalions.[57] But at a further meeting at Comilla on 26 January, crisis point was reached when Slim said that because of the developing situation in the Arakan, only one battalion was now available as back-up for the strongholds. Slim had always made it clear that the offer of four battalions was contingent on the overall picture in the Burma theatre and was a *provisional* offer; Wingate was adamant that he had been made an *unconditional* offer and angrily accused Slim of changing his mind and breaking his word. Slim replied that changed circumstances meant that the four battalions could be provided only if 14th Army had begun a general offensive. Wingate was not interested in an offensive by 14th Army as he thought Special Force the only thing that mattered. Slim, on the other hand, knew that the British *had* to win the battle in Arakan to raise morale and lay the bogey of Japanese invincibility. In a word, he had to be cautious, and here he was preaching caution to the high priest of audacity and even foolhardy recklessness.[58] The two men agreed to sleep on it, but on the 27th, Slim announced that after further reflection he could afford *no* battalions for Wingate. He suggested that Wingate get the men he wanted from the West African Brigade. Wingate confessed that he thought he was going mad, that he now found himself right back at the start, and in a worse situation even than when he emerged from his convalescence at the beginning of December. He composed an angry memo, bitterly critical of Slim, gave one copy to Slim and sent the other to Mountbatten, along with a passionate letter suggesting that Mountbatten cancel Chindit 2 and relieve him of his post.[59]

Mountbatten found himself in exactly the position he had long tried to avoid, caught in the crossfire between Slim and Wingate. Although he had initially been very enthusiastic about Wingate, he gradually came to accept Slim's viewpoint that Special Force was more trouble than it was worth. But he knew he had to tread carefully, for Churchill had expressly appointed him to SEAC so that he could advance Wingate's plans. Pownall agreed with him that Wingate's prerogative of right of appeal to the Prime Minister was a danger to all of them, with the doomsday scenario being that Churchill would replace Slim with Wingate as commander of 14th Army. 'This will bring the PM straight down on Giffard and Slim, for he has already expressed his doubts as to the quality of the military advice that Mountbatten has been receiving. He will jump at the chance of breaking another general or two and will then push very hard, and maybe successfully, to get Wingate installed in command of 14th Army – which would be a most dangerous affair. Wingate may (or may not) be all right as a specialist but he simply hasn't the knowledge or balance to be in high command.'[60] Mountbatten, trying to distance himself from the conflict, ordered Giffard to find a solution. Seeking a compromise, Giffard agreed to supply all the heavy artillery Wingate had been requesting for his strongholds and to release a Gurkha battalion to aid 77 Brigade in garrison work; the rest of the four battalions would be found from the 3rd West Indian Brigade. Initially reluctant – he was known to have peculiar views about the racial composition of the Chindits, accepting

Gurkhas and Burmese alongside the British but no Indians on the ground that they were 'second-rate troops'[61] – Wingate grudgingly agreed. The 81st West African Division had arrived in India in August and would be followed in May 1944 by the 82nd. Wingate was less than impressed by the Africans. On arrival in India they had caused a sensation, with the locals convinced they were cannibals. They caused hilarity by mistaking blood plasma for jam and spreading it on their biscuits.[62] These divisions from Nigeria, the grandiloquently named Royal West Africa Frontier Force, had originally been requested because it was thought that as Africans they would be natural jungle fighters. The reality was that most of them came from the desert areas of northern Nigeria, loathed the jungle and the monsoon and had a particular fear of river crossings. Nevertheless, blooded in the Arakan battles of January–February 1944, they soon proved their merit; eventually the Japanese would come to regard them as the best jungle fighters they ever opposed.[63]

Mountbatten found himself inveigled more and more into the Slim–Wingate conflict when Operation THURSDAY began in earnest in February. The original plan had been an extended version of the first Chindit raid but in two waves, with three brigades making long marches across the Chindwin and into enemy territory; then, two or three months later, the second wave would go in to reinforce the first. But when he learned of the increased availability of transport planes, Wingate became keener on the idea of flying brigades in. One of his first ideas was to fly one brigade to Paoshan in China and then enter Burma from the east across the Salween river. Slim, however, cautioned that all river crossings on the Salween were heavily guarded; he recommended flying the Chindits in directly, saving them the fatigue of getting to the target areas and providing more time for effective operations.[64] Once it was calculated that it would be possible to fly two brigades in at the beginning of March and two more later, Wingate decided that each wave would consist of one brigade marching in and two being flown directly to the target. He then went on a tour of the training areas to exhort the first three brigades that would see action (77, 111, 16). To general surprise, instead of briefing them on the forthcoming operation, he offered a lecture on Cromwell's victory at Dunbar in 1648 and an analysis of Stonewall Jackson's use of troops in the Shenandoah Valley during the American Civil War.[65] Whether this was an unconscious admission of the truth of Slim's observation that the Chindits could never be more than 'strategic cavalry', or mere Wingate eccentricity, his supporters predictably claimed that the men were enthused and invigorated by such a novel approach.

There is continuing evidence of Wingate's mental instability at this time, for it was at this very juncture that he began pushing hard in memo after memo for acceptance of his grandiose plans for an advance to Hanoi, which on his own admission would entail the use of 25 brigades or 100,000 men. Alarmed and alienated, Mountbatten wrote back witheringly that the overall Allied plan for the defeat of Japan would not necessarily permit Wingate to march the width of Indochina. Nothing daunted, Wingate raised his new strategic vision at a plenary session of the chiefs of staff; he told them that he was not interested merely in assisting Stilwell or even 14th Army but had wider ambitions and wanted clarification of this put to the chiefs of staff in London. Mountbatten responded with what one writer has called 'a dignified rebuke': 'I am sure you had no intention of "putting me on the spot" last night but the fact remains that you suggested your LRPG operations should not go on unless the present ideas of world strategy were changed by the Chiefs of Staff!'[66] Ever the master of the 'non-apology apology', Wingate replied that of course he was prepared to implement Operation THURSDAY as it stood. But he followed this letter up with an eight-page sequel on 11 February stressing that his Indochina ambitions were still intact and that he hoped eventually to link up with US forces in the Pacific. Having apparently accepted Mountbatten's reproof at the front door, he attempted to re-enter by the back, asking for extra aircraft to be assigned to him. It was behaviour like this that made it very difficult for Mountbatten to defend Wingate against his many critics. Some Wingate observers claim that the stress of planning Operation THURSDAY was too great for a man not properly recovered from a major illness. Others, more cynically, claim that his essential madness was finally manifesting itself clearly.[67] After further angry exchanges between Wingate and Mountbatten in February, Pownall wrote despairingly: 'Wingate replied with a long-winded diatribe, accusing almost everyone of stupidity, ignorance, obstruction and much else besides . . . I shouldn't be at all surprised if within the next three months it is proved that Wingate is bogus; at any rate he is a thoroughly nasty piece of work.'[68]

So obsessed with his new quixotic plans was he that Wingate did not even see that the future of Special Force had suddenly become secure, since the campaign in Arakan fulfilled the necessary conditions for Chindit activity that both Mountbatten and Auchinleck had agreed on. His mind was elsewhere, dreaming of the temples and pagodas of Indochina. Yet reality soon impinged. Under huge pressure from Mountbatten, Giffard and Slim, he eventually had to accept that the objectives of THURSDAY were more limited than he wanted; Giffard told him that increased numbers were predicable on success alone, that if he wanted more brigades he would have to show significant gains. As a Parthian shot, or to save face, Wingate then demanded more planes. Slim explained that he could not spare aircraft from the Arakan operation, then reaching its climax, while neither Stilwell nor Chiang would agree to diverting aircraft from the Hump; not even Mountbatten had the power to order that. At first Wingate dug his heels in and refused to accept his orders as drafted at a private meeting with Slim, but next morning Slim got Giffard into the office and faced the Chindit leader down. Realising the game was up, Wingate accepted his signed orders with what Slim described as a 'slightly wry smile'.[69] The official aims of THURSDAY were described as: assisting Stilwell's advance; creating favourable conditions for Y-force to cross the Salween; inflicting maximum damage on the Japanese in north Burma. The principal targets would be the Shwebo–Myitkyina railway and the Myitkyina–Bhamo–Indaw road. There would be four strongholds, to be designated Piccadilly, Chowringhee, Broadway and Templecombe (later renamed Aberdeen). The US 900th Airborne Engineer Company would clear strips suitable for Dakotas to land on. As usual, Wingate kept his cards close to his chest. Even to his closest confidants he was secretive and disingenuous. He told Fergusson that something he merely hoped for – that success at Indaw would see Chindit numbers automatically doubled – was actual policy endorsed by Giffard and Mountbatten. He divulged none of his intentions in THURSDAY to potential helpers in SOE, OSS or Force 126 on the grounds that there was too much empire-building, jealousy and *amour-propre* in these organisations (rich, coming from Wingate).[70] Finally, on 4 February he and Stratemeyer issued the essential guidelines for Chindit 2, stressing that this time the wounded would be flown out from the strongholds rather than abandoned, as on the first expedition. Tired of his myriad bosses, Stratemeyer finally exerted himself and decided on support bombing of the stronghold areas prior to their establishment, rather than the deception bombing on Rangoon, Mandalay and Bangkok that Wingate had pressed for.[71]

At last there was action rather than words, as Fergusson's brigade commenced its long march from Ledo, looking more like a mule train than a commando force. Although Special Force was distinguished by its use of animals (apart from elephants it had 250 bullocks, 547 horses and 3,134 mules on its strength), this was the first time on THURSDAY that the efficacy of the mules was tested in operational conditions. Fergusson's brigade, 4,000 strong, took 500 of the mules, fully laden, along with them.[72] The brigade was suitably fussed over before its departure, with Mountbatten, Auchinleck and Giffard all making goodwill visits. All except the muleteers were taken the length of the Ledo road in huge lorries, noting the American blacks still labouring on the road as they passed. The road journey itself gave them an idea of what was up ahead, as it was like a scar cut through the jungle, with ascents up to 5,000 feet, hairpin bends, and half-built bridges taking them over raging torrents. Wingate himself joined Fergusson and his men for the start of the gruelling ascent up the Paktai, wading through mud slides, with the roar of the Ledo road traffic beneath them and deep blue smoke rising from the damp fires of the Chinese labour camps.[73] The brigade had to cross cliffs, hills and ravines, often climbing thousands of feet on one-in-two gradients, then descending as sharply. The heavy loads they carried were made heavier by the torrential rain, rations were short and progress slow, varying between nine and 35 miles a day depending on the condition of the treacherous, slippery hills. Sometimes they reached an altitude of 5,000 feet through varying terrain, jungle or bamboo and teak forests.[74] It could take all day to climb a mountain, and loaded mules often fell headlong to a gory death thousands of feet below. The sappers sometimes tried to ease the uphill climbs by cutting zigzag paths, but the steps usually crumbled before half the column had passed. Sometimes the ascents were so steep that the mules had to be unloaded and their burdens passed upwards by relays of hands. Every day was a living hell, with exhausted men flopping into an instant sleep at night.[75]

It took them all of February to reach the Chindwin, but even then they were still about 200 miles from their target at Indaw. From what he had seen on the first few days before he returned to base, Wingate was secretly cast down, but he put a brave face on it and pretended not to be daunted. At the end of the three-week trek he flew in to observe the crossing of the Chindwin. Although Fergusson had been severely critical of his leader in January and even described him as a liar, he continued to be a true believer and said of Wingate: 'He was sometimes wrong in small things but never in big.'[76] At the time, though, Fergusson was exasperated about the small things. When Wingate touched down on an improvised airstrip on the far side of the Chindwin, Fergusson expected that he would be bringing with him 16 Brigade's second in command and its signals officer. Instead he disembarked with four war correspondents and explained to a furious Fergusson that it was essential to publicise the Chindits' activities.[77] Wingate in turn was infuriated when Fergusson told him that 16 Brigade could not possibly reach Indaw earlier than 20 March, not the date of 5 March Wingate had originally scheduled. The generally sour atmosphere was not improved by Wingate's ardent propagandising for a new fad, turtles' eggs, which he declared provided singular nourishment. Like so many of Wingate's eccentric ideas, this one did not win general approval: turtles' eggs were found to be no more appetising than those of any other reptile, and in fact many of the Chindits experienced stomach pains and other digestive problems after eating them. One positive development was that No. 1 Air Commando successfully dropped rubber boats to supplement the rafts built by the troops on the ground, and it was this that made the crossing of the Chindwin go so smoothly. Otherwise, Fergusson's men were not in good condition, but Wingate ordered them to attack Lonkin, 20 miles west of Kamaing, before proceeding to Indaw; this would be a diversion to help Stilwell.[78] The demoralised and exhausted troops of 16 Brigade accordingly started to veer off towards Lonkin. Matters did not improve. The as-the-crow-flies distance from the Chindwin to Indaw was 150 miles, but the reality was that the Chindits would have to march 300–400 miles up and down razorback ridges, going from tropical storms and mud landslides in the valley to freezing cold but nonetheless flyblown conditions on the heights. Two sentries were found asleep at their posts and punished with a flogging from a massive sergeant major known to the Chindits as 'Captain Bligh'.[79] This was part of the brutal routine of draconian punishment that Wingate, with no legal sanction whatever, had ordained for the Chindit columns, and would lead to court-martial proceedings after the war. Eventually Fergusson decided to detach two columns only for the assault on Lonkin and to proceed towards his objective with the other six. This turned out to be a good decision, for Lonkin was found to be virtually empty of enemy troops.

Back in the world of military politics and intrigue, Wingate continued to exhaust the patience of his nominal superiors, Slim, Giffard and Mountbatten. Both the theory and practice of LRP and Special Force were irreconcilable with the wider aims of Slim and Mountbatten, since Slim wanted to defeat the Japanese at Imphal before proceeding to campaigns in Burma, while Mountbatten still hankered after amphibious operations in southern Burma. Beyond this, ephemeral and contingent factors continued to complicate the triangular relationship – triangular because, in terms of deep dynamic, Giffard was largely a cipher. Having already lost the battle over the four battalions he wanted from Slim's reserve in 26 Indian Division – he had had to make do with 3 West Indian Brigade instead – Wingate was determined to win the second confrontation, over the units in the Chindits' second wave. By mid-March Slim was involved in the massive battle for Imphal and it would have made no sense to leave 14 and 23 Brigades idle and on standby when every last man counted in this mother of battles.[80] Slim proposed to use the two brigades in the defence of Imphal but Wingate, outraged, protested that they were *his* battalions. What was sauce for the goose . . . If Slim could deny him the use of the reserve in 26 Indian Division, then Wingate was entitled to deny Slim the brigades from the second wave. On 9 March he learned that Slim had actually ordered the two brigades into action and flew to Comilla to protest. Patiently Slim explained that Wingate's attitude was dog-in-the-mangerism. It had never been the intention to use the reserve brigades in Burma until two to three months after the fly-in of the first wave, so use of the second-wave brigades in the battle of Kohima did not affect Wingate's plans one iota.[81] To appease the intemperate Wingate, however, Slim agreed to release 14 Brigade to him as soon as the crisis at Kohima eased and the battle stabilised; he was as good as his word. In this confrontation Wingate was being obtuse twice over. It was surely clear that in the dramatically changed circumstances of a major Japanese attack on

278

Assam, it made more sense for the Chindits to be assisting Slim, and to be attempting to cut Mutaguchi's communications rather than helping Stilwell.[82] Moreover, if the Japanese won at Kohima, the British position in Burma would anyway be lost and the Chindit brigades cut adrift, left to wander aimlessly, starve, surrender or stage suicide attacks. Apart from anything else, Japanese victory at Kohima would mean that the Chindits could no longer be supplied from the air, which meant sudden death. Slim later confessed that he had been too soft with Wingate: he should really have cancelled the entire Operation THURSDAY and concentrated on the struggle for Kohima.[83]

Operation THURSDAY's D-Day was 5 March. In the original scheme Fergusson would be attacking Indaw at the very moment of the fly-in of 77 and III Brigades. That morning Slim flew in to the gigantic airstrip at Hailakandi from which the operation would be launched. A massive flotilla of gliders was parked there, and around the edges of the airfield were the Dakotas that would fly them in. The plan was for 77 Brigade to fly in in two halves to establish strongholds on flat stretches of the Kaukwe valley code-named 'Piccadilly' and 'Broadway' north-east of Indaw while III Brigade established itself at 'Chowringee', east of Indaw. All the strongholds would be far from roads and villages but close to plentiful water supplies. Fergusson's overland expedition would meanwhile set up the fourth stronghold at 'Aberdeen', north-west of Indaw.[84] Everything at Hailakandi seemed to be going smoothly until the inevitable hitch occurred. Colonel P.C. Cochran, very sensibly, had taken the precaution of sending his spotter planes out on a reconnaissance of the Kaukwe valley, but Wingate was furious and complained about 'insubordination' (absurdly, as Cochran was not under his command). The aerial photographs clearly showed the putative landing space at Piccadilly covered by teak logs arranged in four symmetrical lines so as to block any aerial put-down; the obvious inference was that the secret of the landings had somehow been blown and the Japanese were waiting for them. Wingate exploded in fury and told Slim that the Chinese must be the traitors.[85] However, since Broadway and Chowringhee had also been photographed by aerial reconnaissance, revealing no blockage, Slim at first suggested diverting the landings there. Wingate's blood was now up and, inconsolable, he declared that the Japanese 'must be' preparing an ambush there also. According to Slim, he took Wingate aside and talked to him calmly, outlining a threefold optimistic scenario: there was only one obstructed airfield; the Chinese were unlikely to have betrayed them; and the Japanese, nervous of Allied airborne assault, had blocked a number of likely sites and by chance hit on one of the correct ones. He probably did not endear himself by pointing out to Wingate that he himself was partly to blame for the blockage of Piccadilly, for it was a site he had used on the 1943 expedition and a photograph of it had appeared in an American magazine – which was how the Japanese knew about it.[86]

Eventually Wingate calmed down, reiterated his feelings about the risk and said to Slim: 'The responsibility is yours.' Slim was uneasy, knowing that a wrong decision might well torpedo the entire Burma campaign. He then consulted Calvert, who said that he was prepared to take the risk. There were just a few nights of the full moon left and the Japanese were massing against Imphal, so this might be the last chance for LRP. Slim then announced that the operation would proceed.[87] His reasoning was fourfold: the Chindits were keyed to a pitch of readiness and would never be able to regain that peak if not used now; he could not let Stilwell down, having promised him a diversionary attack; he could not leave Fergusson and 16 Brigade isolated and twisting in the wind at Aberdeen; if he kept the Dakotas and gliders crowded together on the airfield, it was probable that the Japanese would discover them and destroy them.[88] Wingate seemed to greet the decision with relief, but now another wrangle developed as he announced that the troops originally destined for Piccadilly would go to Chowringhee instead. Slim did not like this, as Chowringhee was on the eastern shore of the Irrawaddy whereas the railway and road links to be cut were on the western side. Another confrontation with Wingate loomed, but fortunately Calvert too opposed Chowringhee, as did Cochran, the US air commander, who pointed out that the new airstrip was very different in configuration and he would not have time to rebrief his pilots. When Air Marshal John Baldwin, in charge of the Tactical Air Force, also opposed Chowringhee, Wingate accepted the majority decision and switched the Piccadilly-destined brigade to Broadway instead. The entire consultation had lasted just 70 minutes. Cochran caught the spirit of the proceedings by jumping on the bonnet of a jeep and calling to his fliers: 'Say, fellers, we've got a better place to go!'[89]

It was decided that the number of gliders should be reduced from 80 to 61 and that they should all go to Broadway. Calvert's men and Cochran's American pilots were quickly rebriefed. The code words SOYA LINK (failure) and PORK SAUSAGE (success) were agreed. Shortly after 6 p.m. the Dakotas took off with their gliders, only 72 minutes behind schedule.[90] Each plane took two gliders. There had been impassioned debate about the wisdom and practicality of this, as the Dakotas had only ever towed one glider before, but Slim, Wingate and Cochran had been among the optimists. It turned out that the pessimists were right. Soon Slim's headquarters received the depressing message SOYA LINK, which was naturally taken to mean that the Japanese had been waiting for the Chindits. Slim reported: 'So the Japanese *had* ambushed Broadway! Wingate was right and I had been wrong. He gave me one bitter look and walked away. I had no answer for him.'[91] Then gradually more and more signals were deciphered and the position became clear. There had been no enemy ambush, but 26 of the 61 gliders had crashed. The Dakotas proved to be unable to tow two gliders after all, and the strain was simply too great. The steep climb at the beginning of the flight – necessary to clear the mountains – put too great a drag on the nylon ropes and some of them snapped. Other aircraft overheated and used more fuel than expected, so some of them had to make emergency landings; a few gliders even had the bad luck to land near Japanese forces. Even those that reached Broadway did not usually escape unscathed; several crash-landed and those coming in after them skidded into the wreckage in a general pile-up. Surprisingly only 23 men were killed, though several were badly injured. On the other hand, 400 Chindits landed safely the first night, along with stores. What triggered the dramatic code word SOYA LINK was that from the air the glider wreckage looked like a Japanese ambuscade.[92] There was further irony. The crashed gliders actually helped with deception and disinformation, for when the Japanese found glider wreckage all the way from Assam to the Irrawaddy, they were at a loss to divine Allied intentions. It later transpired that the 'ambush' at Piccadilly was no such thing. By mere chance the piles of logs had been left there by Japanese woodcutters, who had brought the timber up from the river by elephant for drying. There was universal relief next morning when the codeword PORK SAUSAGE was received and the fly-in could recommence.[93]

Wingate had reached rock bottom on the night of the 5th when SOYA LINK was received. As he retired to bed, Derek Tulloch expressed the hope that tomorrow would bring better things. Wingate dismissed him as a 'bloody optimist'. The most optimistic was Baldwin, who said he would return to Imphal and lay on a fighter sweep for the morning.[94]. By contrast 6 March was a day of triumph, with 55 Dakotas reaching Broadway and the first flights putting down at Chowringhee. Between 5 and 11 March, No. 1 Air Commando and 177 Wing RAF flew 579 Dakota sorties, landing 9,000 men, 1,300 animals and 250 tins of stores without loss.[95] By 11 March all of Calvert's 77 Brigade and half of Lentaigne's 111 Brigade were at Broadway. There was a last-minute decision to scale down the operations at Chowringhee, so after 9 March no more reinforcements were sent there. The idea of establishing a stronghold there was abandoned in favour of something closer to guerrilla activities; for a night or two the other half of Lentaigne's brigade dug in together with the Kachin levies who had been sent to raise the local tribes, then they moved off. It turned out to be a wise decision, for five hours after the Chindits left Chowringhee, the Japanese pulverised the area with saturation bombing. Broadway, on the other hand, conformed to Wingate's dreams. There Calvert set up a true stronghold, complete with a hospital, shops, farms, chicken runs and cultivated fields – for all the world like a permanent settlement. Yet the fire-eating Calvert was not interested in homesteads or colonies. Leaving behind a garrison of two battalions, he took the bulk of his forces on a march across the Gangaw range and the deep Kaukwe Chaung to find a suitable location for a subsidiary stronghold – one that would block Japanese communications to Myitkyina from the south.[96] Within days 77 Brigade collided with the enemy. When the Chindits reached the railway at Kenu on 18 March there ensued a battle as savage as a medieval combat, with ferocious hand-to-hand fighting – 'rifle and bayonet against two-handed feudal sword, kukri against bayonet, no quarter to the wounded, while hand-grenades lobbed over the heads of the combatants incessantly'.[97] The small-scale battle of Pagoda Hill, as it was called, cost Calvert's men 23 dead and 64 wounded (a Victoria Cross was also won), but they counted 42 Japanese dead on the battlefield afterwards. Near the battlefield Calvert founded his second stronghold, codenamed 'White City'.

With 12,000 men now 'inserted in the enemy's guts', to use Wingate's picturesque phrase, and the strongholds seemingly working out well, it was time for triumphalism. On 11 March Wingate issued a self-congratulatory order of the day, full of fustian rhetoric, and next day communicated directly with Churchill in similar mode.[98] The pendulum of the bipolar manic-depressive cycle had now swung back with a vengeance. But Wingate in this mood was almost bound to make enemies, and in a single week he managed to inveigle himself into three separate conflicts. The first, incredibly, was with Colonel Cochran, to whom he owed so much. Many observers thought that Wingate had been simply incompetent in failing to order aerial recon-naissance of his target landing areas, and his later lame excuse that to send out planes on such a mission would alert the Japanese fooled nobody.[99] Cochran had made good his error, but instead of gratitude, Wingate railed at the American's 'insubordination'. To show who was boss, he flew in six Spitfires to Broadway without notifying Cochran. A furious Cochran, who was not in the least overawed by the English prophet, protested vociferously that Wingate had 'bounced' him and was giving the credit due to his fliers to the RAF, whom he described as mere headline-chasers. This was a potential cause célèbre that could have gone all the way up to General 'Hap' Arnold, Wingate's staunch supporter. Swallowing hard, Wingate was obliged to forward Cochran's complaint to Air Chief Marshal Joubert, Mountbatten's talented head of publicity, together with a rare apology.[100] Having shown himself inept at public relations, Wingate then proceeded to hammer the point home with an angry confrontation with Mountbatten. There had been disagreement about whether it was wise to publicise the Chindit oper-ations (Slim thought it a mistake to do so), but the news soon leaked out and was given extensive coverage in Frank Owen's *SEAC* news-paper, though without mentioning Wingate or the Chindits by name. In a towering rage, Wingate ascribed the situation to the usual jeal-ousy and back-stabbing directed against him and issued an order forbidding *SEAC* to be distributed to his men. He had jumped the gun, for Owen was preparing to do a follow-up edition in which Wingate and the Chindits would receive full credit. For his own rather machiavellian reasons, Slim eventually agreed with Owen that Wingate's name should be mentioned; his reasoning was that the Japanese would think it simply a reprise of his small-scale 1943 oper-ation and not take it seriously until it was too late.[101]

Wingate now chose to escalate this dispute with Owen by sending a cable to Joubert saying that he could not answer for the morale of his troops in the light of this overt slap in the face and informing him that *SEAC* was now contraband among the Chindits. In his typical bull-in-a-china-shop way, Wingate had not seen through all the implications of his action and sent the cable *en clair* so that it went through normal channels and was read by cipher and signals staff. As such it was a public attack on Mountbatten's entire organisation. On 19 March the Supreme Commander issued a stiff reprimand:

> Has it not occurred to you that your assumption, that people are going to try and belittle or conceal the doings of your party, makes it all the more difficult for me to ensure that they get the correct measure of credit? For instance, your letter was quite unsuitable for circulating to Air HQ . . . In future I suggest that when you consider a direct response from me is necessary, that this should be written entirely objectively without any note of bitterness being allowed to creep in. If you wish to let off steam I don't mind your doing so in a covering letter which no-one else sees, but if you mix vituperation and factual accounts it merely means that the factual accounts cannot be circulated. Your astounding telegram to Joubert has made me realise how you have achieved such amazing success in getting yourself disliked by people who are only too ready to be on your side.'[102]

Mountbatten was in a peculiarly difficult position. Temperamentally disliking conflict, and knowing that Wingate was Churchill's favourite, he had nonetheless become increasingly disillusioned with him as the loosest of loose cannons, and in any case, the proud and egomaniacal Supreme Commander would never tolerate a challenge to his prestige or *amour-propre*. Wingate's many supporters have always resented Mountbatten's part in his Burma career, accusing him of duplicity and insincerity; it is alleged that he never thought Chindit 2 would get off the ground, but that when it did and achieved initial success, he was keen to take the credit himself. Tulloch was a particular critic of Mountbatten on this score. 'Mountbatten may well have felt a sense of shame in committing his friend to an operation which he himself had opposed and which he had no intention of exploiting even if it was successful.'[103] There was more to it than that. It is doubtful that

Mountbatten ever was a 'friend' of Wingate. Both men wanted to be the supreme figure in Burma and were in a sense competing for the same space. Wingate often complained that Mountbatten did not keep him fully informed about top-level decision-making and signals from Churchill and Roosevelt, but Mountbatten considered that was not Wingate's business; in his view it was part of the definition of a supreme commander that he did not have to share secret information with a subordinate. Wingate, of course, regarded himself as a partner, not a subordinate. There is more merit in the idea that by early March Mountbatten committed himself more strongly to LRP because he was increasingly the target of hostile press criticism in the United States, alleging that he was a 'do nothing' waffler; so concerned was FDR by this that he communicated with Churchill about it on 25 February.[104]

Wingate was always keen to be at the front, so he visited Broadway on 7 March and Chowringhee on the 8th. He would probably have commuted between the strongholds indefinitely, had not Tulloch stressed to him the importance of being at headquarters; if not, hard pressed as they were at Imphal, the trinity of Mountbatten, Giffard and Slim might simply cancel THURSDAY. But it was difficult to keep him away, and the next tour of inspection took him to the subsidiary stronghold that the dauntless Calvert had established from Broadway: the so-called White City. Next (20 March) he flew to the Meza valley, where Fergusson had at last set up Aberdeen.[105] Against Fergusson's protests that his exhausted men needed rest, Wingate insisted that there must be no let-up, as this would allow the enemy, at present unprepared, to build up his strength at Indaw. He sugared the pill by saying that he guaranteed back-up from the reserve 14 Brigade, at which Fergusson reluctantly agreed to attack the Indaw airfields.[106] What Wingate did not tell Fergusson was that his real intention for his reserves was to present Mountbatten with a fait accompli. He had been forced to sign Slim and Giffard's unwelcome orders, but once he had control of 14 Brigade he intended to attack the rear of the Japanese attacking Imphal. In this way the limited aims of THURSDAY he had signed up to would be converted into the more ambitious plans for a general campaign involving Indochina that he had always cherished and in his secret heart never given up.[107] From Aberdeen he flew to Broadway, and then met Tulloch at

Lalaghat. Tulloch gave him the alarming news that the situation at Imphal was so serious that Slim was now seriously considering taking the reserve Chindit brigades (14th and 23rd Brigade) into the 14th Army defending that position. Slim had told Tulloch this in confidence, with strict instructions that he should not alarm Wingate by passing on the news, but Tulloch's loyalty to Wingate overcame all other considerations; besides, he had always disliked Slim.[108] Wingate's immediate reaction was to fly to Comilla for yet another confrontation with Slim. The commander of 14th Army was sympathetic and said he had no desire to stymie the Chindits; but Wingate should understand how serious the situation at Kohima now was. Finally the two men agreed a compromise: 14 Brigade would neither be amalgamated into the 14th Army nor sent to help Fergusson at Indaw. Instead it would proceed to a point 15 miles west of Wuntho and 60 miles south-west of Aberdeen to set up yet another stronghold where it could sever Japanese communications; the luckless Fergusson was to be kept in the dark about the new development.[109]

There was one obvious snag about the compromise plan: it would require aircraft for supply drops, and where were they to come from? Allied airpower was now at full stretch in the defence of Imphal, and the only other source would be the Hump, which would mean a clash with Stilwell, or if not him, with Chiang and 'Hap' Arnold. Wingate thought he saw a chance to turn the tables on Slim, whom he considered had not been straight with him. He told Slim he was going to communicate directly with Churchill; Slim invited him to go ahead. Slim's last view of Wingate was at this meeting on 22 March. 'I said goodbye to him . . . and shook hands with him. As he went to the door he turned towards me again and said, a propos of nothing in particular, "You are the only senior officer in South East Asia who doesn't wish me dead!"'[110] Wingate sent an impassioned cable to London, routed through Mountbatten, claiming to be on the verge of annihilating four Japanese divisions. The cable read in part: 'Get Special Force four transport squadrons now and you will have all Burma north of the 24th parallel plus a decisive defeat . . . General Slim gives me his full backing.'[111] Slim complained to Mountbatten that Wingate had taken his name in vain, but what he really objected to was the hyperbole about four Japanese divisions, which Wingate implied he (Slim) was endorsing. As to the general request for four squadrons of Dakotas or similar, Slim in a separate signal to Giffard also urged this, though his intention was more direct; if he got Churchill's backing for four more squadrons he intended to use them at Imphal, not on LRP operations.[112] Mountbatten, meanwhile, was angry that after his recent pep talks with Wingate, the Chindit leader still seemed to have no conception of loyalty to the overall SEAC command. He called both Giffard and Peirse in for long consultations before sending Wingate's cable on, and when he did so (on 23 March), he added a long covering note to say that neither he, Peirse nor Giffard knew why Wingate was requesting the extra planes. Churchill, however, immediately agreed to provide them and even promised he would mention the Chindits in his next broadcast to the nation.[113]

Meanwhile Fergusson, unaware of all these developments, was labouring with his exhausted troops towards Indaw. Lacking the 900 men who had been detached to Lonkin, his force was 3,000 strong with 400 mules. They reached the outskirts of the airfield but blundered into Japanese outposts and were then ordered back to Aberdeen by Fergusson. The attack on Indaw has always been controversial, but was one of those occasions when everything that could do wrong did go wrong, simultaneously.[114] At least seven different factors can be identified. First, the element of surprise was lost. The initial Japanese reaction to THURSDAY was astonishingly complacent. The commander of the Japanese air force in Burma, Major General Nazoe Noburu, was one of the few to spot the danger and to realise that this was no small-scale raid, like the Chindit incursion of 1943. But the arrogant know-all Mutaguchi dismissed his warnings and described the latest Special Force landings as 'a mouse in a bag'. When the scale and scope of the LRP operation was realised, the Japanese called in reinforcements so that Indaw had been shored up by the time Fergusson got there. Even here, though, Wingate must carry part of the blame. Because he never informed his commanders of his overall plans on the 'need to know' principle and 'for reasons of security', he had not told Fergusson that 116 Brigade, in turn ignorant of Fergusson's intentions, had fed pro-Japanese headmen the 'disinformation' that an attack on Indaw was planned. The 'disinformation' was of course solid intelligence.[115] Second, there was a failure of intelligence and reconnaissance. Fergusson had not realised that there was no water available on the entire stretch between Aberdeen and Indaw, so that his men arrived at the target in an almost terminal state of thirst and exhaustion.[116] Third, by an absurd contretemps Fergusson was out of radio contact with headquarters for 24 hours because Wingate decided to switch his base of operations. Hitherto he had had two different headquarters, one at Imphal and one at Sylhet. When it seemed that the Japanese might overrun Imphal, he switched completely to Sylhet, but the changeover took place on the very days (21–23 March) that Fergusson was attacking Indaw, so there was no proper liaison.[117] Fourth, the Chindits in 16 Brigade turned out to be ill-disciplined and poorly trained and ended up firing on each other during the battle for Indaw.[118] Fifth, Fergusson did not coordinate his attacks properly, so that his assault resembled 'clutching fingers from all sides, and not as a fist'. In self-lacerating mode he later accused himself of not having adequately followed the precepts of the Master.[119] Sixth, and most obviously, Fergusson had been misled and let down by Wingate, since he thought he had a guarantee of back-up from 14 Brigade. When he was later shown Wingate's written order for the deployment of that brigade elsewhere, he remarked bitterly, as so many had before him, on Wingate's mendacity: 'At times the truth was simply not in him.'[120] Finally, and incredibly, Fergusson received a report that the Japanese had sealed off his rear and were attacking Aberdeen. Quickly he called off the retreat and marched back, only to find that the Nigerian reinforcements had arrived in the form of 14th and 3rd West African Brigade.[121]

While all this was going on, the Japanese had launched another ferocious attack against White City, which Calvert and his men beat off, but at the cost of 32 killed and 42 wounded. On 24 March, therefore, Wingate flew down to Broadway and White City on a morale-boosting mission to 77 Brigade. After a side trip to Aberdeen, he flew back to Broadway and then on to Imphal. This was the last time Calvert ever saw him. The flight back to Imphal was in a B-25 Mitchell bomber piloted by Lieutenant Brian Hodges of the USAAF with a crew of five and four passengers, Wingate, his ADC and two war correspondents.[122] The plane reached Imphal at 6.23 p.m. and was closely guarded for the next half an hour before taking off at 8 p.m. for the Hailakandi airfield. Half an hour later it crashed into the Naga hills west of Imphal, near the village of

Thilon. Cochran requested that Special Force send out a search party, which next morning found all the signs of a high-impact crash; almost certainly all the plane's occupants were killed instantly. The usual culprits in the case of an air crash were cited: freak weather, engine failure, pilot error. But because this was Wingate, there was a general reluctance to accept that this was a routine accident, such as had accounted for thousands of airborne combatants in Burma. The official investigation concluded that there had been engine failure and that the pilot had unsuccessfully tried to return to Imphal.[123] Many other theories were tested but found wanting. Sabotage was ruled out, because the B-25 was so closely guarded all the time, and anyway nobody knew Wingate's intentions or flight plans, so there was simply no time for a bomb to have been planted. Thunderstorms or turbulence were cited as possibilities, but all the pilots in the air in the area that day confirmed that all thunderstorms were local and could easily be circumvented. Slim opted for extreme turbulence, even though the pilots' testimony also ruled that out. 'The wreckage was eventually found on the reverse side of a ridge,' he wrote, 'so that it was unlikely that the aircraft had flown into the hill. The most probable explanation is that it had suddenly entered one of those local storms of extreme turbulence so frequent in the area. These were difficult to avoid at night, and once in them an aeroplane might be flung out of control, or even have its wings torn off.'[124] Opinions differ on weather conditions that day, but majority opinion is that they were not too bad. This disposes of the canard that the American pilot, Lieutenant Hodges, had not wanted to take off but the imperious and impatient Wingate browbeat him into doing so. Another view is that the pilot mistook the altitude and was flying too low, and this has some support from eyewitnesses. Yet another theory, based on reports that the plane was on fire when it crashed, was that the B-25 was carrying cluster bombs, which broke loose from the bays, rolled into the fuselage and detonated.[125]

Given human nature, it is a moral certainty that several of Wingate's old foes in the Indian army were glad to see him go, and there were many, whether ironically or not, who cited Shakepeare's words in *Macbeth*: 'Nothing in his life became him like the leaving it.' From those who had known him well the reaction ranged from stupefaction through sadness to stoical acceptance. 'Who will look after us now?' said Captain Richard Rhodes-James. 'Our master was gone and we, his masterpiece, were now ownerless.'[126] Forgetting all his recent strictures and animadversions on his turbulent subordinate, and perhaps with that falsity survivors so often employ towards the troublesome dead, Mountbatten wrote to Edwina: 'I cannot tell you how much I am going to miss Wingate. Not only had we become close personal friends but he was such a fire-eater, and it was such a help to me having a man with a burning desire to fight. He was a pain in the neck to the generals over him, but I loved his wild enthusiasm and it will be difficult for me to try to inculcate it from above.'[127] Others jumped on the bandwagon and claimed they 'knew' Wingate was destined for an early death. Aware of the dangers of air travel, Tulloch never went in the same plane as Wingate and later came forward to say that he had had a premonition of disaster on 24 March and begged Wingate not to fly.[128] Wingate himself had an innate dislike of flying but used willpower to overcome his fear. His attitude was that if he listened to people like Tulloch, he would never be able to board a plane, and that, for the commander of the Chindits, was both intrinsically absurd and likely to turn him and his Special Force into a laughing stock. Although the senior British commanders had disliked Wingate intensely, they had always tried to make allowances for him and to try to value his positive side while ignoring his many blemishes. As Rhodes-James pointed out: 'They also protected him from himself when he did and said things he should not have done or said.'[129] Some thought Wingate lucky in his death, for his premature end meant that his strategic theories were never fully refuted by events, as they would have been had he lived and continued at the helm. This allowed the legend of Wingate the peerless paladin to develop; it is still alive today.[130] Perhaps the most judicious overall estimate came from Slim:

> With him, contact had too often been collision, for few could meet so stark a character without being violently attracted or repelled. To most he was either prophet or adventurer. Very few could regard him dispassionately; nor did he care to be so regarded. I once likened him to Peter the Hermit preaching his Crusade. I am sure that many of the knights and princes that Peter so fiercely exhorted did not like him very

much – but they went crusading all the same. The trouble was, I think, that Wingate regarded *himself* as a prophet, and that always leads to a single-centredness that verges on fanaticism, with all his faults. Yet had he not done so, his leadership could not have been so dynamic, nor his personal magnetism so striking.[131]

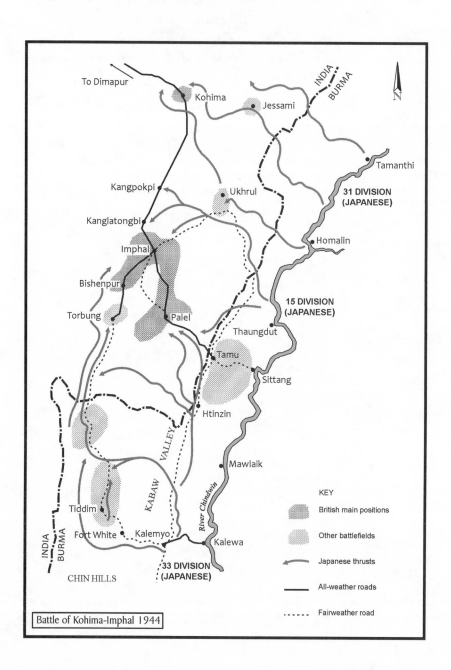

To Dimapur

Kohima

Jessami

INDIA
BURMA

Tamanthi

Kangpokpi

Ukhrul

**31 DIVISION
(JAPANESE)**

Kanglatongbi

Imphal

Homalin

Bishenpur

**15 DIVISION
(JAPANESE)**

Torbung

Palel

Thaungdut

Tamu

Sittang

Htinzin

KABAW VALLEY

River Chindwin

Mawlaik

Tiddim

KEY

British main positions

Other battlefields

Japanese thrusts

All-weather roads

Fairweather road

Fort White

Kalemyo

Kalewa

INDIA
BURMA

**33 DIVISION
(JAPANESE)**

CHIN HILLS

Battle of Kohima-Imphal 1944

Even as Operation THURSDAY began and the campaign in the Arakan continued, simultaneously the Japanese opened a massive offensive in what would prove to be a four-month battle, the Stalingrad of the East. Slim knew that the enemy was planning a great push that they hoped would take them to Delhi, but his intelligence indicated that the battle would be joined on or around 15 March 1944. In fact the Japanese made their move a week earlier. Although Slim's sources were far superior to those of his opponents, whose approach both to intelligence-gathering and its analysis was embarrassingly amateurish, they were, by the standards of the war in Europe, woefully inadequate. Slim sometimes made coded references to the fact that, unlike Montgomery, he was not given access to ULTRA and the other advanced cipher-cracking techniques.[1] Reliant mainly on human intelligence, he faced the problem that the various espionage agencies were almost more interested in stealing a march on each other than fighting the enemy. A major obstacle to clarity was the very plethora of agencies: the American fledgling organisation the OSS (forerunner of the CIA); Force 126, responsible for organising guerrilla bands in the enemy's rear; other irregulars known as V-Force, Z-Force and Detachment 101, which were part intelligence-gathering and part guerrilla; the Indian branch of MI6, known as the Inter-Services Liaison Committee; and especially D Division, the deception branch. There was much duplication of effort, mutual jealousy and a host of abortive or pointless 'operations'; indeed, there was little point in planting double agents or sowing disinformation when the Japanese army paid no attention to reports from its own spies and secret police.[2]

Slim's intelligence, reliable on the enemy's strength and resources, was less so on the intentions of its commanders. Nonetheless, it was obvious that the first target for the Japanese must be Imphal, for this was the key position in Manipur province, on the border with Burma; its capture would allow them to break into the Brahmaputra valley, cut all communications with Ledo, and thus end all prospects of Allied operations in Burma or China.[3] The town of Imphal was now a busy complex of army camps, tarmac roads, cottage hospitals, supply dumps, ordnance depots and engineer parks; some said the 600 square miles of the plain was like a gigantic campsite, but especially vulnerable to land attack, since it was surrounded on all sides by high ground. The geography of Imphal was peculiarly difficult. The great plain, 30 miles long and 20 miles wide, at an elevation of 2,600 feet, was surrounded by jungle-clad mountains: to the north-east were the Naga hills, with summits as high as 5,000 feet, while to the south were the even loftier Chin hills, with peaks between 6,000 and 9,000 feet.[4] The terrain made Imphal difficult to supply, for there were only two roads between Manipur and Assam, only one of which was all-weather. To the north, a road ran through high passes for 148 miles to the key railway terminal at Dimapur via the mountain village of Kohima in the Naga hills. When the first detachment of Japanese crossed the Chindwin on 8 March, aiming for Imphal, they caught Slim unprepared. Part of the problem was that his deputy, Lieutenant General Geoffrey Scoones, who commanded 4 Corps on the Assam front, had been preparing contingency plans for a limited offensive across the Chindwin in spring 1944, to support both Stilwell and Wingate.[5] The result was that two of the three divisions nominally based at Imphal were deployed far to the south: 17 Indian Division, under General 'Punch' Cowan, was at Tiddim, 163 miles south of Imphal in the Chin hills, linked to Imphal by a dirt track that could be cut with ease by an enemy; 20 Indian Division, meanwhile, commanded by Major General Douglas Gracey, was at Tamu, 30 miles south-east of Imphal, whence a metalled road ran 25 miles to the all-important airfield at Palel on the edge of the Imphal plain. Although the two divisions were reasonably close to one another as the crow flies, the mountainous country meant they could not support one another in the event of an attack; both would have to return to the Imphal plain and then re-exit by the other route.[6]

The Japanese attack on Imphal was directed by the wildly ambitious General Mutaguchi Renya, who made the eccentric direction to remain at Maymyo while doing so, out of close contact with his battle-field commanders. Seeing that Scoones had made all the correct defences against expected conventional attacks, Mutaguchi intended to seize Imphal by a combination of guile, surprise and dislocation. He correctly surmised that, if threatened, Scoones would try to hold both Tiddim and Tamu in strength, so disguised his main assault with a subsidiary attack to isolate Cowan at Tiddim by cutting the road to Imphal. He would then attack along the road from Tamu to Palel, forcing Scoones to commit his reserves (23 Indian Division based at Imphal under Major General Ouvry Roberts) to the two threatened sectors of Tiddim and Tamu. When all Scoones's troops were engaged in the south, Mutaguchi would then attack in the north and east.[7] The attack from the east would consist of 6,000 troops travelling with horses and bullocks. These would advance through the wild country between the Chindwin and north-eastern Imphal, following a line through Ukhrul, Sangshak and Litan, block the road north to Kohima, then cross to the west of the road and fall on Imphal from the unex-pected direction of north-west. A back-up force of another 4,000 would pass through Ukhrul and establish itself on the Kohima–Imphal road, blocking any attempt to reinforce Imphal from the north. Meanwhile 20,000 men would attack Kohima to sever the link between Imphal and Dimapur and the Brahmaputra valley. Assailed from four main directions and completely cut off by land, Imphal would be slowly throttled to death. It was a bold and ingenious plan, but Mutaguchi made three unwarranted assumptions: that Cowan and Gracey could be pinned down in the south; that the Anglo-Indian forces would panic and flee when outflanked by the Japanese, as they had in 1942–43; and worst of all, that his troops could hit all these complex targets while travelling light and carrying 100-pound loads.[8] Taking a huge logis-tical risk, Mutaguchi gambled that the element of surprise would outweigh the Japanese lack of heavy artillery, and that his men would be able to live off the land. Overconfident of taking Imphal within a month, he boasted that it would fall in 10 days and therefore provided his units with just 20 days' food supplies. Carrying rice, they could presumably hunt, fish and loot for the rest; or so he assumed.[9]

For his offensive Mutaguchi used three divisions – the 15th, 31st and 33rd – together with some units of the so-called Indian National Army, though these were not used in the front line but mainly in propaganda exercises to persuade Indian troops serving under Slim to desert or join the other side. He began by sending regiments of the 33rd to cut off Cowan at Tiddim. One regiment set out on 7 March and the other the next day, crossing the Manipur river below Tiddim and then moving upstream on the west bank to try to outflank Cowan.[10] The British responded slowly to this threat – so slowly that they only just avoided disaster. Slim had left the decision on the exact date for withdrawing 17 and 20 Divisions back to Imphal to Scoones, but Scoones was un-accountably tardy and even discounted Cowan's reports of enemy activity. Increasingly concerned that he would be cut off, Cowan decided to act unilaterally and gave the order to retreat, in so doing ignoring Scoones's explicit orders to hold firm. By the time Scoones finally woke up to the danger and formally ordered a retreat (13 March), the division was already on its way, whereupon Scoones put in an offi-cial report claiming that Cowan was the one who had moved too slowly.[11] Slim, characteristically, took the blame for this slow reaction, thus covering up for his favourite. To make up for his error, Scoones sent 37 and 49 Brigades to assist Cowan, and Ouvry Roberts sent down reinforcements as well. Even so, it was touch and go for a while. For the next three weeks Cowan's 16,000 troops, 2,500 vehicles and 3,500 mules fought their way northwards; the whole division went on foot, as transport was reserved for stores, ammunition and wounded. The Japanese followed the rear column cautiously, concentrating on working around the division and cutting the road ahead. General Motozo Yanakida, leading the pursuers, was a realist who already considered he was being asked to do far too much with the resources at his disposal, but his chief of staff, Colonel Tanaka, was another gung-ho enthusiast for Mutaguchi and his quixotic ideas and thus inter-preted every piece of caution by Yanakida as cowardice. Angry exchanges between Yanakida and Tanaka hardly helped the Japanese cause.[12]

The retreat from Tiddim constituted what Slim called a 'Neapolitan ice of layers'. What he meant by this was that the two Anglo-Indian brigades, 37 and 49, were pressing down from Imphal on to Japanese forces trying to block the road north, who in turn were between the retreating 17 Indian Division and its pursuers.[13] There was a fierce battle at Tonzang on 17 March, where the Japanese came off second best, and more heavy fighting from 22–25 March along the high ridges lining the road, with the same result, justifying Yanakida's complaint that he had not been given the wherewithal to do his job. All the time divisional engineers were blowing up the road behind them in several places, also leaving 400 booby traps and delayed-action demolitions.[14] When the rearguard crossed the Manipur bridge on 26 March, blowing it up once they were across, the worst was over. Only skirmishes were necessary thereafter to clear the road to the north, and on 5 April 17 Division arrived on the Imphal plain. Theirs was a fine achievement, but the fact remained that Yanakida had come close to encircling an entire Anglo-Indian division because of initial poor intelligence and dithering. It was an inauspicious start to Slim's direction of the campaign, but valuable lessons were learned. The RAF had been instrumental in blunting Japanese initiatives, and it was already apparent that the Japanese had seriously underrated this factor. As Slim said: 'Had not our fighters maintained continuous cover and given quick support at call, the withdrawal, if it could have been carried out at all, would have been a much grimmer and more protracted affair, with serious consequences to the main battle around Imphal.'[15] One can go further and state with conviction that the encirclement and annihilation of Cowan's 17 Division would have made Japanese victory at Imphal a moral certainty. The one thing Mutaguchi could not afford was time. Because of the tenuous supply and logistical situation, 24 hours was a long time in his scheme of things. Even more ominous, could he but have read the runes, was that 17 Indian Division had shown no signs of panic. It was clear that 1942 was not going to be repeated. The ludicrous Japanese ideas of effortless superiority and contempt for their foes, as also their voluntarist belief that the moral can always overcome the material, had taken a serious knock.[16]

There was even heavier fighting in the south-eastern sector, which would develop into one of the main theatres of the entire four-month campaign. Gracey, in charge of 20 Indian Division, had been extremely reluctant to leave his prepared position at Moreh when ordered to do so by Scoones and actually sent in a formal protest.[17] When Scoones repeated the order, 20 Division set about a task of mass destruction, slaughtering cattle and burning oil, destroying in all £1 million worth of supplies to prevent them falling into Japanese hands. The division then completed a 38-mile march north-west along the road through Tamu and Tengnoupal before digging in on the Shennam saddle, holding fortified positions overlooking the road between Tengnoupal and the all-important airfield at Palel, just 25 miles from Imphal. Here they would remain for the next two months, as the Japanese tried to force their way through the intricate network of hills and the British counterattacked; the struggle went on in a see-saw fashion, with hills being taken and retaken, changing hands over and over again.[18] But now the southern front was stabilised to Slim's satisfaction. Despite the numerous blunders that disfigured the first month of the Imphal campaign, Slim was always confident he would win in the long run. The enemy, it seemed to him, was playing into his hands. He had long pondered the conundrum about how, with limited manpower, he could ever get a credible army across the Chindwin into Burma. Now the Japanese were coming to him in a context where he could exploit every advantage of aircraft, armour and artillery, while the enemy was weak on logistics and supply. If only he could keep them in the ring until the monsoon came, Slim was confident that he could destroy the whole of Mutaguchi's 84,000-strong host. He therefore allowed Mutaguchi to advance deep into Manipur province, planning to destroy him on the periphery of Imphal plain.[19] His defence was constructed around self-supporting bastions capable of holding out for 10 days, and in the meantime he intended to flood in reinforcements and bring overwhelming force to bear. He had many winds of fortune at his back. The Japanese military culture, with its hatred of defeat, always led its commanders to take risks with logistics, and Mutaguchi was even more of a headstrong gambler than most other knights of bushido; it was entirely plausible that he would push his troops beyond the limit of their endurance.[20]

Of course Slim was taking risks himself, of which there were glaring ones. The first was that the withdrawal of 17 and 20 Divisions would affect morale adversely; the second was that the defences of Imphal might not be strong enough to withstand Mutaguchi's furious onslaught; and the third, most serious of all, was that he would not be able to reinforce 4 Corps fast enough. When nerves of steel and extreme mental toughness were required, one could ask no better than Slim. Although the stress on him was enormous – shuttling in draughty planes between different command centres while suffering from a bad back, and keeping track not just of the multiple foci in the battle for Imphal but also of Operation THURSDAY and the closing stages of the Arakan campaign – he cultivated a surface of perpetual calm and unflappability. He had a favourite saying: 'Those who matter don't worry, and those who worry don't matter.'[21] Even at this late stage some highly placed Allied commanders urged that the best way to respond to the enemy onslaught at Imphal was a counterattack across the Chindwin. But Slim considered this advice mere armchair generalship, since he had already considered that option and discounted it. Both the Chindwin scenarios – fighting with all available forces on both banks of the river, or a full-scale invasion of Burma – meant confronting the enemy at its strongest where British lines of communication would be precarious. Only the battle on the Imphal plain allowed Slim to fight on ground of his own choosing, where he could be confident of eventually overwhelming Mutaguchi with hugely superior numbers and armament.[22] Nevertheless, he went through some nervous moments in March, when he made three bad errors of judgement: not wishing to act towards Scoones as Noel Irwin had towards him, he refrained from 'micromanaging', only to find that Scoones nearly lost 17 Indian Division by his slowness; he completely failed to anticipate an attack in divisional strength on Kohima; and, it turned out, he had left the eastern approach to Kohima uncovered and undefended.[23]

The last was possibly the most serious mistake. To his everlasting regret, Slim failed to anticipate a thrust by 15 Japanese Division through Ukhrul, Litan and Sangshak. The 15th Division crossed the Chindwin near Thaungdut on the night of 15–16 March as part of Mutaguchi's second wave, and advanced through the hills 'like a ball of fire', making for Sangshak and Litan prior to the attack on Imphal from the east and north. Travelling light and moving fast through the jungle, the Japanese reached Ukhrul late on 18 March, just 50 miles from Imphal. At the same time, 31 Japanese Division crossed the Chindwin in eight columns and spread out like the probing fingers of an extended hand, one column supporting 15 Japanese Division around Ukhrul, another cutting the road to Kohima north of Imphal, another aiming for Jessami, south-east of Kohima.[24] The idea was that in the end the hand would close, and all columns would converge to take out Kohima. The thrust near Ukhrul took the British by surprise; no major attack had been expected in this sector, and there were few defences. Since the original defence force in this area, 49 Brigade, had been rushed south to relieve the pressure on 17 Indian Division, Scoones had to order in the 3,000-strong Indian Parachute Regiment as a makeshift defence. The Indian Parachute Regiment and one brigade of 23 Division dug in to defend Ukhrul, but after two days' hard fighting they were flushed out by the enemy.[25] The Anglo-Indian units then re-formed and made another stand at Sangshak, five miles to the south, where from 21 to 26 March ferocious combat took place. The fighting was at very close quarters, with mortars and mountain batteries blasting away virtually at point-blank range.[26] There was a terrible bloodbath on 23 March, with the Indian Parachute Brigade, commanded by Tim Hope-Thomson, dug in at a position some 800 yards by 300 in the crater of an extinct volcano. The Japanese attacked every night in a vain attempt to dislodge them, but events turned their way when a supply drop dumped most of the food and ammunition on the Japanese lines by mistake. The Japanese were very quick to decipher the colour-coding used on the drops (blue for rations, white for water, red for ammunition) and to anticipate likely dropping zones.[27] With both sides at last gasp, the Japanese finally captured the water supply, and the remnants of the battered British brigade were ordered to disengage and retreat to Imphal. Despite the defeat and the loss of 600 men, the defenders had bought valuable time that the Japanese could not afford. The reason the reluctant Gracey was told to pull out of his favourite position at Moreh and retreat to the Shennam ridges was that he was in danger of being outflanked by Japanese 15 Division after its victory at Sangshak.[28]

Some authorities claim that Sangshak bought a vital five days that ensured that Kohima was besieged just too late. Certainly it was a taster for things to come, a bloody curtain-raiser to the later terrible battles at Kohima and Shennam. When the Japanese took the volcano, what they found stunned them: 'The hill was an appalling sight. The charred ruins of the missionary church looked down on the burned grass and the few trees. Discarded weapons lay everywhere, and scattered shell fragments. The white bodies of British troops lay with the brown and black bodies of the dead Indians, exposed to the sun or lying in heaps in foxholes; corpses with bellies scooped out, or headless, among the mules swelling and heaving with putrefaction.'[29] On the British side, at headquarters there was dismay among many senior officers about Scoones's overall handling of the first weeks of the campaign, for it was felt that the defeat at Sangshak compounded his earlier errors at Tiddim and that the two failures together could have been decisive. As always, Slim defended Scoones and praised his coolness, but Ouvry Roberts was bitter, feeling that Scoones was a congenital slowcoach; others thought Scoones tired after four years of continuous service and temperamentally unsuited to crisis management.[30] In any case, he had his hands full with Gracey, who, having complained about the withdrawal from Moreh, put in a further protest when he was asked to send reinforcements to Sangshak. Not relishing yet another march, Gracey asked rhetorically how men fighting their own Verdun could be expected to help in the Imphal plain also. Scoones replied with some acerbity that if the Japanese succeeded in penetrating the Imphal plain, Gracey's defence at the 'Verdun' on Shennam ridge would become irrelevant.[31]

Slim and Scoones also erred in their assessment of Japanese intentions in the far north. They had not spotted the importance in Japanese thinking of the village of Imphal, set at 5,000 feet on a loop of the Dimapur–Imphal road. Slim, reasonably enough, thought that the seizure of Kohima would be attempted only in conjunction with the much more important target of Dimapur, a huge supply dump on the Ledo–Imphal line, that hub around which Allied activity revolved. If Dimapur fell, the province of Manipur would be indefensible, the Brahmaputra valley interdicted, Stilwell cut off and all overland supply to China at an end. To everyone's surprise, the Japanese decided to aim for Kohima instead of Dimapur and to invest it with an entire division, not just the single regiment Slim was expecting.[32] Slim thought this a fatuous decision by the commander of 31 Japanese Division, General Sato Kotoku, and even asked the RAF not to bomb his headquarters as he wanted to keep such a prize moron in play as his opponent. 'It never struck him that he could inflict terrible damage on us without taking Kohima at all.'[33] More sober judgement underscores that Sato did his best with an impossible brief. The decision not just to mask Kohima and aim for Dimapur – the logical one – was ruled out because the commander-in-chief in Burma, Lieutenant General Kawabe Mazakazu, did not trust Mutaguchi and suspected him (rightly) of harbouring megalomaniac designs to invade India. Operation U-GO had been 'sold' to Tokyo in the first place on the basis that it was a pre-emptive strike to disable 14th Army and make it unable to invade Burma. In Kawabe's view, an attack on Kohima was still within the permissible ambit of a 'defensive' strike, whereas an assault on Dimapur could only be construed as a genuine offensive against Assam and India.[34] The reason for the attack on Kohima in divisional strength thus in the end went back to the long-running feud between the two different cliques in the Japanese army. Sato and Mutaguchi were actually old enemies. In the 1930s Sato belonged to the Tosei-Ha or 'Control' faction in the army, which believed in collaboration with politicians and capitalists. Mutaguchi, on the other hand, belonged to the Kodo-Ha or 'Imperial Way' faction, which was anti-Communist, revolutionary and proto-fascist, prepared to assassinate politicians and businessmen if they stood in the way. Sato was convinced that Mutaguchi wanted to use the Imphal campaign to pursue his own fanatical dreams, and was not prepared to sacrifice his men needlessly for such a cause.[35]

On 29 March the Japanese cut the Kohima–Imphal road. By the end of March Kohima was cut off and Imphal itself under grave threat. Slim had always considered that superior airpower gave him potentially the drop hand at Imphal, but this depended on his actually being given the planes he needed. With the second Japanese wave not yet lauched, on 14 March Slim requested Mountbatten to divert aircraft from the Hump to fly in reinforcements; specifically, he needed 260 Dakota sorties to get the three brigades (9, 123 and 161) of 5 India Division transferred from the Arakan front to Imphal, and he therefore asked for 30 C-47s for the period 18 March–20 April. This was Mountbatten's finest hour, when he demonstrated that he could be both tough and decisive.[36] In February he had asked Washington for 36 DC-3s to cover the emergency in Arakan. FDR gave him 20 C-47s as an emergency measure but expressly warned he was not to ask for any more in the immediate future. Nothing daunted, Mountbatten diverted 30 Hump aircraft to fly in 5 Indian Division from Arakan to Imphal (though he had no authority to do so), then followed this up on 25 March by asking the Combined Chiefs of Staff for another 40 planes.[37] Predictably this was refused, but four days later the Chief recanted under pressure from Churchill and sent the transports, though they were notionally transferred from the Mediterranean theatre; it was stipulated that the loan of the aircraft would run out on 15 June. There had already been contingency planning to transport an entire division by Dakota, and now the plan was triumphantly carried out. It took 758 sorties to transfer two of the brigades of 5 Indian Division to Imphal and one to Dimapur.[38] By 29 March the entire 5 Indian Division had been flown in from Arakan. Mutaguchi had completely underrated the capacity of Allied aircraft to switch entire divisions from one theatre to another. With the first part of the air campaign a success, Slim switched the transports to the supply of Imphal. Five hundred tons a day were dropped – or 150 planeloads, necessitating up to five sorties a day for the air crews, as there were other calls on the transports. Until his reinforcements were fully in place, Scoones cut the ration at Imphal by one-third and sent most non-combatants back to India on returning aircraft.[39]

In this initial phase of the battle for Imphal, both Slim and Mountbatten began to lose confidence in Giffard, who struck them as either unwilling or unable to supply Imphal with what was needed. Even before the Japanese attack, on 5 March, Slim had asked for an extra division to cover Dimapur and Kohima, but Giffard worried about whether the railway could take the strain of transporting 33 Corps from India. Instead Slim was fobbed off with two battalions of 50 Indian Parachute Regiment and a promise of two divisions from 11 Army Group Reserve if it became necessary. He noted with acerbity that this 'was by no means what I asked for' and on 27 March formally requested that 2 British Division be sent to Dimapur.[40] He and Mountbatten became increasingly concerned by Pownall's slowness and lack of urgency, and Slim's previous good opinion evaporated. Mountbatten had already been irritated by Giffard's refusal to yield military precedence to him as supreme commander, and the Imphal crisis brought the latent conflict to a head. Pownall agreed with his boss that Giffard was complacent, arrogant and useless.[41] In May, as the struggle for Imphal still raged, Mountbatten tried to persuade Giffard to resign on grounds of ill-health; when he refused, Mountbatten summarily fired him. Since a suitable replacement could not be found quickly, the absurd situation developed where the dismissed Giffard was asked to stay on as a stopgap. Surprisingly, he accepted, and Slim found him far more useful in this ancillary role than when he had been a superior officer.[42] With Giffard sidelined, Slim and Mountbatten were able to plan the battle more effectively. The basic plan that 4 Corps would hold at Imphal under Scoones while 33 Corps (comprising 2 British Division plus the 5th and 7th Indian Divisions, which had been flown in from Arakan), under the command of General Montagu Stopford, would advance to the relief of Kohima and Dimapur. Even here there were some problems, for Stopford worried that if too many of his troops were thrown in to defend Kohima, there might be nothing left with which to defend the more important Dimapur. Slim agreed that this was a risk, but argued that the tougher a fight Sato had at Kohima, the more time the British would have to arrive at Dimapur. Slim appointed Major General R.P.L. Ranking to the immediate command at Kohima, with orders to hand over to Stopford and 33 Corps when they arrived in April.[43]

The four-month battle of Kohima-Imphal was a conflict of intricate complexity. Even so experienced a commander as Wavell, when he inspected the battlefields later, commented that it seemed to have been fought 'in penny packets'.[44] Unlike a conventional battle such as Alamein, it consisted of hundreds of chance encounters, dozens of disparate setpiece clashes and hand-to-hand conflicts, frontal attacks, desperate defences, ambushes and bombing raids, all of which have been minutely chronicled but whose details nevertheless will probably forever be mysterious. Slim described it as an epic that ran 'across great stretches of wild country; one day its focal point was a hill named on no map, next a miserable unpronounceable village a hundred miles away. Columns, brigades, divisions, marched and countermarched, met in bloody clashes and reeled apart, weaving a confused pattern hard to unravel.'[45] Slim himself tried to elucidate the confusion by using the analogy of the spokes of a wheel, with Imphal as the hub, and reduced the battle to six spokes. Accordingly, the first spoke was the road north from Imphal to Kohima, the second followed the line of the Iril river valley, the third was the track north-east to Ukhrul, the fourth the road to Tamu, the fifth the Tiddim road and the sixth the track running from Bishenpur to Silchar.[46] An even simpler way to view the battle is to see it as a fourfold affair. Spokes two and three form what one might call the central battlefield of Imphal itself; spokes five and six form the southern front and spoke four the south-eastern; while the key event of the entire battle, the struggle around Kohima, represents Slim's spoke one. The only way to present the events of March–June 1944 lucidly is to deal with each theatre in turn, though naturally all these events were going on simultaneously and had mutual influences and impacts; cross-cutting between them merely increases the inherent confusion. Another advantage of viewing the battle as a quartet is that it also aligns with Slim's progressive tetralogy of Kohima-Imphal, when he divided the long battle into four phases: concentration, attrition, counteroffensive and pursuit.[47]

The central front, the one nearest Imphal itself, featured Japanese 15 Division commanded by Lieutenant General Yamauchi Masafumi. The division had performed brilliantly in cutting across near-impossible jungle country from the Chindwin to Kangpokpi and Kanglatongbi and severing the Kohima–Imphal road on 30 March. Yamauchi was a surprising choice of commander, as he was a sophisticate who had lived abroad and served as military attaché in Washington, and was thus yet another who did not see eye to eye with the xenophobic Mutaguchi. Even more bizarrely, he was already mortally ill with tuberculosis. Mutaguchi compounded his problems by assigning to him as his chief of staff another rabid 'Imperial Way' devotee.[48] Aiming directly for Imphal, Yamauchi collided with 5 Indian Division, which had just been flown in from the Arakan and put on frontline duty without a break. Behind them were 17, 20 and 23 Indian Divisions and the 254th Indian Tank Regiment. For the first half of April, Japanese 15 Division fought a titanic struggle with 5 Indian Division for the key position of the 4,000-foot-high peak of Nungshigum, which dominated the northern end of the Imphal plain. Disconcerted to find that the enemy outnumbered them and had tanks and flame-throwers, the Japanese prepared for a grim experience. Scoones directed that 23 Division move up to the support of the Indian 5th, confident that he would break the enemy and then pursue northeast in the direction of Litan and Ukhrul. The gathering crisis at Kohima meant that reinforcements had to be diverted there, which partly accounted for the more evenly matched encounter that ensued. Nungshigum was an uneven ridge three miles long, with two peaks jutting 1,500 feet above the plain, and only five miles from 4 Corps's headquarters in Imphal.[49] The Japanese easily secured the northern peak, but had a hard time with the southern one. First the Indian Brigade secured it but were attacked before they could dig in; forced off the top, they came back next day and recaptured it; but were finally driven back conclusively on 11 April, when Yamauchi attacked it with all his strength. On the 12th, the British retook the southern summit and then lost it again. Finally, on 13 April, they were able to bring to bear their overwhelming superiority in planes and tanks. Bombers dropped their loads almost at treetop level, while all Japanese plans were thrown into disarray when the British scaled both peaks with tanks – something Yamauchi had considered impossible.[50]

Devastated by the defeat at Nungshigum and reluctantly concluding he had no answer to the enemy's tanks, Yamauchi ordered his men to dig in around Sengmai and Kanglatongbi so as to hang on to the Kohima–Imphal road. In April the RAF flew 6,000 sorties and dropped 1,000 bombs in this sector but without making much impression on Japanese bunkers.[51] Meanwhile 23 Indian Division advanced from Nunshigum along the Ukhrul and Iril valley 'spokes', cleaning out pockets of resistance and setting up roadblocks in their rear. Between 16 April and 7 May there was heavy fighting to eject the Japanese from a position on the Mapao spur dividing the Iril valley from the Imphal–Kohima road. Anglo-Indian attacks were met with fierce Japanese counterattacks; 23 Division cleared the enemy from the southern parts of their position, but could not deliver the *coup de grâce*. On 20 May the Japanese evacuated their forward positions after another tremendous struggle, and on the 21st Kanglatongbi, taken by the Japanese on 9 April, was recovered. Still Yamauchi refused to give up. Nevertheless, the Japanese were now beleaguered, Imphal was no longer threatened on its doorstep and the situation on the central front could be regarded as contained and stabilised.[52] Japanese 15 Division had been almost wiped out. Under strength to begin with, Yamauchi's men had then lost heavily at Nungshigum, while the survivors faced starvation as Mutaguchi's promised rations failed to arrive. To cap it all, as Yamauchi admitted, his men simply had no answer to the British attacks, for travelling through the jungle lightly to strike at Imphal had precluded the taking of effective anti-tank weapons. Yamauchi's division was always the Japanese weak spot, but he valiantly refused to lift the roadblock at Kanglatongbi, and it took Ouvry Roberts and 23 Indian Division until early July to open the Kohima–Imphal road. As a last desperate throw, Yamauchi ordered the use of poison gas – a sad end for a man who was always a realist and hence, in this theatre, a pessimist. Despising xenophobic ignora-muses like Tojo and Mutaguchi, Yamauchi knew from his time in the USA how strong the American eagle was; furthermore, without anti-tank weapons he could do little against the British tanks. While the crazed Mutaguchi kept sending him impossible orders to take Imphal, as if he could accomplish it by waving a magic wand, the dying Mutaguchi had to watch forlornly while his brave warriors starved to death or eked a living from bamboo shoots, parsley and lizards.[53]

Since every one of the four fronts saw brutal, vicious and even fanatical fighting, historians and memorialists have long disputed which of the sectors experienced the worst slaughter. Despite the huge loss of life at Kohima, there are those who contend that the battles in the south-eastern theatre, around the Shennam ridge, were the most dreadful of all. Here Gracey with 20 Indian Division (minus one brigade) faced Major General Yamamoto Tsunoru, and the battles raged over a succession of hills on the ridge. With about 25 miles of front to cover, Gracey had taken the decision to defend a number of fortified bastions or 'boxes' and to keep the Tamu road open, rather than try to control the entire theatre (several hundred square miles of broken hill country) – the only rational decision, given that he had just two brigades.[54] The disputed Shennam ridge was a long, uneven ridge running east–west, with a number of hills rising from it, and it was for possession of these hills that both sides fought with tigerish fury. When the Japanese seized Nippon Hill on 1 April, it took nearly three weeks to dislodge them; Gracey needed massive air support to do this, but even so took heavy casualties.[55] He therefore decided to retire into an even tighter defensive perimeter, deeming that possession of the Tamu road was an irrelevance until the struggle for the ridge was resolved. He contented himself with holding the most important heights and all the passes that led to Palel and the Imphal plain. The war in this sector bogged down into a kind of rerun of the Western Front in World War I, with both sides dug in behind bunkers and trenches, fierce attacks taking place every night, and the stench of death everywhere as the corpses piled up in such a restricted area. Every single knoll, eminence or hill was fought over as if the entire campaign hinged on its possession. After Nippon Hill, the next disputed summit was Crete West, the battle for which occupied the 10 days between 21 April and 1 May.[56]

Meanwhile Yamamoto, better equipped with tanks and artillery than all other sector commanders, tried to blast his way up the road to Palel around Tengnoupal, and made some slow progress from 4–11 April. When the British retook the lost ground, Yamamoto ordered his elite squads into action and pushed them back to the starting point. On the night of 19–20 April, three separate attacks by the Japanese with medium tanks were beaten off, and on the 22nd, parts of the British position were overrun. Gracey sensed that his men were becoming exhausted and weary and a further Japanese assault might have led to breakthrough, but by this time they too were exhausted and depleted in numbers. A final ferocious combat on 22 April ended inconclusively.[57] Gracey consoled himself that Bose's Indian National Army had also been in action against his Indians and Gurkhas but had been roughly treated and almost annihilated; when the survivors tried to surrender, they tended to fall foul of the Gurkhas' dreaded kukri. Yamamoto's next move was to send a commando squad against Palel airfield, using 300 members of the INA, on the grounds that they could approach unnoticed. They achieved surprise but failed at the last moment, as did a second INA group, who complained that the Japanese had provided them with no back-up.[58] Desperately seeking to break through somewhere, Yamamoto next launched a massive attack on 'Scraggy' (another hill on the saddle) on 10 May. As with its predecessor, Crete West, the battle for Scraggy went on for 10 days. Simultaneously, Yamamoto once more attacked the Tengnoupal pos-itions on two successive nights (6–8 May) and made a partial breakthrough. A counterattack by 20 Division on 12 May regained some of the ground, but by now Yamamoto's men were once more exhausted. No reinforcements or supplies were reaching them, but meanwhile 20 Indian Division was withdrawn for rest and recupera-tion and Ouvry Roberts's 23 Division moved into the breach in full strength.[59] This was almost the last straw for the Japanese, who regrouped to focus their attention once more on the Shennam ridge. On 23–24 May there was yet more hard fighting for a new hill, Gibraltar, and the Japanese managed to gain a precarious toehold there. There followed a ferocious struggle for Lone Tree Hill on 24 May, followed by a bloodbath over 'Ben Nevis'. The final, futile Japanese attempt on the Shennam ridge took place on 9 June, when Yamamoto made an all-out bid to regain Scraggy. Making a frontal attack on the Gurkhas on that hill, the Japanese took staggering losses from their triple nemeses: heavy artillery, tanks and airpower. Unwilling and, it seemed, incapable of admitting defeat, they kept plugging away until 25 June.[60] But numbers, equipment and morale were telling. Roberts's 23 Division advanced to the point where Palel airfield was no longer within range of Japanese medium artillery, as it had been throughout May, with what Slim in his inimitable way called 'considerable inconvenience'. As a Parthian shot Yamamoto did manage to score one final minor triumph. An eight-strong Japanese commando party raided the airfield on the night of 3–4 July and managed to destroy eight aircraft with torpedoes and magnetic mines – what Slim called 'a very fine effort'.[61]

On the southern sector – Slim's 'Tiddim spoke' – there was ferocious fighting throughout April and May for possession of the track to the west of Bishenpur and for the town itself, 18 miles south of Imphal. Here the Japanese commander was Lieutenant General Yanakida Motozo, another trenchant critic of Mutaguchi. A realist who was sceptical of success given the exiguous resources the Japanese high command was devoting to Mutaguchi's venture, Yanakida inevitably attracted the epithets 'defeatist' and 'cowardly' from Mutaguchi and his fellow fanatics, among whom was the chief of staff (Colonel Tanaka), specially embedded to make sure that Yanakida followed his superior's instructions. Needless to say, his caution was totally justified, but there are even some British commentators prepared to take Mutaguchi's side, on the grounds that, once committed, whatever his reservations, Yanakida should have provided more dynamic leadership.[62] He certainly began well, sending a commando group on a triumphant trek to blow up the bridge over the Iland river in India. Setting out on 29 March, the commandos achieved their objective on 14 April, sending sky-high a 300-foot suspension bridge poised over an 80-foot gorge.[63] Yanakida then concentrated on securing the Bishenpur–Silchar track, hoping to break into the Imphal plain from the west. The threat from the west led Scoones to pull back the 17th Division, which had been operating north of Imphal, and switch it to this front. There ensued a ferocious struggle for the villages northwest of Bishenpur, with a terrible battle waged in mid-April at the so-called Point 5846.[64] No sooner was this concluded than the two hosts clashed again, this time at the village of Ninthoukgong, south of Bishenpur. The Japanese were in possession, and a first attempt by Cowan's 33 Brigade to eject them on 23 April failed badly, as did a follow-up effort by 17 Division two days later. Very bitter fighting at

Ninthoukgong and on the Silchar track west of Bishenpur continued into May. Both sides sustained alarmingly high casualties in gruesome hand-to-hand fighting, with the toll among the British officers of the Indian regiments notably high.[65]

At the beginning of May, 33 Japanese Division and 17 Division remained locked in combat around Bishenpur, with each trying its best to annihilate the other. To Allied surprise, for the first time in the entire Imphal campaign the Japanese air force entered the fray in a significant way, bombing and strafing the Anglo-Indian airfields. Additionally, 25 Zeros raided Bishenpur on 6 May and again on the 10th. While the colossal struggle around Ninthoukgong continued throughout May, the Japanese pushed forward to another village just two miles south of Bishenpur called Potsangbam (inevitably nicknamed 'Pots and Pans' by the British soldiers). The Japanese chose their position well, for they dug in with anti-tank guns in paddy fields and deep water-filled ditches, which made British tanks ineffective. Once again the Anglo-Indian brigades (32 and 63) took heavy punishment and needed truly massive support from fighters and bombers of both the RAF and the USAAF before they were able to winkle the enemy out on 15 May. The dying echoes of the battle were still being heard when the monsoon burst over the combatants, adding another layer of illness, especially foot rot, to the agonies endured by the soldiers, and underlining once again the similarities between the battle of Imphal and the encounters on the Western Front in the Great War.[66] The Japanese 33 Division had fully justified its reputation of being the toughest in the China-Burma-India theatre, but cracks in morale were beginning to show. By the end of April the strength of one of its regiments was down from 3,000 to 800, and even more ominously, a handful of deserters was starting to drift over to the British lines. This was the precise juncture that Mutaguchi chose to put in a personal appearance at the front. A notorious womaniser, he arrived at Yanakida's headquarters on 22 April with 20 geisha girls whom he confidently intended to instal at Imphal once he had won his 'easy' victory. When he reprimanded Yanakida for defeatism and lacking the instincts of a samurai, Yanakida retired hurt, sulking in his tent. The absurd Mutaguchi, genuinely unable to see the force of Yanakida's complaints, promptly sacked him and replaced him with the more biddable Major General Tanaka Nobuo.[67]

Early in May, Cowan tried to seize the initiative with an ambitious and elaborate flanking movement aimed at cutting the Japanese supply line to the south and then encircling 33 Division. The idea was that 48 Brigade of 17 Division would work round to the south and provide the anvil on which the hammer of the other two brigades of 17 Division would strike. Once again there was ferocious but inconclusive fighting, in which Japanese tanks made a rare appearance, but Cowan's manoeuvre essentially foundered because the would-be 'hammer' brigades were themselves swept up in another battle, when Tanaka tried to penetrate Bishenpur and drive a stake right through 17 Division's heart. Between 16 and 20 May he ordered simultaneous assaults on Bishenpur and the gateway to the Imphal plain.[68] Essentially both sides were attempting to go for the jugular at the very same time, and the result was chaos, confusion, slaughter and massacre, with no clear result. Cowan's Gurkhas in 48 Brigade had to fight their way back northward, with some especially bloody clashes around Torbung (20–24 May), while Cowan, taken by surprise at Bishenpur, had to call in 20 Division to extricate himself from a parlous situation.[69] Heavily outnumbered, Tanaka's attacking force was then virtually annihilated. Both sides had failed, but the British could better afford the failure. The Japanese had done all, and more, that valour alone could attain, but they simply lacked the numbers, artillery, tanks and air support for the job. After ten of the most slaughterous days anywhere on the Imphal–Kohima battlegrounds, they withdrew on 30 May.[70] Even Slim, normally a vehement Jap-hater, conceded his admiration for the enemy: 'There can have been few examples in history of a force as reduced, battered, and exhausted as the 33rd Japanese Division delivering such furious assaults, not with the object of extricating itself, but to achieve its original offensive intention.'[71] Yanakida had been proved right, and the mindless dedication to voluntarism by Tanaka and Mutaguchi revealed as the nonsense it was.

Yet the fanatical Tanaka simply would not give up, and ordered his men to hold firm all along the front, even though most of them were starving and morale had plummeted almost to zero point. Cowan slightly played into his hands by trying to recoup the failed attempt to retake Ninthoukgong on 7 April with yet another bid. Bitter fighting in this sector went on from 18 to 29 May. The result was that the Japanese were left in possession but at the cost of a further 1,000 casualties.[72]

Bit by bit Tanaka came to appreciate the wisdom of Yanakida's stance and the truth of his words when he handed over to him: 'It's all hopeless.'[73] He was now prepared to give tacit agreement to the proposition that Mutaguchi's orders to take Bishenpur at all costs simply meant massive casualties for Japan, but unless he was prepared to resign, he had no choice but to obey Mutaguchi's suicidal orders. On 2 June he therefore issued a general order, exhorting his troops to make a last effort to break through to Imphal. The ruthless attitude to human life evinced by the bushido code is well in evidence in Tanaka's alarming words:

> Now is the time to capture Imphal. Our death-defying infantry group expects certain victory when it penetrates the main fortress of the enemy. The coming battle is the turning point. It will denote the success or failure of the Greater East Asia War. You men have got to be fully in the picture as to what the present situation is; regarding death as something light as a feather, you must tackle the task of capturing Imphal. For that reason it must be expected that the division will be almost annihilated. I have confidence in your firm courage and devotion and believe that you will do your duty, but should any delinquencies occur you have to understand that I shall take the necessary action . . . On this one battle rests the fate of the Empire. All officers and men fight courageously![74]

As Slim rightly remarked: 'Whatever one may think of the military wisdom of thus pursuing a hopeless object, there can be no question of the supreme courage and hardihood of the Japanese soldiers who made the attempts. I know of no army that could have equalled them.'[75]

The grim war of attrition continued. By the middle of June the Japanese held only half of Ninthoukgong – they occupied the southern end, separated from the British in the northern part by a muddy stream. Throughout the first half of June the village was the scene of bloody fighting, with an epic encounter on the 7th, when another Victoria Cross was awarded. Ninthoukgong was in fact something of a nursery for these awards, for two more were awarded, to Gurkhas, for the June combats. Still Tanaka urged his battered and bruised men on, and the slugging firefights for individual hills continued: the Japanese took Forest Hill on 20 June but failed against Plum Hill. By now Cowan was confident he had the upper hand – so confident in fact that he had Noel Coward performing cabaret in Bishenpur for his troops. The British superiority in tanks, artillery and airpower was overwhelming, and even the monsoon seemed to take a greater toll on the enemy; by the end of June Tanaka had lost altogether 12,000 dead, 7,000 killed in battle and another 5,000 to disease – an amazing 70 per cent of the division's strength.[76] Slim's tactic of bleeding the enemy dry was rarely seen to more dramatic effect. Yet even at the end of June, the crazed Mutaguchi still clung to the forlorn hope that an eleventh-hour victory at Bishenpur would both retrieve the situation on the southern front and save his face. The real fault, however, must attach to the Japanese commander-in-chief Kawabe. Dithering, ill and decisive, prostrated with amoebic dysentery, he periodically reasoned that he must cancel U-GO in its entirety, but every time he summoned the courage to do so, a cable would arrive from Tokyo stressing the paramount necessity of victory in Burma, to compensate for the disasters in the Pacific. Two-faced also, Kawabe tried to hedge his bets, at once urging Mutaguchi on to even greater efforts and asking Tokyo for permission to cancel the Imphal operation. Even more incredibly, he still hoped for great things from Bose and the INA, despite all the evidence that both were busted flushes. In the end it was a race between Kawabe and Mutaguchi as to who would give up first. On 8 July, just before receiving formal cancellation of U-GO, Mutaguchi himself concluded that the offensive against Bishenpur had failed and ordered the tattered remnants of 33 Division to retreat across the Chindwin.[77]

Despite all the desperate battles fought on the central, southern and south-eastern front, it still remains the case that the heart of the great Imphal-Kohima struggle centred around the village of Kohima itself. The siege of this remote outpost, and subsequent battle, took place so far from the other fronts that some historians, mistakenly, have regarded Kohima as a separate battle.[78] Yet it is very clear that Kohima-Imphal formed an organic whole, that no conflict on any individual front could be properly understood without reference to simultaneous events on the others. Slim's intention always was that the Japanese should be encouraged to believe that victory was imminent on all fronts. This was why, despite Mountbatten's urgings, he did not reinforce Imphal to the point where it was impregnable, for that might have encouraged the Japanese to withdraw. His abiding intention was not just to defeat the enemy but to annihilate him, so that a British invasion of Burma could become a solid reality. Debate has raged over whether Slim initially made a mistake about Kohima, whether his subordinates did, or whether inveigling Mutaguchi into a protracted and impossible campaign in the northern sector was not all part of some machiavellian masterpiece. Slim himself claimed that he was taken by surprise when the Japanese threw an entire division against Kohima,[79] but his autobiographical statements were sometimes misleading – disingenuous, his critics would say. A very good example comes right from the earliest days at Kohima. Slim had originally told Ranking to hold both Dimapur and Kohima until Stopford arrived on the scene. On 3 April Stopford arrived and made what was undoubtedly, from the standpoint of the defence of Kohima, a bad error. He ordered Ranking to pull 161 Brigade out of Kohima and transfer it to Dimapur. Ranking appealed over Stopford's head to Slim to rescind the order but, reluctant as always to overrule his generals, Slim confirmed it.[80] If Slim had overruled Stopford, there is good reason to believe that the ensuing siege of Kohima would not have been so protracted. In *Defeat into Victory*, Slim muddies the waters by claiming that the error was Ranking's, not Stopford's. The usual judgement is that Slim made a mistake and thought Kohima of limited importance compared with Dimapur.[81] Another interpretation is possible: that Slim realised Mutaguchi was playing right into his hands by the assault on Kohima – militarily nugatory alongside the far richer prize of Dimapur – and encouraged him to continue in his folly. This would explain why Slim assigned 161 Brigade to Kohima in the first place, as also the 4th West Royal Kents. Slim's original orders to Ranking were ambiguous and muddled, and this was uncharacteristic of the man. Either his touch in early April was less than sure, or he was playing a very devious game.[82]

The Japanese under Lieutenant General Sato Kotoku launched their attack on the beleaguered Kohima on 4 April, and a famous two-week siege commenced. The defending garrison numbered only some 3,000, of which 1,000 were non-combatants.[83] There was no systematic defence, so the British troops dug in at suitable places along the Kohima ridge. Kohima village, at 5,000 feet, was set in an ocean of peaks and ridges crossed by bridle paths, with some peaks to the west as high as 10,000 feet and those to the north and east reaching 8,000 feet. The village was at the summit of a ridge, where the best road between Assam and Burma goes through a pass. The ridge at Kohima was steep and thickly wooded, creating conditions of pitch blackness for attackers swarming upwards (until the trees were destroyed by artillery). At a right-angled bend of the main road was the deputy commissioner's bungalow, complete with tennis court, to the south of which were small hills on which stood warehouses and supply shacks. With maddening temperatures oscillating between very cool at night and sweaty humidity in the day, this obscure spot was destined to be the scene of 'fighting as desperate as any recorded in history'.[84] Once he had realised his mistake, Stopford sent 161 Indian Brigade back to Kohima. They arrived on 5 April, but there was no room for them on the tightly packed ridge, so they withdrew to Jotsoma, two and a half miles to the north-west, from which they could support the defenders by raining down artillery fire on the attackers. However, by 8 April the Japanese had cut off Jotsoma as well, so there was no direct reinforcement possible from 161 Brigade, which took up a defensive position in a 'box'.[85] From the very beginning the Japanese launched one determined attack after another on Kohima ridge. Sato threw everything he had at the defenders, shelling and mortaring the garrison at dusk, then, after dark, sending in wave after wave of infantry, who clashed with the British in the most terrible and vicious hand-to-hand fighting.

Using both frontal attacks and infiltration, Sato's men gained early success by penetrating as far as the huts on the night of 6–7 April; some of them hid in brick ovens in the field supply depot. They were flushed out from here by an act of courageous self-immolation by a Lance Corporal Harman, who was awarded a posthumous VC.[86] Still the Japanese pressed relentlessly on, nibbling away at the defences on the ridge, taking one small section after another, pressing the garrison into a tighter and tighter defensive circle. On 9 April the British were pushed back to Garrison Hill, while the Japanese took the all-important GPT ridge, which controlled Kohima's water supply; the defenders were now short of water as well as fighting men.[87] As a by-product of their advance, Sato's men seized three months' supply of rice and salt – just as well for them, as they had received no supplies since crossing the Chindwin. Thus fortified, they took Jail Hill to the south, reducing the Kohima defence to a defensive perimeter 700 by 900 by 1,100 yards. The Japanese now had an open field for their guns, so it was exceedingly fortunate for the defenders that the enemy was low on ammunition. Nonetheless, this was the moment when morale was at its lowest, with many soldiers complaining openly that the generals had left them there as sacrificial victims.[88] Although they were being resupplied from the air, the airdrops themselves had disappointing results, increasing the British despondency. Many of the dropped water containers were holed, the wrong ammunition was sent in, the transport planes were highly vulnerable to ground fire as they flew along the floor of the valley, and worst of all, many of the drops fell into the hands of the Japanese, who were overjoyed with this manna from heaven. The one bright spot was that a new water supply was eventually found on the road to the north-west, but this could be used only after dark, with the water-carriers in continual danger of detection and destruction.[89]

No description can do justice to the horrors of the period 4–20 April at Kohima. Every inch of ground was disputed in the bloodiest and most desperate hand-to-hand fighting. Major battles were fought over undistinguished hills on the ridge: Bunker Hill on 11–14 April, Garrison Hill on 17 April; FSD Hill on the same day.[90] There was a grim five-day struggle for the tennis courts of the deputy commissioner's bungalow, which became one of the enduring legends of Kohima. Every night the Japanese repeated their assaults, which the British always knew were coming and could therefore counter with a withering fire from big guns and mortars, followed by deadly fire from Bren guns and grenades at those of the enemy who survived the initial barrage. Every morning the tennis court was festooned with bloated, festering bodies, which provided a smorgasbord for the millions of flies that rose at dawn and were so numerous they covered the corpses like a thick blanket.[91] The physical conditions on the confined battlefield were unspeakable. The defenders on the ridge had to eat, sleep, perform all bodily functions and then fight in slit trenches. It was difficult to sleep much at night, water was always scarce, and when this was relieved by a tropical downpour, everyone ended up soaked to the skin and chilled to the marrow. Dead bodies lay everywhere, and the stench of corpses mingled with that of human faeces and the smell of acrid cordite to produce an unspeakable, noisome fetor.[92]

The wounded fared especially badly, with dying men lying in agony amid the stench of stale sweat, blood and rotting flesh; not surprisingly, many of those wounded, but not mortally, lost the will to live when they were abandoned in the open in such conditions. There was no way to evacuate the wounded, and on the way to the reserve water pipe at night the water-carriers frequently tripped over the bodies of the dead or dying.[93] The Japanese tried to stretch the defenders' nerves to breaking point by attacking at night, using psychological warfare, especially noise and simulated Anglo-Indian panic, but all to no avail, though some of the Indian troops did crack.[94] Yet after a week of the most terrible close combat and carnage, the Japanese managed essentially to slice the British defence in two. Just when hope was fading and success for Sato seemed certain, on 16 April 5 Brigade arrived to relieve Jotsoma, allowing 161 Indian Brigade to advance to the relief of Kohima. The attackers were diverted from their primary task by this new threat, and the sortie from the Jotsoma 'box' allowed 161 Brigade to open the road to Kohima. The Japanese counterattacked vigorously, occupying other hills in their path and inflicting heavy casualties.[95]

Finally, though, heavily outnumbered and starving, the Japanese had to withdraw and lift the siege on 20 April. They had come very close to success, but lack of food and ammunition weighed heavily against them; additionally, the terrain at Kohima made it difficult for them to 'cash' their local numerical superiority. Now the tables were well and truly turned, for Stopford had received four brigades as fresh reinforcements, while the Japanese had no reinforcements, no air support, no tanks, inadequate artillery and a shortage of ammunition. While 2 Division advanced cautiously from Dimapur (most of it had been trained for the wrong kind of warfare – amphibious operations), 7 Indian Division moved to the north of Kohima to pre-empt any enemy move towards the Brahmaputra.[96] For the moment, though, the longer-term prospects were dismissed, while the British enjoyed the triumph of lifting the siege. Although 19 British and Indian regiments would win the battle honours 'Kohima', the more distinguished honour 'Defence of Kohima' would be reserved for the Royal West Kents and the Assam regiment.[97] What the troops of 161 Brigade found when they marched in appalled them. Kohima itself was unrecognisable, its buildings in ruins, its walls pockmarked with bullet holes or shell bursts, all trees stripped of leaves, the wooded slopes of Kohima ridge denuded, and the tattered remains of parachutes hanging raggedly from the few branches that remained. The defenders were like bloodstained scarecrows, in ragged clothes and rotting boots, grimy, bleary-eyed, unwashed, bearded, suffering from shell shock, tinnitus and general alienation, all experiencing sleep deprivation and desperate for slumber. Smelling of blood, sweat and death, they had nothing clean about them except their weapons. It was a scene by Hieronymus Bosch out of Passchendaele.[98] One observer, who had known Kohima when it was a beautifully fresh and green hill station, described it as follows: 'The place stank. The ground everywhere was ploughed up with shell-fire and human remains lay rotting as the battle raged over them. Flies swarmed everywhere and multiplied with incredible speed. Men retched as they dug in . . . the stink hung in the air and permeated one's clothes and hair.'[99] The unsung heroes in keeping the defenders supplied this time had been not so much the Allied air forces as the Naga tribesmen, but it was typical of Slim that he did not neglect this fact either. To show his support for them he sent the 23rd LRP brigade, withheld from Wingate, on a three-month sweep through the Naga hills, gradually flushing the Japanese out of the tribal heartlands all the way to Phek.[100]

Although the siege was over, the battle itself was far from won, for all the gains made by the Japanese had now to be laboriously retaken, inch by bloody inch. A good Japanese commander would have pulled out completely at this moment, and Sato wanted to, but he was under continual pressure from Mutaguchi, always urging him on to one final effort. Absurdly, on 17 April, when the tide was already turning and reinforcements were advancing, Mutaguchi told Sato that he had at all costs to take Kohima by 29 April; naturally he did not say where the necessary food and ammunition were to come from. The publicity-crazed Mutaguchi had hit on the date arbitrarily because it was the emperor's birthday.[101] And so Sato was condemned to continue with a now hopeless fight. Stopford concentrated on removing the Japanese from Kohima ridge before taking the fight to nearby Naga village. He experimented with fighting a holding action in the centre at Kohima with one brigade while outflanking the enemy with the other two, but Sato was no fool (despite Slim's strictures) and the attempt failed.[102] Meanwhile the Japanese, who still held much of Kohima ridge and

were dug in at an extremely strong position 7,000 yards long, counterattacked on Garrison Hill and the defenders were as hard put to it
on the nights of 22–23 April as the orginal besieged troops had been.
On 27 April Stopford switched attention back to the deputy commissioner's bungalow and tennis court (both a shambles by this stage).
After heavy fighting his men took this position and the Japanese counterattack (on the night of 29–30 April), though pressed forward with
all the old ferocity, failed to dislodge them. The fabled tennis court
was once again a no-man's-land, with hand grenades winging from
one side of the court to the other instead of tennis balls. For 16 days
the stalemate around the tennis court continued, until finally the
British were able to move tanks up to the bungalow. As these armoured
behemoths began to devastate the foe, slowly the bloody battle for
the bungalow grounds was won. The Dorset Regiment cleared the
ground of all enemy bunkers and foxholes, using flame-throwers and
showing no mercy; since the Japanese still held the high ground on
three sides of the bungalow, they did not do so without considerable
cost.[103]

Slowly and stubbornly the British began to make inroads on the
Japanese-held hills, although the tightness of enemy discipline and the
brilliance of their interlocking defence systems made progress almost
unbearably painful. The Japanese bunkers and defensive positions,
exhibiting their genius for intersupporting concealed fieldworks, aided
by the natural protection of steep-sided ridges, made them the toughest
of nuts to crack. Unlike the Anglo-Indian troops, who liked to fight
in front, facing the enemy, with the emphasis on individual valour,
the Japanese bunkers were sighted to the flank rather than the rear,
allowing them to fire on their own positions if they were under attack.
Enemy mortars, as lethal and accurate as the legendary German
machine-gunners, time and again prevented the Anglo-Indian attackers
from digging in.[104] Eventually 4th Brigade managed to worm its way
towards GPT Ridge in late April and storm it on 3 May but without
securing the entire position. Unfortunately, 6 Brigade failed to take its
target of Kuki Piquet, which the British had been hammering away
at ever since the raising of the siege. It fared rather better on its second
objective, FSD Ridge, but again, as with GPT Ridge, secured only
part of it.[105] Meanwhile 5 Brigade entered Naga village but was then
thrown out by an enemy counterattack. A British attack on the key

point of Jail Hill was also beaten back with heavy losses on 7 May. As Slim commented: 'Our troops were again discovering that it was one thing to reach a Japanese bunker, another to enter it.'[106] The British were deeply frustrated. Airpower could make no impression on the Japanese positions and the only effective weapon, the tank, was largely impotent because of the impossible gradients of the ridges and the heavy rain that churned everything into liquid mud. Finally in mid-May yet another brigade, from 7th Division, was brought in. Now heavily outnumbered, almost out of ammunition and starving – on a diet of bamboo shoots and wild game – the Japanese also began to sustain high fatalities from beri-beri, dysentery and, especially, malaria. With no quinine, they had no defence against the latter disease. The combination of all these factors finally cracked the warriors of Nippon. Jail Hill, GPT and FSD ridges fell to the British in quick succession during 11–13 May.[107]

Once again Sato pleaded with Mutaguchi for permission to withdraw, but the absurd Mutaguchi asked him to hold on, assuring him that Imphal would fall within 10 days. Sato was at his last gasp but, curiously, the British had almost reached crisis point themselves. Stopford was increasingly worried about the failures and slow progress at Kohima and the seeming ability of the enemy to fight on for ever, simply retreating to another position and digging in there. Even with the airlift, 4 Corps was short of rations, but the real concern was the future of airpower. After 15 June Mountbatten was due to return the 79 transport aircraft, and what would happen then? It was conceivable that if that happened, the intricate design woven by Slim at Kohima-Imphal might unravel. Accordingly, Mountbatten signalled the combined chiefs that if he returned the transport aircraft as agreed, the entire campaign would grind to a halt. What, then, was he to do? He received no answer.[108] Slim was also alarmed by a memo from Peirse, which argued that on one interpretation of the agreement, the aircraft might have to be returned even before mid-June; it depended whether the planes on loan from the Middle East were to be construed as those loaned for the Arakan campaign or as part of a subsequent agreement. He contacted Mountbatten, who once again insisted that the planes were not to be given up and that he would take the responsibility. Mountbatten signalled London, where Churchill agreed that he would oppose any contrary move from FDR and the US Joint

Chiefs, whatever the consequences. As he put it in his inimitable style: 'Let nothing go from the battle you need for victory. I will not accept denial of this from any quarter, and will back you to the full.'[109] This gave Mountbatten the excuse to claim that the retention of the aircraft was the result of his unique genius and strategic insight. In a letter to Edwina he made the absurd boast: 'If the battle of Imphal is won, it will be almost entirely due to Dickie overriding all his generals.'[110] This was of course a grotesque travesty. Slim had asked *him* for the planes, and there were no generals who opposed the move. It is around this time that we first detect a chink in the ostensibly cosy Slim–Mountbatten entente. Always wanting to go faster than conditions or events warranted, Mountbatten told Slim and Scoones that he wished the Kohima–Imphal road opened by mid-June. Slim took the line that he was not going to be hurried by anyone, and this, plus the sacking of Giffard, may have given Mountbatten the idea that Slim too was a sluggard. Certainly Mountbatten's failure to promote Slim to Giffard's old post after the battle was distinctly odd, and we have Alanbrooke's word for it that Mountbatten expressly opposed such a promotion.[111]

However, Slim was grateful that Mountbatten did not make an issue of opening the Kohima–Imphal road, though he did finally issue a directive instructing that the road *must* be opened by mid-July.[112] He knew Imphal would not fall and was far more interested in destroying Mutaguchi's divisions than the formal relief of a place that would survive until he had accomplished his mission. He had every reason for confidence. Mid-May marked the beginning of the end for the Japanese at Kohima. On the 15th, 33 Brigade assaulted the next target, Treasury Hill, and met almost no opposition. Buoyed by these successes, Stopford ordered a twofold assault: on the central Japanese positions around Kohima – Dyer Hill, Pimple Hill and Big Tree Hill – and on the Japanese left in Naga village. Stopford thought enemy resistance was crumbling, but he was soon disabused. On 19 May the attack on Naga village met with initial success, but was then held up by well-concealed Japanese bunkers and finally thrown back in disarray, with heavy casualties. The attack on the centre, by fresh troops from 7 Indian Division, was also repulsed in ferocious fighting from 24 to 30 May.[113] While this slugging match was going on, Stopford tried again at Naga and took Hunter's Hill and Church Knoll, the highest points in the village. At this the Japanese will finally did seem to snap. On 2 June they pulled out of Naga village, meaning that the northern part of the former Japanese positions at Kohima were now in British hands. In the southern sector Stopford tried to take the great Aradura ridge in the last week of May but was thrown back with heavy loss.[114] The fall of Naga village, however, delivered to him a new means of approach to the Aradura, and this plus a change of tactics led to the fall of Big Tree Hill, 2,000 yards north-east of Aradura. As the entire brigade closed in for the kill, the Japanese abandoned their positions and pulled out.[115] The battle of Kohima was now effectively won. Sato, who despised Mutaguchi and was yet another general ideologically opposed to him – Sato belonged to the Tosei-Ha 'Control' faction' – ignored his orders to stay put and signalled to 15 Army his intention to retreat. 'Our swords are broken and our arrows gone. Shedding bitter tears, I now leave Kohima.'[116]

The 64-day battle for Kohima, an epic fully the equal of the Somme or Passchendaele, was finally over, but it still took another 15 days before the road to Imphal was completely open. The Anglo-Indian advance was painful, for they still had to winkle the enemy out of strong positions on the Kohima road, and there was heavy fighting and casualties all the way.[117] On 22 June, 6 Brigade from Kohima joined hands with 9 Brigade from Imphal and Imphal itself was formally relieved, just in time to prevent the 55,000 men and 11,000 animals there from running short of food again. Kawabe came up from Rangoon at the end of May, but spent a lot of time with Yanakida so did not get round to a meeting with Mutaguchi until 6 June, when he found him still in denial about battlefield realities. Even at this late stage Mutaguchi was deluging Sato with impossible orders, which Sato simply disregarded. The first was to send a regiment south from Kohima to assist with 15 Division's attack on Imphal in May, to which Sato signalled that this was impracticable, as his division was approaching exhaustion.[118] The last was one sent after Mutaguchi had thrown in the towel at Kohima, instructing Sato to assist Yamamoto in his last-ditch assault on Palel. Sato ignored this and instead sent his men to search for unhulled rice prior to the retreat to the Chindwin. When Mutaguchi in person gave the order for the exhausted Japanese heroes of Kohima to tackle another impossible task at Palel, they answered with their feet and deserted in droves.[119] Having already replaced Yanakida, Mutaguchi in a fury sacked both Sato and Yamauchi, accusing Sato of insubordination. Sato told Mutaguchi that he was overjoyed at the prospect of a court martial, for the truth about Kohima-Imphal would come out and Mutaguchi would be dragged down into disgrace with him. But Kawabe, who had already decided to end U-GO, did not want the scandal of a court martial, with rival generals washing dirty linen in public. He therefore hushed up the entire controversy. Sato was placed on the reserve and a medical certificate was issued saying that he had had 'a nervous breakdown'.[120] By this time even Mutaguchi had admitted that the game was up, but Kawabe could not formally cancel the operation until he got the all-clear from General Terauchi in Singapore, and this did not arrive until 4 July.[121] Formally dismissed on 7 July, Sato made a moving farewell statement, well within the idiom of that curious amalgam of Buddhism and bushido that was Japanese military culture: 'I ask forgiveness of those who lie dead at Kohima because of my poor talent. Though my body is parted from them, I shall always remain with them in spirit. Nothing can separate those of us who were tried in the fire at Kohima.'[122]

Slim's victory at Kohima-Imphal was total and complete. The casualty figures tell their own story. Of the 65,000 fighting men who crossed the Chindwin in March, the Japanese lost 30,000 killed and 23,000 wounded, and sustained another 15,000 casualties among the 50,000 support staff; in addition 17,000 pack animals died. Such was their fanatical fighting spirit that only 600 prisoners were taken in the entire four-month campaign.[123] The total Allied loss at Kohima-Imphal and Arakan, by contrast, was 24,000. As Mountbatten rightly said in a letter to Edwina: 'It is the most important defeat the Japs have ever suffered in their military career because the numbers involved are so much greater than any Pacific island operations.'[124] Even the monsoon had entered into Slim's calculations: he reckoned that if the garrisons at Imphal and Kohima could stand firm for two months, the Japanese would have to take the main onslaught from the weather when they were ill-equipped and starving. So it proved. Not only did weaponry, radios and everything metallic deteriorate in the rain and rust, but practically everything steamed or turned green, clothes rotted and men's fingers seemed to turn white and wrinkle with age. Even worse, disease became rampant, as mosquitoes multiplied, bringing malaria in their train. At the altitude of Kohima there were times when the combatants could barely see each other and visibility was reduced to 100 yards.[125] By any standards, Slim had planned and executed a military tour de force. Yet even as the Japanese broke off in disarray, and the signs of victory were evident, the military Jeremiahs were still in full cry, nervous about a possible disaster at Imphal. Worst of all offenders was Alanbrooke, a congenital pessimist, who did not even think D-Day would succeed. On 1 June he wrote in his diary: 'In the afternoon, a long meeting with Pownall to discuss the heart breaking situation in Burma. I see disaster staring us in the face, with Mountbatten incapable of realizing it, Pownall clever enough but too lazy to appreciate the danger and Giffard I am afraid lacking the adequate vision to see where he is going to. Oh! How I wish we had some more men with more vision.'[126]

Why did Slim win Imphal-Kohima so decisively? Part of the answer lies in the manifold mistakes made by the Japanese themselves. Their military leaders did not have a clear objective, they were complacent, and they did not plan their offensive meticulously. What was the point of the attack on Kohima, which Slim considered an act of monstrous folly, since it meant he could bleed 33 Division dry while not suffering the kind of real anxiety he would have felt if Dimapur had been under attack? The answer seems to be that it was a compromise between the 'march on India' ideas of Mutaguchi and the more cautious and defensive stance of the higher command. When Tojo gave the go-ahead for U-GO on 9 January 1944, he sanctioned an attack on Imphal not as the prelude to an invasion of India but only as a pious hope that the Imperial Army would be able to report a victory *somewhere* to compensate for the string of defeats in the Pacific.[127] Although Mutaguchi's forces moved at lightning speed once they had crossed the Chindwin, detailed plans had not been laid for trapping and eliminating the three British divisions in the Imphal area. An airborne invasion in the rear of 20 and 17 Divisions, along the line of the Chindits in Operation THURSDAY, would have cut them off from Imphal. The counter-argument would no doubt be that the Japanese lacked the aerial capability for such an operation, but in that case Mutaguchi should have asked himself whether his goals were ever feasible. But he could certainly have prevented the rapid reinforcement of Imphal by 5 and 7 Divisions simply by timing the Arakan operation to coincide more closely with U-GO. By leaving a gap between the two campaigns, he gave Slim the chance to switch these two divisions to the other front.[128] Perhaps an even worse fault was that the Japanese had never really surmounted the 'Pearl Harbor' syndrome – the blitzkrieg campaigns that had won them most of East Asia in five months from December 1941 to April 1942. Just as Napoleon, having defeated the Austrians so many times, fatally underestimated them and nearly came to grief in his 1809 Wagram campaign, so the Japanese totally failed to appreciate that 1944 was not 1942 or even 1943, that the enemy had learned from their mistakes and refashioned their army so that they were now a totally different kind of opponent.[129] The issue of leadership is also salient. Where Slim had the confidence of both his superiors and his ancillary generals, many of whom he had personally trained at military academy, the Japanese leadership was always in disarray, divided between the ideological factionalism of Tosei-Ha and Kodo-Ha. The result was that Mutaguchi ended by sacking three of his four field commanders. That the lack of unity in Japanese command was an important factor can be seen from the sequel to Kohima-Imphal. Mutaguchi was in disgrace and sacked by the end of the year. Tojo resigned as prime minister and chief of the Imperial general staff. At one time Terauchi was tipped as his successor, but Koiso Kuniaki became the new prime minister, while Terauchi stayed in command of the Southern Army.[130]

On the Allied side, airpower was crucial to the victory. General Stratemeyer's Eastern Air Command, one of the units that came under the direction of the Supreme Allied Commander, consisted of the Strategic Air Force, Troop Carrier Command, the Photographic Reconnaissance Force and the 3rd Tactical Air Force, responsible for battlefield back-up. Air Marshal Sir John Baldwin, in charge of the 3rd Tactical Air Force, was an old ally of Slim's who had honed his skills in the Arakan campaign. Baldwin began the airlift to Kohima, code-named Operation STAMINA, on 8 April, but his planes took time to build up to the daily requirement of 540 tons. By 30 June his aircraft had flown in 19,000 troops, 14,317,000 pounds of rations, 1,303 tons of grain for the pack animals, 835,000 gallons of fuel and lubricants, 12,000 bags of mail and 43,475,760 cigarettes, using 404 aircraft from 15 squadrons.[131] All this was done using the airfield at Imphal alone, since the one at Palel was considered too exposed to Japanese artillery fire and commandos. Baldwin was an expert at the fast turn-round of planes, as he had proved when establishing Broadway for Wingate during Operation THURSDAY. His delight in his own expertise is evident: 'Nobody has seen a transport operation until he has stayed at Broadway in the full light of the Burma full moon and watched Dakotas coming in and taking off in opposite directions on a single strip all night long, at the rate of one landing or one taking off every three minutes.'[132] Mutaguchi had not factored into his calculations either the general Allied air capacity or the ability of aircraft to move two divisions from one theatre to another with such speed. While the British were being supplied in this way, the back-up for Mutaguchi's armies was non-existent: they had to survive by hunting, or capturing Allied airdrops. In many respects the ability of the Japanese to fight on for four months at Kohima-Imphal was staggering, for they were without air or armour support, with inadequate artillery, no reinforcements or exiguous ammunition, supplies or rations. At the height of Kohima-Imphal the Japanese were outnumbered two to one, while the Anglo-Indian forces enjoyed a five-to-one superiority in armament. Yet not even this expresses the true disparity, for the two-to-one ratio masks the fact that the British fought in relays, with brigades 'spelling' each other, while the Japanese soldiers were never relieved. Of course it had always been Slim's intention that when he engaged the enemy in a major battle, he would so with crushing superiority at all levels.[133]

All of this has seduced the unwary into asserting that Slim's victory was a foregone conclusion, that a military incompetent could have won Kohima-Imphal with such crushing superiority of resources. This downplays and underrates Slim's talent at every level. At Alamein General Montgomery enjoyed a similar preponderance of power over the Germans, yet the groundwork for his victory had been done by others, notably Auchinleck, whom 'Monty' and Churchill then tried to airbrush out of the picture. The reason the Japanese faced such tough, disciplined and versatile forces at Kohima-Imphal was that Slim himself had forged a 'New Model Army' and had worked for nearly two years on building up equipment, morale, elan and *esprit de corps*. Besides, Slim's personality was ideal for this particular campaign, since he had two great gifts: the ability to turn round a battle that was going in the enemy's favour; and the talent to improvise quickly so that the enemy was soon dancing to his tune. In contrast to the muddled objectives of the Japanese, he knew precisely what his aims were at every hour of every day, and this clarity communicated itself in his lucid and economical strategic briefings, which so impressed all who heard them.[134] A master of timing, he had the art of proceeding neither too fast nor too slow. The war in Burma was bedevilled by leaders who either demonstrated sluggishness and inertia, such as Wavell and Giffard, or were flamboyant bulls-at-a-gate who believed that speed and expedition were everything, notably Churchill, Mountbatten and Wingate. Even Napoleon sometimes came to grief through impatience, but Slim's ability to wait calmly for the right moment was almost Oriental. Ironically, in view of his low opinion of the Japanese, the military leader in history he most resembles is the great sixteenth-century shogun, Tokugawa Ieyasu. Allied to this was a rock-like imperturbability: he was unflappable because he was confident he would win, and he realised that a calm, stoical surface did wonders for morale.[135] None of this made him a plaster saint. He was all too human, and to his officers he could reveal a tetchy side. On one of his visits to Imphal he arrived late for a conference of senior personnel because his escort had lost the way. He told the assembly: 'I know you think the Military Police are bloody awful. Now I know why!'[136] No man can live under permanent stress without cracking sometimes, and despite the great victory at Imphal, there was plenty more stress in store for Slim.

On the nothern front, Stilwell was still trying to trap the Japanese 18th Division at Mainkwan in the Hukawng valley, hooking from the right with his Chinese regulars while the irregulars appeared on the left at Walawbum below Mainkwan to block the enemy retreat. Slim, hoping that his American colleague would enjoy the same numerical advantage he had had in the Arakan, also put under his command the small British garrison at Fort Hertz in the extreme north of the country, which had been holding out since 1942, and the Kachin irregulars. On 19 February Stilwell was reinforced by Galahad force, aka 5307th Composite Regiment of Northern Combat Area Command (NCAC) but better known under their soubriquet 'Merrill's Marauders'. Frank Merrill himself, their commander, was one of Stilwell's favourites, a tall and gaunt-looking man who suffered from poor health, but 'a fine, courageous leader who inspired confidence', as Slim assessed him.[1] At last Stilwell commanded US troops in Burma, 3,000 of them, but this triumph was modified by the personal inadequacy of a number of the Marauders. Recruited from units in the south-west Pacific and the island of Trinidad in the Caribbean, many of the volunteers were psychopaths pure and simple. The 33rd Infantry Regiment was well known as 'the pits of the army', where all the worst problem cases were sent, signing on simply to get out of Trinidad. The Marauders' contract specified a fixed period of three months' training and three months' combat. The training in India had not gone well, with serious disciplinary problems every day apparent. Their three-month stay in India has been described as part terrorising the natives and part keeping the military police busy. Ten per cent of the Marauders went AWOL and the rest amused themselves by shooting at cattle, chickens and birds – virtually anything that walked or crawled, in fact – and even firing at the feet of the locals to make them dance; on the train to Ledo they fired out of the window at any passing 'wogs' that took their fancy.[2] Arrogant, sociopathic, full of blithe self-confidence, the Marauders were a gung-ho outfit whose credo was described as follows: 'My pack is on my back, my gun is oiled and loaded, and as I walk in the shadow of death I fear no sonofabitch.'[3]

The entry of the Marauders into the fray did not impress their commander. Always obsessed by speed – a quality he shared with Mountbatten – Stilwell fretted at the time it took them to cross the 130 miles over the Naga range to the battlefront. Part of the problem was that 5307th Composite was mule-based and had to bring 700 animals with them but none of them knew anything about muleteering. Whatever misgivings Stilwell had when he saw his reinforcements, he kept them to himself and addressed them simply and quietly, explaining that their mission was to hit Walawbum on 3 March.[4] The 3,000 troops were organised in three battalions, each one operating in two columns, known as combat teams, and each with an intelligence and reconnaissance platoon and a pioneer and demolition platoon. Unfortunately the freak rains already experienced by Stilwell continued, so that the Marauders' eight-day, 60-mile trek to Walawbum turned into something of a nightmare. They seized the road as ordered but were then attacked by a large force of Japanese directed by the ubiquitous Tanaka. Fortunately, the assault fell on the 3rd Battalion, which, recruited from New Caledonia and the Pacific south-west, was composed of veterans in jungle fighting. They acquitted themselves so well that Tanaka concluded he could not prevail and prepared to withdraw. Now serendipity took a hand. The Chinese had meanwhile been advancing to Monsum, fighting enemy forces all the way, but the slow progress of the Marauders meant that a Chinese regiment from the 38th Division caught up with its American allies and took Tanaka in the rear. In furious fighting the Japanese lost 1,500 dead and the survivors were harassed all the way on their retreat by Kachin guerrillas.[5] But the temporary collaboration did not presage a wider Sino-American synergy, and the Marauders found operating with their allies a major problem. One issue was disease: the Americans caught dysentery in large numbers and attributed this to the insanitary habits of the Chinese, especially their refusal to boil their water, or to wash their hands after using the latrines. The American K-rations also proved unsatisfactory and unsuitable for jungle warfare, as the Chindits soon discovered.[6]

On 15 March Stilwell ordered the Chinese 22nd Division to its next major objective, the key ridge of Jambu Bum, which separated the Hukawng valley from the Mogaung valley, but the Chinese found it difficult to coordinate attacks by infantry and tanks and suffered badly in a Japanese counterattack. Although in bad health and with a troublesome liver, Stilwell continued undaunted and repeated his favourite credo: 'If the Japanese are behind us, we are also behind them.'[7] Finally, on 19 March, the Chinese 66th Regiment took the Jambu Bum on Stilwell's sixty-first birthday. He celebrated by having a giant cake made and distributing slices to his commanders. The next task for the Marauders involved the 1st Battalion acting as advance guard for the Chinese 113th Regiment advancing to Shaduzup, while the 2nd and 3rd Battalions hit the Kamaing road 20 miles from Kamaing (the central Japanese position in the Mogaung valley) at Inkangahtawng. Once again Stilwell chafed with impatience at the Marauders' slow progress towards Shaduzup; sometimes they managed only five miles a day. They contrived a surprise assault on 28 March, but once again the Japanese counterattacked ferociously. During the bitter fighting an American voice was heard to exclaim: 'Where the hell are the other 5,306 Composite Units?'[8] The other two battalions made a gruelling march in company with 300 Kachin guerrillas, but on the way to Inkangahtawng the two battalions became separated and then realised they would have to cross the Mogaung river, already in full spate. The 3rd Battalion crossed with difficulty but was immediately afterwards halted by heavy opposition, while 2nd Battalion was similarly thrown back outside Inkangahtawng.[9] Reuniting once more, the two battalions withdrew to a suitable defensive position at the hilltop of Nphum Ga, getting a supply drop en route but with the Japanese dogging their heels. On 28 March the Marauders dug in and a week-long firefight commenced. The Japanese managed to drive a wedge between the two battalions and cut off 2nd battalion on the higher slopes of the hill.[10] There was continuous vicious fighting, with both sides short of food, water and ammunition. The Marauders were now in a bad way, as with little drinking water, they were forced to drink from muddy pools, and were surrounded by the stench of dead mules. There was no way to evacuate or help the wounded, who began to die rapidly from disease, especially dysentery, and lack of water. Finally, on 4 April, the 3rd Battalion broke through to link with their comrades. The two battalions then fought their way out, making agonisingly slow progress until on the 7th they joined hands with the 1st Battalion. Next day the Japanese made another attempt to surround the unit and there was more bitter fighting, but the following day they departed. With another of his sudden changes of mind, Tanaka decided that he had to concentrate on Myitkyina and withdrew his attackers there. The extended battle at Nphum Ga and environs had cost the Marauders 59 dead and 379 wounded or disabled, plus a lengthy sickness roster.[11]

While all these military operations were going on, Stilwell had his usual half-dozen political and administrative balls to juggle. At the beginning of March, Slim flew to meet him at Thiphaga: 'Stilwell met me at the airfield, looking more like a duck hunter than ever with his wind-jacket, campaign hat and leggings.' He found his American friend and colleague jumpy and irritable because of both the continuing heavy rain and his uncertainty as to whether the Chinese divisions would coordinate smoothly in a major offensive.[12] Daringly, Stilwell confided to Slim his most secret plan for an attempt to take the key Japanese stronghold of Myitkyina during the monsoon and extracted a promise from him not to speak of it to *anyone*, especially Mountbatten. Stilwell explained to Slim that he was afraid of security leaks in Delhi, though Slim thought he was merely hedging his bets in case of failure. The real reason was that Mountbatten vehemently opposed such a venture and would not have authorised it; he had already told the combined chiefs that any plan to seize northern Burma was fundamentally unsound.[13] It was typical of Slim that he gave Stilwell his solemn word and kept it. The Myitkyina revelation was, however, a diversion from the main purpose of the meeting, which was to brief Stilwell on Operation THURSDAY and the Chindits. Stilwell had never been a Wingate admirer and disagreed at a theoretical and practical level with LRP operations. He expressed doubts about the wisdom of THURSDAY but reluctantly agreed that the enemy might be rattled by having Wingate in his rear. Finally he grinned at Slim over his glasses and said: 'That'll be fine if Wingate does it and stays there, if he goes in for real fighting and not shadow-boxing like last time.'[14] Stilwell's low opinion of Wingate was uncannily like that of a man as unlike him as possible (and who loathed Stilwell for his rudeness), Mountbatten's chief of staff General Pownall, who wrote at about this time: 'If Wingate can be induced (ordered is hardly the word for him) to come westwards towards the Chindwin and if we also hold the Jap in front, we would be in a very good way to eat up two Jap divisions.'[15] Slim replied to Stilwell that his worry was different: not that Wingate would shadow-box but that he would be pinned down in his strongholds. However, on the worst-case scenario he should be able to cut enemy communications for a significant period.

The conference over, Stilwell took Slim on a tour of his headquarters, which Slim found appallingly primitive. He thought the American commander was making a mistake in cultivating a 'just folks' persona and going around dressed like a scarecrow. He himself made a distinction between talking to his men in an avuncular way, eliminating unnecessary distinctions of class and rank – which he approved of – and giving them nothing to take pride in, for Slim, an acute student of human nature, knew that men secretly liked the uniforms, badges and paraphernalia of rank and hierarchy, despite their barrack-room pseudo-egalitarianism. Slim was right. Although the GIs appreciated Stilwell's concern for the 'average Joe', they despised his tatterdemalion appearance, and the spartan lifestyle left them cold. One of the Marauders saw him and said: 'Christ, a duck hunter.' Another remarked, not knowing he was speaking of his commanding officer: 'Look at that poor old man. Some draft boards will do anything.'[16] Gradually in the course of the campaign Stilwell came to realise that the men liked a general to look like a general, so he started wearing his insignia. At this stage, though, Slim thought he was seriously overplaying the image of tough austerity. 'Goodness knows he was tough and wiry enough to be recognised as such without play acting, for it was as much a bit of stage management as Mountbatten's meticulous turn out under any conditions but it achieved its publicity purpose. Stilwell, thank heaven, had a sense of humour which some who practise these arts do not and he could, and did, not infrequently laugh at himself.'[17] It was as well that Stilwell did have a sense of humour, for his enemies and critics liked to deal with him by ridicule for the most part. Mountbatten was fond of an anti-Stilwell story that he confided to his diary: 'The first time that General Stilwell flew over the Hump into China he blew up his Lilo mattress fairly tight and lay down on it to sleep. When the aircraft got to 18,000 feet, the pressure inside the cabin had fallen so much that the Lilo burst and old Vinegar Joe [was] brought down to the deck with a bump. He woke up with a start, drew both his revolvers and looked round to see whom he could shoot. Fortunately at that moment he passed out from lack of oxygen.'[18]

If Slim was always welcome at Stilwell's headquarters, Mountbatten was not, and relations between the Supreme Commander and his deputy steadily declined throughout 1944. On 6 March Mountbatten flew up to Taihpa to review the NCAC. He annoyed Stilwell before a word had been spoken by arriving with an escort of 16 fighters, which, as Stilwell complained to his staff, used enough fuel on the return trip to keep his own campaign going for a week.[19] There were other tensions. Mountbatten had already diverted Hump aircraft to Arakan and would divert more to the Imphal-Kohima battle without informing Stilwell, which rankled with Vinegar Joe. Mountbatten resented both Boatner's secret mission to Washington and the fact that Stilwell was commanding at the front when he should (Mountbatten thought) be attending high-level conferences in Delhi and Chungking, even though Slim agreed that his presence at the front was essential, for otherwise the Chinese would not fight.[20] Behind the scenes the devious Wedemeyer was stirring the pot, and Mountbatten had already complained to Field Marshal Dill in Washington that it was not feasible for Stilwell to fulfil his simulta-neous roles in China, India and Burma; he suggested that he be confined to the role as Chiang's chief of staff while Wedemeyer replaced him in Delhi. Mountbatten mainly considered Stilwell a nuisance: while conceding that he had fire in his belly and was 'a fine old warrior', he complained that he had no understanding of global strategy and was impatient with administration.[21] He was also secretly piqued (prompted by Wedemeyer's leaks from American sources) that Stilwell considered himself the only one fighting a war, that he laboured in the jungle while the Supreme Commander was concerned only with publicity, public relations and his own image – which was true, if not the whole truth.[22] Stilwell's distaste for Mountbatten was more visceral. He disliked him in general terms as an aristocrat, a member of the royal family and a Limey with a cut-glass accent, and in particu-lar terms as a careerist nonentity. As 1944 wore on, Stilwell's animadversions grew more frenetic. 'The more I see of the Limeys, the worse I hate them . . . the bastardly hypocrites do their best to cut our throats on all occasions. The pig-fuckers.' As for Mountbatten himself, he was 'a fatuous ass'; 'childish Louis, publicity crazy'; and 'a pisspot'.[23]

Since Stilwell wore the standard GI trousers and field jacket, without any decorations, when he met the Supreme Commander at the airfield, the sartorial contrast seemed almost to sum up the crevasse that separated the two men. Mountbatten's descent from the plane was described thus: 'In knife-edge, impeccable tan tropical uniform with three rows of campaign ribbons and six-inch shoulder bars encrusted with stars, crowns, crossed swords and batons and royal initials, the Supremo was as elegant in Hukawng as he would have been in Mayfair.'[24] Superficially the two men were correct and even affable. Stilwell began by apologising for the Washington mission – an easy concession to make as he had won the strategic argument. There was a meeting at headquarters where 'Louis made a dumb speech', according to his host. Mountbatten's version was that his speech failed because it was drowned out by the noise of the 16 fighters that insisted on circling round overhead.[25] Then Stilwell whisked the visitor away for a tour of the battlefield at Walawbum, where Mountbatten, to Stilwell's contemptuous disgust, complained about the smell of corpses. Next the Supreme Commander insisted on addressing the Marauders. Stilwell was always unimpressed by 'Louis's rhetoric' but other accounts insist that the speeches went down well and that the GIs were impressed.[26] One exchange with a soldier was reported as follows. Soldier: 'I'm Brown from Texas.' Mountbatten: 'There are a lot of you Texans out here.' Soldier: 'Yes, that's why the war's going so well.'[27] Yet it was clear to all perceptive observers that the two commanders were the proverbial chalk and cheese, separated not just by personal style, method and purpose but by the divergent interests of their two countries. Suddenly Mountbatten decided he wanted to see the fighting currently going on at the front. Stilwell tried to dissuade him, pointing out the danger from snipers and the fluidity of the ebbing and flowing battle. Mountbatten then protested that Stilwell himself was going up to the front, so why could he not go? 'I am an old man and it does not matter about me, whereas I'm responsible for your safety,' Stilwell replied. When Mountbatten insisted that he would take the responsibility, Stilwell tried to dissuade him on other grounds: he had no proper headquarters at the front and nowhere to accommodate Mountbatten's staff. When he received the prompt reply that 'Dicky' would go alone and leave his staff behind, Stilwell concluded that there was no more to be said and he had better play the gracious host.[28]

The Chinese general Liao came forward to be introduced to the Supreme Commander, who decided to take him as his personal guide. The first night they slept in the jungle under parachutes spread on the tops of bamboo poles. Next morning they set out again, but Liao kept stopping every hundred yards, prompting muttered curses from Stilwell: 'Here comes another lecture.' Liao would then proceed to tell the Supremo and his deputy in unnecessary detail exactly what fighting had taken place in each section of jungle. Glad to shake off the attentions of this tiresome dragoman, Mountbatten begged a jeep for a drive through the jungle where Stilwell's Pioneers were clearing the way.[29] Driving too fast, as usual, he ran over a bamboo with his front wheel that ricocheted back into his left eye. At first he thought the bamboo had taken the eye clean out of its socket; it had missed, but for all that he was temporarily blinded. A US missionary who tended him at the scene said: 'Young man, this is plenty serious. You must fly there [Ledo] and as quick as you can.'[30] Mountbatten was at once rushed to Ledo, where a distinguished American eye specialist, Captain Scheie, diagnosed severe internal haemorrhage but said the eye should recover if not subjected to strain. He then endured five days of complete blindness, with both eyes bandaged, during which time he was not allowed to move his head or lie on his side. 'They were the longest 120 hours I can remember,' he confessed.[31] Three nurses did eight-hour shifts, feeding and washing him and reading to him as if he were a baby. It was 19 March, 12 days after the accident, before Scheie pronounced him out of danger. Stilwell showed his humanity by visiting the 'pisspot'. Mountbatten wrote: 'I was much touched that Old Joe Stilwell should have flown up from the front on Sunday to come and pay me a visit in hospital. He and I always get on well personally.'[32] The GIs were less sympathetic. Hearing that Mountbatten was in hospital with optical problems, the Marauders spread the 'scuttlebutt' that 'Uncle Joe busted the Limey in the eye'.[33] There is a particular irony in Mountbatten's accident having happened on the very day the Japanese launched U-GO. It was while he was in bed, still in great pain and unable to read, that (on 14 March) he was told of the desperate need for transport aircraft to relieve Imphal and gave the appropriate orders orally. It is perhaps unnecessary to dwell on Mountbatten's characteristic impetuousness. If he had not insisted on going up to the front, against Stilwell's advice, he would have saved himself days of grief and agony.[34]

When the great crisis of Kohima-Imphal broke, Stilwell did his best to help, although he could not resist a typical crack: 'The Limeys have the wind up at Imphal.' At Slim's urging he decided to make another trip to Chungking to try to get Chiang to commit Y-force; he was also concerned that his Chinese generals were not driving their men hard enough and suspected secret orders were being received from the generalissimo. Chiang had in fact signalled Stilwell when Mountbatten diverted planes from the Hump for the Arakan operation to tell him to halt his advance pending clarification of Allied intentions, but Stilwell had ignored the signal, remarking wearily: 'O Jesus, now *that* starts again.'[35] Slim related that the impact of Arakan on Chiang ruined Stilwell's promising start to his campaign, and the prospects of an early advance on Myitkyina, but that he himself forgave the American for his bitterness 'and he was bitter even for Vinegar Joe'.[36] Stilwell departed for Chungking, flying the usual Hump route via Kunming, in a jaundiced mood: 'If I can't move the Peanut, the jig is up for the season.' He conferred with Chiang next day and found him inflexible on the subject of Y-force, though the generalissimo vaguely promised two divisions for the NCAC push on Myitkyina, which he, like Mountbatten, thought would take place some time in the indefinite future, and certainly after the monsoon. But while he was in Chungking, Stilwell received the unwelcome news that Frank Merrill had had a heart attack and had been rushed from the front to a hospital in Ledo.[37] Before he could take any decision about the future of the Marauders, he had to fly back to India for a conference with Slim and Mountbatten. To his wife he wrote in ambivalent mood about the Supreme Commander: 'Louis and I get along famously even if he does have curly eyebrows ... Just a line before hopping off to see Louis who, to put it mildly, has his hind leg over his neck. If they don't buck up on their side, we will also have our tit in the wringer. What a mess the Limeys can produce in short order.'[38]

Stilwell went to Jorhat for the meeting in gloomy mood, expecting to be stitched up by the Limeys, since his recent request for Anglo-Indian troops to protect US airfields had been turned down – clearly because of the crisis at Kohima-Imphal. He decided, as it were, to get his retaliation in first by offering Slim and Mountbatten the Chinese 38th Division. This of course meant that his own campaign would be over and all hope of reaching Myitkyina before the monsoon gone. He made his magnanimous offer at a pre-lunch meeting with Slim alone (before Mountbatten arrived). Slim thought his old friend looked very tired, but he uttered no anti-Limey reproaches and showed considerable sympathy and understanding for Slim's difficult position. To Stilwell's delight, Slim answered that he was confident that Imphal would hold; he therefore wanted Stilwell to keep the Chinese and launch his attack on Myitkyina as planned, assuming of course that the operation was still on.[39] Stilwell replied that it was very much still on, but that it was more than ever imperative that Slim should keep the secret from Mountbatten. When Slim readily assented, Vinegar Joe tried to press him further, and asked for a guarantee that his communications would not be cut. Slim very correctly replied that this was an impossible demand: he was stretched at Imphal and Kohima so certainly could not vouch for Japanese inability to slip past him into the Brahmaputra valley. What he could promise was that such severance would not last more than 10 days. Stilwell said he'd hoped Slim might reply along those lines and that he should not worry about his previous request for Anglo-Indian troops. He intended to detach a Marauder regiment to guard the airfields, from where they would fly in reinforcements once the attack on Myitkyina began.[40] When Mountbatten arrived after lunch, the two men told him they were completely in agreement, and to the Supreme Commander's surprise, all seemed sweetness and light; naturally they said nothing about Myitkyina. Stilwell wrote to his wife in high delight: 'Much to my surprise, no question of help from us. On the contrary Slim and the Supreme Commander said, go ahead.' This was particularly important to Vinegar Joe, as the Kachins were predicting an early monsoon.[41]

If Slim and Stilwell were behaving like seasoned professionals during the crisis weeks of April, Mountbatten's behaviour was decidedly odd. It was the end of the month before the pain in his eye completely eased, and perhaps this is the explanation for what can only be described as 'inappropriate behaviour'. Pownall had noticed that his boss seemed to be acting strangely, repeating orders that Slim had already given and in general trying to take the credit for his general's success in the field, and took him to task for his micromanaging interventionism. 'I told Mountbatten frankly that he had gone completely off the rails and he had no right to go about things the way he had done . . . I'm bound to say Mountbatten took all this amazingly well, indeed he cried "Peccavi" and apologised. I hope that in the future I shall only have to wag my finger at him and he'll be more careful.'[42] Yet the Supreme Commander drew back from one act of folly only to launch himself into an even greater one: it was a classic instance of *reculer pour mieux sauter*. While the struggle for Kohima-Imphal raged at its most intense, and every plane, piece of equipment and sum of money was vital, he took the extraordinary decision to move his entire headquarters, personnel, equipment, bag and baggage from Delhi to the island of Ceylon (modern Sri Lanka). To all dispassionate observers this seemed indeed a case of a man who could not stand the heat and was therefore getting out of the kitchen. The new headquarters, at Kandy, was 1,600 miles to the south of Delhi and 500 miles farther away from the battlefields of Burma. Mountbatten's only excuse for this piece of egregious idiocy was that Kandy was more suitable as a base for amphibious operations.[43] But if Kohima-Imphal proved anything, it proved that the future of Burma was going to be decided on land, and that all the old Churchill/Mountbatten dreams of seaborne invasions of Sumatra and the like were so much moonshine. The Americans were quite right to see this bizarre decision as a flight from reality, and they were not alone. Auchinleck, Giffard, Slim and Peirse all thought Kandy was much too far from the fighting, and in London alarm signals were raised. Auchinleck was particularly irritated that Mountbatten was breaking a solemn promise he had made to him in October 1943 about eschewing ostentation and an imperial staff.[44]

Yet Mountbatten would not be dissuaded, and on 17 April the mass exodus took place – a criminal waste of resources at such a juncture. Here was the Supreme Commander acting like a Riviera playboy while 14th Army was fighting the battle that would decide the war. And yet Mountbatten had the almost unbelievable gall to claim that he was the architect of victory. His new headquarters in Kandy became a byword for luxury and elegance. Visitors could not get over the general air of affluence and prosperity and the Supreme Commander's sleek fleet of limousines – 'much too grand for me', as one observer waspishly remarked.[45] Mountbatten compounded the problem of being too far from the war and thus being unable to engender any sense of urgency in his personnel by the most grotesque overstaffing. There were now 7,000 men and women on the staff of SEAC and there was not even an operation for them to plan. Soon this incredible figure escalated to 10,000, at the very time commanders in the war theatres were complaining of manpower shortages. Alanbrooke was justifiably incensed when Mountbatten, having quit a perfectly good headquarters in Delhi, then demanded to have his own 'ambassador' there – which, as Alanbrooke saw clearly, would in turn become an excuse for building up another huge staff of drones. As he rightly remarked a little later: 'Seldom has a Supreme Commander been more deficient of the main attributes of a Supreme Commander than Dickie Mountbatten . . . I find it very hard to remain pleasant when he turns up! He is the most crashing bore I have met on a committee, is always fiddling about with unimportant matters and wasting other people's time.'[46] To cap it all, Mountbatten was approaching a state of nervous exhaustion: the incessant travel, the tough decisions he had had to take over Imphal, the pain from his eye all contributed to the crazy decision to relocate to Kandy. This should have provided a rest cure, but observers continued to claim that he looked tired and drawn; his friend Noel Coward was one of these.[47] Wavell, who had more time for him and Wingate than any other senior general, said that he had lost 'that first, fine, careless confidence that caused my predecessor to call him the Boy Champion'.[48]

As if to prove the point, Mountbatten had no sooner moved to Kandy than he was off again, this time on a flying visit to Stilwell's front. A jaundiced Vinegar Joe reported to his wife on the tactlessness of the Supremo and his minions: 'The Glamour Boy was over addressing our troops the other day. His own backyard was on fire and that was the time he chose to make a pep talk to *us*. Impressing his personality on our troops. A Limey forestry official came to our HQ and made the proposition that the US pay the British for the trees we are cutting down in Burma to make a road to China.'[49] As if to thumb his nose at the British, Stilwell sent a message to Stalin, congratulating him on the Red Army's twenty-fifth birthday; not surprisingly,

Soviet sources played this up and the Supreme Leader replied effusively (a case of Uncle Joe to Vinegar Joe).[50] Since Stalin was an ally, there was no reason on the surface why Stilwell should not have congratulated him, but usually the Anglophone Allies, and particularly the British, liked to keep their contacts with the USSR to a formally polite level; by sending this message Stilwell increased the gap between himself and the Red-baiters of the extreme right, such as the devious Wedemeyer. Stilwell was undoubtedly in a strange, unsettled and volatile mood in the spring of 1944. On the one hand he was more vehement and savage than ever. Sharing Slim's loathing for the Japanese, when a (rare) prisoner offered to shake hands with him as a noble opponent, Stilwell raged at him: 'Not with you, you dirty bastard.'[51] On the other, he was far more reflective than usual, setting down on paper his views on a variety of existential matters. Pondering the qualities of a great commander, he concluded that it was 80 per cent character, 10 per cent power of decision, 5 per cent technical knowledge and 5 per cent everything else.[52] Clearly he did not share Napoleon's conviction that the prime requisite was luck. In May he sent his wife a long letter dedicated to the proposition that he was one of life's worriers, but not about himself. 'Strangely enough I do not worry about my own life. It never occurs to me that my plane will crash or that the next bomb has my name on it. The possibility occurs to me, but it does not weigh on my mind at all. I wonder what that indicates.'[53]

Although both Mountbatten and Stilwell in their different ways showed clear signs of exhaustion, probably the toughest decisions that spring were taken by Slim, and not just about Kohima-Imphal. When Wingate died there was the immediate question of who should succeed him, and the subsequent and more important one of just what role the Chindits should now fill. 'It is an interesting sidelight on a strange personality,' Slim wrote, 'that, after his death, three different officers each informed me that Wingate had told him he was to be his successor should one be required. I have no doubt at all that they were speaking the truth.'[54] There were five possible candidates to succeed Wingate: Calvert, Symes, Tulloch, Fergusson and Lentaigne. Tulloch was ruled out at the start because he had never commanded a Chindit column in the field, so Slim used him as a sounding-board and unofficial adviser in the selection process. Symes, who had taken on the post as Wingate's deputy at Auchinleck's urging, as a kind of Indian army 'minder' for the turbulent prophet, was a reluctant Number Two who did the job on the express assurance that he would be a shoo-in to succeed Wingate if anything happened to him. Slim, however, considered that his case was the same as Tulloch's: he had not commanded Special Force in the field. Fergusson and Calvert were both true Wingate believers and disciples, but if one of them was to be chosen it surely had to be Calvert, as his fighting record hitherto was so much more impressive. On the other hand, he was wild and unstable, a fighter but not really a strategic leader and planner; he did not bear the nickname 'Mad Mike' for nothing.[55] By a process of elimination, therefore, Slim came to Lentaigne, who had the considerable advantage of being a Gurkha officer – a breed Slim liked and trusted. Slim told Tulloch that his inclination was to appoint Lentaigne. Tulloch, unaccountably, advised Slim that Lentaigne was the commander most in tune with Wingate – a grotesque and unaccountable travesty of the facts. In fact Lentaigne hated and despised Wingate and thought that all his ideas and theories about Long Range Penetration were arrant nonsense.[56] He was also a heavy drinker, but Slim, following Abe Lincoln's example with General Grant, discounted this as unimportant.

Slim described his selection procedure as follows: 'His [Wingate's] successor had to be someone known to the men of Special Force, one who had shared their hardships, and in whose skill and courage they could trust. I chose Brigadier Lentaigne. He not only fulfilled all these requirements, but I knew him to be, in addition, the most balanced and experienced of Wingate's commanders.'[57] Here Slim was being slightly disingenuous. What he did *not* say was that Lentaigne was the only one, Symes apart, who fully agreed with Slim that the more grandiose plans for Special Force should be wound up, that Long Range Penetration should be wound up and that the Chindits should henceforth function as an adjunct to 14th Army, just as the Marauders did with the Chinese divisions. Slim told Lentaigne forthrightly that the halcyon days were over and that henceforth there would be no special channel to Churchill, bypassing the normal military hierachies. The appointment of Lentaigne was deeply unpopular with some of the Chindit brigades. Calvert felt slighted and Symes, feeling he had been double-crossed, first protested to Giffard, and when that produced no result, put in a formal protest to Alanbrooke in London.[58] His resignation was accepted, and Tulloch became Lentaigne's deputy, as a reward for his services. The effect on the morale of Special Force was palpable, and all the latent fissures, which had been held down because of the sheer domineering force of Wingate's personality, became overt and manifest. There were three factions at large; 77 Brigade under Calvert, which was fanatically loyal to Wingate; III Brigade under Lentaigne and John Masters, where Wingate and all his works were loathed; and a third neutral bloc in 14 Brigade, under Brodie.[59] The Calvert faction thought Lentaigne weak, defeatist and cowardly; he hated Wingate but had never had the guts to stand up to him while he was alive and would similarly let Slim (and later Stilwell) walk all over him.[60] Lentaigne was certainly Slim's man. When Slim announced that he wanted to recall the Chindits to help in the defence of Kohima-Imphal, it was Tulloch who pointed out that they were already fighting a desperate action at White City. Actually, as Tulloch later conceded, Lentaigne's judgement in this instance was sound. If he had agreed without demur to be withdrawn to Imphal, they would not later on have fallen into Stilwell's clutches, with disastrous results for them.[61]

As a result of Tulloch's intervention a compromise was reached, with 14 and III Brigades (those most sympathetic to Slim and Lentaigne's new bearing) ordered to move west towards the Chindwin and block the roads Japanese 15 and 31 Divisions would be using in the Imphal campaign, while Calvert and 77 Brigade were left where they were for the time being pending a visit from Lentaigne.[62] Now nominally under the command of the newly promoted Morris, III Brigade's actual command devolved on John Masters, another Lentaigne loyalist (Lentaigne, Morris and Masters were all Gurkha officers). Meanwhile Calvert and Fergusson had an angry confrontation with their despised superior officer, who flew to 'Aberdeen' to meet them. He gave them the unwelcome news that they would be collaborating in the Imphal battle and were to help take the pressure off 4 Corps. Both the Wingate loyalists protested vehemently. Fergusson wanted another crack at Indaw, while Calvert was adamant that it was madness to abandon White City and Broadway; both men put it to Lentaigne that they were all now being used as Slim's football.[63] When Lentaigne reported back to Slim, he decided to go halfway to meet Calvert and Fergusson (though his critics claim his next action was sheer machiavellianism). He announced that henceforth Calvert and Fergusson would come under Stilwell's command and that their mission was to abandon White City and move towards Mogaung to assist in the operations of the Chinese there. Events prevented the immediate implementation of the new orders. Now finally convinced that the Chindit operation was no mere raid but a genuine cancer 'in their guts' (as Wingate had put it), the Japanese launched a massive attack on Broadway on 27 March.[64] A ferocious running battle went on until 1 April, when the Japanese, worsted, drew off. Broadway was now left in peace until Calvert reluctantly obeyed his orders and withdrew on 13 May, missing what would have been an annihilating attack on the stronghold by 24 hours.[65] Meanwhile the Japanese switched their attention to White City, which was attacked on 6 April. Calvert and his men fought a heroic holding action while reinforcements from the West African Brigade began to arrive. Soon so many Nigerians were in place that Calvert had numerical superiority. Although Calvert had been genuinely delayed by Japanese incursions, Slim and Lentaigne suspected him of stalling. Lentaigne flew in on 11 April and ordered Calvert and 2,400 men to move off into the jungle as a 'floater' column, leaving the Nigerians to man the strongholds.[66]

On 13 April Calvert attacked the village of Sepein near Mawlu but in his usual headstrong way did not time his attack well and went in too soon. Initially repulsed, he returned to the fray with substantial reinforcements from the Nigerians at White City. Caught between Calvert's brigade and the West Africans, the Japanese counterattacked ferociously, and Calvert had to call in an air strike before they were beaten back. At a cost of 100 dead and 200 wounded, Calvert made the unconfirmed claim that he had inflicted 3,000 Japanese casualties and thus could hold White City indefinitely.[67] When Lentaigne repeated the order for a definitive abandonment of Broadway and White City – adding that he was to build a new stronghold called 'Blackpool' 60 miles north (near Hopin and 30 miles south of Mogaung) so as to link with Stilwell – Calvert replied by sending signals that could only be considered insubordinate, making quite clear his contempt for his new commander.[68] To sugar the pill, Lentaigne sent back word that 111 Brigade was also being assigned to the Stilwell theatre and would be blocking the road and railway to Mogaung while 77 Brigade established Blackpool. Calvert, still stalling, pointed out that the new orders would take the Chindits over the 90 days' indenture of active service and then into leave that had been agreed with Wingate. Lentaigne had to fly in again and repeat the order in person on 8 May before Calvert would comply. He pointed out that because of the delay in moving north, the Japanese now had a new division in the Chindit area – 33 Division, under General Honda Masaki. Lentaigne might have expected that Calvert, a member of the enemy faction so to speak, would have opposed his plans, but he was alarmed to find that his loyal ally Masters also had misgivings about the orders for III Brigade. Masters stressed how tired his men were, and Lentaigne promised to send Brodie's 14 Brigade to their support.[69] Both brigades soon had reason enough for their misgivings. Calvert had no sooner founded Blackpool than he was assailed; bitter fighting ensued, with many of the Chindits loudly complaining that they were having to fight for a pointless stronghold.[70] As for Masters and III Brigade, who moved up to relieve their rivals at Blackpool, they too managed to beat off an enemy attack, but prevailed only with the help of Colonel Philip Cochran's Mustangs (Cochran, it will be remembered, was one of Wingate's earliest supporters).[71]

By mid-May the Chindits were in considerable disarray. Fearing even more powerful attacks, Masters flew up to see Lentaigne and complained bitterly that Brodie and 14 Brigade seemed to have vanished into thin air. White City had been abandoned 13 days earlier, so where were Brodie and 14 Brigade? Already the factionalism within the Chindits was becoming more bitter. It was no longer a question of pro-Wingate and anti-Wingate cadres, but brigade against brigade, with each one seeming not to cooperate with the next one. Lentaigne lamely said that he understood the stress that all Chindit units were under and suggested that if Masters found the pressure of the enemy at Blackpool too great, he should simply pull out. After the relative success story of Broadway and White City, Blackpool was proving a disappointment. The monsoon, thick churning mud and the gradual build-up of Japanese forces with heavy artillery were all making the position untenable. A further attack on 17 May was beaten off, but then came a more sustained one a week later. Short of food and ammunition, Masters had no choice but to pull out, but the order to withdraw was given late, when the Japanese had already occupied positions forward of the stronghold, so that the retreating Chindits took terrible losses.[72] Masters decided to head back towards the 'Aberdeen' area, and after a three-day march they made contact with the Nigerians and regrouped, now 2,000 strong. By this time everyone was exasperated by the continued non-appearance of 14 Brigade, and Masters was angry with Lentaigne also for his supposed indifference.[73] The Kilkenny cats syndrome in Special Force was now threatening to tear the Chindits apart. Everyone was exhausted, morale was low, and even Cochran's pilots were starting to complain about the non-stop operations.[74] If the leadership from Lentaigne was weak, that from Stilwell was worse and verged on indifference. He had never wanted the Chindits under his wing in the first place, fearing that the Limeys would be insubordinate. He also disagreed with Lentaigne's dispositions, particularly the order to abandon White City, curiously concurring with Calvert on this point if on no other. He also feared that if all the Special Force brigades moved north towards him, as Lentaigne had ordered, they would simply drag Honda's 33 Division in their wake while he already had his hands full with Tanaka's 18 Division.[75]

In any case, Stilwell's attention was now elsewhere, focused on the epic trek by the Marauders towards Myitkyina, the key objective of the entire campaign. If he could take Myitkyina and improve its airfield to all-weather status, the Hump cargoes would be dramatically improved. Moreover, building a road and pipeline from Myitkyina to Bhamo would see an eventual link-up with the old Burma road to Kunming and Chungking. Meanwhile the main Chinese force would advance down the Mogaung valley to Kamaing, which Tanaka had orders to hold on to at all costs. Although he had only one division against five similar Chinese formations, he hoped to be reinforced by Japanese 53rd Division, at which point he would counterattack. Sadly for him, the high command assigned him just two extra battalions, which meant his main hope for the defence was the monsoon itself. It did not occur to the Japanese that Stilwell would attempt a wide flank march on Myitkyina, because the steep Kumon mountains barred the way and even the Kachins declared them uncrossable.[76] Yet this was precisely Stilwell's intention. As he had earlier told Slim, the secret was to be kept from Mountbatten, and early in May he received implicit backing from Washington for his independent action. On 4 May the US Joint Chiefs of Staff decided they would land on Formosa, the

Philippines and the Chinese mainland, thus highlighting the importance of Myitkyina to the wider US strategy and meaning that Stilwell had implicit consent to sideline Mountbatten and SEAC.[77] Nimitz, Spruance and all the best naval minds had wanted to bypass the Philippines but MacArthur, who had rashly promised 'I shall return' when he left the islands ignominiously in 1942, had his 'face' to save. Confronted with a blizzard of rhetoric about MacArthur's 'sacred obligations . . . redemption of seventeen million people . . . blood on his soul', etc., FDR gave in and let him have his way, partly in fear that the general might otherwise resign and challenge him in the 1944 presidential election.[78] Stilwell accordingly prepared his assault force. Although the Marauders were in poor shape after the gruelling campaigns of the previous three months, he assured them that he needed just one final effort to take the airfield at Myitkyina, after which they would enjoy a well-deserved furlough. Only 1,400 Marauders were now effective, and Stilwell proposed that they march in the vanguard of 4,000 Chinese troops, using 600 Kachin rangers as their eyes and ears. Already his man-management was attracting adverse comment. While he lauded and cajoled the Chinese, he refused to praise the heroic members of Galahad force, mindful of General Pershing's dictum that American troops should always fight without being wheedled, coaxed or cosseted. His coldness and insouciance were the beginning of an alienation between him and the Marauders that would end in their hating him.[79]

On 28 April the 6,000-strong assault force set out for Myitkyina under the command of Frank Merrill, who had made a miraculous (it turned out to be temporary) recovery from his heart attack. The going was every bit as difficult as the Kachins had predicted. The Marauders and Chinese slogged over precipitous slopes in the monsoon rains, regularly losing mules and their loads as they toppled over cliff edges into deep gorges or simply sank down dead with exhaustion. The Marauders later claimed that dealing with the mules was far more onerous than fighting the enemy. Climbing up to 6,000 feet, then descending, then ascending again often in the teeth of bitterly cold winds, they eliminated small Japanese garrisons in mountain villages as they went. Clambering and crawling, often on hands and knees, they painstakingly cut steps into the steepest, muddiest ascents. With constant heavy rain, they sometimes made no more than four or five miles all day. Two of the teams ran out of rations and had to wait at prearranged clearings for an airdrop. Still the Marauders plodded on, sustained by the thought that after a short battle they would all be going home.[80] They had one great advantage that the Chindits never had, in the shape of a good number of Nisei (Japanese-American) soldiers who knew the language and OSS operatives who were able to tap Tanaka's phones and learn his battle plans. This was yet another example of the overwhelming Allied superiority over the Japanese in intelligence of all kinds – signals, disinformation, espionage.[81] Finally, on 14 May, Merrill sent Stilwell the signal that they were 48 hours from their target; the Kachins had reported that there were no more than 700 Japanese at Myitkyina and they were totally unprepared. The 24-hour codeword STRAWBERRY SUNDAE was transmitted on 15 May, and then, two days later, the codeword Stilwell had been waiting for – IN THE RING – which meant that the attack was starting. The Marauders launched their assault on the airfield at 10 a.m. on 17 May, and 50 minutes later it was entirely in their hands. The jubilant code-word MERCHANT OF VENICE was sent. Stilwell enjoyed an ecstatic moment of triumph. 'Will this burn up the Limeys!' he wrote jubilantly in his diary.[82] Next morning he arrived at the airstrip with 12 reporters. He and Merrill hugged each other with joy before Stilwell departed, confident that the town itself would fall within hours.

Yet this was to be the classic case of hubris followed by nemesis. The seizure of the airfield should have been followed by the fall of Myitkyina itself, but the town proceeded to hold out for another 10 weeks, even though in the first few days they did have just 700 men to pit against Merrill's nominal strength of 6,000. As so often happens, several things went wrong at once. Most of the Marauders were no longer battleworthy, many of them suffering from scrub typhus, foot rot, jungle sores and dysentery – 'a pitiful but splendid sight', as Merrill called them,[83] and those who were still effective took the line that their task was over: they had taken the airfield and were now due furlough as promised. Merrill therefore sent the Chinese troops to take the town, but this operation turned into fiasco when two of their battalions ended up fighting a pitched battle with each other on the 18th and did exactly the same thing next day, with the additional refine-ment that a third battalion joined in. When it turned out that no detailed plans of any kind had been made to take Myitkyina town,

Merrill called for reinforcements urgently. Instead of infantry, Stilwell sent engineers and anti-aircraft guns, reasoning that the essential thing was to hold the airfield.[84] With Stilwell ignoring his pleas and the Chinese engaging in fratricide, Merrill succumbed to another heart attack on the 19th. His place was taken by Brigadier General Hayden Boatner, Stilwell's chief of staff, who turned out to be a hopeless field commander. Worst of all, Stilwell was offered the fresh troops of the British 36th Division, but pigheadedly turned down the offer, as he did not want to be beholden to the Limeys; Myitkyina, in his view, had to be an all-American operation.[85] Stilwell would hear no excuses about how exhausted the Marauders were; in his view their failure meant they were lazy, disaffected or 'yellow' – one of his perennial obsessions. He insisted on rousting out the seriously ill from hospital and getting them back on the front line, and pressed his engineers into combat roles, at which they proved useless.[86] Another piece of 'treachery' (in his view) was that one of his most talented officers, Colonel Charles Hunter, braved his wrath by sending in a hard-hitting report stressing that the Marauders were at the end of their tether and particularly disillusioned by the favouritism shown by Stilwell's officers to the Chinese.[87] While all this was going on, General Maruyama, leading the defence in Myitkyina, was building up his strength; within a week, reinforcements from 56 Division on the Salween front had arrived to swell his numbers to 3,000, and shortly afterwards another detachment pushed the tally up to 4,500.

The failure to take Myitkyina town after the walkover victory at the airfield turned into one of Stilwell's greatest humiliations. But in the first heady 48 hours he saw only a great victory, as did the rest of the world. Mountbatten was stupefied to learn of the Marauders' exploit when he did not even know Stilwell was aiming at Myitkyina, and his fury deepened when a signal arrived from Churchill demanding to know how 'the Americans by a brilliant feat have landed us in Myitkyina'.[88] Mountbatten had to suppress his anger and send Stilwell a congratulatory order of the day: 'By the boldness of your leadership you have taken an enemy completely by surprise and achieved an outstanding success by seizing the Myitkyina airfield.' After describing the crossing of the Kumon mountains as 'a feat which will live in military history', he tried to rationalise his own humiliation by claiming that the Chindit destruction of Japanese communications had made the exploit possible – a tall story, as he must have known. Mountbatten also used one of his most cherished ploys: taking the credit for all the bright ideas and great achievements of his generals. He wrote to his daughter: 'Isn't the news of the capture of Myitkyina airfield great? It is one of my most interesting fronts, commanded by my deputy General Stilwell.'[89] Despite the tribulations to come, the operation had momentous consequences. Long-term, it shortened the Hump route. Between May and October 1944, 14,000 transport planes took off from the airfield bearing 40,000 tons of supplies to China.[90] Any thought of a seaborne invasion of Sumatra was permanently shelved, making Mountbatten's move to Kandy an even more absurd and unnecessary extravagance. And the convergence of Myitkyina with the victory at Kohima-Imphal meant that Slim would go on to greater things – an interesting historical irony in light of the fact that the overland Allied invasion of central and southern Burma was about to be shelved permanently until the Japanese launched U-GO. Possibly the greatest beneficiary of all these fluke occurrences was Mountbatten. The man who had no interest in crossing the Chindwin and the Irrawaddy and instead wanted to nibble round the edges with amphibious operations ended up as Earl Mountbatten of Burma, as if he had masterminded the entire operation from the beginning.[91]

One of the most dramatic impacts of the congruence of Myitkyina and Kohima-Imphal was on the attitude of Chiang Kai-shek. Since the beginning of the year FDR had been pressing Chiang hard to commit Y-force, which still languished in idleness on the Chinese side of the border. The generalissimo gave his now-clichéd answer: that China was too weak to undertake a major campaign, being at once under threat from the Japanese in the east of the country and the Communists in the north.[92] Even Roosevelt could see that this was disingenuous, since in addition to outnumbering the Japanese along the Salween front by about ten to one, the generalissimo had 400,000 troops facing Mao's Communists. Faced by blatant mendacity, he sent back a dusty reply. Marshall urged him to go further and tell Chiang that unless Y-force was sent into action, Lend-Lease would be cut off immediately. As ever, this was a psychological bridge too far for FDR. When he received another bland message from Chungking, he sent Chiang his sharpest message yet, but still stopping short of the 'or else no Lend-Lease' proviso Marshall wanted. Chiang predictably took FDR's reproof as loss of 'face' and did not reply. Roosevelt then took Marshall off the leash, and the President's chief of staff finally sent the rocket he had always wanted to deliver to Chungking.[93] Shocked into action, Chiang with much fanfare ordered Y-force into action, but delayed it behind the scenes. Yet when the British relieved Kohima on 20 April, he was genuinely impressed and gave the nod to his commanders to proceed in earnest but slowly – *festina lente*, to adopt the famous slogan of the emperor Augustus. It was only when the sensational news of the seizure of Myitkyina airfield came in in the third week of May that the generalissimo finally took his foot off the brake. Y-force turned out to be 115,000 men short of the official complement; Chiang promised 95,000 replacements, but only 23,000 arrived.[94] Nonetheless, General Wei Li-huang was eager to see action after so much enforced idleness. Going much faster than in the generalissimo's original timetable, he directed the crossing by 32,000 Chinese troops on rubber boats and bamboo rafts of the 60-foot-deep Salween, a maelstrom of treacherous whirlpools. One Chinese observer claimed that such an exploit had not been achieved by Chinese armies in 1,000 years.[95] Once over the gorges and into the 10,000-foot Kaoliikung mountains – another range considered impassable – they swiftly overran the totally unprepared Japanese outposts. Elated, they pressed on along a spur of the Himalayas and took Lungling on 10 June, only to be driven out a week later by a fierce enemy counterattack. There ensued a two-month struggle for Lungling, a crucial objective if the land route from Burma to China was to be opened.[96] Now both Y-force and X-force at Myitkyina were bogged down.

Hard pressed in Myitkyina as Japanese reinforcements built up, Stilwell asked Lentaigne to relieve the pressure by ordering Calvert to take Mogaung. Tanaka's original thinking had been to hold the 30-mile stretch betwen Kamaing and Mogaung as long as possible, reasoning that as long as his 18 Division was blocking Stilwell's advance in the Mogaung valley, there could be no attack on Myitkyina. His tactics were to hold Kamaing until the monsoon, when he hoped the elements would do his job for him and the enemy forces would be trapped in flooded valleys. By mid-June the monsoon rainfall would be one inch a day and tanks would be unable to move. All the time he was walking a tightrope, as his men were on one-eighth rice rations and his guns limited to four rounds a day.[97] This smoke-and-mirrors act was to some extent duplicated in Calvert's 77 Brigade, though unlike the Japanese, they received airdrops. However, Tanaka's carefully laid plans began to unravel when the Marauders arrived at Myitkyina like a thunderbolt. On 27 May Lentaigne signalled Calvert to take Mogaung; 'Mad Mike' replied that he hoped to have completed the job by 5 June. This was no more than a pious hope. From the very beginning of his trek to Mogaung, Calvert ran into far heavier resistance than expected. In ferocious fighting to seize the Mogaung bridge, the Chindits were at first thrown back, losing 130 killed and wounded, and prevailed only by calling up massive air strikes.[98] When Major Archie Wavell, the viceroy's son, was not flown out immediately when wounded, as ordered, a furious Lentaigne threatened Calvert with dismissal.[99] But Calvert had more pressing problems than another row with Lentaigne. His own men in 77 Brigade were suffering grievously in the chaos of the monsoon. Men soaked and shivering slithered through mud; packs doubled their weight in the wet; the rain made jungle tracks impassable and the mists made it easy for units to get lost: one detachment was said to have spent three days crawling around in mud before finding itself back where it started. The monsoon had a multiplier effect on diseases, especially malaria and dysentery, but the Chindits found the worst enemy was scrub typhus, which killed large numbers of both Special Force and the West African brigade; even those who survived the horrible malady were often left with such severe depression that they committed suicide soon after 'recovering'.[100]

Grimly struggling on, Calvert's Chindits successfully assailed the village of Naungkyaikthaw after an aerial blitz on the Japanese bunkers. Calvert claimed that he killed 100 Japanese that day, but his own numbers were diminishing alarmingly, with disease and battle vying to notch up the greater tally of dead. Just when his situation was beginning to seem desperate, his Gurkhas made contact with the Chinese on 18 June at Lakum village, two miles from the town of Mogaung.[101] Calvert conferred with the Chinese commander, but found his allies curiously reluctant to make a frontal attack and excessively concerned about casualties. They considered the Chindit method of fighting headstrong, reckless and wasteful. In a curious reversal of the usual stereotype, it was the British, not the Chinese, who seemed to hold human life cheap.[102] What followed was one of the most bloody and savage battles even by the gruesome standards of the Burma campaign. After a massive artillery barrage, Calvert called down an air strike by seventy Mustangs on the enemy position. On 23 June battle was joined with mortars, anti-tank grenades and flame-throwers. The carnage on the 23rd was terrific, and the Gurkhas won two Victoria Crosses in a single day for conspicuous valour. Another assault next day was largely carried out by the Chinese and their heavy artillery.[103] By noon on the 25th the Japanese were effectively beaten, but the Gurkhas did not begin to edge cautiously into the town until the next day. They found the enemy fled.[104] Mogaung was one of the great infantry battles of the war, but it was effectively 77th Brigade's last hurrah, for casualties were enormous. Calvert lost 800 men dead and wounded – almost half his force – and his brigade was no longer an effective fighting force. Only 300 men were left who could walk, let alone march. In some accounts of the battle, the Chinese and the American airpower tend to get written or airbrushed out, but to his great credit, in his own version of the battle, Calvert gave them full credit.[105] Victorious but at their last gasp, the Chindits blamed Stilwell for much of what had gone wrong. Unaccountably, some pro-Chindit authors write as if the mere fact of being under Stilwell's command of itself generated the huge casualties, which is absurd. But they are on firmer ground in complaining that planes failed to arrive regularly to ferry out the wounded, which may well have been the result of incompetence at his headquarters.[106] Certainly Stilwell showed himself an ingrate on this occasion. There were no messages of congratulation, just a curt 'we have it' in his diary. He compounded his sins by claiming later that the victory at Mogaung had been a walkover, won against starving Japanese with few Allied casualties.[107] He also briefed the BBC correspondents that the battle had been won by his Chinese. This was presumably his revenge for the many times the BBC had written him out of their reports or changed purely American successes into 'Allied victories'. Calvert was incandescent with fury when he heard on the radio that Chinese-American forces had taken Mogaung. He wrote: 'The Chinese-American forces having taken Mogaung, 77 Brigade has taken umbrage.'[108]

It is often alleged by the pro-Wingate coterie of historians that Slim and Stilwell were particularly hard on Calvert, as he was a Wingate loyalist and therefore the butt of their displaced (and posthumous) dislike of the prophet of the Chindits. This view can hardly survive an examination of Stilwell's treatment of Lentaigne, Morris and Masters, the so-called anti-Wingate Chindits. The truth is that Stilwell piled unacceptable pressure on *all* the Chindit brigades and set them impossible tasks because he feared the domino effect of allowing them to retire with their hard-won battle honours. The reasoning was that if he let the Chindits return to India on furlough, he would then have to do the same with the Marauders while Myitkyina was still in enemy hands, and in that case what about the Chinese, who had been in the field longer than either?[109] Certainly his treatment of Morris and his Chindit detachment, known as MorrisForce, was even worse than that he had meted out to Calvert and 77 Brigade. A close friend and ally of Lentaigne, Morris, described as 'peppery, authoritarian, obstinate and impetuous', loathed Wingate and seems to have had an almost paranoid fear of him.[110] Like Lentaigne, he attracted obloquy from critics, who said he was weak and indecisive, and both Stilwell and his chief of staff Boatner seemed to have played on this. Boatner ordered MorrisForce to assail the Japanese formations east of the Irrawaddy and Morris's men made eight separate attacks on well-entrenched enemy positions. Morris signalled that he was losing one third of a platoon daily from sickness and asked permission to pull out and go to India on furlough.[111] Boatner refused in Stilwell's name, having asked the Chinese what they thought and received the negative answer he expected. Soon Morris's strength was down to three platoons, and his men cursed the very names of Boatner and Stilwell. Boatner actually went down to MorrisForce and 77th Brigade to tell them to their face that he thought they were 'yellow' – faithfully echoing his master, with whom real or alleged cowardice was an obsession.[112] A Chindit colonel was said to have remarked: 'Boatner will kill us all before he is finished' and fulfilled his side of the prophecy by being killed in action next day.[113] It was only after massive pressure from Mountbatten that Lentaigne was finally permitted to agree to Morris's request on 21 July, by which time MorrisForce was a skeleton crew in more senses than one.

Basically Stilwell would not or could not grant the Chindits or the Marauders furlough while Myitkyina still stood defiant, though it was his fault and that of his commanders and planners that this was the case. Furiously pressing the attack without success, Stilwell was reduced to shuffling his deck of cards pointlessly, first replacing Boatner with Brigadier General Wessels temporarily, then replacing him with Hunter, and finally reinstating Boatner. Stilwell himself flew in to the airfield on several occasions, tearing his hair out about the rain, the poor morale of his men, the mutual recrimination of the commanders, the fact that aircraft had to land supplies and reinforcements even though they could not see the ground, and the general failure to make progress. His jotted pronouncements have all the hallmarks of a mind at the end of its tether. 'Good God, what goes on in Mitch? . . . Rain – if we can't land planes we can't land troops . . . this is one of those terrible days when you wish you were dead . . . GALAHAD is shot . . . the wear and tear on the nerves continues. Are we attempting too much? Can they hold us? Is there a surprise ready? Counterattack? Will our people stick it out? Casualties too heavy? I can tell I've nearly had enough of this.'[114] A contingent of 2,600 volunteers arrived from the USA to replace the Marauders, some of them used to jungle conditions as they were veterans from Panama, bored with the chore of guarding the canal. Rushed from Bombay to Ramgarh for a perfunctory week's training, they were then hustled to 'Mitch', where, instead of replacing the Marauders, they were amalgamated with them. They entered a nightmare world of rain and mud, where most of the old Galahad men were so tired that they fell asleep even during battle or leaned over the trenches vomiting up their K-rations.[115] Scrub typhus had by now become endemic, with 100 men a day going down. One regimental colonel was at his post with a temperature of 103° F and the men were not allowed to report sick unless they had run a temperature of 102° F for three days. The new recruits were largely hopeless. At least 50 were classified by the medical examiners as irremediable sociopaths, while the rest seemed frozen with terror at the mere thought of the Japanese.[116] Ill-trained, the newcomers gave fresh meaning to the notion of a 'scratch unit', and some had their first taste of how to load and fire a rifle on the plane to Myitkyina. While Hunter was solicitous for the men and complained of their poor treatment (and was later sidelined for having done so), both Stilwell and Boatner came across as uncaring, indifferent and even cruel. Stilwell's behaviour was untypical, for in normal circumstances he was no soldier-slapping Patton. This and his demeanour towards Mountbatten and Slim (described below) suggests that he might have had a mental breakdown at Myitkyina – not surprisingly, as the stress would have finished off most men in their sixties. Whatever the truth, he became as much a hate figure for the Marauders as he already was for the Chindits. Fuelled by marijuana, the Galahad men referred to their commander and his staff as 'stuffed baboons' as well as more obscene and unprintable things.[117] 'Bloodless and utterly coldhearted, without a drop of human kindness' was one of the milder criticisms of Stilwell. Two direct quotes from individual Marauders convey the general loathing. One said: 'That bastard ain't no American. He was born in his goddam Myitkyina and I hope he dies there.' Another put it more graphically: 'I had him in my rifle sights. I coulda squeezed one off and no one woulda known it wasn't a Jap that got the sonofabitch.'[118]

Fighting in the monsoon with demoralised troops against a determined and well-entrenched enemy, Stilwell had to endure 10 weeks of mental turmoil until Myitkyina finally fell on 3 August. As if the stress of 'Mitch' was not enough, he also had to visit Chiang in Chungking in early June, when the generalissimo reverted to the old Chennault mantra about winning the war with airpower alone if only he had enough planes and fuel. Stilwell was gloomy: 'The situation in China looks pretty bad. I believe the Peanut is going to pay dearly for being stupid and stubborn . . . Peanut much surprised over North Burma success.'[119] Back at Myitkyina the battle went from bad to worse. Well-aimed Japanese mortars were now seriously interrupting the air traffic over the airfield and at one time the Chinese-American force was down to a single day's rations. It seemed entirely plausible that the Japanese might soon be able to take the runways. 'There were days when a *banzai* charge by General Mizukami's garrison or a determined push by 53 Division, which had been ordered to lift the siege, would in all probability have swept right over the airstrip.'[120] By now the undisciplined Marauders were refusing to take orders and even threatening to 'frag' their officers. The entire weight of the fighting fell on the Chinese, who were predictably angry about having to sustain all the casualties, thus involving Stilwell in a further round of stress. The Allies did not win Myitkyina; the Japanese lost it when they were forced to pull out through sheer lack of food and ammunition. Mizukami committed suicide, and his body was found in the ruins when the Allies entered.[121] Kamaing, Mogaung and Myitkyina were all lost at root through Nippon's lack of resources. Yet the victories at Mogaung and Myitkyina decisively broke the Japanese hold on north Burma, and the results were dramatic, and not just in the increased tonnage flown over the Hump. US engineers were able to start work on a road through the Hukawng and Mogaung valleys through Kamaing to Myitkyina and then repaired the road south to Bhamo, which the Chindits had destroyed. From Bhamo the road ran northeast to link up with the old Burma road going up to Yungling and Kunming and eventually, 600 miles later, Chungking itself. The consequences of Myitkyina were thus momentous, but the cost had been high: 272 Marauders were killed and another 955 wounded, with 980 invalided out, even under Stilwell's draconian strictures on illness. The Chinese lost 972 dead and 3,184 wounded and the Japanese 790 dead and 1,180 wounded.[122] At last the desperate Marauders were homeward bound and officially disbanded in August, albeit later reconstituted as 75th Infantry Regiment. Unlike the Chindits, they were given a Distinguished Unit Citation for their pains.

It is a nice question whether Stilwell was more hated by the Marauders or the Chindits, but at least the Chinese factor could be adduced in mitigation of his treatment of his own countrymen. There was less justification for his attitude to the Chindits, which led to major confrontation with Mountbatten and Slim and extinguished the last embers of a dying relationship. The first great row came over Calvert and 77 Brigade, but this was resolved amicably after some tense moments. After the signal victory at Mogaung, Stilwell ordered Calvert to advance to Myitkyina and join in the siege there. Calvert, feeling that 77 Brigade had already performed far beyond the call of duty, ignored the order and shut down all radio contact with Chindit HQ. He then marched to Kamaing, expecting to be evacuated to India. He forgot that it would have been far easier to be flown out from Myitkyina.[123] Stilwell was furious about the insubordination and there was talk of a court martial. Eventually Lentaigne managed to get in touch with Calvert and tell him it was imperative he faced the music. Despite the fact that Lentaigne and Calvert loathed each other, the new Chindit commander had been defending him to the best of his ability, but Stilwell's detestation of Lentaigne did not help. Arriving at headquarters, Calvert was ushered into a room where Vinegar Joe, his son, Boatner and Lentaigne were sitting. The following conversation ensued:

STILWELL: Well, Calvert, I have been waiting to meet you for some time.

CALVERT: I have been waiting to meet you too, sir.

STILWELL: You send some very strong signals, Calvert.

CALVERT: You should see the ones my brigade-major won't let me send.

STILWELL (laughing): I have just the same trouble with my own staff officers when I draft signals to Washington.[124]

Whether by luck or calculation, Mad Mike had struck just the right note to appeal to Vinegar Joe, and the ice was broken. There was no more talk of court martials. When Calvert launched into a detailed account of the Mogaung campaign, Stilwell kept saying: 'Why wasn't I told?' It turned out he knew nothing of the history of 77 Brigade and was totally unaware that it had been in the field for four months.

Yet if relations with Calvert were resolved amicably, Stilwell could not be appeased about the rest of the Chindits and continued to complain about Lentaigne and the various ways in which Special Force had let him down: the unilateral abandonment of Blackpool, the poor and 'cowardly' showing of MorrisForce, the alleged 'malingering' of the other brigades, the many acts of 'insubordination' and defeatism by Chindit commanders, especially Lentaigne. Things got so bad that Mountbatten spent a lot of time flying up to the front to try to pour oil on the turbulent waters. A visit on 30 June is of peculiar interest, as both men recorded impressions in their diaries. Here first is Stilwell: 'Mountbatten has been up again. He had the nerve to make a speech at our headquarters but he doesn't fool our GIs much. They are getting a look at the British Empah with its pants down and the aspect is not so pretty. You can imagine how popular I am with the Limeys. I have been thinking of Mountbatten as a sophomore but I have demoted him to freshman.'[125] Mountbatten's 'take', as so often, was more Panglossian. He recorded the address to the GIs and continued thus:

After this we lunched in his tent with the rain beating down on us and the temperature inside so great that we were as wet from sweat as if we had been sitting in the monsoon rain outside . . . Although Stilwell has always shown himself quite remarkably friendly to me the meeting was not easy as there were several points of difference to be cleared up. However, he met me very handsomely more than half way (the problem is that Stilwell wants to be able to direct Lentaigne's special forces). If only I could see him every day there would never be any difficulties in this command between the Americans and ourselves. Not that we do have many difficulties, as our relations on the whole are now very good.[126]

The diary entry smacks of humbug on two counts. By this time Mountbatten was actively intriguing to have Stilwell replaced as his deputy (see below). And if he wished for close contact with his commanders, why on earth had he relocated to Ceylon, which ruled out such contact? The visit ended on a disappointing note for the Supreme Commander. He expressed a desire to see Myitkyina, but both Stilwell and Lentaigne protested vehemently that this was too perilous. Mountbatten insisted he had to go, and the others reluctantly acquiesced. Suddenly the trip was cancelled. The Japanese had chosen that very day to make a massive fighter sweep over the battleground, and with only four Mustangs to protect him, Mountbatten would have been in serious danger.[127] Mountbatten, it seemed, was damned if he did and damned if he didn't. The time he had arrived with 16 Mustangs he had brought too many escorts and attracted ridicule; this time he brought too few.

Continually plagued by Stilwell's complaints about Lentaigne, Mountbatten tried using Slim as an intermediary, knowing that he and Vinegar Joe got on well. Yet even Slim hit a brick wall. The talks between the two started amicably enough. Slim jokingly reminded Stilwell that now that Kamaing had fallen, as per their agreement he was no longer the American's commanding officer. 'Well, general,' said Stilwell, 'I've been a good subordinate to you. I've obeyed all your orders.' Slim replied: 'Yes, you old devil, but only because the few I did give you were the ones you wanted!'[128] Having, as he thought, got Stilwell in a good mood, Slim gently suggested that he might now agree to come under Giffard's command, especially as Giffard would be in Burma only for a short time in a caretaker role. Stilwell adamantly refused; his contempt for Giffard had lost none of its old bite. This issue was patched up in a face-saving way: Mountbatten himself took over Giffard's military role. Next Stilwell launched into a series of grouses about the Marauders and the Chindits. Cast down by the protracted siege of Myitkyina, 'he was extremely caustic about his unfortunate American commanders, accusing them of not fighting and killing the same Japanese over and over again in their reports'.[129] The complaints about the Chindits were the most difficult issue. Slim had a series of meetings with both Lentaigne and Stilwell, and tried to work out the rights and wrongs of Vinegar Joe's lamentations. Lentaigne was bitter and told him that Stilwell was a hard driver who always asked the impossible, demanding that all the Chindit columns be simultaneously engaged and refusing to evacuate casualties. It was impossible to remonstrate with Stilwell, said Lentaigne, because he now refused any personal contact with the Chindit leader. Slim likened Stilwell and Lentaigne to Agamemnon and Achilles, this time with both men sulking in their tents: 'I found Stilwell bitter and Lentaigne indignant and very understandably suffering from prolonged strain.'[130] Trying to act the honest broker, Slim went back to Stilwell with his findings. His conclusion was that in many instances the Chindits had not carried out Vinegar Joe's orders because they were incapable of having done so. When he heard this, Stilwell began to vaunt the achievements of the Marauders over those of the Chindits. Slim would have none of it. Calmly he pointed out that Galahad had been behind Japanese lines a much shorter time and had sustained higher casualties. As for MorrisForce, why accuse a unit of a few hundred of failing to achieve what 30,000 Chinese and Marauders had not been able to do? Expecting Myitkyina to fall imminently, Slim unwisely agreed to Stilwell's suggestion that he retain the Chindits until that time and then release them.[131] The problem was that 'Mitch' took until 3 August to surrender, and no one had foreseen this.

As July began, the monsoon continued to howl and there was still no sign of any crack in Myitkyina's defences, both Lentaigne and Mountbatten became ever more agitated. Worried about the knock-on effect on the morale of the Marauders and the Chinese, Stilwell simply would not agree to send the Chindits on furlough. Early in July he sent 14 Brigade and the West Africans to take Taugni, which they accomplished brilliantly, a fourth Special Force Victoria Cross being won in the engagement.[132] Lentaigne then told Stilwell that his men had had enough and that 111 Brigade must be flown home at once. Stilwell objected that this meant his agreement with Slim was being broken, and both sides appealed to Mountbatten. The Supreme

Commander sent up what Stilwell scathingly referred to as 'another circus from Kandy', this time a deputation consisting of Wedemeyer, Frank Merrill and Major General I.O.S. Playfair. Another face-saving agreement was patched up: 111 Brigade was allowed to leave but 14 Brigade had to stay for mopping-up operations around Taugni.[133] Mountbatten was furious about Stilwell's attitude, but as Pownall pointed out, he had to balance the exhaustion of the Chindits against the attitude of the 'cousins': 'Whatever happens, we are in danger of this affair embittering Anglo–US relations. If we pull them out, the Americans (especially Stilwell) will say we ratted on them. If we leave them in, the British commanders will know why and will say so.'[134] Finally Mountbatten's patience snapped. He told Stilwell that in the interests of humanity, all the medically unfit must leave at once. Stilwell flatly refused to concede. Mountbatten tried to force his hand by ordering a medical inspection of the remaining Chindits. The inspection of Masters's brigade on 17 July found only 118 fit for active service out of 2,200 officially rostered in four and a half battalions. Many had lost up to 45 pounds in weight, suffered at least three bouts of malaria, foot rot, septic sores, prickly heat or typhus. Masters sarcastically minuted Stilwell to enquire what their duties were, and Stilwell rewarded the sarcasm by sending them to guard a Chinese artillery battery, to the fury of the Chinese gunners, who construed this as loss of face.[135] It was 1 August before Stilwell allowed Masters's brigade and the other Chindits to leave, and probably only then because on this date he was promoted to four-star general. Whatever debate there may be over the initial merit of Special Force, by the end it was little short of a disaster. The last time a Chindit unit fired a shot in anger was 7 August, when 36 Division – the one originally spurned by Stilwell – took over the duties of Special Force.[136] As a distinct entity the Chindits ceased to exist in February 1945. Operation THURSDAY had seen 1,034 Chindits killed and 2,572 wounded, but it inflicted 10,000 Japanese casualties, including an estimated 5,764 killed. In other words, Special Force lost one fifth of its total strength and most of those who survived never fought again; poor rations and a high sickness rate – themselves consequences of Wingate's fanatical voluntarism – were largely to blame.[137] Yet because Wingate vanished from the scene early and the Chindits came under Stilwell's command, he was the one who attracted their censure and hatred. Tulloch, lamenting that Stilwell had 'his evil way with us', thought he should have been exterminated like a mad dog.[138]

Stilwell's bruising encounters with the British over Lentaigne and the Chindits both increased his anti-Limey censoriousness and convinced Mountbatten that his so-called deputy commander would have to go. It is hard to overstate how deeply feelings ran on both sides, and there is circumstantial evidence that the Slim–Stilwell rapport was never the same again. Even those who were accustomed to treat Stilwell's Anglophobe rants with detached and ironical amusement began to come round to the view that he had gone too far; perhaps it was not just a Stilwell trope, Vinegar Joe rhetoric; perhaps he really did in some pathological way hate the British. Others thought that what in Stilwell himself was a rather tiresome running joke was with his acolytes and close aides a genuine and deadly animus. Boatner and Brigadier General Benjamin Ferris, chief of staff of Stilwell's rear echelon in Delhi, were considered the prime exponents of an irrational Anglophobia.[139] On 22 June, the ever-loyal Frank Merrill radioed Stilwell to tell him that Mountbatten, together with Stilwell's deadly enemy Wedemeyer, was intriguing to have him replaced as his deputy commander by either Wedemeyer himself or General Daniel Sultan. The slippery Wedemeyer was playing a double game, determined to bring Stilwell down but secretly disloyal to Mountbatten and briefing against him in Washington, as he did during a trip there in June when he was supposed to be promoting the Supreme Commander's interests.[140] Mountbatten's main hopes for ousting Stilwell were focused on Alanbrooke in London. Alanbrooke agreed, as did many, that Stilwell wore too many hats, and when General Marshall visited London in mid-June, suggested that the Americans 'rationalise' the situation. Marshall correctly read this as part of a devious intrigue against his favourite, and reacted angrily: 'Brooke, you have three C-in-Cs in India; none of them want to fight. We have one man who will fight and you want him taken out. What the hell kind of business is this?'[141] A sadder and wiser man, Alanbrooke later reflected:

Marshall had originally asked us to accept this Stilwell-made set up to do him a favour, apparently as he had no one else suitable to fill the gaps. I was therefore quite justified in asking him to terminate a set up which had proved itself as quite unsound. I had certainly not expected him to flare up in the way he did and to start accusing our commanders of a lack of fighting qualities, and especially as he could not have had any opportunities of judging for himself and was basing his opinions on reports he had received from Stilwell. I was so enraged by his attitude that I had to break off the conversation to save myself from rounding on him and irreparably damaging our relationship.[142]

For the moment, then, Mountbatten was stymied. The incandescent state of Anglo-American relations in Burma in summer 1944 was hardly the right context in which he should have been asking favours of the 'optional extra' kind, but tact was never his strong point. At some stage he had got it into his head that a touring concert party by his old friend Noel Coward would be a great morale-booster for Allied troops and cabled Coward, then in South Africa, to come on to Ceylon. Perhaps Mountbatten was misled by the signal successes scored by very different kinds of entertainers, such as Vera Lynn, and the Cockney gossiping duo 'Gert and Daisy', who had made a great hit with 14th Army.[143] Coward duly sailed in the destroyer *Rapid* and arrived in Ceylon on 28 May. There was an inauspicious start to his tour when among the guests at a reception Mountbatten held for him was Admiral Sir James Somerville, the navy commander-in-chief and the Supremo's old foe. Somerville, who had a wonderful gift for repartee, spent the evening sparring waspishly with Coward and, in the opinion of some, emerged the victor in the verbal duel.[144] Clearly this was some form of transmogrified aggression towards Mountbatten, for three weeks later Somerville wrote formally to the Admiralty to protest about the Supreme Commander's use of his planning staff, accusing him of seeking 'a form of absolute control usually exercised by dictators'.[145] Mountbatten next asked Stilwell to provide transport for Coward and his troupe at the very moment the American was close to nervous breakdown because of the stalemate at Myitkyina. Vinegar Joe abruptly refused, 'either from simple prejudice or perhaps on the theory that Coward's talents would not be appreciated by Chinese and American GIs'.[146] Feeling insulted and humiliated, Mountbatten complained both to Lieutenant General Raymond Wheeler, a trusted American aide, and to Stilwell himself. Wheeler suggested that Stilwell send a message of regret, which he did, and the Coward tour headed for Ledo. Coward's first performance, in front of the black troops building the Ledo road, was a total disaster. They had never heard of the 'Limey piano-tinkler', thought his would-be sophisticated cabaret both patronising and boring, and gave him the slow handclap. Coward himself blamed his poor reception on having to belt out his songs from a platform high above the Ledo road, along which lorries and heavy transports continued to thunder. He added that only the RAF were sophisticated enough to enjoy his shows.[147] The first performance was so embarrassing that Mountbatten was soon contacting Stilwell again, trying to save his friend's face. When a second performance was given at Ledo's general hospital, Stilwell had to order his men to show approval, whatever their real feelings. Coward, disappointed by his reception on a long tour of Delhi, Bombay and Madras, returned to Ceylon and collapsed. He got his revenge later – and created an international incident – by referring in his *Middle East Diary* to 'mournful little Brooklyn boys, lying there in tears amidst the alien corn' – which was, rightly, read as an insult to American servicemen.[148] Stilwell was thoroughly disgusted by the entire fiasco and radioed his friend General Daniel Sultan: 'If any more piano players start this way, you know what to do with the piano.'[149] The entire episode was a suitable black-comedy summation of the lamentable state of Stilwell–Mountbatten relations in the summer of 1944.

After the great victory of Kohima-Imphal, Slim had two main tasks: to pursue the enemy and to decide his future strategy. Although utterly defeated on all four fronts, the retreating Japanese fought tenacious rearguard actions and they were assisted by a variety of factors. At first Slim and his generals did not realise the scale of the enemy's defeat and even in late June they could not be entirely certain that the Japanese were not regrouping for a counterattack. Part of this was sheer bad intelligence. Slim was later to complain that he never received the help from ULTRA intercepts that other generals (he was particularly thinking of Montgomery) did.[1] Additionally, the intelligence he could garner in the battle theatre itself was limited not only by the paucity of prisoners taken (at least until 1945) but by an acute shortage of Japanese-speaking linguists who could read and interpret captured enemy documents.[2] As late as 24 June 1944, when the battle of Kohima-Imphal was in its terminal stages, with a badly beaten Japanese army on the run, Scoones still thought they had the capability to launch a major attack from both Tamu and Bishenpur.[3] In the immediate aftermath of the Imphal battle, Slim was not in the director's chair, having been laid up with malaria; he broke his own rules, took a bath after sunset and was bitten by a mosquito.[4] Overwhelmingly, though, the factor that inhibited close pursuit of the beaten enemy was the weather. Torrential rain slowed operations on all fronts in Assam and Manipur, while the exhausted heroes of Kohima-Imphal needed rest and recreation in India before they could play any further part in hostilities. Slim described the terrible conditions in mud and rain the pursuers had to endure: 'Hill tracks in a terrible state, either so slippery that men can hardly walk or knee-deep in mud. Administrative difficulties considerable. Half a company took ten hours to carry two stretcher cases four miles. A party of men without packs took seven hours to cover five miles.'[5]

Beset by the monsoon and malaria – 9 Brigade of 5 Division lost only nine killed and 85 wounded in fighting in July, but 507 to sickness and disease – Slim's army dogged the enemy's heels from July to November but always cautiously, for the Japanese were expert at holding up their progress with well-placed snipers and booby traps. Although victorious, the men of 14th Army found the pursuit demoralising work, feeling particular anticlimax when they finally entered some strategic objective that had been fought over for months. 'There was for the victors none of the thrill of marching through streets which, even if battered, were those of a great, perhaps historic, city – a Paris or a Rome. There were no liberated crowds to greet the troops.'[6] When 11 East African Division entered Tamu, the effect was profoundly depressing: 'The place was a charnel house, of a macabre eeriness hard to describe. 550 Japanese corpses lay unburied in its streets and houses, many grouped grotesquely around stone Buddhas which looked blandly out over the sacrifices huddled at their feet. Dozens more, over a hundred, lay in indescribable filth, dying of disease and starvation, among the corpses.'[7] Everywhere they went, the Anglo-Indian troops found evidence that the Japanese had suffered the most colossal defeat, far greater than Slim at first realised. Yet Slim had to proceed with circumspection. His men were suffering badly from malnutrition, not just from the shortage of food but because of its very nature, with no fruit or fresh vegetables. Also, medical research was beginning to throw up the alarming discovery that because of the stress of combat, food passed rapidly through the body without the extraction of the necessary vitamins and minerals – one of the by-products of a metabolism traumatised by battle. After clearing the enemy presence from Dimapur and Kohima and then the Imphal plain farther south in mopping-up operations in July, Slim made an important decision. Once the Japanese were completely cleared out of the Tamu and Tiddim areas, he would get his pioneers and engineers to concentrate on building roads in the Kabaw valley in preference to the Tiddim road, and would introduce the East African division there on the grounds that, though it was a hotbed of malaria, the East Africans should be more resistant to it; they were, though they still took losses from the disease. In many ways it was a more deadly enemy than the Japanese. In the first six months of 1944, the entire South-East Asia Command lost 40,000 killed and wounded in battle but 282,000 to various tropical diseases, and in October, 14th Army had a malaria rate of 84 per cent. The snag about abandoning the Tiddim road was that henceforth casualties would either have to accompany the columns or be dumped in the villages they passed through; they could no longer be evacuated by air.[8]

While the pursuit went on, Slim turned his mind to the issue of future strategy. After nagging the combined chiefs for six months for a clear directive on priorities and strategy for SEAC, Mountbatten got a shock when it finally arrived on 3 June. There was nothing about his beloved amphibious operations and nothing relevant to Slim's ambition for an invasion of central Burma. Instead – and clearly reflecting that by 1944 the USA easily had the whip hand in Allied decision-making – all the emphasis was on China, as the main adjunct to the war in the Pacific. SEAC was directed to increase air supplies over the Hump and to open land routes to China.[9] It is interesting that this disappointing response did not even satisfy Stilwell's aims and objectives. Mountbatten quickly took the decision to ignore the feeble response from the combined chiefs and discussed with Slim and Giffard the three main possibilities, as they saw it. One was a limited crossing of the Chindwin by 14th Army, designed to link up with Stilwell and the Chinese. The second was an amphibious assault on Rangoon, after whose fall the Allies would march to Mandalay. This was Mountbatten's favourite, and the British chiefs of staff favoured it as an easy option; the Supreme Commander gave it the code name DRACULA.[10] The third was code-named CAPITAL and was Slim's brainchild. This was an overland invasion of central and southern Burma, crossing the Chindwin and the Irrawaddy and taking 14th Army to Mandalay and Lashio. Slim, whose strategic brain was greatly superior to his colleagues', knew that only his overland advance would work. It must be stressed that, regardless of what was later claimed by bandwagon jumpers (Mountbatten included), this was entirely Slim's idea and no other commander envisaged it. As the military historian Ronald Lewin has accurately remarked, Slim was an artist whose inner eye saw the aesthetic curve from Imphal though the Irrawaddy to Rangoon.[11] But Mountbatten and Giffard were highly dubious, especially when Slim insisted he could achieve his goal with the existing 14th Army and without extra resources. Slim allowed himself a rare moment of bitterness about the general defeatism in Kandy and Delhi concerning his plans. Nevertheless, he was given the green light and began planning CAPITAL in July; his staff called the project to capture Rangoon overland SOB (Sea or Bust).[12]

July was a difficult month for Mountbatten. Not only were there the continual wrangles with Stilwell about Lentaigne and the Chindits, but, having sacked Giffard, he was running out of patience with both Peirse and Somerville as well. On the other hand, if he sacked them too, he would be in danger of losing credibility in London. Meanwhile Slim and Giffard were insisting that 14th Army should move forward and undertake CAPITAL even if DRACULA was approved, but Mountbatten suspected that if that operation was too far advanced by the time he got the approval for his amphibious assault on Rangoon, the combined chiefs would use that as an excuse to cancel DRACULA later. In addition, there were ominous rumblings from Churchill. Still obsessed with an attack on Sumatra – which would of itself preclude DRACULA – he was also hankering after supporting MacArthur's left flank in the Pacific by a massive effort from Australia. The idea had been broached that Mountbatten might be reassigned to Australia as MacArthur's deputy – not at all what the Supreme Commander wanted, even if he could overcome the hostility of the Admiralty to the idea of him as commander of the British fleet in the Pacific, which was what such a position would entail.[13] For all these reasons Mountbatten decided his presence in London was essential; he needed to 'pitch' for DRACULA and get all rival ideas scotched. Stilwell came down to Kandy for a 'difficult' meeting on 1 August and to take over as acting supreme commander while Mountbatten was away.[14] The Supreme Commander flew off and arrived in London on 5 August. He linked up with Wedemeyer, who, in Washington in June, had been secretly rocking the boat and backing the official US line that only China mattered, and that DRACULA and all operations of its ilk were simply about restoring the British Empire, which should form no part of US policy. Nevertheless, Mountbatten took him to the meetings with Alanbrooke and other military commanders, on the assumption that he was loyal and would back his amphibious plans. At a conference on 7 August, Alanbrooke agreed that the capture of Myitkyina had changed everything, that the British would therefore have to go on campaigning in Burma and that the best way forward was the airborne attack on Rangoon.[15]

The next day, 8 August, was a critical day for Mountbatten. A full conference was held on the entire British strategy in South-East Asia and the Far East, attended not just by Alanbrooke and the chiefs of staff plus Mountbatten and Wedemeyer, but also by Churchill himself, Attlee, Eden and Oliver Lyttelton. The meeting was exhausting, not just because of its seven-hour length but because it had to be scheduled to fit in with Churchill's peculiar and eccentric timetable. It began at 11 a.m. and went on until 1.30 p.m., when it was adjourned to accommodate the Prime Minister's habitual bibulous lunch and post-prandial nap. It resumed at 6 p.m., went on until 8.30 p.m., was adjourned again for dinner and then resumed at 10.30 p.m. for another two hours.[16] Mountbatten found himself under fire from two directions: from Churchill, who was still adamant that he wanted an invasion of Sumatra; and from the service chiefs, who wanted all resources to be concentrated on a purely Pacific strategy. His only real ally was Eden, who championed the attack on Rangoon as the best chance for a quick end to the war in Burma, but his idea that the Australians might be willing to take part in this was quickly rebutted by a negative cable from Canberra. Nonetheless, Eden recorded that Mountbatten, who had begun the day very unhappy, finished it very content, confident that DRACULA was making progress.[17] Although he supported Mountbatten on this issue, Alanbrooke had found the day a severe ordeal.

Just back from our evening conference with the PM. It was if anything worse than any of the conferences of the day. I believe he has lost the power of giving a decision. He finds every possible excuse to avoid giving one. His arguments are becoming puerile, for instance he upheld this evening that an attack on the tip of Sumatra would force a withdrawal of Japanese forces in northern Burma and would liquidate our commitment in this area. We have conferred for seven hours !!! with him today to settle absolutely nothing. Nor has he produced a single argument during the whole of that period that was worth listening to. I am at my wits' end and can't go on much longer!'[18]

Although Alanbrooke supported DRACULA, he found the opposition of Churchill *and* the military planners in the War Office hard to overcome, while feeling his customary disillusionment about the Supreme Commander himself. On 11 August he reported a busy day, 'culminating with quite hopeless letters from Dickie Mountbatten to Marshall, which he sent me to look at!! I had to tell him that he could not send *any* of them and should attend COS on Monday with Wedemeyer and we could tell the latter what he should say to Marshall.'[19] From Alanbrooke's tone, one can infer that at least part of Mountbatten's rejected correspondence had to do with Stilwell, for Brooke knew from his own bruising encounter with Marshall in June what his American counterpart's reaction would be to any criticism of his protégé. On 17 August he noted in his diary the obstructionism of the War Office over the Rangoon project. The planners flatly declared impossible the date of March 1945 for an assault on Rangoon, but in a two-hour meeting Alanbrooke adequately refuted their claims. However, he was disillusioned about having to browbeat the people who were supposed to be on his side, in addition to his violent conflicts with Churchill. 'There are moments when I would give anything just to get in a car and drive home, saying I was fed up with the whole show and they could look for someone else to fill my job!'[20] His final meeting with Mountbatten laid down the parameters for DRACULA. On the assumption that the European war would be over by the end of 1944, he would begin transferring troops to Burma on 1 October: 'It is a gamble, but I believe one worth taking.'[21] While Mountbatten flew back to Ceylon, Alanbrooke departed in the *Queen Mary* with Churchill for the second Quebec conference. This was to doom DRACULA. The Americans were lukewarm about the project from the start, but grudgingly said they would go along with it provided northern Burma was not starved of resources as a result. Half-promises were made about withdrawing six divisions from the Italian campaign, but Pownall presciently warned Mountbatten not to get his hopes up.[22] He was right. The go-ahead for DRACULA had always been predicated on the assumption that Germany would be defeated by the end of 1944, but by the latter stages of the year, with Allied setbacks at Arnhem and later in the Battle of the Bulge, such a prediction looked increasingly chimerical. At a cabinet meeting on 2 October, Churchill announced that no forces could be diverted for the Rangoon venture and that it would have to be postponed until after the 1945 monsoon. Alanbrooke, however, knowing Churchill's pathological fondness for peripheral operations, suspected that the Prime Minister would backslide and attempt to do something for his protégé Mountbatten.[23]

While Mountbatten was in London, Stilwell flew down from Myitkyina to Ceylon to exercise his prerogative as deputy supreme commander and take the chair while the Supreme Commander was away. The decision surprised everyone, as Myitkyina still held out, but by now Stilwell was convinced its fall was imminent. At first there was some apprehension, as 'the announcement that he actually intended to do so aroused in Kandy the emotions of Rome awaiting Alaric the Hun [sic]'.[24] Stilwell was full of confidence, knowing that Myitkyina was on the brink of surrender, with the defenders on a quarter of a bowl of rice a day, and unfazed by Mountbatten's hostility (by this time he knew his SEAC boss was intriguing to have him removed). He wrote blithely: 'At one time or another all the best people have attempted to get the can attached, but have somehow slipped up on it – up to now anyway.'[25] He showed exactly what he thought of Mountbatten when he was met at the airport in Ceylon by a showy official limousine (a black Cadillac). Demonstrating enormous contempt, he barked: 'Get me a jeep.' He then drove up the mountain to Kandy in the jeep with the Cadillac behind with all his luggage, playing the gallery touch, 'with his leg hanging over the side in what seemed to some a petty and unnecessary show of disdain'.[26] He joined Mountbatten for an uneasy farewell lunch in the King's Pavilion (the Supremo's official residence), and remarked afterwards: 'I've got to quit eating with Louis. I actually like those rum cocktails.' The next three weeks were something of an idyll after the stress of Chungking and the hardships of Myitkyina. The Japanese duly surrendered there on 3 August, and a few days later came official confirmation of Stilwell's promotion to four-star general. The congratulations poured in. One NCAC regiment, presumably changing its tune now that victory had been achieved, sent a message to say that nothing like Myitkyina had been achieved in military annals since the *Iliad*. Stimson sent him a message of congratulation, saying: 'I never signed a commission which has given me greater satisfaction.' Stilwell told his wife that Ceylon was a paradise, like Hawaii, and something akin to Shangri-La after the rigours of northern Burma.[27]

Stilwell made a point of underlining the contrast between himself and Mountbatten. He abolished the daily conferences and excoriated the rare planning meetings in his diary as 'dumb', 'sad', 'zero', 'make-believe acts' and 'crappier than usual'.[28] According to his account, as the days of laid-back *dolce far niente* continued, Mountbatten's staff started to dread their boss's return: 'I have let them do their own work and cancelled most of their belly-ache meetings. Now they realise they must again face the daily blast of wind and paper, and they don't relish the idea. We almost had it on a commonsense basis.'[29] In a letter to his wife he was exultant about the fall of Myitkyina: 'We finally got Mitch. It was a bitch of a fight and with the raw troops we had, full of anxiety, but we are sitting pretty now. What a bitter dose that was for the Limeys. They said it was impossible so often and so vehemently that they just couldn't believe it was true.' He also told her of Mountbatten's arrival from London at Ceylon on 24 August: 'I went down to Colombo to welcome Mountbatten on his return. I went to the zoo first to look at the monkeys just to get in the mood. He was not at ease with me, which is not surprising because his trip had to do with an operation on his deputy's throat. Maybe the fourth star threw a monkey wrench into the machinery.'[30] In glaring and blatant contrast to Stilwell's account of his time at Kandy and his joyous reception by the SEAC staff, Mountbatten had this to say: 'All my senior staff, British and American, reported to me on my return that he had been quite incapable of taking charge or giving any useful directions at theatre level.'[31] When historical accounts clash as violently as this, it is worth asking whether either version expresses the truth. As so often, both were right and both were wrong, depending on their premises. It was an open secret that Stilwell was bored by logistics, administration and committee meetings, and it may well be believed that all the staff at Kandy except the very highest echelons welcomed the holiday from paperwork. It was the top brass, with their status diminished by Stilwell's reforms, who complained to Mountbatten. His liking for daily conferences and committees is at first sight puzzling in so impatient a man, for such characters usually like to speed through meetings in half an hour, ruthlessly using their own chairman's guillotine. In Mountbatten's case, the lust for speed and 'cutting through' was at war with an equal and opposite relish for micromanagement, which only the daily conference could satisfy.

With the Supreme Commander back, Stilwell did not tarry long, and on 30 August left Ceylon for Delhi and thence, a week later, Chungking. By this time Mountbatten's suspicion and paranoia about his deputy was such that when he was out of touch, en route for Chungking, he at first imagined Stilwell had secretly stolen off to the second Quebec conference. He got his own back by finally visiting Myitkyina and seeing the Irrawaddy from the air for the first time.[32] But soon he had more serious matters to attend to. Following the Cabinet decision on 2 October, the bad news about DRACULA was conveyed to him, and at first he was prostrated with shock, scarcely able to believe what he was being told. He wrote to Edwina in something like terminal despair, and then indited a long letter to his ally Eden, explaining why the Rangoon operation was so crucial. It was clear, he wrote, that DRACULA could not now take place before January 1946 at the earliest, which was not only a betrayal of the hundreds of thousands of British troops in the India-Burma theatre but an abandonment of the British Empire. If Britain failed to reconquer at least one former colony by the end of the war, its prestige would be rock bottom and irremediable. The jealousy of the United States was the main culprit, along with their absurd concentration on China, which was now irrelevant to the outcome of the war in the Pacific anyway.[33] Feeling that he could not just sit idly by while epoch-shaking decisions were being made by world leaders, Mountbatten decided he would have to attend a conference in Cairo in mid-October, which, in a bizarre replay of 1943, immediately followed a conference at Quebec. The so-called second Cairo conference, however, turned out to be no more than a 24-hour stopover for Churchill, Alanbrooke and the rest of the prime-ministerial party. For Alanbrooke indeed it was of even shorter duration, as he told his wife on 8 October: 'It is hard to believe that I dined comfortably in England yesterday, had breakfast in Naples today and may have my dinner in Cairo, and possibly breakfast in Crimea tomorrow with lunch in Moscow!!'[34] By the time Mountbatten reached Cairo, Churchill and the others were in Moscow. Mountbatten sought official permission to follow them there but was warned off by Churchill in no uncertain terms. Since Stalin was not at war with Japan, the presence there of the SEAC commander would flout all the protocols of international diplomacy.[35] A despondent Mountbattten moped about Cairo for a while, feeling himself to be in a time warp, since in 1943 Churchill had also flown on for a conference with Stalin, leaving him behind (on that occasion the conference was in Tehran). To make matters worse, Mountbatten was informed by his friends in Churchill's inner circle that the cancellation of DRACULA was going to be used as a pretext to get him to cut his staff at Kandy, and there was going to be enormous pressure on him to move to Calcutta. The only consolation was Churchill's remark to Eden, which he passed on: 'I give Dickie full marks. We gave him a lousy job but he has performed it splendidly.'[36] The Supremo had to take what pleasure he could from a meeting with King Farouk. He reminded the portly monarch that they had met in London in 1937 at the screening of a Ginger Rogers film. 'He informed me that he had met her in person since then, and had been very thrilled. I was able to counter that I had also met her in person since then, and had not been very thrilled.'[37]

While Mountbatten was thus occupied, Slim was pressing ahead with detailed planning for CAPITAL. The first stage was completing the rout of the enemy, and the second was detailed planning for what would happen once 14th Army was across the Chindwin. As his field commander in the pursuit he used Stopford. With 4 Corps resting at Imphal, 33 Corps would advance along the Tiddim road, with 5 Indian Division in the van, to destroy the remnants of Japanese 33 Division. Meanwhile 11 East African Division would advance along the Tamu road to destroy the vestiges of Japanese 15 and 31 Division. The two Anglo-Indian divisions would then converge at Kalemyo, at which point the Tiddim road would be abandoned as a supply route in favour of the Kabaw valley and airdrops. At the beginning of August 11 East African Division entered Tamu, to find it a chaos of corpses, the dying and the diseased.[38] The pursuit along the Tiddim road was led by 5 Indian Division, with the enemy fighting delaying actions all the way and the road resembling a gigantic rubbish dump as the fleeing Japanese jettisoned a variety of impedimenta: postcards and letters from home, souvenirs, family photographs and curious cartoons exhibiting everyday life in a Japanese home.[39] The regular troops were immensely assisted in this sweeping operation by Slim's own hand-picked force of irregulars – the Lushai Brigade, consisting of Indian soldiers, Chin levies and British officers, Slim's version of LRP and in his view far superior to the Chindits. The brigade operated with great success in the wild country south of the Tiddim road, acting as a gadfly on the enemy flanks and cutting the Japanese communications.[40] The Japanese evacuated Tiddim on 6 October, but there was hard fighting in this sector all the way to the Chindwin, where 5 Indian Division was to make for Kalewa, with another Victoria Cross being earned. The pathetic remnants of Japanese 15 and 31 Divisions managed to struggle across the Chindwin with their foes in hot pursuit. More and more prisoners were falling into Allied hands by now, mainly those too weak and starved to go on; the British tended to be sympathetic to these scarecrow starvelings but the Indians went in for atrocities in revenge for previous wrongs.[41] Next Slim sent units across the Chindwin to test enemy strength on the other side, preparatory to building bridge-heads for a general crossing. First across were the East Africans of the King's African Rifles, marching east from Tamu to Sittang, aiming for the Kabaw valley and Kalewa, but they immediately ran into much stiffer resistance, especially from elite units among the retreating Japanese, who felt new confidence once over the river.[42] Resistance also stiffened on the Tiddim–Kalemyo road when the strongpoint of Kennedy Peak, 8,800 feet high, was reached. Kalemyo was occupied on 14 November, at which point Slim ordered 4 Corps to cross the Chindwin and capture Pinlebu, while Scoones sent 19 Indian Division across at Sittang. A ferocious three-week struggle for Pinwe ensued, with the Japanese losing large numbers of their precious tanks; in this battle they had four main enemies to contend with: heavy artillery, devastating airpower from the RAF and USAAF, disease, and the monsoon itself. Finally the key position of Kalewa was captured on 28 November, again after heavy fighting.[43]

What sounds like a smooth and streamlined operation on paper was not accomplished without terrific losses and significant setbacks. Slim was lucky that DRACULA was knocked on the head, as Mountbatten had intended to order 14th Army back to Imphal so that the men could be rested preparatory to the amphibious attack on Rangoon, and had issued contingency orders to this effect. Determined to present him with a fait accompli, Stilwell, Giffard and Slim all opposed this idea, and as acting supreme commander Stilwell had the clout to implement their wishes.[44] Yet most of the obstacles were more mundane, many of them the effects of the monsoon, which was due to last until mid-November. Traversing the Manipur river was itself an ordeal, even though there were no Japanese to contest the crossing. One hundred yards wide, the river boasted a raging torrent, swollen by the monsoon floods, which ran at 12 knots, sweeping away the first flimsy ferries and drowning their occupants. Stouter ferries were built to defy the Manipur in spate, and the crossing was finally effected on 16–19 September.[45] As the troops advanced, pioneers and engineers built supply roads behind them, often cantilevering sections of the track from cliff faces. Casualties, too, were not insignificant. Half of 33 Corps's total strength of 88,500 men were engaged in the post-Imphal pursuit of July–November 1944, and they sustained about 80 per cent losses, while 5 Indian Division counted 88 killed, 293 wounded and 22 missing during their progress from Imphal to Kalemyo, but killed 1,316 of the enemy and took 53 prisoners.[46] Total casualties in both 4 and 33 Corps amounted to 50,300, but at least 47,000 of these succumbed to serious tropical diseases, including 20,000 malaria cases.[47] The malaria rate in 14th Army at this stage was 84 per cent, but a dramatic turn-round was at hand in the shape of new drugs, new treatments and new preventive measures, so that by March–April 1945, the sickness rate from malaria had come down to an almost incredible one in a thousand.[48] All that, however, lay in the future. By late November 1944, Slim could congratulate himself on a superbly efficient advance conducted in the teeth of the monsoon, and in the face of mud, torrential rain, bridgeless streams and the inroads of disease. As has been well said: 'It was an achievement that would have been unimaginable two years or perhaps even one year previously – the achievement of an army whose commander inspired it to feel at home with the impossible.'[49]

Naturally Slim was secretly pleased that DRACULA had been knocked on the head, as it competed for scarce resources with CAPITAL. In this regard the signal sent from the Quebec conference on 16 September was crucial: 'Your object is the recapture of all Burma at the earliest possible date.' This final paragraph of the Quebec directive was the historical covenant, so to speak, that enabled Slim to realise his aspirations. But it must be stressed that Slim, unlike Wingate, was always prepared to put his ambition on hold for the greater good; he never forfeited his integrity. As his biographer has commented: 'Slim was no Patton, seeking personal glory. If a viable DRACULA could have been mounted, promising genuine success, he was too good a soldier and too dedicated to his country's interests not to have welcomed it.'[50] Mountbatten, though sometimes ambivalent about Slim, was on this occasion gracious in defeat, and on his return from Egypt, he relieved him of responsibilities in the Arakan sector so that he could concentrate on CAPITAL. Mountbatten did of course have an ulterior motive, for if he was to be denied amphibious glory at Rangoon, he could use combined operations to secure a minor victory at Arakan. Accordingly, on 8 November, he ordered an attack on the Japanese positions there by the end of January at the latest, and assigned the task to 25 Indian and 2 West African Divisions.[51] Slim was glad to be relieved of overseeing Arakan, as throughout September and November he faced the massive job of retraining and restructuring his army. Fighting around the Irrawaddy would be very different from that at Kohima-Imphal, and not just because it would be an offensive campaign of movement as against the defensive, First-World-War-style attrition waged in March–June. Predominantly hill and jungle warfare would give way to fighting in the open country, where Slim hoped to use his tanks decisively. The rethinking and retraining was rigorous, but was never imposed in an authoritarian way from above. Not only were Slim's 'cabinet meetings' of his senior officers very democratic, with everyone being allowed a full say, but Slim was a good delegator. He always allowed his generals to show initiative in the field, and never breathed down their necks – an indispensable attribute in an army commander directing a campaign over such vast distances; a micromanager would have been a disaster. As a result of his laid-back attitude, great trust was established between Slim and his corps and divisional commanders.[52]

By this time Slim had built up the organisation of 14th Army to the point where every cog in the overall mechanism worked in a streamlined way. Scoones was expecting to direct 4 Corps (the battle-hardened 7 Indian Division and the 'virgin' 19 Indian Division) in the Chindwin crossing, but Slim thought him too slow and ponderous for the campaign of movement to come, and kicked him upstairs as Commander-in-Chief, Central Command, India. He replaced him with a personal favourite, Frank Messervy, and ensured that he had a similar hard-driving deputy in Peter Rees to head the greenhorn 19 Indian Division. Slim had an uncanny ability to read men's strengths and weaknesses, and realised that Messervy, despite his Patton-like qualities as a fighting general, was not stable and balanced enough in judgements calling for nuance and discrimination. He therefore appointed Brigadier Eddie Cobb as his chief of staff. Messervy read the runes correctly and construed this as a veiled criticism, with Cobb functioning as a brake to curb his excesses. He protested to Slim that he knew nothing of Cobb, that Cobb did not fit his requirements as a chief of staff. Slim's curt response to this was Attlee-like. 'Very well,' he said, 'no Cobb, no Corps.' Messervy accepted defeat. To sugar the pill, Slim told him that he was allowed to take risks in the campaign, as the enemy was demoralised.[53] Yet Slim did not just concentrate on his field commanders. He also had a wonderful hand-picked support team, among whom Colonel Alf Snelling (chief quartermaster), Brigadier 'Tubby' Lethbridge (chief of staff) and Major General W.F. Hasted (chief engineer) featured prominently. Like all great commanders, Slim was a master of logistics, and he understood perfectly the constraints he would be operating under once in Burma. Staff studies showed that the maximum force supportable beyond the Chindwin – 400 miles from the Dimapur railhead and 200 miles from the nearest air-supply base – was four divisions.[54] Slim had to balance the realities of airpower against the numbers he needed to penetrate Burma, while also bearing in mind that the numbers themselves might be difficult to attain, for 14th Army was being crippled by malaria, battalions were falling in numbers, and reinforcements were not coming through fast enough.[55]

Slim also had to appraise the balance of power, both his own strengths and weaknesses and those of the enemy. After Imphal, the Japanese had implemented a major personnel change, against all tenets of their military culture and almost unprecedented at such a high level; such was the trauma of their defeat on the plains of Manipur. Both Mutaguchi and Kawabe were transferred to staff jobs in Tokyo. Heading their army in Burma now was General Kimura Kyotaro, a shrewd, tactically skilful and flexible commander; Lieutenant General Tanaka Shinichi was transferred from 18 Japanese Division in north Burma to be his chief of staff.[56] By the end of October 1944, the Japanese were on the run in all theatres and had just sustained a catastrophic naval defeat at Leyte Gulf in the Philippines. Their new conception was to have Siam (Thailand) and Malaya as the outer periphery of a fortress zone, even though it was cut off from Japan by aggressive and highly successful US submarine warfare against the sea lanes to the homeland. The combination of Kohima-Imphal with Mogaung and Myitkyina mean that by autumn 1944, Kimura's role was reduced to defending southern Burma as the northern flank of their new 'South-East Asia defence zone'. With few reinforcements or supplies to look forward to, Kimura had grim prospects. On paper he had ten divisions (2, 15, 18, 31, 33, 49, 53, 54, 55, 56), though this was really seven, since little remained of the three divisions that had been devastated at Kohima-Imphal. He also had the dubious support of Bose's INA and Aung San's seven-battalion Burma National Army, but the civilian population was increasingly going over to the side of the likely winners.[57] Unexpectedly, Kimura received 30,000 fresh troops in the period June–October, but his problem was more commissariat than raw numbers, since he was rapidly running out of supplies. Even those he had – 45,000 tons of food, 500 lorries and 2,000 pack animals – were difficult to get to the front, and Kimura was painfully aware that the situation could only get worse. The South-East Asia zone was slowly being throttled by the Allied naval blockade, all approaches to Rangoon were mined, and in 1944 total Japanese shipping losses amounted to 2. 3 million tons. Even those ships that ran the blockade would proceed no farther than Penang in Malaya.[58]

On some indices, Japan had already reached the stage of total desperation, for the number of boys aged 12–14 pressed into military service in Tokyo rose from 700,000 in October 1944 to one and a quarter million by February 1945.[59] Nonetheless, Slim had some difficult calculations to make. By stretching airpower to the limit and beyond, he reckoned that he could put four and two thirds divisions across the Chindwin, plus two tank brigades. This was where the Arakan operation would be vital. The maximum range of the Dakotas was 250 miles, but if the Anglo-Indian forces were able to seize the islands off the Arakan coast – Akyab, Cheduba, Ramree – they would acquire air bases that would bring southern Burma within range.[60] Even though 15, 31 and 33 Japanese Divisions had ceased to exist, and Kimura had to keep some troops back to deal with Stilwell in the north (and later the incursion in the Arakan), the enemy should be able to put five and one third divisions and one tank regiment in the field. Would this be enough to secure victory? Once again airpower would be crucial and decisive, and the extent to which the Allies dominated the skies in South-East Asia was almost laughable in its crushing superiority.

They had more than 1,300 planes, while the Japanese had just 64. The RAF had 627 aircraft in Burma in December 1944 and the USAAF 691. By March 1945 these figures had increased to 772 and 748 respectively.[61] As always, war had engendered some quantum leaps in technology, so that the picture of aerial warfare was changing rapidly. By installing extra fuel tanks and cruise controls, USAAF Liberators were now capable of a bomb load of 8,000 pounds over a maximum range of 1,100 miles.[62] The RAF Beaufighters meanwhile proved an ideal aircraft for attacking railway locomotives and rolling stock, as their rockets could penetrate railway sheds and hangars. Strategic Air Force Operations to destroy Japanese transport systems and infrastructure would seriously reduce their military power.[63] And in December, with the end of the rains, the well-known perils of the monsoon for fliers would no longer manifest themselves; the worst were the terrifying thunderstorms in cumulonimbus clouds that no plane could climb above and which were capable of tearing apart even a huge aircraft like the Liberator.

Until December 1944 Slim had a clear-cut strategy. Having established bridgeheads at Sittang, Mawlaik and Kalewa, he intended to cross the Chindwin and engage Kimura between there and the Irrawaddy. His guess was that the Japanese would dig in along the formidable jungle-clad mountains of the Zibyutaungdan range (2–2, 500 feet high), 25 miles east of the Chindwin and running parallel to it for 120 miles. Slim intended to prise them out by piercing this defence in two places, with Messervy's 4 Corps (7 and 19 Indian Divisions, plus 255 Tank Brigade) on the left and Stopford's 33 Corps (2 British Division, 20 Indian Division and 254 Tank Brigade) on the right. Messervy's 4 Corps would break out of the Sittang bridgehead, strike east through the mountains, take Pinlebu and then come in on the Shwebo plain from the north, while 33 Corps would advance from Kalewa, following the course of the Chindwin south-east to Yeu and Monywa – all of them places well known to 14th Army from their ignominious retreat nearly three years earlier. Once the Japanese were winkled out on to the open plain, Slim's vast superiority in planes and tanks would enable him to annihilate them.[64] He was relying on the usual Japanese psychology, the reluctance to admit defeat, the desire to go down fighting and, most of all, the almost certain refusal to give up Mandalay without a fight. But Kimura was a wily bird and quickly divined Slim's intentions. Why should he fight on the Shwebo plain, where Slim had a clear comparative advantage; was that not the sort of madness that had dragged Mutaguchi down to disaster at Kohima-Imphal? To Slim's intense disappointment, it soon became clear that Kimura had no intention of being gulled so easily.[65] From the ease with which his troops penetrated the Zibyutaungdan range, it soon became clear that Kimura would not be fighting on the Shwebo plain. Instead he left small forces to delay the British and withdrew across the Irrawaddy, intending to counterattack when the British crossed that river. Basically his intention was to pull off an Imphal in reverse, exhausting the Anglo-Indians by attrition and then destroying them as they retreated in the monsoon of May 1945. He ordered his men to dig in at two points, leaving himself free to manoeuvre, both at the curve of the Irrawaddy at Sagaing, opposite Mandalay, and down-stream from Mandalay; both positions gave him the option of a further defence in the triangle of the Irrawaddy delta. Slim would now have to make the difficult traverse of the Irrawaddy and then defeat the Japanese – a much tougher proposition than his original estimate.[66] So far Kimura, having been dealt a very bad hand, was performing brilliantly. What would Slim do next?

The first weeks of December were anxious ones for him. It did not help that the entire senior personnel of SEAC were in a state of flux, largely because of Mountbatten's megalomania. October was a key month for 'Dickie', as he saw the back not only of Stilwell (against whom he had intrigued assiduously) but the three chiefs of staff who had 'defied' him. All the problems basically arose from the fact that the creation of the post of Supreme Commander, South-East Asia, was a nonsense that had never been properly thought out and was simply one of Churchill's 'bright ideas'.[67] Mountbatten, with his vaulting ambition, always wanted to be a generalissimo, not a mere committee chairman, in which case, as the chiefs of staff ruefully concluded, what was the point of them and what was their role supposed to be? Either they or the supreme commander were an unnecessary layer in the military hierarchy. In land warfare the complex system would work only if the supreme commander, the army commander and the general actually directing the campaign were all of one mind. Mountbatten and Slim meshed perfectly, and Slim and Giffard collaborated well because Giffard always gave his subordinate his head. But Mountbatten and Giffard was an impossible mixture.[68] Temperamentally poles apart, they seemed to differ at every conceivable level. For Giffard fighting during the monsoon was dangerously irresponsible, personal visits to buck up the men's morale were mere grandstanding, and Mountbatten's entire style was personally and aesthetically repugnant. Detesting Stilwell as he did, Giffard thought that both Slim and the Supreme Commander deferred to him too much. Resenting the entire system that had made him Mountbatten's underling, and disliking the man personally, Giffard habitually sided with the other commanders, Peirse and Somerville, who both felt exactly as he did.[69] Whatever Mountbatten proposed, the trio opposed as if by reflex action. Sacked in May, Giffard was still in post in October because of the difficulty of finding someone to replace him; a general had to be found who was both competent and could put up with Mountbatten, and this was never going to be easy. The obvious solution was for Slim to take over Giffard's role, but the Supreme Commander opposed this, ostensibly because Slim was too valuable where he was. This argument might have worked in March–June 1944 during Kohima-Imphal, and again after December when Slim was engaged in CAPITAL, but had no validity whatever in the intervening period. The suspicion arises that, consciously or unconsciously, Mountbatten was jealous of Slim. Already in the habit of taking credit for the other man's achievements, Mountbatten may have felt that this would be impossible if Slim was at the very nerve centre of power. The suspicion is enhanced by Mountbatten's refusal to have Slim in either Giffard's job or that of Pownall, as his chief of staff, when Pownall retired in the autumn.[70]

The reason Giffard was not replaced more rapidly can be laid at the door of Mountbatten's prima-donna antics. Both the replacements for Giffard and Pownall became snarled up in wrangles about who should get the jobs. For the Pownall post Generals Swayne, Nye and Lushington were all proposed and rejected by one side or the other. To supplant Giffard, Pownall had very early identified Oliver Leese as the likely candidate, but he was heavily involved in operations in Italy and could not be switched immediately. Leese was a Montgomery protégé who had commanded 30 Corps at Alamein and then the 8th Army in Italy.[71] The obvious unsuitability of a man with a background in European and desert warfare for the very different campaigns in

Burma seems to have troubled no one in London, though Churchill, for reasons of his own, did not confirm the appointment until 14 September; there was then another six-week hiatus before the Prime Minister officially informed Leese of his promotion. Giffard returned to London, where he put his side of the story to Alanbrooke; having heard both his and Mountbatten's version of events, the CIGS was in no doubt that Giffard had had 'a very raw deal. I blame Henry Pownall for a great deal of it, for he should certainly have been able to control Dickie better than he did. In any case I feel certain that most of the credit for the Burma success is due to Giffard.'[72] Having removed one of the incubuses who so tasked him, Mountbatten used the excuse of Peirse's adultery with Lady Auchinleck to get rid of him.[73] It seemed that adultery was a heinous crime when committed by Peirse but not by Mountbatten or Edwina. Peirse was replaced by Air Chief Marshal Trafford Leigh-Mallory, but he was killed almost at once and replaced by the unknown New Zealander Keith Park.[74] The most persistent thorn in Mountbatten's side, possibly because he was the most intelligent of the three chiefs of staff, Admiral James Somerville, also moved on, and was replaced by Bruce Fraser. The Supreme Commander was mightily relieved to see depart the sea dog of the old school who had always regarded him as an upstart, overpromoted pup, but Fraser was a stopgap appointment, and was transferred almost immediately to command the new British Pacific fleet. Mountbatten wrote on 15 November: 'I shall miss Bruce Fraser so much; he has been such a wonderful change after James Somerville and has produced an entirely new atmosphere throughout the whole of the Eastern Fleet staff.'[75] Fraser in turn was replaced by Admiral Arthur Power. Although he had merely the ships left behind by Fraser to form the so-called East Indies Fleet, his force was far better integrated into SEAC than the Royal Navy ever had been before. Churchill had made it a point of understanding with the Admiralty that whoever was appointed this time had to defer to Mountbatten. Superficially pleased, Mountbatten suspected that the new dispositions were a mere sop to him while the Admiralty transferred its real affections to the new Pacific fleet.[76] At least he could now visit the fleet, whereas under Somerville all his attempts to do so had been sabotaged.[77]

Mountbatten's precious behaviour continued to grate on Alanbrooke, and the London–Kandy correspondence quickly became acidulous, the CIGS taking the Supreme Commander to task for seeming to imply that the Burma war was the only one being waged. The tedious negotiations for Pownall's replacement finally bore fruit when Lieutenant General Frederick 'Boy' Browning, veteran of the Arnhem campaign, was appointed. Pownall hardly helped matters by advising Mountbatten that Browning was not really up to the job, but Browning himself regarded the posting as a bed of nails. Alanbrooke noted that he was not exactly overjoyed by the assignment: 'he took it well, but I doubt whether in his heart of hearts he was thrilled.'[78] Always conscious of his age, and the lack of gravitas this conferred, Mountbatten consoled himself with the thought that Browning was only three years older than he was; in fact he later turned out to be one of the Supremo's favourite officers.[79] If he had been lucky so far with the replacements, Mountbatten fell spectacularly at the final hurdle. He had allowed his personal exasperation with Giffard and his wounded *amour-propre* to override the consideration that the really important military relationship, that between Giffard and Slim, had worked smoothly and effectively. Two out of three of the core relationships had been successful. Now he had engineered a situation where only one of the three elements, the Slim–Mountbatten nexus, was functional. The new army commander-in-chief, Oliver Leese, got on neither with Mountbatten nor with Slim. He seems to have been appointed almost entirely on the good word of Pownall and because of Mountbatten's irritation with Giffard, not on any real merits. Alanbrooke, who was always very shrewd about British officers, while being hopelessly at sea in his judgement of Americans (because he did not understand them), had long had doubts about Leese and thought he would not get on with Mountbatten. 'He is certainly not anything outstanding as a commander,' he wrote in August.[80]

Leese's early contacts with Mountbatten and Slim were not auspicious. He arrived in Delhi on 8 November, then flew down to Ceylon, where Mountbatten whisked him off to his birthday party in a ballroom. Leese was shocked by the permissive atmosphere. A very pretty Wren kissed the Supreme Commander passionately in a long clinch, while the band played 'Happy Birthday'. Leese looked on, starchily unimpressed, and later wrote to his wife: 'They were at extreme pains to explain that it did not happen very often. But I doubt that. It was gay and full of life – full enough of drink – and very odd. Most girls were U's [Mountbatten's] and other secretaries and they seemed to spend their time sitting on the arms of U and others' chairs. It all seemed a pity somehow, as it gives the Playboy atmosphere, in terrible contrast to those from the battle.'[81] On 12 November Leese was appointed Commander-in-Chief, Allied Land Forces South-East Asia (ALFSEA), which included all American forces in action in Burma (but not China), and three days later set up his HQ at Barrackpore, where he met Slim and Christison. Forthcoming operations in the Arakan were assigned to Christison, with an independent command, to free Slim entirely for the campaign beyond the Chindwin. The encounter with Slim was superficially friendly, though it was obvious that the two men did not get on at any profound level. Leese's impressions were not particularly favourable, although he patronisingly remarked that Slim was a good tactician. Slim showed no signs of being glad to have Leese in Burma and, according to Leese, 'belly-ached' a lot.[82] Leese was one of those curious individuals who regarded any mounting of a critique, however sensible, as 'whingeing'. Slim's misgivings were intensified when Leese began to pack his HQ administration with 8th Army veterans. Even in his autobiography, where Slim in Thumper-like mode barely breathes a word of criticism of anyone, there is a hint of the underlying tension: 'His staff . . . had a good deal of desert sand in its shoes and was rather inclined to thrust Eighth Army down our throats.'[83] This was deeply resented by 14th Army, which considered itself at least the equal of 8th Army. Slim took to bombarding Leese's staff with gratuitous praise of 14th Army, and so the tensions escalated. Leese was heard to say that he did not consider Kohima-Imphal in the same class as the victories in North Africa and Italy, claimed that Slim considered himself a better general than Montgomery, and in general ludicrously underrated the brilliant commander of 14th Army.[84]

Unlike Giffard, who always supported Slim, gave him his head and basically let him do what he wanted, Leese was another micromanager in the Noel Irwin mould, who wanted to be the true commander; in a curious way, he had a similar personality to the Supreme Commander, whom he rapidly came to loathe, and described as 'crooked as a corkscrew'.[85] He failed to understand that most of the pieces in the Burma jigsaw puzzle were already in place by the time he arrived, and that nobody needed his input. He resented the special rapport between Slim and the soldiers of 14th Army, and even more the close working relationship between Mountbatten and Slim, to say nothing of the offence Mountbatten gave by stating in private that it was harder to win the Victoria Cross in Burma than it was in Europe, and that the individual warriors of 14th Army, man for man, outclassed those of 8th Army.[86] Idiotically, Leese would often issue 'new' orders, identical to those Slim had given weeks and months ago. He was an incubus Slim could well have done without as he planned the final stages of CAPITAL. On 14 December, Slim and his three key corps commanders, Scoones, Stopford and Christison, were all knighted in a special ceremony at Imphal by Wavell, who appeared in the regal role by special permission of the King. Observers at the ceremony thought Slim looked tired and drawn.[87] Quite apart from the Leese factor, the reason for tension was obvious. Slim realised he would have to slow down the speed of his advance and restructure CAPITAL or risk a premature assault on the wide and strongly defended waterway. While he considered his options, he put the final touches to the Chindwin operations. Five new Bailey bridges were built, including the longest floating in the world at that time (1,154 feet), which was assembled and installed on the Chindwin on 7–10 December.[88] Elephants were crucial in the task of moving timber as trees were felled, bridges built and new airstrips laid. At the Chindwin Slim put on an impressive display of river power as part of the infrastructure for his onward march. Five hundred river barges were constructed at Kalewa, and gunboats bristling with machine guns and cannons launched to protect the river traffic.[89] All that was needed now was Slim's revised strategy to outwit Kimura so that he could reach Rangoon before the monsoon began.

When Stilwell returned to China in early September, having visited Chungking just twice since he went to the front in January as a battle commander, he found things as bad as ever but the labyrinthine web of intrigue and jockeying for advantage even more complex and Byzantine. Ever since the failed army coup by young officers the year before, the iron fist of the KMT had clamped down even more tightly. It was typical of Chiang that, after seeing off a grave challenge to his position, he should then settle back into his old ways and do nothing about the circumstances that had caused the coup in the first place. With morale low, corruption rampant and increasing, the economy stagnating and even the old warlords of the 1920s and 1930s enjoying a revival, all the generalissimo could think of was that perennial obsession the threat from the Communists. It never seemed to occur to him that all his policies – conscription, confiscations, compulsory levies on rice, widespread corvées, trying to buck the market and beat inflation with a compulsory freezing of prices – all alienated the peasantry even further and thus played into the hands of Mao Tse-tung and the Red Army.[1] What kind of resistance to the famous Eighth Route Army was likely when the Kuomintang soldiers were not paid and scarcely even fed? Since all copy by foreign journalists was censored, it was difficult for the outside world to get a line on the true state of affairs, but those in power in Washington who were really interested could have read Ambassador Gauss's lucid reports, where the entire fiasco was analysed. The trouble was that Gauss was telling FDR and Cordell Hull, the Secretary of State, things they did not want to hear. He did not exactly help his case by constantly predicting the downfall of the KMT, which, however, managed to limp on from month to month.[2] The atmosphere of a topsy-turvy Alice-in-Wonderland failed state and all its attendant absurdities was well caught by Mountbatten in a diary entry on 18 July. The rumour reached him that Chiang was to become a father again but no one knew who the mother was, since his wife, the much-admired Madame Chiang, had walked out on him in July and gone to Brazil after he refused to banish a concubine; she did not return until September 1945. Mountbatten commented: 'In the western world the reverse is often enough true but it takes China to turn the facts of Nature inside out.'[3]

Gauss and Stilwell had long argued that in China the only people doing any real fighting and killing Japanese were the Communists, and that therefore Washington should consider cutting Chiang adrift and supporting Mao and the Red Army. Stilwell was a Republican and a man of conservative views (Roosevelt was too liberal for him), but as a battling general he had no interest in ideology and was concerned only with the most effective fighters. The situation was almost exactly analogous to that in Yugoslavia at the same time. Both Churchill and his envoy, the 'Balkan brigadier' Fitzroy MacLean, were vehement anti-Communists, but in wartime their only interest was which Yugoslav faction was killing the most Germans. When MacLean found that this was Tito and his Communist partisans, Allied aid was directed to them. The reluctant Serbian nationalist fighters, the Cetniks, under their leader Mihailovic, were cast adrift because they shirked from battle with the Germans and often actively collaborated with them.[4] If reason alone was the lodestar for US foreign policy, this is what should have happened in China. Gauss had long urged Chiang to forge an alliance with the Communists so that both could fight the Japanese; if Chiang refused, he recommended his Lend-Lease be discontinued. Growing impatience with the generalissimo, and the evidence of their own eyes at the Cairo conference in 1943, led key decision-makers in Washington eventually to investigate the fighting potential of Mao and the Red Army. On the Yugoslav analogy and example, it was obvious that US support should have been switched immediately to the Communists. In northern China, where there was the greatest concentration of Japanese troops and industry in the entire country, the Reds controlled 155,000 square miles and 54 million people and had a well-trained and disciplined army of 475,000, to say nothing of the impressive inroads they were making on the hearts and minds of the Chinese peasantry. Clearly nationalists and Communists ought to collaborate against the common enemy, but this was not Chiang's agenda. Fearing that he was growing comparatively weaker day by day, he wanted to attack the Communists while FDR's attention was elsewhere, focused on Europe, before US reinforcements arrived in China or Russia entered the war by invading Manchuria. Finally, in late 1943, Chiang gave three American correspondents permission to visit Mao.[5]

The journalistic mission was headed by the Chinese-speaking Colonel David Barrett, famous as the only American who could tell jokes in Chinese convincingly to the Chinese themselves. Stilwell thoroughly approved of the mission, perhaps mindful that Chou En-lai had said in 1942: 'I would serve under General Stilwell and I would obey.'[6] He became more and more excited by the idea of a combined force, with 20 Communists in each company of 100 men. The chief of staff of Y-force, Hsiao I-shu, cautioned him that that meant the entire company would be 'Red' within a fortnight. A military mission to the Communists in Yenan was ready to go in February 1944, but the generalissimo, as usual, stalled and, when FDR repeated his request in March 1944, used his back-up ploy of simply making no answer. FDR responded by sending the mission anyway: this was the famous 'Dixie mission'.[7] Yet it was clear that the way forward in China was to bring Mao and the Communists into an anti-Japanese united front. This was the pretext for the Wallace mission to China, when Roosevelt sent out Vice President Henry Wallace to persuade Chiang to negotiate with Mao.[8] There was the usual FDR machiavellianism at play here also, as the President wanted his unpopular 'veep' out of the country when the Democrat convention met in June. Careful preparations were made for the visit. Wallace was given the assistance of experienced China hands like Owen Lattimore, and Stilwell's political adviser John Service prepared a long, lucid and cogent memo on the true state of affairs in Chiang's China.[9] Yet Wallace was made of crooked timber, only too willing to heed the anti-Stilwell faction. As soon as his embassy was announced, the Alsop–Chennault axis went into overdrive, arguing for Stilwell's recall and absurdly talking up the achievements of Chennault's air force.[10] From 21 to 24 June Wallace parleyed with Chiang in Chungking. At first the generalissimo flatly refused to allow a formal, authorised military mission, then he backtracked and said he would authorise it if, as a quid pro quo, both

Stilwell and Gauss were dismissed. Wallace was taken in by all Chiang's nonsense and declared himself moved by his 'distress'. Four of Stilwell's deadly enemies – Chennault, Wedemeyer, Soong and Joseph Alsop – all buttonholed Wallace with demands that Stilwell should go.[11] In his cable to FDR, Wallace accepted all their diaphanous special pleading at face value, and even suggested that Wedemeyer should be Stilwell's replacement. Wallace and Stilwell did not meet each other. Stilwell despised him as a moron, and was anyway preoccupied with the struggle for Mogaung and Myitkyina. He did suggest that Wallace fly down to meet him in the Mogaung valley, but this was too close to the sound of gunfire for the fastidious Wallace. When Wallace's ridiculous suggestions were discussed in Washington, Marshall, knowing only too well their provenance, made short work of them.[12]

Yet another anti-Stilwell intrigue had flopped, so badly that the *New York Times* took up with avidity the idea of Mao and the Communists being partners in the anti-Japanese alliance.[13] Indeed, so far were Marshall and the Joint Chiefs from heeding Wallace's advice that they were working in the opposite direction: they wanted to enlarge Stilwell's authority in China, not remove him. China was no longer important as an air base for raids on Japan once Saipan, taken in July after a bloody three-week struggle with fanatical Japanese defenders, became available. On the other hand, the Joint Chiefs took seriously Stilwell's warning that the large Japanese armies in China might decide to fight on even if Nippon itself was successfully invaded – doing by analogy what the British intended to do in 1940 if they had lost the Battle of Britain, carrying the struggle over into Canada.[14] A protracted war on the Chinese mainland would involve the USA in two deadly dangers. If they transferred war-weary GIs from Europe to China, the American public would not wear it; even worse, the appearance of the Soviet Union in Manchuria would become a 'racing certainty', and this was diametrically opposed to US interests. Making Stilwell the commander of all Chinese forces, without any interference from Chiang, would also remove him from SEAC and stop the whispering campaign against him by Mountbatten and Alanbrooke. The US War Department wanted to promote Vinegar Joe to 'Field Chief of Staff' – a field marshal in all but name – in China.[15] A memo on 30 June, strongly backed by Stimson, argued (correctly) that Stilwell had welded a proper and credible Chinese army in Burma in the teeth of unbelievable obstacles, and that the taking of Myitkyina airfield was an amazing feat of arms. Marshall wrote to Stilwell to suggest that after his stint at Kandy he should base himself permanently in Chungking so as to be ready to wage the expected long land war against the Japanese, pointing out that his absence from the SEAC theatre would both placate the British and transfer the pressure on to Chiang. Stilwell replied briefly: 'I'll go where I'm sent,' but suggested to Marshall that it would be better if FDR read the riot act to Chiang first.[16]

The main factor pushing Washington in the direction of Stilwell's promotion was the alarming success of a new Japanese offensive in China opened in June and code-named I-CHIGO. This was a last-ditch attempt by Tokyo to defeat China before US bombers came within range of the homeland but, ironically, it was launched just before the Americans invaded Saipan on 16 June and achieved that capability anyway. I-CHIGO, involving half a million Japanese troops – the largest numbers ever deployed in the whole of Japanese military history – was nothing if not ambitious. Japanese merchant navy losses were by now restricting the flow of raw materials from South-East Asia, so the response of strategists in Tokyo was to try to forge a continental corridor, linking Korea, Manchuria and East China with Thailand, Malaya and Singapore. Sweeping the demoralised Chinese before them, the Japanese took Honan, then turned south from Hankow to strike at the air bases in eastern China.[17] Changsha, the capital of the rice-bowl region, fell on 18 June, sparking the bitterest phase of the Chennault–Stilwell feud. Chennault virtually provided the refutation of his own tenets when his fabled 14th Air Force could not prevent the enemy advance, though they did slow it. He claimed that his failure was simply because of shortage of supplies, and tried to shift the blame to Stilwell and the Hump. Vinegar Joe rightly saw this as a campaign 'to duck the consequences of having sold the wrong bill of goods'.[18] He was livid with Chennault after an article appeared in the Saturday Evening Post stating that Chennault was the only man of genius in Asia and Stilwell a mere World War I foot soldier.[19] Under extreme pressure from Chiang, Stilwell agreed to divert 1,500 tons of cargo from the B-29s to Chennault if Washington consented. Marshall, knowing full well that the Flying Tigers were more in the nature of a paper tiger and that Chennault was a charlatan, abruptly refused. By this time both he and many others had become convinced that the slow progress of the war in Europe was because so much materiel had been diverted to the Hump at Chiang's request, in vain, pointlessly and uselessly. Stimson said of the Hump: 'It has been bleeding us white in transport airplanes.'[20] As for Chennault, he had already lost credibility and 'got across' MacArthur by boasting that he could bomb the Philippines from China. In MacArthur's view, the Philippines were his personal bailiwick, and Stilwell chortled: 'MacArthur in a sweat over Chennault trying to bomb Manila.'[21] Marshall explained in his rejection note that nothing must interfere with the B-29s. Stilwell replied: 'Instructions understood and exactly what I hoped for.' Now definitively rejected by the Joint Chiefs, Chiang and Chennault spewed out their rage towards Stilwell, whom they held responsible for their humiliation. Stilwell remained unfazed by I-CHIGO, reasoning that the Japanese would soon outrun their lines of communication. Meanwhile he intended to unite Y-force and his own NCAC, get more reinforcements from the USA, and then move into south-west China. With an army of 250,000 under his command he was confident that he could drive the enemy into the sea.[22]

The collective denial of the Roosevelt administration about the reality of Chiang's regime received a bad jolt in May when the well-known journalist Theodore White blew the lid off the Kuomintang in an article in Life. Describing the KMT as 'a corrupt political clique that combines some of the worst features of Tammany Hall and the Spanish Inquisition', he argued that it was madness to give the regime a 'prolonged kiss of death' by continuing to prop it up.[23] This was an open endorsement of what Stilwell had been saying for years. Perhaps encouraged by the new mood in the USA, from the beginning of September onwards Stilwell's diaries became full of sombre reflections on the nature of the Kuomintang and its leader. Why were the Allies fighting the Nazis in Europe, with their one-party system, use of terror and the Gestapo, yet backing to the hilt the selfsame fascist system in China? Why had Roosevelt never demanded a quid pro quo from Chiang for the Lend-Lease supplies that flooded into his country? The choice between the Kuomintang and the Communists was a classic 'no-brainer', the contrast between corruption, neglect, chaos, heavy taxation, hoarding, the black market and trading with the enemy on the one side, and the reduction of taxes, rent and interest and an increase in production and the standard of living on the other. The

Communists practised what they preached; the KMT utterances were mere meaningless words. Above all, there was the personality of the generalissimo. 'I have never heard Chiang Kai-shek say a single thing that indicated gratitude to the President or to our country for the help we were extending to him. Invariably, when anything was promised he would want more. Invariably he would complain about the small amount of material that was being furnished. Always complaints about the vast amount going to Britain and the trickle to China . . . The cure for China's trouble is the elimination of Chiang Kai-shek.'[24] Even Stilwell's promotion to de facto field marshal was problematical, for the Chinese army – or at least those portions that had not been trained at Ramgarh – was seriously deficient. On paper it contained 324 divisions plus another 60-odd specialist brigades and 89 so-called guerrilla units, which should have made it by far the most formidable army in the world. Unfortunately the paper strength masked the reality. Chinese divisions, supposed to be 10,000 men, rarely had more than 5,000, casualties were never replaced, all the officers were place men and political appointees, the troops were unpaid, unfed, sick and undernourished, training was non-existent and equipment antiquated or unserviceable, and there was no artillery, transport or medical corps worth the name. This was to say nothing of the fact that Chiang habitually kept at least 20 divisions as reserves, facing north to deal with the Communist menace, and refused to release them to any other theatre. Above all, Chinese culture itself worked against military prowess. Taoism taught one to go with the flow, accept fate and never take risks, for if you did nothing, you couldn't be blamed for whatever happened.[25]

In the privacy of his journal Stilwell took what comfort he could from Brit-bashing. Even when the Limeys tried to be accommodating, they managed only to be patronising. Mountbatten had told him that, as an American, he did not have to join in singing 'God Save the King' but he should at least stand up when the National Anthem was played. Stilwell took a sour view of this advice: 'I don't mind standing up. All I object to is 1) standing on my knees and 2) having my feet kicked out from under me when I do stand up.'[26] Always obsessed with the view that the British did not pull their military weight and that the war in Asia was simply a device whereby American blood and treasure rescued the moribund British Empire, he oddly took up the discredited

Wingate–Churchill line that the Indian army was a bloated bureaucracy of bullet-dodging loafers. Auchinleck had already refuted this, demonstrating that 400,000 was the maximum fighting strength of his army, not the one million confidently bruited by Wingate. Churchill in fact, with his lifelong contempt for the Indian army, tied himself into knots on this issue, both accepting the Wingate figure and then telling Auchinleck that he should slim down his army by about a million men.[27] Most of the anti-Limey effusions were standard diatribe. 'I see that the Limeys are going to rush to our rescue in the Pacific. Like hell. They are going to continue this fight with their mouths. Four or five old battleships will appear and about ten RAF planes will go to Australia but in twenty years the schoolbooks will be talking about "shoulder to shoulder" and "the Empire struck with all its might against the common enemy" and all that crap. The idea of course is to horn in at Hong Kong again, and our Booby [FDR] is sucked in.'[28] The main enemy, of course, was always Mountbatten, who by this time was a positive bête noire for Stilwell. He was highly amused when a *March of Time* documentary entitled 'Background Tokyo' implied that the Americans were doing all the fighting in Burma and portrayed the Supreme Commander in a poor light as a mere playboy, with carefully edited footage showing him apparently being sycophantic to Madame Chiang.[29] He was not so happy when the boot was on the other foot, and wrote in outrage to his wife: 'Did you see Churchill's speech about Louis's great campaign in Burma? They apparently feel it necessary to pump a little prestige into him. Today's news is that Eden announced that the "beloved" commander of the SEAC was in London. He didn't tell me he was going so I suppose there is more skulduggery afoot.'[30] This was a curious mirror-image version of Mountbatten's paranoia. When Stilwell went to Chungking in September, Mountbatten imagined that he was stealing off to the Quebec conference; when Mountbatten went to Cairo, Stilwell imagined that he had gone to London. In fairness to Mountbatten, he was more meticulous about keeping his deputy informed than Stilwell was with him.[31]

While Stilwell amused himself with these lucubrations, the great crisis with Chiang approached. Stilwell had told Marshall it was essential that FDR read the riot act. Marshall drafted a very stiff memo arguing that in the light of the Japanese I-CHIGO campaign, Stilwell had been right after all and Chiang and Chennault wrong. By now disillusioned with Chiang, Roosevelt signed it. His memorandum of 4 July 1944 has been described as 'in effect a scorecard totting up Chennault's failures and Stilwell's triumphs'.[32] After reminding the generalissimo that the future of Asia was at stake, he proceeded to an encomium of the Chief of Staff in China:

> While fully aware of your feelings regarding General Stilwell, never-theless . . . I know of no other man who has the ability, the force and the determination to offset the disaster which now threatens China and our over-all plans for the conquest of Japan. I am promoting Stilwell to the rank of full general and I recommend for your most urgent consideration that you recall him from Burma and place him directly under you in command of all Chinese and American forces and that you charge him with full responsibility and authority for the coordin-ation and direction of the operations required to stem the tide of the enemy's advances.

FDR signed off with a contemptuous dismissal of the Chiang–Chennault thesis of victory through airpower: 'Please have in mind that it has clearly been demonstrated in Italy, in France, and in the Pacific that airpower alone cannot stop a determined enemy.'[33] To make sure there would be no suppression, doctoring, bowdlerisa-tion or spinning of this stark document, Marshall bypassed Soong and had the senior US permanent officer in Chungking, Major General Benjamin Ferris, deliver it in person, together with a translation by John Service, Stilwell's political adviser. As has been well said, this thunderbolt called Chiang 'the Peanut' by implication.[34] It certainly put the generalissimo on the spot for, as Barbara Tuchman has sagely remarked: 'It can be said that regardless of Stilwell's faults and offenses, even if he had the tongue of angels, the temperament of a saint and the professional charm of a Japanese geisha, the generalissimo would still have had no more intention of giving him command of his armed forces than of giving it to Mao Tse-tung.'[35]

The Roosevelt memorandum constituted not so much a loss of face as a direct slap in the face. Chiang's worst enemy had been promoted four-star general, one of only five in the entire US army (the others being Marshall, MacArthur, Eisenhower and 'Hap' Arnold). Fuming impotently – he knew that any overt expression of anger might mean the severance of Lend-Lease – Chiang searched the arsenal of Chinese cunning for a riposte, and came up with a brilliant solution. His initial reaction was typical: stall, stall, stall.[36] First, he claimed that 'political limitations' in the Chinese army would make it impossible for the moment to appoint a supreme commander with plenipotentiary powers. What that meant in fact was that, with Stilwell as a real commander, he, Chiang, would be unable to manipulate his generals. Then he played his ace. He asked FDR for a 'mediator' who would resolve the differences between him and Stilwell – in effect asking for a superior officer to be appointed above Stilwell.[37] Amazingly, Roosevelt took the bait, and a sanguine Chiang moved in for the kill, intending to use the envoy to dilute the new system into meaninglessness. With Mountbatten requesting that Stilwell be transferred from SEAC to China, Wallace advocating his total recall and Chiang unwilling to grant him supreme military power in China, FDR fatally took his foot off the gas pedal and looked around for some sort of intermediate solution. Instead of reading the riot act to Chiang, he sent an emollient reply. The stupidity of this response should have been obvious, for it was only when the President had sent an 'or else' message and threatened to cut off Lend-Lease unless the generalissimo sent Y-force across the Salween that Chiang finally buckled. A disappointed Marshall was reduced to cabling Stilwell to ask feebly what parts of his command he might be prepared to give up. Yet by suggesting Sultan as the commander of US and Chinese forces in Burma with Wedemeyer as deputy commander, SEAC, *at the very time* Chiang was refusing Stilwell supreme command in China, Marshall was in effect proposing that Vinegar Joe be reduced to a cipher. That was not his personal intention but simply the logic of FDR's appeasement of the anti-Stilwell faction.[38]

On 23 July, encouraged by FDR's conciliatory response, Chiang named four further conditions for accepting the American terms. He demanded that Stilwell be barred from commanding the Red Army in the field unless the Communists acknowledged him (Chiang) as the ruler of the Chinese state; that Stilwell command only those armies currently in the field against the Japanese and not those that were held in reserve; that Lend-Lease be entirely in the hands of the Chinese government; and that there should be a detailed protocol to define the limits of Stilwell's powers vis-à-vis the generalissimo. It should have been obvious to everyone in Washington that Chiang was not negotiating seriously, but, incredibly, they allowed matters to drift. Vinegar Joe himself remained pessimistic that anything would change. As one of the Chinese generals sympathetic to him remarked: 'We will only have real command in the field when all telephone lines to Chungking are cut' or, as Stilwell himself put it a little later: 'The cure for China's trouble is the elimination of Chiang Kai-shek.'[39] When Chiang asked him for an increase in Lend-Lease supply, he pounced, determined that the generalissimo and Chennault should not get away with the lies of the past, which FDR had endorsed; he wanted them out in the open. Blithely he replied that since Chiang had in the past asked that all US aid should go to Chennault and not Burma, the generalissimo should address his request to Chennault, who had just received a consignment of 12,000 tons. Stilwell had hoped that Chennault would be recalled in disgrace after I-CHIGO had revealed all his tenets about airpower as nonsense, but FDR had given too many hostages to fortune by his earlier praise of the Flying Tigers. In retaliation for the snub over Chennault and Lend-Lease, Chiang tried to open a second front in Washington through his foreign minister T.V. Soong. Their target was once again Harry Hopkins, the President's 'grey eminence', who was known to be unsympathetic to Stilwell and to consider that relations with China would improve only when he was recalled.[40] Chiang's brother-in-law, H.H. K'ung, based in Washington, was the main conduit for these intrigues.

On 9 August, nudged by Hopkins, FDR offered Chiang General Patrick Hurley as an intermediary and Chiang accepted with alacrity. Marshall, determined to keep one step ahead of Hopkins, was opposed to the very idea of an intermediary as an obvious cuttlefish tactic by Chiang, but hearing that Hopkins was going to offer one of his own 'creatures' to the President, he got in first by recommending Hurley, thought to be friendly to Stilwell. Patrick Hurley was a controversial and, by all accounts, highly dislikeable character. A man of the far right, he had been born in poverty in Oklahoma next to a Choctaw reservation, made a fortune as an attorney and been Secretary of War during the Hoover administration of 1928–32. Roosevelt used him as a 'fixer', and he had organised the American end of the Tehran conference in 1943 entirely to FDR's satisfaction. Variously described as handsome, talkative, irascible, suave, worldly, vain, arrogant, 'simple minded and Reaganesque before his time' (and memorably by Theodore White as an 'ignoramus'), Hurley was said once to have killed a fractious mule with a hammer. Later he revealed himself as a notable pro-Chiang figure, but in 1944 he was best known as a vituperative critic of the British Empire and European colonialism.[41] Donald Nelson, his fellow intermediary, was a chemical engineer who had just resigned as chairman of the War Production Board. Doubtless groaning inwardly that yet another mission was to come out to have the wool pulled over its eyes by Chiang, Stilwell replied meekly to Marshall's news that Hurley was visiting China yet again. Marshall stressed that no firm decision had yet been taken on the CBI theatre or Chiang's demand for a political commissar and insisted that Hurley was a mere stopgap. In his reply, Stilwell even managed a joke with reference to his own nickname: 'I would welcome the help of your candidate. It takes oil as well as vinegar to make good French dressing.'[42]

Even while Hurley and Nelson were en route to India, on 23 August, Washington replied to Chiang's four further conditions and rejected them all, except to say that Lend-Lease would shortly be removed from Stilwell's control and the generalissimo would be informed of the new arrangements in due course. Marshall cabled Stilwell that the intended reforms in his theatre were now clearer. He would in future no longer be in charge of Lend-Lease for China, and would cease to be Mountbatten's deputy. The Burma-India part of the CBI theatre would be hived off, and Stilwell would be supreme commander in China. Stilwell knew well enough how little that meant and accepted his obvious demotion with good grace, remarking that nothing could be worse than the present situation.[43] All the top analysts in the State Department could see clearly that Chiang was stalling, hoping to sit out the war, fearful of American landings in his country and wishing Japan to be defeated outside his borders so that he did not have to use his reserves. The problem was that Roosevelt could never quite overcome his ingrained 'China complex' and the conviction that Chiang was an important player.[44] On 30 August Stilwell left Kandy for Delhi, where he met Hurley and Nelson. Hurley at first seemed all Stilwell could wish for. His extrovert, rambunctious manner, not to mention his cowboy boots, convinced Stilwell that he was a no-nonsense down-to-earth and non-ideological fellow spirit. Hurley told him that Mountbatten had repeatedly tried to ditch him only to be blocked by FDR, and that Marshall was four-square behind him and appreciated all his difficulties.[45] He did not of course tell him that Vice President Wallace, in order to get Chiang's agreement for US envoys to visit Mao in Yenan, had gone out on a limb and promised him Stilwell's dismissal in return – the true reason Chiang agreed to the so-called Dixie Mission.[46] But Stilwell might have heeded the warning signs when Hurley told him that he understood Chiang's cautious approach and declared that the British were even greater double-crossers than the Chinese: 'The Limey reverse Lend-Lease,' said Hurley, 'is a racket. They refuse cost figures and are purposely gumming up the accounts so the snarl can never be untangled.'[47] Perhaps because he was so impressed by the anti-Limey rhetoric, Stilwell did not pick up the ominously pro-Chiang subtext.

The three men flew to Chungking and talks began. On 7 September Chiang saw Stilwell alone at 9.30 in the morning and tried to 'soft soap' him ahead of the plenary meeting with Hurley and Nelson at 11 a.m. He talked to Stilwell emolliently, appearing to accept that his command of all Chinese armies on FDR's terms was already a settled thing. Stilwell was naturally suspicious and wrote: 'Well, here it is . . . Now what do I do?'[48] The issue of Lend-Lease was touched on at the later conference, but Stilwell pointed out that the fall of Myitkyina had changed the picture entirely; US planes could fly to Chungking without the interception of Japanese fighters, and therefore he expected the supplies to exceed anything Chiang would need. There was much truth in this. Supplies to Chungking increased from 29,000 tons in August and 30,000 in September to 35,000 in October and 39,000 in November. Stilwell did not fail to make the point that this break-through had not come about because of Chennault's much-vaunted airpower but because of the heroic efforts of Stilwell's infantry.[49] Vinegar Joe did not attend all the conferences as he found them tedious and disingenuous. On the occasions he was absent, Chiang habitually complained that Stilwell was more powerful in China than he was, and instead of dismissing this as claptrap, Hurley listened sympathetic-ally. When Vinegar Joe did attend he was both bored and disgusted: 'One and a half hours of crap and nonsense. Wants to withdraw from Lungling, the crazy little bastard. So either X attacks in one week or he pulls it out. Usual cockeyed reasons and idiotic tactical and strategic conceptions. He is impossible.'[50] At the various meetings, Chiang kept insisting that Lend-Lease had to be turned over to him to run, and even Hurley, absurdly sympathetic to the generalissimo, had to remind him that he was talking about American property. Yet Hurley was beginning to worry Stilwell by his constant conciliation of Chiang: 'Pat much impressed with the antics of the Peanut,' he wrote. 'What they ought to do is shoot the Generalissimo and [General] Ho and the rest of the gang.'[51] Hurley seemed unconcerned when Chiang sucked him into a whirlpool of irrelevancies or discussed quixotic fantasies such as damming the Yangtze instead of dealing with the present urgent military crisis. When Soong came out with his unctuous bromides about the 'dignity of a great nation', Hurley listened sympathetically. Stilwell was revolted by the humbug: 'We must not look while the customer puts his hand in our cash register, for fear we will offend his "dignity" ... The picture of this little rattlesnake being backed by a great democracy, and showing his backside in everything he says and does, would convulse you if you could get rid of your gall bladder. What will the American people say when they finally learn the truth?'[52]

The first great crisis of September arose over the battle of Lungling. Y-force was still doing well on the Salween front and massive Chinese forces blasted their way into the cities of Sungshan and Tengchung, an ancient settlement said to have been visited by Marco Polo. Even so, they succeeded only because of large-scale backing from the USAAF. To their stupefaction, the victors found dead Japanese soldiers chained to their positions.[53] Lungling was another matter. There, having driven the Chinese out, 56 Japanese Division was reinforced on 26 August by 6,000 fresh troops, who pushed Y-force back so convincingly that some units retreated at once to the Salween.[54] Chinese casualties were mounting rapidly, though losses were terrific on both sides. In the battles for Tenchung and Lungling, the Chinese lost 37,133 dead and the Japanese 13,620.[55] Although the Japanese had no intention of penetrating any deeper into south-west China, Chiang panicked, fearing an enemy drive on Kunming and the Hump airfields. On 8 September he ordered Stilwell (or rather he told Hurley to order him) to attack with X-force southwards towards Bhamo. Stilwell refused, pointing out that his men were exhausted and they had yet to clear the route of the Ledo road south from Myitkyina, adding for good measure that he did not want to get into another row by infringing on Mountbatten's sphere of influence.[56] The entire Chiang-Hurley-Stilwell triangle was bedevilled by mutual incomprehension and failure to communicate. Chiang assumed that Hurley was Stilwell's superior, when that was not the case at all. He also thought that Stilwell's role as his chief of staff should trump his position as commander of all American troops in the CBI theatre; in fact Stilwell was under explicit orders from Washington to prioritise the two roles the other way round.[57] Despairing of getting his own way, Chiang began to bluster. First he said he would withdraw the whole of Y-force to a defensive ring around Kunming. Then he backtracked and said he would leave it around Lungling in exchange for his having complete control of Lend-Lease. Stilwell exploded: 'The crazy little bastard. The little matter of the Ledo road is forgotten. The only point on the whole trace we do not control is Lungling and he wants to give that up and sabotage the whole God-damn project – men, money, material and sweat that we have put in for two and a half years just to help China. Unthinkable . . . It does not even enter that hickory nut he uses for a head.'[58]

On 13 September, two of the envoys from Mao and the Red Army conferred with Stilwell and told him that their leader was quite prepared to fight under him but not in any circumstances under Chiang; still less would Mao acknowledge Chiang as head of state. Stilwell made it clear to the KMT bureaucrats that as the Reds were the only Chinese prepared to take on the Japanese in serious fighting, he would be supplying them with American arms and equipment and intended to go to Yenan shortly to finalise this.[59] Chiang was now desperate, for the day was fast approaching when the Chinese Communists would get access to Lend-Lease, and then the preponderance of power, already only just to Chiang's advantage, would shift to Mao. Fortunately, he had an ace in the hole that Stilwell knew nothing of. While Vinegar Joe thought that 'Pat' was an ally, the devious and scheming Hurley was advancing his own design to replace Gauss as the US ambassador to China, and letting Chiang know he was sympathetic to his problems with Stilwell. By being charming and accommodating to the generalissimo, the envoys increased his confidence that in a trial of strength with the hated Stilwell he might prevail.

Chiang even tried on Nelson (he considered Hurley too smart an operator) that tired old Chinese shtick: 'Most foreigners don't understand us, but you do.' It is not surprising that Slim's biographer has referred to 'the bone-headed Patrick Hurley'.[60] Hurley was so inept he did not even send his cable to Washington through secure channels, so that the serpentine Tai-li knew everything that was going on.[61]

While Chiang and Hurley intrigued full-time to compass his downfall, Stilwell had a war on two fronts to attend to. Apart from the Salween front, the Japanese advance in China proper was giving cause for concern. On 14 September he flew to Kweilin, 'the Paris of the South', where the Japanese had just launched an offensive and were throwing back the Chinese with ease. As usual when Stilwell was not at the helm, the Chinese fought with a kind of stoical defeatism tinged with bitterness.[62] Regarding as suicidal Chiang's orders to hold the city at all costs, Stilwell ordered the evacuation of the air base and the destruction of all gasoline his soldiers could not take away – so much for the Chiang–Chennault thesis that the KMT armies could defend air bases. The situation on this front continued critical. By November both Kweilin and Liuchow had fallen and the Japanese were almost knocking on the gates of Chungking itself.[63]

Meanwhile, Stilwell's strongly worded protest to Washington about Chiang's behaviour on Lungling and the Salween front had deeply impressed Marshall. He believed implicitly the Stilwell thesis that the generalissimo did not want to fight so much as to sit out the war and watch 'until one barbarian defeats the other'.[64] When Stilwell's latest cable reached him, Marshall was at the Octagon conference, the second conclave at Quebec between Roosevelt and Churchill on the post-war future of Germany. Primed by Marshall, an angry and exasperated FDR sent a message to Chiang saying that the withdrawal from the Salween was unacceptable and that if he persisted, he would have to take the consequences; this was a thinly veiled threat to withdraw Lend-Lease. After stating categorically that the generalissimo was obliged to play his full part in the war, FDR added that there must be no further stalling about the status and nature of Stilwell's command; he must be given 'unrestricted' powers as supreme commander. The memo was nothing less than an ultimatum, and could not be construed in any other way.[65] Whooping with delight, Stilwell refused all attempts by Hurley and others in Chungking to soften the message and insisted on taking it to Chiang in person.[66] On 19 September he enjoyed his greatest hour of triumph when he 'handed this bundle of paprika to the Peanut and then sank back with a sigh. The harpoon hit the little bugger right in the solar plexus and went right through him. It was a clean hit, but beyond turning green and losing the power of speech, he did not bat any eye. He just said to me, 'I understand.'[67] In a state of hubris, Stilwell went home and composed some lines of doggerel:

> I've waited long for vengeance –
> At last I've had my chance,
> I've looked the Peanut in the eye
> And kicked him in the pants
>
> The old harpoon was ready
> With aim and timing true,
> I sank it to the handle
> And stung him through and through.
>
> The little bastard shivered,
> And lost his power of speech,
> His face turned green and quivered
> And he struggled not to screech.
>
> For all my weary battle,
> For all my hours of woe
> At last I've had my innings
> And laid the Peanut low.
>
> I know I've still to suffer
> And run a weary race
> But O! The blessed pleasure!
> I've wrecked the Peanut's face.[68]

The immediate impact of Roosevelt's message was all that Stilwell could have hoped for. After the words 'I understand', Chiang abruptly ended the meeting and retired to his private quarters, where he burst into 'compulsive and stormy sobbing'.[69] A jubilant Stilwell heard about the lachrymose outburst and wrote to his wife: 'Rejoice with me. We have prevailed . . . his head is in the dust. The dope is that after I left, the screaming began and lasted into the night.'[70] Yet Stilwell's gloating was premature. The fantasy of landing a lethal blow on 'the Peanut', as in Ahab's imaginings on the death of Moby-Dick, was, sadly, just that. Nemesis followed the hubris. When Hurley went in to see Chiang on 23 September about the participation of the Red Army in a joint campaign against the Japanese, the generalissimo brushed the subject aside as of no importance; the important thing, he said, was that at all costs he had to get rid of Stilwell. Hurley reported to Stilwell that Chiang had accused him of 'preemptorily refusing' an order to make a feint on Bhamo from Myitkyina and said that China could no longer have two masters: it had to be either Chiang or Stilwell. By a curious coincidence, next day there was a broadcast on Japanese radio claiming that Stilwell was actively seeking to oust Chiang and set himself up as tsar or proconsul in China; from the smooth congruence of events, Stilwell suspected a set-up job. Hurley further reported that Chiang had accused Stilwell of persuading FDR to send the humiliating cable, that the President would not have done it on his own initiative.[71] The generalissimo had by now divined Hurley's ambitions and was determined to use him and Nelson. He persuaded them to contact Roosevelt and claim that recent verbal exchanges on China rested on a misunderstanding; there was no real tension between the war aims of China and the USA but only a 'personality clash' between him and Stilwell. Hurley added his own spin, that he had attempted to be diplomatic by delivering the President's ultimatum himself, but that Stilwell had insisted on taking it. Roosevelt, always weak and neurotic about China, took the blame-shifting line that he had been 'bounced' into sending the tough telegram by Marshall when his mind was elsewhere at Quebec.[72] Chiang's sources, who had an excellent line to the White House via Harry Hopkins, told him that provided a face-saving deal could be concocted, FDR would agree to Stilwell's dismissal; T.V. Soong and Alsop worked hard on drafting a convincing proposal. Thus encouraged, Chiang upped the ante by convening the standing committee of the KMT and telling them that unless Stilwell was sacked, China would no longer be a sovereign nation. At the end of the month FDR concluded that Vinegar Joe would have to go. Two factors weighed with him. He was beginning to grow bored with

China, especially as it no longer mattered for the successful conclusion of the war; all American efforts were now going into island-hopping in the Pacific and the invasion of the Philippines. Perhaps even more importantly, the 1944 presidential election was just a month away, and he certainly did not want some cause célèbre, involving his own credibility, to erupt at a critical moment in the voters' decisions.[73]

On 1 October, Stilwell began to get some inkling of the danger he confronted and wrote at length on the situation both in his diary and to his wife. The interesting thing is that, less shrewd about the evil in men than Chiang, he still had not divined Hurley's true aims. 'FDR proceeds to cut my throat and throw me out. Pat feels very low about it. I don't. I don't. They just can't hurt me. I've done my best and stood up for American interests. To hell with them . . . It looks very much as though they have gotten me at last. The Peanut has gone off his rocker and Roosevelt has apparently let me down completely.'[74] This was honest and wholly consistent with his earlier remarks. He always said he 'was willing to be ditched . . . if at any time the pressure grew too heavy. It was always his secret ambition to be a sergeant in a machine gun company.'[75] But his great ally Marshall was not finished yet. For three weeks he fought a bitter and protracted battle to call Chiang's bluff and bring him to heel. He put to the President all the bitterness occasioned in US military circles by the materiel supplied to Chiang and Chennault over the Hump – which he claimed prolonged the war in Europe for at least a year because of the shortage of air transport. He begged and pleaded with the President to rescind Lend-Lease to China, but FDR would not take that final, irrevocable step, as Chiang had gambled he would not.[76] By their stupid and sycophantic softly-softly diplomacy, Hurley and Nelson had given Chiang the clear impression that, as the President's envoys, they, not Stilwell, must be expressing his true thoughts. Chiang could therefore sit down for a long poker game, confidently expecting that his opponent would blink first. As before, Marshall's great ally was Stimson, who was particularly indignant that Chennault had corralled all those tens of thousands of tons of supplies and had achieved nothing, whereas Stilwell, the hero of Myitkyina, was now to be made the victim.[77] Under pressure, FDR agreed a compromise. On 5 October he told Chiang he would agree to Stilwell's ousting as chief of staff and director of Lend-Lease, but he insisted that he stay on as commander of Chinese forces in Burma and Yunnan; moreover, there would be no US commander in China. But compromise was the wrong ploy to use with Chiang; he read it as weakness. There was no mention in the latest message of the one thing he really feared – the end of Lend-Lease. Although the generalissimo's face was now more than adequately saved, he sensed FDR's weakness and pressed on for total victory. Only the complete removal of Stilwell from China would satisfy him. Absurdly, he claimed in his adamant reply that the Burma campaign had drained China's resources, without mentioning that the USA had provided those resources in the first place; he even had the gall to suggest that it was Stilwell's fault that the airfields in eastern China had been lost. On 11 October, Hurley finally showed his hand and told the White House that he backed Chiang completely. Marshall continued to fight hard, but FDR had essentially buckled and caved in. It was the final manifestation of his China neurosis. Contrary to all reason and a mountain of evidence, he was determined to champion Chiang, shrinking from the obvious alternative of embracing Mao. Given his premises, the only logical conclusion was that Stilwell had to be dismissed.[78]

On 19 October, Roosevelt formally recalled Stilwell from China and ordered him to relinquish all his roles there. Marshall sent a radio message to Stilwell to confirm that the deed was done. During these first 19 days of October, Vinegar Joe had been mournful and resigned. He wrote with great bitterness about being 'ignored, insulted, double-crossed, delayed, obstructed for three years . . . The Peanut sits on his hands and watches with great glee the fool Americans who actually get out and fight.'[79] Marshall informed him of the new dispositions in the CBI theatre, which itself ceased to exist because of the restructuring. General Daniel Sultan would take over his former duties in the India-Burma sector while General Raymond Wheeler would become Mountbatten's deputy in SEAC.[80] The worst blow for Stilwell was the appointment of Wedemeyer as Chiang's chief of staff and commander of US forces in China. He had come to have an almost visceral loathing for the 'ambitious and conceited' Wedemeyer, with his would-be movie-star looks (tall, elegant, aquiline, luxuriantly haired) and his almost monomaniacal self-regard. In June he had noted in his diary: 'Good God – to be ousted in favour of Wedemeyer – that would

be a disgrace.'[81] Stilwell fought hard not to accept this futher humiliation and, when asked by Marshall for his recommendations as his
replacement, named six undistinguished officers, some of whom had
already been recalled from other posts in disgrace; Marshall declared
himself shocked by his friend's irresponsible suggestions, which by
their very implausibility actually strengthened the case for the detested
'Al'.[82] Wedemeyer would later complain that Stilwell made no formal
handover, left him no notes or instructions and refused even to see
him, but after his treachery and backstabbing he should surely not
have been surprised.[83] Hurley achieved his aim when he was appointed
ambassador to replace Gauss, who resigned when Stilwell was
dismissed; the State Department pretence that his resignation was a
completely separate matter fooled no one.[84]

Now that he had what he wanted, Chiang tried to sugar the pill by
offering Stilwell a decoration, but Stilwell abruptly declined. His diary
entry reads: 'Told him to stick it up his ass.'[85] At 5 p.m. on 20 October
he made a farewell call on the generalissimo and reminded him that
all he had done had been for the good of China. Madame was not
there, since she had left for a two-month stay in Brazil in July 1944
and then proceeded to the USA. Tired of Chiang's relentless woman-
ising, she appears to have departed with no intention of returning,
giving out publicly that she needed to consult American specialists for
her health.[86] Stilwell stayed just 48 hours in Chungking after his recall;
Marshall, knowing his gaffe-prone nature, wanted him back in
Washington as soon as possible, and warned him he was not to say
a word about his dismissal to anyone, especially the press.[87] He left
Chungking on the afternoon of 21 October and proceeded in a leisurely
way to Delhi, taking three days, with stopovers at Kunming, Paoshan,
Myitkyina and Ramgarh. Once back in the United States, he at first
seemed under virtual arrest, being accompanied everywhere by Secret
Service men. He was effectively gagged by Marshall and Roosevelt
until after the presidential election, even though many newspapers
and US public opinion were affronted by this 'truckling' to Chiang.[88]
Only when FDR returned as president in triumph for an unprecedented (and never to be repeated) fourth time did Stilwell's plight
become generally known.[89]

Stilwell's Anglophobia was not forgotten. In November, a
Conservative MP, Mr Reginald Purbrick, proposed in the House of

Commons that Stilwell be declared *persona non grata* anwhere British troops were engaged. His old enemy General (by this time Field Marshal) Alexander said after the war: 'Dear Old Joe – he could be mighty naughty at times.'[90] Mountbatten used the opportunity to claim that only his intervention had kept the Stilwell–Chiang show on the road so long – another of his blatant, self-preening exaggerations. And there was more than a smidgin of humbug in his public comments. To Vinegar Joe himself he wrote: 'Most Englishmen, as you yourself undoubtedly know, find you a difficult man to deal with, but, with the exception of the trouble over Lentaigne . . . I can testify that I have found you both easy and helpful in all matters which I raised in person with you.' To FDR he wrote: 'I was sorry to see Stilwell go not only because I personally like him, but because it meant that I lost my beloved Al Wedemeyer.'[91] Yet it is significant that the only Briton Stilwell wrote to was Auchinleck, for whom he seems to have developed an unexpected fondness: 'This is goodbye to you and Lady Auchinleck, with my very best wishes for the future. The sheriff has caught up with me and I have been yanked out, but whatever my glaring deficiencies as a diplomat, I hope you will remember me, as I remember you, as a friend and that we will meet again, as you have promised, in California.'[92] The notable absentee in all this farewell correspondence was Slim, and the suspicion arises that some sort of personal Rubicon was crossed in the relations between the two men over the issue of Lentaigne and the Chindits. Certainly Slim's comments in his autobiography are all positive: 'When all was said and done, the success of this northern offensive was in the main due to the Ledo Chinese Divisions – and that was Stilwell . . . In the 14th Army and, I think, throughout the British forces our sympathies were with Stilwell – unlike the American 14th Air Force who demonstratively rejoiced at his downfall . . . We saw him go with regret, and he took with him our admiration as a fighting soldier.'[93]

However, in later comments Slim was less generous, and he was particularly irked by the publication of the *Stilwell Papers*, which his wife rushed through after his death.

It was a pity that the book was published as it was. Such papers, written in the heat and exasperation of the moment, in spite of their salty humour, did not do him justice. He was much more than the bad-tempered, prejudiced, often not very well-informed and quarrel-some man they showed him to be. He was all that, but in addition he was a first-class battle leader up to, I should say, Corps level and an excellent tactician, but a poor administrator. At higher levels he had neither the temperament not the strategic background or judgement to be effective. Even in the tactical field he hampered himself by, I believe, deliberately employing only mediocre American subordinate commanders and a good deal of nepotism on his staff. His dislike, openly expressed and shown, of all 'limeys', which at times did not make for cooperation, was, I always found, if not taken too seriously more amusing than dangerous. I used to tease him about it and he took it very well. Yet his distrust of the British was deeply rooted, and on what grounds I could not discover.'[94]

Some comments are in order. The charge of nepotism was, sadly, true. Stilwell used his mediocre son, Colonel Joseph Stilwell, as his head of intelligence (G2), and it was the son who badly underestimated the Japanese potential at Myitkyina. He also employed two of his sons-in-law as liaison officers with the Chinese.[95] As for employing only mediocrities, even Slim's biographer is moved to protest at this point. Not only did Slim forget that he had already described Frank Merrill as a brilliant officer, but most of the high talents in the US military were employed in the Pacific and thus unavailable. As Lewin rightly comments: 'Stilwell had to make bricks out of what was sometimes straw.'[96] On Stilwell's alleged strategic incapacity, Slim again goes too far. It is true that he was bored by logistics and administration and that his theories of using Chinese armies to win the war in China were in their own way as far-fetched as Chennault's notion of victory through airpower alone. But he was no fool, and could scarcely have become a four-star general (the US equivalent of a field marshal) if he was. Moreover, Marshall, who saw through the egotistic antics of Patton and MacArthur, rated Stilwell as the best of the best; Marshall, too, to put it mildly, was no fool, and in the opinion of some good judges was *the* great strategic planner of the Second World War. No man had more faults than Stilwell: he was ruthless, overcynical, drove men too hard, was tactless, abrasive and foolish. Later traduced by the China lobby, absurdly, as an agent in delivering China to the Communists, he was in fact a great patriot, who ardently desired to defeat the enemy, told the unvarnished truth exactly as he saw it and was a man of real integrity. He was also an historical figure of some importance, for until the drama of the Nixon–Mao meeting in 1972, he represented America's 'supreme try' in China.[97]

One final and very important point is salient in any overall consideration of Stilwell. Although stabbed in the back by FDR, he never made public the dark side of that enigmatic character, which might have done irretrievable harm to the President's reputation. On his return from the Cairo conference in late 1943, Stilwell confided to Colonel Frank Dorn, his chief of staff, an extraordinary conversation he had had with FDR in Egypt. As Stilwell expressed it: 'The Big Boy's fed up with Chiang and his tantrums, and said so. In fact he told me in that Olympian manner of his: "If you can't get along with Chiang and can't replace him, get rid of him once and for all. You know what I mean. Put in someone you can manage."' Stilwell confessed he was shocked by the order. Although Chiang was a 'pain in the neck' and Stilwell agreed with Dorn that everyone who knew him, including Madame and his generals, must at one time or other have wished him dead, assassination was not in the American tradition ('the United States doesn't go in for this sort of thing') and was against his own code of ethics.[98] It should be remembered that this was before the crazier antics of Wild Bill Donovan and the OSS were known about and long before the truly dark era of the CIA. Nevertheless, having been given an order by his commander-in-chief, Stilwell duly passed it on to Dorn. He instructed him to prepare contingency plans for a 'hit' on the generalissimo, all naturally on a 'deniable' basis, with the proviso that any attempt to liquidate Chiang had to be 100 per cent sure to succeed before he, Stilwell, would give it the nod. He signed off by telling Dorn that he doubted whether anything would ever come of it or that FDR would ever give him the green light, and so it proved. The conscientious Dorn and his officers worked through a number of scenarios – shootings, bombings, poisonings, a palace revolution – and eventually hit on a wild scheme to fly Chiang to inspect his troops at Ramgarh and crash the plane en route. The American pilots would be given sealed orders to be opened over the Hump and provided with reliable parachutes; those donned by the generalissimo and his entourage would be faulty.[99] Amazingly, this was not the only assassination plan Stilwell had been ordered to cooperate with. Colonel

Carl Feifler, the senior OSS officer in the CBI theatre, was told by Stilwell that orders had come from on high to prepare a contingency plan to liquidate the generalissimo using Botulinus toxin. Stilwell told Feifler he disapproved of the idea but that the orders had come from 'the man above'.[100] Truly it was the case that in Kuomintang China actuality was reversed, the real became the surreal, and the dream world of Chungking bade fair at any moment to turn into nightmare.

Stilwell was an authentic American hero sent on a mission impossible. Both he and his supporter Marshall – and Stimson also, who was shocked and disillusioned by his dismissal – had to deal not only with the egomania and mindlessness of Chiang but the wilful and disingenuous stubbornness of FDR. Roosevelt treated Stilwell worse than any other theatre commander.[101] None of his other generals had to put up with a constant stream of interrupting meddlers (Lauchlin Currie, Wendell Wilkie, Henry Wallace, Donald Nelson and Patrick Hurley, twice) 'whose chief qualifications were ignorance of China or, in some cases, Roosevelt's desire to get them out of the country'. As has been well said, 'An Eisenhower or a MacArthur would have blown his stack; Stilwell patiently put up with it.'[102] Marshall too, without whom Roosevelt would have been at sea in the Second World War, was severely taxed by Roosevelt's duplicity, dishonesty and insensitivity. On the issue of China particularly, the President often overruled Marshall with almost studied rudeness, as when he turned down Marshall's relatively trivial request not to appoint Wedemeyer as Stilwell's replacement.[103] A particular irritant was the way FDR would not reply to a minute from Marshall, file it or otherwise place it on the record, but simply send it back if he did not like the contents.[104] Then there was the way Roosevelt would arbitrarily change or doctor a carefully composed Marshall statement. In pique at Chiang's attitude towards Stilwell, FDR appointed Wedemeyer purely as the generalissimo's chief of staff and announced grandly that there would be no overall American commander in China. This fit of irritation simply played into Chiang's hands, for he had accepted the principle of a US commander only under duress in the first place. So far from punishing him, the White House restored the status quo ante with a mere US chief of staff – exactly the outcome Chiang wanted. To the woefully inept presidential performance over Stilwell can be added the hate-laden campaign of the generalissimo over three years – a hatred driven purely by the base factor that Stilwell would not allow him a free hand to channel US Lend-Lease into his own coffers. Naturally none of this weighs with the purblind China revisionists who want to rehabilitate Chiang as a statesman.[105] On the relationship with Chiang, the last word should go to Stilwell, expounding his credo: 'The trouble was largely one of posture. I tried to stand on my feet instead of my knees. I did not think the knee position was a suitable one for Americans . . . If a man can say that he did not let his country down, if he can live with himself, there is nothing more he can reasonably ask for.'[106] And when the corrupt Kuomintang finally succumbed to Mao and the Communists in 1949, had Stilwell still been alive he would have been justified in saying: 'I told you so.'

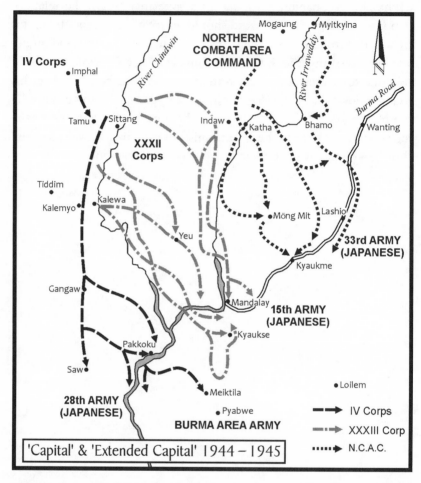

The tension observable on Slim's face at the investiture ceremony at Imphal on 14 December was not the result only of Kimura's disappointing decision not to fight at Shwebo. Already facing massive logistical problems, Slim was in effect stabbed in the back by Chiang and Wedemeyer. Shortly after Stilwell's departure, Kweilin fell to the Japanese, exposing once again the deficiencies of Y-force and the generalissimo's home-based troops vis-à-vis the Ramgarh-trained and Stilwell-nurtured X-force.[1] A few days later the city of Liuchow, 100 miles south of Kweilin, also capitulated, underlining the poverty of

Chennault's thinking; contrary to all his assurances – and exactly as Stilwell had predicted – the Japanese were now overrunning his airfields. Chiang, predictably, panicked and turned to Wedemeyer for a solution. Wedemeyer was in a trap of his own devising; he was getting what he thought he wanted but quickly found he did not like it at all. Planning to use 'honey rather than vinegar' in his dealings with the generalissimo – and with this in mind he had filed away all the correspondence between Vinegar Joe and the 'Peanut' so that prying eyes could never find it[2] – he soon discovered that Chiang was an impossible ingrate who expected his US chief of staff to have a magic wand that would spirit away all problems. Marshall took great satisfaction in, in effect, replying 'I told you so' to Wedemeyer's querulous reports to Washington about the Kuomintang.[3] Desperate for some expedient that would shut the generalissimo up, at least temporarily, Wedemeyer peremptorily ordered 75 Dakotas, vital to the supply of Slim's 14th Army, back to China to assist on the home front. What made this particularly treacherous was that Wedemeyer knew, from his long association with Mountbatten, just how vital airpower was for success in Burma. The Supreme Commander learned with a shock that the man he had called his 'beloved Al Wedemeyer' had gone native and was now a fully paid-up member of the KMT tendency.[4] The first Slim knew of this development was at dawn on 10 December, when he was woken at his HQ by the roar of aircraft engines. The supplies for 14th Army, already in the planes, had simply been taken off and dumped on the airstrip before the Dakotas took off.[5]

The departure of the 75 planes caused an immediate administrative crisis in a 14th Army HQ already stretched to the limit by logistical problems. As Slim pointed out, 14th Amy by this time had a ration strength of 750,000 in a force scattered over an area as large as Poland, and this was *before* it commenced offensive operations. Before troops can fight, they have to be fed, clothed, housed, equipped, paid, doctored, policed and transported by other personnel, all of whom in turn have to be fed, paid, housed, etc.[6] As for CAPITAL, and even more, the refinements Slim made in EXTENDED CAPITAL, airpower was crucial, and his staff had calculated, before the Wedemeyer debacle, that the aircraft available to them would *just* suffice, provided there was no significant enemy interception or any sustained patches of bad weather. Road and rail transport, they hoped, would become available to them once they had conquered areas the enemy currently controlled, but meanwhile inadequate roads would have to do. The railhead at Dimapur was linked to Tamu via Imphal through a 206-mile all-weather road, and then by another recently constructed all-weather highway from Tamu to Kalewa (a further 112 miles). If they could capture Shwebo and Mandalay, they would have further all-weather roads that could be reached by transport across the Chindwin's Bailey bridge, but short of that, all other supplies would have to be by river.[7] An explosion in boat-building on the Chindwin, especially rafts and barges, was the result – most existing craft had been destroyed by the retreating Japanese. Yet fundamentally 14th Army had to reach the Irrawaddy, 600 miles from a railhead, cross the mighty river itself and then gamble on getting all the way to Rangoon before the monsoon broke in May. This was the context in which Wedemeyer withdrew the Dakotas. It sounded like the definition of mission impossible. Slim dealt with the immediate crisis by cutting down on the planes that would be available for Christison's invasion of the Arakan (later, by intense lobbying, Mountbatten managed to get two thirds of the departed aircraft back), but for anyone but a superlative commander, the position on paper at the beginning of December would have seemed dire. All reports indicated that Kimura was waiting on the other side of the Irrawaddy with eight divisions, ready for the mother of all battles, what he had already called 'the battle of the Irrawaddy shore'. Even with five divisions, a British assault across the river seemed suicidal.[8]

Slim went into conference with his corps commanders Stopford and Messervy on 18–19 December and explained to them his new conception of EXTENDED CAPITAL. Where the original CAPITAL had aimed merely at the defeat of the enemy in central Burma, the new plan envisaged total defeat in the country and the occupation of Rangoon by early May. He made it plain to his two commanders that the plan would not be discussed with or even referred to Leese, who was likely for one reason or other to ruin it if put in the picture.[9] Seeking for somewhere other than Shwebo where he could engage Kimura on terms of comparative advantage, Slim hit on the idea of making a secret dash for Meiktila, 70 miles south of Mandalay, the supply town for the Japanese 33 and 15 Army and the 'beating heart' of their entire war effort in Burma. Since the railway and main road north from Rangoon ran through Meiktila, the position was a key, nodal one, and without it Kimura could not hold Mandalay. Moreover, if Slim could get one of his corps down to Meiktila in secret while the other crossed the Irrawaddy where Kimura expected the British to cross, the Japanese would be effectively encircled.[10] Since Meiktila contained supply bases, ammunition dumps, airfields, depots and hospitals, the Japanese armies in the north were like the extended fingers of a hand, with Meiktila its wrist. In Slim's words: 'Crush that wrist, no blood would flow through the fingers, the whole hand would be paralysed, and the Japanese armies on the arc from the Salween to the Irrawaddy would begin to wither.'[11] Slim intended to use 4 Corps for the secret march and 33 Corps for the Irrawaddy assault Kimura expected. It was hammer and anvil once again, with 33 Corps the hammer from the north and 4 Corps, at Meiktila, the anvil. EXTENDED CAPITAL was thus a war-winning stratagem of extreme genius, if Slim could pull it off. But how to move an entire corps, with tanks and heavy armour, through jungle without alerting the enemy? It was obvious that the most massive programme of deception, disinformation and obfuscation would have to be attempted. In the first place, 33 Corps would have to perform heroically in the north, keeping up constant pressure so that Kimura would never smell a rat. Then he would have to be convinced that he was being attacked on the Mandalay/Irrawaddy front by both corps.[12]

Messervy's 4 Corps would be advancing south through the Gangaw valley and along the Myittha river – following the route Slim had taken in the opposite direction during the 1942 retreat – aiming to cross the Irrawaddy at Pakkoku and then launch itself on Meiktila. In accordance with his master plan, on 26 December Slim temporarily assigned 19 Division and 268 Tank Brigade from 4 Corps to 33 Corps, so that any Japanese agents would be able to report that the two British corps were indeed working together and massing on the other side of the river near Mandalay.[13] While the real 4 Corps would maintain radio silence on its long trek, a dummy headquarters for a bogus 4 Corps would be set up at Tamu, complete with radio and signals. There would be deliberate 'indiscreet' talk by officers that pro-Japanese informants could pick up on, and an increase in radio traffic in the

Shwebo area. Fake airdrops to fake agents would increase the confusion.[14] Elaborate deception exercises were given grandiose titles such as STENCIL and CLOAK. Lieutenant Colonel J.H. ('Elephant Bill') Williams was instructed to go 40 miles up the Yeu river with a huge party of elephants, to suggest that a large force (possibly another detachment from 4 Corps) was about to cross the Chindwin there.[15] Another advantage the deceivers had was that any force aiming at Meiktila would be expected to proceed on the Kalewa-Yeo-Shwebo approach. RAF planes would have to patrol the area around Pakkoku constantly to make sure that no Japanese aircraft got close enough to the area to report the secret advance of 4 Corps. The big obstacle that lay in 4 Corps' path was the town of Gangaw. It was well defended, but if Slim committed too many men to capture it, the Japanese might be alerted to the clandestine march of Messervy's corps, and it would be disastrous if any of Messervy's men were questioned and interrogated in the fighting. To 'take out' this obstacle, therefore, Slim relied on a massive aerial bombardment by RAF 221 Corps, followed by an attack by the Lushai Brigade. The Japanese were familiar with this unit and knew that it was Slim's version of the Chindits; if they were reported in the Gangaw valley, it would be clear that Slim was playing at being Wingate and the attacks read as those by loose cannon. It was inconceivable that the Lushai Brigade would be deployed in the same area as regular troops, as this seemed to make no sense at all; the obvious inference the Japanese were to draw was that Slim was feinting down the Myittha river in a vain attempt to disguise the intended attack on Mandalay. Using them in the Gangaw valley thus constituted a deception within a deception. As a final twist, Slim had Messervy send 28 African Brigade ahead of his corps. If they observed these troops, the Japanese were sure to take them for 11 East African Division, recently active in the Kabaw valley.[16]

Having to his own satisfaction masked the operation by 4 Corps, Slim then had to solve the details of getting his troops and tanks across 'impossible' country. Major General Bill Hasted, 14th Army's chief engineer, estimated that he could build a road along the Kabaw and Myittha valleys using bithess, extensively used for aircraft runways. Bithess was hessian in rolls 50 yards long and one yard wide, treated with bitumen to look like a long carpet of oilcloth. Strips were laid to overlap by eight inches and the road, levelled and packed tight, was cambered by laying the two outside strips first and then building the road up from edge to centre.[17] Hugely expensive, the process used up a gallon of petrol and a gallon of diesel for every yard of road laid, and to build 100 miles of bithess road took 1,000 vehicles a day. At first, Hasted estimated the road would take a day for every mile built, but Slim dismissed this as impossibly slow. The two men took a flight to examine the terrain, but even after flying low over the jungle, Hasted still had no real idea and plucked the figure of 42 days out of the air. Slim replied: 'God help you, Bill, if it takes more than fifty.'[18] Even so, no one knew for certain whether such a road would stand up to the wear and tear of tanks and heavy vehicles. Since Slim had always been a great proponent of tanks as *the* strike weapon in land warfare and was almost obsessive in his concern for their reliability in difficult terrain, he inspected 255 Brigade shortly before the jump-off towards Meiktila. He quizzed the brigade major about his Sherman tanks and was irritated by the bland replies he received. 'The most important thing is reliability,' he snapped. 'Mechanical failure could make them a liability. How reliable are those Shermans?' 'Very, sir,' was the reply. 'Given sufficient fuel, some essential spares and some time at night to do maintenance on them.' Slim seemed unconvinced. 'You had better be right,' he growled.[19] When it came to efficiency, the otherwise affable 'Uncle Bill' could be a hard driver. He told Hasted at the start of the operation that he wanted 500 tons of supplies delivered down the Chindwin in two months' time. Hasted produced a familiar 14th Army cliche: 'The difficult we will do at once; the impossible will take a little longer ... For these miracles we like a month's notice.' 'You're lucky,' Slim replied. 'You've got two.'[20] Hasted, as ever, performed brilliantly. Cutting down teak, using elephants to haul logs to the riverside and using a variety of boatmaking skills, by May 1945 he had built 541 new rafts. This was important, as in the latter stages of the march on Meiktila, 4 Corps was to be supplied by river from Myingyan, near Pakkoku and at the confluence of the Chindwin and the Irrawaddy.

Messervy took some time assembling his corps for the secret march, since when Slim told him about EXTENDED CAPITAL on 18 December, almost none of his regiments was at the jump-off zone – with the Africans at Imphal and 7 Indian Division at Kohima. Finally the great trek south began on 19 January. The campaign that followed to seize both Meiktila and Mandalay had three stages for each corps: the operations en route to the Irrawaddy; the crossing of the mighty river; and the two great battles that followed on either front. It will be convenient to follow the fortunes of 33 Corps (2, 19 and 20 Divisions) first, since on their sustained and continuous aggression the success or failure of Slim's great bluff would depend. The first steps were taken on 3 December when a brigade of 20 Division crossed the Chindwin with little opposition – perhaps surprisingly, since the east bank of the river was thick jungle covering steep hills and ridges. On 19 December 2 Division relieved the brigade and began the push towards Shwebo, the initial target, 40 miles north-west of Mandalay. Major General 'Pete' Reese commanding 19 Division meanwhile left the Sittang bridgehead, aiming for Pinlebu and Pinbon; it was this division's rapid progress in the first few days that convinced Slim the enemy had no intention of fighting on the Shwebo plain.[21] After taking Wuntho on 19 December, 19 Division clocked up an amazing 200-mile advance in 20 days through difficult terrain from the Chindwin by 23 March. Both 2 and 20 Division were also accelerating as they converged on Yeu and Monywa. Their advance was from Mawlaik and Kalewa, through an undefended Pyingaing on 23 December, sweeping aside a Japanese rearguard at the end of the month and then sending a mechanised column to secure the Kabu weir on the Shwebo plain, which the Japanese had planned to blow up. On 2 January 2 Division reached Yeu and crossed the Mu river; engineers then built a bridge so that other detachments, especially 268 Tank Brigade, could follow.[22] Now 2 Division and 19 Division raced each other for Shwebo. Advance patrols were in the outskirts by 7 January. As they proceeded, each division built airstrips at 50-mile intervals, to land supplies and evacuate the wounded. Constant bridge-building was also a feature; between January and April it is estimated that 14th Army built 145 bridges.[23] Finally 19 Division narrowly won the race for Shwebo, with a disappointed 2 Division trooping in on 9 January. Japanese opposition here was light; only 58 enemy dead and ten prisoners were recorded.[24]

From Shwebo, 19 Division turned east to the Irrawaddy and prepared to cross at two places north-west of Mandalay, forever trying to keep a high profile so that Kimura always believed Mandalay was the British Holy Grail. Once the Anglo-Indians neared the Irrawaddy, the hostilities intensified: there was particularly bitter fighting at Kabwet on the west bank on 25 January, where 2 Royal Berkshires lost 100 men in a five-day running battle.[25] To the west, 20 Division pounded both Budalin and Monywa, the last riverside port on the Chindwin, but got bogged down by tough resistance from Japanese 33 Division and had to call up rocket strikes from the air force. Two hundred planes flew three days of non-stop missions on 18–20 January before 20 Indian Division subdued the port on 22 January.[26] Myinmu fell next day, but not before some bloody combat with a large party of Japanese who were trying to cross the river. After resisting stubbornly and being close to annihilation, the Japanese survivors committed suicide by walking into the river to drown.[27] Opposition had been tough on the west bank of the Irrawaddy, but essentially Kimura had failed to stop the British in the Chindwin-Irrawaddy loop. He was not especially anxious, since his main effort was reserved for destroying the enemy during the river crossing or when they landed on the east bank. But first there was something of a lull, as Slim slowed 33 Corps down so as to give river transport and airlift priority to 4 Corps in the south. He had to time the two different crossings of the Irrawaddy perfectly. If 4 Corps appeared on the east bank too soon, Kimura would spot the danger and move his reserves to Meiktila; but if 4 Corps crossed too late, he might already have defeated 33 Corps with the local preponderance of force he enjoyed and prevented the diversionary attack on Mandalay.[28] The progress of 4 Corps was smoother than that of 33 Corps and they encountered only light opposition. On 28 January they took Pauk and on 3 February Messervy ordered the attack on Pakkoku on the west bank, with diversions made at Chauk and Pagan – all to make the enemy think a crossing would be attempted at Pakkoku. There was another calculated piece of deception in the form of a simulated crossing at Seikpyu opposite Chauk, using 28th East African Brigade, complete with a dummy parachute drop and maps showing Yenangyaung as the objective. The Africans arrived at Seikpyu on 8 February with much fanfare and hullabaloo, drawing a counterattack as planned.[29] Kimura learned of these activities, but, relying on past intelligence, assumed it was irregulars like the Lushai Brigade trying to distract him from concentrating farther north.

Slim now faced the great, and some thought insuperable task: the crossing of the Irrawaddy by two corps at different points on the river.

In the north, where 33 Corps had to make the traverse, Kimura was supremely confident, with eight divisions plus one and a third divisions of Bose's Indian National Army; even if Slim could put five divisions into the field against him, he should have the edge. Then there was the obstacle of the mighty river itself. One of the great rivers of the world, 1,300 miles long and navigable for 1,000 miles of its length, the waters were at their lowest level in January and February but would rise dramatically in March–September with the heavy rains. The current that 33 Corps would have to contend with was just 1–2 mph in strength (as against 6 mph in high season), but against this was the stark geographical fact that the river was 2,000 yards wide where they intended to cross, and 4,000 yards wide at the confluence with the Chindwin, where 4 Corps would be operating.[30] The Japanese had no intention of defending all 200 miles of the river at the battle front, even if they had had the colossal manpower this would take, but sensibly concentrated on the most likely crossing spots. Though short of planes with which to devastate the enemy actually during the traverse, Kimura was confident he could destroy whatever units got across. Slim, on the other hand, suffered from a dire shortage of equipment; with so few boats, his men had to cross 'on a couple of bamboos and a bootlace'. As he remarked: 'I do not think any modern army has attempted the opposed crossing of a great river with so little.'[31] Juggling the shortage of boats with the problem of timing, Slim decided that he should concentrate on getting 4 Corps across before landing the entire 33 Corps on the other side, as the chance of major debacles was high while 4 Corps, the vital force for the successful outcome of the campaign, remained on the west bank. He also resolved that the crossing by 4 Corps should be made in a concentrated span of time, as against the piecemeal traverse of 33 Corps.

Arriving early at the Irrawaddy because of their rapid progress through the Chindwin-Irrawaddy loop, 33 Corps spent a month getting across the Irrawaddy. In order to convince Kimura that Mandalay was his objective, Slim sent his divisions across in both a westerly and a northerly direction, indicating a pincer movement on Mandalay. Coming from the north, 19 Division began its crossing on the night of 14–15 January around Kyaukmyaung, 20 miles south of Thabeikkyin. The Japanese were slow to respond, and not until the 17th did they realise that a serious passage of the river was afoot. While they massed for the counterattack, 64 Brigade established a bridgehead, just in time to receive the first wave of a ferocious onslaught that saw vicious hand-to-hand fighting going on all night on 20–21 January. This was now to be the pattern: every single traverse of the Irrawaddy would be met with concentrated force. But Slim took comfort from the tardy Japanese response: 'The Japanese, confused by the numerous feints and patrol crossings elsewhere, had not been quick to decide which were the real crossings, and even then they took some time to concentrate against them.'[32] At first it was thought that the whole of 4 Corps was crossing, for the transfer of divisions between the two corps certainly had its obfuscating effect on the Japanese. The thrust from the north by 19 Division was also helped by a major blunder on Kimura's part, as he read the crossings as an attempt by the division to link up with 36 Division, still operating in the north in the former Stilwell domain from Bhamo to Lashio. Even so, Kimura pressed the two brigades now on the east bank very hard with his 15th and 33rd Divisions. His attempts to destroy the bridgehead were blunted by the common Japanese error of launching their troops piecemeal as they arrived instead of building up for a single, devastating onslaught. For three weeks 19 Division withstood everything that was thrown at them – massive artillery barrages, suicide squads, infiltration forces.[33] Very gradually, as the corpses of the attackers piled up, the attacks began to lose their bite, and at the beginning of February, there was a lull of two days and two nights. Sensing the pulse of the enemy attack weakening, Slim seized the moment and got his tanks across the river, ready for the breakout. After the lull, the enemy resumed their attacks, but they were no longer pressed with the same elan as before. Bit by bit the British were growing stronger and the enemy weaker. Slim visited the precarious bridgehead and found his men exhausted but in good heart. 'The fighting had been severe, the casualties to our men considerable, and the strain of fighting in these restricted places, with their backs to the river no light one.'[34]

Since airpower was crucial to the successful British defence of the Kyaukmyaung bridgehead, the other divisions in 33 Corps had to an extent to mark time while 19 Division fought the enemy to a standstill. After taking Yeu and Shwebo, Stopford and 2 Division had to wait for supplies from the Dimapur railhead, since all the airdrops were going to 19 Division. But as soon as Pete Reese's men were ready to break out (11 February), Slim ordered 20 Division across the Irrawaddy. They had reached the river at Myinmu on 22 January and paused, ready for the signal to traverse. Ordered to cross on the night of 12–13 February, they breasted 1,500 yards of river with strong currents running. Held up by partially submerged sandbanks, they landed virtually unopposed and achieved almost total surprise. Once again it took the Japanese time to react, and their real counterattack did not begin until the 15th.[35] When they did move, the impact was devastating, for they struck with two weapons unusual for the Japanese: fighter planes and flame-throwers. Ferocious combat ensued, with the enemy at first trying to drive a wedge between the two brigades, but once again the Japanese made their old mistake of throwing in each new wave of reinforcements piecemeal instead of accumulating for a single devastating onslaught. The initially worrisome Zeros, strafing the eastern shore, were soon cleared away by vastly superior Allied airpower, and rocket-firing Hurricanes knocked out 13 enemy tanks in one day.[36] Soon the Japanese were reduced to banzai attacks and suicide missions. Almost indescribably ferocious combat went on continuously during 21–26 February; two Japanese battalions totalling 1,200 men lost an incredible 953 killed in these five days. It was some of the hardest fighting in the entire Burma campaign. It took three weeks of bitter bloodletting before 20 Division established its bridgehead.[37] The Allies now had two secure bridgeheads on the eastern shore, but Kimura still had some grounds for hope. It seemed that 14th Army were overwhelmingly concentrated in the Chindwin-Irrawaddy loop, and the two bridgeheads were still some way from Mandalay, respectively 45 miles north and 30 miles west of the city. The 'battle of the Irrawaddy shore' had not gone according to expectations so far, but the British seemed bogged down on the banks of the river. There was reason to hope that if he recalled his forces from all other theatres and concentrated them at Mandalay, he might still achieve a resounding eleventh-hour victory. When 2 Division crossed on the night of 24–25 February at Ngazumi, to the east of 20 Division's bridgehead, they found their crossing bitterly contested and had a hard time of it. For a moment Slim's optimism faltered: 'The crossing, if not a failure, was near to becoming one.' A strong recovery by 2 Division and a strange, faltering passivity by the enemy after the first onrush saw all of 2 Division safely across by 26 February. As Slim gleefully related:

'Kimura was in fact pausing to regroup for a final effort on the Irrawaddy shore. He did not know it, but the real storm had not yet broken on him.'[38]

The crossing of the Irrawaddy by 4 Corps far to the south was even more of a saga. One of the intrinsic problems was that, like most large rivers, the Irrawaddy bore little resemblance to the blue waterway shown on maps. Each monsoon altered the channel and sandbanks, and accurate information about the river at any given point could be obtained only by divers and thus would risk alerting the enemy across the water. Even so, frogmen and SBS specialists were used to chart the only practicable channels.[39] The shortage of river craft and their inherent unreliability compounded the difficulty. Outboard engines on the boats proved only about 50 per cent reliable, and the shortage of boats meant that assault crossings had to be timed precisely, so that craft could be switched from one crossing site to another.[40] For all these reasons 7 Division would now have to make the longest river crossing in any theatre anywhere in World War II. Because of the sandbanks, the traverse would have to be oblique, and the crossing was therefore almost 2,000 yards long. After a hard fight for Pakkoku by 114 Brigade, which lasted for a week until 10 February (and was meant to convince the enemy that Slim intended to cross there), the various units made their way to the river by three different routes. The entire operation by 4 Corps was planned in four phases: first would be the assault crossing by 7 Division on the night of 13–14 February and in silence, with landfall just above Nyaungu, where four beaches and the surrounding cliffs would be seized; then some battalions of 33 Brigade and some tanks would be ferried over ready for the assault on Meiktila; next would be a rapid advance from the bridgehead to take Nyaungu itself; and finally a new bridgehead at Nyaungu to take 17 Division across by the direct route.[41] The initial landfall would be three miles upstream from Pagan, the ancient capital of Burma, with its 1,200 red, white and gleaming gold pagodas and temples.

Unfortunately phase one badly miscarried, possibly because Messervy had grown overconfident.[42] His boats proved inadequate to deal with the strong current, and an enemy machine gun opened up on the first men across, causing panic. A company of South Lancashires got across, but in the confusion the crossing was aborted and the

Lancashires were left high and dry on the far side.[43] As the British contemplated the inevitable massacre of their comrades, a boat arrived from the holy city of Pagan with two of Bose's INA men, or 'Jiffs' as they were known to the Allies. Brandishing a white flag, the Jiffs told the British that the Japanese had abandoned their positions on the other side. When it was discovered that the Lancashires had not been attacked, the commanders recovered their wits and decided to reinforce them. A battalion of Punjabis crossed unopposed, and then another two,[44] while 33 Brigade dug in and improvised a bridgehead, expecting imminent enemy attack, but none came. On the 15th, therefore, there were more crossings, and by the 16th the bridgehead had linked up with the Sikhs detailed to take Pagan. To general stupefaction, the surprise had been total; Japanese intelligence, as usual, had proved atrocious, and the feints at Pakkoku and Chauk completely successful.[45] On 16–17 February, 17 Division crossed, ready for the strike at Meiktila. Only on the 17th did the Japanese launch savage counterattacks on the bridgehead at Nyaungu, as they finally realised that the troop movements reported around Pagan were not quasi-touristic irregulars but two entire divisions. Beaten back by superior numbers, the Japanese dug in at Nyaungu town in a labyrinthine network of tunnels and catacombs. When repeated air strikes, rockets and even napalm could not shift these doughty defenders, the British solved the problem in a ruthless but effective way by sealing up the tunnels and burying them alive.[46] Pagan, defended only by the feckless INA, surrendered without a fight. Victorious on all fronts, Slim on one of his flying visits was able to revel in the beauty of Burma's ancient capital: 'Its 1200 temples, madder red or ghostly white, rise, some like fantastic pyramids or turreted fairy castles, others in tapering pagoda spires, from the sage green mass of trees against the changing pastel blues, reds and golds of sunrise. As a foreground flows the still dark yet living sweep of moving water.'[47]

Both Slim's 14th Army corps were now across the Irrawaddy and he dominated the river along a 200-mile front from a point about 20 miles south of Pakkoku to Thabeikkyin, north of Mandalay. He had put five divisions across one of the widest rivers in the world in the teeth of enemy opposition. What he had achieved was terrific and fantastic. As his biographer points out:

It serves to emphasise his achievement if one draws a contrast with Montgomery's advantage at the Rhine crossing [a virtually simultaneous event]. Behind his 21 Army Groups lay the vast and efficient road and rail network of North-West Europe. He had airborne divisions on his immediate front. His technical equipment – the continuous smokescreen, amphibious vehicles, etc. – was lavish and up-to-date. An enormous artillery pool, rich in ammunition, gave him unlimited support. Compared with the Irrawaddy, the Rhine is narrow and its behaviour readily calculable.[48]

A portrait of Slim at this moment of triumph has been provided by the popular writer George MacDonald Fraser:

The biggest boost to morale was the burly man who came to talk to the assembled battalion [of the Border Regiment] . . . I'm not sure when, but it was unforgettable. Slim was like that: the only man I've ever seen who had a force that came out of him, a strength of personality that I've puzzled over since . . . His appearance was plain enough: large, heavily built, grim-faced with that hard mouth and bulldog chin; the rakish Gurkha hat was at odds with the slung carbine and untidy trouser bottoms . . . Nor was he an orator . . . His delivery was blunt, matter-of-fact, without gestures or mannerisms, only a lack of them. He knew how to make an entrance – or rather, he probably didn't, and it came naturally . . . there was no nonsense of 'gather round' or jumping on boxes; he just stood with his thumb hooked in his carbine sling and talked about how we had caught Jap off-balance and were going to annihilate him in the open; there was no exhortation or ringing clichés, no jokes or self-conscious use of barrack-room slang – when he called the Japs 'bastards' it was casual and without heat. He was telling us informally what would be, in the reflective way of intimate conversation. And we believed every word – and it all came true. I think it was that sense of being close to us, as though he were chatting offhand to an understanding nephew (not for nothing was he 'Uncle Bill') that was his great gift . . . You knew, when he talked of smashing the Jap, that to him it meant not only arrows on a map but clearing bunkers and going in under shell-fire; that he had the head of a general with the heart of a private soldier.[49]

Between 18 and 21 February, the rearguard of 17 Division and the all-important 255 Tank Brigade were ferried across the river. The advance on Meiktila, 80 miles from the bridgehead, began on 21 February, with 4 Corps dividing: most of 17 Division was aiming for Kamye and the rest for Seiktein, with a possible pincer movement on Taungtha in mind. The 63rd Brigade rolled up the opposition, marched rapidly to Welaung and then took Taungtha on 24 February. There was heavy resistance at Oyin on 20 February, and in a vicious encounter 70 Rajputs and 200 Japanese were killed. It was noticed, however, that even though the enemy soldiers fought with all their old fanaticism, their actual fighting skills and tactics seemed below their 1944 level; this was read as demoralisation and, by the same token, gave an enormous fillip to the Anglo-Indians.[50] Thereafter the going became much tougher, since the whole of 'Snipers' Triangle' between Welaung and Meiktila had to be cleared of suicide squads. Japanese tactics against the irresistible tanks were to hurl themselves under the tracks with a box of explosives, usually picric acid, attached to their chest, which would then be detonated, wiping out both the attacker and the entire tank and crew.[51] The tanks found the going heavy, as they slid into dry ravine beds and clambered up the other side through clouds of dust; this was no longer jungle warfare but more like the desert kind. Eight miles from Meiktila, 63 Brigade became snarled up in a bitter struggle to overcome the enemy in well-dug-in positions, but now Slim's prophecy about the efficacy of tanks in this kind of open country was fulfilled.[52] Cowan used his armour to punch (the pun is irresistible) his way to the airfield. The plan was to have a more successful kind of Myitkyina operation: Cowan would take the airstrip, while Messervy took the town. Slim was pleased with the way things were working out. As he remarked grimly: 'The Japanese had no experience of these massed armoured attacks and seemed quite incapable of dealing with them.'[53]

But although the tanks had proved to be a veritable miracle weapon in the open country, at Meiktila itself the situation was different. As Cowan and Messervy closed in on this beautiful town with its elegant red-brick buildings, tree-lined avenues and villas set between two lakes, they found the local Japanese commander, General Kasuya, and his 13,500-strong garrison determined to fight to the last. Kasuya's elite troops, probably no more than 3,200 in all, were dug in in terrain unsuitable for tanks, under houses, in the banks of the lakes, in concrete- and earth-covered timber-clad strongpoints and behind piled-up rice sacks. Meiktila was a good place to defend, as the approaches from west and south were along the lakes so that the entry roads were in effect causeways; and from the lakes ran deep irrigation channels and ditches. Slim's strategy was to take Meiktila quickly, then, when Kimura turned to deal with this new and unexpected threat, to hit him with all the might of 33 Corps.[54] It was a tense moment, as every division of 14th Army was now committed along the Irrawaddy, all at the limits of Allied airpower and supply. Cowan surrounded the town, then laid down a heavy bombardment and artillery barrage before sending in the tanks on 1 March. The battle was watched by Slim himself, who insisted on being present, determined that Meiktila should not become another Myitkyina. The RAF refused to fly him in on a 'dangerous and foolhardy mission' but the Americans were more insouciant and a B-25 of the USAAF got him to the front.[55]

Cowan's armoured onrush was countered by a stubborn Japanese defence from a deep screen of mutually supporting bunkers and fortified houses, using heavy artillery, machine guns and anti-tank weapons. Resistance was as fanatical as anything the Allied armies had seen in three years of warfare: snipers, concealed in the most unlikely places, picked off dozens of infantrymen slowly making their way down the rubble-strewn streets.[56] Only very slow progress was made, and at dusk Cowan pulled out his tanks, ready for a fresh start in the morning. Next morning the slaughterous duel of tank versus bunker recommenced, with the same pattern of methodical, house-by-house, almost inch-by-inch, combat. The entire town seemed one enormous booby trap, with every house a strongpoint, every water channel containing its own hidden bunker, every ruined building or pile of bricks concealing a sniper, and every heap of rubble another anti-tank gun or machine gun. The implacable battle raged for three whole days. Japanese 75 mm guns engaged the Anglo-Indian tanks and infantry at point-blank range but were gradually and painfully eliminated one by one.[57] Six p.m. on 3 March saw the end of the fighting in the centre of the town, when the last 50 Japanese left on their feet committed mass suicide by running into the lake and drowning. In the outer environs of the town there were the same terrible scenes of bloodshed, the same determined resistance and identical savage slaughter during the ensuing days (4–5 March).

Slim hailed the capture of Meiktila in four days as a magnificent feat of arms that in effect sealed the fate of the Japanese in Burma. The slaughter was terrific. The Japanese had been determined to go down fighting, and even their sick and wounded left their hospital beds to make a last-ditch stand armed only with sharpened bamboo poles. The official body count spoke of over 2,000 Japanese dead in the town centre and 47 prisoners taken, but their fatalities were far higher, because large numbers of them had been buried alive in underground tunnels and bunkers, the ruins and the rubble concealed other corpses, many suicides had crawled away to make an end, and the lake continued to disgorge bodies for weeks afterwards. Slim himself testified to 876 Japanese dead in a single area of town just 200 yards long and 100 wide.[58] Too late Kimura saw how he had been hoodwinked and diverted large portions of the army he had been preparing to repel 33 Corps in a desperate attempt to retake Meiktila. The victorious British found themselves besieged, but Slim was as confident of the outcome as he had been at Kohima-Imphal. Kimura would have needed massive slices of luck to retrieve the situation, and even though he dispatched formidable forces to the siege of Meiktila, they arrived piecemeal, from many different directions and many different formations. Slim meanwhile could bask in the superior morale of his victorious troops, the fact that the Japanese were trying to counterattack on terrain that overwhelmingly favoured the British, and most of all, his massive air superiority. Incessant Allied air attacks played havoc with enemy communications, and Slim's efficient signals corps was able to pinpoint the various Japanese headquarters, which were relentlessly bombed. Forced to observe radio silence so as not to call down this aerial wrath, the Japanese found themselves unable to communicate effectively with their commanders in the field. Additionally, Cowan sent out armoured formations to assail and harass incoming Japanese regiments so that they could not coordinate with their colleagues and form up into a cohesive force.[59] Nevertheless, Kimura's counteroffensive was deadly and vicious and came uncomfortably close to an unlikely success. His obvious target was the airfield, the vital artery that supplied the defenders. From 6 to 12 March the Japanese probes in this area were ineffective, but after 12 March they became much more serious, making ingenious use of anti-tank weapons, mines and 'human mines' – suicide fighters crouched in foxholes who would detonate 100 kilo aircraft bombs when a tank rolled overhead. After three weeks of remorseless attrition, the Japanese were close enough to the airfield that Allied flights had to cease; thereafter there was no supply, no reinforcements and no evacuation of the wounded.[60]

Slim hit back in two main ways. First, he committed his remaining reserves, 5 Indian Division, which arrived by air on 17 March – just before the suspension of flights.[61] Then he ordered Messervy to take Myingyan, the vital riverhead on the Chindwin, which would allow large-scale riverine supply. Myingyan proved a tough nut to crack, and a first assault failed, but it finally fell on 18 March, the day after the reserves arrived, though the British had to survive another four days of banzai charges and suicide attacks before their position there was secure. Once Myingyan was open, 14th Corps engineers and pioneers began constructing wharves, bridges and new roads, and soon there was another supply line to Meiktila. The Japanese hit back by temporarily severing the communications with the Nyaungu bridge-head, but their attempts to retake Nyaungu and Chauk failed, mainly because Bose's much-vaunted INA proved to have no stomach for a fight against their tougher compatriots.[62] Despite titanic efforts on all fronts in the circular siege of Meiktila, the Japanese just lacked that last ounce of resources and self-belief that might have secured victory even against enormous odds. The confusion in the Japanese high command did not help. Kimura had put Lieutenant General Honda Masaki in charge of retaking Meiktila, but Honda considered his mission both impossible and pointless; he thought the Imperial Army should regroup for a sustained defence farther south.[63] Eventually, on 29 March, the Japanese abandoned the hopeless task of recapturing Meiktila. Sheer logic, and even basic arithmetic, dictated the decision. By the end of that month the Japanese had destroyed 50 British tanks and inflicted 300 casualties, but in the same period had sustained 2,500 casualties and had 50 big guns destroyed. This meant that to knock out one tank they would need one gun and 50 men; to retake Meiktila they would need 5,000 men and 100 guns, but they had just 20 guns and half the required number of effectives. Finally Kimura's chief of staff, Tanaka Shinichi, visited the headquarters of 33 Japanese Army and on his own responsibility ordered 33 Army to disengage and cover the retreat of the Japanese 15th Army.[64] The battle for Meiktila was finally and conclusively over.

Once Kimura shifted his resources to meet the new threat at Meiktila, Slim ordered a general advance on Mandalay by 33 Corps, and on 26 February the three divisions in the corps began their breakout from the bridgeheads. The battle for Mandalay was always going to be a tough one, even though the Japanese commander there, Major General Yamamoto Seiei, like Honda Masaki at Meiktila, thought its defence pointless, something he was commanded to perform purely for the city's prestige value. Interestingly, Slim shared this view, remarking that Mandalay was a news item but not a strategic target.[65] The two strong points were Mandalay Hill and Fort Dufferin. Mandalay Hill was a great rock rising steeply from the plain to a height of nearly 800 feet, and dominated the north-eastern quarter of the city. Its steep sides were covered with temples and pagodas – it was something of a mini-Pagan, in fact – but the Japanese had honeycombed them with machine-gun nests. Pete Reese, to his great credit, refused to order bombers to pound the sacred places but ordered them taken by the infantry. Many observers contrasted his scrupulousness with the philistine and barbaric approach of the American troops at Monte Cassino in Italy.[66] On 8 March 19 Indian Division began its cautious advance towards the hill, and on the 9th was engaged in heavy fighting with Japanese fighters concealed in cellars on the lower slopes. The Anglo-Indians proceeded up the flanks on 10–11 March, painfully winkling out and then exterminating the enemy among the Buddhist temples. As so often, the main opposition came from sharpshooters and elite units in tunnels, which the grim-faced attackers dealt with by pouring barrels of tar, petrol and oil into the access points and then igniting them with tracer bullets.[67] Fort Dufferin was a much tougher proposition. A great rectangular walled enclosure, containing one and a quarter square miles of parkland, dotted with official residences, barracks and office blocks, it also boasted the royal palace of Theebaw, the last Burmese king. Essentially a medieval castle, with crenellated walls 2,500 yards long and 30 feet high, faced with thick brickwork and backed by earth embankments 70 feet wide at their base, the fort was protected in front of the thick wall by a 75-yard-wide moat, with the water crossed by railway and road bridges. By any standards it was a formidable obstacle to an army in a hurry.

After the inevitable slog through the city of Mandalay, beset by snipers all the way and with the tanks in response blasting at anything that moved, the attackers completely surrounded the fort on 15 March. Many observers thought that the ensuing siege was like something out of the Middle Ages, although old Indian army hands inclined to analogies drawn from the Indian Mutiny.[68] Huge guns were brought up to breach the walls, rafts and scaling ladders prepared, while aerial bombardment with 500 lb bombs opened up gaps in the walls but could not even put a dent in the great bank of earth. The scale of the problem soon became apparent: howitzers could make no impression on the defences, while the RAF bombardment, though causing damage, did little to shake the resolve of the defenders; the air force even sent in bombers equipped with the 2,000 lb skipping bombs used on the 'dambusters' raid on the Mohne dam in the Ruhr in 1943, but to no effect. On 16–17 March, attacks on the north-western and north-eastern sections of the wall were beaten off with heavy loss, and on the 18th and 19th four separate attempts to cross the moat failed badly.[69] Finally the Mitchell bombers did manage to bounce one bomb off the moat on to the walls and tore open a 15-foot hole, but Slim, who arrived to witness this battle just as he had at Meiktila, decided a direct assault would be far too costly. Slim was minded to bypass the fort and press on south, but Reese persuaded him to wait for the results of a commando attack through the sewers. This was just about to be launched, on 20 March, when the Japanese suddenly appeared with white flags.[70] Although 19 Division had borne the brunt of the fighting, 2 and 20 Divisions had also played an honourable part, so Slim decided that there would be a formal ceremony, something like a Roman triumph, in which all three divisions would take part. These arrangements were made without any reference to Mountbatten and Leese, who were both angry and resentful when told. The reaction of 14th Army to this peevishness was a metaphorical shrug of the shoulders. One of Slim's aides wrote waspishly: 'It was apparently resented that those who were actually responsible had taken the credit.'[71]

The victories at Mandalay and Meiktila (especially the latter), as Kimura later admitted, were the masterpiece of Allied strategy in the battle for Burma, which ensured Slim's final triumph over the Japanese.[72] Slim's encirclement of Kimura by the brilliant march on Meiktila was both a triumph of logistics and a tour de force of military imagination. As a piece of pure deception it can be rated, as Slim's biographer argues, ahead even of the concealment of the 6th

Panzer Army in the Ardennes before the Battle of the Bulge, or the disinformation that convinced the Wehrmacht that there was a huge Allied army in south-east England under General Patton, ready to cross to the Pas de Calais – one of the ruses that allowed the D-Day OVERLORD landings to succeed.[73] It is also true that the Japanese colluded in their own destruction by their certainty that no Anglo-Indian army could reach Meiktila by any but the conventional route – a certainty so adamantine that Field Marshal Count Terauchi, commander-in-chief of the entire South-East Asian theatre, actually transferred Japanese 2 Division from Meiktila to Indochina just before Cowan and Messervy struck. Yet to characterise Slim's achievement at Meiktila and on the Irrawaddy as mere deception is subtly to downgrade his brilliance. There are solid grounds for asserting that when all due allowances have been made, and *mutatis mutandis* (for until the twentieth century most battles were one-day or at least two-day affairs), Slim's encirclement of the Japanese on the Irrawaddy deserves to rank with the great military achievements of all time – Alexander at Gaugamela in 331 BC, Hannibal at Cannae (216 BC), Julius Caesar at Alesia (58 BC), the Mongol general Subudei at Mohi (1241) or Napoleon at Austerlitz (1805). The often made – but actually ludicrous – comparison between Montgomery and Slim is relevant here. Although unkind critics say that Kohima-Imphal was a mere matter of slugging attrition, where even a mediocre general enjoying Slim's superiority in manpower, artillery, resources and airpower would have prevailed, exactly the same thing could be said, *a fortiori*, about Montgomery's over-hyped victory at Alamein in November 1942. Even if we allow Alamein and Kohima-Imphal to be achievements at the same level, there is no Montgomery equivalent of the Irrawaddy campaign. His one attempt to prove himself a master of the war of movement – Operation MARKETGARDEN against Arnhem – was a signal and embarrassing failure. Montgomery was a military talent; Slim was a military genius.

It was typical of the modest and unassuming Slim that he never sought to claim all the credit for his great victory. He was lavish in his praise of his field commanders and said of 'Punch' Cowan: 'To watch a highly skilled, experienced and resolute commander controlling a hard-fought battle is to see, not only a man triumphing over the highest mental and physical stress, but an artist producing his effects in the most complicated and difficult of all the arts.'[75] Slim always made a point of mentioning everyone who played a part in his victories: engineers, lorry drivers, boffins, back-room boys, even paper-pushers. Most of all he constantly stressed the importance of airpower and was impatient with those, like Churchill, who tried to airbrush this factor out of victory in Burma (presumably, mainly, because the Prime Minister did not want to have to acknowledge the contribution of *American* airpower).[76] There was always very close rapport between Slim and Baldwin on one hand and Stratemeyer on the other. During EXTENDED CAPITAL, Allied air forces flew 7,000 sorties a day to sustain the offensive, and by April, 90 per cent of 14th Army's supplies (or 1,200 tons a day) were provided by air.[77] It was particularly crucial, after Wedemeyer's unforgivable withdrawal of the 75 aircraft in December, that a much greater American, General 'Hap' Arnold, made another 145 transport planes available; without these, EXTENDED CAPITAL could not have succeeded. Unlike Churchill, Slim had no narrow, chauvinistic concerns about acknowledging the huge contribution of his major ally: 75% of the 88,500 tons that reached 14th Army in March and 70% of the 80,000 tons supplied in April came from the USAAF.[78]

The nearer 14th Army got to Rangoon, the more salient the issue of air supply, which was why Christison and the 12th Army had been assigned the task of conquering the Arakan peninsula and the offshore islands in the Bay of Bengal, to bring Rangoon within easy range of Allied aircraft. Their offensive opened on 12 December 1944 and achieved the capture of Akyab by 2 January 1945. Thereafter Christison's advance slightly bogged down. A terrible battle for Kangaw, involving sanguinary hand-to-hand fighting, went on from 22 January to 2 February before the Japanese were subdued.[79] The island of Cheduba was occupied without opposition, but Ramree island, 50 miles long, 20 miles wide and fringed by miasmal mangrove swamps, took longer than expected to succumb. The first landings took place on 21 January, but as Slim reported: 'It was not until six weeks later that the last enemy fugitives fell victims to the naval patrols – and the sharks – as they attempted in small craft or on rafts to reach the mainland.'[80] After mopping up in northern and central Arakan, Christison had to seize a bridgehead at Taungup prior to opening up the Taungup–Prome road before the monsoon. However, by the time Slim was advancing south from Mandalay and Meiktila, the all-weather airfields at Akyab, Cheduba and Ramree islands were either in full operation or close to it.

The Arakan campaign was essentially a sideshow for Slim, but events on the Chinese front in the north were altogether more ominous and could conceivably have derailed his entire strategy. At the beginning of the year the omens were propitious. On 27 January 1945 came the historic moment when X-force, now under General Sultan, driving the Japanese before them up the Burma road to the border with China, made contact with their comrades in Y-force pushing south under General Sun.[81] Sultan and Sun were supposed to be cooperating to take some of the pressure off Slim, and at first this seemed to be working out, for Y-force took Lashio on 7 March, while Sultan's forces occupied Hsipaw, 35 miles south-west of Lashio but, more significantly, just 100 miles from Mandalay, where 33 Corps was even then pulverising Fort Dufferin.[82] Meanwhile Colonel Lewis Pick reported to Sultan that the Ledo road had been cut through to Bhamo to meet the Burma road and was at last open. The first overland convoy, of 113 vehicles, from India to China left Ledo on 12 January and arrived at the Chinese border 16 days later, having covered 478 miles from Ledo; it then ate up the remaining 566 miles to Kunming on the Burma road in another eight days.[83] This should have meant the end of the Hump, but the aerial route was not closed until November 1945, and in July, 71,042 tons of supplies were still being flown to China by that route. Stilwell was proved right about the Hump as about so much else. Given that 1,074 planes and their crew were lost on this perilous trans-Himalayan passage – or roughly one plane for every day the Hump was open – it was sheer madness for the USA to have supplied Chiang by this route without asking anything in return.[84] In any case, suddenly all the sweetness and light on the Chinese front became the blackest darkness. Wedemeyer, whose idea of diplomacy was to give Chiang whatever he wanted without demur, backed the generalissimo when without warning on 23 February he ordered the immediate return of all Chinese and American forces operating under the NCAC umbrella. The direct consequence was that any chance of Slim using Sultan's forces for the advance on Rangoon were gone, but even worse, Kimura could now withdraw all Chinese forces in the north for the campaign against Slim in central and south Burma; there were at least 6,000 unscathed Japanese soldiers in the hills of the Shan states. Slim responded by asking for the use of British 36th Division, which had been operating in the north with NCAC forces; fortunately Leese made no difficulty about this.[85]

Yet the real threat to EXTENDED CAPITAL at the exact point when the struggle for Meiktila was just beginning was Chiang's demand that all his troops be flown out *immediately* in US planes of the 10th Air Force nominally designated for his use; if complied with, this demand would derail Slim's entire strategy. Slim appealed to Mountbatten, who urgently contacted Churchill, who in turn contacted Marshall. The US army chief made the statesmanlike decision that the aircraft Slim needed would not be withdrawn until 1 June or the fall of Rangoon, whichever was the sooner.[86] The crisis came as an annoying distraction for Mountbatten, who was enjoying his wife's visit to him, going to see George Formby shows in Bombay and acting like an aerial sightseer as he observed Slim's troops advancing from the Chindwin.[87] Mountbatten decided that a visit to Chungking to beard the generalissimo in his lair was imperative. Wedemeyer, alarmed that his erstwhile boss would learn the extent to which his former deputy had double-crossed him with Chiang, hurriedly arranged an 'urgent' meeting in Washington that he and Ambassador Hurley had to attend. When Mountbatten suggested that he postpone his visit until his American 'friends' got back to China, the machiavellian Wedemeyer replied that Chiang would take umbrage if Mountbatten did not make the visit as arranged.[88] No longer with any illusions about the generalissimo, Mountbatten did not enjoy his trip to Chungking. Chiang insulted his intelligence by trying the same nonsensical blandishments that had worked temporarily in 1943. When Mountbatten cut through this brusquely and asked why he had issued his unhelpful orders, Chiang replied that he was unwilling for Chinese troops to fight south of Mandalay. That would make Slim's task very difficult, Mountbatten pointed out. That was his problem, said Chiang. Why did he not just rest content with Mandalay?[89] Testily Mountbatten pointed out the obvious, that it was no longer a question of fighting south of Mandalay but fighting *anywhere* in Burma, since the generalissimo was recalling all his troops to China. It would be better, therefore, he added with asperity, for the Chinese to depart as soon as possible – the British were tired of the expense of feeding them –

and leave the rest of South-East Asia to the Supreme Commander. That did not suit the dog-in-the-manger Chiang either; he did not want the British in Siam or Indochina since he considered that his sphere of influence.[90] The exasperated Mountbatten was reduced to making notes in his diary about the superior charm (but lesser beauty) of Madame Sun Yat-sen as compared with her sister.[91] He was also far from happy to learn that the old American suspicion of the British Empire was alive and well even among his so-called friends. General Raymond Wheeler told him that he backed Wedemeyer and Hurley completely in their desire to abandon Burma, while Sultan was on record as having said that the precarious Anglo-American entente would fracture completely if the British conquered Burma and pressed on to Malaya.[92] Similar suspicions were entertained towards French colonialism. When Mountbatten recommended involving the French in the reconquest of Indochina, the Americans declared themselves totally opposed. The egregious Wedemeyer even tried to turn the conflict between Chiang and his US advisers on one hand and the British on the other into an excuse for self-pity: in a typical piece of over-the-top Wedemeyer rhetoric, he complained that he was subject to snarls from both the lion and the dragon.[93]

None of this was of much interest to Slim, now that he had the assurance of the airpower he needed to complete the drive to Rangoon. He was full of confidence, knowing that the campaign was essentially won but aware that there must be much more vicious fighting before he could enter Rangoon. The casualties at the two battles of Meiktila and Mandalay had been relatively light on the British side – just 10,000 for the entire 14th Army[94] – but against this Slim was aware that henceforth he would be fighting with five divisions instead of the seven (5, 7, 17, 2, 19, 20, 36) he disposed of in March during the struggle for Mandalay and Meiktila. The exhausted 2nd Division was being returned to India, while 36 Division was too dependent on logistical support from the NCAC forces that had now been withdrawn to China; it was even conceivable that, fighting on just one front, the regrouped Japanese might enjoy local superiority in infantry.[95] Speed would be Slim's secret weapon – a rapid advance by motorised and armoured units over open country that would leave the enemy gasping. He tried out his ideas in March even while the battles for Meiktila and Mandalay were raging. He ordered Gracey and 20 Division to strike south at the stricken Japanese 33rd Army as it retreated to the Shan hills and Toungoo. Gracey and his men followed a line from Kyaukse to Meiktila, 'killing lavishly as they went'[96] in a campaign reminiscent of General Phil Sheridan's in the Shenandoah valley in 1864. They killed more than 3,000 Japanese and captured 50 guns, leaving the Japanese 33rd Army as the flimsiest of paper tigers, down to just 8,000 men and a handful of guns. Meanwhile, immediately after the fall of Mandalay, 19 Division struck south-east at Maymyo, the old summer capital of Burma set in the hills, and achieved total surprise, overwhelming the garrison and cutting the rail link between the Japanese in central Burma and those fighting the Chinese in the north. In 10 weeks of hard fighting since reaching the Irrawaddy the redoubtable 19 Division had killed 6,000 of the enemy. Kimura's original fallback plan of trying to halt the British on a line running south-west from Kyaukse was in ruins.[97] Slim's idea of sending out full brigades to harry and pester the enemy was bearing fruit: further prizes to come his way in March were the towns of Myotha and Wundwin. These fell to brigades of 20 Division, which also took Kyaukse itself on 30 March. Slim paid eloquent testimony to these exploits: 'This breakout of the 20th Division was a spectacular achievement which only a magnificent division, magnificently led, could have staged after weeks of the heaviest defensive fighting.'[98] In three weeks the division had cleaned out an area 45 miles by 40, controlling a 50-mile stretch of the Rangoon–Mandalay railway; in their wake the Japanese had left behind 2,000 dead and 50 guns. Finally 2 Division, the last across the Irrawaddy and soon to be retired to India, while not meeting the determined opposition 19 and 20 Division had run into, was still held up by a series of stubborn enemy rearguard actions; nevertheless, by mid-March they had taken Kyauktalon, Myinthi and the Ava bridge. In sum, by the end of March both banks of the Irrawaddy from Mandalay to Chauk, plus the main road and railway route to Rangoon as far south as Wundwin, were securely in British hands.[99]

All eyes were now on Rangoon, 320 miles from Meiktila by rail and 370 from Chauk via the Irrawaddy valley. With seven divisions Slim had originally planned a double advance by both itineraries, using a corps in each, but with his slimmed-down manpower he opted to concentrate on the railway route. The strike force would be led by Messervy and 4 Corps, but Slim detached a division west across the hills to follow the course of the Irrawaddy south to Prome, whence another road and railway ran south to Rangoon. This task he gave to Montagu Stopford, whose 33 Corps was now in effect reduced to 20 Division, since 2 Division was leaving and 19 Division had been assigned to Messervy.[100] Reese and Messervy were commanders after Slim's heart, but he seems to have experienced increasing difficulties with Stopford, whose assignment can in part be read as a form of relegation. Tension between the two had been noticed by Mountbatten on 19 February, when Slim rather patronisingly remarked to the leader of 33 Corps: 'Well, goodbye Monty, good luck to your attack and don't make a balls of it.'[101] Stopford chafed under Slim's leadership and had one of his staff officers send a complaint to Mountbatten that he was being starved of supplies, bypassing Slim altogether. An angry Slim summoned him to Pagan for a tense interview, where Stopford convinced Slim he had never seen the offending paper with the complaints to SEAC. This may have been a classic case of telling the truth but not the whole truth. It was the only occasion hitherto when command relations in 14th Army resembled the disastrous state of affairs in the Imperial Japanese army.[102] Slim assured a dejected Stopford that his depleted 33 Corps might still get to Rangoon ahead of Messervy. If the contretemps with Stopford introduced a sour note into the general atmosphere of 14th Army triumphalism, this was counterbalanced by the good news that Aung San, leader of the anti-British Burmese National Army and generally considered a Japanese puppet and quisling, had fallen out with his masters and declared them the BNA's enemy. Slim was not convinced by Aung San's sudden enthusiasm for the British and read his apostasy, correctly, as a simple calculation that they, not the Japanese, were going to win. Although foreseeing that Aung San and his army would be a major headache after liberation, Slim thought it was better to have them on his side; Mountbatten agreed.[103]

Another factor complicating the advance on Rangoon was the sudden, and final, revival of DRACULA. Even while Slim and the 14th Army were achieving stunning victories in central Burma, the Supreme Commander was still not convinced this was the way to subdue the country, and continued to hanker after his perennial obsession – amphibious operations – which would, after all, make him, not Slim, the real conqueror of Burma. Never interested in such glory-hunting demarcation disputes, Slim was in favour of a modified DRACULA, as he feared Kimura would pack Rangoon with suicide squads that would hold out until the monsoon, and could therefore do with all the help he could get. Yet in January–February 1945, both Mountbatten and Leese, in a rare show of unanimity, agreed that they should be looking ahead to the reconquest of Singapore and therefore that the first target for a joint naval and airborne attack should be the island of Phuket; in a ridiculous pun, which works only through gross anglicisation, a wag on Mountbatten's staff had dubbed the modified DRACULA 'Operation ROGER'. [104] With an amphibious assault on Rangoon seemingly ruled out, Slim was more concerned by the calendar and the likely irruption of the monsoon in mid-May than by Japanese opposition, at any rate short of the capital city itself. When he ordered the advance south, the men of 14th Army found the going tough. They were marching in intense humidity, crippling heat and savage pre-monsoon storms – always the harbinger of the main deluge to come. The change in weather as March merged into April made flying difficult and dangerous, with planes particularly liable to be thrown around in mountainous cumulus clouds. As Slim said over and over again, the role of the RAF and the USAAF in the final month of his campaign has never been fully recognised. The infantry and tanks fought a blitzkrieg war, seizing airstrips then passing on to allow aircraft to land in their rear, still cleaving to the original plan of building an airfield every 50 miles.[105] Suddenly it was announced that 14th Army would not just be racing the monsoon to Rangoon but an amphibious operation as well. The British chiefs of staff unknowingly came to Slim's assistance by deciding that the attack on Phuket island should not be attempted until the capture of Rangoon was accomplished fact. Reversing his earlier decision, on 2 April Mountbatten announced that the original DRACULA would take place after all, using a division of paratroops, and that the assault would take place no later than 5 May. Now 14th Army had both the weather and the amphibious 15 Corps as competitors in the race for the Burmese capital.[106]

At first Slim planned to leave substantial enemy forces in his rear and mop up once Rangoon was taken, concentrating all his resources on a sustained dash south. In the light of the revised DRACULA, he changed his mind and decided to make 33 Corps responsible for what he called 'Union Jack' sweeps diagonally across designated squares.

Doubtless Stopford thought his boss had been disingenuous in his earlier assurances of a fair crack at Rangoon. The Union Jack operations saw 33 Division pitted against staunch and often fanatical resistance at Prome, Salim, Padan, Magwe, Yenangyaung, Allanmyo and at Mount Popa, where 500–600 crack Japanese troops made a heroic stand that took the British from the end of March to 19 April to overcome.[107] The encounters in all these places were all the more bitter as the originally retreating Japanese were joined by their comrades fleeing south after the rout in the Arakan. What made the 'Union Jack' operations so successful was the lightning speed of Slim's mechanised forces. On 11 April, one of the mechanised brigades was 60 miles from Taungdwingyi but three days later took the enemy by surprise and seized the town. Similarly 7 Division's blitzkrieg caught the Japanese napping at Yenangyaung on 22 April, and this was a key target because of the oilfields. Slim was exultant: 'The Japanese were bewildered by the speed, strength and direction of 20th Division's thrust. Their whole plan for the defence of the oilfields had collapsed; even their retreat was cut off.'[108] Allanmyo fell to Stopford on 28 April, but on 1 May he was no farther south than Magwe, though with the road clear to advance south from Allanmyo to Prome and Rangoon. An unexpected bonus had come his way in mid-April when the pro-British Karens finally rose in open rebellion against the Japanese, further impeding enemy attempts to halt the dash to Rangoon. The Karens fought ferociously and mercilessly and in one guerrilla operation were estimated to have inflicted 4,000 casualties for the nugatory loss of just 70 irregular fighters. Altogether in the Karen hills Stopford estimated that his guerrilla allies were responsible for 10,000 casualties, more even than his own troops.[109]

While 33 Corps was performing such heroic 'back-room' tasks, 4 Corps began the dash south for Rangoon at the beginning of April, aware that to beat Mountbatten's DRACULA assault to the capital they would have to cover the 338 miles from Meiktila to Rangoon in 35 days. The units involved in the great push were 17 Division, 5 Division, 19 Division and 255 Tank Brigade. Slim aimed to smash through fast before the enemy could dig in at strongpoints. This worked well at Thazi, but around Pyabwe, 4 Corps ran into its first major obstacle. General Honda had built an impressive defensive line around Pyabwe and the surrounding villages, making them both mutually supportive and self-supporting from arms dumps within the villages. The road south of Pyabwe was cut by 255 Tank Brigade and on 10 April, Messervy's men attacked. The first assault failed against a heavily bunkered position around the waterworks, and a second took 12 hours of desperate close fighting to make any headway. Finally, in some of the most vicious and sanguinary hand-to-hand combat yet seen, 48 Brigade took the heavily defended railway station and railway embankment areas.[110] By dawn on 11 April, Pyabwe was in British hands, and 2,000 Japanese dead were counted in the town and surrounding villages. Slim noted grimly: 'For its size, Pyabwe was one of the most decisive battles of the Burma war. It shattered Honda's army, but it did more, it settled the fate of Rangoon.'[111] Further to the north, 99 and 48 Brigades became bogged down around Yindaw where, on 7 April, the Japanese had a 1,000-strong garrison dug in behind a lake, protected by water channels and earthen banks, and defences bristling with mines, barbed wire and anti-tank guns. For three days the British could make no impression, so finally Slim ordered the two brigades to break off the engagement and bypass it, leaving the next attack to 5 Division coming up behind them. It became clear that the enemy was determined to contest every mile of the route to Rangoon, for 5 Division had no sooner reached Yamethin, a short distance to the south of Pyabwe, than they were hit by a 400-strong suicide squad, which infiltrated the town at night and then dug in for a kind of terrestrial kamikaze. Once again the delay was effective, and it took a further three days to wipe the defenders out.[112]

Anxious about the relatively slow progress being made, Slim urged 5 Division on at record speed to Shwemyo, which they entered on 16 April, moving so fast that they caught the next would-be suicide squads only just starting to dig in. By nightfall on 16 April, 4 Corps' vanguard was only 240 miles from Rangoon. Finding the next town on the railway line, Pyinmana, strongly defended, the armoured group bypassed it and seized the airfield at Lewe, 10 miles farther south, so that 5 Division could be resupplied by air. The next task was to dash for Toungoo, to get there before the Japanese could concentrate and dig in, and to seize the airfield that would bring Rangoon within range.[114] Moreover, in a worrying communication, Slim was informed that DRACULA was now definitely scheduled for 2 May because of bad weather forecast thereafter; this left 4 Corps just 11 days to cover

over 200 miles – about 20 miles a day – and the previously confidently quoted odds of 3–1 on for the corps to beat 15 Corps to Rangoon were now lengthened. Realising that he would have to take multiple short cuts now, and that in normal circumstances the Japanese could be expected to beat his men at Toungoo, Slim launched the Karen guerrillas on them, with predictable consequences: 'The Japanese, driving hard through the night down jungle roads to Toungoo, ran into ambush after ambush; bridges were blown ahead of them, their foraging parties massacred, their sentries stalked, their staff cars shot up.'[115] Hammered by the Karens and assailed from the air by fresh RAF attacks, the Japanese lost the race for Toungoo. On 22 April, 5 Division, in the van of 4 Corps, entered Toungoo having covered 50 miles in three days and delighted with their swift and easy victory. Now there were just 160 miles to cover, but only eight days left before DRACULA. On 23 April, at Pyu, 30 miles south of Toungoo, they received the lame surrender of the 1st Division of Bose's Indian National Army, together with 150 officers and 3,000 men. The INA, always an object of derision for their countrymen in the Indian army, had taken a leaf out of Aung San's book and decided that further resistance was hopeless.[116]

On 24 April, 5 Division clocked up another 20 miles to Penwegu; they were 140 miles from Rangoon with seven days to go but utterly exhausted. They handed over the baton next day to 17 Division, who took it up and roared on to Daiku by the evening of 26 April, now just 80 miles from Rangoon with five days to go. But now came Kimura's last hurrah. Deciding that the defence of Rangoon was impossible, he assembled every last man for a determined defence at Pegu, hoping to hold on there until the monsoon broke.[117] On 27 April 17 Division got a whiff of things to come when they had to clear minefields and then tangle with suicide squads before they could proceed, but not before they had counted another 500 enemy dead on the line of march. Most of the next day they battled against stiff enemy resistance north of Pegu, until they arrived at nightfall to find Pegu a veritable fortress. Just 47 miles north of Rangoon, it was an ideal defensive position, as the town stood on both banks of the winding Pegu river with bridges conveying road and rail links to Rangoon. The Japanese had demolished both railway bridges and used the folds of the river to build a cunningly entrenched redoubt within the town.[118] A two-pronged assault by 17 Division on 29 April was easily beaten off. Next day the British gained a precarious foothold on the west bank of the river, but the Japanese still dominated the intact road bridge and even audaciously tried to sever the road link to Toungoo in the rear of the attackers. Frustrated, Slim once again flew to the front and found morale encouragingly high. When the Japanese counterattack was finally beaten off, he spoke to one of the British gunners. 'I'm sorry you've got to do all this on half rations,' he said. 'Don't you worry about that, sir,' came the answer. 'Put us on quarter rations, but give us the ammo and we'll get you into Rangoon!'[119] There was now no more than 24 hours to get to Rangoon before the paratroops landed, but as the British tentatively advanced through the ruins of Pegu, they found the place honeycombed with mines and booby traps, causing further delays. Finally ready to advance on 2 May, they were overwhelmed by the torrential rains of an early-breaking monsoon (two weeks earlier than expected). Even as they sat down in the rain, word came in that, as Slim's biographer rather glibly put it: 'DRACULA had beaten EXTENDED CAPITAL by a short head.'[120] Slim was stoical: 'On the evening of the 2nd, when news of the successful landing south of Rangoon and the Japanese evacuation had been received, the 17th Division was halted in drenching rain 41 miles by road from its goal.'[121] Kimura had lost at Pegu but he caused a delay that led 14th Army to lose as well. The 17th Division had to take what comfort it could from statistics. Since crossing the Irrawaddy, it had lost 719 men killed, 2,767 wounded and 71 missing, but had killed over 10,000 of the enemy, taking only 167 prisoners.[122]

Operation DRACULA had been a marked success. Setting out from Akyab and Ramree island, six convoys sailed between 27 and 30 April. An immense flotilla accompanied them: four aircraft carriers, two battleships (one British, one French), two British and Dutch cruisers, two escort carriers, six destroyers (joining them from Trincomalee in Ceylon), 12 bomber squadrons and a screen of fighters. After a bombing blitz on 1 May, a battalion of Gurkhas was dropped, followed by fighters from the 50 Indian Parachute Brigade, in what some observers described as the last echo of the vanishing Raj, the last exploit of the once glorious Indian army.[123] Meanwhile a pilot flying over the city saw written in large letters on the roof of the gaol: 'JAPS GONE. EXDIGITATE' (arch RAF cod-Latin for 'Get your fingers out!').[124] Accordingly on 2 May, in worsening weather, a brigade of 26 Division landed on each bank of the river. The brigade from the east bank entered the city on 3 May to find the Japanese indeed gone; after the usual divided counsels in the Japanese high command, the realists had prevailed over the last-ditchers.[125] Yet the first attacker into Rangoon was probably the pilot from 14th Army's 221 Group who landed at Rangoon airfield on his own initiative during the limbo period and found the enemy gone. Slim always took comfort from the thought that the first 'liberator' into Rangoon had come from 14th Army. In his desire to beat 15 Corps to the punch, he himself acted irresponsibly and flew ahead of proper air cover with Messervy and an American pilot, Captain Robert Fullerton, plus a couple of staff officers, on 1 May. The plane came under anti-aircraft fire and Fullerton was hit in the leg. He landed the plane at Pegu, but the wound proved serious and the leg had to be amputated. Slim was remorseful: 'I felt – and still feel – very guilty about this. I had no business as Army Commander to go where I did, and, if I was so stupid as to go, I had no excuse for taking Messervy or the others with me.'[126] Messervy, however, was phlegmatic and speculated that they could conceivably have landed at Rangoon airfield and found the Japanese gone. That would have put Slim's experience on a par with that of MacArthur in the Philippines. As Messervy drily remarked: 'Bill Slim could have occupied Rangoon.'[127]

The campaign to reconquer Burma had come to a triumphant conclusion, but about 60–70,000 Japanese troops still remained at large in the country. There followed three months of hard fighting while 14th Army dealt with the enemy rearguards and residues, of which the most formidable formations were in the Karen hills and along the Sittang river towards Siam. Stopford and 33 Corps did a good job of clearing the remaining Japanese units out of the Irrawaddy valley, but all operations between May and August 1945 were hampered by the monsoon, which made flying, land transport, communications and supply all very difficult. Slim concentrated on preventing any enemy build-up in the Moulmein area and sealing off the eastern bank of the Sittang.[128] The first objective was secured only after further sanguinary battles, principally those at Allanmyo from 11 to 15 May and Kama near Prome, where the remains of Yamamoto's forces were destroyed in a running fight from 21 to 30 May; after the battle, 1,400 Japanese corpses were counted. The killing continued in June and July, with a further 11,500 Japanese dead, while just 96 Anglo-Indians died.[129] The only vestige of pride the Japanese were able to salvage was in their heroic breakout from the densely wooded Pegu Yomas, an area running along the Sittang for 75 miles north–south and 30 miles west–east. Here on 28 July, 27,000 men of the Japanese 28th Army began the long march to Siam. Aiming to intercept them between the Yomas and the Sittang and between the Sittang and the Salween, the British doled out fearful punishment, killing another 12,000 enemy and taking 740 prisoners (by this time the despondent Japanese were more prepared to be taken captive) for the loss of just 95 killed and 322 wounded on their own side. Nevertheless, the Japanese survivors did get to Siam by late August, only to discover that their divine emperor had surrendered.[130] The Pegu Yomas engagement took place while Slim was already on leave and before the full extent of his military genius was realised in Britain. In time his calibre was appreciated and his importance in the theory of war, for he had demonstrated the credibility of the 'indirect approach' – aiming primarily not at the physical destruction of the enemy so much as breaking his will to fight. Slim had proved himself a true master of war, always concentrating on enemy weaknesses, always coordinating land, sea and airpower. Only the very rare captain has all the virtues – the total mastery of logistics, superb imagination and creativity, the ability to use deception, spring surprises, take calculated risks and remain permanently flexible, all the time pursuing single-minded objectives and inspiring the ordinary soldier to great feats with an avuncular, sangfroid leadership. William Slim had all these qualities.[131]

Epilogue

While these final operations were going on, Slim in Rangoon tried to set up a civilian administration. It helped that many Burmese bureaucrats and officials, unwilling to serve the Ba Maw puppet government under the Japanese, had gone into hiding and now emerged to report for duty. What did not help was that Mountbatten had identified yet another man in his long list of personal bêtes noires – this time the civilian governor of Burma, Sir Reginald Dorman-Smith.[1] As a soldier, Slim was mainly concerned with how to integrate Aung San and the previously pro-Japanese Burmese National Army. He met Aung San at Meiktila on 16 May and found him a man he could do business with, both a genuine patriot and a realist.[2] Since it was clear that Aung San had been bitterly anti-British in 1942, had ambushed Anglo-Indian forces, committed atrocities and was now collaborating only because the British were clearly the winning side, not all Slim's staff, to say nothing of his political superiors, took his sanguine view of the future of this man in Burmese politics. There was some bitterness that he was being rewarded essentially for no good reason, while the steadfastly loyal British allies, particularly the Karens and the Kachins, were being offered no guarantees for the future when Burma might become independent.[3] Aung San was, however, only one side in Slim's polygon of concerns. He had to ponder the political implications of the new mood of brimming confidence among his own Indian soldiers. After their great martial prowess and stirring victories, was it at all plausible that such men would return meekly to be ruled by the British Raj? Was not one implication of the victory in Burma that Indian independence now became something that could not be delayed? There was a curious sense in which Churchill had been right to distrust the Indian army.[4] Besides, Slim had to plan for the forthcoming invasion of Malaya. The idea was that Operation ZIPPER, codeword for the Malayan campaign, would be the province of 14th Army, while the smaller 12th Army took over mopping-up operations and the final pacification of Burma. This idea in turn was seriously jeopardised when yet another of Mountbatten's most vociferous critics took a hand. P.J. Grigg, Secretary of State for War, although beloved by Alanbrooke,[5] loathed Mountbatten with a rare detestation. It particularly galled him that Mountbatten – and indeed Alanbrooke and Churchill – had played no part in the conception of EXTENDED CAPITAL, and had opposed it almost to the end, but were now taking credit for it as if the whole operation had been planned in London. Casting around for a way to cut Mountbatten down to size, he announced that the period soldiers had to serve abroad before exercising a right of repatriation should be reduced from three years and eight months to three years and four months. This meant that tens of thousands of 14th Army veterans qualified for immediate home leave, with the further implication that ZIPPER could not get off the ground because of manpower shortages.[6]

Yet Slim soon had more immediately pressing and personal problems to settle. One would have thought that a man who had just brought off one of the great military achievements of the ages would have been feted, lionised and lauded to the skies. That is not what happened. His immediate boss, Oliver Leese, finally reached snapping point with the Slim–Mountbatten axis, nutmegged as he was between a military genius and a showman who specialised in taking the credit for anything extraordinary or praiseworthy that happened. His exasperation seems finally to have boiled over. On 3 May, the very day Slim entered Rangoon in triumph, Leese came to Kandy to see Mountbatten, who was then recovering from a bad attack of amoebic dystentery, and put it to the Supreme Commander that Slim had been working at white heat for more than a year now, ever since the beginning of Kohima-Imphal, was tired and should therefore be relieved by a fresher man for Operation ZIPPER; he suggested Christison as his replacement.[7] Self-contradictorily, he added that Slim was the right man to stay on and oversee the peacetime administration of Burma – a job at least as onerous as planning ZIPPER. Mountbatten said he was not keen on the idea but raised no objection to sounding Slim out about the proposal. It was quite clear that he did not express clearly enough his opposition to the idea of replacing Slim, and the obvious question arises: why not?[8] Three different answers have been given. Mountbatten supporters claim that he was ill and did not fully realise what was on Leese's mind. This explanation has not found favour with more cynical historians, who suggest that Mountbatten was actuated by one of two considerations. It was well known that he disliked Leese and wanted rid of him, and he saw this as a bed of nails on which the blundering Leese would impale himself. Others say that he was by now wildly jealous of Slim and realised that the full truth about the Burma campaign would come out; this would show that the Supreme Commander, far from being an all-wise, all-seeing generalissimo, had consistently backed the wrong horse (amphibious warfare) and then at the eleventh hour disingenuously tried to take credit for EXTENDED CAPITAL. The disgrace of Slim would muddy the waters and enable him to continue his mythical pose as 'king of Burma'; the real king would have been deposed.[9] Of course it was possible that Mountbatten, who possessed all the peasant cunning of a true machiavellian, could see advantages to him however the Slim–Leese clash turned out; whoever lost the struggle, it would mean one fewer thorn in the Supremo's side.

Thinking he had been given the green light, Leese flew to Akyab to tell Christison that he was to be the new commander of 14th Army; Slim would be assigned to the lesser 12th Army in Burma.[10] The element of chicanery in Leese was clear from three separate false statements: he said that Slim had already left 14th Army when in fact he had not even spoken to him yet; he said that Stopford would be replacing him; and he added that Mountbatten had given the order for Slim's sacking but did not want the unpleasant chore of a personal confrontation and insisted it was Leese's job.[11] The elated Christison said goodbye while Leese flew on to Meiktila for his meeting with Slim on 7 May. Thinking this was routine, Slim was flabbergasted by Leese's opening words: 'Before we talk of anything else, I must tell you that I have decided to give Christison command of the 14th Army . . . I do not consider you capable of planning a large-scale amphibious operation, so I do not think it would be fair either to 14th Army or yourself to leave you in charge of it.'[12] When he offered Slim the command of the peacetime 12th Army in Burma, Slim rightly read this as an insult and indignantly rejected the offer. He said he would rather resign and return to Britain. Still unaware of the enormity of his action, the obtuse Leese signalled Alanbrooke in a matter-of-fact way, announcing that he had replaced Slim. On 9 May Slim told his senior staff that he had been sacked, and soon the news leaked out to the other ranks.[13] Predictably, 14th Army was incandescent at the news of the sacking of their beloved 'Uncle Bill'. The feeling among Slim's staffers was well summed up by his aide Jim Godwin: 'Oliver Twist [Leese] and Mountbatten must be out of their minds. I never trusted that affected silk-handkerchief-waving guardsman.'[14] The general feeling was that Mountbatten was behind it all, and the resulting wave of resentment hit Kandy like a tsunami. Mountbatten saw that he had miscalculated and quickly tried to distance himself from the decision, declaring himself very worried about it and telling Alanbrooke he would be taking the matter up with Leese.[15] In London, Alanbrooke was stupefied when he got Leese's signal. In fairness to Leese, he had sent an earlier cable raising in general terms the possibility of replacing Slim, but Alanbrooke either ignored it or was too busy to read it. Now, however, he reacted angrily. On 14 May he sent the bluntest of blunt signals to Leese with a severe reprimand. What did he mean by dismissing the most successful general in the East? How dare he take such unilateral action? Was he not aware that only Mountbatten could make such a decision, and then only after the closest consultation with the chiefs of staff in London? Leese should not even have discussed the matter with Slim; it was far outside his powers. In sum he would agree to Slim's departure only if he and Mountbatten could produce the strongest possible reasons.[16]

Alanbrooke's feelings were confirmed by a meeting with Auchinleck, who also happened to be in London at the time. 'The Auk' told Churchill at lunch on 20 May that Slim was the finest general in the entire Far East and South-East Asia theatre and strongly recommended him as his successor as Commander-in-Chief, India.[17] Feeling himself to be in the frame also, Mountbatten summoned Leese to Kandy for another dressing-down, telling him that he had blundered and that his earlier orders must be countermanded.[18] Now in the most terrible mess, Leese tried one last time to get Slim to accept the post as head of 12th Army, but once again Slim refused adamantly. Although Slim had appeared poker-faced and phlegmatic at the interview with Leese on the 7th, in private he was fuming. The public Slim was still playing the role of the bluff professional soldier: 'It was a bit of a jar as I thought 14th Army had done rather well. However he [Leese] is the man to decide. I had to sack a number of chaps in my time, and those I liked best were the ones who did not squeal. I have applied for my bowler [hat] and am awaiting the result.'[19] In private, though, Slim told Brigadier 'Tubby' Lethbridge that the incident was a replay of his conflict with Noel Irwin in 1943 and he was confident he would ultimately prevail: 'This happened to me once before, and I bloody well took the job of the man that sacked me. I'll bloody well do it again.'[20] Mountbatten was reluctant to dismiss Leese, having so recently got rid of Giffard, as he feared for his own credibility: the obvious inference, if he got rid of two army commanders-in-chief as well as his other commanders and so many key personnel at Kandy, would be that the Supreme Commander was impossible to work with. However, Alanbrooke gave him no choice. In 'I told you so' mood – for the CIGS had never had a high opinion of Leese – he told Mountbatten that after such a grotesque error of judgement, Leese was no longer a credible commander and should be sent home.[21] This order was confirmed after a meeting between Alanbrooke and Churchill on 29 June. Slim was on home leave at the time, and Alanbrooke called him to tell him the good news; not only was Leese sacked, but Slim was to be promoted to full general and given Leese's job as Commander-in-Chief, Allied Forces, South-East Asia. Stopford was given command of 14th Army and General Miles Dempsey sent out to command 12th Army.[22] Christison was left high and dry, humiliated and let down by Leese, who failed to console him but simply moaned to him that he was being made the 'fall guy' for the real villain, 'Dickie'.

Slim was on his way back from the UK to take up his new command when, on 14 August, he learned that Japan had surrendered unconditionally after the two devastating atomic bomb attacks on Hiroshima and Nagasaki. Emperor Hirohito was forced to 'endure the undendurable', but still managed to achieve a classic of Oriental face-saving: 'The war has developed, not necessarily to our advantage.' Two days later Slim was at the headquarters of ALFSEA, and on 12 September sat on Mountbatten's left to receive the official surrender of all Japanese forces in South-East Asia. Slim's hatred of the Japanese had not abated; rather it had increased once he learned the fate of Allied prisoners of war. MacArthur, already looking forward to his entente with Hirohito and his long tenure as an 'American Caesar' in Japan, decreed that Japanese officers should not be asked to give up their swords at the surrender, for otherwise there might be mass suicide. MacArthur had his agenda, but Slim had his. He felt very strongly that if the Japanese officer class was not made to swallow the bitter pill of sword surrender, the legend would grow that they had never really been beaten, simply betrayed, in the same way as the German officer class after World War I. He therefore disregarded MacArthur's ban on the archaic ceremony; all the swords were given up, there was no mass suicide, and Slim always thereafter kept General Kimura's sword on his mantelpiece.[23] He did not stay in Burma long, and returned to Britain in 1946 as Commandant of the Imperial War College. His main lieutenants all played a part in post-war reconstruction in South-East Asia. Messervy administered Malaya, Stopford took over as supremo at SEAC after Mountbatten's departure in June until the command was wound up in November, while Christison was Mountbatten's agent in Indonesia in the short-lived British intervention there in 1945–46, spent nearly half a century in retirement and died in 1993 aged 100. Intending to retire in 1948, Slim was brought back to eminence by Prime Minister Clement Attlee, who appointed him Chief of the Imperial General Staff in 1948 to replace Montgomery. 'Monty' had already hand-picked his putative successor, John Crocker, but Attlee slapped him down as only Attlee could. After the Prime Minister gave him the news, Monty protested: 'But I've already told Crocker.' 'Well, you'll have to untell him,' replied Attlee curtly.[24] Promoted to field marshal, Slim served as CIGS for three years and then in May 1953 was appointed Governor General of Australia, where he remained until 1959. Created Viscount Slim in 1960, he was made Constable and Governor of Windsor Castle and died in London in December 1970 aged 79.

Stilwell did not simply fade away and brood in California after FDR made him the sacrificial victim of his unwise China policy. When he heard that Chiang had renamed the Burma–Ledo road the 'Stilwell highway', his reaction was one of amused contempt: 'I wonder who put him up to that' was his only comment.[25] By 1945 Vinegar Joe was back in the ring punching. Always a fighting soldier and forever in search of a command berth, he arrived in Manila on 25 May and was greeted cordially by Douglas MacArthur. He toured the Okinawa battlefields and on 18 June, the day before he was due to fly back to California, MacArthur offered him a prestigious job as his chief of staff. Although touched and gratified, Stilwell declined on the grounds that he was no great administrator and was anyway looking for a position as a field commander. MacArthur queried whether a four-star general would really consent to serve as a front-line commander; Stilwell replied that he would be glad to command a single division as long as he was allowed to fight.[26] MacArthur replied that he could do better than that; as commander of an army he knew no better than Vinegar Joe. Stilwell flew out to Honolulu, but when he got there, a cable from MacArthur was waiting for him, offering him the command of 10th Army, one of the spearheading forces for the coming invasion of Japan. On 23 June Stilwell assumed command: he was to command the second wave of the invasion with 25 divisions. Among those he had under him were Canadian, Australian and Indian units that had been taken away from SEAC after the Japanese defeat in Burma. Stilwell chuckled: 'Mountbatten has to give up units for this operation! Life is funny.'[27] The Japanese surrender ended hopes of further martial glory, but there were compensations in the news from China. Wedemeyer, even with his sycophantic approach, was finding Chiang impossible, while an alliance between Marshall and 'Hap' Arnold had finally removed Chennault from any real power over the air force in China; these duties devolved on the much more rational and trustworthy Stratemeyer. With Truman in the White House after FDR's death in April 1945, US policy in China became much more hard-headed and empirical. Public opinion in the USA dramatically turned against the generalissimo as more and more stories about the corruption of the Kuomintang were printed in the press. What Theodore White had been in the Roosevelt era, the witheringly anti-Chiang drama critic turned war correspondent Brooks Atkinson, writing in the New York Times, was in the Truman years.[28] Truman made Marshall his Secretary of State, and after a tour of inspection in China that confirmed in detail everything Stilwell had said about Chiang – and the moral and military supremacy of Mao and the Communists – the President ended by cutting off aid to the nationalists and embargoing arms sales. In 1949 Mao achieved complete victory in the Chinese civil war, forcing Chiang to flee to Taiwan.

452

Alas, Stilwell did not live to see Chiang's downfall. Determined to die with his boots on, in November 1945 he headed a War Department Equipment Board, which showed a prescient interest in ballistic missiles. He died of liver cancer in October 1946 aged 63, at the Presidio, San Francisco, while still on active service.

Shortly after MacArthur entertained Stilwell and gave him the Okinawa appointment, he had another distinguished visitor, none other than the Supreme Commander, SEAC, himself. The omens were not propitious for a favourable outcome, since both men were outrageous prima donnas – Eisenhower said he had spent five years in the Philippines studying dramatics under Doug MacArthur – and the American had initially opposed the creation of SEAC, fearing it would limit his own independence of action. Mountbatten made his mark, as he so often did, by exuding charm, especially the old-fashioned kind of British charisma that so appealed to Americans. For once he was prepared to play second fiddle, and the tactic paid off. On 12 July he wrote in his diary about his meeting with the American Caesar in Manila: 'I had a long and interesting conversation with MacArthur. Or, to be more precise, I listened to a fascinating monologue, and found the same difficulty in trying to chip in as I have no doubt most people find in trying to chip in to my conversation.' Two days later the lustre had not worn off and Mountbatten confessed that he was completely under the older man's spell:

Contrary to popular conception, he gives the impression of being a rather shy and sensitive man, who regards compliance with the needs of publicity as a duty . . . he does not look at all fierce or commanding until he puts his famous embroidered cap on. As we went out together to face the photographers, and he pulled his cap on, his whole manner changed. His jaw stuck out, he looked aggressive and tough, but as soon as the photographers had finished, he relaxed completely, took off his hat, and was his own charming self . . . he is one of the most charming and remarkable characters I have ever met, and so sympathetic and friendly towards the SEAC.'[29]

It is a fair comment that Mountbatten's enthusiasm was based on recognition of strengths and weaknesses like his own. Mountbatten was selfish and vain but not remote or cold, ambitious but with a cocksure personality leavened with common sense. He would not have made flowery speeches referring pleonastically to 'divine God' as MacArthur did and, unlike the American Caesar, he could laugh at himself. Impetuous, impressionable, overexcited by 'experts', Mountbatten was a liberal-left personality who believed in human goodness; MacArthur was a hardline right-winger who believed in main force. As Mountbatten's biographer has shrewdly remarked: 'It is doubtful if MacArthur's opinion of his visitor was as flattering as his guest's.'[30] Yet the differences between the two men should not be overstated. Both considered themselves born to rule, reverenced monarchical and hereditary principles, were supreme commanders and proconsuls or viceroys (MacArthur in Japan, Mountbatten in India) and were cordially loathed by many of their colleagues (Eisenhower found MacArthur unspeakable, while Marshall summed him up crisply as 'never any good . . . always a four-flusher').[31] Curiously, both men ended their lives speaking out strongly against the use of nuclear weapons in combat.

Once Japan had surrendered, the position of supreme commander seemed less attractive to Mountbatten, for he was happy backing neither the neo-colonial position of the Dutch in Indonesia nor that of the French in Indochina. Because the British were the only credible military presence in South-East Asia, he had to spend the latter part of 1945 and early 1946 using British forces to hold the ring and keep at bay the nascent nationalist movements headed by the Viet Minh in Vietnam and Sukarno in Indonesia. This was not the kind of work Mountbatten relished, so he was delighted to be offered the post of Viceroy of India, succeeding Wavell. Where Wavell had put together a thoughtful programme for gradual British withdrawal from the subcontinent and the gradual phasing in of the Congress party of Nehru and Gandhi in India and the independent Muslim state of Pakistan under Muhammad Ali Jinnah, Mountbatten reverted to his destroyer mode and decided that everything had to be done with unconscionable haste. The famous declaration that the British would quit India 'by August 1947 at the latest' was mainly Mountbatten's work. Many historians have therefore held him responsible for the terrible Hindu–Muslim communalist massacres that followed the lightning British departure.[32] After the debacle in India, Mountbatten returned to his first love the sea, first commanding a cruiser squadron, then climbing the final rungs of naval promotion until he became First Sea Lord in 1954–59, almost the exact period that Slim was in Australia as governor general. Even though it gradually became obvious that Slim was the true military genius in Burma, and that Earl Mountbatten of Burma was a solecism as a title, Mountbatten tried to recoup some of the glory for himself by co-opting Slim and insinuating that he and the field marshal were equal partners in the enterprise. His later career was controversial at many different levels. Edwina died in 1960 at the age of 58 from a heart attack, but not before very strong rumours began to circulate that in the 1946–47 viceroyalty period she and Nehru had been lovers. Then in 1968, as the beleaguered Labour government of Harold Wilson struggled with economic crisis, the newspaper proprietor Cecil King intrigued with the intelligence services, trying to plot a *coup d'état* that would make Mountbatten a British dictator.[33] The details of this conspiracy are still far from clear, but it seems that Mountbatten, after some dithering, had the good sense to turn down the proposed role. Even his death in 1979 became controversial. The official story was that the Provisional IRA assassinated him and others in Sligo when they blew up a motorised fishing boat, and an IRA member, Thomas McMahon, was later jailed for the crime.[34] Yet the late Enoch Powell, himself a controversial figure, always maintained that the CIA had assassinated Mountbatten because he had just spoken out against nuclear weapons.[35] According to this version of his death, the CIA engineered a set-up job that would look like an IRA assassination, and the Provisional IRA, for propaganda reasons and to enhance its own credibility, was happy to take responsibility. It seems that even in death Mountbatten divided opinion sharply. All four of Burma's 'musketeers' – Slim, Stilwell, Mountbatten and Wingate – were larger-than-life characters, all incredibly working in the same theatre. They seem more creatures of myth than of history, and it is unlikely that we shall ever see such a quartet juxtaposed again.

Finally, we must ask the 64,000-dollar question: was the Burma war worth it? There is a persuasive school of thought that holds that all twentieth-century wars, except the Spanish Civil War and the Second World War in Europe, were avoidable conflicts, that they were not waged for vital national interests but were the result of stupidity, miscalculation and irrationality. The First World War, the Korean war and the Vietnam conflict of 1965–75 fit well enough into this category. What about the war between the Allies and Japan, and particularly the war in Burma? The aggressive foreign policy of FDR and Secretary of State Cordell Hull, complemented by the equally aggressive policies of Prince Konoye and General Tojo, produced a kind of irresistible force versus immovable object scenario, but it could hardly be said that vital national interests were at stake. Japan went to war in defence of the Greater East Asian Co-Prosperity Sphere, perceived to be vital to her national survival; post-war events and the Japanese economic miracle showed clearly that the narrowly defined economic autarky of the Sphere was *not* essential for economic survival. The United States basically went to war because she would not accept an Asian Monroe doctrine, with Japan having hegemony in China, but by her own errors (principally the mindless and irrational support given to Chiang) lost all influence in China for 25 years. Cynics would say the Americans might just as well have let Japan have its fervently desired hegemony. The Burmese, in so far as they took part in the war in their own country, fought for independence. Yet the history of Burma after independence in 1948 has been singularly unhappy, to the point where it would be a brave man who would assert that the present-day despotic regime represented for ordinary people any advance at all on British colonialism. By a huge irony, Burma since 1948 has espoused exactly the kind of paranoid xenophobia that brought the Japanese empire to grief in the 1930s. The British fought in Burma to preserve and restore the British Empire in the East, yet within two years of the end of the war, India, the fulcrum and axis of the whole system, was independent, with Burma following a year later, and Malaya and Singapore limping through years of 'emergency' before also relinquishing the imperial bonds. We have made great claims for Slim, but a further one must be that his military genius and the encirclement of the Japanese on the Irrawaddy meant that Britain relinquished its empire at the moment of its most glorious military success, and allowed her to retreat from the imperial arena with pride.

Notes

Guide to abbreviations used in Notes:

CAB. Cabinet Papers in the National Archives
DIV. William Slim, *Defeat into Victory* (1956)
MP. *The Papers of George Caflett Marshall*, ed. L. Bland & S.R.S. Stevens (Baltimore, 1991)
SP. *The Stilwell Papers*, ed. T. White (1949)
WO. War Office Papers in the National Archives

Chapter One   pp. 1–15

• 1. In savage wars casualties are difficult to estimate exactly, and so the gruesome scholarly arguments about war dead continue; the fate of the Soviet Union in the 'Great Patriotic War' of 1941–45 is the best known case. Louis Allen, *Burma. The Longest War 1941–45* (1984), p. 640, puts the Japanese dead at 185,149. For his general survey of casualties see ibid. pp. 637–45. For British casualties see Martin Brayley & Mike Chappel, *The British Army 1939–45* (2002), p. 6; Jon Latimer, *Burma. The Forgotten War* (2004), p. 1. For the Burmese civilian casualties see Vadim Erlikman, *Poder i narodon as el eniia V XX veke spravochnik* (Moscow, 2004), pp. 74–5 and, more generally, R.J. Rummel, *Statistics of Democide. Genocide and Mass Murder since 1900* (Charlottesville, Va., 1998). • 2. Walter La Feber, *The Clash: US–Japanese Relations throughout History* (1998). • 3. See Philip Payson O'Brien, ed., *Britain and the End of the Anglo-Japanese Alliance 1902–1922* (2004). • 4. Erik Goldstein & John Maurer, eds., *The Washington Conference, 1921–22. Naval Rivalry, East Asian Stability and the Road to Pearl Harbor* (1994). • 5. Elting E. Morrison, *The Letters of Theodore Roosevelt* (Cambridge, Mass., 1954) pp. 829–30. See also H.R. Brands, *TR. The Last Romantic* (NY, 1997), p. 530. • 6. W. Elsbree, *Japan's Role in South East Asian Nationalist Movements 1940–1945* (Harvard, 1953), pp. 8–11; see also Michael

A. Bamhart, *Japan Prepares for Total War: The Search for Economic Security 1919–1941* (Ithaca, NY, 1987). • 7. R. Dallek, *Franklin D. Roosevelt and American Foreign Policy, 1932–35* (Oxford, 1979). • 8. F. Dorn, *Walkout. With Stilwell in Burma* (NY, 1971), p. 20. For the Chinese factor more broadly see D. Borg & S. Okatmoto, *Pearl Harbor. A History. Japanese-American Relations 1931–1941* (NY, 1973). • 9. These stories about the wives are told in Jonathan Fenby, *Generalissimo Chiang Kai-shek and the China He Lost* (2003). For the hostage tale see D. Wilson, *When Tigers Fight. The Story of the Sino-Japanese War 1937–1945* (1982), pp. 9–10. The most recent, and in some quarters considered definitive, biography of Chiang is Jay Taylor, *The Generalissimo. Chiang Kai-shek and the Struggle for Modern China* (2009), though to this reader it seems highly biased in favour of Chiang and prepared to give him the benefit of every doubt. • 10. Allen, *Burma*, op. cit., pp. 284–5. • 11. Even though some revisionist historians claim, unconvincingly, that war could have been avoided if FDR and Cordell Hull had been more flexible (see Keiichiro Komatsu, *Origins of the Pacific War and the Importance of 'Magic'* (NY, 1999). • 12. J.C. Hsiung & S.I. Levene, *China's Bitter Victory: The War with Japan 1937–1945* (NY, 1993). • 13. M. Collis, *First and Last in Burma* (1956), pp. 22–5. • 14. Ba Maw, *Breakthrough in Burma* (1968), pp. 61–2, 78, 114–15. • 15. D.J. Taylor, *Orwell. The Life* (2003); Bernard Crick, *George Orwell. A Life* (1980). For a modern 'footsteps' journey in Burma in search of Orwell see Emma Larkin, *Secret Histories* (2004). • 16. H.G. Wells, *Travels of a Republican Radical in Search of Hot Water* (1939), pp. 84–8. • 17. M. Collis, *The Outward Journey* (1952), pp. 121–2. • 18. J.F. Cady, *A History of Modern Burma* (Ithaca, NY, 1958), pp. 156–63. • 19. Ibid., pp. 170–5. • 20. M. Collis, *Trials in Burma* (1945), p. 209; N.R. Chakravarti, *The Indian Minority in Burma. The Rise and Decline of an Immigrant Community* (Oxford, 1971). • 21. For this war see Anthony Stewart, *The Pagoda War* (1972); George Bruce, *Burma Wars 1824–86* (1973). • 22. D.G. Hall, *Burma* (1950), p. 167; Godfrey Harvey, *British Rule in Burma 1824–1942* (1942). • 23. For the Kachins and Shan (with some additional material on the Mon) see the classic study by E.R. Leach, *The Political Systems of Highland Burma* (1973). • 24. Frank Kingdon-Ward, *Return to the Irrawaddy* (1956), pp. 157–76; E.H.M. Cox, *Farrer's Last Journey* (1926) pp. 219–42. • 25. Kingdon-Ward, *Return*, op. cit., pp. 67, 78. • 26. The classic work on ornithology is Bertram E. Smythies, *Birds of Burma* (1940), which still holds its place despite recent competition from the disappointing volume by Kyaw Nyunt Lwin & Khin Mama Twin, *Birds of Myanmar* (2005). • 27. Christopher Sykes, *Orde Wingate* (1959), p. 422. • 28. Latimer, *Burma*, op. cit., p. 321. • 29. And hence, perhaps, the total absence of such mention in Mountbatten's diaries, in contrast to the observations of Slim, Stilwell and Wingate. For the proposition in general, see Latimer, *Burma*, op. cit., p. 21. • 30. See e.g. Kingdon-Ward, *Return*, op. cit., p. 67. • 31. J.H. Williams, *Elephant Bill* (1950), pp. 84–5, 123. • 32. Sykes, *Wingate*, op. cit., p. 422. • 33. See U. Toke

Gale, *The Burmese Timber Elephant* (1974). • 34. Williams, *Elephant Bill*, op. cit., p. 107; Larkin, *Secret Histories*, op. cit., p. 175. • 35. Williams, *Elephant Bill*, op. cit., pp. 94–9. • 36. Trevor Royle, *Orde Wingate. Irregular Soldier* (1995), p. 242. • 37. Williams, *Elephant Bill*, op. cit., p. 105. • 38. Frank McLynn, *Carl Gustav Jung* (1996), pp. 146–7. • 39. E. Leviton et al., 'The Dangerously Venomous Snakes of Myanmar', *Proceedings of the California Academy of Sciences* 54 (2003), pp. 407–62. • 40. Henry Park Cochrane, *Among the Burmans. A Record of Fifteen Years of Work* (NY, 1904), p. 257. For more modern figures see S. Swaroop & B. Grab, 'Snakebite Mortality in the World', *Bulletin of the World Health Organisation* 10 (1954), pp. 35–75 (at pp. 64–5). • 41. Williams, *Elephant Bill*, op. cit., p. 106; Latimer, *Burma*, op. cit., p. 64. • 42. Leviton, op. cit., see also Herndon G. Dowling & Jannon U. Jenner, *Snakes of Burma: Checklist of Reported Species and Bibliography* (Washington DC, 1988). • 43. The great American expert on Burmese snakes, Joseph Slowinski, died in 2001 at the age of 38 from a bite from a many-banded krait: Jamies James, *Snake Charmer. A Life and Death in Pursuit of Knowledge* (NY, 2008). • 44. Latimer, *Burma*, op. cit., p. 322. • 45. William Slim, *Defeat into Victory* (1956), p. 417 (hereinafter DIV). • 46. T.H. White, ed., *The Stilwell Papers* (1949), p. 285 (hereinafter SP). • 47. It is extremely disappointing that the reputable and normally reliable military historian Jon Latimer accepts this story (Latimer, *Burma*, op. cit., p. 370). But it is reproduced straightfacedly and uncritically in a number of books. See Robert Farquharson, *For Your Tomorrow. Canadians and the Burma Campaign 1941–1945* (2004), p. 131. • 48. See S.K. Kar and H.R. Bustard, 'Saltwater crocodile attacks on man', *Biological Conservation* 25 (1983), pp. 377–82. • 49. The identical account is reproduced in volume after volume but always without any reliable source being cited. It is put in context in A.C. Pooley, T. Hines & J. Shields, *Crocodiles and Alligators* (NY, 1989), pp. 172–86. • 50. The most telling critiques of the story known to me are: Steven G. Platt et al., 'Maneating estuarine crocodiles: the Ramree Island Massacre revisited', *Herpetological Bulletin* 75 (2001), pp. 15–18; and David Finkelstein, 'Tigers in the Stream', *Audubon Magazine* 86 (May 1984), pp. 98–111. • 51. For the official British account see *London Gazette* 23–26 April 1948. • 52. Peter Haining, *The Banzai Hunters* (2006), pp. 133–4. For W.O.G. 'Bill' Potts see the obituaries in *The Times*, 19 July 1997, and *Independent*, 12 July 1997. • 53. Of course one has no objection to a fiction being used as the launch pad for another fiction. The Ramree crocodile story has produced at least two novels incorporating the sensational story: Robert Appleton, *Sunset on Ramree* (2008), and Yasuyuki Kasai, *Dragon of the Mangroves* (2006). • 54. B. Towill, *A Chindit's Chronicle* (Lincoln, Nebraska, 2000), p. 72. • 55. Allen, *Burma*, op. cit., p. 194. • 56. Quoted in Latimer, *Burma*, op. cit., p. 384.

• 1. For some aspects of Slim's early life see his *Unofficial History* (1959).
• 2. Ronald Lewin, *Slim. The Standard Bearer* (1976), pp. 35–6. • 3. Ibid, pp. 49–53.
• 4. Robert Lyman, *Slim, Master of War: Burma and the Birth of Modern Warfare*
(2004), pp. 265–8. • 5. Adrian Fort, *Archibald Wavell. The Life and Times of an
Imperial Servant* (2009), p. 55. • 6. Victoria Schofield, *Wavell. Soldier and
Statesman* (2006) pp. 113, 118, 122, 281. • 7. Richard Mead, *Churchill's Lions*
(2007), pp. 473–5. • 8. S.W. Kirby, ed., *The War Against Japan* (1960), i, p. 56;
W.S. Churchill, *The Second World War* (1950), iii, pp. 161–72; J. Kennedy, *The
Business of War* (1957), p. 108. • 9. P. Lowe, *Great Britain and the Origins of the
Pacific War* (Oxford 1977), pp. 8–10, 134–5; F. Lin, *A Military History of Modern
China 1924–1949* (Princeton, 1956), pp. 175–6. • 10. Brian Connell, *Wavell, Supreme
Commander, 1941–1943* (1969), p. 29. • 11. B. Prasad, ed., *The Retreat from Burma
1941–42* (Delhi, 1952), p. 31; T. Carew, *The Longest Retreat. The Burma Campaign*
(1969), p. 11; J.F. Cady, *A History of Modern Burma* (Ithaca, 1958), pp. 412–19.
• 12. Fort, *Wavell*, op. cit., p. 250. • 13. Churchill, *Second World War*, op. cit.,
iii, p. 564. • 14. Fort, *Wavell*, op. cit., p. 254. • 15. Connell, *Wavell*, op. cit., p. 62.
• 16. Fort, *Wavell*, op. cit., pp. 256–7. • 17. Jonathan Fenby, *Generalissimo Chiang
Kai-shek and the China He Lost* (2003); Brian Crozier, *The Man Who Lost China*
(1976). I find unconvincing the exhaustive attempt by Jay Taylor, *The
Generalissimo: Chiang Kai-shek and the Struggle for Modern China* (Harvard, 2009),
to rehabilitate Chiang. It skates over Chiang's deficiencies and exhibits signs
of 'historical contrarianism' – the desire to knock orthodox views simply
because they are orthodox. • 18. Ronald Lewin, *The Chief. Field Marshal Lord
Wavell, Commander in Chief and Viceroy, 1939–1947* (1980), p. 159. • 19. Barbara
Tuchman, *Sand against the Wind. Stilwell and the American Experience in China,
1911–45* (1971), p. 234. • 20. For General George Marshall, one of the towering
figures of the Second World War, see the four-volume biography by Forrest
Pogue (1963–87), especially Volume 2, *Ordeal and Hope 1939–1943* (1966), and
Volume 3, *Organizer of Victory 1943–1945* (1973). • 21. Alex Danchev & Daniel
Todman, eds., *The War Diaries of Field-Marshal Lord Alanbrooke, 1939–1945*
(2001), pp. 219, 223–4 (hereinafter Alanbrooke Diaries). • 22. Fort, *Wavell*,
op. cit., pp. 259–61. • 23. Allen Warren, *Singapore 1942. Britain's Greatest Defeat*
(2003). • 24. Connell, *Wavell*, op. cit. • 25. Churchill certainly held Wavell
responsible: Churchill, *Second World War*, op. cit., iv, p. 127. • 26. J.B. Haseman,
The Thai Resistance Movement during the Second World War (De Kalb, Illinois,
1978), pp. 35–6; see also E.B. Reynolds, *Thailand and Japan's Southern Advance,
1940–1945* (Basingstoke, 1994). • 27. J. Smyth, *Milestones* (1979), p. 169. • 28. Jon
Latimer, *Burma. The Forgotten War* (2004), pp. 46–7. • 29. P.F. Geren, *Burma*

Diary (1968), pp. 3–7. • 30. J. Lunt, *Hell of a Licking. The Retreat from Burma 1941–42* (1986), pp. 95–100. • 31. See the extended treatment in Louis Allen, *Burma. The Longest War 1941–45* (1984), pp. 26–34. • 32. Lunt, *Hell of a Licking*, op. cit., pp. 120–3; Connell, *Wavell*, op. cit., p. 133. • 33. Alanbrooke Diaries, p. 229. • 34. Kirby, *War Against Japan*, op. cit., iv, p. 88. • 35. John Connell, *Auchinleck. A Biography of Field-Marshal Sir Claude Auchinleck* (1959), p. 192. For the battle of Sittang see Allen, *Burma*, op. cit., pp. 36–44, where he sidetracks into a long digression on the blowing of the Sittang bridge. • 36. Latimer, *Burma*, op. cit., pp. 63–4. • 37. Connell, *Wavell*, op. cit., pp. 181, 190–200. • 38. Alex Nicholson, *The Life of Field-Marshal Earl Alexander of Tunis* (1973). • 39. John Keegan, *Churchill's Generals* (1991); Richard Mead, *Churchill's Lions* (2007), pp. 41–46. • 40. Latimer, *Burma*, op. cit., p. 68. • 41. T. Carew, *The Longest Retreat* (1969), pp. 155–7. • 42. Lunt, *Hell of a Licking*, op. cit., pp. 167–8. • 43. Allen, *Burma*, op. cit., pp. 44–57. • 44. Lewin, *Slim*, op. cit., p. 84. • 45. John Masters, *The Road Past Mandalay* (1961), p. 44. • 46. DIV, pp. 10–11, 28–30. • 47. Ibid., pp. 90–1. • 48. Connell, *Wavell*, op. cit. • 49. I. Lyall–Grant & K. Tamaya, *Burma 1942: The Japanese Invasion – Both Sides Tell the Story of a Savage Jungle War* (Chichester, 1999), p. 70; M. Caidin, *Zero Fighter* (1970), pp. 100–4. Slim's estimate is at DIV, p. 7. • 50. Fort, *Wavell*, op. cit., p. 279. • 51. DIV, pp. 41–3. • 52. W. Elbree, *Japan's Role in South-East Asian Nationalist Movements* (Harvard, 1953), pp. 32–4; G.R. Collis, *The Eagle Soars* (Bishop Auckland, 1998), p. 25. For a full study see Michael Tomlinson, *Most Dangerous Moment* (1979). • 53. G. Tyson, *Forgotten Frontier* (Calcutta, 1945), p. 35; M.C. Nickolson, *Burma Interlude* (Honolulu, 1989), p. 105; Lunt, *Hell of a Licking*, op. cit., p. 173. • 54. L. Stowe, *They Shall Not Sleep* (NY, 1945), p. 116. • 55. G. Evans & A. Brett-James, *Imphal. A Flower on Lofty Heights* (1962), pp. 42–3. • 56. Allen, *Burma*, op. cit., pp. 62–3. • 57. P. Carmichael, *Mountain Battery* (Bournemouth, 1983), pp. 75–7. • 58. Lunt, *Hell of a Licking*, op. cit., pp. 202–3; G. Fitzpatrick, *No Mandalay, No Maymyo* (Lewes, 2001), pp. 110–11; G.M.O. Davy, *The Seventh and Three Enemies: the story of World War Two and the 7ᵗʰ Queen's Own Hussars* (Cambridge, 1952), p. 294; J.F. Cady, *A History of Modern Burma* (NY, 1958), p. 440. • 59. For a general survey see Alan K. Lathrop, 'The Employment of Chinese Nationalist Troops in the First Burma Campaign', *Journal of South-East Asian Studies* 12 (1981), pp. 409–32. • 60. DIV, pp. 52, 64. • 61. Harold Alexander, *The Alexander Memoirs* (1962), p. 94. • 62. DIV, pp. 64, 87. • 63. Ibid., p. 72. • 64. Latimer, *Burma*, op. cit., p. 93. • 65. Prasad, ed., *Retreat from Burma*, op. cit., p. 69. • 66. G. Rodger, *Red Moon Rising* (1943), p. 98. • 67. Latimer, *Burma*, op. cit., p. 95. • 68. Quoted in ibid., p. 96. But better is A. Wagg, *A Million Died. The Story of the War in the Far East* (1943), pp. 84–98. • 69. DIV, pp. 60–62. • 70. P. Carmichael, *Mountain Battery* (Bournemouth, 1983), pp. 167–8; M. Farndale, *History of the Royal Regiment of Artillery. Far East Theatre 1939–1945* (2002), pp. 98–100; E.W.C. Sandes, *From Pyramid to Pagoda* (1952), pp. 29–31.

• 71. DIV, p. 67. • 72. Lunt, *Hell of a Licking*, op. cit., pp. 212–13. • 73. Latimer, *Burma*, op. cit., pp. 98–9. • 74. DIV, p. 69. • 75. Ibid., pp. 74–5. • 76. Latimer, *Burma*, op. cit., p. 101. • 77. DIV, pp. 80–1, 86. • 78. Mike Calvert, *Fighting Mad* (Shrewsbury, 1996), p. 77. • 79. DIV, pp. 83, 87–8. • 80. Lunt, *Hell of a Licking*, op. cit., pp. 241–3; DIV, pp. 92–5. • 81. DIV, pp. 95–9. • 82. Ibid., pp. 102–7. • 83. Carew, *Longest Retreat*, op. cit., p. 255. • 84. Latimer, *Burma*, op. cit., p. 110. • 85. DIV, p. 108. • 86. Ibid., p. 109. • 87. Hugh Tinker, 'The Indian Exodus from Burma 1942', *Journal of South-East Asian Studies* 6 (1975), pp. 1–14. • 88. Latimer, *Burma*, op. cit., pp. 120, 461; DIV, p. 114. • 89. Latimer, *Burma*, op. cit., p. 116. • 90. DIV, pp. 115–20. • 91. Cady, *History of Modern Burma*, op. cit., p. 440. See also WO 203/5716. • 92. DIV, pp. 120–1. • 93. Geoffrey Evans, *Slim as Military Commander*, (1969) p. 84; Lewin, *Slim*, op. cit., pp. 98, 102–3. • 94. Alexander, *Memoirs*, op. cit., pp. 92–5. Alanbrooke's assessment of Alexander is more than just interesting: 'It is too depressing to see how Alex's deficiency of brain allows him to be dominated by others! He must have someone else to lean on! He has *no* personality of his own and lets anyone else climb into his skin! In Africa, Sicily and South Italy he was carried by Montgomery. In central Italy by Oliver Leese and Harding and failed badly, and now he has selected MacMillan as his mount.' That was written on 18 January 1945. Later Alanbrooke added the following: 'I think that in my criticism of Alex, I was certainly wrong in saying that "he has no personality of his own". He most certainly had a definite personality of exceptional charm, of outward calm which engendered confidence, of exceptional bravery and of great attractiveness. One could not help being fond of Alex and of enjoying being with him. I think, however, that it was just on account of all these outward qualities that on knowing him one realized the deficiency of brains and character. I have often described him as being a beautiful Chippendale mirror, with the most attractive and pleasant frame, but when you look into the mirror you always find the reflection of some other person who temporarily dominates him, be it a Monty, an Oliver Leese or a MacMillan.' (Alanbrooke Diaries, pp. 646–7.) • 95. DIV, p. 118. • 96. John Kennedy, *The Business of War* (1957), p. 210. • 97. Alexander to Wavell, 10 March 1942, WO 259/62. • 98. Fort, *Wavell*, op. cit., p. 295.

Chapter Three   pp. 42–68

• 1. Forrest C. Pogue, *George C. Marshall. Organizer of Victory* (NY, 1973), pp. 78, 257; Eric Larrabee, *Commander in Chief. Franklin Delano Roosevelt, His Lieutenants, and their War* (1987), p. 518. • 2. Pogue, *Marshall*, op. cit., p. 77. • 3. SP, pp. 5–12. • 4. For the first 50 years of his life see Barbara

Tuchman, *Sand against the Wind. Stilwell and the American Experience in China 1911–45* (1971), pp. 9–142. • 5. N.N. Prefer, *Vinegar Joe's War: Stilwell's Campaigns for Burma* (Novato, CA, 2000), p. 14. • 6. Tuchman, *Sand against the Wind*, op. cit. • 7. Stilwell despised Drum and was amused by his prima donna antics while deciding whether to take the post (Larrabee, *Commander in Chief*, op. cit. • 8. L.I. Bland & S.R.S. Stevens, ed., *The Papers of George Catlett Marshall* (Baltimore, 1991), iii, p. 140 (hereinafter MP). • 9. C.T. Liang, *General Stilwell in China 1942–1944. The Full Story* (NY, 1972), pp. 24–5. • 10. Tuchman, *Sand against the Wind*, op. cit., p. 243. • 11. SP, p. 50. • 12. Stimson diary, 14 January 1942 quoted in Henry L. Stimson & McGeorge Bundy, *On Active Service in Peace and War* (NY, 1949), pp. 298–9. For Stimson see also Godfrey Hogson, *The Colonel. The Life and Times of Henry Stimson 1867–1950* (1990); Elting E. Morison, *Turmoil and Tradition: A Study of the Life and Times of Henry L. Stimson* (1960); David F. Schmitz, *Henry L. Stimson. The First Wise Man* (2000). • 13. SP, pp. 50–3. • 14. Ibid., p. 58; Tuchman, *Sand against the Wind*, op. cit., p. 250. • 15. Francis, L. Loewenheim, Harold D. Langley & Manfred Jonas, eds., *Roosevelt and Churchill. Their Secret Wartime Correspondence* (NY, 1975), p. 206. • 16. SP, pp. 41, 43. • 17. Tuchman, *Sand against the Wind*, op. cit., p. 253. • 18. Larrabee, *Commander in Chief*, op. cit., pp. 183–5. • 19. Derek Tulloch, *Wingate in Peace and War: An Account of the Chindit Commander* (1972), p.102. • 20. SP, p. 43. • 21. Ibid., pp. 44, 54. • 22. Tuchman, *Sand against the Wind*, op. cit., pp. 236–7. • 23. Chiang's vision and perception have also been defended by other friendly critics, notably Hans Van de Ven, 'Stilwell in the Stocks: the Chinese Nationalists and the Allied Powers in the Second World War', *Asian Affairs* 34 (2003), pp. 243–59. See also Van de Ven, *War and Nationalism in China, 1942–1945* (2003). Less notice has been taken of his bizarre behaviour in manoeuvring towards war in Tibet in 1942–43 as a pre-emptive strike in his struggle against the Communists, hoping for direct control over China's south-western provinces. That such a probe, if seriously carried out, would have brought Chiang into conflict with the British, who claimed Tibet as part of India, seems to have bothered him not at all: Lia Hsiao-Ting, 'War or Strategy? Reassessing China's Military Advance towards Tibet, 1942–1943', *China Quarterly* 186 (2006), pp. 446–62. • 24. Tuchman, *Sand against the Wind*, op. cit., p. 322. • 25. Jay Taylor, *The Generalissimo* (Harvard, 2009), pp. 176–7. • 26. Tuchman, *Sand against the Wind*, op. cit., p. 197. • 27. J.A. Goette, *Japan Fights for Asia* (1945), p. 79. • 28. R.J. Aldrich, *Intelligence and the War against Japan: Britain, America and the Politics of Secret Service* (Cambridge, 2000), pp. 201–2. • 29. SP, pp. 54, 57. • 30. Ibid., p. 56. • 31. Forrest Pogue, *Ordeal and Hope 1939–1942* (1966), pp. 355–9. • 32. Stephen C. Shadegg, *Clare Booth Luce* (NY, 1970), Wilfred Sheed, *Clare Booth Luce* (NY, 1982). • 33. SP, p. 67. • 34. Ibid., p. 68. • 35. Ibid., p. 71. • 36. For the Chiangs' visit to India see Hannah Pakula, *The Last Empress. Madame Chiang Kai-shek and the Birth of Modern China* (2010),

pp. 377–8; Taylor, *Generalissimo*, op. cit., pp. 195–6. • 37. SP, pp. 70, 72–3.
• 38. Pakula, *Last Empress*, op. cit. See also Laura Tyson Li, *Madame Chiang Kai-shek: China's Eternal First Lady* (NY, 2006); Sterling Seagrave, *The Soong Dynasty* (NY, 1996); Emily Hahn, *The Soong Sisters* (1942). Clare Booth Luce declared that Madame was the nearest thing to a Joan of Arc or a Florence Nightingale that the decade had produced (Pakula, *Last Empress*, op. cit., p. 379).
• 39. See Martha Byrd, *Chennault – Giving Wings to the Tiger* (Tuscaloosa, 2003); Martin Caidin, *The Ragged Warriors* (NY, 1978); and the book by Chennault himself, *Way of a Fighter* (NY, 1949). Cf. also Robert Hebgen, ed., *General Claire Lee Chennault. A Guide to his Papers* (Palo Alto, 1993). • 40. Daniel Ford, *Flying Tigers: Claire Chennault and his American Volunteers 1941–42* (Washington DC, 2007), pp. 30–4, 45. • 41. O.J. Greenlaw, *The Lady and the Tigers* (NY, 1943), pp. 148–9. • 42. Leland Stowe, *They Shall Not Sleep* (1945), pp. 62–85. • 43. Ford, *Flying Tigers*, op. cit., pp. 333–4; Robert Lee Scott, *Flying Tigers. Chennault and China* (Santa Barbara, 1973), pp. 61–5. For Chiang's obsession with airpower see Guangqiu Xu, *War Wings: the United States and Chinese Military Aviation, 1929–1949* (NY, 2001), p. 182. • 44. Larrabee, *Commander in Chief*, op. cit., p. 545.
• 45. SP, p. 69. • 46. Stowe, *They Shall Not Sleep*, op. cit., pp. 21–5. For a description of Stilwell's house in Chungking see Larrabee, *Commander in Chief*, op. cit., pp. 538–9. • 47. See Frederic Wakeman, *Spy Master. Dai Lai and the Chinese Secret Service* (Berkeley, 2003). Tai-Li famously got his comeuppance eventually at the hands of the legendary head of the OSS, 'Wild Bill' Donovan (Richard Dunlop, *Donovan. America's Master Spy* (Chicago, 1982), pp. 426–7.
• 48. Tuchman, *Sand against the Wind*, op. cit. • 49. O.C. Spencer, *Flying the Hump: Memories of an Air War* (Texas, 1992), p. 40. • 50. Tuchman, *Sand against the Wind*, op. cit., p. 267. • 51. Liang, *General Stilwell in China*, op. cit., pp. 33–5.
• 52. Taylor, *Generalissimo*, op. cit., pp. 55–6, 257–9. • 53. SP, p. 79. • 54. Ibid., p. 78. • 55. Tuchman, *Sand against the Wind*, op. cit., p. 270. • 56. F. Eldridge, *Wrath in Burma* (NY, 1946), pp. 47, 92; Ho Y-c, *The Big Circle* (NY, 1948), p. 5; M. Collis, *Last and First in Burma, 1941–1948* (1956), p. 122. • 57. SP, p. 78. • 58. Ibid., p. 80. • 59. Ibid., pp. 81–9. • 60. Tuchman, *Sand against the Wind*, op. cit., p. 271. One man who may not have liked the new entente was Churchill: he intensely disliked the Stilwell–Alexander dual command (W.S. Churchill, *The Second World War* (1950), iv, pp. 169–70. • 61. P. Carmichael, *Mountain Battery* (Bournemouth, 1983), pp. 75–7; T. Carew, *The Longest Retreat* (1969), pp. 204–5; Jack Belden, *Retreat with Stilwell* (NY, 1943), p. 215. • 62. Tuchman, *Sand against the Wind*, op. cit., p. 274. • 63. SP, p. 89. • 64. For Merrill see N. Boatner, *The Biographical Dictionary of World War Two* (Novato, CA, 1996), pp. 361–2.
• 65. Tuchman, *Sand against the Wind*, op. cit., p. 275. • 66. DIV, p. 51. • 67. SP, p. 90. • 68. Ibid., p. 92. • 69. Tuchman, *Sand against the Wind*, op. cit., passim.
• 70. SP, pp. 93–4. See also Pakula, *Last Empress*, op. cit., pp. 387–8. • 71. Liang, *General Stilwell in China*, op. cit., p. 37. • 72. SP, pp. 96–9; Tuchman, *Sand*

464

against the Wind, op. cit. • 73. Tuchman, *Sand against the Wind*, op. cit., p. 282. • 74. SP, p. 99; Tuchman, *Sand against the Wind*, op. cit., p. 284. • 75. SP, pp. 100, 104. • 76.Tuchman, *Sand against the Wind*, op. cit., p. 285. • 77. Ibid., p. 276. • 78. DIV, p. 76. • 79. SP, p. 103. • 80. DIV, p. 77. • 81. Ronald Lewin, *Slim. The Standard Bearer* (1976), p. 65. • 82. DIV, p. 108; Tuchman, *Sand against the Wind*, op. cit., p. 276. • 83. DIV, p. 82. • 84. John Masters, *The Road Past Mandalay* (1961), pp. 265, 309–10; Robert Farquharson, *For Your Tomorrow. Canadians and the Burma Campaign 1941–45* (2004), p. 59. • 85. Which in no way invalidates his critique of Chiang. Taylor, *Generalissimo*, op. cit., thinks it does, but his work is vitiated by a systematic no-holds-barred attempt to discredit Stilwell in order to bolster his unconvincing 'rehabilitation' of Chiang (see ibid., pp. 191–295). Unhappily for him, most of Taylor's critique subsists at the level of mere assertion, not scholarship. • 86. SP, p. 99. • 87. Ibid., pp. 100, 104. • 88. Alanbrooke Diaries, pp. 442–3. • 89. SP, pp. 106–7. • 90. Ibid., pp. 107, 109. • 91. Ibid., p. 109. • 92. Ibid., p. 106. • 93. See Duane Schultz, *The Doolittle Raid* (NY, 1988); Carroll V. Glines, *The Doolittle Raid* (NY, 1988). • 94. Carroll V. Glines, *Doolittle's Tokyo Raiders* (Princeton, 1964), p. 6. • 95. Quoted in Jon Latimer, *Burma. The Forgotten War* (2004), p. 113. • 96. F. Dorn, *Walkout. With Stilwell in Burma* (NY, 1971), esp. pp. 152–64, 206–11, 237–43. See also the account by the surgeon Gordon Seagrave, with whom Stilwell enjoyed a close entente: Seagrave, *Burma Surgeon* (NY, 1943), pp. 210–11. • 97. Tuchman, *Sand against the Wind*, op. cit., p. 296. • 98. SP, p. 111. • 99. Ibid., p. 113. • 100. Ibid., p. 114. • 101. Ibid., p. 115. • 102. E.V. Fischer, *The Chancy War. Winning in China, Burma and India in World War Two* (NY, 1991), pp. 108–13; W.G. Burchett, *Trek Back from Burma* (Allahabad, n.d.), p. 272. • 103. SP, p. 116. • 104. C.F. Romanus & R. Sunderland, *Stilwell's Mission to China* (Washington DC, 1953), p. 139; Liang, *General Stilwell in China*, op. cit., p. 41. • 105. Chennault, *Way of a Fighter*, op. cit., p. 161. • 106. Pakula, *Last Empress*, op. cit., p. 392.

Chapter Four   pp. 69–89

• 1. Christopher Sykes, *Orde Wingate* (1959). • 2. David Rooney, *Wingate and the Chindits: Redressing the Balance* (1994), p. 15. • 3. John Bagot Glubb, *Arabian Adventures* (1978), p. 9. • 4. Sykes, *Wingate*, op. cit., pp. 52–82. • 5. It is instructive to contrast the lucid and convincing account in Trevor Royle, *Orde Wingate* (1995), pp. 79–81, with the vague and evasive version of events in Sykes, *Wingate*, op. cit., pp. 84–8. • 6. Royle, *Wingate*, op. cit., pp. 87–8. • 7. John Connell, *Wavell. Scholar and Soldier* (1964), pp. 183–94. • 8. John Rose, *The Myths of Zionism* (2004), pp. 130–1. • 9. Norman Finkelstein, *Image and Reality in the Israel–Palestine Conflict* (1995), p. 113. • 10. Tom Seger, *One Palestine*

Complete (2000), pp. 430–1. • 11. Leonard Mosley, *Gideon Goes to War* (1955), p. 58.
• 12. Ibid., pp. 38–72. See also the generous assessment in Simon James Angrim,
'Orde Wingate and the British Army 1922–1944. Military Thought and Practice
Compared and Contrasted', PhD thesis, University of Wales, 2007; Chapter
Four. • 13. Royle, *Wingate*, op. cit., p. 109. • 14. Mosley, *Gideon*, op. cit., p. 76;
see also *Sunday Express*, 6 March 1954. • 15. Norman Rose, *Chaim Weizmann.
A Biography* (1986), pp. 257–88. • 16. Royle, *Wingate*, op. cit., p. 158. • 17. Sykes,
Wingate, op. cit., pp. 109–26. • 18. Royle, *Wingate*, op. cit., pp. 97–9. • 19. Sykes,
Wingate, op. cit., pp. 209–10. • 20. Derek Tulloch, *Wingate in Peace and War:
An Account of the Chindit Commander* (1972), pp. 285–6. • 21. Mosley, *Gideon*,
op. cit., pp. 97–144. • 22. Sykes, *Wingate*, op. cit., pp. 245–6, 302–7, 318–19. See
also Angrim, 'Orde Wingate and the British Army', op. cit., Chapter Five.
• 23. Mosley, *Gideon*, op. cit., pp. 149–58; Sykes, *Wingate*, op. cit., pp. 324–8.
• 24. John Masters (1979), p. 161; Rooney, *Wingate*, op. cit., p. 73; Mosley,
Gideon, op. cit., pp. 159–72; Royle, *Wingate*, op. cit., pp. 216–20; Sykes, *Wingate*,
op. cit., pp. 331–6. • 25. Shelford Bidwell, *The Chindit War* (1979), p. 39. • 26.
Sykes, *Wingate*, op. cit., pp. 335–41. • 27. The 'all or nothing' personality often
co-exists with religious mania, as has been brilliantly demonstrated by Erik
Erikson in *Young Man Luther* (1958). • 28. Mosley, *Gideon*, op. cit., p. 170; Royle,
Wingate, op. cit., pp. 186–7. • 29. Royle, *Wingate*, op. cit., pp. 94, 129, 160–3.
• 30. Wilfred Thesiger, *The Life of My Choice* (1987), pp. 318–22, 327–28, 350–54;
Michael Asher, *Thesiger: a Biography* (1994), pp. 191–205. • 31. Mosley, *Gideon*,
op. cit., p. 116; Royle, *Wingate*, op. cit., p. 188; Sykes, *Wingate*, op. cit., p. 250.
• 32. Mosley, *Gideon*, op. cit., p. 170; Royle, *Wingate*, op. cit., pp. 235, 237.
• 33. Royle, *Wingate*, op. cit., pp. 19, 56, 93–4, 125, 162, 186. • 34. Ibid., pp. 129,
241, 254; Sykes, *Wingate*, op. cit., pp. 339–40. • 35. Charles M. Wilson, *Churchill:
Taken from the Diaries of Lord Moran* (1966). • 36. Mosley, *Gideon*, op. cit., p. 157.
• 37. Royle, *Wingate*, op. cit., pp. 232, 241–3. • 38. Ibid., p. 241. • 39. Ibid., pp. 30,
54, 67, 84, 92, 113, 232, 273–4. • 40. Mosley, *Gideon*, op. cit., pp. 176–8. • 41. For
the SOE see Charles Cruickshank, *SOE in the Far East* (Oxford, 1983); Ian
Fellowes-Gordon, *The Battle for Naw Seng's Kingdom* (1971). • 42. R. Dunlop,
Behind Japanese Lines. With the OSS in Burma (Chicago, 1979), esp. pp. 29–41,
121–35, 151–64, 206–8; M. Miles, *A Different Kind of War* (NY, 1967), pp. 76–8.
• 43. A. Irwin, *Burmese Outpost* (1945); B. Phillipps, *KC8 Burma* (NY, 2000).
• 44. See David Rooney, *Mad Mike. A Life of Michael Calvert* (1996). • 45. Mike
Calvert, *Fighting Mad* (Shrewsbury, 1996), pp. 55–66. • 46. DIV, p. 162. • 47. Calvert,
Fighting Mad, op. cit., p. 77; Mosley, *Gideon*, op. cit., p. 179. • 48. Mike Calvert,
Prisoners of Hope (1971). • 49. Mosley, *Gideon*, op. cit., pp. 180–1. • 50. Sykes,
Wingate, op. cit., p. 364. • 51. Calvert, *Fighting Mad*, op. cit., p. 76, Calvert;
Prisoners of Hope, op. cit. • 52. Sykes, *Wingate*, op. cit., pp. 367–9. • 53. Royle,
Wingate, op. cit., pp. 235–6. • 54. Louis Allen, *Burma. The Longest War 1941–45*
(1984), p. 120. • 55. Bernard Fergusson, *Beyond the Chindwin* (1995), p. 20.

• 56. Bidwell, *Chindit War*, op. cit., p. 25; Tulloch, *Wingate in Peace and War*, op. cit., p. 71. • 57. Calvert, *Prisoners of Hope*, op. cit.; Sykes, *Wingate*, op. cit., p. 371. For these early days of Special Force and the evolution of 77 Indian Brigade into the Chindits see (in great detail) Wo 172/611 and 106/4670. • 58. Royle, *Wingate*, op. cit., p. 238. See also WO 172/2107; 106/46; 106/51. On the more general issues of integrating Asian units see Tarak Barkawi, 'Culture and Combat in the Colonies: the Indian Army in the Second World War', *Journal of Contemporary History* 41 (2006), pp. 325–55. • 59. Calvert, *Fighting Mad*, op. cit., p. 123. • 60. John Connell, *Auchinleck: A Biography of Field-Marshal Sir Claude Auchinleck* (1959), p. 743. • 61. Byron Farwell, *The Gurkhas* (1984), p. 217. • 62. Calvert, *Prisoners of Hope*, op. cit., p. 12. • 63. David Halley, *With Wingate in Burma* (1945), pp. 30–2. • 64. Bernard Fergusson, *Wavell: Portrait of a Soldier* (1961), p. 72. • 65. Sykes, *Wingate*, op. cit., p. 376. • 66. Fergusson, *Beyond the Chindwin*, op. cit., p. 24. • 67. Royle, *Wingate*, op. cit., p. 241. • 68. C.J. Robb, *Wingate's Raiders* (1944), pp. 761–62. • 69. Connell, *Auchinleck*, op. cit. • 70. Royle, *Wingate*, op. cit., p. 244. • 71. Bidwell, *Chindit War*, op. cit., p. 40. • 71. Bidwell, *Chindit War* p. 40. • 72. Royle, p. 226. • 73. Rooney, *Wingate* op. cit. p. 76. • 74. ibid. p. 77. • 75. Sykes, p. 378. • 76. ibid. p. 375. • 77. P. Chinney, *March or Die* (1997) p. 29. • 78. Mosley, op. cit. pp. 188–89; J.S.G. Blair, *In Arduis Fidelis* (Edinburgh 1998) p. 358. • 79. John Masters, *The Road Past Mandalay* (1961) p. 157. Virtually identical sentiments were expressed by Terence O'Brien, *Out of the Blue. A Pilot with the Chindwins* (1984), p. 22. • 80. P. Stibbe, *Return via Rangoon* (1995) p. 25. • 81. Latimer, *Burma*, p. 158. • 82. Fergusson, *Beyond the Chindwin*, op. cit. p. 47. • 83. Sykes, p. 379.

Chapter Five   pp. 90–109

• 1. J. Lunt, *Hell of a Licking. The Retreat from Burma 1941–42* (1986), p. 263. • 2. Ronald Lewin, *Slim. The Standard Bearer* (1976), p. 105. • 3. William Fowler, *We Gave Our Today* (2009), p. 85. • 4. M. Maybury, *Heaven Born in Burma. Vol. 2. Flight of the Heaven Born* (Castle Cary, 1985), p. 168; A.J.F. Doulton, *The Fighting Cock* (Aldershot, 1956), pp. 20–1. • 5. Jon Latimer, *Burma. The Forgotten War* (2004), p. 112; Louis Allen, *Burma. The Longest War 1941–45* (1984), pp. 83–5. • 6. DIV, pp. 112–13. • 7. Latimer, *Burma*, op. cit., p. 111. • 8. Mike Calvert, *Fighting Mad* (Shrewsbury, 1996), p. 107. • 9. Roy McKelvie, *The War in Burma* (1948), pp. 44–5. • 10. See, for example, G. Fitzpatrick, *No Mandalay, No Maymyo* (Lewes, 2001), pp. 261–5. • 11. G. Seagrave, *Burma Surgeon Returns* (NY 1946), p. 30. • 12. Barbara Tuchman, *Sand against the Wind* (1971), p. 277. • 13. Ho Y-c, *The Big Circle* (NY, 1948), pp. 23–4. • 14. DIV, p. 114. • 15. R. McKie, *Echoes from Forgotten Wars* (Sydney, 1980). • 16. Patrick Davis, *A Child at Arms* (1970).

• 17. Lewin, *Slim*, op. cit., p. 141. • 18. Stephen Roskill, *The War at Sea* (1961), ii, p. 30. • 19. G. Moorehouse, *India Britannica* (1983), p. 242. • 20. Peter Clarke, *The Cripps Version. The Life of Sir Stafford Cripps 1889–1952* (2002), pp. 292–302. • 21. This issue is dealt with at exhaustive length in Nicholas Mansergh, ed., *Constitutional Relations between Britain and India. The Transfer of Power*, 12 vols. (1982). • 22. Brian Connell, *Wavell, Supreme Commander, 1941–1943* (1969), p. 23. • 23. H. Evans, *Thimmaya of India. A Soldier's Life* (NY, 1960), pp. 180–1; C. Sommerville, *Our War: The British Commonwealth and the Second World War* (1998), pp. 11–12; P. Hart, *At The Sharp End* (Barnsley, 1998), pp. 119–20. • 24. A. Stewart, *The Underrated Enemy. Britain's War with Japan, December 1941–May 1942* (1987), p. 199; DIV, p. 136. • 25. Adrian Fort, *Archibald Wavell* (2009), pp. 302–3. • 26. DIV, p. 137. • 27. Ibid., pp. 142–3. For a detailed examination of these points see T.R. Foreman, *The Jungle, the Japanese and British Commonwealth Armies at War, 1941–45* (2005). • 28. Fowler, *We Gave Our Today*, op. cit., p. 31. • 29. Lunt, *Hell of a Licking*, op. cit., • 30. J. Becka, *The Nationalist Liberation Movement in Burma during the Japanese Occupation Period, 1941–1945* (Prague 1983), pp. 81–101. • 31. F.C. Jones, *Japan's New Order in East Asia: Its Rise and Fall 1937–1945* (NY, 1978), pp. 333–7. • 32. W. Elsbree, *Japan's Role in South East Asian Nationalist Movements, 1940–1945* (Harvard, 1953), pp. 18–41. • 33. For full details see Latimer, *Burma*, op. cit., pp. 133–6. • 34. DIV, p. 151. • 35. Geoffrey Evans, *Slim as Military Commander* (1969), p. 86. • 36. Cecil Beaton, *Far East* (1945), p. 29. • 37. DIV, p. 150. • 38. Allen, *Burma*, op. cit., pp. 94–5. • 39. Ibid., p. 95. • 40. Lewin, *Slim*, op. cit., p. 105. • 41. Robert Lyman, *Slim, Master of War* (2004) p. 75. • 42. Allen, *Burma*, op. cit., p. 97. • 43. DIV, p. 152. • 44. B. Prasad, ed., *The Arakan Operations, 1942–45* (Delhi, 1954), pp. 24–9. • 45. B. Perrett, *Tank Tracks to Rangoon* (1978), p. 80. • 46. Allen, *Burma*, op. cit., p. 106. • 47. 'The conspiracy theorist might conclude that Irwin was quietly lining Slim up to be the scapegoat for the campaign, knowing that disaster was looming.' (Lyman, *Slim*, op. cit., pp. 91–2). • 48. Lewin, *Slim*, op. cit., p. 121. • 49. DIV, pp. 153–4. • 50. Connell, *Wavell*, op. cit., p. 252. • 51. S.W. Kirby, ed., *The War against Japan* (1960), ii, p. 339. • 52. DIV, pp. 155–7. • 53. Prasad, ed. *Arakan Operations*, op. cit., pp. 81–8. • 54. DIV, pp. 159–60. • 55. Quoted in Latimer, *Burma*, op. cit., pp. 148–9. • 56. Allen, *Burma*, op. cit., p. 114. • 57. Lewin, *Slim*, op. cit., pp. 123–4. • 58. Michael Calvert, *Slim* (1973), p. 53. • 59. DIV, p. 161. • 60. Connell, *Wavell*, op. cit., p. 255. • 61. J.S.G. Blair, *In Arduis Fidelis: Centenary History of the Royal Medical Corps* (Edinburgh, 1998), pp. 328–9; G. Armstrong, *The Sparks Fly Upwards* (East Wittering, 1991), pp. 138–40. • 62. Eric Munday, USAAF *Bomber Units Pacific, 1941–45* (1979). • 63. Fowler, *We Gave Our Today*, op. cit., pp. 90–1. • 64. N.R.L. Franks, *Hurricanes over the Arakan* (Wellingborough, 1989), p. 210; M.C. Cotton, *Hurricanes over Burma* (1995), p. 175. • 65. D. Anderson, 'Slim', in John Keegan, *Churchill's Generals* (1991), p. 305. For Slim's own account of Gallabat see his *Unofficial History* (1959), pp. 127–48. • 66. Robert Lyman, *The Generals*, pp. 143–86, esp. pp. 141, 151–2. • 67. Ibid., p. 148. • 68. Lyman, *Slim*, op. cit., p. 75. • 69. George MacDonald Fraser, *Quartered Safe Out Here* (1992), pp. 35–6. • 70. Fowler, *We Gave Our Today*, op. cit., p. 8. • 71. Ibid., pp. 8–9. • 72. Evans, *Slim*, op. cit., p. 27; Michael Carver, ed., *The War Lords: Military Commanders of the Twentieth Century* (1976), p. 377. • 73. Lyman, *Slim*, op. cit., p. 2. • 74. DIV, p. 164. • 75. Lyman, *Slim*, op. cit., p. 5. • 76. R. Lewin, *The Chief* (1980), pp. 215–20; Arthur Bryant, *The Turn of the Tide* (1956), p. 624. • 77. DIV, p. 121. • 78. John Marsh, ed., *Alexander. The Memoirs 1940–1945* (1962), p. 92; Nigel Nicolson, *Alex: The Life of Field-Marshal Earl Alexander of Tunis* (1973), p. 137; Lunt, *Hell of a Licking*, op. cit., p. 160; W.G.R. Jackson, *Alexander as Military Commander* (1971). • 79. J. Hedley, *Jungle Fighter* (Brighton, 1996), p. 26. • 80. DIV, p. 119; Lunt, *Hell of a Licking*, op. cit., p. xviii.

Chapter Six   pp. 110–134

• 1. David Rooney, *Stilwell* (1971), pp. 40–1. • 2. SP, p. 119. • 3. C.T. Liang, *General Stilwell in China* (NY, 1972), p. 44. • 4. Barbara Tuchman, *Sand against the Wind* (1971). • 5. The probability is that Chiang knew only too well but shut his eyes and ears to inconvenient truths. His champion, Taylor, exposes his breathtakingly ostrich-like approach to the graft, peculation and racketeering of the KMT regime: 'Corruption, he believed was a problem best addressed in a fundamental way once peace and unity had been secured': Jay Taylor, *The Generalissimo* (Harvard, 2009), p. 222. • 6. SP, p. 122. • 7. Ibid., p. 123. • 8. Tuchman, *Sand against the Wind*, op. cit., p. 307. • 9. Ibid., p. 262. • 10. Ibid., pp. 260, 263. • 11. For Clarence Gauss see John L. Durrence, 'Ambassador Clarence E. Gauss and US relations with China, 1941–1944', PhD thesis, University of Georgia, 1971. • 12. Hannah Pakula, *The Last Empress* (2010), pp. 365, 379, 417, 420, 422, 432, 435, 437–8. • 13. John Morton Blum, *From the Morgenthau Diaries. Years of War 1941–1945* (Boston, 1967), pp. 87–102; John Morton Blum, *Roosevelt and Morgenthau* (Boston, 1970), pp. 269, 463–79. • 14. Henry L. Stimson & McGeorge Bundy, *On Active Service in Peace and War* (NY, 1949), p. 299. • 15. SP, p. 122. • 16. Ibid., pp. 124–6. • 17. Tuchman, *Sand against the Wind*, op. cit., p. 309. • 18. C.F. Romanus & R. Sunderland, *Stilwell's Mission to China* (Washington DC, 1953), pp. 104–8. • 19. See Thomas M. Coffery, *Hap. The Story of the US Air Force and the Man Who Built It* (1982); Bernard C. Nalty, *Winged Shield, Winged Sword. A History of the US Air Force* (1997). • 20. Tuchman, *Sand against the Wind*, op. cit., pp. 310–11. • 21. Jon Latimer, *Burma. The Forgotten War* (2004), p. 127. Stilwell also resented the switch of airpower to the Middle East (SP, p. 126). • 22. SP, p. 127. • 23. Ibid.,

p. 128. • 24. Ibid., p. 129. • 25. Tuchman, *Sand against the Wind*, op. cit., p. 313. • 26. SP, p. 129. Hopkins disliked Stilwell, manipulated as he was by T.V. Soong (Pakula, *Last Empress*, op. cit., p. 413). • 27. Romanus & Sunderland, *Stilwell's Mission*, op. cit., pp. 104–8. • 28. 'Reconquest of Burma, July 1942–June 1943', CAB 121/681. • 29. SP, p. 132. • 30. Romanus & Sunderland, *Stilwell's Mission*, op. cit., pp. 227–8. • 31. See Roger Sandilands, *The Life and Political Economy of Lauchlin Currie* (Duke, NC, 1990); John E. Haynes & Harvey Klehr, *Venona: Decoding Soviet Espionage in America* (Yale, 2000). • 32. Tuchman, *Sand against the Wind*, op. cit., p. 324. Currie strongly disliked Stilwell (Pakula, *Last Empress*, op. cit., pp. 396, 402). • 33. SP, pp. 135–6. • 34. See Ross Y. Koen, *The China Lobby in American Politics* (NY, 1974). • 35. SP, p. 133. • 36. Ibid., p. 131. • 37. Gauss was an important diplomat with twenty years' experience of China. See John S. Service, *The Amerasia Papers: some problems in the history of US–China relations* (1971); Paul A. Varg, *The Closing of the Door. Sino–American Relations 1936–1946* (NY, 1973). For particular episodes when Gauss made an anti-Chiang intervention or recommendation to his superiors in Washington see Robert Dallek, *Franklin D. Roosevelt and American Foreign Policy 1932–1945* (1995), p. 489; Akira Iriye, *Power and Culture. The Japanese–American War 1941–1945* (1981), p. 156. • 38. Tuchman, *Sand against the Wind*, op. cit., p. 320. For other critiques of KMT corruption see T. White & A. Jacoby, *Thunder out of China* (NY, 1946); pp. 105, 140, 170, 178, 187–8, 256; George H. Kerr, *Formosa Betrayed* (Boston, 1965). • 39. The British even disliked the training of the Chinese at Ramgarh (WO 106/3547). For an American view of Ramgarh see MP, iii, pp. 384–5, 393–4. The Chinese army at Ramgarh was so impressive that Taylor (*Generalissimo*, op. cit., p. 253, momentarily forgets his defence of Chiang, right or wrong: 'The Chinese Army in India . . . numbered some 30,000, all healthy and each carrying a modern weapon – a unique experience for a Chinese army.' Why was this, pray, if the KMT was not corrupt and Chiang always a peerless leader? •40. SP, pp. 137–8. • 41. See Jung Chang & Jon Halliday, *Madame Sun Yat-sen* (1986); Israel Epstein, *Woman in World History: The Life and Times of Soong Ching-Ling* (1993); Sterling Seagrave, *The Soong Dynasty* (1996). • 42. White & Jacoby, *Thunder out of China*, op. cit., p. 154. • 43. SP, pp. 140–2. • 44. Tuchman, *Sand against the Wind*, op. cit., pp. 326–31. • 45. Ibid., p. 364. • 46. F.F. Lin, *A Military History of Modern China* (Princeton, 1956), p. 137. • 47. John King Fairbank, Albert Feuerwerker, et al., eds., *Cambridge History of China* (1986), p. 575. • 48. Tuchman, *Sand against the Wind*, op. cit., p. 265. • 49. Ibid; see also Liang, *General Stilwell in China*, op. cit., pp. 129–32; Eric Larrabee, *Commander in Chief* (1987), p. 562. • 50. Rooney, *Stilwell*, op. cit., p. 64. • 51. Lin, *Military History*, op. cit. • 52. DIV, p. 144. • 53. F. Eldridge, *Wrath in Burma. The Uncensored Story of General Stilwell and International Maneuvers in the Far East* (NY, 1946), p. 146. • 54. SP, pp. 121–2. • 55. Ibid., pp. 143–50. • 56. Ibid., pp. 153–4. • 57. William Manchester, *The*

Glory and the Dream. A Narrative History of America, 1932–1972 (1974), p. 226.
For the entire convoluted Wilkie story see Ellsworth Barnard, *Wendell Wilkie, Fighter for Freedom* (NY, 1966); Steve Neal, *Dark Horse. A Biography of Wendell Wilkie* (1989); Charles Peters, *Five Days in Philadelphia: 1940, Wendell Wilkie and the Political Conventions that Freed Franklin Delano Roosevelt to Win World War Two* (NY, 2006). • 58. For the Wilkie tour of China see Gardner Cowles, *Mike Looks Back* (NY, 1985), pp. 65–89; Graham Park, *Two Kinds of Time* (Boston, 1950), pp. 429–30; Pakula, *Last Empress*, op. cit., pp. 405–12. • 59. Cowles, *Mike Looks Back*, op. cit., p. 90; Pakula, *Last Empress*, op. cit., pp. 433–4. • 60. Tuchman, *Sand against the Wind*, op. cit., p. 337. For Chennault's side of the story see his *Way of a Fighter* (NY, 1949), pp. 212–16. • 61. SP, pp. 157–9. • 62. Tuchman, *Sand against the Wind*, op. cit., p. 338. • 63. SP, pp. 159, 161. • 64. Ibid., p. 161. • 65. Ibid., p. 162. • 66. Latimer, *Burma*, op. cit., p. 130. • 67. Michael Howard, *Grand Strategy* (1972), iv, pp. 39–91. • 68. J.W. Dunn, 'The Ledo Road', in B.W. Fowle, ed., *Builders and Fighters. US Engineers in World War Two* (Virginia, 1992), p. 329. • 69. L. Anders, *The Ledo Road. General Joseph W. Stilwell's Highway to China* (Norman, OK, 1965), pp. 37–41. • 70. C.F. Romanus & R. Sunderland, *Stilwell's Command Problems* (Washington, 1956), p. 10. • 71. SP, p. 164. • 72. Eldridge, *Wrath in Burma*, op. cit., p. 149. • 73. SP, p. 165. • 74. Tuchman, *Sand against the Wind*, op. cit., p. 344. • 75. Ibid. Madame Chiang was given the codename 'Snow White' by the US Secret Service: Pakula, *Last Empress*, op. cit., p. 415. • 76. SP, p. 167. • 77. For Madame's visit to the USA see Pakula, *Last Empress*, op. cit., pp. 412–42. • 78. Romanus & Sunderland, *Stilwell's Mission*, op. cit., p. 244. • 79. SP, p. 171. • 80. Latimer, *Burma*, op. cit., pp. 131, 464. • 81. Tuchman, *Sand against the Wind*, op. cit., p. 345. • 82. SP, pp. 172–5. • 83. Romanus & Sunderland, *Stilwell's Mission*, op. cit., p. 244. In order not to complicate an already fiendishly complex story I omit the detail of the mission sent to Chiang after conferring with Wavell. This consisted of Hap Arnold, General Brehon Somervell and British Field Marshal Dill. By common consent it was the master diplomat Dill who persuaded Chiang to sign up to ANAKIM: H.H. Arnold, *Global Mission* (NY, 1949), pp. 407–27; MP, iii, pp. 584–6. • 84. Ibid., p. 259. • 85. Liang, *General Stilwell in China*, op. cit., p. 104. • 86. SP, pp. 176–9.

Chapter Seven   pp. 136–158

• 1. David Rooney, *Wingate and the Chindits* (1994), pp. 77–8; 82; WO 203/2082–2084; 172/611. • 2. John Bierman & C. Smith, *Fire in the Night. Wingate of Burma, Ethiopia and Zion* (2001), p. 234; WO 203/4376. • 3. Bierman & Smith, *Fire in the Night*, op. cit., p. 265. • 4. Mike Calvert, *Fighting Mad* (Shrewsbury, 1996), p. 134; Ronald Lewin, *The Chief. Field-Marshal Lord Wavell*.

Commander-in-Chief and Viceroy 1939–1947 (1980), pp. 207–8. • 5. Christopher Sykes, Orde Wingate (1959), pp. 379–81. • 6. Leonard Mosley, Gideon Goes to War (1955), pp. 190–1. • 7. Sykes, Wingate, op. cit., pp. 384–5; B. Prasad, ed., Reconquest of Burma (Delhi, 1958), i, p. 99. • 8. Louis Allen, Burma. The Longest War 1941–45 (1984), p. 126. • 9. Bernard Fergusson, Beyond the Chindwin (1995), p. 59; Mosley, Gideon, op. cit., pp. 193–4; Sykes, Wingate, op. cit., pp. 386–7; Allen, Burma, op. cit., p. 126. • 10. Bierman & Smith, Fire in the Night, op. cit., p. 271. See also Simon James Angrim, 'Orde Wingate and the British Army', PhD thesis, University of Wales, 2007, Chapter Seven. • 11. C.J. Rolo, Wingate's Raiders (1944), p. 61; Fergusson, Beyond the Chindwin, op. cit., pp. 58–9; CAB 106/204. • 12. Rolo, Wingate's Raiders, op. cit. pp. 47–52. • 13. Sykes, Wingate, op. cit., pp. 390–1. • 14. P. Stibbe, Return via Rangoon (1995), p. 51; D. Halley, With Wingate in Burma (1945), p. 54. • 15. Prasad, ed., Reconquest of Burma, op. cit., i, p. 107. • 16. WO 106/4670. • 17. Fergusson, Beyond the Chindwin, op. cit. • 18. Ibid. • 19. Sykes, Wingate, op. cit., p. 394. • 20. Ibid, p. 396. • 21. Stibbe, Return via Rangoon, op. cit., p. 78. • 22. WO 106/4827. • 23. P.D. Chinnery, March or Die (Shrewsbury, 1997), pp. 38–42; Jon Latimer, Burma. The Forgotten War (2004), p. 162. • 24. Sykes, Wingate, op. cit., p. 403. • 25. Ibid. • 26. David Rooney, Mad Mike. A Life of Michael Calvert (1996), passim. • 27. H. James, Across the Threshold of Battle (Lewes, 1993), p. 90. • 28. Fergusson, Beyond the Chindwin, op. cit., p. 101; Bernard Fergusson, The Trumpet in the Hall 1930–1958 (1970), p. 148; Chinnery, March or Die, op. cit., pp. 44–5. • 29. Sykes, Wingate, op. cit., pp. 405–6. • 30. Allen, Burma, op. cit., pp. 133–5. • 31. Sykes, Wingate, op. cit., p. 405; WO 203/5953. • 32. Fergusson, Beyond the Chindwin, op. cit., p. 101; Fergusson, Trumpet in the Hall, op. cit., p. 350. • 33. Calvert, Fighting Mad, op. cit., pp. 134–7. There is considerable controversy about the fate of the wounded. Allen, Burma, op. cit., p. 133, says the Japanese responded to this appeal to their honour. But Donovan Webster, The Burma Road (2004), p. 99, says: 'The soldiers abandoned on that island were never heard from again. Their loss haunted Mike Calvert to the day he died.' • 34. Sykes, Wingate, op. cit., p. 410. • 35. Derek Tulloch, Wingate in Peace and War (1972), p. 66; Calvert, Fighting Mad, op. cit., p. 85. • 36. Mike Calvert, Prisoners of Hope (1971), p. 16; Calvert, Fighting Mad, op. cit., p. 139. • 37. Prasad, ed., Reconquest of Burma, i, p. 122; James, Across the Threshold of Battle, op. cit., p. 122. • 38. Rolo, Wingate's Raiders, op. cit., p. 113. • 39. Prasad, ed., Reconquest of Burma, op. cit., i, p. 130. • 40. Sykes, Wingate, op. cit., p. 411. • 41. Bierman & Smith, Fire in the Night, op. cit., pp. 286–7. • 42. Trevor Royle, Orde Wingate (1995), p. 251; WO 172/2107. • 43. Sykes, Wingate, op. cit., pp. 414–15. • 44. Bierman & Smith, Fire in the Night, op. cit., pp. 286–7. • 45. Latimer, Burma, op. cit., pp. 164, 472. • 46. Fergusson, Beyond the Chindwin, op. cit., p. 143. • 47. Sykes, Wingate, op. cit., pp. 416–17. • 48. Allen, Burma, op. cit., p. 139. • 49. Fergusson, Beyond the Chindwin, op. cit., p. 151. • 50. Prasad, ed.,

Reconquest of Burma, op. cit., i, p. 127. • 51. Fergusson, *Trumpet in the Hall*, op. cit., p. 158. • 52. Fergusson, *Beyond the Chindwin*, op. cit., pp. 153–4; WO 106/4670. • 53. Allen, *Burma*, op. cit., p. 142. • 54. J.P. Cross & B. Gurung, eds., *Gurkhas at War* (2000), p. 73; R. Painter, *A Signal Honour. With the Chindits and the 14th Army in Burma* (1999), p. 55; P. Narain, *Subedor to Field-Marshal* (New Delhi, 1999), p. 171. • 55. Bierman & Smith, *Fire in the Night*, op. cit., pp. 299–301. • 56. Sykes, *Wingate*, op. cit., pp. 422–4. • 57. Ibid., p. 424. • 58. W.G. Burchett, *Wingate's Phantom Army* (Bombay, 1944) pp. 154–6. • 59. Rolo, *Wingate's Raiders*, op. cit., pp. 119–45. • 60. Sykes, *Wingate*, op. cit., p. 426. • 61. Allen, *Burma*, op. cit., pp. 144–5. • 62. Sykes, *Wingate*, op. cit., pp. 429–30. • 63. Rolo, *Wingate's Raiders*, op. cit., pp. 47–52; Burchett, *Wingate's Phantom Army*, op. cit., pp. 154–56. • 64. Julian Thompson, *The Imperial War Museum Book of War Behind Enemy Lines* (1998), pp. 142, 157. • 65. Fergusson, *Beyond the Chindwin*, op. cit., p. 142. • 66. Allen, *Burma*, op. cit., p. 138. • 67. Bierman & Smith, *Fire in the Night*, op. cit., pp. 288–9; Tulloch, *Wingate in Peace and War*, op. cit., p. 85. • 68. Sykes, *Wingate*, op. cit., p. 432; Royle, *Wingate*, op. cit., p. 253. • 69. Prasad, ed., *Reconquest of Burma*, op. cit., i, p. 136; G.R. Stevens, *History of the 2nd King Edward VII's Own Goorkha Rifles* (Aldershot, 1952), iii, p. 231; CAB 106/41; WO/203/5954; 203/25. • 70. DIV, p. 162. • 71. Burchett, *Wingate's Phantom Army*, op. cit., p. 180. • 72. Fergusson, *Beyond the Chindwin*, op. cit., p. 240. • 73. Allen, *Burma*, op. cit., p. 147. • 74. Michael Howard, *Grand Strategy* (1972), iv, p. 548. • 75. Bierman & Smith, *Fire in the Night*, op. cit., p. 308.

Chapter Eight   pp. 159–182

• 1. SP, pp. 185–6. • 2. Barbara Tuchman, *Sand against the Wind* (1971), p. 348. • 3. SP, pp. 180–1; Hannah Pakula, *The Last Empress* (2010), pp. 425–6. • 4. See Warren F. Kimball, *The Juggler. Franklin Roosevelt as Wartime Statesman* (Princeton, 1991), pp. 139–43; Keith Sainsbury, *Churchill and Roosevelt at War* (1994), pp. 160–78; David Stafford, *Roosevelt and Churchill. Men of Secrets* (1999), pp. 249–63. • 5. Tuchman, *Sand against the Wind*, op. cit., p. 355; Paul Fussell, *Wartime* (NY, 1989), pp. 161–2. • 6. C.F. Romanus & R. Sunderland, *Stilwell's Mission to China* (Washington DC, 1953), p. 270. • 7. Arthur Bryant, *The Turn of the Tide* (1956), p. 494. • 8. Thomas M. Coffery, *Hap* (NY, 1982) op. cit.; H.H. Arnold, *Global Mission* (NY, 1949), pp. 407–27. • 9. Tuchman, *Sand against the Wind*, op. cit., p. 357. • 10. SP, p. 190; Tuchman, *Sand against the Wind*, op. cit., p. 358. • 11. Tuchman, *Sand against the Wind*, op. cit., pp. 359–61. • 12. Romanus & Sunderland, *Stilwell's Mission*, op. cit., pp. 279–82; Jay Taylor, *The Generalissimo* (Harvard, 2009) pp. 227–8. • 13. SP, pp. 191–6. • 14. David Rooney, *Stilwell* (1971), p. 80. • 15. Marshall's consistent checkmating of Chennault can be followed in great detail in MP, iii, pp. 502–3, 641–3, 672–6. • 16. Tuchman, *Sand against the Wind*, op. cit., p. 368. • 17. Ibid., p. 269. • 18. Robert E. Sherwood, *Roosevelt and Hopkins* (NY, 1948), p. 716. • 19. Rooney, *Stilwell*, op. cit., pp. 80–2. • 20. MP, iii, pp. 674–5; Romanus & Sunderland, *Stilwell's Mission*, op. cit., p. 323. Predictably, the violently anti-Stilwell Taylor makes great play of the general's lacklustre performace in Washington: Taylor, *Generalissimo*, op. cit., p. 231. • 21. Claire Lee Chennault, *Way of a Fighter* (NY, 1949), p. 220. • 22. Tuchman, *Sand against the Wind*, op. cit., pp. 369–73. • 23. Alanbrooke Diaries, p. 403. • 24. Sherwood, *Roosevelt and Hopkins*, op. cit., p. 958. • 25. SP, p. 198. • 26. Ibid., p. 200. • 27. Ibid. • 28. Ibid., pp. 201–2. • 29. Tuchman, *Sand against the Wind*, op. cit., pp. 379–81. • 30. Ibid., pp. 378, 381. • 31. SP, pp. 204, 206. • 32. Ibid., p. 206. • 33. Tuchman, *Sand against the Wind*, op. cit., p. 377. • 34. William R. Pears & Dean Brelis, *Behind the Burma Road* (Boston, 1963), pp. 107–9; F. Eldridge, *Wrath in Burma* (NY, 1946), pp. 174–6. The corruption on the Hump and the Burma Road was egregious even by Kuomintang standards. Sixteen different Chinese agencies supervised the arriving Lend-Lease materiel, all the directors of which had been appointed by nepotism. Much of the supplies simply did not arrive, being appropriated by the KMT 'rake-off'. One estimate was that for every 14,000 tons that left India and Burma, only 5,000 tons reached China. When American journalists tried to report this, Roosevelt made sure the reports were suppressed: Leland Stowe, *They Shall Not Sleep* (1945), pp. 74–7. • 35. Tuchman, *Sand against the Wind*, op. cit., p. 377. • 36. Donovan Webster, *The Burma Road* (2004), p. 128. • 37. Eric Sevareid, *Not So Wild A Dream* (NY, 1976), p. 247; Don Moser, *China, Burma, India* (1978), p. 84. • 38. Tuchman, *Sand against the Wind*, op. cit., p. 365. • 39. W.S. Churchill, *The Second World War* (1950), v, pp. 560–1. • 40. Webster, *Burma Road*, op. cit., p. 149. • 41. DIV, p. 249. • 42. Richard Rhodes-James, *Chindit* (1980), p. 77; David Rooney, *Wingate and the Chindits* (1994), pp. 131–5, 174; Shelford Bidwell, *The Chindit War* (1979), p. 207. • 43. Christopher Sykes, *Orde Wingate* (1959), pp. 433–9. • 44. Trevor Royle, *Orde Wingate* (1995), pp. 259–62. • 45. Churchill, *Second World War*, op. cit., v. • 46. Leonard Mosley, *Gideon Goes to War* (1955), p. 211. • 47. Alanbrooke Diaries, p. 436. • 48. Sykes, *Wingate*, op. cit., p. 451. • 49. Alanbrooke Diaries, pp. 438–9. • 50. Ibid., pp. 438, 441. On the floods see Wavell to War Office, 17 August 1943, WO 106/3810. • 51. Derek Tulloch, *Wingate in Peace and War* (1972), pp. 114–25; Alanbrooke Diaries, p. 443. • 52. Auchinleck memo, 19 August 1943, WO 203/5214; cf. also John Connell, *Auchinleck* (1959), pp. 743–5. • 53. Kirby to Alanbrooke, 3 April 1959, CAB 101/82. • 54. Sykes, *Wingate*, op. cit., pp. 460–1; WO 203/5213; 172/2658; 172/4261–4277 • 55. Mosley, *Gideon*, op. cit., p. 213. • 56. Sykes, *Wingate*, op. cit., p. 468. • 57. Ibid., p. 472. • 58. Royle, *Wingate*, op. cit., pp. 274, 277. • 59. Sykes, *Wingate*, op. cit., pp. 473–4. • 60. Royle, *Wingate*, op. cit., p. 276. • 61. Mosley, *Gideon*, op. cit., pp. 220–2. • 62. Robert

Lyman, *Slim, Master of War* (2004), p. 121. • 63. Ibid. • 64. DIV, pp. 182–7.
• 65. Ibid., p. 188. • 66. A.J. Barker, *The March on Delhi* (1963), p. 75. • 67. M.R.
Roberts, *Golden Arrow. The Story of the 7th Indian Division in the Second World
War* (Aldershot, 1952), p. 12; H. Maule, *Spearhead General. The Epic Story of
General Sir Frank Messervy and his men at Eritrea, North Africa and Burma* (1961),
p. 225. • 68. A. Brett-James, *Report My Signals* (1948), p. 81. • 69. Lyman, *Slim*,
op. cit., pp. 125, 281. • 70. A. Brett-James, *Ball of Fire* (Aldershot, 1951), p. 252.
• 71. Messervy's biography is Maule, *Spearhead General*, op. cit. • 72. DIV,
pp. 170–1. • 73. Connell, *Auchinleck*, op. cit., pp. 735–6. • 74. DIV, pp. 172–6.
• 75. Ibid., p. 177. • 76. J.S.G. Blair, *In Arduis Fidelis* (Edinburgh, 1998), pp. 328–9;
F.A.E. Crew, *The Army Medical Services: Campaigns. Vol. 5 Burma* (1966), pp. 122–3;
S.W. Kirby, ed., *The War Against Japan* (1961), iii, pp. 32–3; G. Armstrong, *The
Sparks Fly Upwards* (East Wittering, 1991), pp. 138–40. • 77. DIV, pp. 178–80.

Chapter Nine   pp. 183–208

• 1. A.N. Wilson, *After the Victorians* (2005), pp. 493–4. • 2. Philip Ziegler,
Mountbatten (1985), pp. 126–7. • 3. Ibid., p. 146. • 4. Ibid., p. 172. • 5. Ibid., p. 146.
• 6. C.P. Stacey, *Official History of the Canadian Army in the Second World War*
(Ottawa, 1966), i, pp. 340–99. • 7. Julian Thompson, *The Royal Marines* (2001),
pp. 263–9. • 8. This issue and all others concerning Dieppe is examined
exhaustively in Brian Loring Villa, *Unauthorised Action. Mountbatten and the
Dieppe Raid* (Toronto, 1989). • 9. Nigel Hamilton, *Monty. The Making of a General*
(1981), pp. 547–56. • 10. R. Lyman, *The Generals* (2005), p. 190. • 11. Alanbrooke
Diaries, pp. 242, 357, 388. • 12. This was the operation Mountbatten dubbed
'Habbakuk' (ibid., p. 438). • 13. Ibid., pp. 445–6. • 14. Ibid., pp. 400–1. • 15. David
Faber, *Speaking for England: Leo, Julian and John Amery: The Tragedy of a Political
Family* (2005), pp. 374–76. • 16. Victoria Schofield, *Wavell. Soldier and Statesman*
(2006), p. 279; Arthur Bryant, *The Turn of the Tide* (1956), p. 612. • 17. Trevor
Royle, *Orde Wingate* (1995), p. 270. • 18. For American opposition to Sholto
Douglas and enthusiasm for Tedder see Forrest Pogue, *George C. Marshall.
Organizer of Victory 1943–1945* (1973), p. 258. For all the rejected candidates see
John J. Sbrega, 'Anglo-American Relations and the Selection of Mountbatten
as Supreme Allied Commander, South East Asia', *Military Affairs* 46 (1982),
pp. 139–45. For FDR's dislike of Sholto Douglas see Pogue, *Organizer of Victory*,
op. cit., p. 259. Tedder has had several biographies. See Vincent Orange,
Tedder (2004); Roderick Owen, *Tedder* (1952). Sholto Douglas has fared less
well, but see K. Probert, *High Commanders of the RAF* (1991). • 19. Oliver
Warner, *Cunningham of Hyndhope* (1967), p. 222; cf. also Michael Simpson, *A
Life of Admiral of the Fleet Andrew Cunningham* (2004); John Winton,

Cunningham. *The Greatest Admiral since Nelson* (1998); Stephen Roskill, *Churchill and the Admirals* (1977). • 20. Wilson was described by Richard Mead in *Churchill's Generals* (2007), p. 496, as 'sound but not spectacular'. His own account of these years is in *Eight Years Overseas, 1939–1947* (1948). • 21. Anthony Eden, *The Reckoning* (1965), p. 404. • 22. Ronald Lewin, *Churchill as Warlord* (1973), p. 214. • 23. Alanbrooke Diaries, p. 437; Bryant, *Turn of the Tide*, op. cit., p. 693. • 24. Ziegler, *Mountbatten*, op. cit., p. 220. • 25. John Connell, *Auchinleck* (1959), pp. 749–51; Ziegler, *Mountbatten*, op. cit., p. 222. • 26. Alanbrooke Diaries, p. 441. For Churchill's earlier promises see pp. 420, 427, 429. • 27. John Harvey, ed., *The War Diaries of Oliver Harvey* (1978), p. 286. • 28. Elliott Roosevelt, *As He Saw It* (NY, 1946), pp. 71–2. • 29. H.G. Nicholas, *Washington Despatches* (1981), pp. 248–52. • 30. Peter Lyon, *Eisenhower, Portrait of a Hero* (NY, 1974), p. 69. • 31. Albert Wedemeyer, *Wedemeyer Reports!* (NY, 1958), pp. 136, 250, 273. • 32. Michael Gannon, *Operation Drumbeat* (NY, 1991), p. 168. • 33. See Thomas B. Buell, *Master of Sea Power. A Biography of Fleet Admiral Ernest J. King* (Annapolis, 1995); John Lehmann, *On Seas of Glory: Heroic Men, Great Ships and Epic Battles of the American Navy* (NY, 2002). See also John Ray Skates, *The Invasion of Japan. Alternatives to the Bomb* (SC, 2000). • 34. Alanbrooke Diaries, p. 359; Pogue, *Organizer of Victory*, op. cit., p. 305. • 35. Buell, *Master of Sea Power*, op. cit., p. 487. • 36. Ziegler, *Mountbatten*, op. cit., p. 217. • 37. Ibid. pp. 223–4. • 38. Alanbrooke Diaries, pp. 451–2. • 39. SP, p. 209. • 40. Ziegler, *Mountbatten*, op. cit., p. 235. • 41. Philip Mason, *A Shaft of Sunlight* (1978), pp. 177–8. • 42. Philip Ziegler, ed., *Personal Diary of Admiral The Lord Louis Mountbatten, Supreme Allied Commander, South East Asia, 1943–1946* (1988), p. 6 (hereinafter Mountbatten Diary). • 43. Brian Bond, ed., *Chief of Staff: The Diaries of Lieutenant-General Sir Henry Pownall. Vol. 2 1940–1944* (1974), pp. 110–11 (hereinafter Pownall Diaries). • 44. Connell, *Auchinleck*, op. cit., p. 762. • 45. Pendell Moon, ed., *The Viceroy's Journal* (1973), p. 15. • 46. Mountbatten Diary, pp. 7–8; Wedemeyer, *Wedemeyer Reports!*, op. cit., p. 252. • 47. Pownall Diaries, p. 117. • 48. Roger Parkinson, *The Auk* (1977), p. 245. • 49. Ziegler, *Mountbatten*, op. cit., pp. 231–4. • 50. Bryant, *Turn of the Tide*, op. cit., p. 693; Lewin, *Churchill as Warlord*, op. cit., p. 214; Eden, *Reckoning*, op. cit., p. 404. • 51. Moon, ed., *Viceroy's Journal*, op. cit., p. 15. • 52. Wedemeyer, *Wedemeyer Reports*, op. cit., p. 255. • 53. Pownall Diaries, 11 March 1944. • 54. Ziegler, *Mountbatten*, op. cit., pp. 239–40. • 55. Mountbatten Diary, p. 8. • 56. Ziegler, *Mountbatten*, op. cit., p. 212. • 57. SP, p. 218; Mountbatten Diary, p. 10. • 58. Donovan Webster, *The Burma Road* (2004), pp. 271–2. • 59. Barbara Tuchman, *Sand against the Wind* (1971), p. 385. • 60. Ibid. • 61. Webster, *Burma Road*, op. cit., p. 147. • 62. This section is based on knowledge gleaned from the following sources: Daniel Marston, *The Pacific War Companion: From Pearl Harbor to Honolulu* (2005); John H. Bradley, Thomas B. Buell & Thomas E. Griers, eds., *The Second World War: Asia and the Pacific* (2003). • 63. F. Eldridge,

Wrath in Burma (NY, 1946), p. 200. • 64. Pownall Diaries, p. 139. • 65. Alanbrooke Diaries, p. 404. • 66. SP, p. 211. • 67. MP, iv, pp. 158–9. • 68. Ibid., iv, pp. 135, 139, 200; C.F. Romanus and R. Sunderland, *Stilwell's Personal File. China-Burma-India 1942–1944*, 5 vols. (Wilmington, Del., 1976), iii, 950. • 69. Jay Taylor, *The Generalissimo* (Harvard, 2009), p. 239. • 70. Tuchman, *Sand against the Wind*, op. cit., pp. 389–92; Hannah Pakula, *The Last Empress* (2010), pp. 462–5. • 71. SP, p. 217. • 72. Hsi-heng Ch'i, *Nationalist China at War: Military Defeats and Political Collapse* (Ann Arbor, Mich., 1982), pp. 113–14. Taylor, *Generalissimo*, op. cit., p. 256, notes the attempted coup but quickly moves on. Once again, he cannot explain why, if Chiang was a peerless leader and there was no corruption in KMT China, there should have been a coup attempt in the first place. • 73. Joseph W. Alsop, *I've Seen the Best* (NY, 1992), pp. 224–5. • 74. SP, pp. 213–20. • 75. Mountbatten Diary, p. 12. • 76. SP, p. 218. • 77. Ibid., p. 220. • 78. Tuchman, *Sand against the Wind*, op. cit., p. 394. • 79. Ziegler, *Mountbatten*, op. cit., p. 244. • 80. SP, p. 221. • 81. Ziegler, *Mountbatten*, op. cit., p. 245. • 82. Mountbatten Diary, p. 13. • 83. Tuchman, *Sand against the Wind*, op. cit., p. 395. • 84. Ziegler, *Mountbatten*, op. cit., p. 243. • 85. Mountbatten Diary, p. 11. • 86. Ibid., p. 15. • 87. Ziegler, *Mountbatten*, op. cit., p. 245. • 88. Mountbatten Diary, pp. 16–17. • 89. Pownall Diaries, p. 116. • 90. Elliott Roosevelt, ed., *The Personal Letters of Franklin Delano Roosevelt*, 2 vols. (NY, 1950), ii, p. 1468. • 91. Ziegler, *Mountbatten*, op. cit., p. 247. • 92. SP, p. 223. • 93. Ibid., p. 222; Mountbatten Diary, p. 21. • 94. SP, p. 222; Tuchman, *Sand against the Wind*, op. cit., p. 396.

Chapter Ten   pp. 209–231

• 1. DIV, p. 169. • 2. Mountbatten Diary, p. 19. • 3. Robert Lyman, *The Generals* (2005), pp. 211–16. • 4. DIV, pp. 192, 202. • 5. David Rooney, *Wingate and the Chindits* (1994), p. 211. • 6. DIV, pp. 202–3; Lyman, *Generals*, op. cit., p. 205. • 7. Ronald Lewin, *Slim. The Standard Bearer* (1976), pp. 128–9. • 8. DIV, pp. 199–201. • 9. Lewin, *Slim*, op. cit., p. 132. • 10. Michael Howard, *Grand Strategy* (1972), iii; p. 578. • 11. S.W. Kirby, ed., *The War against Japan. The Decisive Battles* (1961), Appendix 3. • 12. Lewin, *Slim*, op. cit., p. 129. • 13. Mountbatten Diary, pp. 22–3. • 14. Ibid., pp. 27–8; Christopher Sykes, *Orde Wingate* (1959), pp. 476–81. • 15. Barbara Tuchman, *Sand against the Wind* (1971), p. 397. • 16. Robert Dallek, *Franklin Roosevelt and American Foreign Policy, 1932–1945* (Oxford, 1979), pp. 406–41. • 17. See Don Lohbeck, *Patrick J. Hurley* (Chicago, 1956); Russell D. Buhite, *Patrick J. Hurley and American Foreign Policy* (Ithaca, NY, 1973). For his rigidly anti-Communist and pro-Chiang posture see T. White & A. Jacoby, *Thunder out of China* (NY, 1946) pp. 199, 208–11, 249–52; Michael Schaller, *The United States and China in the Twentieth Century* (NY, 1979), p. 99.

For Hurley's errands for FDR see Lohbeck, *Patrick J. Hurley*, op. cit., pp. 15–86, 159–64. • 18. Tuchman, *Sand against the Wind*, op. cit., p. 397. • 19. SP, p. 226. • 20. Ibid., p. 224. • 21. Ibid., p. 227. • 22. Tuchman, *Sand against the Wind*, op. cit. • 23. Ibid. • 24. Brian Crozier, *The Man Who Lost China* (1976), p. 249. • 25. Hannah Pakula, *The Last Empress* (2010), p. 469. • 26. Harold Macmillan, *The Blast of War* (NY, 1967), p. 357. • 27. C.F. Romanus & R. Sunderland, *Stilwell's Mission to China* (Washington DC, 1953), pp. 56–7, 352. • 28. Alanbrooke Diaries, p. 477. • 29. Mountbatten Diaries, p. 31. • 30. Arthur Bryant, *Triumph in the West* (1959), p. 44. • 31. W.S. Churchill, *The Second World War* (1950), v, p. 78. • 32. Stephen Roskill, *Churchill and the Admirals* (1977), p. 219. • 33. Churchill, *Second World War*, op. cit., iv, p. 119. • 34. Elliott Roosevelt, *As He Saw It* (NY, 1946), p. 144; William D. Leahy, *I Was There* (NY, 1950), p. 236. • 35. SP, p. 230. • 36. Philip Ziegler, *Mountbatten* (1985), pp. 260–1. • 37. Alanbrooke Diaries, p. 478. • 38. Ibid., pp. 277–8. • 39. Tuchman, *Sand against the Wind*, op. cit., p. 403. • 40. Mountbatten Diary, p. 43. • 41. Alanbrooke Diaries, pp. 479–80. • 42. Tuchman, *Sand against the Wind*, op. cit., p. 403. • 43. Churchill, *Second World War*, op. cit., v, pp. 328–9. • 44. Alanbrooke Diaries, p. 480. • 45. SP, p. 232; Tuchman, *Sand against the Wind*, op. cit., p. 403. • 46. SP, p. 232. • 47. Tuchman, *Sand against the Wind*, op. cit., p. 404. Needless to say, Chiang's great admirer Jay Taylor denies the truth of the story. He says Chiang knew all about rainy seasons but was simply ignorant of the particular word 'monsoon'. As a secondary defence he blames the quality of Madame's interpreting: Taylor, *The Generalissimo* (Harvard, 2009), p. 248. • 48. Ziegler, *Mountbatten*, op. cit., p. 262. • 49. Mountbatten Diary, p. 34. • 50. Ibid., p. 35; Alanbrooke Diaries, p. 481. • 51. Tuchman, *Sand against the Wind*, op. cit., p. 405. • 52. SP, p. 232. • 53. Mountbatten Diary, p. 36. • 54. Ibid., pp. 37–8. • 55. Ibid., pp. 39–40. • 56. SP, pp. 233–5. • 57. Churchill, *Second World War*, op. cit., p. 328. • 58. The Tehran conference is very well covered in the Alanbrooke Diaries, pp. 482–92. • 59. Pug Ismay, *Memoirs of Lord Ismay* (1960), pp. 336–42; Ziegler, *Mountbatten*, op. cit., p. 263. • 60. Churchill, *Second World War*, op. cit., p. 412; Pendell Moon, ed., *The Viceroy's Journal* (1973), pp. 39–40. • 61. Robert E. Sherwood, *Roosevelt and Hopkins* (NY, 1948), pp. 773–9; Sumner Welles, *Seven Decisions that Shaped History* (NY, 1950), p. 151; Roosevelt, *As He Saw It*, op. cit., p. 154; Ross T. McIntyre, *White House Physician* (NY, 1946), p. 167. • 62. Tuchman, *Sand against the Wind*, op. cit., p. 409. • 63. Ibid, p. 411. • 64. There is very good coverage of all this in John Blum, *From the Morgenthau Diaries* (Boston, 1967), iii, pp. 103–19. • 65. Ibid., pp. 110–19. • 66. SP, pp. 236–9; Tuchman, *Sand against the Wind*, op. cit., pp. 409–10. • 67. SP, p. 233. • 68. Ibid., pp. 246–7. • 69. Ibid., p. 248. • 70. Ibid., pp. 249–50. • 71. Herbert Feis, *The China Tangle. The American Effort in China from Pearl Harbor to the Marshall Mission* (Princeton, 1953), pp. 120–1; Arthur Young, *China and the Helping Hand, 1939–1945* (Harvard, 1963), p. 40. • 72. Feis, *China Tangle*, op. cit., p. 127; C.F.

Romanus & R. Sunderland, *Stilwell's Command Problems* (Washington, 1956), pp. 298–301. • 73. F. Dorn, *Walkout. With Stilwell in Burma* (NY, 1971), p. 145. • 74. Larry I. Bland, ed., *George C. Marshall. Interviews and Reminiscences for Forrest C. Pogue* (Lexington, VA, 1996), p. 605. • 75. Sherwood, *Roosevelt and Hopkins*, op. cit., pp. 408, 513, 706–7, 739. • 76. MP, iv, pp. 302–3. Here was Marshall at his angriest. Referring to Alsop's correspondence with Soong, he wrote to FDR: 'It means to me that Alsop is either more competent as a commander than Stilwell or as a General Staff expert than the officers we have out there (which would continue him in the class with some other columnists and commentators), or that he is a seriously destructive force . . . I am of the opinion that we will be placing our command and control in the Burma-China theatre on a foundation of sand if we accept subordinates who are determinedly critical and disloyal to the commander whom we charge with the responsibility for our soldiers and operations in that theatre.' • 77. Ibid., iii, p. 482. • 78. Albert Wedemeyer, *Wedemeyer Reports!* (NY, 1958), pp. 246–9. • 79. Ibid., pp. 222–5.

Chapter Eleven   pp. 232–257

• 1. DIV, pp. 204, 214. • 2. M. Boatner, *The Biographical Dictionary of World War Two* (Novato, CA, 1996), p. 429; E.L. Fischer, *The Chancy War. Winning in China, Burma and India in World War Two* (NY, 1991), pp. 30–1; L. Anders, *The Ledo Road, General Joseph W. Stilwell's Highway to China* (Norman, OK, 1965), pp. 88–104. • 3. 'The North Burma Campaign: Ledo to Myitkyina. A Background History', WO 203/2672; Anders, *Ledo Road*, op. cit., pp. 101–3; E.R. Craine, *Burma Roadsters* (Tucson, AZ, 1992), pp. 85–7. • 4. Ho, Y-c, *The Big Circle* (NY, 1948), pp. 64–6. • 5. Ronald Lewin, *Ultra Goes to War* (1978), pp. 254–5; Lewin, *The Other Ultra* (1982), p. 244. For the OSS operations among the Kachins see R. Hilsman, *American Guerrillas. My War Behind American Lines* (Washington DC, 1990), pp. 137–8, 297–8; W.R. Peers & D. Breslis, *Behind the Burma Road* (1963), pp. 120–32; R. Dunlop, *Behind Japanese Lines. With the OSS in Burma* (Chicago, 1979), pp. 21–3; W. Langer, *In and Out of the Ivory Tower* (NY, 1977), p. 187; cf. also J.S. Fletcher, *Secret War in Burma* (Austell, GA, 1997); Sharon E. Karr, *Traveller of the Crossroads* (Jacksonville, OR, 1996). • 6. SP, p. 255. • 7. DIV, p. 252. • 8. G.S. Seagrave, *Burma Surgeon Returns* (NY, 1946), p. 94; DIV, p. 253. • 9. C.F. Romanus & R. Sunderland, *Stilwell's Command Problems* (Washington, 1956), pp. 122–8. • 10. Barbara Tuchman, *Sand against the Wind* (1971), p. 420. • 11. DIV, p. 254. • 12. Sun Tzu, *The Art of War*, trans. S.B. Griffiths (Oxford 1963), p. 109. • 13. Tuchman, *Sand against the Wind*, op. cit., p. 419. • 14. David Rooney, *Stilwell* (1971), p. 97. • 15. Tuchman, *Sand against the Wind*, op. cit., p. 423. • 16. F.F. Lin, *A Military History of Modern China 1924–1949* (Princeton, 1956), p. 189. • 17. Tuchman, *Sand against the Wind*, op. cit., p. 432. • 18. For Wedemeyer's key role in Sino-American relations see Herbert Feis, *The China Tangle* (Princeton, 1953); William Strueck, *The Wedemeyer Mission. American Politics and Foreign Policy during the Cold War* (Georgia, 1984); Tang Tsou, *America's Failure in China 1941–50* (NY, 1963); cf. also Tang Tsou, 'The Historians and the Generals', *Pacific Historical Review* 31 (1962), pp. 41–8. • 19. Carton de Wiart, *Happy Odyssey* (1950), p. 259. • 20. Pownall Diaries, p. 32. • 21. Philip Ziegler, *Mountbatten* (1985), pp. 248–9. • 22. Ibid., p. 252. • 23. Owen's account of his time with Mountbatten is in *The Campaign in Burma* (1946). For his career in general see Michael Foot's reflections in Bill Hagerty, 'The real commander', *British Journalism Review* 13 (2002), pp. 19–31. See also S.P. Mackenzie, 'Vox Populi: British Army Newspapers in the Second World War', *Journal of Contemporary History* 24 (1989), pp. 665–81. • 24. Michael Edwardes, *The Last Years of British India* (1963), p. 147. • 25. John Connell, *Auchinleck* (1959), p. 777. • 26. Lowell Thomas, *Back to Mandalay* (1952), pp. 118–19. • 27. Ziegler, *Mountbatten*, op. cit., p. 256. For Joubert see his own autobiography *The Fatal Sky* (1952). For his work with RAF Coastal Command see Roy Conyers Nesbit, *RAF Coastal Command in Action 1939–45* (1997), and Andrew Kendrie, *The Cinderella Service; RAF Coastal Command 1939–1945* (2006). • 28. Mountbatten Diary, pp. 55, 68. • 29. Cunningham diary, 11 December 1945, Add. MSS 52, 578. • 30. Ziegler, *Mountbatten*, op. cit., p. 248. • 31. Mountbatten Diary, pp. 40–1. • 32. W.F. Craven & G.L. Crate, *The Army Air Forces in World War Two. Volume 4. The Pacific. Guadalcanal to Saipan* (Chicago, 1950), p. 450. • 33. SP, p. 256. • 34. Mountbatten Diary, p. 54. • 35. SP, pp. 258–9. • 36. Shelford Bidwell, *The Chindit War* (1979), p. 32. For Stilwell's obsession with what he perceived as cowardly behaviour see Robert Farquharson, *For Your Tomorrow. Canadians and the Burma Campaign 1941–45* (2004), p. 59; John Masters, *The Road Past Mandalay* (1961), pp. 309–10. • 37. Tuchman, *Sand against the Wind*, op. cit., pp. 423–4. • 38. DIV, p. 205. • 39. Ibid., p. 206. • 40. Ibid., pp. 206–7. • 41. Tuchman, *Sand against the Wind*, op. cit., p. 424. • 42. DIV, p. 207. • 43. Ronald Lewin, *Slim. The Standard Bearer* (1976), pp. 141–2. • 44. Don Moser, *China, Burma, India* (Alexandria, VA, 1978), p. 119. • 45. Ziegler, *Mountbatten*, op. cit., p. 264. • 46. Alanbrooke Diaries, p. 521; Arthur Bryant, *Triumph in the West* (1959), pp. 147–8. • 47. C.F. Romanus & R. Sunderland, *Stilwell's Mission to China* (Washington DC, 1953), p. 164. • 48. Tuchman, *Sand against the Wind*, op. cit., pp. 427, 430. • 49. Albert Wedemeyer, *Wedemeyer Reports!* (NY, 1958), p. 258. • 50. SP, p. 259; Tuchman, *Sand against the Wind*, op. cit., p. 230. • 51. W.S. Churchill, *The Second World War* (1950), v pp. 560–573. • 52. SP, p. 259. • 53. Tuchman, *Sand against the Wind*, op. cit., pp. 430–1. • 54. Romanus & Sunderland, *Stilwell's Command Problems*, op. cit., pp. 161–3. • 55. Tuchman, *Sand against the Wind*, op. cit., p. 425. • 56. The order from

Marshall to eat humble pie is at MP, iv, pp. 321–2. • 57. Ziegler, *Mountbatten*, op. cit., pp. 266–7. • 58. Tuchman, *Sand against the Wind*, op. cit., p. 432. • 59. SP, p. 258. • 60. Romanus & Sunderland, *Stilwell's Command Problems*, op. cit., pp. 162–3, 171–2. • 61. MP, iv, p. 250. • 62. Warren F. Kimball, ed., *Churchill and Roosevelt. The Complete Correspondence*, 3 vols. (Princeton, 1984), ii, pp. 690, 694. • 63. MP, iv, pp. 372–3; 500–5; C.F. Romanus & R. Sunderland, *Stilwell's Personal File. China-Burma-India 1942–1944*, 5 vols. (Wilmington, Del., 1976), iv, 1554. • 64. MP, pp. 365–7. • 65. DIV, p. 184. • 66. Lewin, *Slim*, op. cit., p. 136. • 67. Geoffrey Evans, *Slim as Military Commander* (1969), p. 87. • 68. Pendell Moon, ed., *The Viceroy's Journal* (1973), pp. 73–77. • 69. DIV, p. 226. • 70. M.R. Roberts, *The Golden Arrow* (Aldershot, 1952), p. 39. • 71. For the Admin Box see Louis Allen, *Burma. The Longest War 1941–45* (1984), pp. 179–80; Jon Latimer, *Burma. The Forgotten War* (2004), p. 228. • 72. Robert Lyman, *Slim, Master of War* (2004), pp. 151–2. • 73. Lewin, *Slim*, op. cit., p. 139. • 74. 'Report by HQ 5th Indian Division on the first attack on Razabil Fortress', WO 203/1793. • 75. G. Betham & H.V.R. Geary, *The Golden Gallery: the Story of the 2nd Punjab Regiment 1761–1947* (Oxford, 1956) pp. 276–9. • 76. DIV, pp. 231–5. • 77. A. Swinson, *Four Samurai: A Quartet of Japanese Commanders in the Second World War* (1968), pp. 115–50. • 78. Allen, *Burma*, op. cit., pp. 150–73. • 79. Ibid., pp. 182–6. • 80. Ibid., p. 185. • 81. G. Evans, *The Desert and the Jungle* (1959), pp. 134–9; E.W.C. Sanders, *From Pyramid to Pagoda* (1952), pp. 171–2. • 82. K. Tamayama & J. Nunnerley, *Tales by Japanese Soldiers of the Burma Campaign 1942–1945* (2000), p. 148. • 83. DIV, pp. 240–3. • 84. There are accounts of the later Razabil operations at WO 203/1793 and 203/1175. See also Roberts, *Golden Arrow*, op. cit., pp. 107–8; D.P. Marston, *Phoenix from the Ashes: The Indian Army in the Burma Campaign* (Westport, CT, 2003), pp. 132–4. • 85. DIV, p. 230. • 86. Marston, *Phoenix*, op. cit., pp. 134–7. • 87. Mountbatten Diary, p. 66. • 88. DIV, pp. 246–7. • 89. Mike Calvert, *Slim* (1973), p. 83; A.J. Barker, *The March on Delhi* (1963), p. 92. • 90. Lewin, *Slim*, op. cit., p. 157; Lyman, *Slim*, op. cit., pp. 162–3. • 91. DIV, p. 233. • 92. N.R.L. Franks, *Spitfires over the Arakan* (1988), pp. 50–9, 114, 137, 145. • 93. H. Probert, *The Forgotten Air Force: the RAF in the War against Japan, 1942–1945* (1995), pp. 168–72; N.R.L. Franks, *First in the Indian Skies* (1981), pp. 104–6; D.J. Innes, *Beaufighters over Burma* (Poole, 1985), p. 93; H. St G. Saunders, *Royal Air Force 1939–1945* (1975), iii, pp. 318–22. • 94. Allen, *Burma*, op. cit., p. 178. • 95. Probert, *Forgotten Air Force*, op. cit., pp. 158–60. • 96. DIV, p. 240.

Chapter Twelve   pp. 258–291

• 1. Christopher Sykes, *Orde Wingate* (1959), p. 486. • 2. Trevor Royle, *Orde Wingate* (1995), p. 281. • 3. Ibid., p. 277. • 4. David Rooney, *Wingate and the Chindits*

(1994), p. 208. • 5. John Connell, *Auchinleck* (1959), pp. 748, 756–7. • 6. Ibid., pp. 761–2. • 7. DIV, p. 256. • 8. Royle, *Wingate*, op. cit., p. 275. For the re-organisation of the LRP forces and the six brigades see WO 106/4683–84; 172/2237–2240. • 9. DIV, pp. 21–7. • 10. Sykes, *Wingate*, op. cit., pp. 483–4. In February Special Force was rather unnecessarily redesignated 3rd Indian Division, much to Wingate's annoyance, as this made it sound like the despised Indian army (WO 203/5219). • 11. For the Chindits' training and Wingate's idiosyncratic contribution see WO 203/5216. For the air support see P.D. Chinnery, *Any Time, Any Place, Anywhere. 50 Years of the USAF Air Commando and Special Operations Forces 1944–1992* (Shrewsbury, 1994), pp. 17–27. For the role of the United States in the Chindit campaigns see WO 203/4214. • 12. L.J. Thomas, *Back to Mandalay* (Worcester, 1952), pp. 14–19. • 13. R.D. Wagner, *Any Place, Any Time, Anywhere. The 1st Air Commandos in World War Two* (Atglen, PA, 1998), p. 52. • 14. Leonard Mosley, *Gideon Goes to War* (1955), pp. 224–8. • 15. Philip Ziegler, *Mountbatten* (1985), p. 277. • 16. Sykes, *Wingate*, op. cit., p. 487. • 17. Ibid. • 18. Royle, *Wingate*, op. cit., p. 296. • 19. Rooney, *Wingate and the Chindits*, op. cit., p. 227. • 20. Mountbatten Diary, p. 50; Sykes, *Wingate*, op. cit., p. 491. • 21. Charlton Ogburn, *The Marauders* (NY, 1959), p. 60. • 22. Sykes, *Wingate*, op. cit., p. 499. • 23. Rooney, *Wingate and the Chindits*, op. cit., p. 157. • 24. Sykes, *Wingate*, op. cit., pp. 499–500. • 25. Barbara Tuchman, *Sand against the Wind* (1971), p. 426. • 26. Derek Tulloch, *Wingate in Peace and War* (1972), pp. 147–8. • 27. Quoted in Jon Latimer, *Burma. The Forgotten War* (2004), p. 240. • 28. Sykes, *Wingate*, op. cit., p. 494. Additionally Fergusson was disillusioned about the rations issued to his troops. Fergusson had told Wingate he would not again put his troops through the 1943 ordeal, and Wingate had promised to issue credible rations. But all he did was to substitute American K-rations, replacing bully beef with egg and bacon and hard tack with more palatable biscuits. Overall, there were just a few more calories than in the 1943 ration packs. Fergusson felt that Wingate had lied to him. According to the best sources it was not so much Wingate's bad-tempered confrontation as Mountbatten's soothing words that made Fergusson change his mind: Bernard Fergusson, *The Trumpet in the Hall 1930–1958* (1970), pp. 175–6; Julian Thompson, *The Imperial War Museum Book of War Behind Enemy Lines* (1998), p. 179. • 29. Tulloch, *Wingate in Peace and War*, op. cit., p. 136. • 30. Royle, *Wingate*, op. cit., pp. 288–9. For the complete Wingate–Mountbatten correspondence see WO 203/5215. For a detailed examination of other issues involved see WO 203/3267. • 31. Sykes, *Wingate*, op. cit., pp. 493–4. • 32. Ronald Lewin, *Slim. The Standard Bearer* (1976), p. 154. • 33. DIV, pp. 218–19. The incident left Slim with a deep loathing for Wingate, which he covered up in his memoirs. The feeling was reciprocated. To his officers in a public session Wingate referred to Slim as 'a stupid ass'. James Angrim has commented: 'In actuality there seems to have been a deep animosity, personal and mutual, which, in Slim's case, appears to have hardened in the decade after Wingate's death': Angrim, 'Orde Wingate and the British Army', PhD thesis, University of Wales, 2007, Chapter Seven. • 34. Wingate to Mountbatten, 5 January 1944, WO 203/517. Sykes, *Wingate*, op. cit., pp. 492–3. The resignation threat 'did little to sweeten his relationship with Slim': Royle, *Wingate*, op. cit., p. 288. • 35. Sykes, *Wingate*, op. cit., p. 497. • 36. CAB 106/206. • 37. Royle, *Wingate*, op. cit., p. 289; see also WO 203/5219, 4212. • 38. Sykes, *Wingate*, op. cit., p. 498. • 39. CAB 106/41. • 40. Royle, *Wingate*, op. cit., p. 289. • 41. Sykes, *Wingate*, op. cit., p. 510. • 42. DIV, p. 216. • 43. There is a very good assessment of all this in Robert Lyman, *Slim, Master of War* (2004), pp. 177–89. • 44. DIV, p. 217. • 45. Royle, *Wingate*, op. cit., p. 323. • 46. DIV, p. 218. • 47. Lewin, *Slim*, op. cit., p. 153. • 48. Ibid., p. 182. • 49. Ibid., pp. 183–4. See also the comments in CAB 106/41. • 50. Rooney, *Wingate and the Chindits*, op. cit., p. 215. • 51. Bernard Fergusson, *Beyond the Chindwin* (1995), pp. 241–2. • 52. C.J. Rolo, *Wingate's Raiders* (1944), p. 23; Peter Meade, *Orde Wingate and the Historians* (1987), p. 142. • 53. DIV, p. 217. • 54. Lewin, *Slim*, op. cit., p. 163. • 55. Ibid., p. 143. • 56. Tulloch, *Wingate in Peace and War*, op. cit., p. 190. 'It is difficult to see this enigmatic figure as the plain man he depicted in his autobiographical memory of the Far Eastern War': Sykes, *Wingate*, op. cit., p. 497. • 57. Lyman, *Slim*, op. cit., p. 186. • 58. Sykes, *Wingate*, op. cit., pp. 500–1. • 59. The entire correspondence can be followed at WO 203/5217–5218. For a convenient summary see Royle, *Wingate*, op. cit., pp. 291–2. • 60. Pownall Diaries, p. 113. • 61. R. Callahan, *Burma 1942–1945: The Politics and Strategy of the Second World War* (1978), p. 101. • 62. C. Somerville, *Our War* (1998), pp. 204–5; Rooney, *Wingate and the Chindits*, op. cit., p. 171. • 63. Somerville, *Our War*, op. cit., p. 222; Rooney, *Wingate and the Chindits*, op. cit., p. 171. • 64. DIV, p. 219. For the evolution of the fly-in plans see WO 203/4620. • 65. Sykes, *Wingate*, op. cit., pp. 498–9. • 66. Ibid., p. 510. • 67. Ibid., p. 511. • 68. Pownall Diaries, p. 142. • 69. DIV, p. 220. • 70. Peter O'Brien, *Out of the Blue* (1984), p. 186. See also WO 203/5222; 203/4260; 203/5216; 203/5220. • 71. Sykes, *Wingate*, op. cit., p. 508. • 72. J. Clabby, *History of the Royal Army Veterinary Corps 1919–1961* (1963), pp. 124–6. • 73. Sykes, *Wingate*, op. cit., pp. 505–7. • 74. W.J. Cooper, *Desert Sand to Jungle Trail* (Minster Lovell, 1997), p. 135. • 75. Shelford Bidwell, *The Chindit War* (1979), p. 136. • 76. Bernard Fergusson, *The Wild Green Earth* (1946), p. 74. • 77. Sykes, *Wingate*, op. cit., p. 514. • 78. Bidwell, *Chindit War*, op. cit., pp. 134–6. • 79. Rooney, *Wingate and the Chindits*, op. cit., p. 159. • 80. Lyman, *Slim*, op. cit., p. 187. • 81. Geoffrey Evans, *Slim as Military Commander* (1969), p. 163. • 82. Bidwell, *Chindit War*, op. cit., p. 150. • 83. DIV, p. 268. • 84. Ibid., pp. 260–1. For the detailed planning of air support see WO 203/5220. • 85. Tulloch, *Wingate in Peace and War*, op. cit., p. 148. Wingate had something of an obsession about the 'treacherous Chinaman': see John Bierman & C. Smith, *Fire in the Night* (2001), pp. 381–4. It is true, however, that Chinese security was lax: B. Prasad, ed., *Reconquest of Burma* (Delhi, 1958), i, p. 337. • 86. Bidwell, *Chindit War*, op. cit., p. 104; DIV, pp. 261–2. Slim's account has been disputed by the pro-Wingate faction. See Bierman & Smith, *Fire in the Night*, op. cit., pp. 348–50, and Tulloch, *Wingate in Peace and War*, op. cit., pp. 200–1. • 87. Mike Calvert, *Prisoners of Hope* (1971), p. 23; Lewin, *Slim*, op. cit., p. 163; Calvert, *The Chindits. Long Range Penetration* (1973), p. 27. • 88. DIV, pp. 262–3. • 89. DIV, p. 263. For Cochran's participation in THURSDAY see MP, iv, pp. 343–4. Surprisingly, Marshall had a high opinion of Wingate: Forrest Pogue, *George C. Marshall. Organizer of Victory 1943–1945* (1973), p. 257. • 90. Tulloch, *Wingate in Peace and War*, op. cit., pp. 200–1. • 91. DIV, p. 264. • 92. Sykes, *Wingate*, op. cit., p. 518. • 93. DIV, p. 265. • 94. Tulloch, *Wingate in Peace and War*, op. cit., p. 202. • 95. Bidwell, *Chindit War*, op. cit., p. 110. • 96. J. Lunt, *Imperial Sunset* (1981), p. 318. • 97. Sykes, *Wingate*, op. cit., p. 521; Mike Calvert, *Fighting Mad* (Shrewsbury, 1996), p. 153; Calvert, *Prisoners of Hope*, op. cit., p. 51. • 98. R. Rhodes-James, *Chindits* (1980), p. 79. • 99. O'Brien, *Out of the Blue*, op. cit., pp. 56–9; L.J. Thomas, *Back to Mandalay* (1952), pp. 161–6; E.R. Evans, *Combat Cameraman. China-Burma-India* (Pittsburgh, 1996), pp. 77–81. • 100. Sykes, *Wingate*, op. cit., p. 524. The Spitfires at Broadway have generated their own controversy. Slim says 30 Japanese planes raided Broadway but got the shock of their lives when RAF planes took to the air against them and shot down 15: DIV, p. 266. Either these figures are wrong or there must have been more than six Spitfires at Broadway; not even the RAF would accept suicidal odds of five to one. What is certain is that a few days later (19 March), another Japanese raid caught the Spitfires napping; all were either shot down or destroyed on the ground: Tulloch, *Wingate in Peace and War*, op. cit., p. 219. • 101. DIV, p. 266. • 102. Ziegler, *Mountbatten*, op. cit., pp. 275–6. • 103. Tulloch, *Wingate in Peace and War*, op. cit., p. 192. • 104. A.J. Barker, *The March on Delhi* (1963), p. 96; Tulloch, *Wingate in Peace and War*, op. cit., p. 259; Royle, *Wingate*, op. cit., p. 283. • 105. Sykes, *Wingate*, op. cit., p. 527. • 106. Fergusson, *Wild Green Earth*, op. cit., pp. 96–117; Fergusson, *Trumpet in the Hall*, op. cit., pp. 199–200. • 107. Royle, *Wingate*, op. cit., p. 304. • 108. Tulloch, *Wingate in Peace and War*, op. cit., p. 209; Royle, *Wingate*, op. cit., p. 306. • 109. Sykes, *Wingate*, op. cit., p. 528. • 110. Lewin, *Slim*, op. cit., p. 146. • 111. Ibid., p. 181. • 112. Royle, *Wingate*, op. cit., pp. 306–7; Sykes, *Wingate*, op. cit., p. 529. • 113. Tulloch, *Wingate in Peace and War*, op. cit., pp. 223–5; Lewin, *Slim*, op. cit., p. 183. • 114. Bidwell, *Chindit War*, op. cit., pp. 134–42. • 115. There is excellent coverage of the Japanese reaction in Louis Allen, *Burma. The Longest War 1941–45* (1984); pp. 326–8. The fiasco caused by Wingate's pathological secretiveness is touched on by his most fervent advocate but quickly skated over: Rooney, *Wingate and the Chindits*, op. cit., p. 161. • 116. Allen, *Burma*, op. cit., p. 342. • 117. Sykes, *Wingate*, op. cit., p. 530. • 118. Bidwell, *Chindit War*, op. cit., pp. 142–6. • 119. Calvert, *Prisoners of Hope*, op. cit., p. 97; Fergusson, *Wild Green Earth*, op. cit., p. 121. • 120. Fergusson, *Trumpet in the Hall*, op. cit., p. 177. There are those who say that Wingate's order of 23 March to 14 Brigade, instructing them to cut Japanese communications between Wuntho and the Chindwin, was a misunderstanding or complete disregard of Slim's actual orders (S.W. Kirby, ed., *The War against Japan* (1961), iii, pp. 212, 218). • 121. Jon Latimer, *Burma. The Forgotten War* (2004), p. 250. • 122. For a full account see Allen, *Burma*, op. cit., pp. 346–8. • 123. 'Death of Wingate', WO 203/4881; D. Hanley, *The Death of Wingate and Subsequent Events* (Braunton, 1994), esp. pp. 66–76. • 124. DIV, pp. 268–9. • 125. Royle, *Wingate*, op. cit., pp. 310–12. • 126. Rhodes-James, *Chindits*, op. cit., p. 206. • 127. Ziegler, *Mountbatten*, op. cit., p. 276. • 128. Royle, *Wingate*, op. cit., p. 310. • 129. Rhodes-James, *Chindits*, op. cit., p. 89. • 130. For various views see Rooney, *Wingate and the Chindits*, op. cit., pp. 115, 131–5, 139, 150, 219, 228, 230, 235; Tulloch, *Wingate in Peace and War*, op. cit., p. 190; Royle, *Wingate*, op. cit., p. 326; Allen, *Burma*, op. cit., pp. 345–6. • 131. DIV, p. 269.

Chapter Thirteen   pp. 293–327

• 1. DIV, p. 289. • 2. A. Clayton, *Forearmed: A History of the Intelligence Corps* (1993), pp. 183–9. For V-force see WO 203/464. For the groups in general see D.G. Morris, *Beyond the Irrawaddy and Salween* (Gardendale, Vic., 1996). • 3. Lyall Grant, *The Turning Point* (Chichester, 1993), p. 54. • 4. Louis Allen, *Burma. The Longest War 1941–45* (1984), pp. 193–5. • 5. DIV, p. 286. • 6. Robert Lyman, *Slim, Master of War* (2004), pp. 165–70. • 7. Ibid., pp. 175–7. • 8. A.J. Barker, *Japanese Army Handbook 1939–1945* (Shepperton, 1979), p. 116; K. Tamayama & J. Nunnerley, *Tales by Japanese Soldiers of the Burma Campaign 1942–1945* (2000), p. 175. • 9. Tamayama & Nunnerley, *Tales*, op. cit., p. 175. • 10. S.W. Kirby, ed., *The War against Japan* (1961), iii, p. 193. • 11. WO 72/4188; G. Evans & A. Brett-James, *Imphal. A Flower on Lofty Heights* (1962), p. 114; B. Prasad, ed., *Reconquest of Burma* (Delhi, 1958), i, p. 190. • 12. Allen, *Burma*, op. cit., pp. 198–205. • 13. DIV, p. 301. • 14. Grant, *Turning Point*, op. cit., p. 62; Kirby, ed., *War against Japan*, op. cit., iii, p. 450. • 15. DIV, p. 303. • 16. Evans & Brett-James, *Imphal*, op. cit., pp. 122–6; David Rooney, *Burma Victory: Imphal and Kohima March 1944 to May 1945* (1992), p. 35; Grant, *Turning Point*, op. cit., p. 62. • 17. Allen, *Burma*, op. cit., pp. 210–11. • 18. Rooney, *Burma Victory*, op. cit., pp. 42–5. • 19. Lyman, *Slim*, op. cit., pp. 172–5. • 20. Ronald Lewin, *Slim. The Standard Bearer* (1976), pp. 176–82. • 21. Ibid., p. 176. • 22. DIV, pp. 290–1. • 23. Lyman, *Slim*, op. cit., pp. 165–99. • 24. DIV, pp. 298–300. • 25. WO 203/36. • 26. The entire battle has been well described by Harry Seaman, *The Battle at Sangshak* (1989). • 27. Tamayama & Nunnelly, *Tales*, op. cit., p. 161. • 28. Seaman, *Battle*, op. cit., p. 32. • 29. Allen, *Burma*, op. cit., p. 219. • 30. DIV, p. 299; Seaman, *Battle*, op. cit., p. 56; Grant, *Turning Point*, op. cit., p. 61. • 31. Lyman, *Slim*, op. cit., p. 156. • 32. Ibid., pp. 199–200. • 33. DIV, p. 311. • 34. A. Swinson, *Four Samurai* (1968), pp. 115–50. • 35. Allen, *Burma*, op. cit., pp. 284–6. • 36. DIV, p. 306; Philip Ziegler, *Mountbatten* (1985), p. 271. • 37. C.F. Romanus & R. Sunderland, *Stilwell's Command Problems* (Washington, 1956), p. 175. Marshall was particularly reluctant to divert planes to Imphal, for he feared it would set a precedent whereby Mountbatten would gradually acquire carte blanche to do what he wanted with the aircraft of USAAF: MP, iv, p. 354. • 38. N.R. Franks, *The Air Battle at Imphal* (1985), p. 37; A. Brett-James, *Ball of Fire* (Aldershot, 1951), pp. 300–1. • 39. M.R. Roberts, *Golden Arrow* (Aldershot, 1952), p. 299; Evans & Brett-James, *Imphal*, op. cit., p. 157; H. Probert, *The Forgotten Air Force* (1995), pp. 188–94; H.G. Sanders, *The Royal Air Force* (1975), iii, pp. 318–23. • 40. Lyman, *Slim*, op. cit., p. 203. • 41. Pownall Diaries, p. 151. • 42. Ziegler, *Mountbatten*, op. cit., p. 272. • 43. DIV, p. 308. • 44. Lyman, *Slim*, op. cit., p. 189. • 45. Lewin, *Slim*, op. cit., p. 173. • 46. DIV, p. 323. • 47. Ibid., p. 296. • 48. Allen, *Burma*, op. cit., p. 247. • 49. There is a detailed account of the battle in A.F. Freer, *Nunshigum. On the Road to Mandalay* (Bishop Auckland, 1995). • 50. Allen, *Burma*, op. cit., pp. 253–60. • 51. Evans & Brett-James, *Imphal*, op. cit., p. 112. • 52. DIV, pp. 325–6. • 53. Allen, *Burma*, op. cit., pp. 295–301. • 54. Ibid., p. 223. • 55. Evans & Brett-James, *Imphal*, op. cit., p. 233. • 56. Jeremy Taylor, *The Devons. A History of the Devonshire Regiment 1685–1945* (Bristol, 1951), pp. 181–7. • 57. DIV, pp. 327–8; Evans & Brett-James, *Imphal*, op. cit., p. 233. • 58. Evans & Brett-James, *Imphal*, op. cit., p. 327; Allen, *Burma*, op. cit., pp. 226–7. • 59. DIV, p. 328. • 60. Jon Latimer, *Burma. The Forgotten War* (2004), pp. 280–2. • 61. DIV, p. 334. • 62. Allen, *Burma*, op. cit., pp. 203–6. • 63. DIV, p. 329; Evans & Brett-James, *Imphal*, op. cit., pp. 244–5; Rooney, *Burma Victory*, op. cit., pp. 244–5. • 64. Latimer, *Burma*, op. cit., pp. 282–3. • 65. DIV, p. 330. • 66. Evans & Brett-James, *Imphal*, op. cit., pp. 246–65; B.R. Mullaly, *Bugles and Kukri* (1957), pp. 224–30. • 67. Evans & Brett-James, *Imphal*, op. cit., pp. 251–61. • 68. Allen, *Burma*, op. cit., pp. 278–81. • 69. Rooney, *Burma Victory*, op. cit., pp. 159–61; Evans & Brett-James, *Imphal*, op. cit., p. 264. • 70. Rooney, *Burma Victory*, op. cit., pp. 162–4. • 71. DIV, p. 336. • 72. A.J. Barker, *The March on Delhi* (1963), p. 139; Prasad, ed., *Reconquest of Burma*, op. cit., i, p. 227. • 73. Allen, *Burma*, op. cit., p. 280. • 74. Evans & Brett-James, *Imphal*, op. cit., pp. 105–6. • 75. DIV, p. 337. • 76. Allen, *Burma*, op. cit., p. 284. • 77. Lyman, *Slim*, op. cit., p. 223; Allen, *Burma*, op. cit., pp. 310–11. • 78. Lewin, *Slim*, op. cit., p. 184. • 79. DIV, p. 305. • 80. Lyman, *Slim*, op. cit., pp. 206–7. • 81. DIV, p. 310; G. Evans, *Slim as Military Commander* (1969), p. 161. • 82. Lewin, *Slim*, op. cit., p. 178, opts for the former explanation. • 83. The exact number of effectives at Kohima during the siege, like so much else in the Burma campaign, is disputed. For the differing estimates see Arthur Campbell, *The Siege. A Story from Kohima*

(1956), p. 53; Brett-James, *Ball of Fire*, op. cit., p. 306; Barker, *March to Delhi*, op. cit., p. 173; Prasad, *Reconquest of Burma*, op. cit., i, p. 306. • 84. Compton Mackenzie, *All Over the Place* (1949), p. 77. • 85. The indecision about 161 Brigade, its mixed fortunes and its to-and-from itinerary, can be followed in WO 172/4507, 172/4884; CAB 44/190. See also Kirby, ed., *War against Japan*, op. cit., iii, p. 301; A. Swinson, *Kohima* (1966), pp. 51–6. • 86. Campbell, *Siege*, op. cit., pp. 55, 81; J. Colvin, *Not Ordinary Men. The Story of the Battle of Kohima* (1995), pp. 86–8; C.E. Lucas-Phillipps, *Springboard to Victory* (1966), pp. 149–51. • 87. WO 172/4884; Barker, *March on Delhi*, op. cit., p. 174. • 88. Barker, *March on Delhi*, op. cit., p. 171; Colvin, *Not Ordinary Men*, op. cit., pp. 42–52. • 89. N.R.L. Franks, *The Air Battle of Imphal* (1985), p. 124; Probert, *Forgotten Air Force*, op. cit., p. 187. • 90. Kirby, ed., *War against Japan*, op. cit., iii, p. 303. • 91. Latimer, *Burma*, op. cit., p. 268. • 92. R. Humphreys, *To Stop a Rising Sun* (Stroud, 1996), p. 29. • 93. Prasad, ed., *Reconquest of Burma*, op. cit., i.p. 269; Brett-James, *Ball of Fire*, op. cit., p. 321. • 94. Campbell, *Siege*, op. cit., pp. 66–73, 203. • 95. WO 203/2683; 172/4451. • 96. J. Thompson, *The Imperial War Museum Book of the War in Burma 1942–1945* (2002), pp. 138–40. • 97. P. Steyn, *The History of the Assam Regiment. Vol. 1 1941–1947* (Calcutta, 1959), pp. 70–4. • 98. See the various descriptions in Lyman, *Slim*, op. cit., p. 209; Allen, *Burma*, op. cit., p. 238; Latimer, *Burma*, op. cit., p. 271. • 99. Swinson, *Kohima*, op. cit., p. 103. • 100. Ibid., pp. 116–25; P. Hart, *At The Sharp End* (Barnsley, 1998), pp. 153–6; see also J. Nunnelly, ed., *Tales from the Burma Campaign 1942–45* (Petersham, 1998); D.R. Mankekar, *Leaves from a War Reporter's Diary* (New Delhi, 1977); W.A. Wilcox, *Chindit Column 76* (1945). • 101. Allen, *Burma*, op. cit., p. 287. • 102. DIV, p. 319. • 103. WO 203/4367. • 104. Latimer, *Burma*, op. cit., p. 299. • 105. Swinson, *Kohima*, op. cit., pp. 126–72. • 106. DIV, p. 321. • 107. Swinson, *Kohima*, op. cit., pp. 175–84. • 108. Ibid., p. 143. • 109. Kirby, ed., *War against Japan*, op. cit., iii, p. 310. • 110. Ziegler, *Mountbatten*, op. cit., p. 272. • 111. Alanbrooke Diaries. • 112. DIV, p. 342. • 113. Swinson, *Kohima*, op. cit., pp. 202–7. • 114. Colvin, *Not Ordinary Men*, op. cit., pp. 197–206. • 115. E.V.P. Bellers, *The History of the 1st King George V's Own Gurkha Rifles. Vol 2. 1920–1947* (Aldershot, 1956). • 116. Allen, *Burma*, op. cit., p. 289. • 117. W.L. Hailes & J. Ross, *The Jat Regiment* (1965), pp. 297–300. • 118. Swinson, *Four Samurai*, op. cit., p. 135. • 119. Allen, *Burma*, op. cit., p. 311. • 120. Ibid., pp. 308–9; Lewin, *Slim*, op. cit., p. 186. • 121. Evans & Brett-James, *Imphal*, op. cit., pp. 312–14. • 122. Swinson, *Kohima*, op. cit., p. 245. • 123. Ibid., pp. 242–3; Lyman, *Slim*, op. cit., p. 225. • 124. Lyman, *Slim*, op. cit., pp. 224–5. • 125. Humphreys, *Rising Sun*, op. cit., p. 12. • 126. Alanbrooke Diaries, p. 553. • 127. R.J.C. Butow, *Japan's Decision to Surrender* (Stanford, CA. 1954), p. 31; F.H.C. Jones, H. Borton & B.R. Pearm, *The Far East 1942–1946* (1955), p. 123. • 128. Lewin, *Slim*, op. cit., pp. 176–82. • 129. Ibid. • 130. Swinson, *Four Samurai*, op. cit., p. 252; M. Boatner, *The Biographical Dictionary of World War Two* (Novato, CA, 1996), pp. 267, 275, 287, 387, 1555. • 131. Evans & Brett-

James, *Imphal*, op. cit., p. 204. • 132. Quoted in Royle, *Wingate*, op. cit., p. 302. • 133. See DIV, *passim*. • 134. Brett-James, *Ball of Fire*, op. cit. • 135. A. Brett-James, *Report My Signals* (1948), pp. 29–30. • 136. Lewin, *Slim*, op. cit., p. 168.

Chapter Fourteen pp. 328–363

• 1. DIV, p. 254. For a full assessment of Merrill see M. Boatner, *Biographical Dictionary of World War Two* (Novato, CA, 1996), pp. 361–2. • 2. Charlton Ogburn, *The Marauders* (1960), pp. 72, 79. For the poor calibre of the Marauders see also MP, iv. pp. 516–17. • 3. For various views of the Marauders' personalities, all tending in the same direction, see Ogburn, *Marauders*, op. cit., p. 61; F. Owen, *The Campaign in Burma* (1946), p. 84; J.B. George, *Shots Fired in Anger* (Washington, 1981), p. 460. For the Marauders' view of their own excellence see Ogburn, *Marauders*, op. cit., p. 285. • 4. N.N. Prefer, *Vinegar Joe's War: Stilwell's Campaign for Burma* (Novato, CA, 2000), pp. 82–3. • 5. Ibid. • 6. J. Girsham & L.J. Thomas, *Burma Jack* (NY, 1971), pp. 145–6. • 7. Prefer, *Vinegar Joe's War*, op. cit., pp. 100–1. • 8. A.D. Baker, *Merrill's Marauders* (1972), pp. 74–89; Ogburn, *Marauders*, op. cit., p. 183. • 9. C.N. Hunter, *Galahad* (San Antonio, TX, 1963), p. 88. • 10. Prefer, *Vinegar Joe's War*, op. cit., pp. 103–8; George, *Shots Fired in Anger*, op. cit., pp. 524–6. • 11. Prefer, *Vinegar Joe's War*, op. cit., pp. 114–22; Baker, *Merrill's Marauders*, op. cit., pp. 90–109; C.F. Romanus & R. Sunderland, *Stilwell's Command Problems* (Washington, 1956), p. 191 • 12. DIV, pp. 254–5. • 13. Romanus & Sunderland, *Stilwell's Command Problems*, op. cit., p. 200. • 14. DIV, p. 256. • 15. Pownall Diaries, pp. 152–3. • 16. F. Eldridge, *Wrath in Burma* (NY, 1946), p. 216; *Time*, 21 October 1946. • 17. DIV, pp. 256–7. • 18. Mountbatten Diary, p. 108. • 19. Eldridge, *Wrath in Burma*, op. cit., p. 229. Mountbatten himself claimed that he was embarrassed and annoyed that the fighters had accompanied him: Mountbatten Diary, p. 77. • 20. DIV, p. 252. Mountbatten was right to be suspicious of the Boatner mission. In February 1944 Boatner told FDR that the British were soft-pedalling on the Burma war and their contribution was negligible: MP, iv, p. 300. This was of course before Kohima-Imphal. • 21. C.F. Romanus & R. Sunderland, *Stilwell's Mission to China* (Washington DC, 1953), p. 170. Wedemeyer had full scope for his intrigues, since he went to England to discuss CULVERIN (February 1944), met Eisenhower, Churchill and King George VI, then went on to Washington to brief Roosevelt: *Wedemeyer Reports!* (NY, 1958), pp. 258–64. • 22. Ralph Arnold, *A Very Quiet War* (1962), p. 153. • 23. Quoted in Philip Ziegler, *Mountbatten* (1985), p. 247. • 24. Barbara Tuchman, *Sand against the Wind* (1971), p. 436. • 25. SP, p. 263; Mountbatten Diary, p. 77. • 26. J.E.T. Hopkins & J.M. Jones, *Spearhead: A Complete History of Merrill's Marauders*

Rangers (Baltimore, 1999), pp. 113–15, 135–7; L.E. Weston, *The Fightin' Preacher* (Cheyenne, 1992), pp. 124–5. • 27. Carton de Wiart, *Happy Odyssey* (1950), p. 251. • 28. Mountbatten Diary, p. 77. • 29. Ibid., p. 78. • 30. Ibid., p. 79. • 31. Ibid., p. 80. • 32. Ibid. • 33. Eldridge, *Wrath in Burma*, op. cit., p. 202. • 34. Ziegler, *Mountbatten*, op. cit., p. 271. • 35. Romanus & Sunderland, *Stilwell's Mission*, op. cit., p. 176. • 36. DIV, p. 271. • 37. SP, p. 266; Tuchman, *Sand against the Wind*, op. cit., p. 441. • 38. SP, pp. 263, 267. • 39. DIV, pp. 271–2. • 40. Ibid., pp. 272–3. • 41. SP, pp. 267–8. Even Derek Tulloch, no great admirer of Slim, says the decision to turn down Stilwell's offer was 'one of the most important and far-reaching decisions made by the Army commander during the whole campaign'. Tulloch, *Wingate in Peace and War* (1972), pp. 242–3. • 42. Pownall Diaries, p. 128. • 43. Ziegler, *Mountbatten*, op. cit., pp. 278–9. • 44. John Connell, *Auchinleck* (1959), p. 760. • 45. Arnold, *Very Quiet War*, op. cit., p. 130. • 46. Alanbrooke Diaries, pp. 715–16. Biting criticisms of Mountbatten are a staple of these diaries. See also pp. 551, 553. • 47. Noel Coward, *Future Indefinite* (1954), p. 304. • 48. Pendell Moon, ed., *The Viceroy's Journal* (1973), p. 304. • 49. SP, p. 270. • 50. Ibid., p. 264. • 51. Tuchman, *Sand against the Wind*, op. cit., p. 435. • 52. SP, p. 272. • 53. Ibid., p. 278. • 54. DIV, pp. 269–70. • 55. Shelford Bidwell, *The Chindit War* (1979), p. 161; Rhodes-James, *Chindit*, p. 87; Fergusson, *The Trumpet in the Hall*, p. 179 • 56. Bidwell, *Chindit War*, op. cit., pp. 160, 207; Tulloch, *Wingate in Peace and War*, op. cit., p. 236. Slim is also said to have confided that he had no choice, as Lentaigne was the only Chindit leader who wasn't mad: Royle, *Wingate*, op. cit., p. 316. For Lentaigne's conception of LRP and the Chindits see CAB 106/171. • 57. DIV, p. 269. • 58. Louis Allen, *Burma. The Longest War 1941–45* (1984), p. 351. • 59. David Rooney, *Wingate and the Chindits* (1994), p. 170. • 60. Robert Thompson, *Make for the Hills* (1989), p. 54. For the most extraordinary no-holds-barred attack on Lentaigne see Rooney, *Wingate and the Chindits*, op. cit., pp. 131–5. • 61. Tulloch, *Wingate in Peace and War*, op. cit., p. 239. • 62. S.W. Kirby, ed., *The War Against Japan* (1961), iii, p. 247; WO 203/5221; CAB 106/203. • 63. Bidwell, *Chindit War*, op. cit., p. 169. • 64. Mike Calvert, *The Chindits* (1973), pp. 82–3. • 65. Christopher Sykes, *Orde Wingate* (1959), p. 536. • 66. Mike Calvert, *Fighting Mad* (Shrewsbury, 1996), p. 21; Calvert, *Chindits*, op. cit., p. 99. • 67. Calvert, *Fighting Mad*, op. cit., pp. 186–7; Calvert, *Chindits*, op. cit., p. 105. • 68. Rooney, *Wingate and the Chindits*, op. cit., p. 136. • 69. John Masters, *The Road Past Mandalay* (1961), p. 219; R. Rhodes-James, *Chindits* (1980), p. 109. • 70. Rooney, *Wingate and the Chindits*, op. cit., p. 139. • 71. Rhodes-James, *Chindits*, op. cit., p. 125. • 72. Masters, *Road Past Mandalay*, op. cit., p. 259; Bidwell, *Chindit War*, op. cit., p. 233; Rhodes-James, *Chindits*, op. cit., pp. 141–5. • 73. Masters, *Road Past Mandalay*, op. cit., p. 267. • 74. Rhodes-James, *Chindits*, op. cit., p. 125. • 75. Bidwell, *Chindit War*, op. cit., p. 208. • 76. Romanus & Sunderland, *Stilwell's Command Problems*, op. cit., p. 200. • 77. Tuchman, *Sand against the Wind*, op. cit., pp. 446–7;

E.J. King & W.M. Whitehall, *Fleet Admiral King* (NY, 1952), p. 541. • 78. Larrabee, *Commander-in-Chief*, op. cit., pp. 342–48. • 79. Ogburn, *Marauders*, op. cit., pp. 5, 26. • 80. Ibid., p. 207. • 81. Douglas Ford, 'Strategic Culture, Intelligence Assessment and the Conduct of the Pacific War: the British–Indian and Imperial Japanese Armies in Comparison, 1941–1945', *War in History* 14 (2007), pp. 63–95. • 82. Ian Fellowes Gordon, *The Battle for Naw Seung's Kingdom: General Stilwell's North Burma Campaign and its Aftermath* (1971), p. 120; SP, p. 275. • 83. Romanus & Sunderland, *Stilwell's Command Problems*, op. cit., p. 230. • 84. Ibid., p. 228–33. • 85. Ibid., p. 233. • 86. Ibid., p. 240. • 87. Ibid., p. 237. • 88. W.S. Churchill, *The Second World War* (1950), v, p. 569. • 89. Ziegler, *Mountbatten*, op. cit., p. 275. • 90. Romanus & Sunderland, *Stilwell's Command Problems*, op. cit., pp. 228–30. • 91. Tuchman, *Sand against the Wind*, op. cit., p. 431. • 92. Romanus & Sunderland, *Stilwell's Mission*, op. cit., p. 308. • 93. Ibid., p. 310; Romanus & Sunderland, *Stilwell's Command Problems*, op. cit., pp. 310–14, 329, 340–1; see also MP, iv, pp. 417–18. • 94. The offensive by Y-force is covered in detail by Romanus & Sunderland, *Stilwell's Command Problems*, op. cit., pp. 329–60. • 95. F.F. Lin, *A Military History of Modern China 1924–1949* (Princeton, 1956), p. 216. • 96. C.T. Liang, *General Stilwell in China* (NY, 1972), p. 176. • 97. Allen, *Burma*, op. cit., p. 364. • 98. W.F. Jeffrey, *Sunbeams like Swords* (1951), pp. 142–5; Bidwell, *Chindit War*, op. cit., p. 269. • 99. Mike Calvert, *Prisoners of Hope* (1971), p. 211. • 100. J. Shaw, *The March Out* (1953), p. 150; B. Towill, *A Chindit's Chronicle* (Lincoln, NE, 2000), p. 72; Rooney, *Wingate and the Chindits*, op. cit., pp. 173–74. • 101. Calvert, *Prisoners of Hope*, op. cit., pp. 218–23; Calvert, *Fighting Mad*, op. cit., pp. 197–8; Jeffrey, *Sunbeams*, op. cit., p. 160. • 102. Bidwell, *Chindit War*, op. cit., pp. 272–3. • 103. Calvert, *Prisoners of Hope*, op. cit., pp. 224–36. • 104. Bidwell, *Chindit War*, op. cit., pp. 273–4. • 105. Calvert, *Fighting Mad*, op. cit., p. 176. • 106. Allen, *Burma*, op. cit., p. 374; Rooney, *Wingate and the Chindits*, op. cit., p. 193. • 107. SP, p. 283. • 108. Rooney, *Wingate and the Chindits*, op. cit., p. 196. • 109. MP, iv, pp. 436–7; Romanus & Sunderland, *Stilwell's Command Problems*, op. cit., pp. 196–9, 220–1; Tulloch, *Wingate in Peace and War*, op. cit., p. 250. • 110. Peter O'Brien, *Out of the Blue* (1984), pp. 35, 139. • 111. Romanus & Sunderland, *Stilwell's Command Problems*, op. cit., pp. 243–4. • 112. Peter Lane, *Chinese Chindits*, pp. 37–9; Ogburn, *Marauders*, op. cit., p. 289; Masters, *Road Past Mandalay*, op. cit., pp. 286–9; Rooney, *Wingate and the Chindits*, op. cit., p. 150. • 113. O'Brien, *Out of the Blue*, op. cit., p. 256. • 114. Tuchman, *Sand against the Wind*, op. cit., pp. 449–52. • 115. J.P. Davies, *Dragon by the Tail* (NY, 1972), pp. 242, 293. • 116. Romanus & Sunderland, *Stilwell's Command Problems*, op. cit., p. 242. • 117. Ogburn, *Marauders*, op. cit., p. 289. They and the Japanese also liked to hurl insults at each other on the front line. Many of these jibes, some infantile, others obscene or scatological, are collected in WO 203/468. • 118. O'Brien, *Out of the Blue*, op. cit., p. 31; Ogburn, *Marauders*, op. cit., p. 279. • 119. SP, p. 279. • 120. Romanus &

Sunderland, *Stilwell's Command Problems*, op. cit., p. 244. • 121. Allen, *Burma*, op. cit., pp. 381–5. • 122. Ogburn, *Marauders*, op. cit., p. 277. • 123. Calvert, *Prisoners of Hope*, op. cit., pp. 249–51. • 124. Ibid., p. 252. • 125. SP, p. 283. • 126. Mountbatten Diary, p. 114. • 127. Ibid., p. 115. • 128. DIV, p. 279. • 129. Ibid. • 130. Ibid. • 131. Allen, *Burma*, op. cit., pp. 376–7. • 132. J.A.L. Hamilton, *War Bush* (Norwich, 2001), pp. 301–5. • 133. Romanus & Sunderland, *Stilwell's Command Problems*, op. cit., pp. 243–4. • 134. Pownall Diaries, pp. 182–3. • 135. Masters, *Road Past Mandalay*, op. cit., pp. 278–82. • 136. Bidwell, *Chindit War*, op. cit., p. 279. • 137. Calvert, *Fighting Mad*, op. cit., p. 183; M. Hickey, *The Unforgettable Army* (Tunbridge Wells, 1992), pp. 138–9; WO 203/4610. • 138. Tulloch, *Wingate in Peace and War*, op. cit., pp. 101–2; Rooney, *Wingate and the Chindits*, op. cit., p. 212. • 139. Pownall Diaries, p. 32; O'Brien, *Out of the Blue*, op. cit., p. 217; Lane, *Chinese Chindits*, op. cit., p. 39; Rooney, *Wingate and the Chindits*, op. cit., p. 155. • 140. SP, p. 283; Ziegler, *Mountbatten*, op. cit., p. 274. • 141. Arthur Bryant, *Triumph in the West* (1959), p. 162; Tuchman, *Sand against the Wind*, op. cit., p. 467. • 142. Alanbrooke Diaries, p. 559. • 143. P. Humphreys, *To Stop a Rising Sun* (Stroud, 1996), pp. 74–6. Doris and Ethel Waters were the sisters of the actor Jack Warner, famous on British television in the 1950s and 1960s as PC Dixon of Dock Green. • 144. Mountbatten Diary, p. 110. • 145. Ibid., p. 112. • 146. Tuchman, *Sand against the Wind*, op. cit., p. 452. • 147. Sheridan Morley, *A Talent to Amuse* (1969), p. 250; R. Arnold, *A Very Quiet War* (1962), pp. 122–3; Coward, *Future Indefinite*, op. cit., p. 304. • 148. Philip Hoare, *Noel Coward* (1995), pp. 350–1. • 149. Tuchman, *Sand against the Wind*, op. cit., p. 452.

Chapter Fifteen   pp. 364–385

• 1. DIV, p. 221; Ronald Lewin, *Ultra Goes to War* (1980), p. 139. • 2. G. Evans & A. Brett-James, *Imphal* (1962), pp. 76–83. • 3. WO 203/56. • 4. DIV, p. 345; Mountbatten Diary, pp. 119, 128. • 5. DIV, p. 349. • 6. Ronald Lewin, *Slim. The Standard Bearer* (1976), p. 199; DIV, p. 351. • 7. DIV, p. 351. • 8. Lewin, *Slim*, op. cit., p. 191. • 9. S.W. Kirby, ed., *The War Against Japan* (1961), iv, pp. 14–16. • 10. Ibid., v, p. 419. • 11. Lewin, *Slim*, op. cit., p. 192. • 12. Bernard Fergusson, *The Trumpet in the Hall* (1970), p. 190; DIV, pp. 373–5. • 13. Pownall Diaries, pp. 176–7. • 14. John Connell, *Auchinleck* (1959), p. 775; Mountbatten Diary, p. 121. • 15. Alanbrooke Diaries, p. 578. • 16. Ibid. • 17. Anthony Eden, *The Reckoning* (1965), p. 267. • 18. Alanbrooke Diaries, p. 579. • 19. Ibid., p. 580. • 20. Ibid., p. 581. • 21. Ibid., p. 582. • 22. Pownall Diaries, p. 187. • 23. Alanbrooke Diaries, p. 599; Arthur Bryant, *Triumph in the West* (1959), p. 300. • 24. Barbara Tuchman, *Sand against the Wind* (1971), p. 473. It is disappointing that so distinguished a historian as Barbara Tuchman should be guilty of this howler.

Alaric, who sacked Rome in 410, was a Goth. The better known Attila the Hun marched on Rome in 452 but turned back before reaching the Eternal City. • 25. SP, p. 289. • 26. Tuchman, *Sand against the Wind*, op. cit., p. 473. • 27. Ibid., pp. 473–4; SP, p. 287. • 28. Tuchman, *Sand against the Wind*, op. cit. • 29. SP, p. 289. • 30. Ibid., pp. 289–90. • 31. Philip Ziegler, *Mountbatten* (1985), p. 281. • 32. Mountbatten Diary, pp. 130, 132–3. • 33. Ziegler, *Mountbatten*, op. cit., pp. 282–3. • 34. Alanbrooke Diary, p. 601. • 35. Mountbatten Diary, p. 141. • 36. Ziegler, *Mountbatten*, op. cit., pp. 283–4. • 37. Mountbatten Diary, p. 142. • 38. G. Hanley, *Monsoon Victory* (1958), pp. 20–7. • 39. A. Brett-James, *Ball of Fire* (Aldershot, 1951), pp. 365–6; Brett-James, *Report My Signals* (1948), p. 197. • 40. Robert Lyman, *Slim, Master of War* (2004), p. 238. • 41. Evans & Brett-James, *Imphal*, op. cit., pp. 76–83; Jon Latimer, *Burma. The Forgotten War* (2004), pp. 349–50. • 42. J. Nunnelly, *Tales from the King's African Rifles. A Last Flourish of Empire* (NY; 1988), pp. 140–89; H.Moyse-Bartlett, *King's African Rifles. A Study of the Military History of East and Central Africa 1890–1945* (Aldershot, 1956), pp. 617–34. • 43. Kirby (ed.), *War against Japan*, op. cit., iv, pp. 143–5. • 44. DIV, p. 377. • 45. Ibid., p. 361. • 46. Ibid., p. 364. • 47. R. Callahan, *Burma 1942–1945. The Politics and Strategy of the Second World War* (1978), p. 141. • 48. Lewin, *Slim*, op. cit., p. 191. • 49. Ibid., pp. 199–200. • 50. Ibid., p. 198. • 51. B. Prasad, ed., *The Arakan Operations 1942–45* (Delhi, 1954), pp. 213–14. • 52. Brett-James, *Report My Signals*, op. cit., pp. 29–30; G. Evans, *Slim as Military Commander* (1969), p. 215. • 53. Lewin, *Slim*, op. cit., pp. 206–7. • 54. Ibid., p. 200. • 55. DIV, p. 376. • 56. Louis Allen, *Burma. The Longest War 1941–45* (1984); p. 387. • 57. Ibid., pp. 390–1. • 58. M. Parillo, *The Japanese Merchant Marine in World War Two* (Annapolis, 1993), pp. 137–43. • 59. D. McIsaac, ed., *The United States Bombing Survey* (NY, 1976), ix, p. 104. • 60. DIV, p. 383. • 61. Allen, *Burma*, op. cit., p. 393; H. Probert, *The Forgotten Air Force* (1995), pp. 232–5. • 62. Probert, *Forgotten Air Force*, op. cit., pp. 203–9. • 63. See Latimer, *Burma*, op. cit., pp. 347–8, 522, for massive detail on the war in the air. • 64. Lyman, *Slim*, op. cit., p. 239. • 65. DIV, pp. 390–2. • 66. Allen, *Burma*, op. cit., pp. 392–4. • 67. The Americans had always been sceptical. Wags dubbed SEAC 'Saving England's Asian Colonies' or 'Supreme Example of Allied Confusion': E.P. MacIntosh, *Sisterhood of Spies. The Women of the OSS* (Annapolis, 1998), p. 191. • 68. Lewin, *Slim*, op. cit., p. 203. • 69. Pownall Diaries, pp. 166–7. • 70. Alanbrooke Diary, p. 616. • 71. For a full biography see R. Ryder, *Oliver Leese* (1987). • 72. Alanbrooke Diaries, p. 727. To blame Mountbatten is one thing; to cut Slim out of the loop and not give him any credit shows how badly informed the CIGS often was. • 73. P. Warner, *Auchinleck. The Lonely Soldier* (1981), pp. 263–4. • 74. Probert, *Forgotten Air Force*, op. cit., pp. 223–5. • 75. Mountbatten Diary, p. 151; Richard Humble, *Fraser of the North Cape* (1983), p. 245. • 76. Ziegler, *Mountbatten*, op. cit., p. 285. • 77. Mountbatten Diary, p. 167. • 78. Alanbrooke Diaries, pp. 627, 633.

For a sketch of Browning see M. Boatner, *Biographical Dictionary of World War Two* (Novato, CA, 1996), p. 66. Browning was married to the novelist Daphne du Maurier, who famously made a public protest at the portrayal of her late husband by Dirk Bogarde in the 1977 Richard Attenborough film *A Bridge Too Far*. • 79. Ziegler, *Mountbatten*, op. cit., pp. 286–7. • 80. Alanbrooke Diaries, pp. 582, 671. • 81. Ryder, *Oliver Leese*, op. cit., pp. 200–1. • 82. Ibid., p. 203. • 83. DIV, p. 385. • 84. Lyman, *Slim*, op. cit., pp. 236–7. • 85. Ibid., p. 237. • 86. Mountbatten Diary, p. 145. • 87. Kirby, ed., *War against Japan*, op. cit., iv, p. 161; Mountbatten Diary, pp. 148–9, 156–7. For Slim looking under par see Lewin, *Slim*, op. cit., p. 208. For those interested in such things, Slim was awarded the KCB and the others the KBE. • 88. Latimer, *Burma*, op. cit., pp. 357–8. • 89. J.H. Williams, *Elephant Bill* (1950), p. 130.

Chapter Sixteen   pp. 386–411

• 1. Graham Peck, *Two Kinds of Time* (Boston, 1950), pp. 417, 450, 476, 514, 533–4; T. White & A. Jacoby, *Thunder out of China* (NY, 1946), p. 197. • 2. Hollington Tong, *Dateline China* (NY, 1950), pp. 242, 247–50. • 3. Mountbatten Diary, p. 121. For Madame Chiang's departure see *New York Times*, 30 November, 11 December 1944. • 4. See Frank McLynn, *Fitzroy Maclean* (1992), pp. 158–63. • 5. C.F. Romanus & R. Sunderland, *Stilwell's Mission to China* (Washington DC, 1953), pp. 302–3. • 6. Barbara Tuchman, *Sand against the Wind* (1971), p. 463. • 7. MP, iv, p. 387; C.F. Romanus & R. Sunderland, *Stilwell's Personal File* (1976), v, 1913–18. For the Dixie Mission see John Service, *Lost Chance in China* (NY, 1974), esp. pp. 179–81, 196–7; David D. Barrett, *The Dixie Mission: the US Army Observer Corps in Yenna, 1944* (Berkeley, 1970). • 8. For Wallace see John Maze & Graham White, *Henry A. Wallace: His Search for a New World Order* (S. Carolina, 1995); John C. Culver & John Hyde, *American Dreamer: The Life and Times of Henry A. Wallace* (2002). For details of the Wallace mission see Henry A. Wallace, *The Price of Vision: The Diary of Henry A. Wallace 1942–1946* (Boston, 1973), pp. 349–51; Owen Lattimore (with Fujiko Isono), *China Memories* (Tokyo, 1990), p. 186. • 9. Lattimore, *China Memories*, op. cit., pp. 181–6. Service made four valuable points: 1) The USA had spoiled China with an open-ended Lend-Lease cornucopia. The Stilwell approach of provisional aid was the correct one. 2) It was vital to recognise other elements in China such as Madame Sun Yat-sen and the Communists. 3) Washington should stop lying about Chiang and the KMT – by this date essentially irrelevancies anyway – and educate US public opinion towards a realistic assessment of China: Joseph W. Esherick, *Lost Chance in China: the World War Two Dispatches of John S. Service* (NY, 1974), p. 153. Above all, secret service collusion between Tai-li and the Secret Service US Naval Group China under Commander Milton E.Miles should be discontinued. Miles, who later had a nervous breakdown, was a maverick operator who got across Wild Bill Donovan and worked as his own spy network: Milton Miles, *A Different Kind of War* (Garden City, NJ, 1967), pp. 115–16; Michael Shaller, *The US Crusade in China, 1938–1945* (NY, 1979), pp. 248–50. For Donovan's activities in North Burma see MP, iv, pp. 498–9. • 10. Herbert Feis, *The China Tangle* (Princeton, 1953), pp. 145–51; Claire Lee Chennault, *Way of a Fighter* (NY, 1949), p. 266. For the Chennault exaggerations see MP, iv, pp. 256–7. • 11. Samuel Rosenman, *Working with Roosevelt* (NY, 1952), pp. 438–9; Eugene L. Rasor, *The China-Burma-India Campaign 1931–1945* (1998), p. 39; Ke-Wen Chang, *An Encyclopedia of Chinese History, Culture and Nationalism* (1998), p. 332. • 12. Tuchman, *Sand against the Wind*, op. cit. • 13. *New York Times*, 9, 21 June, 22 August, 6 October 1944. • 14. Jon Latimer, *Burma. The Forgotten War* (2004), p. 338. • 15. Tuchman, *Sand against the Wind*, op. cit., p. 468. • 16. Ibid. • 17. White & Jacoby, *Thunder*, op. cit., pp. 181–3; cf. MP, iv, p. 503; C.F. Romanus & R. Sunderland, *Stilwell's Command Problems* (Washington, 1956), pp. 316–28, 371–4. • 18. Tuchman, *Sand against the Wind*, op. cit., p. 458. Chennault's complaints to Marshall are at MP, iv, p. 475. Yet even he admitted the heavy loss of his planes during I-CHIGO (Chennault, *Way of a Fighter*, op. cit., pp. 287–92). • 19. SP, p. 282. • 20. MP, iv, pp. 472–3; Romanus & Sunderland, *Stilwell's Command Problems*, op. cit., pp. 367–9; Tuchman, *Sand against the Wind*, op. cit., p. 259. • 21. SP, p. 288. • 22. C.F. Romanus & R. Sunderland, *Time Runs Out in CBI* (Washington DC, 1959), p. 57. • 23. Peck, *Two Kinds of Time*, op. cit., p. 498; for White see Joyce Hoffmann, *Theodore H. White and Journalism as Illusion* (NY, 1995). • 24. SP, pp. 291, 295, 296. • 25. Ibid., pp. 292–3. • 26. Ibid., p. 292. • 27. Stilwell's comments on this are at ibid., p. 296. For Churchill's comments see *The Second World War* (1950), v, pp. 600–1. For the Auk's refutation see John Connell, *Auchinleck* (1959) p. 743. • 28. SP, p. 304. • 29. Philip Ziegler, *Mountbatten* (1985), p. 284. • 30. SP, p. 310. • 31. See, for instance, the letter Mountbatten sent Stilwell from London on 14 August (WO 203/3331). • 32. MP, iv, pp. 417–18; Romanus & Sunderland, *Stilwell's Command Problems*, op. cit., pp. 309–10. The quotation is from Eric Larrabee, *Commander-in-Chief* (1987), p. 572. • 33. Tuchman, *Sand against the Wind*, op. cit., p. 470. • 34. Ibid. • 35. Ibid., p. 471. • 36. This is admitted even by Chiang's most ardent defender: Jay Taylor, *The Generalissimo* (Harvard, 2009) pp. 278–80. • 37. MP, iv, p. 510. • 38. Ibid., iv, pp. 500–7; Romanus & Sunderland, *Stilwell's Command Problems*, op. cit., pp. 374–8. • 39. Romanus & Sunderland, *Stilwell's Command Problems*, op. cit., p. 472; SP, p. 296. • 40. Larrabee, *Commander-in-Chief*, op. cit., p. 568. • 41. The standard account of Hurley is Patrick D. Buhite, *Patrick J. Hurley and American Foreign Policy* (Ithaca, NY, 1973). For some anecdotes about him see John Pen La Farge, *Turn Left at the Sleeping Dog* (NM, 2006), p. 103; T. Christoper

Jesperson, *American Images of China 1931–1949* (1999), p. 136; Arnold A. Other, *Another Such Victory. President Truman and the Cold War 1945–53* (NY, 2002), p. 311. • 42. MP, iv, pp. 544–5, 554. • 43. Ibid., iv, pp. 563–6. • 44. Tuchman, *Sand against the Wind*, passim. • 45. SP, p. 290. For the Hurley mission in late 1944 see Lattimore, *China Memories*, op. cit., p. 85; John Paton Davies, *Dragon by the Tail* (NY, 1972), p. 342; White & Jacoby, *Thunder*, op. cit., pp. 199, 208–11, 249–52; Michael Schaller, *The United States and China in the Twentieth Century* (NY, 1979), p. 99; Jonathan Fenby, *Chiang Kai-shek: China's Generalissimo and the Nation He Lost* (NY, 2004), p. 438. • 46. Carolle J. Carter, *Mission to Yenan. American Liaison with the Chinese Communists 1944–1947* (Lexington, KT, 1997), p. 23. For the so-called Dixie Mission see Wilbur J. Peterkin, *Inside China 1943–1945: An Eyewitness Account of America's Mission to Yenan* (Baltimore, 1992); William P. Head, *Yenan! Colonel Wilbur Peterkin and the American Military Mission to the Chinese Communists 1944–1945* (Chapel Hill, NC, 1987). • 47. SP, p. 300. • 48. Ibid., p. 299; Tuchman, *Sand against the Wind*, op. cit., p. 482. • 49. Tuchman, *Sand against the Wind*, op. cit. • 50. SP, p. 303. • 51. Ibid., p. 300. For Hurley's very strong pro-Chiang position see Lohbeck, *Patrick J. Hurley* op. cit., pp. 285–6. • 52. SP, pp. 303–4. • 53. Webster, *Burma Road* (2004), pp. 275–6. • 54. C.T. Liang, *General Stilwell in China* (NY, 1972), pp. 176–7. • 55. Romanus & Sunderland, *Time Runs Out*, op. cit., pp. 354–60, 394–8. • 56. SP, p. 299. • 57. Liang, *General Stilwell*, op. cit., pp. 24, 50, 64, 77. • 58. Tuchman, *Sand against The Wind*, op. cit., p. 489. • 59. Romanus & Sunderland, *Stilwell's Command Problems*, op. cit., p. 429. Feis, *China Tangle*, op. cit., pp. 222–63. • 60. Ronald Lewin, 'World War Two. A Tangled Web', *Journal of the Royal United Services Institute* 127 (1982), p. 19. • 61. Larrabee, *Commander-in-Chief*, op. cit., p. 574. • 62. White & Jacoby, *Thunder*, op. cit., pp. 187–8. • 63. Ibid., pp. 190–4. • 64. Tuchman, *Sand against the Wind*, op. cit., p. 489. • 65. MP, iv, pp. 585–6; also Romanus & Sunderland, *Stilwell's Command Problems*, op. cit., p. 546. Hurley naturally wanted to shield Chiang from the full blast of FDR's invective: Lohbeck, *Hurley*, op. cit., pp. 292–3. • 66. Liang, *General Stilwell*, op. cit., pp. 239–41. The receipt of the famous telegram has often been described as Chiang's greatest humiliation. See White & Jacoby, *Thunder*, op. cit., pp. 220–1; Fenby, *Chiang Kai-shek*, op. cit., pp. 428–9; Feis, *China Tangle*, op. cit., p. 189. • 67. Taylor, *Generalissimo*, op. cit., p. 289; Romanus & Sunderland, *Stilwell's Command Problems*, op. cit., pp. 443–53. • 68. SP, pp. 305–6. In his rage Chiang threatened to have Stilwell assassinated: Taylor, *Generalissimo*, op. cit., p. 289. • 69. SP, p. 305. • 70. Ibid. • 71. Ibid., pp. 307–9. • 72. Tuchman, *Sand against the Wind*, op. cit. • 73. The most detailed study of FDR in the 1944 elections is Samuel Rosenman, *Working with Roosevelt* (NY, 1952). • 74. SP, p. 310. • 75. Romanus & Sunderland, *Stilwell's Mission*, op. cit., p. 278. • 76. Tuchman, *Sand against the Wind*, op. cit., pp. 499–500. • 77. Henry L. Stimson & McGeorge Bundy, *On Active Service in Peace and War* (NY, 1949), pp. 303–4, 535–6. Stimson thought

Stilwell's subsequent dismissal a bitterly unjust outcome: Feis, *China Tangle*, op. cit., pp. 194–5. Marshall prepared a draft signal to Chiang, dated 16 October 1944 (MP, iv, pp. 627–8), which, while accepting Stilwell's withdrawal, nonetheless slapped the generalissimo down when he claimed that Stilwell was unsuitable for the proposed new command. He also added that the charge that Stilwell had lost eastern China was absurd. As for the attack in northern Burma, that was a joint decision by the US president and the British prime minister. He also warned Chiang that Stilwell's dismissal would adversely affect the reputation of the Kuomintang in the USA. Needless to say, FDR himself altered the minute, heavily diluting the doughty defence of Stilwell. The final version appears in Romanus & Stilwell, *Stilwell's Command Problems*, op. cit., pp. 460–2, 468–9. • 78. For the protracted negotiations see Tuchman, *Sand against the Wind*, op. cit., pp. 498–500. • 79. SP, pp. 312–15. • 80. For these two see M. Boatner, *Biographical Dictionary of World War Two* (Novato, CA, 1996), pp. 549–50, 608–9. • 81. SP, p. 283; Allen, *Burma*, op. cit., p. 387. As Webster (*Burma Road*, op. cit.) rightly remarks, what kind of man would call his autobiography *Wedemeyer Reports!*, complete with exclamation mark? • 82. Albert Wedemeyer, *Wedemeyer Reports!* (NY, 1958) pp. 65–7. • 83. MP, iv, pp. 578–9. • 84. See *Time*, 13 November 1944. • 85. Tuchman, *Sand against the Wind*, op. cit., p. 467. • 86. Lara Tyson Li, *Madame Chiang Kai-shek*, op. cit., p. 258; Sterling Seagrave, *The Soong Dynasty* (NY, 1986) pp. 412–13; Hannah Pakula, *The Last Empress* (2010), pp. 504–8. • 87. MP, iv, p. 631. • 88. There was a particularly lucid, incisive and passionately pro-Stilwell article in the *New York Times*, 31 October 1944. • 89. Tuchman, *Sand against the Wind*, op. cit., pp. 507–9. • 90. Ibid., p. 467. • 91. Mountbatten Diary, pp. 147–8; Ziegler, *Mountbatten*, op. cit., pp. 284–5. • 92. Connell, *Auchinleck*, op. cit., p. 777. • 93. DIV, pp. 281, 383–4. • 94. Ronald Lewin, *Slim. The Standard Bearer* (1976), pp. 141–2. • 95. Louis Allen, *Burma. The Longest War 1941–45* (1984), p. 367. A G-2 was an officer belonging to Military Intelligence at the division level or higher. • 96. Lewin, *Slim*, op. cit., p. 142. • 97. The phrase is Barbara Tuchman's (*Sand against the Wind*, op. cit., p. 531). For a defence of Stilwell on the above lines see David Rooney, *Stilwell the Patriot* (2005). • 98. F. Dorn, *Walkout. With Stilwell in Burma* (NY, 1973). • 99. Pakula, *Last Empress*, op. cit., p. 485. • 100. Thomas Moor & Carl F. Feifler, *The Deadliest Colonel* (NY, 1975), pp. 145–6, 184, 193; cf. Maochun Yu, *OSS in China. Prelude to Cold War* (Yale, 1996), p. 113. Some have alleged that Feifler devised the plan on his own and then unjustly implicated Stilwell as 'legitimator'. His motive was that he detested Wild Bill Donovan and wanted to achieve an exploit that would blow Donovan out of the water. It *is* known that he angered Donovan by reminding him that he came under Stilwell's command. • 101. Stimson & Bundy, *On Active Service*, op. cit., pp. 303–4, 535–6. • 102. Larrabee, *Commander-in-Chief*, op. cit., p. 578. • 103. Forrest Pogue, *George C. Marshall. Organizer of Victory* (NY, 1973), pp. 354–5. • 104. Thompson Parrish, *Roosevelt and Marshall. Partners in Politics and War* (NY, 1985), pp. 443–4. • 105. To my mind the prime offender is Jay Taylor. His pro-Chiang excesses can be seen at all stages in his book, but there is a particularly shaky defence of Chiang's almost psychotic changes of mind at pp. 249–52 of *Generalissimo*, op. cit. Taylor actually gives the game away by the tell-tale phrase 'to conjecture' on p. 250. • 106. SP, pp. 348–9.

Chapter Seventeen pp. 412–445

• 1. T. White & A. Jacoby, *Thunder out of China* (NY, 1946), pp. 190–3. • 2. Albert Wedemeyer, *Wedemeyer Reports!* (NY, 1958), pp. 301, 305. • 3. C.F. Romanus & R. Sunderland, *Time Runs Out In CBI* (Washington DC, 1959), pp. 52, 165. • 4. Wedemeyer as good as admits this himself: *Wedemeyer Reports!*, op. cit., p. 291. • 5. DIV, pp. 395–6. • 6. Jon Latimer, *Burma. The Forgotten War* (2004), p. 378. • 7. DIV, pp. 397–400. • 8. Ronald Lewin, *Slim. The Standard Bearer* (1976), p. 210. • 9. R. Callahan, *Burma 1942–1945* (1978), pp. 156–8. • 10. WO 203/298. • 11. DIV, p. 393. • 12. Lewin, *Slim*, op. cit., pp. 209–13. • 13. DIV, p. 401. • 14. T. O'Brien, *The Moonlight War* (1987), pp. 169–73; G. Hartcup, *Camouflage* (Newton Abbot, 1979), pp. 115–16; S.W. Kirby, ed., *The War against Japan* (1961), iv pp. 501–5. • 15. J.H. Williams, *Elephant Bill* (1950), p. 279. • 16. DIV, pp. 404–6. • 17. Louis Allen, *Burma. The Longest War 1941–45* (1984), pp. 399–400. • 18. Lewin, *Slim*, op. cit., p. 217. • 19. Allen, *Burma*, op. cit., p. 416. • 20. DIV, p. 398. • 21. Ibid., pp. 401–2. • 22. Ibid. • 23. G. Evans, *Slim as Military Commander* (1969), p. 190. • 24. Kirby, ed., *War against Japan*, op. cit., iv, p. 177. • 25. Ibid., iv, p. 186; Allen, *Burma*, op. cit., pp. 403–5. • 26. Allen, *Burma*, op. cit., pp. 409–11. • 27. DIV, p. 418. • 28. Robert Lyman, *Slim, Master of War* (2004), p. 247. • 29. Malcolm Page, *KAR. A History of the King's African Rifles and East African Forces* (Barnsley, 1998), pp. 160–3; DIV, pp. 422–3. • 30. James R. Penn, *Rivers of the World* (Santa Barbara, CA, 2001), p. 115. • 31. DIV, pp. 409–10. • 32. Ibid., p. 415. • 33. Kirby, ed., *War against Japan*, op. cit., iv, pp. 184–6. • 34. DIV, p. 415. • 35. Ibid., pp. 420–1. • 36. C.L. Proudfoot, *We Lead* (New Delhi, 1991), pp. 85–8. • 37. DIV, p. 421. • 38. Ibid., pp. 433–6. • 39. Michael Roberts, *Golden Arrow* (1952), p. 76. • 40. Lewin, *Slim*, op. cit., p. 221. • 41. G. Evans, *The Desert and the Jungle* (1959), p. 141. • 42. J. Nunnelly, ed., *Tales from the Burma Campaign 1942–45* (Petersham, 1998), pp. 87–8. • 43. Evans, *Desert and the Jungle*, op. cit., p. 146. • 44. J. Thompson, *The Imperial War Museum Book of the War in Burma 1942–1945* (2002), pp. 298–302. • 45. Evans, *Desert and the Jungle*, op. cit., p. 151. Evans, who went up in a plane to reconnoitre, narrowly missed being shot down. • 46. B. Prasad, ed., *Reconquest of Burma* (Delhi, 1958), ii, pp. 286–8. • 47. DIV, p. 429. • 48. Lewin, *Slim*, op. cit., pp. 221–2. • 49. George MacDonald

Fraser, *Quartered Safe Out Here. A Recollection of the War in Burma* (1995), pp. 35–6. • 50. H. Smaule, *Spearhead General* (1961), pp. 351–2. • 51. Miles Smeeton, *A Change of Jungles* (1962), pp. 89–90. • 52. The history of tank warfare in the Burma campaign almost merits a study to itself. There is copious material on the use of heavy armour in the period January–April 1945 in WO 203/1795 and 203/354. • 53. DIV, p. 442. • 54. Ibid., p. 443. • 55. Ibid., pp. 442–3, 446–7. • 56. For a complete description of the battle see Smeeton, *Change of Jungles*, op. cit., Allen, *Burma*, op. cit., pp. 436–9. • 57. J.P. Cross & B. Gurung, eds., *Gurkhas at War* (2002), p. 99. • 58. Allen, *Burma*, op. cit., pp. 439–40; DIV, p. 451. • 59. DIV, pp. 452–4. • 60. A. Brett-James, *Ball of Fire* (Aldershot, 1951), p. 402. • 61. Lyman, *Slim*, op. cit., p. 251. • 62. DIV, pp. 456–7. • 63. Allen, *Burma*, op. cit., p. 450. • 64. Ibid., p. 454. • 65. Ibid., p. 407; DIV, p. 469. • 66. Compton Mackenzie, *All Over the Place* (1949), p. 110. • 67. John Masters, *The Road Past Mandalay* (1961), p. 308; Prasad, ed., *Reconquest of Burma*, op. cit., ii, p. 354. • 68. DIV, p. 469. • 69. Prasad, ed., *Reconquest of Burma*, op. cit., ii; pp. 354–9; Kirby, ed., *War against Japan*, op. cit., iv, p. 299. • 70. Prasad, ed., *Reconquest of Burma*, op. cit., pp. 361–3. • 71. Latimer, *Burma*, op. cit., p. 395. • 72. E.K.G. Sixsmith, *British Generalship in the Twentieth Century* (1970), p. 290; J. Gooch, ed., *Decisive Campaigns of the Second World War* (1990), p. 168. • 73. Lewin, *Slim*, op. cit., pp. 214–15. • 74. For Terachi and Meiktila see ibid., p. 216. On Slim as military genius: 'In so defeating the Japanese Slim earned a Chinese accolade, for Sun-Tzu would surely have recognised him as a "heaven-born captain"': ibid., p. 213. • 75. DIV, p. 447. • 76. Ibid., pp. 410–11, 413, 416; Lyman, *Slim*, op. cit., p. 245. • 77. Lewin, *Slim*, op. cit., p. 217; Lyman, *Slim*, op. cit., p. 245. • 78. WO 203/866. See also C.F. Romanus & R. Sunderland, *Stilwell's Command Problems* (Washington, 1956), p. 299. • 79. Latimer, *Burma*, op. cit., pp. 359–73; Allen, *Burma*, op. cit., pp. 456–8. • 80. DIV, p. 462. • 81. Herbert Feis, *The China Tangle* (Princeton, 1953), p. 275; White & Jacoby, *Thunder*, op. cit., p. 260; Don Moser, *China, Burma, India* (VA, 1978), pp. 190–1. • 82. Romanus & Sunderland, *Time Runs Out*, op. cit., p. 141; Kirby, ed., *War against Japan*, op. cit., iv, p. 194. • 83. Webster, *Burma Road*, pp. 318–19, 324–7. • 84. E.L. Fischer, *The Chancy War* (NY, 1991), pp. 49–60; O.C. Spencer, *Flying the Hump* (TX, 1992), p. 174. • 85. DIV, pp. 443–4, 464–6. • 86. W.S. Churchill, *Second World War* (1950), vi, p. 535. • 87. Mountbatten Diary, pp. 168–77. The flight over the battlefield was typical Mountbatten: 'Beneath was a most inspiring sight – an army in hot pursuit of a beaten enemy . . . Down the river Chindwin an endless stream of DUKWs and other crafts were carrying soldiers; along the track on the river bank lorries and motor vehicles of all types were ploughing on in an endless stream like the traffic leading to Epsom on Derby Day. Alongside them marched the infantry in single file, interspersed with mule trains. It is just one vast forward surge, and one of the most exhilarating sights I have ever seen': Philip Ziegler,

Mountbatten (1985), p. 288. • 88. Mountbatten Diary, p. 186. • 89. Ibid., pp. 192–3; DIV, p. 444. • 90. Ziegler, *Mountbatten*, op. cit., pp. 293–4. • 91. Mountbatten Diary, pp. 193–4. • 92. Romanus & Sunderland, *Time Runs Out*, op. cit., pp. 324–5. • 93. Ziegler, *Mountbatten*, op. cit., pp. 293–4. • 94. Lewin, *Slim*, op. cit., p. 228. • 95. DIV, p. 482. • 96. Allen, *Burma*, op. cit., p. 454. • 97. DIV, pp. 470–2. • 98. Ibid., pp. 473–4. • 99. Ibid., pp. 474–5. • 100. Lewin, *Slim*, op. cit., pp. 231–2. • 101. Mountbatten Diary, p. 181. • 102. Lewin, *Slim*, op. cit., p. 233. • 103. Allen, *Burma*, op. cit., pp. 582–4. • 104. Latimer, *Burma*, op. cit., p. 407. • 105. Lewin, *Slim*, op. cit., pp. 232–3. • 106. DIV, p. 487. Slim was told by Mountbatten at Monywa on 19 March that DRACULA would go ahead, but Leese then spent 11 days dithering over the details. Finally he refused to authorise certain airborne troops whose participation was essential for success. Mountbatten had to fly to Calcutta in person to reprimand Leese and countermand his orders: Lewin, *Slim*, op. cit., p. 231. • 107. DIV, pp. 488–9. • 108. Ibid., pp. 489–92. • 109. WO 203/53. • 110. Allen, *Burma*, op. cit., pp. 464–7. • 111. DIV, p. 496. • 112. Ibid., p. 497. • 113. Lewin, *Slim*, op. cit., pp. 233–4. • 114. Kirby, ed., *War against Japan*, op. cit., iv, pp. 249–50. • 115. DIV, p. 499. • 116. Prasad, ed., *Reconquest of Burma*, op. cit., ii, p. 402. • 117. WO 208/1057. • 118. Allen, *Burma*, op. cit., pp. 477–8. • 119. DIV, p. 504. • 120. Lewin, *Slim*, op. cit., p. 234. • 121. DIV, p. 505. • 122. Thompson, *Imperial War Museum Book of the War in Burma*, op. cit., p. 383. • 123. Though the trope was originally used about Slim's dash south to Rangoon: Masters, *Road Past Mandalay*, op. cit., p. 312. • 124. DIV, p. 506. • 125. For the discussions see Allen, *Burma*, op. cit., pp. 481–4. • 126. DIV, pp. 504–5. • 127. Lewin, *Slim*, op. cit., p. 236. • 128. DIV, pp. 510–13. • 129. Latimer, *Burma*, op. cit., p. 422. • 130. The entire story is told in Allen, *Burma*, op. cit., pp. 488–534, and at greater length in his *Sittang. The Last Battle* (1976). • 131. Lyman, *Slim*, op. cit., p. 254; Lewin, *Slim*, op. cit., p. 210.

Epilogue   pp. 446–456

• 1. Mountbatten Diary, p. 209. • 2. DIV, pp. 516–20. Slim probably overrated Aung San, to judge from the following hyperbolic statement: 'I have always felt that, with proper treatment, Aung San would have proved a Burmese Smuts': ibid., p. 520. • 3. See 'Patriotic Burmese Forces and Anti-Fascist Organisations, Burma', WO 203/4404. • 4. Jon Latimer, *Burma. The Forgotten War* (2004), p. 409. • 5. See Alanbrooke Diaries, pp. 713, 721. • 6. Mountbatten Diary, p. 211; DIV, pp. 521–2. • 7. Leese. • 8. Robert Lyman, *Slim, Master of War* (2004), p. 256, says: 'Mountbatten's instructions had either not been clear or else Leese was so determined to remove Slim from command of 14th Army that he was prepared simply to ignore them.' • 9. Philip Ziegler,

Mountbatten (1985), p. 295. • 10. One version of the Leese–Christison conference is that the army to invade Malaya would be a completely new force but would have the title of 14th Army to utilise its propaganda value, while the real 14th Army was rebranded as 12th Army: Lyman, *Slim*, op. cit., p. 256. • 11. Later in life Leese admitted that Mountbatten had given no such order and could not be held accountable for his own blunder: Ronald Lewin, *Slim. The Standard Bearer* (1976), p. 238. • 12. Ziegler, *Mountbatten*, op. cit., p. 294. • 13. M. Hickey, *The Unforgettable Army* (Tunbridge Wells, 1992), p. 231. • 14. Ziegler, *Mountbatten*, op. cit., p. 294. • 15. On which one can only comment that if he was worried about it, he should have given clear and unambiguous instructions in the first place. • 16. Lewin, *Slim*, op. cit., p. 243. • 17. A. Greenwood, *Field Marshal Auchinleck* (Durham, 1991), p. 256. • 18. Mountbatten Diary, p. 207. • 19. Lewin, *Slim*, op. cit., p. 241. • 20. D. Smuthwaite, ed., *The Forgotten War. The British Army in the Far East 1941–1945* (1992), p. 49. • 21. Alanbrooke Diaries, p. 698; Mountbatten Diary, p. 220. • 22. Alanbrooke Diaries, pp. 700–1. • 23. DIV, pp. 531–4. • 24. Lewin, *Slim*, op. cit. • 25. Barbara Tuchman, *Sand against the Wind* (1971), p. 511. • 26. Ibid., p. 519. MacArthur seems to have harboured no grudge that in 1944 Stilwell turned down his request for manpower from China. He wanted 50,000 labourers from Chiang for backup operations but Stilwell told him that the Chinese economy was so fragile it could not sustain such a loss, adding, however, that if China was properly run, there would be no problem about meeting the request: C.F. Romanus & R. Sunderland, *Stilwell's Personal File: China-Burma-India 1942–44* (1976), v, 2448. • 27. Tuchman, *Sand against the Wind*, op. cit., p. 520. • 28. Philip Knightley, *The War Correspondent as Hero and Mythmaker from the Crimea to Iraq* (2004), p. 303. Wedemeyer complained to Marshall in December 1944 along identical lines to Stilwell, making it clear that the problems in China were not due to a Stilwell–Chiang personality clash and thus exposing the 'big lie' of the pro-Chiang apologists; C.F. Romanus & R. Sunderland, *Time Runs Out in CBI* (Washington DC, 1959), pp. 165–6. • 29. Mountbatten Diary, pp. 221–3. Here Mountbatten displays rare self-knowledge, as Pownall often accused him of liking the sound of his own voice: Ziegler, *Mountbatten*, op. cit., pp. 339–41. • 30. Mountbatten Diary, p. 225. • 31. Ziegler, *Mountbatten*, op. cit., p. 297. • 32. Larrabee, *Commander in Chief*, op. cit., p. 309. • 33. This case is strongly argued in Andrew Roberts, *Eminent Churchillians* (1994). • 34. See David Leigh, *The Wilson Plot* (1988). • 35. Simon Heffer, *Like the Roman* (1998).

Index